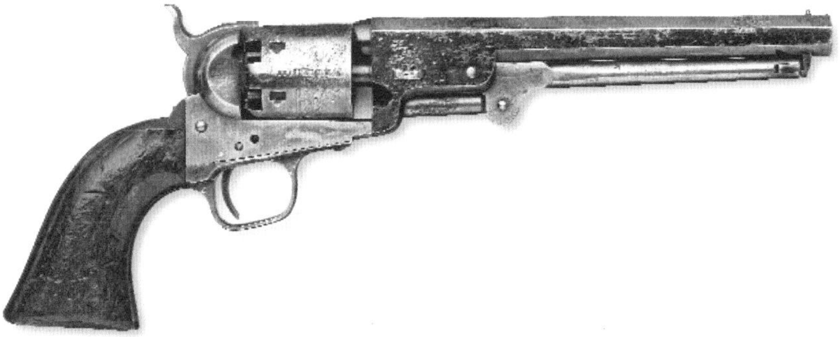

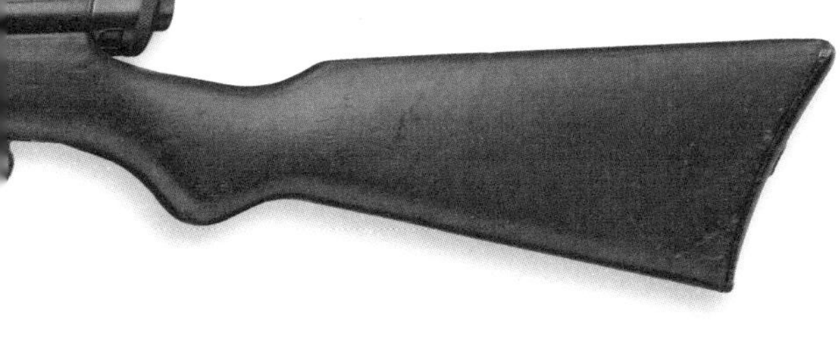

THE WORLD ENCYCLOPEDIA OF

# PISTOLS REVOLVERS AND SUBMACHINE GUNS

AN ILLUSTRATED HISTORICAL GUIDE TO OVER 500 MILITARY, LAW ENFORCEMENT AND ANTIQUE FIREARMS

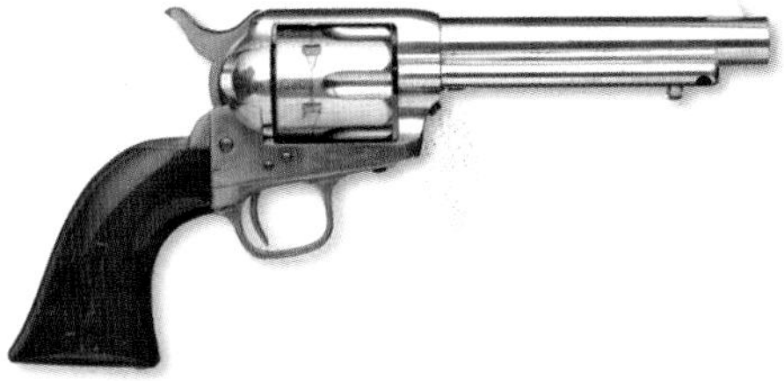

WILL FOWLER, ANTHONY NORTH & CHARLES STRONGE, WITH T. LOGAN METESH

LORENZ BOOKS

This edition is published by Lorenz Books
an imprint of Anness Publishing Ltd
info@anness.com
www.lorenzbooks.com
www.annesspublishing.com



A CIP catalogue record for this book is available from the British Library.

Originally designed and produced for Anness Publishing by THE BRIDGEWATER BOOK COMPANY LIMITED.

Publisher: Joanna Lorenz
Editorial Director: Helen Sudell
Project Manager: Sarah Doughty
Photography: Gary Ombler
Designer: Alistair Plumb
Art Director: Lisa McCormick
Production Controller: Ben Worley



# Contents

# Introduction

Although the firearm has a long history, the amount of technical progress that took place in the first 500 years is relatively small. The earliest evidence of the handgun, whether in illuminated manuscripts or as archaeological artefacts, gives us clues to its development from an unwieldy vase-shaped object to a straight-barrelled version similar to the barrel of a modern firearm. The first section of this book spans the entire history of small arms development, from the origins of gunpowder to the most up-to-date weapons of the 21st century. There then follows two unparalleled visual directories of significant pistols and submachine guns from around the world, from the 19th century to the present day.

### The beginnings of arms development

The first chapter of this book, *The Early History of Arms,* is a comprehensive history of the technical development of early arms. It opens with an exploration of the very earliest inventions from the 11th century. Always improving on previous models, various techniques were subsequently developed to ignite and fire prototype guns in the most efficient way possible, while allowing the user to hold the weapon by a wooden stock (the handle). While early guns were often ignited by a burning tinder or a red-hot iron, the serpentine system allowed an arm (the holding "serpentine") a match to ignite the powder in the touch-hole. This developed into the matchlock system, whereby the arm was held clear of the powder by a spring. To fire the gun, the spring was released by means of the action of the trigger and the powder in the priming pan was lit. The wheel-lock worked very much like a flint lighter, whereby a wheelspring mechanism helped the arm to move to ignite the powder in the pan by means of friction. The 17th-century flintlock developed this idea further and a flint was struck against steel to produce a spark. The invention of the flintlock was so successful that it formed the basis of all military, naval and personal firearms for the best part of 200 years.

The percussion system was an ingenious development that saw the end of the flintlock, first by replacing the traditional locks (flintlocks or wheel-locks) on existing weapons and then by being fitted to new firearms. The percussion cap was a system using

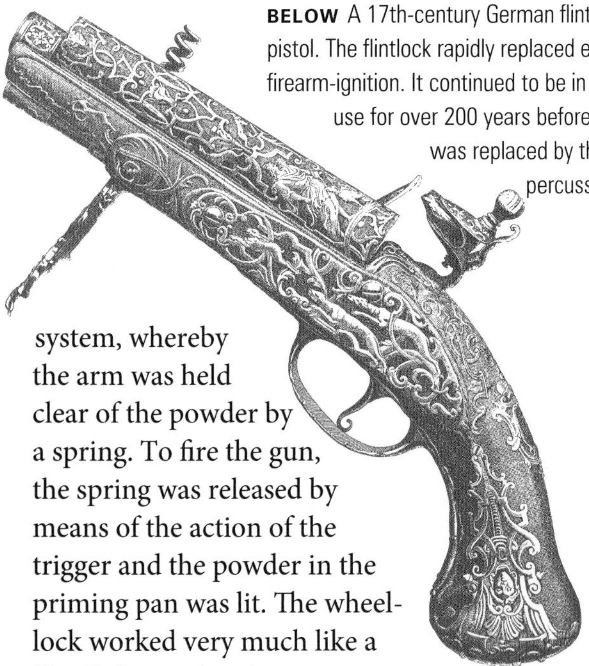

**BELOW** A 17th-century German flintlock pistol. The flintlock rapidly replaced earlier firearm-ignition. It continued to be in common use for over 200 years before it was replaced by the percussion cap.

**LEFT** Handguns in use in a 15th-century siege. As technology improved, guns and cannons took over from traditional medieval weapons such as crossbows and combat became more impersonal and mechanical.

a cap containing fulminate of mercury, a chemical compound which exploded when struck, that was attached to the barrel of the gun by a simple tube. The subsequent experiments with percussion caps, early cartridges and breech-loading rifles (loaded from the rear rather than the front) gave rise to the modern firearm. Different trades, influenced by increasing industrialization in Europe, contributed to its manufacture, whether lock, stock or barrel.

### The 20th century and beyond

The second chapter, *Into the Modern Age,* examines the development of firearms in the modern day. Of particular significance was the invention of the revolver by Samuel Colt, which had a critical influence on American history as it was played out in both the "Wild West" (real and mythical) and the American Civil War (1861–65).

The turn of the 20th century also saw the introduction of one of the most important handgun designs of modern history, John Moses Browning's M1900 automatic pistol, later refined to become the Colt M1911. The original automatic pistols were so ingeniously designed that their derivates have remained in service with major military forces to the present day.

The beginning of World War II (1939–45) saw an acceleration of handgun and submachine-gun design. The British Sten gun was conjured up in the dark days of 1940, while the Soviet PPS-43 was born from the wreckage of Leningrad in 1942–43.

In the post-war era, further revolver, pistol and submachine-gun designs were developed, in response to international warfare, the needs of police forces, and the growing threat of international terrorism. Also covered in this section of the book is the advent of non-lethal weapons, as security forces explore the options of stunning or anaesthetizing their opponents rather than using lethal force.

**ABOVE RIGHT** The Micro Uzi is used for covert operations that require a weapon that can be easily concealed and deployed while providing an effective rate of fire and accuracy. While classified as a submachine gun, Micro Uzi is small enough to sometimes be designated as a pistol.

**ABOVE** The .45 Colt M1911, regarded as the most successful automatic pistol of all time. Adopted by the US Army in 1911, the pistol was still in service in 1985. There are many copies still in use.

### The directories

The two directory chapters encompass both significant and less well-known firearms from both major and minor national producers. Organized by country and then alphabetically by manufacturer in date order (except where a chronological order shows the development of a gun), the directories provide a concise description of each firearm and its vital specifications. The weapons are mainly 20th-century firearms but the directory also includes weapons from the 19th century, as well as the latest developments in the firearms industry. The most eminent firearms manufacturers in the world today include some of the world's oldest industrial corporations. Beretta of Italy was established as far back as the 16th century, in 1526. In 1984 the company celebrated securement of one of the world's most valuable military handgun orders from the US Army. Likewise, Colt, Smith & Wesson, Remington and Ruger, all of whom helped to shape early American history, continue to produce state-of-the-art pistols and revolvers for today's security forces. The precision engineering and high-quality manufacturing of German, Swiss and Austrian firms is catalogued in the products of firms such as Steyr Mannlicher and SIG Sauer (SIG). The directories chart their developments from the steel creations of early years to the polymer-framed modular products of the 21st century. They also include a wide range of entries from smaller manufacturers across the globe, such as the family firm Para-Ordnance of Canada, who have built on classic designs like the Browning M1911 and improved them, while developing an array of other mission-specific firearms.

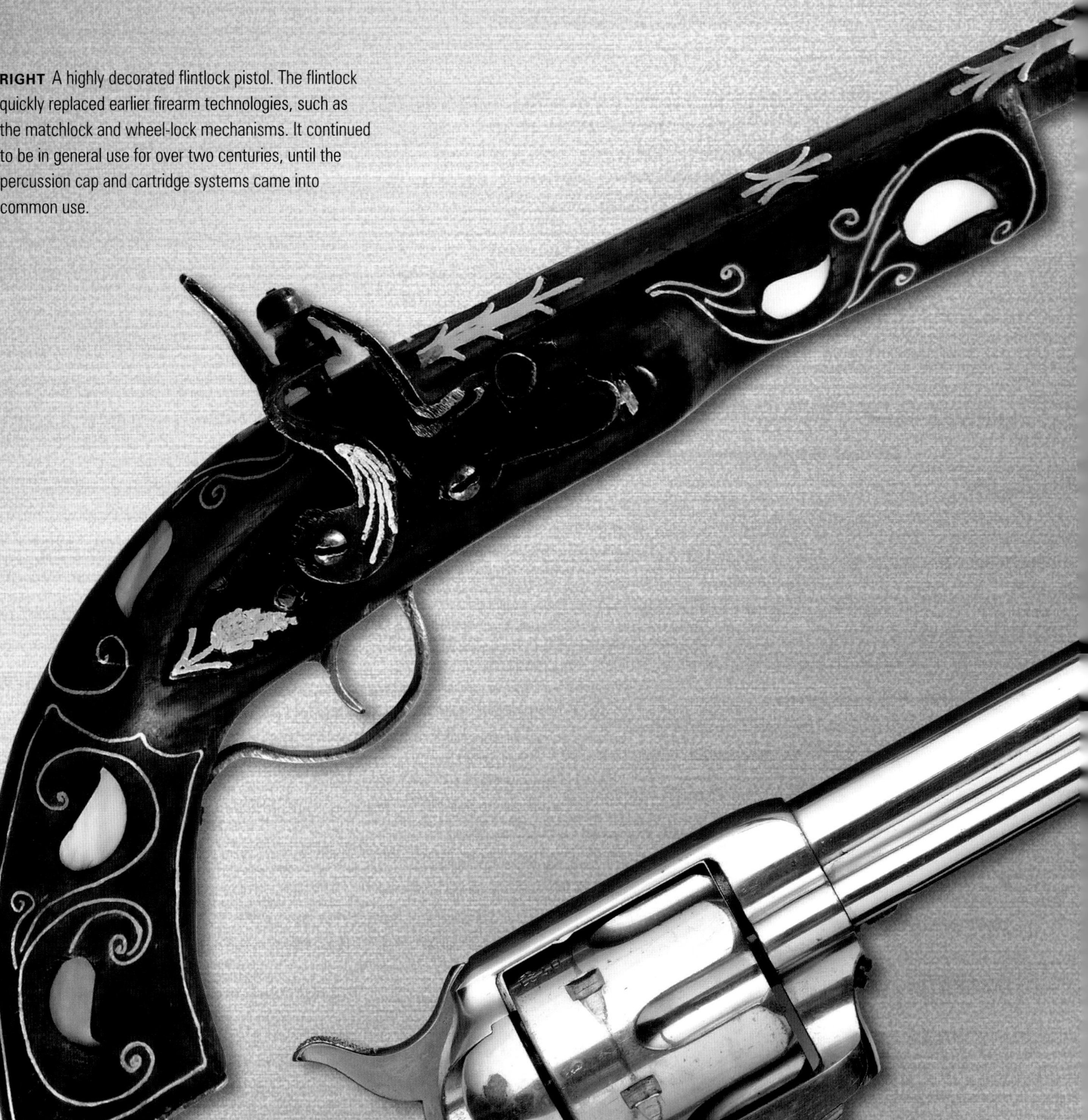

**RIGHT** A highly decorated flintlock pistol. The flintlock quickly replaced earlier firearm technologies, such as the matchlock and wheel-lock mechanisms. It continued to be in general use for over two centuries, until the percussion cap and cartridge systems came into common use.

**RIGHT** This was one of the most famous revolvers of the American Wild West. Designed for the US Cavalry, it was first produced in 1873 and is often known as the "Colt 45".

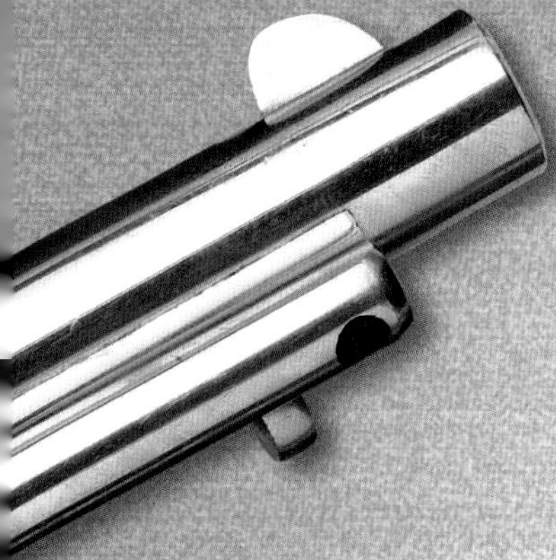

# The early history of arms

This chapter provides a colourful journey, from the early discoveries of chemical compounds that would explode when lit and the use of these powders to fire a projectile, through the development of ever more sophisticated systems for firing weapons. This included matchlock and flintlock mechanisms, and the early forms of today's firearms that are loaded from the rear of the barrel (the breech) and use metal cartridges containing bullet, gunpowder and primer. This section also covers such aspects as the use of firearms for duelling, examines the unique nature of handguns produced by the mostly Islamic countries of the East, and reflects on the arts of ornamentation and engraving that were to complement handgun design and development through the ages.

**ABOVE** From the 18th century, duels could be fought using pistols. Special sets of duelling pistols were crafted for wealthy noblemen. A pistol duel normally took place at dawn. The parties would be placed back to back with loaded weapons in hand. They would walk a set number of paces, turn to face their opponent and shoot. Many pistol duels were to first blood (such as a minor wound) rather than to death.

# The first firearms

The invention of the gun was the logical consequence of the discovery of gunpowder. Once the knowledge of its powerful explosive forces had spread to Europe, probably from China via Islamic Spain, the next challenge was to contain the force and to use it to propel a missile.

### The discovery of gunpowder

Gunpowder was known to the Chinese by the 11th century and the knowledge of it probably came to Europe through Moorish Spain. The earliest definite reference to guns comes from Florence in Italy in the 14th century and the earliest illustration of a gun is to be found in a 14th-century English royal manuscript. These early guns have characteristics that can be traced throughout the history of firearms.

**ABOVE** Roger Bacon, English experimental scientist, philosopher and Franciscan friar. His 13th-century manuscript included an anagram which contained the formula for gunpowder. Scholars such as Bacon received much knowledge from the East via Moorish Spain.

The early history of gunpowder is as confusing as it is interesting. India, China, the Arabs and Western Europe have all laid claim to its invention. Gunpowder was more widely known to consist of saltpetre, charcoal and sulphur. Sifting through the evidence reveals that, while gunpowder was known to Chinese alchemists as early as the 11th century, they were looking for a material that burned rather than propelled missiles. While alchemists of different cultures may have known about gunpowder they may not have understood the correct proportions to use to create explosions.

### Early evidence

The earliest hard evidence for gunpowder is found in European manuscripts of the 13th century. There are references to gunpowder in the *Liber Ignium* of Marcus Graecus, which dates from about 1300, and in the treatise *De Mirabilium Mundi* of Albertus Magnus who died in Cologne in 1280. The best known is in a manuscript of Roger Bacon, written in about 1260. In this *Epistolae de secretis operibus artis et naturae et de nullitate magial* is a Latin anagram that, when solved, can be translated as "seven parts of saltpetre, five of new hazelwood and five of charcoal". This is an effective recipe for gunpowder. There are also references in the *Opus Majus* of 1267, and in the *Opus Tertium* of *c.*1266–68 which describes a form of firework. The method calls for the powder to be enclosed in an instrument of parchment the size of the little finger, somewhat reminiscent of later paper cartridges.

If gunpowder originated in China, it probably came to Western Europe through the alchemical works of Moorish Spain during the first half of the 13th century. The role of the Arabs in the early history of gunpowder and firearms has probably been underestimated. An Arabic treatise found in Leningrad describes arrows or bullets being fired through a tube by gunpowder, but the date of the manuscript has been disputed, so the claim that firearms were invented by the Arabs cannot, at present, be substantiated.

## The Milemete gun

Some early references to guns related to military campaigns. In one of his early incursions into Scotland in his campaign to take the Scottish crown, Edward III of England may have had with him an early form of gun. In a manuscript dated 1326, its author, scholar Walter de Milemete, included a depiction of a vase-shaped gun supported by a trestle. This type of gun was to become more and more commonplace. Protruding from the vase was a large metal arrow. Some kind of wadding was probably placed around its shaft in order to maximize the propellent force. The vase itself would have been formed from cast iron or bronze. The weapon was fired by applying a red-hot iron or something similar to a touch-hole to ignite it. Such devices would come into ever more frequent use from this time onwards.

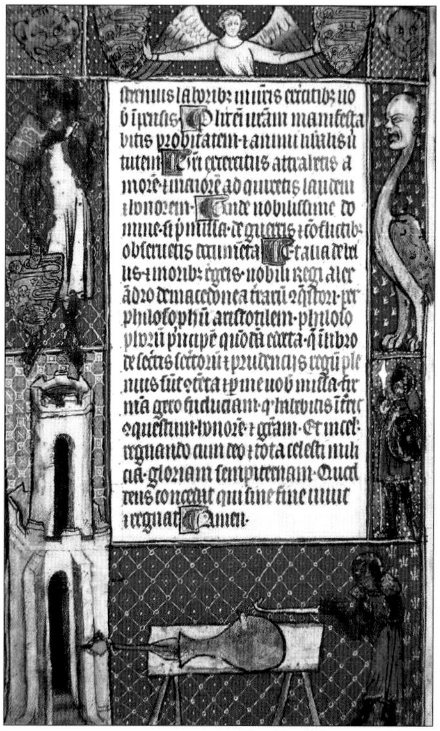

**RIGHT** The earliest-dated picture of a gun, from *De Notabilitatibus, Sapientis et Prudentia* of Walter de Milemete, 1326. More efficient systems of firing guns were soon devised.

### The first gun and prototypes

According to legend, the gun was invented by a German monk known as "Black Berthold", who came from Freiburg in southern Germany. While he was making gunpowder with a mortar and pestle, the mixture exploded, propelling the pestle from the mortar like a bullet, thus giving him the idea for a gun. The monk is a purely legendary figure, but this story of the introduction of firearms may contain an element of truth as it is recorded as early as the 15th century.

There are early accounts of prototype guns in both Chinese and Arab sources. From a 12th-century Chinese source is a description of a bamboo tube filled with gunpowder, which fired arrows. It was mentioned in a military treatise of the 17th century but is based on much earlier sources. Here it was described as a long copper tube containing an arrow, the stock being a short pole. A very similar primitive gun is shown in a 14th-century Arabic manuscript. Many of the early guns were designed to fire arrows rather than other missiles.

In 1326 the Council of Florence decreed that two men should be appointed to manufacture "iron bullets or arrows and metal cannon". Further references of the same year, also from Florence, mention "cannon, iron balls and gunpowder". The earliest precisely datable illustration of a gun, the Milemete gun, also dates from 1326.

The very marked flask-shape of the gun is not just artistic licence but is based on the sound principal of reinforcing the gun at the back, where the initial explosion happens. This lesson was learned the hard way, when guns had burst at this weak point.

**RIGHT** Berthold Schwartz was a fictitious German monk known as "Black Berthold". He was said to have discovered gunpowder around 1320 after experimentation with solidifying quicksilver.

# Early cannons and handguns

It was soon discovered that the vase-like shape of the early guns, like the Milemete gun, was not the most efficient, and that a traditional projectile like an arrow was not best suited to the new invention. A straight, metal tube was soon developed. The next step was to find the most efficient method of lighting the gunpowder. A method of absorbing "recoil" – the force of the gun going backward after the shot was fired – also needed to be found. The effectiveness of these weapons was growing – the handgun, as we know it, had arrived.

**ABOVE** An early iron gun. This long, thin hand cannon is from Vedelspang Castle, Copenhagen. Dated around 1400, it was more dangerous if used as a club.

### First developments

The Milemete gun demonstrated a stage in development whereby the notion of an arrow as a projectile is still in mind. The shape of the arrow, however, was not suited to maximizing the propellant effect of the explosion and, by the end of the 14th century, stone cannon balls were almost always used.

### The Loshult gun

The vase-like feature occurs on the earliest known hand cannon, the Loshult gun, excavated in Sweden in 1861. Cast in bronze, it has a distinctive flask-like shape and also a simple counter-sunk pan around the touch hole to help ignition. It has been dated to the first half of the 14th century. A gun found in the sea near Morko, Sweden, has also been dated to the 14th century. Cast in bronze with a two-stage polygonal barrel, there is a cast bearded figure behind the square pan or touch-hole and a projecting hook below the breech. The hook stopped the recoil when the gun was fired, hence the name "hakenbüchs" (hook can). The surface was engraved with religious texts. The gun was very short and was clearly made as a handgun.

Another early handgun was excavated from Tannenberg Castle in Germany, destroyed in 1399. Made of cast bronze, the gun had a two-stage polygonal barrel. The bore, in front of the powder-chamber where the missile is held, has deliberately been made narrow, probably to increase the force of the explosion. The Tannenberg gun dates from about 1350.

**BELOW** An early gun, dated around 1350, was found near Loshult, Sweden. The Loshult gun looked like a miniature cannon and would have been fired in much the same way as the gun depicted in the Milemete manuscript, i.e. from a trestle.

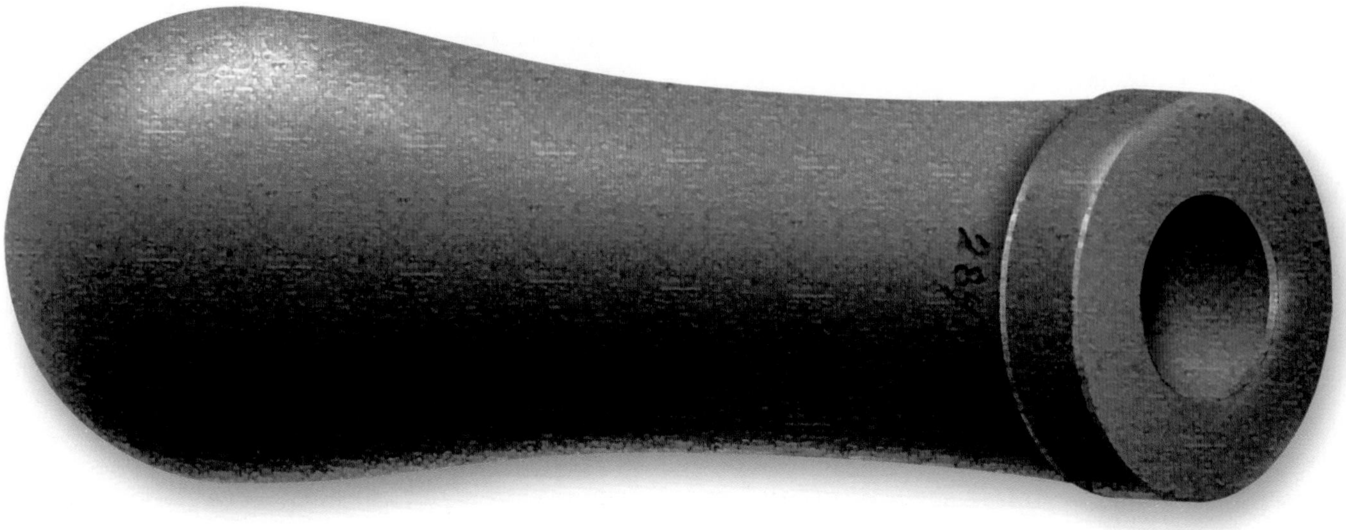

**BELOW** The Morko gun was found on the bed of the Baltic Sea. The hexagonal barrel was similar to many of the early small arms. This gun marks an important stage in the development of the handgun – it does not have the bulbous shape of a small cannon, but instead has a "modern" straight barrel.

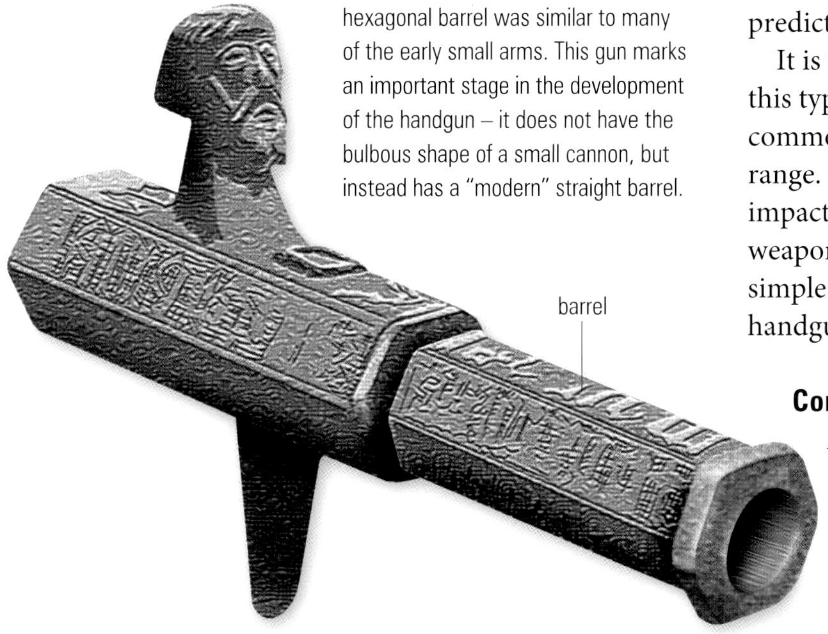


## Design and construction

Both the Milemete and Loshult guns looked more like cannons than handguns and they also comprised a bulbous area at the back. The Morko gun, dating from about the middle of the 14th century, was more recognizable as a handgun, with a straight firing tube, and it was designed to be fired without the use of any supports, such as a trestle. The Morko gun, like the Tannenberg gun, was a straightforward metal tube attached to a wooden stock, which was either a pole or a construction similar to that used for a crossbow. Weapons such as these may have been designed to accept a metal bolt but the Tannenberg gun when excavated was found to be loaded with a lead bullet. A variety of ancient handguns has been found in various locations, some of them in Spain, others in Switzerland, Sweden and England.

## Firing the early guns

The metal tube (or barrel) of a handgun such as the Morko gun or the Tannenberg gun was about 300mm/12in in length. The bore (the interior diameter of the barrel) was about 17mm/0.67in. A handgun had a powder chamber, which was linked to a small hole drilled at right angles. The gunpowder and propellant would have been inserted through the muzzle (the forward end). The gun was probably fired by inserting a red hot wire poker into the touch-hole. Another way of firing would have been to use a slow-burning match fuse. The slow match was usually made up of cord or twine soaked in a potassium nitrate solution. It was then left to dry. When lit, it would burn at a predictably slow rate.

It is thought that a bullet fired from a gun of this type was capable of penetrating the steel armour commonly used at the time, within a reasonable range. This was in addition to the psychological impact on the enemy of the noise and flash of the weapon. The effectiveness of these comparatively simple weapons was not underestimated and the handgun was here to stay.

## Continuing development

As the understanding of the forces involved grew, so did the power and size of the weapons. In due course new designs began to appear to deal with the force of the recoil. Sometimes the handgun was supported on a tripod. Occasionally the stock was not made of wood but was instead formed of a curled metal extension to the main barrel.

**ABOVE** Use of handguns in the 15th century as depicted in *Rudimentum Noviciorum*, Lubeck, 1475. This gun was mounted on a pole and appeared to be lit through a touch-hole.

# Matchlocks

**The matchlock was the first major step forward in developing an efficient firing mechanism that would allow the user to concentrate on holding his weapon with both hands and aiming it effectively. As the power and efficiency of the handgun increased, the wooden stock began to be developed, so that the recoil could be effectively absorbed. Increased weight meant that a pike or forked support between the weapon and ground were used.**

### The serpentine lock

The method of manually igniting the charge by means of a rod that held a piece of metal or glowing tinder, was superseded in the early 15th century by a device known as a serpentine (an angled arm) or serpentine lock. The first mechanical firing mechanism was the matchlock, the basis of which was the serpentine. The mechanism had to be both efficient and robust.

The early matchlock was operated by pressing the lever up to the stock so the match or tinder was pushed into the touch-hole. Unlike the now-traditional ignition designs where the hammer falls forward when the trigger is acted upon, the matchlock's serpentine actually moves backwards to reach the touch-hole. Since the pole stock could be placed under the arm at the shoulder, the gun could now be aimed properly. This development led to changes in the shape of the stock, which became polygonal. Some handguns, however, retained the pole-stock until well into the 15th century. It is possible that the serpentine lock was suggested by the trigger action of a crossbow, which, like the serpentine, was a long lever under the stock which was pressed upwards to release the cord. The polygonal

**BELOW** A drawing of parts of a matchlock. The simple mechanism could work well as long as match and powder were dry.

### Serpentine development

The first recorded illustration of a serpentine lock is from a manuscript dated 1411 (Codex Vindobana 3069) which can be found in the Austrian National Library. This shows the simplicity of the serpentine system, and the straightforward operation of the lever mechanism. The man firing the weapon is able to keep both hands on the stock making aiming and firing easier. It is known that stocks grew in length in order to absorb recoil from firing, and they ranged between just under a metre to 1.5 metres (1.64 yards) in length. As stocks developed, different methods of holding the weapon also evolved.

**LEFT** The gun-wielder from this 14th-century manuscript is firing the weapon from under his arm, but over time firing from the shoulder became more common. The kneeling figure is in the process of casting bullets.

profile of some early gun stocks also resembles those of crossbows. The crossbow was the most powerful hand-held missile weapon then in use, so it was logical for early gunmakers to copy its features.

Some matchlock serpentines included a spring, which would move the arm holding the match more rapidly into the pan. The "match" was normally a length of woven hemp cord boiled in a solution of saltpetre and then allowed to dry. It was literally looped around the fingers. It was carried lit, smouldering ready to ignite the gunpowder. The invention of the matchlock allowed mechanical means to press the glowing end into the touch-hole. In addition the matchlock was a simple mechanism, easy to make and repair and reasonably reliable. It did not, however, resolve the problem of how to ignite the powder without having to carry a constantly glowing match. It also could give away the position of the user to the enemy.

### Fifteenth-century improvements

During the 15th century a number of improvements were made. The touch-hole was moved from the top of the barrel to the side. This led to an improved pan, which was mounted on the side of the barrel and had a hinged cover to protect the powder. As the arm holding the match descended, the flash pan cover moved aside exposing the powder in the pan. Once the powder had been ignited and the gun fired, the pan cover would return to its original position. This ingenious system gave the powder in the pan much greater protection from the effects of wind or rain or from being inadvertently tipped out of the pan. It also meant that the weapon was safeguarded against sparks inadvertently firing the gun before the firer was ready. More rapid action was achieved by the development of the "snap-matchlock" in which the serpentine arm was replaced by a curved match-holder driven by a spring.

**ABOVE** A handgun being discharged. This is a matchlock handgun with a pike rest. Some matchlocks had a disproportionately large stock requiring a support to take the weight.

**BELOW** An ornate matchlock mechanism from the 18th century. Despite the ornate design, the matchlock was operated by the simple process of a lit match igniting the gunpowder.

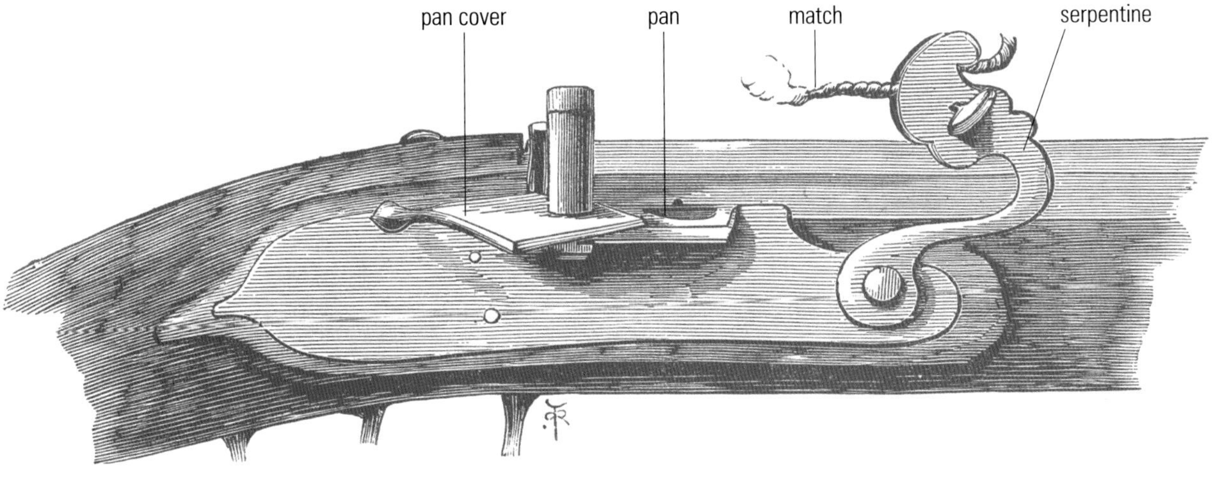

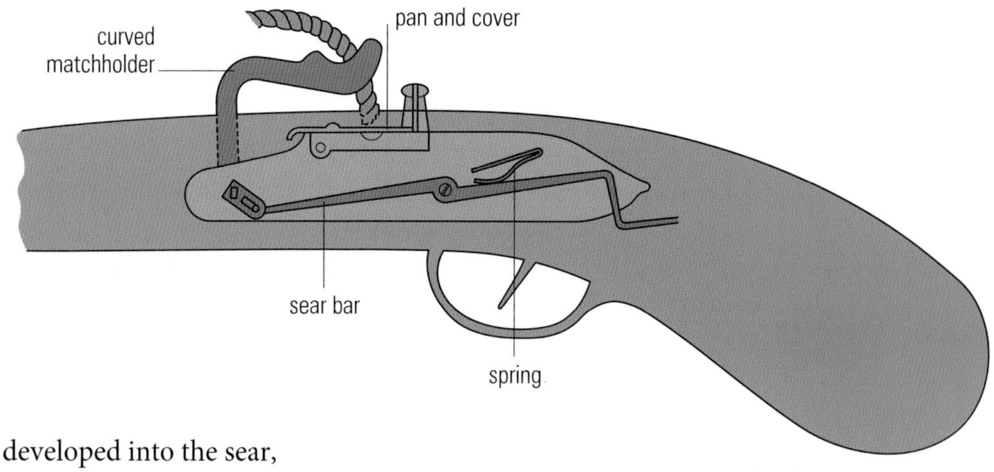


**RIGHT** Cross-section through a firearm showing the internal workings of the snap-matchlock: when the trigger lever was pressed the lighted match fell into the powder in the pan and ignited the charge. The curved matchholder was drawn back against a spring so that when the trigger was pulled the match came down very quickly to the powder.

## The snap-matchlock

By about 1470 the system had developed into the sear, or snap-matchlock. The serpentine was replaced by a curved matchholder driven by a spring. When the trigger lever was pressed, the lighted match fell into the powder in the pan and ignited the charge. The match was held down in the pan through the action of springs and levers mounted on the inside of the lock-plate. The matcholder was then pulled back manually and was held by the sear (a lever or catch). When the trigger was pulled, the sear was withdrawn and the matcholder snapped back into the pan. The mechanism was soon superseded by new inventions in Europe, but was taken to Japan by Portuguese traders in the 16th century and used in Japan until the 19th century. The Japanese snap-matchlock pistol is a scaled-down version of a long arm, fitted with a wide barrel and the matchlock on the side of the stock.

## Advances in gunpowder

The gunpowder used at the time was also known as serpentine. One defect of serpentine powder was that its different constituents, of different mass, tended to separate over time or during movement. The saltpetre and sulphur would settle at the bottom and the charcoal element at the top. This was likely to make ignition less efficient. It was only with the invention of "corned" powder in the early 15th century that this problem was addressed. In this process, the ingredients were all ground and mixed together and then sieved to make sure that all the constituent particles were the same size.

**LEFT** An early 17th-century musketeer fires a matchlock musket. The musket replaced the arquebus, a firearm used from the 15th to the 17th centuries. The matchlock gradually became lighter and more compact in design and more efficient to use.

## The matchlock in warfare

By the 15th century firearms were used to an increasing extent on the battlefield. Improved systems of ignition such as the serpentine lock and the snap-matchlock, together with changes in the shape of guns, made them lighter and easier to use. Improved methods of making barrels included the introduction of rifling within the barrel of the firearm. Rifling refers to the grooves that were created in the barrel of a firearm to produce a spin on the projectile to improve accuracy of the shot.

By the end of the 15th century firearms were playing an increasing role in warfare. The matchlock musket gave the common footsoldier a much better chance of bringing down a swordsman without either of them having to be in contact. The weapon stock began to change to a flattened form that could be placed against the shoulder, one hand gripping the butt and operating the trigger while the other supported the barrel. Assuming the powder did not simply "flash in the pan" (the explosion of gunpowder in the pan), but ignited the charge, in the breech, the bullet was propelled in a cloud of smoke and with a loud bang.

However, the disadvantage was that the matchlock musket was much better suited to use by the infantry than the cavalry. The cavalry needed pistols that could be fired on horseback and could be lit without using

**ABOVE** Matchlock musket from around the late 17th century as painted by the circle of the Master of Calamarca.

a constantly glowing match that was exposed to the weather. However, matchlocks were cheap and simple to produce, and so stayed as part of armed warfare on the battlefield for over 200 years. Although considered obsolete in the 16th century, some matchlocks were still being used during the 18th century.

### Fire-lock mechanisms

Throughout history gunmakers have attempted to improve their weapons and make them easier to hold and shoot. After the development of the matchlock there was a move towards producing something more elegant with a more effective method of ignition. What was required was a device to produce a fire on demand. In the 16th century matchlocks were replaced by fire-lock mechanisms (so-named because they created fire by striking pyrite against steel). Early versions used the wheel-lock mechanism, but the more efficient flintlock mechanism soon followed.

### Development of the pistol

Although some of the early matchlocks were small, essentially they were not "small arms". They were more closely aligned with small shoulder – or long arms. Early pistols were often referred to as "small arquebusses". The arquebus was a small firearm used during the 15th to 17th centuries, using the matchlock mechanism. The arquebus would later slowly be succeeded by the larger musket, a muzzle-loading shoulder gun with a long barrel, beginning in the 16th century. Surviving examples of small handguns or pistols fitted with matchlocks are extremely rare and were not widely used, except in Japan where the snap-matchlock was in common use. The term "pistol" did not come into general use before the 16th century. Its origins are unclear. It may have developed from the word *pistolet* which in the 14th century meant both a dagger and a firearm.

**ABOVE** A Japanese matchlock musket from the 18th century. The snap-matchlock mechanism was used in Japan until the 19th century.

# The wheel-lock

In the early years of the 16th century there came an invention that was a milestone in the history of firearms – the wheel-lock. The matchlock had relied on a lighted match which was awkward to hold and entirely susceptible to the weather. It was normally held between the fingers and was dangerous to use. Seventeenth-century accounts tell of careless gunners going to replenish powder, forgetting that they were holding a match, and as a result blowing up entire powder magazines. The wheel-lock solved this problem, as the gun could simply be aimed and fired. It remained in use until about 1650.

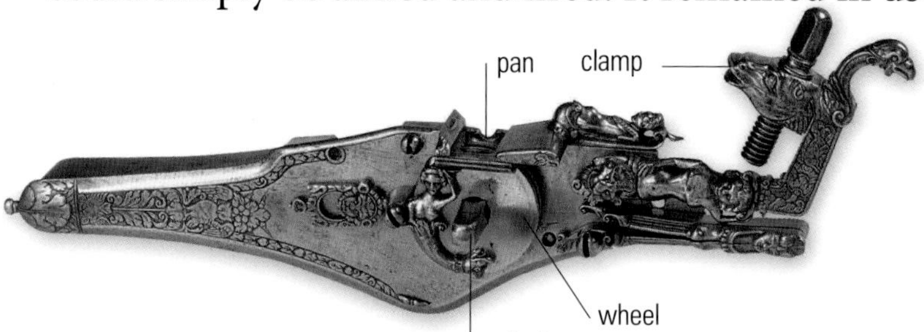


**LEFT** An example of the revolutionary wheel-lock mechanism. Invented in the early 16th century, this development represented a firearm milestone. It was safer and more convenient than a matchlock, since there was no longer a need to keep a smouldering match close to loose gunpowder.

### How a wheel-lock worked

Whereas the matchlock was an incredibly simple design, the wheel-lock's internal workings were much more complicated. The wheel-lock worked like a giant cigarette lighter. A wheel cut with slots turned against a piece of iron pyrite, producing a shower of sparks that ignited the powder in the pan. The wheel was turned by a short chain. Protruding from the wheel was a spindle. A spanner was used to wind the mechanism and this depressed the spring and wound the chain round the spindle. When the wheel was fully wound it was locked by a series of levers. Pulling the trigger withdrew the locking lever and the wheel then revolved around the pyrite. The pyrite was held in jaws at the end of a curved arm, which was lowered manually against the wheel. The pan had a sliding cover operated by a button. In later wheel-locks the pan-cover slid back automatically when the trigger was pulled.

### An Italian invention

Recent research by arms historian Claude Blair has established that the wheel-lock was almost certainly invented and first used in the province of Friuli in north-east Italy, in the early years of the 16th century. The letters of Luigi da Porto (1485–1529), an author and military commander in Venice, provided the evidence. In 1510 he was on campaign in Friuli and visited the city of Cividale where he observed some of the citizens using handguns for "shooting little birds high in flight" and also fish in clear water. He also describes an action between Venetian and Imperial German forces in which "little guns", which resembled iron maces, were used to great effect. He describes the guns as being "three spars long", although this does not translate to any known measurement.

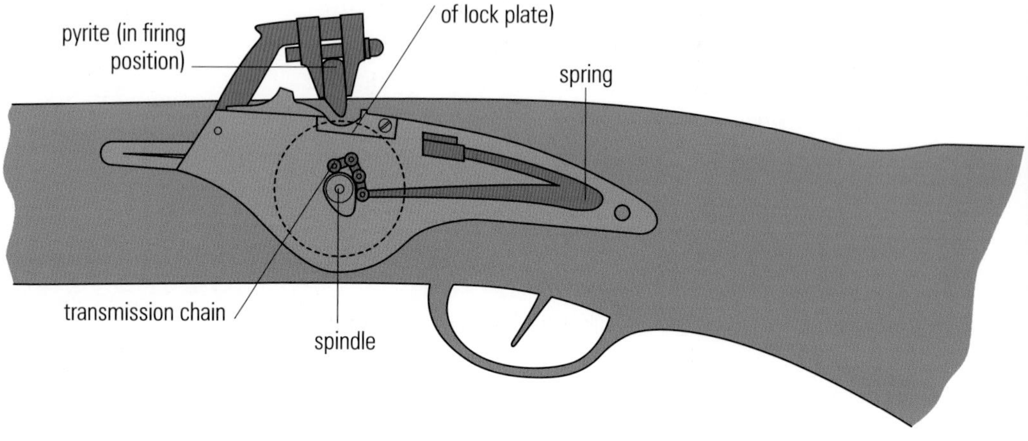


**RIGHT** Cross-section through a firearm showing the workings of the wheel-lock. A spring was connected to the wheel's axle by a short length of chain. The axle was wound back to put the spring under tension. When ready to fire, the trigger was pulled. The wheel was released and would spin rapidly, scraping against the pyrite. White-hot particles from the pyrite fell into the flash pan, igniting its powder and then the main charge.

**BELOW** French wheel-lock pistol. The elaborate engraving and high-quality materials are typical of French pistol manufacture. They reflect the complexity of the wheel-lock mechanism, which required a high level of craftsmanship.

**RIGHT** Wheel-lock six-shot revolver from Germany, dated around 1600. This multi-barrelled firearm has a six-chambered cylinder that needs to be rotated by hand.

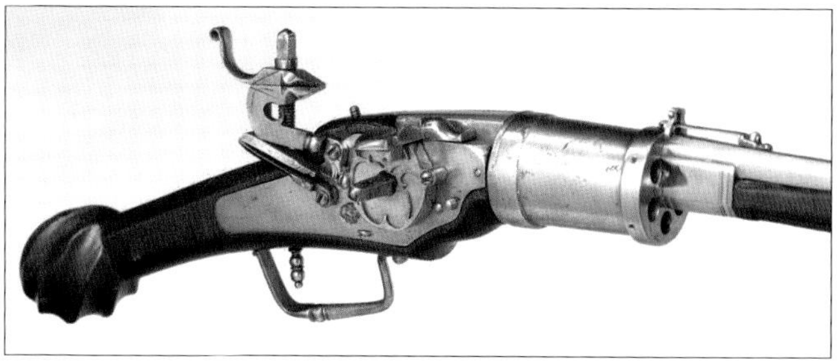

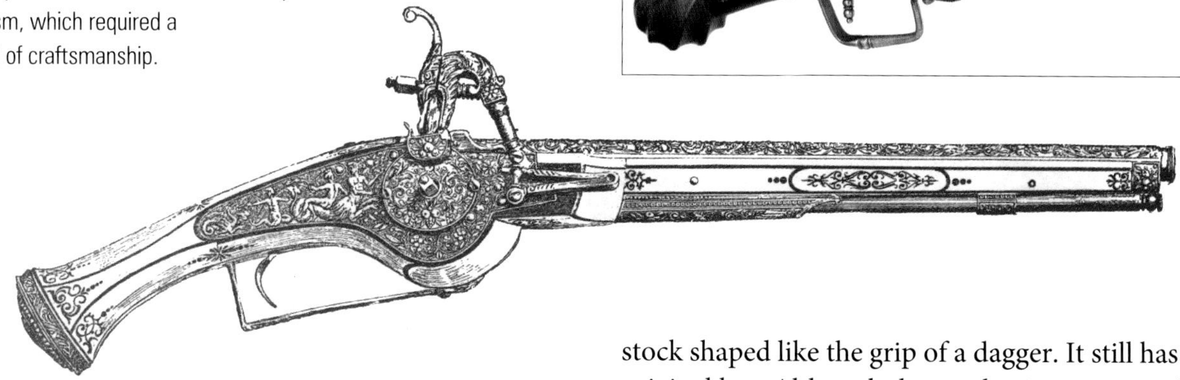

It is almost impossible to shoot birds in flight or fish in water with a matchlock, as the "flash in the pan" (the explosion of gunpowder in the pan) acted as a warning. This led inevitably to the conclusion that the little guns must have been wheel-locks. As Friuli province belonged to Venice, it also explains why some of the earliest examples of the wheel-lock are to be found in the Doge's armoury in the Palazzo Ducale, Venice. Two of these are horseman's axes, perhaps the "iron maces" that Luigi da Porto saw in Cividale. These have been dated to about 1520.

### The wheel-lock in Germany

German gunsmiths also seem to have adopted the wheel-lock early in the 16th century, as there is an account in 1507 of a servant being given money by the steward of Cardinal Ippolite d'Est to go to Germany and buy "a gun of the type that is ignited with a stone". Another reference dating from 1515 describes a young German accidentally shooting a girl in the neck with a gun that "fired itself". An indication of how novel and dangerous wheel-locks were considered to be in the early 16th century is the edict issued in 1517 by Maximilian I (1459–1519) banning their use in the Habsburg empire.

The earliest-dated wheel-lock pistol was made for the Emperor Charles V (1519–56), almost certainly by a German gunsmith. It is dated 1534 and has a stock shaped like the grip of a dagger. It still has its original key. Although the mechanism remained basically the same, there were changes to the shape of the stock of wheel-lock pistols. By the end of the 16th century the stock was angular; one type of German wheel-lock, the "puffer", which was fashionable in the 1580s, had a stock terminating in a large ball. This allowed it to be drawn from large holsters, which were then fashionable. Wheel-locks were in use until the last quarter of the 17th century, but were being superseded by other forms of ignition by the 1650s.

**RIGHT** A horse soldier with a wheel-lock pistol, from the *Kunstbuchlin* by Jost Amman, Frankfurt, 1599. Although the development of the wheel-lock was not widely adopted because they were expensive to produce, they allowed pistols to be aimed and fired with one hand.

# The snaphance

An important development in the history of firearms, the snaphance led directly to the invention of the flintlock. The snaphance was an improvement on most of the previous systems of ignition. It was almost certainly a German invention based on the snap-matchlock. Invented in the 1540s, it was rapidly adopted throughout Europe. Local variants of the snaphance lock were developed throughout the 17th century.

## Early snaphance designs

In the 16th century a suitable replacement for the wheel-lock needed to be found for military use. It required something cheaper and simpler than the wheel-lock. The snaphance lock was invented in about 1540. A Florentine ordnance dated 1547 describes some guns having locks of this form. The earliest snaphance lock known is to be found on a gun in the Royal Armoury, Stockholm. This is one of a group of thirty-five documented as having been fitted with these new locks at the Royal workshops at Arboga in central Sweden in 1556. The miquelet was a Mediterranean version of the snaphance lock. Both the snaphance lock and the miquelet played an important part in the development of the flintlock, the next step forward in the development of firearms.

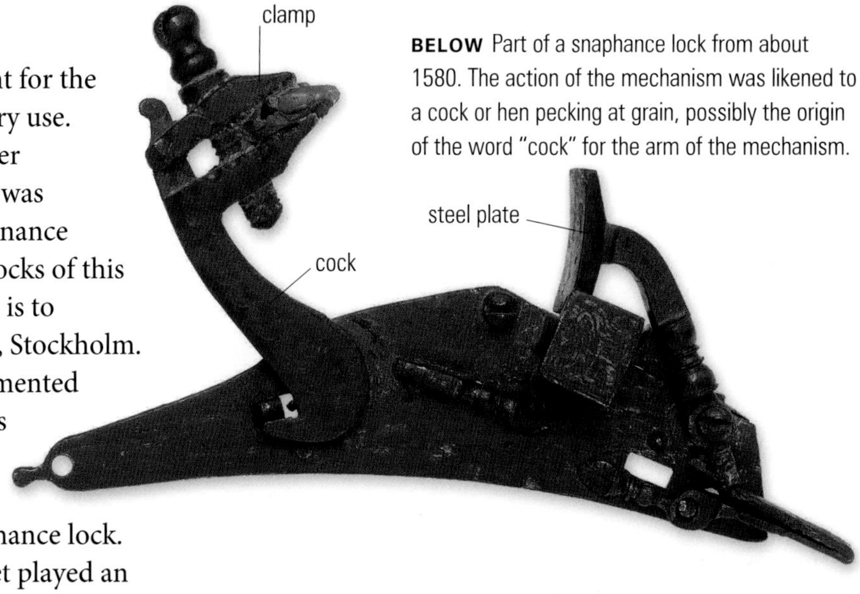


**BELOW** Part of a snaphance lock from about 1580. The action of the mechanism was likened to a cock or hen pecking at grain, possibly the origin of the word "cock" for the arm of the mechanism.

The name of the snaphance lock probably derived from a Dutch expression describing its action – like that of a pecking hen or cock ("snap haan"). Although this suggested a Dutch origin for the lock, the evidence seems to contradict this, as some of the earliest known snaphances are German and this type of lock was almost certainly a German improvement on the earlier snap-matchlock.

**BELOW** Cross-section through a firearm showing the workings of the snaphance lock. The lock was invented in around 1540. In the snaphance system, the flint was held in a clamp at the end of the cock. Once the trigger was pulled, the cock was released and, under strong pressure, the flint struck against the steel plate (or battery). White-hot steel shavings were produced that fell into the flash pan and ignited the priming powder. The steel could be retained in a "safe" position, forward of the pan if required. The cock could not then cause a spark if accidentally released.

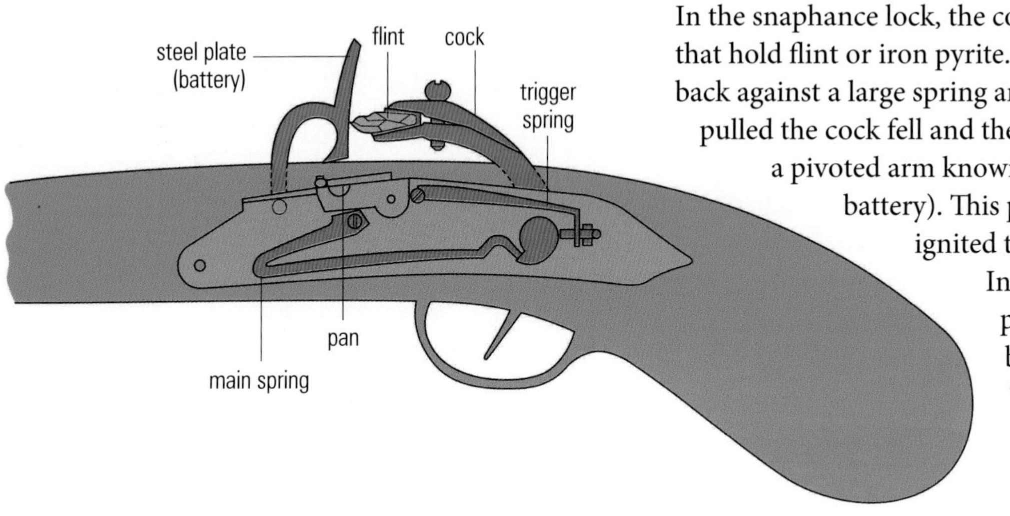


## The workings of the snaphance

In the snaphance lock, the cock was fitted with jaws that hold flint or iron pyrite. The cock was pulled back against a large spring and when the trigger was pulled the cock fell and the pyrites or flint struck a pivoted arm known as the steel plate (or battery). This produced sparks which ignited the powder in the pan. In its earliest form the pan-cover had to be opened before pressing the trigger. There were variations of the lock throughout Europe.

### The miquelet or patilla

Another form of snaphance was the Mediterranean lock or miquelet, widely used in southern Europe and northern Africa. The Spanish version of this lock was known as a patilla lock. At least one writer on Spanish firearms in the late 18th century declared that the miquelet was a Spanish invention, although the evidence contradicts this. The snaphance was probably introduced to Spain in the 1570s. The main characteristics of the Spanish snaphance were the large external mainspring, which acted on the heel of the cock, and the steel plate (battery) made in two parts so that the front could be replaced. The steel plate was cut with a series of vertical grooves. The most noticeable feature, however, is the form of the jaws, which were long and rectangular and held together by a screw with a large open ring at the top.

The snaphance was most widely used in Italy. It had its own local variation – the Roman lock – which had a mainspring operating on the end of the cock, and two sears to allow for the half-cock and full-cock position. It had a horizontal sear and the usual separate pan-cover and steel plate. This type of lock possibly derived from English locks, which were very popular in Italy in the 17th century.

### The Baltic lock

Snapping-lock guns were mechanically simpler and much more reliable than wheel-locks. One of the earliest forms of snaphance was known as the Baltic lock, characterized by prominent jaws held by a screw, a cock formed as a long bar with shallow downward curve and an extension at the back. This extension caught on a sear which operated horizontally through the lock. The mainspring was mounted on the outside of the lock-plate.

### The Netherlandish lock

There were local variations of the snaphance produced in the Low Countries, and in England and Scotland. The Netherlandish lock had a cock with a projection at the rear, which connected with a sear. The pan-cover opened automatically when the lock fell and the steel was attached to the end of a pivoting arm. The Netherlands developed a trade in the lock.

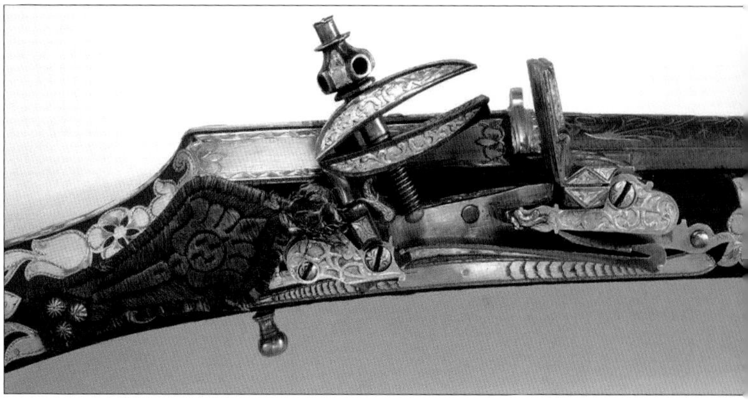

**ABOVE** A miquelet lock sporting gun from Algeria. Sometimes known as the Mediterranean lock, the miquelet was characterized by large jaws that held the flint, and by a large main spring.

### The Scottish lock

There is some evidence to show that the snaphance was known in the early 17th century as a Scottish lock. With their engraved brass stocks and locks, Scottish firearms have always been appreciated as curiosities and enjoyed wide distribution in the 16th and 17th centuries. The two earliest Scottish snaphances known are a pair with left- and right-handed locks in the armoury of the Electors of Saxony in Dresden. They are dated 1598.

### The English lock

A type of snaphance found on English firearms of the 1630s is known as the English lock. This could be engaged at the half-cock position. This was a safety device for the lock. Like the Baltic lock, the English lock has a back-catch, which is caught in a notch cut into the back of the cock.

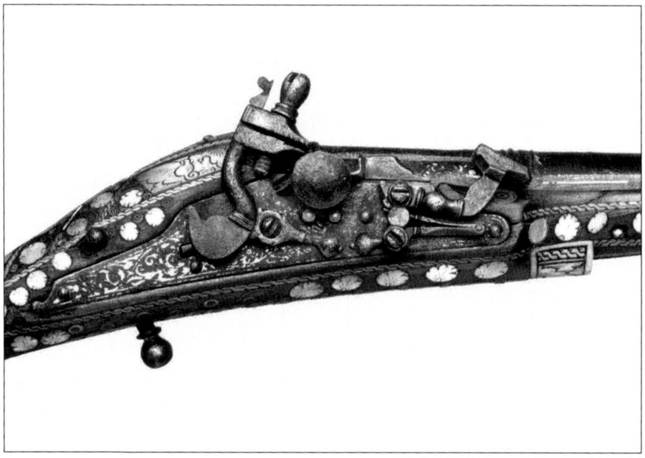

**ABOVE** A highly decorated 16th-century snaphance.The pistol shows the mechanism's high level of sophistication. The flintlock that was developed during the 17th century was less complex to produce.

# The early flintlock

**The invention of the flintlock in the early 17th century brought together the best features of the local snaphance designs. The flintlock was comparatively simple and very efficient, and was widely used on pistols and long guns. It originated in France but, by the middle of the 17th century, it was in use in most European countries. Because of its popularity the flintlock was in service for over 200 years and was still being made in the 1830s.**

### The first flintlocks

The flintlock was a development of the earlier snaphance. The early mechanism, sometimes called a doglock, has the steel and pan-cover made as one unit. The sear moves vertically, engaging in two notches cut in the tumbler (a steel cam attached to the axis shaft of the cock). These notches give either half-cock or full-cock as required, the safety position being half-cock.

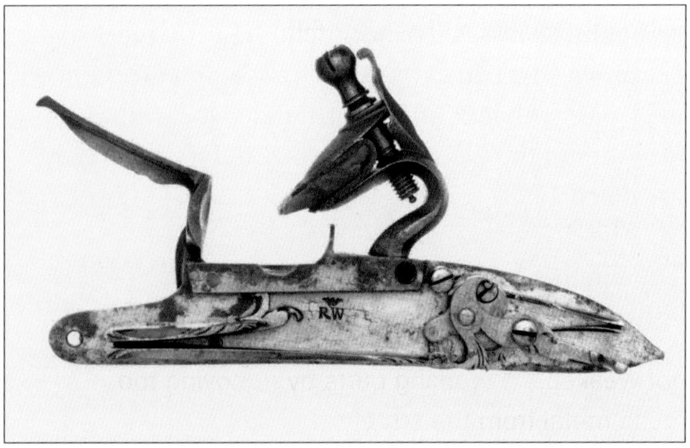

**ABOVE** An English flintlock mechanism from London of around 1775. The flintlock mechanism was relatively straightforward and reliable. It became the primary means of ignition for muskets and pistols for the best part of 300 years.

To fire the weapon the cock was pulled back to full-cock and the trigger was pulled.The flint struck the steel, which opened the pan lid and created a spark which fell into the powder. The powder ignited and set off the main charge of powder which was placed in the barrel, with the propellant, such as a ball.

The flintlock was almost certainly invented by a member of the le Bourgeoys family who worked in Lisieux, Normandy. Jean, Pierre and Marin le Bourgeoys had a workshop which specialized in the production of mechanical devices such as locks and watches, and Marin was mechanic to the king. The earliest datable flintlock mechanism is to be found on a French royal gun from the famous cabinet d'armes of Louis XIII. The stock was inlaid with the royal cipher and the barrel was stamped with the mark of Pierre le Bourgeoys. As Pierre died in 1627, the flintlock is likely to have originated sometime in the 1620s.

The earliest recorded pistol using the flintlock system is a revolver in the Kremlin armoury, Moscow. It was made by a Russian gunmaker named Pervusha Isaev who worked in the Kremlin armoury around 1625 and had clearly come across contemporary French flintlocks.

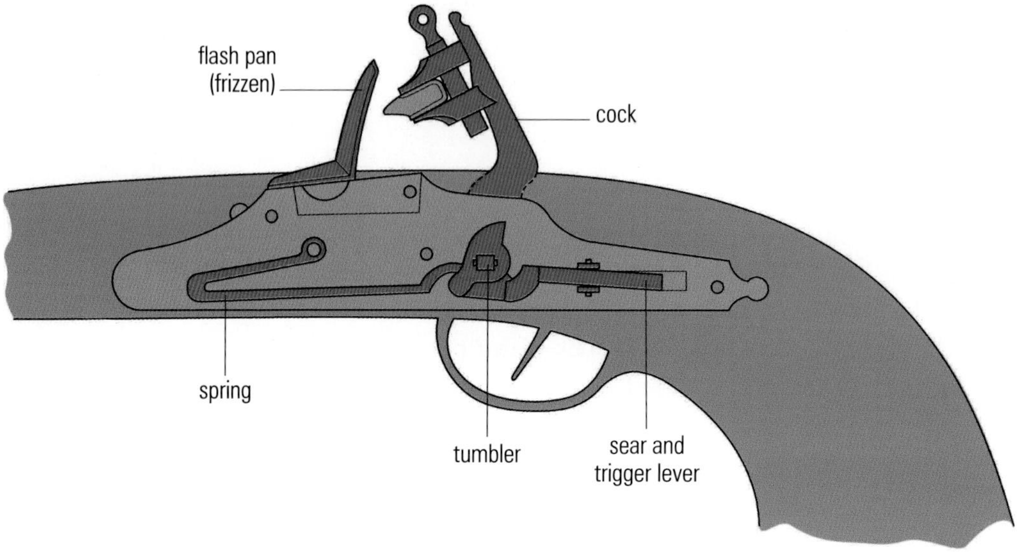


**RIGHT** Cross-section through a firearm showing the workings of the flintlock. The flash pan, or frizzen, is filled with priming powder and then closed to protect it.The cock holding the flint is then drawn back to half-cock. In this mode the weapon cannot be fired. To fire the weapon the cock is pulled back to full-cock. When the trigger is pulled the flint strikes the steel, which opens the pan lid and creates a spark which falls into the powder. The powder ignites and sets off the main charge, which has been placed in the barrel.

### Common features

Flintlocks dating from the first half of the 17th century have several easily recognizable characteristics. The lock-plate was flat, attached to the stock by two screws, and the upper and lower edges were usually parallel. In early examples the lock-plate extended downwards at the centre, revealing a feature found on the earlier wheel-locks. The cock was flat, with a long, curved narrow neck and forward jaws to hold the flint. Early flintlock pistols were very long, the barrels supported by a full stock which was flat and curved gently at the butt-end, which made the early pistols appear very graceful. Initially the butt-cap (its base) had a short spur extending down the stock. By the end of the 17th century this spur extended almost to the lock-plate. In about 1630 a lock-plate and cock of concave section were introduced, for added strength. After 1660 the profile of the lock-plate became concave. It is these features that enable the specialist to date flintlock pistols accurately.

### National characteristics

With the spread of the flintlock across Western Europe after the 1630s, national characteristics began to emerge. Each workshop had its own special, easily recognizable style. France dominated the firearms trade in the early 17th century and many fine flintlock pistols that are preserved in the famous armouries of Europe were made by the gunmakers of Paris.

In Scotland the true flintlock was not introduced until about 1700, the earlier snaphance being preferred. The shape of Scottish pistols was always very distinct and the flintlock is found on pistols with the characteristic heart-shape and ram's horn butt.

By the middle of the 17th century the form of the flintlock was fully developed and it changed little over the next century. One technical feature that was found on some later flintlocks was the *detent*. This was a small, hinged lever attached to a tumbler, the mechanism which held or released the power of the mainspring on the cock. The *detent* stopped the sear from going to the half-cock position as the cock fell.

### Decoration

The stock of a flintlock pistol could be elaborately carved and decorated. One very distinctive group of pistols made by the gunmakers of Maastricht in the Low Countries in the 1650s have stocks of carved ivory, the butt-caps terminating in carved classical heads with helmets in the Baroque style.

Italian flintlock pistols of the latter part of the 17th century are also very distinctive. Gunmaking centres like Brescia in northern Italy were famous for their firearms. A feature of their work is the use of chiselled, engraved and pierced steel to decorate the stock. The locks are chiselled in low relief with flowers and animals, and the butt-plates are decorated with finely pierced and engraved mounts. Engraving was a decorative technique widely used on the mounts and locks of firearms because it did not weaken the working parts by removing too much metal from the structure.

Compared to the work of continental gunsmiths, the products of English makers during the 17th century were comparatively modest, the decoration being usually limited to rather naïve engraving, although pierced silver butt-caps are occasionally found on late 17th-century English flintlocks.

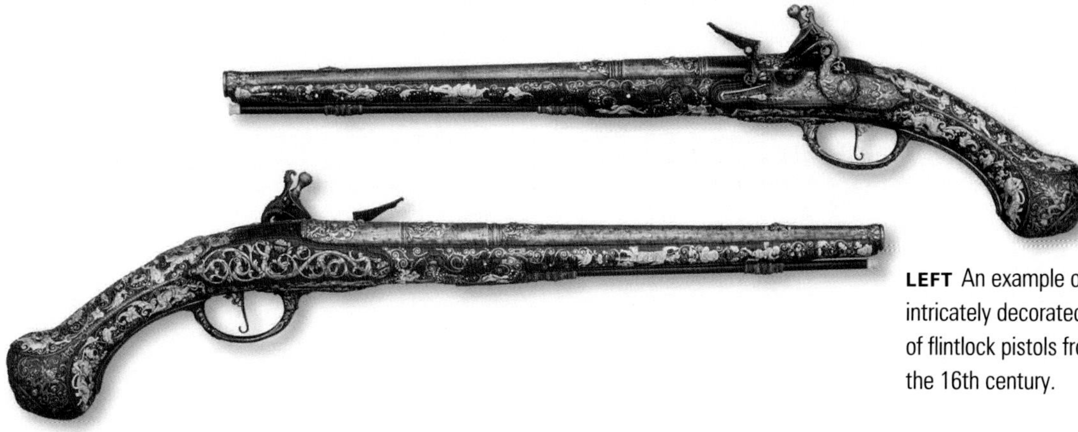

**LEFT** An example of an intricately decorated pair of flintlock pistols from the 16th century.

# Breech-loaders and early revolvers

As the development of the handgun continued, the minds of both craftsmen and gun-users turned to the problem of how to fire more shots while taking the least amount of time to reload. Both the breech-loading system for pistols and early revolvers were attempts to improve efficiency in this area.

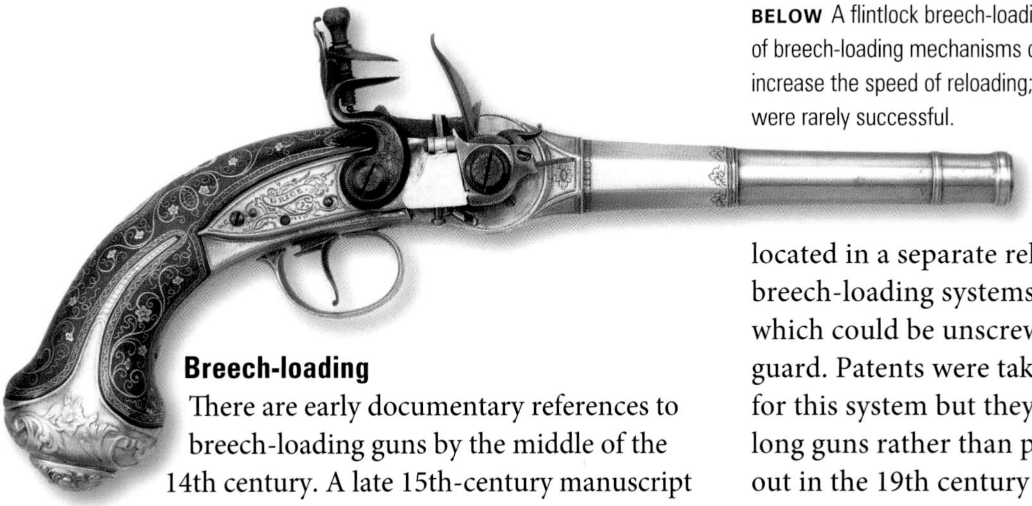

**BELOW** A flintlock breech-loading magazine pistol from 1780. The use of breech-loading mechanisms demonstrated the continual quest to increase the speed of reloading; however, with powder and ball they were rarely successful.

### Breech-loading

There are early documentary references to breech-loading guns by the middle of the 14th century. A late 15th-century manuscript from the University Library at Evlangen in Germany illustrates some breech-loading handguns with separate reloadable chambers. The earliest surviving breech-loading firearms date from the early 16th century. These generally have a hinged section at the breech which can be opened to allow a reloadable chamber containing powder and ball to be inserted. A carbine (a small firearm) made for Henry VIII of England, dated 1537, is of this type.

### The turn-off barrel

Another form of breech-loader used a system in which the barrel could be unscrewed. This was widely used in England during the 17th and 18th centuries, particularly on "Queen Anne"-style flintlock pistols. It became apparent that greater accuracy could be achieved if a large ball was used with a rifled barrel that unscrewed. A rifled barrel had a number of grooves that have been cut, pressed or forged into the barrel of the weapon to stabilize the projectile. It is recorded that Prince Rupert hit the weathercock of St Mary's church in Stafford, England in 1642, twice in succession, using rifle-barrelled pistols.

Barrels could also be hinged so that they "broke" rather like a modern shotgun. When the trigger-guard was pulled back it revealed a locking-catch on the top of the barrel. The charge and ball were located in a separate reloadable chamber. The best breech-loading systems relied on a vertical plug which could be unscrewed by turning the trigger-guard. Patents were taken out in the 18th century for this system but they were used almost entirely on long guns rather than pistols. Patents were also taken out in the 19th century for barrels that swivelled and chambers that pivoted.

### The Roman-candle system

The problem of making a firearm that could fire a series of shots was solved initially by increasing the number of barrels. One such firearm with multiple barrels was known as the "infernal machine", and its use in 1835 shows that creating a multi-shot firearm was a long and imperfect process. The infernal machine was a 25-barrel volley gun built by Giuseppe Marco Fieschi in his failed assassination attempt on King Louis Philippe I of France on 28 July 1835. The original gun is now on display at the Musée des Archives Nationales in Paris, France. However, by the 16th century the idea of the super-imposed load was developed. It was known as the "Roman-candle system", named after a firework that threw out a series of burning balls. A series of charges were placed next to each other, the bullets being pierced and loaded with fuse. In theory, when the first charge was fired, the ignition should have passed to the one behind it, firing the charges in a measured series. This system was used on specially designed wheel-lock pistols which fired three shots, but needed three separate locks. A 16-shot repeating rifle dating to 1580 that uses two flintlock mechanisms to set off the super-imposed shots is in the collection of the National Firearms Museum in Fairfax, Virginia.

### French four-shot repeater

In the 1630s a clockmaker of Grenoble in France produced a repeater that could fire four shots from a single barrel. In order to prevent all the charges going off together – a major problem with superimposed loads – the pistol had to be carefully loaded with tight-fitting wads and balls to separate each charge.

### The sliding lock

Another system developed in the 1780s for flintlock pistols was known as the sliding lock. Four shots could be fired from four touch-holes, the lock being slid along the lock plate on a bar to connect with each touch-hole.

### Magazine systems

Before the invention of the cartridge that contained powder, ball and primer, a repeater had to have separate "magazines" for the powder and ball. In the mid-17th century a Florentine gunmaker, Michele Lorenzoni, developed a repeating system for pistols that used separate magazines for the powder and ball. It also had a priming magazine on the lock. The pistol was primed and cocked by means of a lever on the side, powder and ball passing into the chamber when the pistol was raised and lowered. Versions of this system were made in England as late as 1800.

The magazine system developed by the Kalthoff family in the 1640s is only found on long guns, although a version was used on pistols made by the German gunsmith Sigmund Klett.

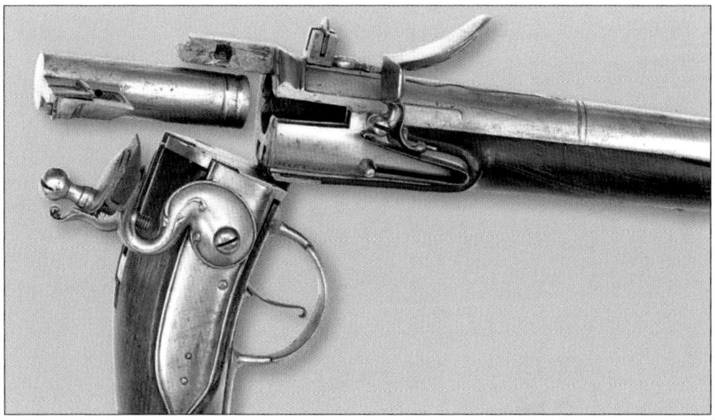

**ABOVE** A flintlock breech-loading gun from around 1690. Breech- loading of the powder and ball led the way to new developments such as the metal cartridge, shown above, which would replace the powder, ball and primer and eventually make the flintlock mechanism obsolete.

### The early revolver

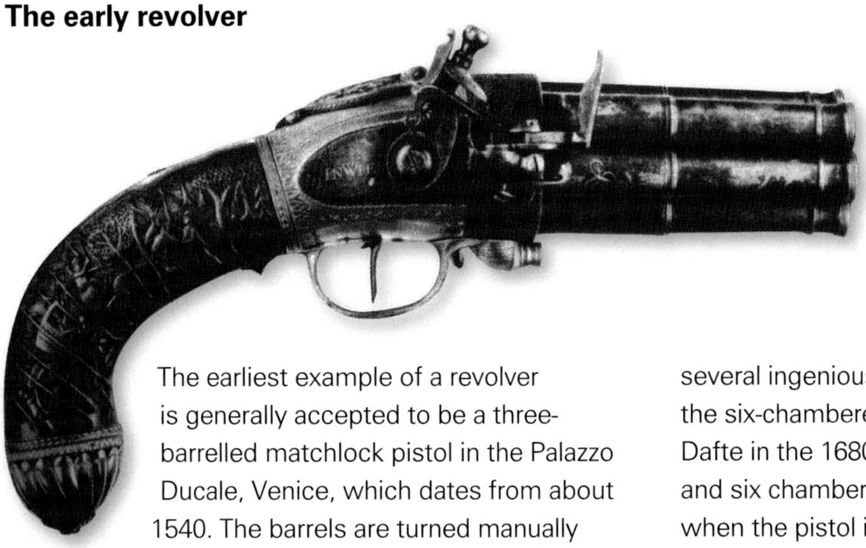

**LEFT** The seven-barrel revolving flintlock. The introduction of revolving barrels meant it was no longer necessary to reload after each shot, though the primer had to be replaced in the flash pan. The system would work better with the percussion cap lock.

The earliest example of a revolver is generally accepted to be a three-barrelled matchlock pistol in the Palazzo Ducale, Venice, which dates from about 1540. The barrels are turned manually and locked in place by a spring catch. Another early revolver is the three-barrelled wheel-lock pistol etched with devices associated with the Emperor Charles V. The pistol is of steel and fires steel darts from small-calibre barrels. A wing-nut at the end of the stock allows the barrels to be moved and locked. Firearms with revolving cylinders and single barrels were known by 1600, and the 17th and 18th centuries saw several ingenious versions. One of the best known is the six-chambered snaphance revolver made by John Dafte in the 1680s. It has a brass barrel and cylinder and six chambers, each of which aligns with the barrel when the pistol is cocked. The Swiss gunsmith James Gorgo also made a revolver in the late 17th century with three chambers, the cylinder being released by pulling up the trigger guard. The late 18th century saw the development of the pepperbox (an early form of revolving repeating pistol), but it had been anticipated in the 1730s with the five-barrel pistol made by Johan Gottfried Kolbe. It was manually cocked for each shot, the barrels rotating when the pistol was cocked.

# Flintlock development

The invention of the flintlock was to have a transforming effect on world history. Although imperfect in many ways and liable to misfire, the flintlock's success was based on its essential simplicity and ease of maintenance. The testament to its success was that the flintlock remained the basic ignition system for a pistol or musket for over 200 years.

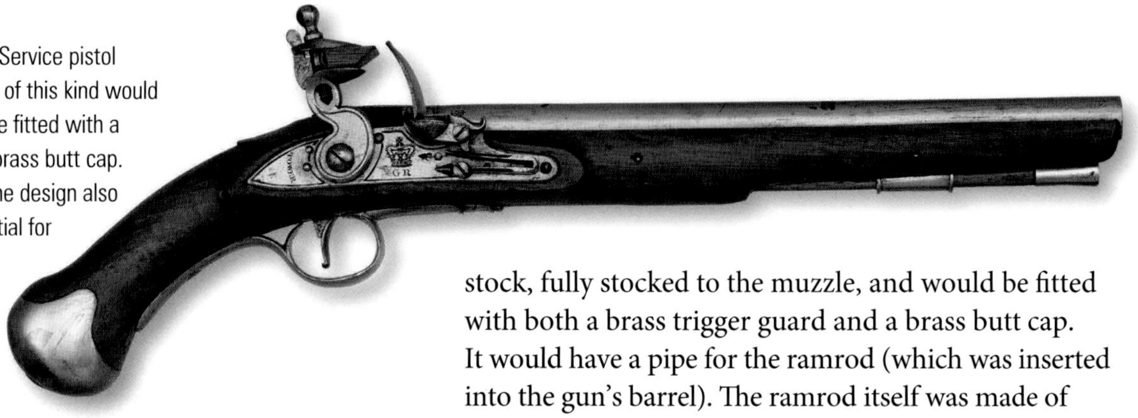

**RIGHT** A Royal Navy Sea Service pistol from 1805. A typical pistol of this kind would have a walnut stock and be fitted with a brass trigger guard and a brass butt cap. The elegant simplicity of the design also speaks of reliability, essential for seamen in battle.

### Flintlock pistols

The flintlock pistol had a comparatively short range and, as it was often not rifled, it was also not very accurate. It was normally used as a close-range back-up to the sword or cutlass, as a self-defence weapon, or for duelling.

During the 18th century, a pattern of Sea Service pistols began to emerge in the Royal Navy, and these were often used by boarding parties, in addition to the cutlass, or they could be used to repel boarders. These pistols, some of which were manufactured by Richard Wilson in England, were either produced in 300mm/12in long form or 225mm/9in short form, the latter being better suited to the mêlée of a boarding party. A typical Sea Service pistol would have a walnut stock, fully stocked to the muzzle, and would be fitted with both a brass trigger guard and a brass butt cap. It would have a pipe for the ramrod (which was inserted into the gun's barrel). The ramrod itself was made of wood and had a brass tip. The pistol would have a steel trigger and there was also a steel belt hook fitted on the side. The hook would have made the pistol easy to carry and to replace on the belt when it had been fired.

**ABOVE** The flintlock pistol was highly regarded by pirates and carried when boarding ships. However, reloading was so slow that pirates often used the pistol's butt as a club.

Apart from its use by the navy, the flintlock pistol was also used by cavalry in the 18th and 19th centuries. It was, of course, impossible to reload while in the midst of a charge or a mêlée with the enemy, so the pistol would normally be fired in the first instance when reasonably close to the enemy lines, to cause as much damage and confusion as possible, and the cavalry cutlass (a short, curving sword) would then be used for close-quarter action.

Like the Sea Service Pistol, the British also introduced a standard type of cavalry pistol in 1796. Called the New Land Cavalry Pistol, it was designed for units such as the Royal Horse Artillery. Fitted with a flat butt and a ring to make it easy to carry when not in use, it also had a ramrod that swivelled to make it easier and quicker to reload when on horseback.

### Huguenot gunmakers in England

Compared with guns made in France, which was one of the chief centres of gunmaking in Europe, English guns were relatively plain in design. Strangely enough, this characteristic may not be entirely native to England for many Huguenot gunmakers came to England as refugees in the 17th century and they would have had a significant influence on the design of English guns.

### Pocket pistols

Flintlock pistols, however, were not all designed for the derring-do of the battlefield or the high seas. Gunmakers were also conscious of a market that continues to be lively today – for discreet, elegant weapons to be used in self-defence. In the days of highwaymen, this was a useful asset. Bunney of London, for example, is known to have manufactured a 150mm/6in ladies' gold pistol with an elegantly worked stock. Such a weapon could be easily concealed about the person and used to devastating effect if necessary. There is also a man's version in plainer style of the same proportions.

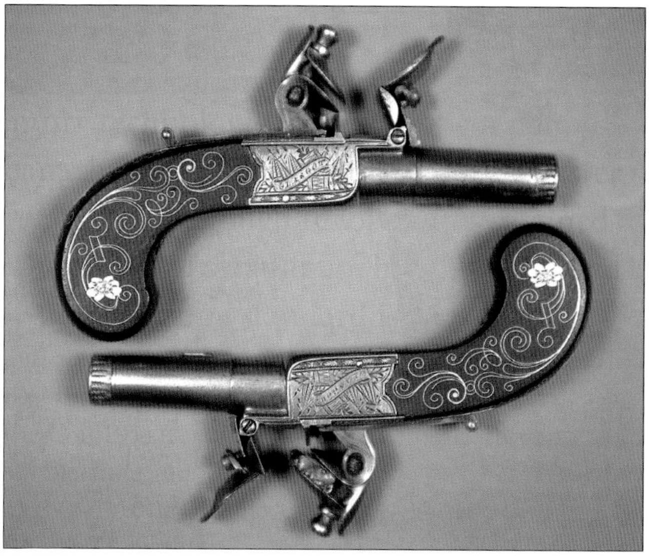

**ABOVE** A pair of 18th-century lady's muff pistols made by Charles Gourley of Glasgow. The length of each gun was under 125mm/5in so could be carried easily. They were also louder than the average pistol to frighten off assailants, but would be unlikely to cause serious damage.

### The box lock

Concealment of a flintlock pistol threw up an obvious difficulty. The mechanism was large and unwieldy and would be liable to get snagged, making quick deployment difficult. Gunmakers therefore developed what is known as the "box lock". This was a system whereby the cock and frizzen were removed from the sides and concealed in the body of the pistol, only emerging once the trigger was pulled. The pan was taken away leaving only a saucer-shape depression surrounding the touch-hole. In some versions, the trigger and trigger guard were also concealed in the body of the weapon, making it a very easy armament to carry. In this case the trigger was revealed once the weapon was cocked.

### Flintlocks in America

The flintlock mechanism in Europe was the mainstay of military forces both on land and at sea for several centuries. It was also hugely important, as a musket or rifle, in colonial America. Although the flintlock mechanism was complex, it was also relatively easy to manufacture, maintain and highly reliable. For the colonists who lived in America in the 17th century it had a huge influence on their ability to survive and to expand westwards. They were used to kill game to feed their families, defend the homestead and to exert dominance over the native American population.

The American flintlock musket evolved from the colonists' weapons. It was effectively used by US forces in the American War of Independence (1775–83) and in the War of 1812, against the English army where it was nicknamed the "Kentucky rifle". The rifle was also the friend of the solitary backwoodsman.

**ABOVE** *Trade from the Monongahela* by Gayle Hoskins, showing American backwoodsmen buying and testing Kentucky rifles. Whereas blacksmiths had previously been concerned exclusively with horseshoes and similar requirements, the growing importance of firearms led to the development of a skilled cottage industry.

# The percussion system

Although the flintlock was a successful mechanism, it also had its limitations. Two factors led to the replacement of the flintlock by a more efficient system. One was the creation of fulminate of mercury and the other was the ingenuity of a Scottish pastor, Alexander John Forsyth, who developed its use in the new percussion system.

## Early gunpowder experiments

From the early 17th century, chemists and military specialists had been experimenting with ways to increase the explosive power of gunpowder. Giuliano Bossi, writing in 1625, recommended adding antimony or mercury precipitated with acid. A German alchemist, Johann Kunchel (1630–1703), is thought to have discovered fulminate of mercury, which was later used in the percussion system. There were a number of experiments by French chemists in the 18th century that replaced gunpowder with fulminate of mercury. These were unsuccessful as the fulminates were highly volatile and either detonated too quickly or burst the cannon or firearm in which they were used.

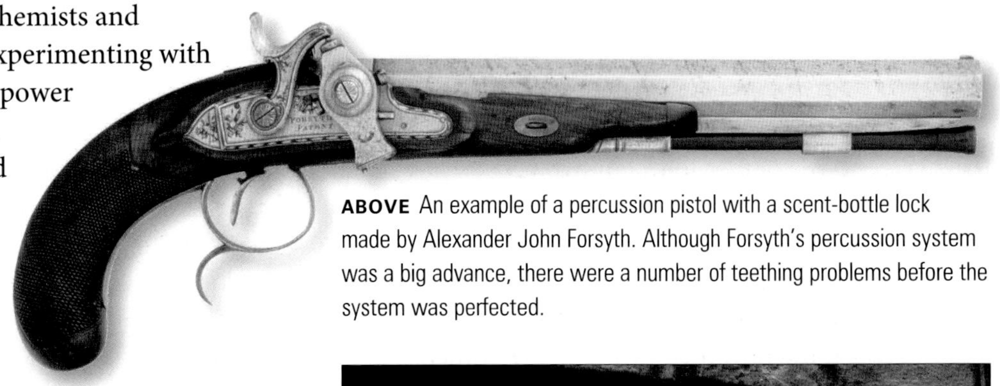

**ABOVE** An example of a percussion pistol with a scent-bottle lock made by Alexander John Forsyth. Although Forsyth's percussion system was a big advance, there were a number of teething problems before the system was perfected.

## The work of Forsyth

In 1800 Edward Howard published a paper on mercury fulminate in the *Philosophical Transactions of the Royal Society*. His work came to the notice of

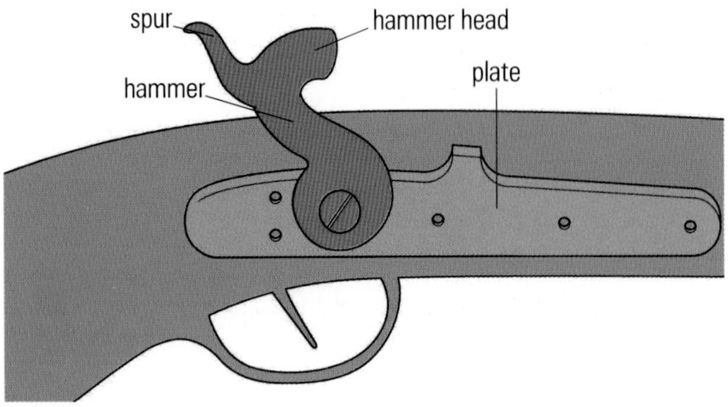


**ABOVE** Diagram showing the external view of the percussion system. The system was developed to overcome the disadvantages of the flintlock ignition. Many flintlocks were converted to the percussion system. The system is exactly the same as the flintlock in terms of its internal mechanisms and, like the flintlock, the hammer used could be held in uncocked, half-cocked and fully-cocked positions.

**ABOVE** Wall tablet memorial to Alexander John Forsyth, inventor of the firearm percussion system, in 1807, Tower of London. Forsyth invented the system as a result of a logical necessity to reduce the delay in setting off the main charge.

**LEFT** A four-barrelled percussion pistol made in Belgium around 1750 as a flintlock and later converted. The percussion system enabled flintlock pistols to be easily adapted to the new mechanism.

an amateur chemist and mechanic of Aberdeen, the Reverend Alexander John Forsyth (1768–1843). Forsyth was also a keen sportsman. Although the flintlock was reliable, it had its faults. The priming powder was easily affected by damp, but more serious from the sporting point of view was the problem of the delay between the priming powder being ignited in the pan and the main charge in the barrel being set off. The puff of smoke from the priming powder frequently alerted the game as well.

### Using fulminate

Forsyth realized that if fulminate could be used instead of priming powder, a gun could be fired very quickly once the trigger had been pulled. He had already written a paper on fulminate in 1799 and by 1805 had developed a lock, which used fulminate of mercury instead of priming powder to detonate the main charge. The old flintlock mechanism could be converted to the new percussion system very easily and cheaply. The cock was replaced by a hammer, the steel and spring were removed. The priming pan would be replaced by the circular plug around which the scent-bottle magazine revolved. It was not necessary to alter the interior working of the lock as the hammer, like a cock, was operated by the mainspring.

Forsyth was cousin to the influential characters Henry and James Brougham, who introduced him to Sir Joseph Banks, a patron of science and Member of Parliament. This led to an introduction to Lord Moira, Master General of the Ordnance. Moira realized how useful firearms using the new percussion system would be to the British army, and arranged for Forsyth to have a workshop at the Tower of London. Although initially he received some financial support, Forsyth had difficulty in getting anyone to make the new lock, and also in obtaining sufficient fulminate. A gun-lock and a lock for a small cannon were tried out at Woolwich but the results were disappointing, and an unfavourable report about the new lock was made to the Board of Ordnance. Forsyth was aware that the military potential of his invention could not be immediately realized, especially when a new Master of the Ordnance stopped his work at the Tower. The Earl of Chatham was the new Master of Ordnance and he did not share Lord Moira's enthusiasm for the new design. He ordered Forsyth to remove his "rubbish" from the Tower. After leaving the Tower of London, Napoleon Bonaparte supposedly offered Forsyth £20,000 if he would bring his invention to France, but Forsyth declined.

### The 1807 patent

On 11 April 1807 Forsyth took out a patent for the new lock and in 1808, established a business with James Brougham in London at the Forsyth Patent Gun Co. Much of his later career was spent protecting his patent from infringement by competitors.

#### The scent-bottle lock

To hold the fulminate powder, Forsyth used a container shaped like a flat scent-bottle. It held enough to prime 30 shots. At the top was a striking pin operating against a spring. The container was attached to the lock by a round plug, which allowed it to rotate, and had a channel that led to the touch-hole. The scent-bottle magazine was rotated to drop some fulminate into a cavity on the top of the plug. It was then returned to its original position so that the striker was at the top. Instead of a cock with jaws holding flint, Forsyth devised a hammer that hit the striking pin when the trigger was pulled.

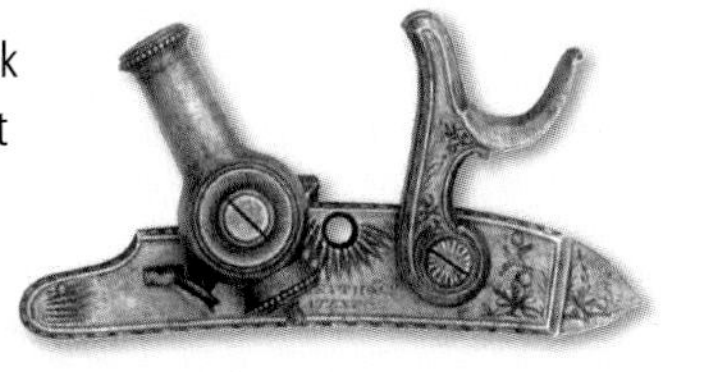

**RIGHT** The scent-bottle lock was an ingenious device but also potentially dangerous, as the contents could ignite and explode.

# The percussion cap

In Britain the percussion lock took some time to establish itself and it was not until about 1820 that it began to replace the flintlock on a large scale. On the Continent, however, the virtues of the new lock were immediately recognized and Parisian gunmakers were soon making copies and taking out patents based on the design of the Forsyth lock. One of the problems of the new percussion lock was how to control the rate of flow of the fulminate, and this led to another significant development – the percussion cap.

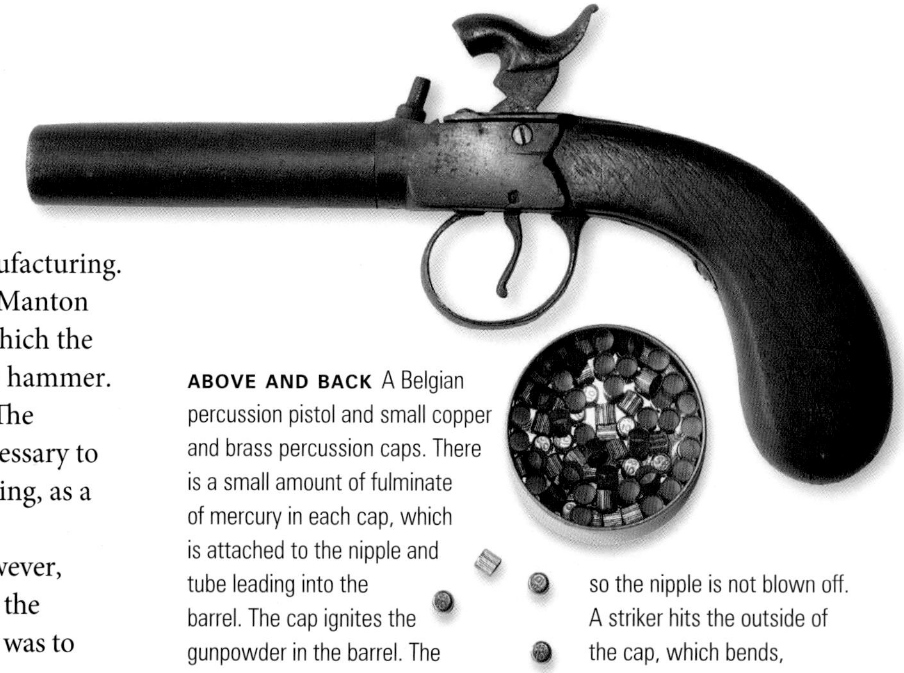

**ABOVE AND BACK** A Belgian percussion pistol and small copper and brass percussion caps. There is a small amount of fulminate of mercury in each cap, which is attached to the nipple and tube leading into the barrel. The cap ignites the gunpowder in the barrel. The hammer is shaped to strike the cap on the nipple and cover it so the nipple is not blown off. A striker hits the outside of the cap, which bends, and the primer is crushed, so it explodes.

### The tube lock

The London gun trade was initially very reluctant to accept the new percussion lock, principally because its craftsmen had spent their working lives on flintlocks and the change constituted an upheaval in manufacturing. However, in 1816 British gunsmith Joseph Manton took out a patent for a percussion lock in which the fulminate was contained in a tube set in the hammer. The tube could be taken out and reloaded. The disadvantage of the lock was that it was necessary to carry a number of loaded tubes when shooting, as a new one was needed for every shot.

The problem of the volatile fulminate, however, remained unsolved. One solution was to put the fulminate between two paper discs. Another was to make the fulminate into pellets covered with wax or iron oxide. Fulminate was very susceptible to damp and deteriorated quickly, so it had to be carefully stored.

In 1818 Joseph Manton took out another patent, this time for a tube lock in which the fulminate was contained in a copper tube. A section of the tube went directly into the touch-hole, and the hammer fell on the exposed section. This was held in place on a flat pan by a cover and spring. The detonation was very rapid but it tended to blow the tube to fragments – a danger to both the shooter and his immediate neighbours.

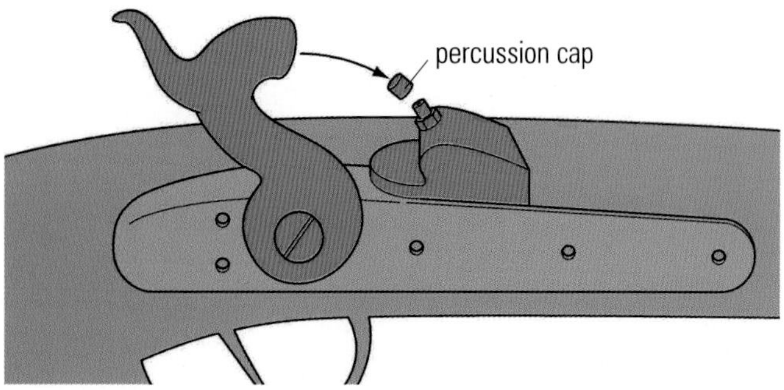


**ABOVE** Diagram showing the positioning of the percussion cap. The percussion system was relatively straightforward. The hammer struck a nipple on top of which was placed a copper cap containing the priming charge. This exploded on impact and set off the main charge.

The problem of safely housing the fulminate was only solved with the invention of the percussion cap. This was made in the form of a small cylinder shaped like a top hat, which contained the fulminate. The lock was fitted with a nipple which was adjacent to the barrel, and had a channel leading directly into it. The cap fitted over the nipple and was detonated by the hammer when it fell.

### Various claims for the invention

The percussion cap was so successful that many of the prominent sportsmen and gunmakers of the day claimed to have invented it. Colonel Hawker wrote an account in *Instructions to Young Sportsmen*, published

in 1830, saying it was his idea and that the gunmaker Joe Manton had altered a pellet-lock gun to his design. Gunmaker Josef Egg claimed to have made a copper cap out of an old penny piece while James Purdey claimed a cap out of the brass ferrule of an umbrella. The most likely inventor, however, is English-born Joshua Shaw (1776–1860), who claimed to have made a series of percussion caps, first in steel, then in pewter, then in copper, in 1816. He went to America in 1817 and was finally granted a patent in 1822. The patent office must have believed his claim because in 1847 Congress awarded him $18,000 for the invention.

The earliest European patent for a percussion cap was granted to François Prelat, a Parisian gunmaker, in 1820 as an addition to another patent issued in 1818. However, as Prelat is known to have copied other gunmakers' discoveries, it is unlikely that he actually invented it, and Joshua Shaw is the most likely inventor.

**ABOVE** Shooting was to become a fashionable activity. This is a shooting gallery in a smart part of London, *c.* 1825–1830.

### Adopting the new system

One of the reasons why the percussion cap was slow to be adopted was the composition of the fulminate. The most commonly found priming powder used in early percussion locks was made from potassium chlorate, sulphur and charcoal, along with some other ingredients. The mixture gave very variable results and it also quickly corroded the nipple and the gun barrel.

In 1824 a London chemist took up the manufacture of percussion caps. He based the priming on fulminate of mercury, following a paper published in the *Philosophical Magazine and Journal* by E. Goode Wright, who advocated the use of fulminate of mercury because of its ease of manufacture and relative stability compared with other methods.

### The under-hammer lock

The development of the percussion lock led to major changes in the design of firearms. One result was the under-hammer lock. The percussion lock was usually located on the top of the firearm, but on the under-hammer lock it was located on the underside. Under-hammer locks, however, were rare. Their advantage was that during shooting, the flash did not impair vision.

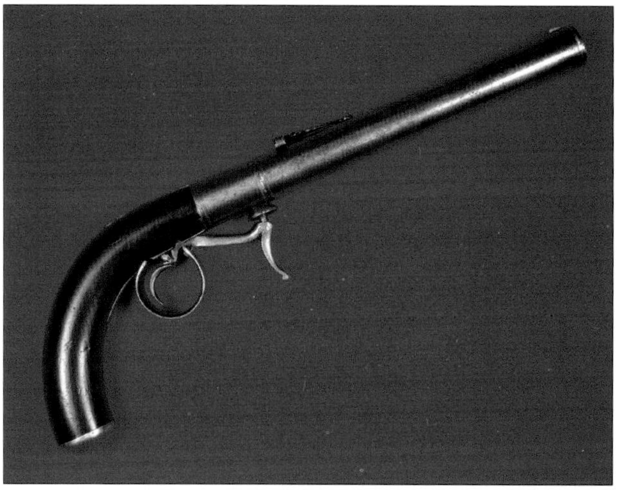

**RIGHT** Under-hammer box lock percussion pistol, of around 1850 with a turn-off rifled barrel. New designs allowed for a cleaner exterior and greater ease of concealment.

# The development of cartridges

As with many handgun developments, there was one overriding criterion. This was the time it took to reload. Soldiers under fire were under pressure to reload as quickly as possible before the enemy was upon them. Sportsmen also needed to reload quickly before their prey escaped. The answer was the cartridge, where all the elements required for firing were contained in a single package.

### Loading the gunpowder

In the early days of firearms, gunpowder was loaded into the muzzle of a barrel, followed by cloth and wadding, and then a lead ball. Hunters carried a powder flask, while the military used paper cartridges. The cartridge began as a thick paper tube, which contained both powder and the ball. When it was used with a muzzle loader, the base of the cartridge would be ripped off and the powder poured down through the muzzle into the barrel. The ball would then be inserted and the paper would be shoved down on top of the ball with the use of a ramrod, in order to keep powder and ball in place.

In the days before the flintlock, serpentine powder was used to prime the pan. Later, serpentine was no longer used and the user would prime the pan with some of the powder from the cartridge before pouring the remainder down the barrel. The flintlock

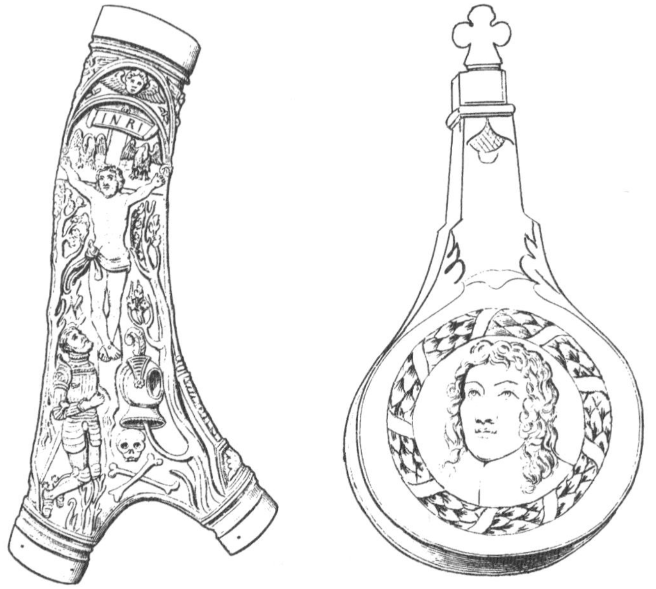


**ABOVE** 17th-century English powder flasks. The ritual of loading a flintlock musket, or pistol, with powder from a flask and a separate bullet came to an end with the invention of the cartridge.

### Priming the flintlock

To prime the flintlock with a cartridge, the lock was half-cocked. The cartridge was torn open and enough powder was used to half fill the pan, away from the touch-hole. The pan was then shut and the remaining charge was poured down the barrel, followed by the paper and ball pushed into position by a ramrod. Once ignited, the flash shot through the touch-hole into the main charge in the barrel. The flintlock was a fairly reliable system, but it could fail in adverse weather.

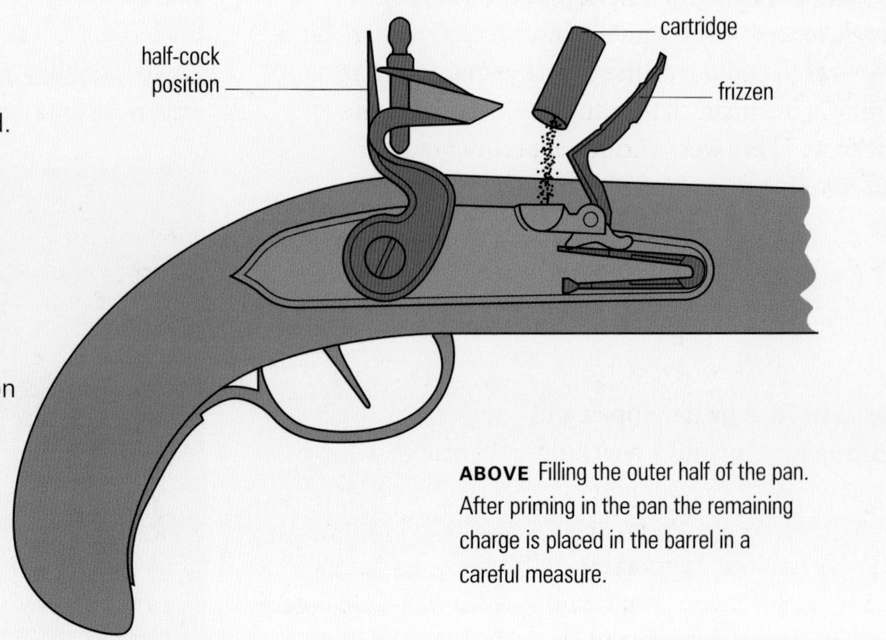


**ABOVE** Filling the outer half of the pan. After priming in the pan the remaining charge is placed in the barrel in a careful measure.

**RIGHT** A Belgian pinfire six-shot revolver from *c.*1865. This revolver was designed to take a metallic cartridge based on Lefaucheaux's design.

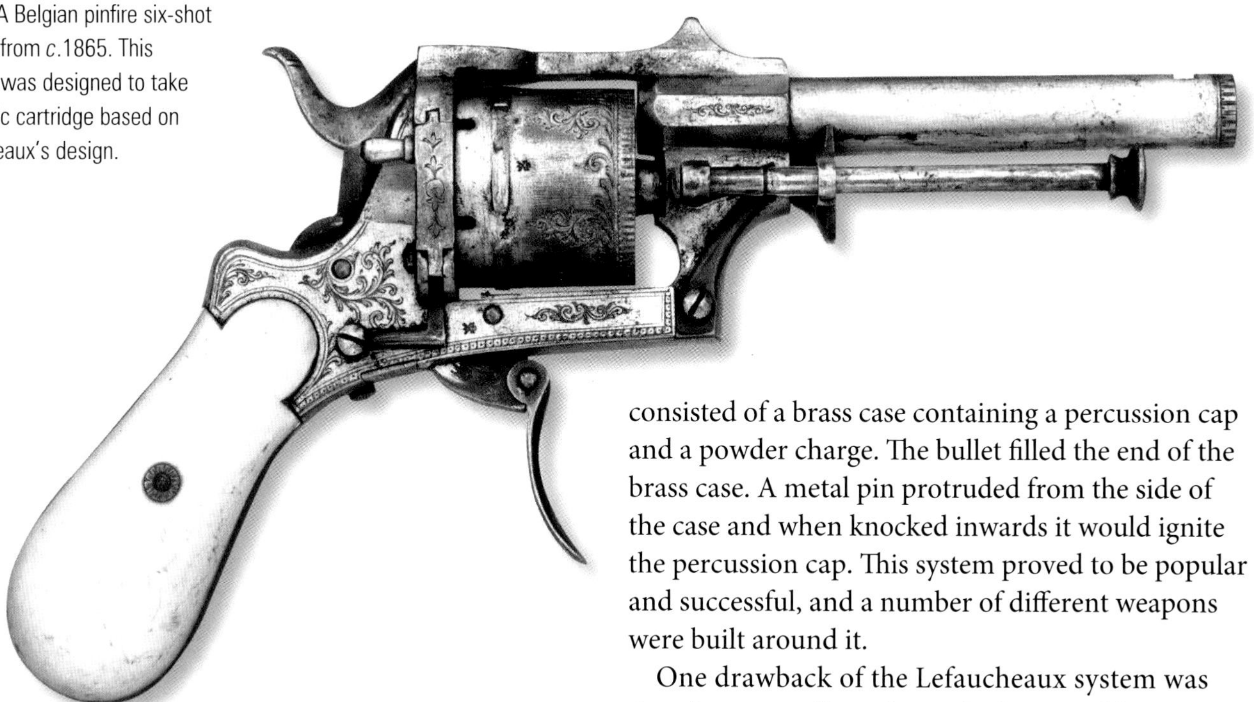

mechanism obviated the need to prime the pan as a separate operation, as a certain amount of powder would run through from the base of the barrel into the covered pan. This system was to prevail during most of the extensive flintlock era, and was mostly reliable as long as the powder in the flash pan stayed dry. This, of course, was not always the case, and on average three out of ten times the flash-pan powder would fail to ignite or the flash pan would ignite without setting off the main charge in the barrel.

After the development of the percussion system by John Forsyth and others, and the parallel development of fulminate of mercury, the next logical step was to contain all the various elements – the ignition, the main charge and the bullet – in one package. There were various experiments with different forms of cartridge, and there were also different schools of thought about the position of the percussion cap in the cartridge.

## The pinfire cartridge

Johannes Pauly was a Swiss gunmaker working in Paris. In 1812 he developed and patented a breech-loading firearm and a new kind of cartridge, which was the early development of the pinfire cartridge. These designs were very well thought out, but for various reasons, gunmakers of the time did not follow up his ideas. Work continued in this field, and the pinfire cartridge was invented by a Frenchman called Casimir Lefaucheaux in 1835. The cartridge consisted of a brass case containing a percussion cap and a powder charge. The bullet filled the end of the brass case. A metal pin protruded from the side of the case and when knocked inwards it would ignite the percussion cap. This system proved to be popular and successful, and a number of different weapons were built around it.

One drawback of the Lefaucheaux system was that the protruding pin made the round less convenient to handle than the later rimfire or centrefire cartridges. The pin needed to be aligned correctly in a slot in the chamber, and it could cause the round to detonate if it were accidentally knocked. Lefaucheaux's son Eugene continued to improve both the cartridge and the design of the weapon after his father died in 1852. The system was refined and patented by another Frenchman, Clément Pottet, in 1855, and further work was carried out in London by Colonel Edward Boxer, who patented a centrefire cartridge with a metal base and coiled brass body.

**BELOW** The kit of an American Civil War cavalryman included French pinfire pistols and a cartridge case.

Paris gunsmiths such as Lefrancheaux were influential in the development of composite cartridges comprising paper and brass. A similar version was successfully used by gunsmith Johann Nikolaus van Dreyse for a needle gun – so named because of the extended pin that ran through the centre of the bolt to ignite the percussion cap. The most notable development was the placement of the percussion cap in the centre of the base of the brass cartridge, which is the same system used in modern centrefire cartridges.

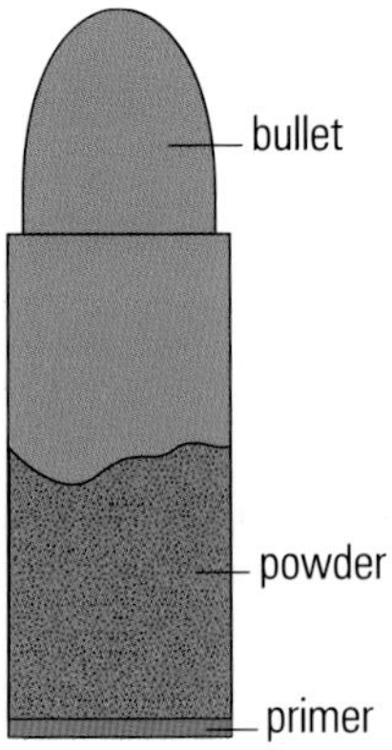


**ABOVE** The first rimfire cartridge was essentially just a percussion cap with a projectile pressed in the front, and a rim to hold it securely in the chamber.

## The rimfire cartridge

The rimfire cartridge developed in the 1830s, although it was not started commercially until 1845. The rimfire cartridge was essentially a large percussion cap which contained not only the priming compound, but also the propellant powder and bullet. One disadvantage of the rimfire system was that the cartridge is rendered useless by the impact of the hammer and it could not be re-used (unlike other cartridges which could be reused by replacing the primer, gunpowder and bullet). It also had a shorter range. Due to the thin case they are limited to light, low pressure calibres (calibres relate the diameter of the inside of the barrel). If the calibre measurement is in inches then the calibre is quoted as decimal of an inch, so a gun with a diameter of 0.22in is a .22 or "twenty-two calibre". In the past, rimfire calibres up to .44 were common. Today's rimfires are of calibre .22 (around 5.5mm) or smaller.

## The centrefire cartridge

In 1854 Charles Lancaster invented a cartridge which was sealed in a brass case. The brass at the base was thin enough for the pin to activate the percussion cap contained in the base of the cartridge.

**ABOVE** Pinfire pistols were used during the American Civil War (1861–65), although they were not always highly regarded because of their low power compared with other percussion revolvers, such as Colts, which were widely used on the battlefield.

This was a centrefire cartridge, which proved to be the most successful cartridge type and is one of the most commonly used for all large-calibre weapons today. There is some discussion as to the original patent for the centrefire cartridge, which is in itself an indication of the significance of the invention. It is said to have been invented in 1861 by the English gunmaker G. H. Daw, but Clément Pottet of Paris is also mentioned, and a London firm, the Eley Brothers, successfully won the patent.

In 1867 an Eley–Boxer centrefire cartridge was adopted by the British War Office for use in Enfield rifles. The original Eley–Boxer cartridge was made of solid brass. In 1870, Colonel Hiram Berdan of the US Ordnance Department developed a bottle-shaped brass cartridge with a cap and chamber at the base and flash holes drilled on either side. Modern cartridges are made from a brass and metal alloy. Centrefires today also are generally capable of higher-powered loads than rimfire.

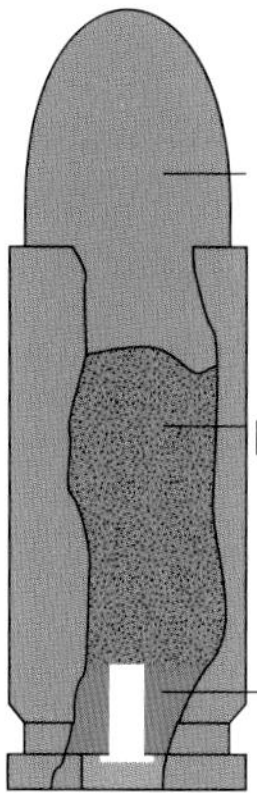


**ABOVE** A centrefire cartridge has the primer located in the centre of the base. Centrefires are generally capable of high-powered loads.

### The advantages of a metal cartridge

The beauty of a metal case for some types of cartridges was that it expanded under the heat of the explosion and thus created a seal in the chamber. This increased the energy of the bullet towards the muzzle of the gun. It also prevented the gun user from being injured by escaping high-pressure gases as the trigger was pulled. The brass case of a centrefire cartridge could also be re-used once it had been ejected from the chamber. It had to be precisely manufactured to suit the dimensions of the particular gun for which it was intended. This entailed precision machining to fine tolerances of the parts integral to the gun and the cartridge itself. Different cartridges would be designed to carry different loads, and it would be important to match the right cartridge load to the pistol, otherwise the pistol would be liable to explode when it was fired. Cartridges are manufactured and named in imperial or metric sizes.

### The needle gun

Johann Nikolaus Dreyse was a Prussian gunsmith who invented a military breech-loading needle gun. The system involved the use of a bolt which was used to open and close the breech, through which the cartridge was loaded. The bolt was locked by pulling it down in front of a lug in the frame. The "needle" was an extended firing pin that passed through the centre of the bolt. When released by the trigger, the needle would fly forward, pass through the paper cartridge and ignite a percussion cap at the base of the bullet.The cartridge used in this system was made up of four separate elements: the paper case itself, the powder charge, the priming cap and the bullet. The primer was placed between the bullet and the main powder charge so that the needle passed through the powder charge before igniting the primer.

Although it was a clever design and was highly effective for its time, the needle gun also had some inherent weaknesses. The fact that the needle had to pass through the bolt meant that, unless the parts were extremely well fitted and sealed, a certain amount of gas would leak through the bolt. Also, as the needle was present when the explosion took place, it was quickly subjected to wear and tear and would sometimes break.

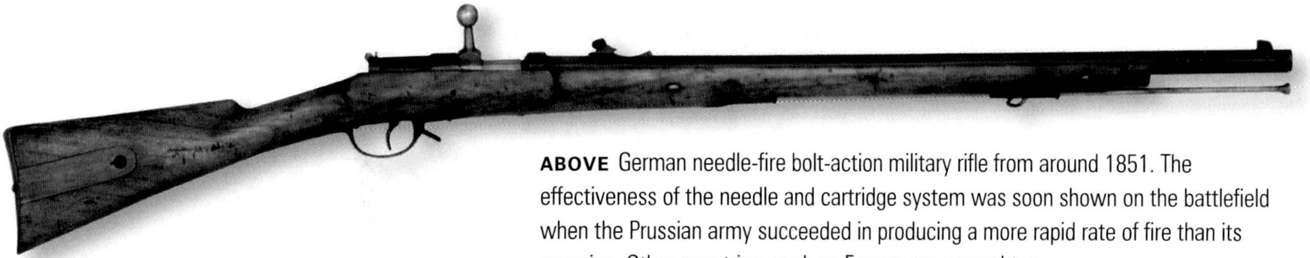

**ABOVE** German needle-fire bolt-action military rifle from around 1851. The effectiveness of the needle and cartridge system was soon shown on the battlefield when the Prussian army succeeded in producing a more rapid rate of fire than its enemies. Other countries, such as France, soon caught up.

# Manufacture, proof and trade

The term "lock, stock and barrel" is a reminder that the firearm was made up of several different components, each of which required different materials and different craftsmanship skills. The inherent and increasing complexity of the firearm was to pose a growing technological challenge to gunmakers, while the organization of the different trades was to become both a stimulus to and a sign of the growing process of industrialization, first in Europe and then elsewhere.

## Craftsmanship

The manufacture of a firearm was a complex process and involved a number of different specialist trades relevant to the different parts of the firearm. The 16th-century origins of the firearm manufacturer Beretta, for example, lie in precision forging of steel barrels. As firearms became more complex, they not only called on the skills of metalworkers and forgers but also of woodworkers to develop the stock and experts in precision mechanisms to create the trigger and lock systems.

Each part of the lock mechanism for a flintlock pistol would have been hand-made. The trigger, powder pan, springs and screws would have been individually forged and filed.

**ABOVE** A gun is assembled at the Beretta gun factory in Italy. Craftsmanship skills would prove to be compatible with the advent of the machine age, and successful firearms manufacturers would find the right balance between the two.

Although early stocks for such weapons as the arquebus or matchlock were fairly rudimentary, later stocks for flintlocks, percussion weapons and breech-loaders were an integral part of the weapon. These needed to be worked with skill so that the metal parts fitted correctly and in alignment with each other, and so that the stock itself was strong enough to both support the weapon and absorb recoil.

Stocks were often made of well-seasoned hardwoods such as English walnut, although this did not necessarily always come from England. In addition to their utilitarian value, stocks were sometimes engraved to underline their fine workmanship. The barrel itself was often forged from a flat wrought-iron bar. Metalworking skills that included heating, hammering and boring would result in a smooth-bore interior. A separate process was used for rifling.

The quality of weapons depended to a large extent on developments in metallurgy. Weapons could not be made to fine tolerances if the metal could not be worked precisely. Due to the high pressures involved when a weapon was fired, this was of some significance.

The art of gunmaking had to take many factors into account. It needed to be fitted to its purpose, to have the right balance and "feel", and such details as the quality of the trigger pull would also be noticed. The craftsmanship of the gun evolved in the manufacture of finely weighted barrels, the creation of smooth-functioning locks and triggers and the sculpting of a fine stock. Alongside this individual craftsmanship came the advent of the machine age. Machines were designed to produce parts in greater volumes, though without the individual touch. The two processes could be successfully combined by bespoke gunmakers while volume manufacturers could claim that their products were often on a par with their handmade competitors.

### The Birmingham Gun Quarter

The different skills required in the manufacture of a firearm were part and parcel of the process of industrialization in England. Different craftsmen focused on their individual products and they were brought together by the gun manufacturers to assemble the finished product. It made sense to keep the different trades as close together as possible in order to cut down on time and expense and as a result areas such as Birmingham's Gun Quarter became recognized as specialist areas for gunmaking. Not all of the parts were produced in the Gun Quarter, however. Locks, for example, often came from elsewhere.

In 1767 Birmingham in England had 35 gun and pistol manufacturers, 8 gun barrel manufacturers and filers, 5 gun barrel polishers and finishers, 11 gun lock manufacturers, forgers and finishers, and three gun-swivel and stock makers. The different parts were often sent to London to be made up by "fabricators" who assembled and sold the weapons.

**LEFT** Manufacture of arms around 1862. The organization of craftsmen and machinery to satisfy the demand for firearms was a significant stage in the Industrial Revolution.

## Proving

The Birmingham Proof House is evidence of another important stage in gunmaking – the proving (testing) of barrels. The gun barrel would have a charge fired through it that was significantly more powerful than the one it was designed to fire. If there was any sign of weakness, such as distortion or cracking, the gun would fail the test. Otherwise, it would be awarded an official proof mark to prove its worthiness. The Birmingham Proof House was established in 1813 by Act of Parliament, and it became illegal to trade in arms without the award of a proof mark.

Due to the particular nature of gunmaking, it both thrived upon and contributed to the greater sophistication of the nascent industrial age. With the growth of large cities and, in the case of England, with labourers beginning to leave the land to seek work in the towns and cities, there was great scope for the development of a thriving gun trade.

## The United States

In colonial America, gunsmiths also sprang up, though initially many of these would either assemble or repair firearms imported from England and elsewhere. In due course, the United States would be the pioneer of some of the most important small-arms designs of all time and would develop its own thriving gun trade.

**ABOVE** Smith & Wesson's revolver factory: *Scientific American* 24 January, 1880. Like Colt, Smith & Wesson soon became a major industrial concern with growing markets both at home and overseas.

# Duelling pistols

As firearms became more accurate, they were used for hunting and for sport. In due course, the handgun in particular came to be used in duelling, a practice that had its roots in a warped code of honour. While an "honourable scar" might be obtained from the slash of a sword, firearms were inherently less difficult to control and the results were almost invariably fatal. In order to meet the ongoing demand, specialist manufacturers began to emerge who prided themselves in the sophistication and accuracy of their products.

## A code of honour

Duelling has had a long and undistinguished history that pre-dates the medieval era. The throwing down of a gauntlet was the traditional challenge that would be followed in the pre-firearms era by a fight with swords. In England there was such a thing as a judicial duel, dating from the 11th century, which was only abolished by English law in 1819.

The nature of duelling, however, is such that it tells us less about the law of the state than it does about individual codes of honour. So precarious was the notion of honour that the offended person was "honour bound" to demand satisfaction for even the smallest slight, or risk a disastrous decline in his status. Similarly, the accused would either have to accept the challenge or risk being branded a coward. It was the direct opposite of the Christian teaching of "turn the other cheek".

**ABOVE** A matched pair of flintlock duelling pistols made by London gunmakers in 1805. Duelling pistols were designed to be identical in every way to give both contestants an even chance.

The use of pistols for duelling became more common from about the middle of the 18th century and, in order to ensure that the duellists should have an equal chance, the pistols were often designed as matching pairs and presented in a box. In some cases the box also contained miniature pistols to be used by the "seconds" (trusted representatives of each party who may stand in for the dueller). This would allow the seconds to defend themselves or to intervene if there should be any unorthodox behaviour.

## Early makers of duelling pistols

The first set of duelling pistols was probably made in England, to very high specifications. As duelling was supposedly the preserve of "gentlemen", it was appropriate that the design and finish of duelling pistols should be suitably lavish, and this was particularly the case for French pistols. It was also important that the pistols should be both reliable and accurate. In the days of flintlocks, great care was taken to minimize the chances of a misfire by careful loading.

There were a number of pistol makers in both Europe and America who acquired considerable reputations for the quality of their products. These included Durs Egg, John Manton, John Twigg and Robert Wogdon of England; Gastinne Renette, Le Page and Nicolas Beutet of France; Auguste Francotte of Belgium; Continner of Vienna; and Simeon North, James Haslett and R. Constable of America.

Early duelling pistols tended to be lightweight designs, but heavier designs began to emerge. Part of the extra weight was in the barrel, which was designed to reduce recoil and improve accuracy. As with many flintlock firearms, duelling pistols were often converted to the percussion system, which radically increased their reliability.

## Code Duello

Duelling was controlled by elaborate codes, which included the French Renaissance code, and an Irish code agreed at the Clonmel Summer Assizes in 1777 which was to some extent based on the French code. The Irish code had over 25 rules that stipulated how a duel should be managed and what constituted satisfaction for an insult.

The basis of any code was that, once an insult had been made, a challenge would be given and a place agreed where the duel could take place. Normally the contestants would bring seconds as well as a physician. The seconds might try to arrange a reconciliation between the parties and, if an apology was accepted, the duel would be called off.

The duel would be carried out on a piece of measured ground and details such as the number of paces between the contestants would be agreed. Sometimes the contestants would "delope", which meant firing into the air so as not to wound the other party. This practice was, however, forbidden in the Irish code.

**ABOVE** Pistols were increasingly used for duelling from the mid-18th century.

**RIGHT** Normally duels were carefully stage-managed. The "quick draw" from a holster belonged to the Wild West.

## Famous duels

There have been a number of notable duels through the ages. In 1598 the playwright Ben Jonson killed the actor Gabriel Spenser. In 1796 William Pitt the Younger had a duel with George Tierney. In 1809 George Canning had a duel with Lord Castlereagh and, in 1829, the Duke of Wellington had a duel with the 10th Earl of Winchelsea.

The duel between the duke and the earl followed public criticisms of the duke by the earl. The two met in Battersea Fields and the duke fired wide. Winchelsea returned the compliment, after which he agreed to publicly retract his accusations. The duel damaged the reputation of the Duke of Wellington and underlined public distaste for the practice of duelling. It is a good indication of the level to which the code of honour had become ingrained that, in two countries where the practice of duelling had been declared illegal, the Prime Minister of Great Britain and two leading American politicians should use the duel to seek their satisfaction. At the height of its notoriety, hundreds of duels per year were fought between less well-known individuals.

### The Hamilton–Burr duel

In 1804 the United States Vice-President, Aaron Burr, fought a duel with the former United States Treasury Secretary, Alexander Hamilton. By the time the Hamilton-Burr duel was fought, duelling had been declared illegal in New York, so the two men and their accomplices secretly crossed the Hudson River to a remote rocky ledge in New Jersey. It is said that Hamilton may have deliberately aimed wide with his first shot, though another view is that, the bullet from Hamilton's gun was launched too early and went high. Burr is also said to have tried a non-fatal shot, but it did enough damage to Hamilton's internal organs to kill him.

**ABOVE RIGHT** The 1804 duel between Aaron Burr and Alexander Hamilton in which Hamilton was killed. The guns were a pair of .54-calibre flintlock pistols made by Robert Wogdon and owned by Hamilton's brother-in-law, John Barker Church. The guns were purchased by Chase Manhattan Bank in 1930 and are on display in their New York City headquarters.

# Eastern pistols and handguns

Firearms from the East have a rich and distinctive history. They are recognizable, both for their unique shapes and also for the characteristically rich decoration that distinguish them from more sober European products. Although some of these firearms were decorated European derivatives, many fine and original products were also developed in the East.

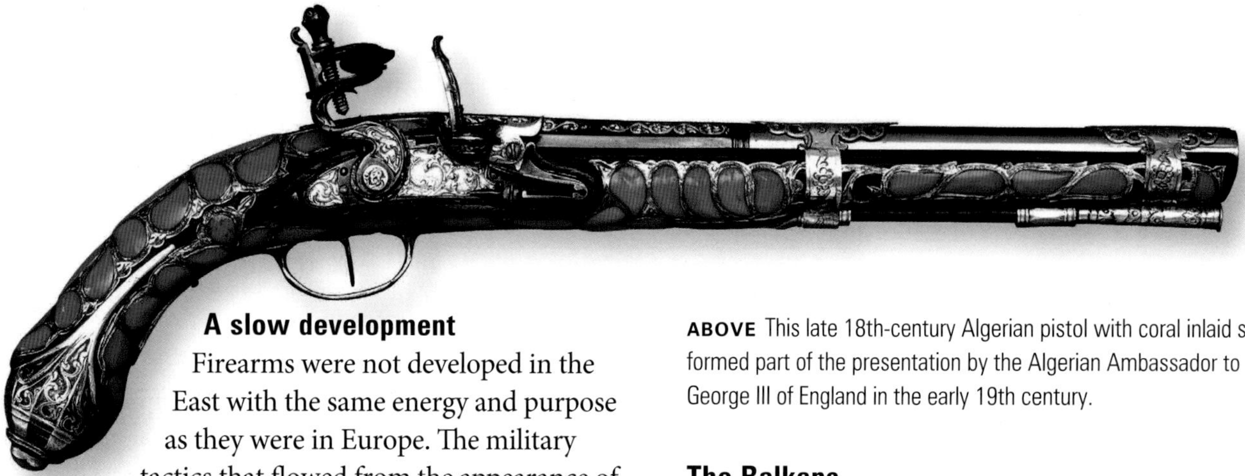

**ABOVE** This late 18th-century Algerian pistol with coral inlaid stock formed part of the presentation by the Algerian Ambassador to King George III of England in the early 19th century.

### A slow development

Firearms were not developed in the East with the same energy and purpose as they were in Europe. The military tactics that flowed from the appearance of firearms were slow to develop. Codes of honour and concepts of how a warrior should behave meant that the sword was often preferred to the firearm. Moreover, unlike Europe, where a process of industrialization complemented firearms development, the manufacture and maintenance of firearms in the East was not as well developed.

However, it is almost certain that gunpowder was invented in the East, and the knowledge of its secrets are said to have been transmitted to Europe via Iran and India, where they are likely to have been recorded in Sanskrit, and then to the Maghrib (the West), which included Moorish Spain. In the 13th century the Arab alchemist Hasan al-Rammah wrote a description of how to make gunpowder, and Roger Bacon and Albertus Magnus visited the Spanish-based centres of learning to find out about it.

Despite its Eastern origins, the conservatism of the Ottoman Empire was such that little was done to take the next logical step – to develop the means by which the gunpowder could be used. It is said, however, that the Arabs fired a missile from a sealed tube of bamboo, filled with black powder, and the Chinese are believed to have developed one of the first metal handguns.

By the time of the Siege of Algeciras in southern Spain by Alfonso XI in 1343, the Christians discovered to their cost that the Muslims were armed with cannon.

### The Balkans

The transfer of firearms technology from the West to the East largely took place via the Balkans. The Venetians are said to have taken firearms to the Balkans in 1352 and the Ottomans used firearms to defeat Christian crusaders at battles such as the Battle of Kosovo (1448).

Due to the ongoing threat of Muslim expansion, a Papal Bull of 1444 banned the trade of firearms with the Ottomans, but this and other bulls do not appear to have had much effect. After the dissolution of the monasteries in England in 1541, lead and bronze from the destroyed buildings were sold to the Turks, some of which may have been used for making weapons and ammunition.

The elite Ottoman corps known as the janissaries were the soldiers most likely to be equipped with firearms. The janissaries included a large proportion of young, originally Christian men from the Balkans who had converted to Islam, and they largely replaced the traditional cavalry, the spahis, as footsoldiers.

By the beginning of the 16th century, handguns were widely in use in the Ottoman Empire, but many of these were of European origin or were inspired by European designs and it is said that European-sourced firearms were preferred to the local variety by those who could afford them. It was soon discovered that when they malfunctioned there was little or no native expertise or backup from armourers to put them right.

**ABOVE** Siege of Belgrade, 1521, from *The Military Campaigns of Suleyman I*. The exchange between East and West in the Balkans would also include the transfer of knowledge about firearms.

A pistol might become little more than an ornate and expensive club. As in Europe, homemade firearms were made by different craftsmen and there was a system of testing and approval among the Turks, with the appropriate mark made on the pistol once it had been passed.

In the 18th and 19th centuries firearms continued to be imported into the Ottoman Empire in ever-greater numbers, and it provided a valuable market as the Industrial Revolution gathered pace. English firms such as the Birmingham Small Arms Company won substantial orders from the Ottoman Government.

## The Maghrib

As European nations such as Portugal pushed down the west African coast in their quest for the route to India, and as France and Spain extended their influence in North Africa, the development of firearms in the Maghrib was duly influenced by European designs. Again, innate conservatism led to the retention of certain archaisms in design, and local influence was seen largely in the style of decoration, which might include gold and silver wire or gold and silver damascene. In some parts, notably Algeria, coral was also widely used. Again, different craftsmen would produce parts of the firearm, and often these were manufactured to a high standard.

## The Caucasus

Like the Balkans, the Caucasus is a link between Europe and Asia, and the region has its own tradition of weapon-making which speaks of a high level of craftsmanship and enjoys a high reputation. Typical pistols from the region from the beginning of the 19th century would have ivory ball butts and black, leather-covered stocks. Decoration with niello (an alloy used as an inlay in a design) was common.

## Japan

Firearms were first introduced into Japan in 1542 by the Portuguese. The local warlords were keen to trade for more arms, and they also ordered local swordsmiths to copy the weapons. By 1575, at the Battle of Nagashino, Japanese battle tactics had changed to suit the introduction of firearms. By 1587, however, it was thought they might give too much power to the peasantry. Under the military dictatorship of the Tokugawa Shogunate, which lasted until 1868, firearms were believed to have been suppressed as part of a wider plan to maintain stability, but this was mostly notional, and on the whole they continued to be used.

**ABOVE** *Geijutsu Hideu Hue* (Accomplishments in the Secret Arts) by Japanese Ohmori Sakou, illustrated by Kuniyoshi, reveals the Japanese use of firearms in the mid-19th century.

# The art of the gunmaker

Early firearms were sophisticated pieces of workmanship and the owners of these treasured possessions were invariably wealthy. Alongside the craftsmanship required to produce a firearm there grew the craft of decoration. The more complex the firearm was, the more elaborate was the decoration. The level of decoration, however, varied between different countries, with France producing some of the most lavish handguns and England the most sober. Gunmaking centres created their own styles.

## Early decorated handguns

Even in their very earliest forms, firearms were sometimes decorated. The barrel of the late 14th-century cast-bronze handgun from Morko is roughly engraved with religious texts on the barrel and has the bust of a bearded man adjacent to the touch-hole. Bronze barrels were made in late medieval times, by founders used to producing decorated bronze wares, so it was no wonder the barrels were often ornate.

The earliest examples of decorated handguns date from the 1530s, including wheel-locks made for the Emperor Charles V (1519–56). The number of finely decorated wheel-lock guns far outnumbers those with matchlock mechanisms – this expensive, complicated mechanism was deemed to deserve rich decoration. Craftsmen from various traditions, specializing in decoration, therefore found themselves practising their skills on firearms. Barrels were chiselled and gilded, and wooden stocks inlaid with engraved staghorn.

**ABOVE** A pair of pistols by N. Boulet made for Murat in 1805, Musée de L'Armée, Paris. France produced some of the most lavishly decorated firearms, with French gunmakers dominating the trade in the 17th and early 18th centuries. It was a celebration of craftsmanship.

There has always been a link between the craftsmen who worked on gun-stocks and those who worked on small items of furniture such as cabinets and desks, because of the use of materials such as staghorn and ebony which were widely used for inlaid wood in the 16th and 17th centuries. The craftsmen who decorated high-quality firearms were careful to avoid techniques that would weaken either the stock or the barrel. For this reason, in the 16th century, etched decoration was always preferred to chiselling, and inlaid decoration to carving.

## Sources of ornament

It seems from surviving examples that highly decorated firearms first began to be produced in quantity in the first quarter of the 16th century. Elaborate decoration was based upon the engraved sheets of designs which circulated in the workshops of different gunmakers. The craftsmen employed on the decoration of a gun would reflect elements of an engraved design, fitting them into the space available on a gun-stock or barrel. It is possible therefore to see the influence of artists such as German artist Virgil Solis and French goldsmith Etienne Delaune on firearms decoration.

A finely decorated firearm was the work of several craftsmen. The wooden stock was made by the stock-maker, the barrel maker produced the barrel, and the lock was made by yet another craftsman. Engraved designs made specifically for firearms were not apparent before the last quarter of the 16th century. After this period they become common.

It is from the 17th and 18th centuries that most surviving pattern books date, and it is possible to relate engraved and chiselled work from these periods to the pattern books of particular artists. Among the more notable are François Marcou (*c.*1657), Jean

Berain (*c.*1650) and De Lacollombe (*c.*1730). All three artists were French, but as French gunmakers dominated the trade in the 17th and early 18th centuries this is not surprising.

### Gunmaking centres

Various gunmaking centres had their own particular decorative styles. Northern Italy, especially Brescia, used pierced steel and chiselled work; French gunmakers used chased gold; and the gunmakers of Tula in Russia used blued steel overlaid with tiny flowers in gold. By contrast, the best English makers used decoration very sparsely – the maker's name and some simple engraved scroll-work is often the only ornament. Silver mounts are frequently found on firearms, usually cast from moulds and applied to the stock. For the highest-quality work cast gold was used. The neo-classical presentation pistols by the French gunmaker Boutet are often mounted in gold. Five pistols made for the 19th-century exhibitions of 1851 and 1882 also by French gunmakers, were highly decorative and cannot have been intended for use. Some fine early Colt revolvers are richly engraved, but had the overall sense of design of the earlier periods.

### Decorative techniques

A variety of techniques was used over the centuries to decorate firearms. The metal parts such as the barrel, lock, butt-cap and mounts were etched and gilded, damascened (inlaid) in gold and silver and chiselled. Some of the first chiselled work was done by Daniel and Emmanuel Sadeler, who worked for the Elector of Bavaria in the 1620s. The designs were usually based on the engravings of Etienne Delaure and were in low relief against a gold background, the relief decoration being coloured dark blue to make a vivid colour contrast. The stocks of pistols were inlaid with a variety of metals, especially brass and silver. The subjects were drawn from mythology or from the chase. Firearms were widely used for hunting, especially in the 16th and 17th centuries.

Gunmakers followed contemporary ornamental styles extremely closely. French Rococo and Neo-classical styles are all found on firearms and there are even pistols made for presentation in the 19th century that are decorated in the style of the gothic revival, the stocks being set with medieval knights in architectural niches of carved ivory.

**BELOW** Dutch gunsmiths at work, *c.*1695.

# Combined weapons

The somewhat unpredictable nature of early firearms, added to the elaborate and lengthy process of reloading, gave rise to the notion that the firearm should be combined with an edged weapon or another form of defence.

### Early inventions

The idea of combining the mechanism of a firearm with another weapon was thought of as early as the 15th century. Some of the earliest wheel-locks were found on three crossbows in the Arsenale at Venice, dating from about 1510. Another interesting group of combined weapons are the gun-shields from the armoury of Henry VIII of England, many of which are preserved in the Tower of London and Windsor Castle, in England. Supplied in 1544 by an Italian merchant in Ravenna, these consisted of a steel-faced circular shield, fitted in the centre with a short, heavy, breech-loading pistol operating on the matchlock principle.

In addition to guns combined with maces and axes, firearms were also combined with a dagger. The wheel-lock mechanism was mounted on the face of the blade and the barrel was formed of the central section of the blade. The dagger became a gun when the tip of the blade was pulled out to reveal the barrel.

Different gunmaking centres produced their own distinctive combination arms. One such was the *fokos*, an axe with a small blade, mounted on an elaborately inlaid wooden shaft, on which is set a flintlock mechanism. The *fokos* was a speciality of the gunmakers of Teschen in Silesia and was popular in the late 17th century, mainly in Eastern Europe.

### Hunting swords

Where combined weapons were most widely used was in the hunting-field. Hunting was a most important occupation, especially before the 19th century. Elaborate costumes and equipment were designed specifically for the chase. Included in this equipment were combined arms. These included spears combined with guns and, in particular, sword gun combinations. There are a number of short hunting swords dating from the 18th century which have short barrels mounted on the blade with a small

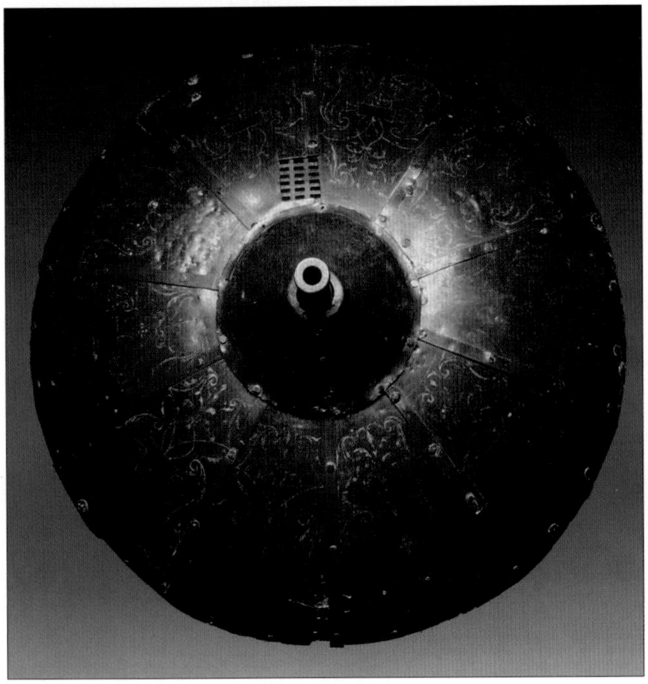

**ABOVE** Gunshield with a short barrelled breech-loading matchlock gun in its centre. Stored in the Tower of London since the 16th century, the shield was mentioned in an inventory dated 1547.

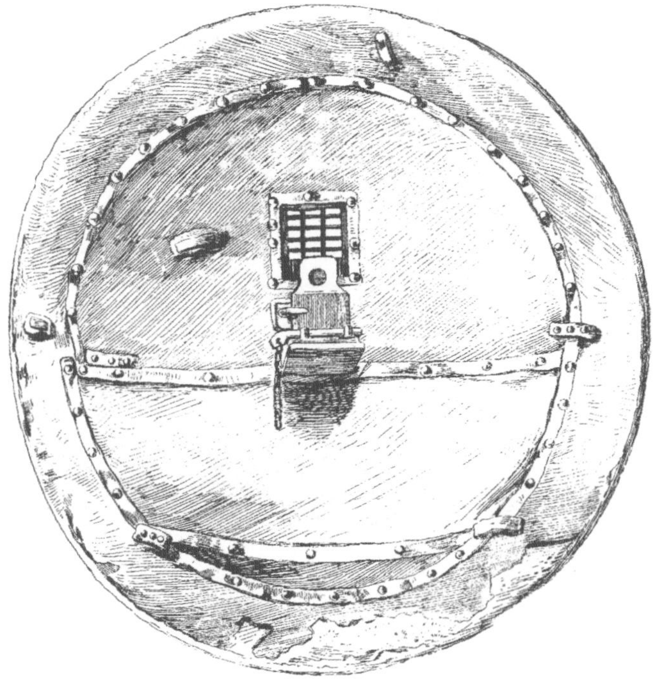

**ABOVE** Rear view of a 15th-century English shield with a gun. The small trellised window would have been used for aiming. Such designs were impractical and short-lived.

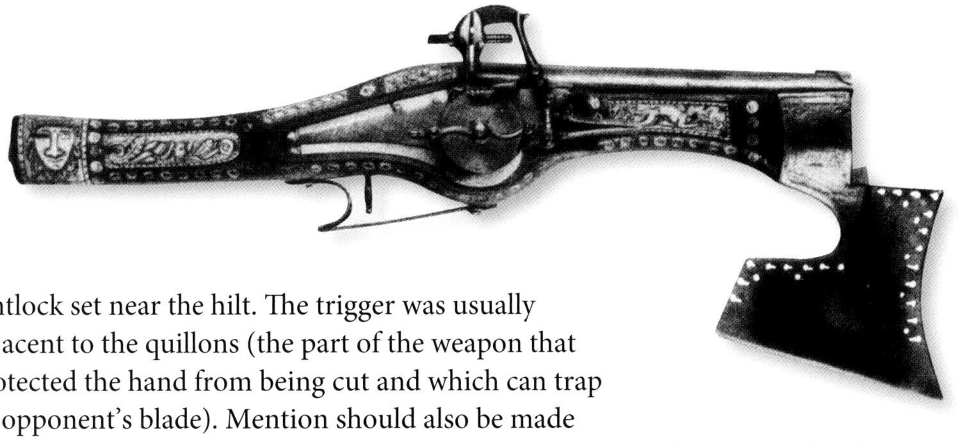

**LEFT** A German 17th-century wheel-lock pistol with battleaxe. Apart from the sword or knife, most combination weapons such as these were clumsy and inefficient and have never been very successful in use.

flintlock set near the hilt. The trigger was usually adjacent to the quillons (the part of the weapon that protected the hand from being cut and which can trap an opponent's blade). Mention should also be made of the series of flintlock firearms produced at the end of the 18th century that had a bayonet folded under the barrel which snapped forward into place when the trigger guard was pulled back.

### Combining with furniture

One of the most unusual examples of a firearm combined with a piece of furniture is a 19th-century steel chest made to contain valuables which has four percussion pistols mounted inside. If the lid is opened without setting a special catch, the pistols fire. An examination of the barrels of the steel chest indicated that all four pistols had been fired at some time.

### Other combinations

Pistols have been combined with keys, with knives, forks and spoons, and with truncheons. An inventor from Barnstaple in Devon, England, patented a metal truncheon with a percussion lock in 1823. An American patent of 1837 obtained by George Elgin of Georgia was a single-shot percussion pistol combined with the blade of a Bowie knife (a stout hunting knife). These were made in some quantity and were clearly very popular. In Sheffield a knife-pistol known as the "self protector" was made by the cutlery firm of Unwin and Rogers. These were made from about 1845 and were large pen-knives set with a barrel.

## Wheel-lock combination axe and pistol

This was possibly a novelty or curiosity weapon, which fired from five barrels from the axe-edge end of the weapon. The muzzles of these five barrels were concealed by a hinged cover which formed the edge of the axe-blade at the right. The topmost barrel was ignited by a matchlock (not visible) fitted on the left side – the mechanism was concealed by a brass plate. The second barrel was visible from the right side of the weapon and ignited by a wheel-lock. This mechanism occupied most of the outer surface of the axe-head on the right side. The gunpowder in the pan was ignited by the pyrites held in the jaw. There was a tubular extension to the pan of the wheel-lock to hold a length of match which would be ignited by the flash of the priming and then withdrawn to ignite the remaining three barrels. The remaining three barrels were ignited by the hand-held match, as was the sixth barrel forming the handle or shaft.

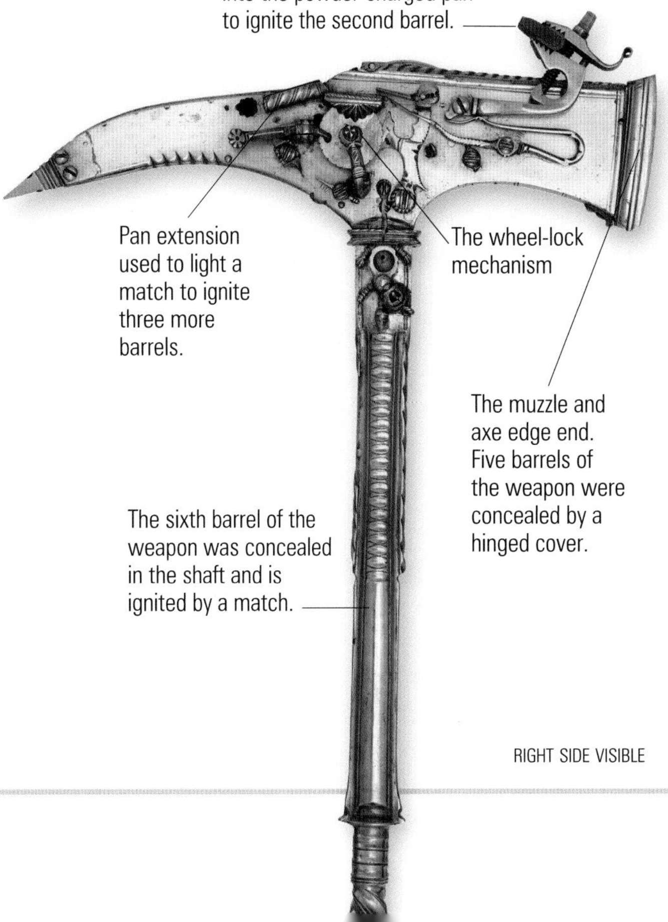


**RIGHT** This unusual weapon is believed to be Iberian or German, dating from the early 17th century.

# "The gun that won the West"

The handgun most widely associated with the opening up of the American West in the mid and late 19th century, and the books and films that have been based on this period, will always be the Colt revolver in its various forms. If this was the gun used by the "good guy" in a Hollywood Western movie, the weapon of choice of the villain was the pocket sized Deringer pistol. In the 1890s Smith & Wesson, a company with a fine pedigree in small-arms design would produce the revolver that would replace the Colt for the US Navy and Army.

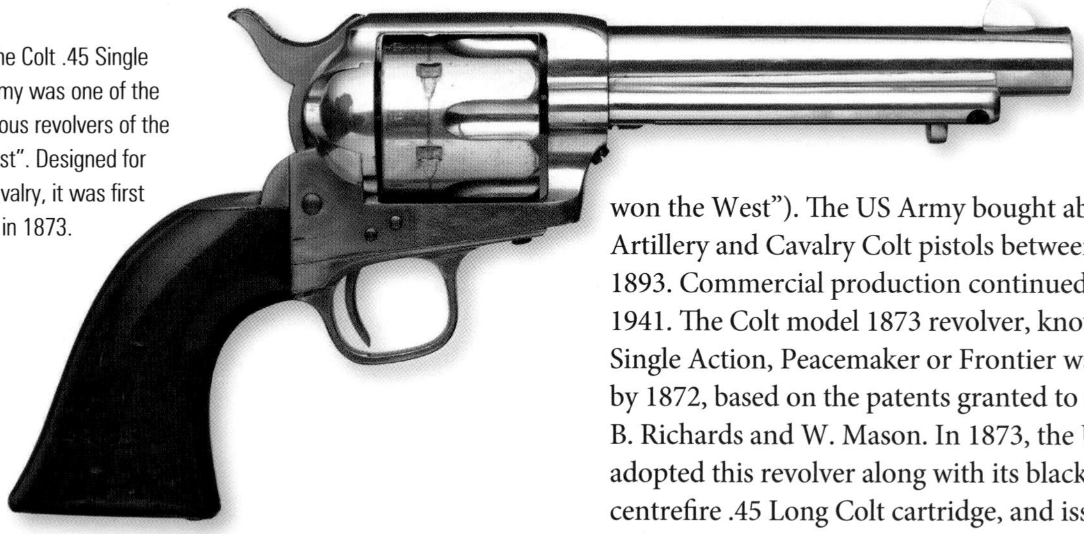

**RIGHT** The Colt .45 Single Action Army was one of the most famous revolvers of the "Wild West". Designed for the US cavalry, it was first produced in 1873.

## Samuel Colt's innovation

The style of revolver that was popular in the 1840s and 1850s had six bored holes in the barrel. It could be loaded with six shots in one go, which could be fired one after the other. It continued to be used until the 1860s in both Europe and the United States. In 1835 Samuel Colt took out a patent for a weapon with a rotating cylinder. He established the standard of a cylinder with multiple chambers, each of which successively locked in position behind the barrel and was discharged by pressure on the trigger. In Colt's early revolvers, the cylinder revolved as the hammer was cocked manually. Later revolvers, in which the hammer was cocked and the cylinder revolved as the trigger was pulled, were developed soon afterwards.

## The .44/40 Colt

Colt initially produced the same gun in a variety of calibres and barrel lengths, ranging from a stubby 4.75in/120mm up to 12in/305mm for the civilian market. The .44/40 Colt was particularly popular because the ammunition was compatible with that of the Winchester carbine (known as "the gun that won the West"). The US Army bought about 37,000 Artillery and Cavalry Colt pistols between 1873 and 1893. Commercial production continued, but ceased in 1941. The Colt model 1873 revolver, known as the Colt Single Action, Peacemaker or Frontier was developed by 1872, based on the patents granted to Charles B. Richards and W. Mason. In 1873, the US Army adopted this revolver along with its black powder centrefire .45 Long Colt cartridge, and issued the Army or Cavalry model with two different lengths of barrel.

The advent of films and television Westerns in the 1950s prompted the Colt company to bring the Single Action back into production for the commercial market in 1956. The 1957 film *Gunfight at the O.K. Corral*, depicting a fight on a chilly day in 1881, is an interesting example of the realities of gunfights in the Wild West. Handguns were notoriously difficult to fire at close range. The accepted wisdom is the classic pose of a gun at arm's length and shoulder height. The quick-firing hero fanning the hammer of his Colt as he "shoots from the hip" and hits his adversaries with lethal shots is pure Hollywood.

## Deringer pocket pistols

At the far end of the scale from the Colt revolver was the little single-shot pocket pistol developed by Henry Deringer of Philadelphia. Versions of the Deringer were made by numerous gunsmiths, including Colt. It achieved its greatest popularity in the United States in the years leading up to the Civil War. It was a favourite of men and women who wanted a compact, easily concealed firearm for personal defence, and so 15,000 were produced between 1850 and 1866.

## The Colt factory

Samuel Colt, the son of a factory owner, was born in Hartford, Connecticut, on 19 July 1814. After leaving school, Colt worked at his father's textile mill. He was fascinated with machinery and spent his spare time disassembling and reassembling his father's guns. When only 16, he designed a fireworks display for the Fourth of July celebrations. Unfortunately, the school building burned to the ground. Fearing expulsion, Colt ran away to sea in 1829. While at sea Colt got the idea of designing a handgun with a revolving cylinder containing several bullets which could be fired through a single barrel. On his return he continued his work and the five-shot revolver was patented in the mid-1830s. In 1836 Colt established his Patent Arms Manufacturing company in Paterson, New Jersey.

However, sales were generally slow, and in 1842 he was forced to close down his factory. In 1847 Colt designed a six-shot Walker revolver. Soon afterwards the US government ordered 1,000 revolvers for use in the Mexican War. Colt was now in a position to establish a new factory in Hartford, Connecticut. By 1856 Colt had the largest private arms' manufacturing facility in the world. Colt, who skilfully promoted the gun culture that endures in America to this day, died on 10 January 1862. The Colt industry thrived and its handguns would arm the US Armed Forces and Police for many years.

**LEFT** The inventor and industrialist Samuel Colt. By 1856 Colt owned the largest private arms manufacturing facility in the world.

Although the .41 Deringer pistol was somewhat limited by its single-shot capacity, its light weight and small size gave it a distinct advantage over bulkier weapons like the 1873 Colt. To compensate for the single shot, many people simply carried two pistols. The Deringer became notorious when it was used in a number of Californian murders in the 1850s, as well as its later use in the assassination of President Lincoln. In Hollywood films about the West the little pistol would be used by sneaky gamblers, though in John Ford's 1939 classic film *Stagecoach* the southern gambler produced a Deringer as an act of mercy to kill the wife of a US Cavalry officer and spare her from capture by Apache Indians.

### The test of war

In 1892 the US Army retired the Colt .45 Single Action Army Model revolver and decided to re-equip with a more modern revolver. They selected a .38 revolver built on a robust frame and both Colt and Smith & Wesson made versions of these firearms. In 1889 the US Navy adopted the revolver, followed by the US Marine Corps in 1905.

However it was during the Philippine Insurrection of 1899–1900 that showed that the .38in cartridge was not powerful enough. To rectify this, in 1908 a .38 Special cartridge was developed and the .38 Army Special revolver. Though it was superseded by a .45 model of similar design in 1909 the Special remained in production until 1928 for the commercial market and police, with some 220,000 being made.

**LEFT** *Gunfight at the O.K. Corral,* 1881, as depicted in a painting by Terence Cuneo. It gives a good idea of the close range at which many of these shootouts took place. In this gunfight one participant – John "Doc" Holliday – used a shotgun that he had kept hidden under his coat.

# Innovations

The final years of the 19th century saw innovations in the way pistols and revolvers were designed. Among them were firearms made by Leopold Gasser who operated factories across Europe, which reputedly turned out 100,000 revolvers annually in the 1880s and 1890s. In 1907 the Austrian Roth-Steyr self-loader was the first such weapon to be adopted for military service. The huge British Gabbet-Fairfax Mars semi-automatic (also called self-loading) pistol, though novel, was destined never to be used by the British Army.

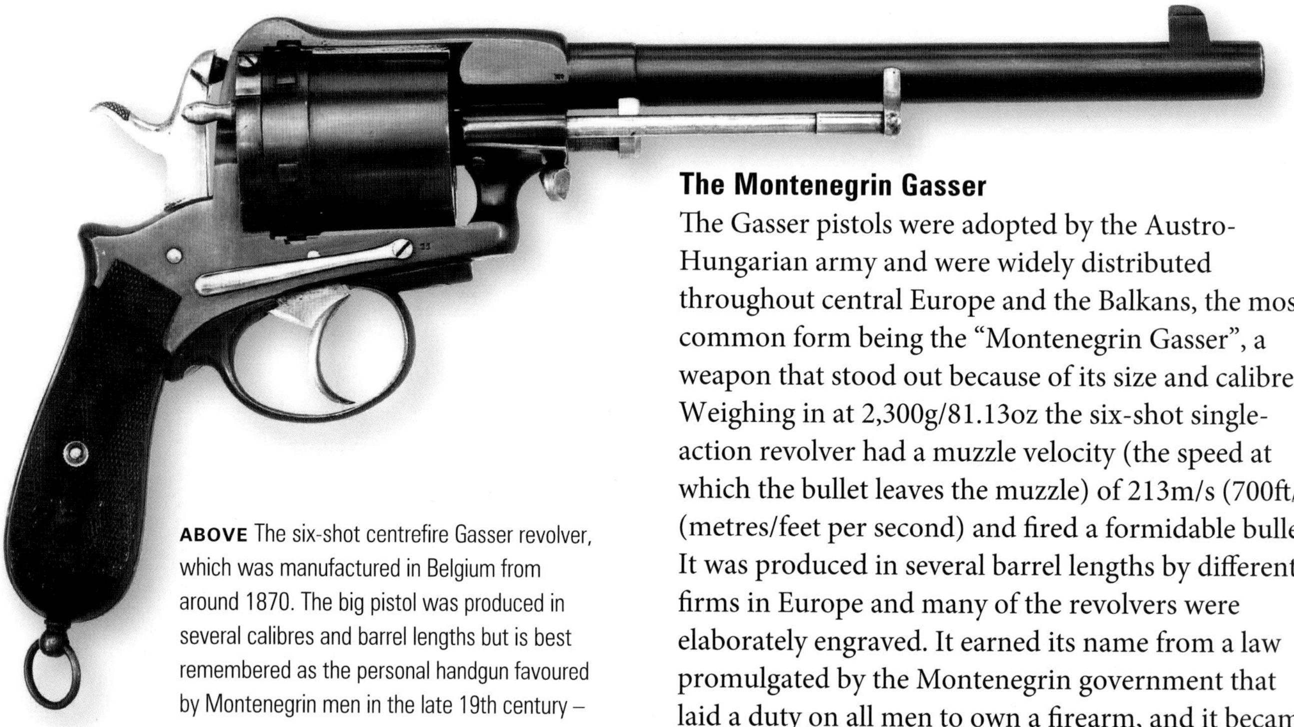

**ABOVE** The six-shot centrefire Gasser revolver, which was manufactured in Belgium from around 1870. The big pistol was produced in several calibres and barrel lengths but is best remembered as the personal handgun favoured by Montenegrin men in the late 19th century – earning it the sobriquet "Montenegrin Gasser".

### The Montenegrin Gasser

The Gasser pistols were adopted by the Austro-Hungarian army and were widely distributed throughout central Europe and the Balkans, the most common form being the "Montenegrin Gasser", a weapon that stood out because of its size and calibre. Weighing in at 2,300g/81.13oz the six-shot single-action revolver had a muzzle velocity (the speed at which the bullet leaves the muzzle) of 213m/s (700ft/s) (metres/feet per second) and fired a formidable bullet. It was produced in several barrel lengths by different firms in Europe and many of the revolvers were elaborately engraved. It earned its name from a law promulgated by the Montenegrin government that laid a duty on all men to own a firearm, and it became the weapon of choice for the men of Montenegro.

### The single-and double-action revolver

A revolver works by having several firing chambers arranged in a circle in a cylindrical block. These are brought into alignment with the firing mechanism and barrel one at a time. In early revolvers, a shooter had to pull the hammer back before each shot and then pull the trigger to release the hammer. These are called single-action revolvers.

An innovation in lock-work arrived in the 1850s, which allowed firing by single- or double-action. The hammer could either be cocked and then released by a light trigger pressure, or the trigger could be pulled right back in a "long pull" action to rotate the cylinder and raise and release the hammer. This meant it did not need to be manually cocked between shots. Double-action is used on most present day revolvers. The first revolvers used gunpowder, balls and caps like the early percussion-cap pistols. The shooter would load each of the six chambers in the cylinder with gunpowder and a projectile, and fire using the percussion caps. In the 1870s, these early models were replaced by revolvers that used bullet cartridges instead of gunpowder and caps. Revolvers passed through the pinfire and rimfire stages to use the centrefire metallic cartridge case. The breech-loading revolver has a gate in the rear part of the frame (which backs up the cylinder) for loading and ejecting.

## Young cannon

ABOVE Different designs of the Gabbet-Fairfax Mars could fire 8.5mm, 9mm or .45 ammunition. The recoil force from the .45 round was such that the firer found his arm jerked vertically upright on firing.

In the world of big self-loaders, the British Gabbet-Fairfax Mars reigned supreme. Different marks designed by H.W. Gabbet-Fairfax could fire 8.5mm, 9mm or .45 calibre ammunition. However, it was the .45 that really had a punch. It had a muzzle velocity of 381m/s (1,250ft/s) while the 8.5mm produced an incredible 533m/s (1,750ft/s). It was rejected by the British War Office as a service weapon because of the requirement for special ammunition and the excessive recoil caused by the powerful cartridges and complex long recoil mechanism, which did not lend itself to cost-effective production. Another drawback of the design was that the cases were ejected out of the back of the pistol directly into the face of the firer. The design did not prove to be a commercial success. It is not known exactly how many Mars pistols were manufactured, most estimates being around 70, although one pistol is known with a serial number of 195. It is an indication of the rarity of these weapons that when one came up for auction in 2015, it sold for US $46,000.

ABOVE The Roth-Steyr Model was developed by George Roth and first issued to the Austro-Hungarian cavalry in 1907. The design included a bolt that extended the full length of the receiver.

## Cavalry pistols

The Roth-Steyr Model is an early 20th-century pistol. It was the first self-loader to be adopted by a major power as a service weapon when it entered service with the cavalry arm of the Austro-Hungarian army in 1907. It was a large and heavy pistol that fired a unique rimless 8mm cartridge. The barrel and breech were locked together and are separated during recoil by a cam action that rotated the barrel through 90 degrees to unlock the bolt. Though the pistol had 10-rounds of ammunition, this was not housed in a removable magazine and they had to be loaded into the butt (grip) from the top using a charger (a device to load a magazine). The pistol had a rather complex safety system: the pistol would reload after it had been fired, but would not recock. The bolt had to be pulled back by hand to reset the mechanism if there was a misfire. This was a deliberate feature as a pistol with a conventional pull would have been too light and prone to accidental discharge if the horse shied or bucked.

**ABOVE** The 1908 Bergmann-Bayard. German industrialist, Theodor Bergmann, hired a gun designer and developed a series of automatic pistols at the turn of the 20th century. It used its own 9mm Bergmann-Bayard cartridge.

**ABOVE** The 1935 Browning 9mm GP or Grand Puissance (High-Power) pistol. The pistol had been designed a decade earlier in 1925 by the weapons engineer John Moses Browning.

# Into the modern age

During the 20th century technological improvements in weapons design meant that they became more reliable, faster and ultimately more deadly. Although revolvers maintained a steady following, the automatic handgun, initially designed by John Moses Browning, became standard issue for police and security forces around the world. Many have become classics: the Luger, Beretta and Browning High-Power remain highly regarded weapons. Two world wars and countless smaller conflicts have only encouraged arms manufacturers to produce lighter, quieter and more powerful weapons. From the Mauser and Tommy gun, via the Sten gun to the Uzi, successive generations have produced ever more efficient weapon systems. In the early years of the 21st century, the wheel seems to have gone full circle. Fail-safe firepower is still critical, but there is now a demand for non-lethal ammunition that will fell an opponent without causing permanent damage.

**ABOVE** Weapons training for women in 1941. The submachine gun in the foreground is a Sten Mark III and the Sten in the background is a Mark I. The Mark I had a wooden foregrip and forward handle. The Mark III is a simplified version of the Mark I and II.

# Guns of the Empire

The weapons of empire used by soldiers and adventurers were often large-calibre revolvers that could be used quickly in a confined space such as a tent or cabin, and long-range rifles used in engagements on the North-West Frontier of India or the open veldt of South Africa. A classic example was the British Webley .455 revolver developed by Webley & Son (Webley & Scott Revolver and Arms Company Ltd from 1897) in the 1870s. A few years later the French Army adopted an 8mm revolver, the Modèle d'Ordonnance (Lebel); it was a revolver that would be taken into the 20th century.

**LEFT** The Webley Mark I, adopted by the Royal Navy in 1887, was the first in a series of revolvers produced by this British company.

## Webley revolvers

The British Webleys were the first "top-break" revolvers with a two-piece frame, which hinged (or broke) at the forward low end for the ejection of cartridge cases and loading. The ejector operated automatically when the frame was broken open and all six empty cases were ejected simultaneously from the cylinder. The cartridges could then be inserted by hand. Designers of revolvers in all calibres adopted the top-break system, as it made for quick reloading – crucial in a short-range firefight. Webleys that had been rechambered for the .45 ACP (a calibre known as .45 Automatic Colt Pistol) round used two three-round half-moon clips (to hold enough ammunition to half-fill the cylinder). This further speeded up reloading.

**BELOW** The last stand of a British officer at the Battle of Isandlwana in 1879. He has only six rounds in his Webley revolver and little scope to reload quickly.

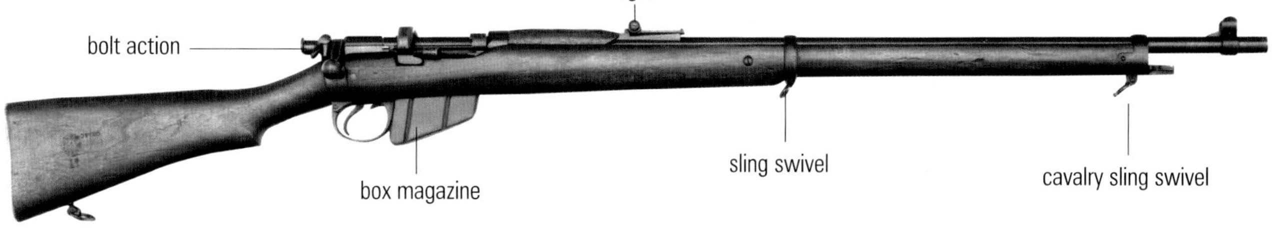


**ABOVE** The British eight-round .303 Lee Metford, the first repeater rifle. Adopted by the British military in 1888, it encouraged development in small-arms design which, in the case of the Lee Metford, resulted in the introduction of the No. 4 Rifle.

### Personal choice

British Army officers and colonial administrators of the Empire would often buy private weapons. Winston Churchill purchased a Webley Wilkinson revolver in 1893 and carried it during his early military career. His later private purchases were a C96 Broomhandle and a Colt 1911. The penalty for this personal choice could be finding ammunition if the weapon was of an unusual calibre. In a remote outpost of the Empire this could literally be a matter of life and death and persuasive words of a salesman in a London gunsmith would ring hollow as the officer looked at his emptying ammunition pouch in a firefight.

In 1887, the British Army and Royal Navy took the first Webley revolver as its official service revolver. This six-shot, double-action revolver was engineered to take the black powder .455 British service cartridge. This cartridge fired a large lead bullet, but because it used black powder it had a relatively slow muzzle velocity of 180m/s (590.55ft/s). Although a smokeless cartridge was then developed, the velocity remained low and could also be fired in early revolvers.

All Webley revolvers were double-action or double-action-only, with a very distinctive barrel shape, a frame lock with lock lever on the left side of the frame, and V-shaped lock spring at the right side.

### Trench raids

The generals and political leaders who took Europe to war in August 1914 had not anticipated the possibility of trench warfare, but as the stalemate on the Western Front continued, compact and handy weapons such as the Webley became highly valued by the combatants. The long bolt-action rifles carried by most infantry in European armies (the exception was the British, with their compact Short Magazine Lee Enfield), were ideal for long-range engagements in open country, but were impractical in the confines of a trench. In the quick, violent fighting patrols known as "trench raids" soldiers carried clubs, knuckle-dusters and knives – silent weapons that could be used in hand-to-hand combat. The revolver or semi-automatic pistol were the only useful firearms in these confined spaces. This was the battleground that would spawn a new weapon: the submachine gun.

### The French army revolver

The French 8mm Modèle d'Ordonnance (Lebel) 1892 revolver enjoyed a remarkable longevity in service with the French Army. Adopted in 1892, it was still in service in World War II. The pistol had a conventional swing-out cylinder, with the release button on the right, which made it a user-friendly weapon for left-handed shooters. It had an ingenious system that allowed the left-hand plate to swing forward on a hinge to expose the mechanism for cleaning. Like many weapons developed in the late 19th century the revolver used its own special 8mm ammunition.

**LEFT** The Webley Mark VI was first produced in 1915 and remained in service until World War II. The revolver, similar in many ways to the Mark V Webley, was issued to British and Commonwealth forces.

# Classic revolvers

Revolvers were the classic handguns of the 19th and early 20th centuries. Although they were reliable and robust, reloading under pressure always presented a problem, and the weapon could become clogged by dirt or grit.

**ABOVE** The 7.62mm Nagant Model 1895 was a Belgian pistol, but it was later produced in the USSR and Scandinavian countries.

### The Nagant Model 1895

Widely regarded as a Russian revolver, the Nagant Model 1895G was actually designed in the early 1890s by the Belgian brothers Emile and Leon Nagant. It was first manufactured and used in Russia and adopted by other countries, including Sweden and Poland and, later, the USSR. Local production began in 1898 after the Imperial Russian government had received shipments from Belgium. Technically, the Nagant was almost obsolete when it was adopted in 1895, since revolvers like the American Smith & Wesson Hand Ejectors and Colts with side-opening cylinders were much faster to reload. However, it was not until 1930 that the Nagant Model 1895 finally became obsolete in Russia, enduring as the standard sidearm for more than thirty years. It was widely used and manufactured during World War II, and production finally ceased in the 1950s. The Nagant Model 1895 had some distinctive features, such as the gas-sealed cylinder, which, almost uniquely, made it a revolver suitable for mounting a silencer. A special silencer, called the "Bramit device", was designed by the Mitin brothers, and was used by the Russian NKVD secret police and some Red Army special forces during World War II.

### The Webley-Fosbery model 1901

Designed by George Fosbery, a Victorian hero who at the age of 31 had won the Victoria Cross, the Webley-Fosbery is a remarkable weapon. In effect it is an automatic revolver. It opens, loads and unloads like other contemporary Webley revolvers. However, when the pistol is fired, the recoil from the cartridge moves the receiver back in its frame. At this point

**RIGHT** The original caption for this American poster reads: "Cowboy spurring on horse to escape Indians, while shooting it out with a Smith and Wesson pistol." The poster was created in the late 19th century in order to promote Smith & Wesson revolvers.

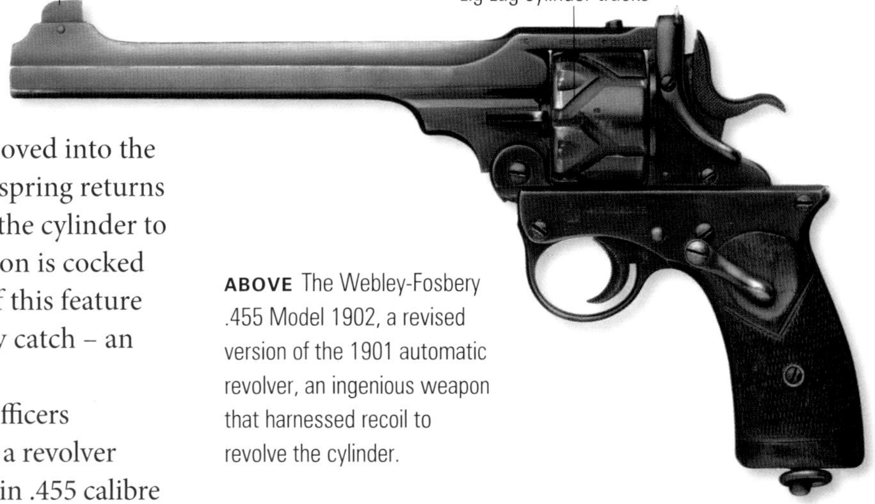


**ABOVE** The Webley-Fosbery .455 Model 1902, a revised version of the 1901 automatic revolver, an ingenious weapon that harnessed recoil to revolve the cylinder.

a cam pin fixed in the frame engages in zigzag slots in the outer surface of the pistol cylinder, and revolves it half-way toward the next chamber. Simultaneously the pistol's hammer is moved into the cocked position. As the frame-mounted spring returns the receiver forward, the cam pin forces the cylinder to revolve the rest of the way, and the weapon is cocked and ready to fire its next shot. Because of this feature the Webley-Fosbery is fitted with a safety catch – an unusual feature in revolvers.

The weapon was popular with British officers before World War I, who could purchase a revolver made to order. The Webley was available in .455 calibre for the British service cartridge, and later in .38 ACP. With a ready supply of six-round clips, a marksman could attain a rate of fire of 70 rounds per minute (rpm).

### The Colt model 1917

With the United States' entry into World War I, manufacturers of the Colt 1911 with the .45 ACP cartridge could not keep up with the demand of the US Army. Two pistols were chosen as a stopgap measure: the Colt New Service pistol and the Smith & Wesson New Century, both of which had been used in action by the British Army on the Western Front. In the light of this combat experience the design of the Smith & Wesson was modified. The Colt New Service was chambered in the .45 ACP cartridge and known as the Colt Model 1917. It could be quickly loaded or unloaded by either three-round stamped metal half-moon clips or six-round full-moon clips.

### The "Three Eight"

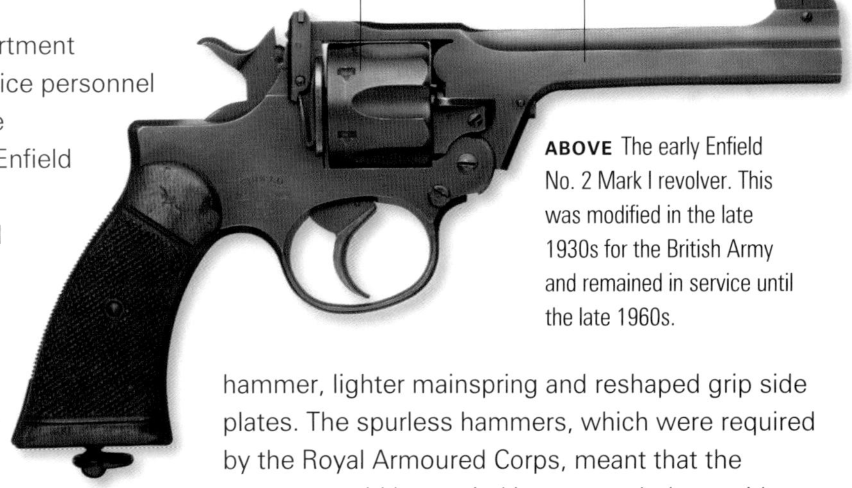


**ABOVE** The early Enfield No. 2 Mark I revolver. This was modified in the late 1930s for the British Army and remained in service until the late 1960s.

After World War I the British War Department decided that tank crews and other service personnel who required a sidearm needed a more compact handgun. The result was the Enfield No. 2 Mark I .38 revolver developed at the Royal Small Arms Factory in Enfield between 1926 and 1927. The design was a scaled-down Webley Mark VI with its "break-top" frame and cylinder chambered for six rounds and firing a heavy-grain bullet. The hammer/trigger group was redesigned, with a manual hammer safety lock added, as well as a separate cylinder lock. This revolver was adopted for British military service in 1932 as the Enfield revolver, .38 No. 2 Mark I. After 1938, almost all No. 2 Mark Is were converted into No. 2 Mark I* configuration.

The Enfield No. 2 Mark I* was developed in the late 1930s for the British Tank Corps (part of the Royal Armoured Corps) and was distinguished from the early Mark I by a spurless, double-action-only hammer, lighter mainspring and reshaped grip side plates. The spurless hammers, which were required by the Royal Armoured Corps, meant that the weapon could be carried in an open holster without snagging on controls or cabling inside the tank.

The Enfield No. 2 Mark I** appeared in 1942 as a simplified, wartime design. These revolvers were similar to the No. 2 Mark I*, but without the hammer stop. After 1945, all the Enfields were recalled and converted into No. 2 Mark I* configuration. Known informally as the "Three Eight" in the British army, the revolver was robust and comfortable to fire.

# Enter the semi-automatic

To men who carried revolvers, the semi-automatic pistol initially seemed over-engineered and too complex. It would, however, supersede the revolver in almost all roles in the 20th century. Among its attractions were a more compact shape and ease of reloading.

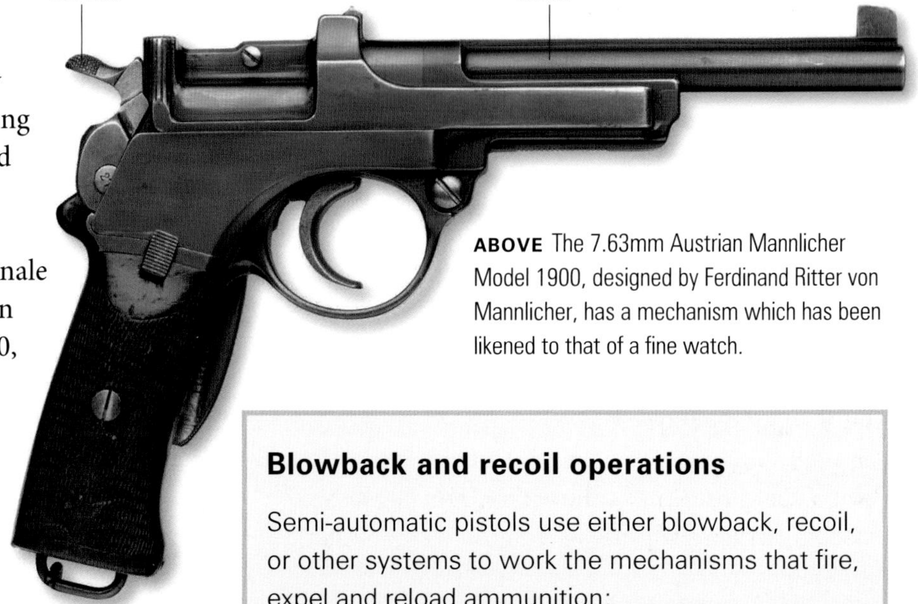


**ABOVE** The 7.63mm Austrian Mannlicher Model 1900, designed by Ferdinand Ritter von Mannlicher, has a mechanism which has been likened to that of a fine watch.

### The John Moses Browning

The first semi-automatic pistol, the FN Browning M1900, was designed by American firearms maker J.M. Browning in *c.*1896, and followed by an improved version in 1897. In 1898, Browning's design was accepted by the Belgian firearms manufacturer Fabrique Nationale de Herstal (FN), who began production of the 1899 model. A year later, in 1900, Belgium adopted the FN Browning M1900, a modified version with a shorter barrel. Use of the Browning Number 1 pistol, as it was also known, spread across Europe as a civilian and police sidearm. The chamber was designed for the 7.6mm x 17mm round, which is also known in the Americas as the .32 AC, a new smokeless round. Manufactured until about 1911, more than 700,000 FN Browning M1900 pistols were made.

### An Austrian aristocrat

The 7.63mm Austrian Mannlicher Model 1900 has all the elegance of a duelling pistol from an earlier century. Designed by Ferdinand Ritter von

**ABOVE** The FN Browning M1900 was one of the most commercially successful semi-automatic pistols produced before World War I. It was widely used by police forces and bodyguards.

### Blowback and recoil operations

Semi-automatic pistols use either blowback, recoil, or other systems to work the mechanisms that fire, expel and reload ammunition:

**Blowback-operated weapons** use the pressure created from the fired round to push a bolt, located directly behind the round, back and forth against a spring. Its pressure pushes the bolt backwards against the spring and also ejects the spent round from the gun. A new round enters the weapon, and as the compressed spring pushes the bolt forward, the bolt pushes the round into the breech. A pin on the end of the bolt strikes the round and fires it, beginning the cycle again. Blowback weapons are simple and reliable, but they do not form a complete seal at the breech when firing.

**Recoil-operated weapons** push the barrel and the breech backwards as a unit, along with the bolt. The ejection and reloading cycles are completed during this recoil, and the breech remains sealed during firing. Recoil-operated have more moving parts than blowback-operated weapons. The weapons are heavy but very reliable. As a result, they have relatively low rates of fire.

Mannlicher, it is a well-balanced, light pistol with a mechanism that has been likened to that of a fine watch for its precision and action. Von Mannlicher had a good design but knew that it could be improved. The 1900 model was followed by the 1901 with a longer barrel and a repositioned rear sight. In 1903 he produced a model with a box magazine (a device for holding ammunition via a slot on the receiver) in front of the trigger guard and a new mechanism. Although European armies did not take up the 1900 and 1901 models, they became popular in South America. One of the drawbacks of this pistol was that it used a special cartridge made only in Austria, and, to add to the logistic problems, the 1903 pistol had its own specialized ammunition.

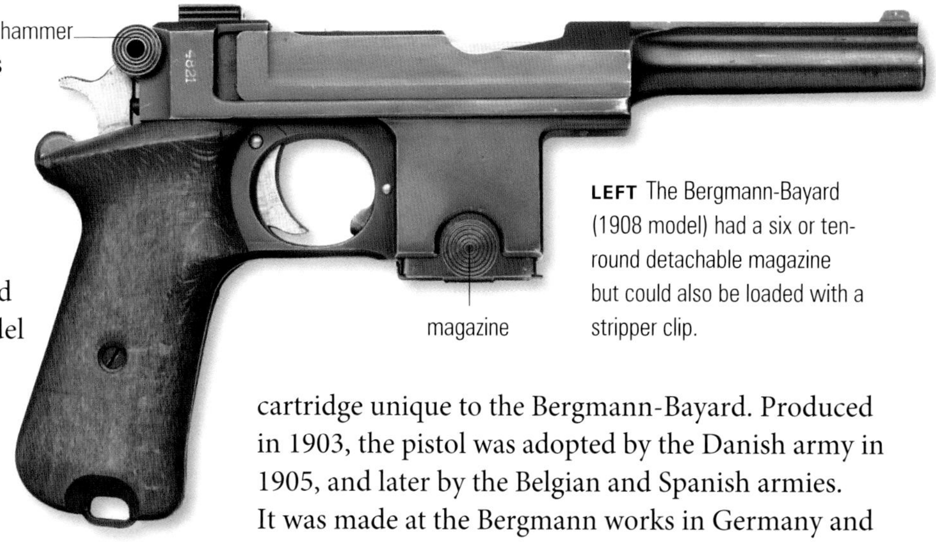


**LEFT** The Bergmann-Bayard (1908 model) had a six or ten-round detachable magazine but could also be loaded with a stripper clip.

### The Bergmann-Bayard

This German pistol was one of the first pistols developed to use 9mm calibre ammunition, although this was not Parabellum but a round with a larger cartridge unique to the Bergmann-Bayard. Produced in 1903, the pistol was adopted by the Danish army in 1905, and later by the Belgian and Spanish armies. It was made at the Bergmann works in Germany and also mass-produced by Peiper of Herstal in Belgium. Although the pistol looks like a Mauser, it has a simpler trigger mechanism and the magazine can be removed. To reload, the magazine can either be filled by hand or, with the action open, a charger can be inserted and the rounds pushed into the magazine – an obvious advantage in a military pistol. Like other weapons of this period it could be fitted with a holster stock that was clipped to the bottom of the butt to convert it into a light carbine (automatic rifle).

### The Luger Model 1908

The German Luger self-loading pistol, known in German army service as the Pistole 08 from its year of adoption, was named after George Luger, a designer at the Ludwig Löwe small-arms factory in Berlin. Hugo Borchardt based the Luger's design on an earlier idea, but Luger re-designed the Borchardt locking system (called lock-out) into a much smaller package. The toggle-lock mechanism was complex, but it made the weapon comfortable to fire and therefore more accurate. The first military Lugers were made in 1900 to a Swiss order. The original calibre was 7.65mm, but in 1902 at the request of the German navy, the firm of Deutsche Waffen und Munitionsfabriken (DWM), along with Luger, designed a bigger round. By re-necking the case of the 7.65mm Luger round the 9mm Luger/Parabellum was developed. The standard pistol had an eight-round box magazine and fired the Parabellum round with a maximum effective range of 70m/230ft.

**ABOVE** The Luger Model 1908, also known as the Pistole 08.

In the 1920s the British firm Vickers manufactured Lugers for export to the Netherlands. The shortest pistol had a 103mm/4.06in barrel, an overall length of 222mm/8.75in and weighed 875g/30.9oz.

The Naval Luger weighed 1,043g/36.8oz, had a 198mm/7.8in barrel, a tangent sight, and could be fitted with a 32-round "snail" magazine, effectively making it a light submachine gun.

# Semi-automatic innovation

The German Luger was an elegant design. However, the first .455in self-loading pistol produced in 1904 by the prolific British firm Webley & Scott Revolver and Arms Company Ltd did not have the same appeal, nor was it a commercial success. The American Colt M1911 self-loading pistol, however, proved to be the era's great survivor: with its rugged design and reliability in the front line it remained in service until the Vietnam War.

### The .455 Webley & Scott 1910

An improved version of the .455 Webley & Scott pistol introduced in 1910 proved a real success. It was the Royal Navy's standard pistol until the end of World War II and was used by the Royal Air Force, the Metropolitan Police and throughout the Empire. The pistol had a grip safety (a safety mechanism that prevents a gun from being fired, unless the grip is held firmly). On firing the ejection port threw the empty cases upwards and forwards. An ingenious system with the magazine allowed a user to fire hand-loaded single shots with the magazine partially inserted – if he needed a full magazine he simply had to push it completely home and six rounds were immediately available.

**LEFT** The Italian Glisenti Model 1910, sometimes referred to in early records as the Brixia, fired a low-powered 9mm round.

At the same time, the Italian Glisenti M1910 became the first semi-automatic pistol to be adopted by the Italian military. Although a later version was chambered to use the same cartridge case as the 9mm Luger, it was largely replaced by the 9mm Beretta Model 1915 in World War I.

Introduced in 1912, the Austro-Hungarian forces in World War I preferred the Steyr Model 1912 pistol over the range of other standard issue pistols. It was also used by the Romanians and Germans. Officially named "Selbstiade Pistol M12" by the Austrian Army, the pistol was also informally known as the Steyr-Hahn ("Steyr with a hammer") to distinguish it from the Roth-Steyr. During World War II, a number of weapons were re-barrelled for use by the German Army to take the 9mm Parabellum cartridge. About 250,000 of the pistols were made before production ceased in 1919.

**ABOVE** A British sergeant armed with a Colt .45 M1911A1 semi-automatic pistol stalks a German sniper in Italy, 1943. The American-made Colt was widely issued to Allied forces and was a popular sidearm. Its .45 rounds made it highly effective at short range.

### The .45 Colt 1911

The giant in the world of self-loading or semi-automatic pistols is the .45 Colt 1911, a US government model developed from a Browning design. It is a much more reliable pistol under muddy or sandy conditions than weapons like the Luger, because it does not have so much of its working mechanism exposed. The United States adopted this pistol in 1911 and modified it in 1921. It was redesignated the M1911A1. American servicemen carried the .45 Colt through World War II, the wars in Korea and Vietnam, and it was also widely issued to Allied forces. The 1911 was supplanted by the Beretta M9 in 1985, ending the 1911's record-setting 74-year-run as the longest service length for an American sidearm. It was 215mm/8.46in long, weighed 1,105g/39oz, had a seven-round magazine,

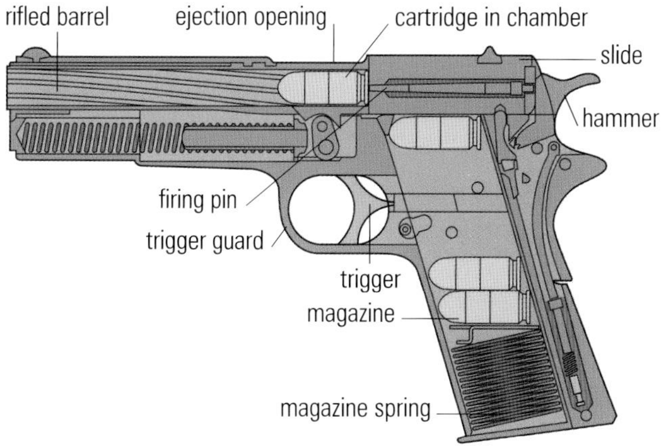


**ABOVE** A cross-section of a .45 Colt pistol. The rounds are held under compression in the magazine and each time the slide moves to the rear – either on firing or when the pistol is cocked, a round is fed into the chamber. Pressing the trigger releases the mechanism that allows the spring-loaded hammer to hit the firing pin.

**ABOVE** The Austrian Steyr Model 1912 was converted by the Germans in World War II to take 9mm Parabellum.

and a muzzle velocity of 262m/s (860ft/s). Ammunition from the Colt 1911A1 was compatible with the Thompson submachine gun Model 1928A1.

## Soviet TT pistols

About this time in the Soviet Union, Fedor V. Tokarev began developing a series of pistols with the prefix TT for Tula-Tokarev, or Tulskiy Tokarev (meaning Tokarev from Tula). The 7.62mm TT-33 was developed in 1930 and adopted by the Soviet Army the same year. In 1933, the pistol was improved with a new locking system and a different disconnector (used to prevent the gun from firing unless a magazine is inserted). It looked rather like the 1903 Colt .38 Pocket Automatic Pistol and could be disassembled (field stripped) in a similar way to the Colt 1911. The pistol was single-action, and recoil-operated in the same way as the Browning design, with an eight-round single-stack magazine.

## Japanese Nambu Type 14

Across the Pacific, the 14th Year Pistol designed by Japanese General Kijiro Nambu was an improved and cheaper version of an earlier, similar Japanese pistol. Externally it looked like a Luger, but the locking system was based on a different system. The Imperial Japanese Army adopted it in 1925 as the official sidearm with the designation Type 14 Pistol. One unusual version, nicknamed "Kiska", had a very large trigger guard designed for use by a soldier wearing thick gloves in the bitter winters of northern Japan, mainland China and Korea.

The Nambu Type 14 was maligned as a very poorly designed weapon. It fired an underpowered 8mm cartridge with a muzzle velocity of 290m/s (950ft/s). It was difficult to reach and operate the safety catch, and if the magazine release catch became clogged it was very difficult to remove the magazine. However, the Nambu also functioned very well, was very accurate, and had an excellent natural point of aim and trigger pull.

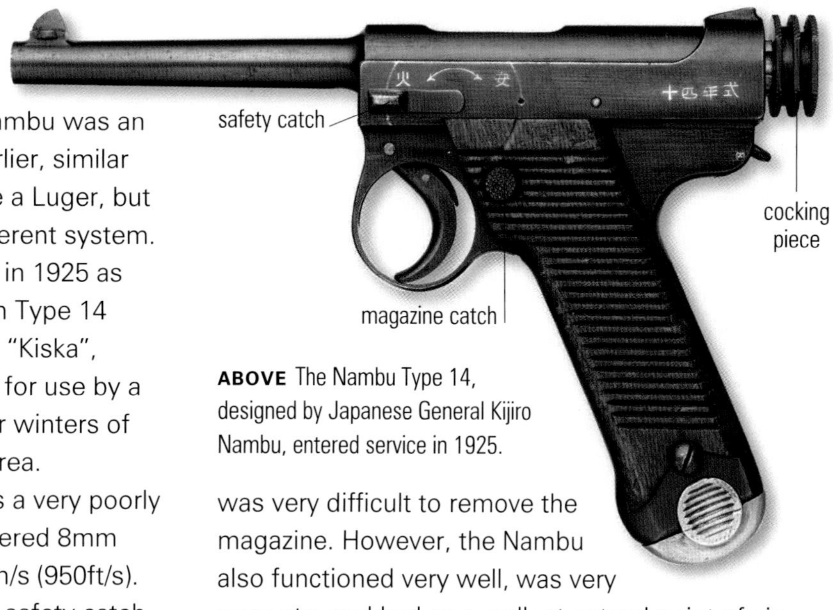


**ABOVE** The Nambu Type 14, designed by Japanese General Kijiro Nambu, entered service in 1925.

# The submachine gun

The need for a submachine gun had its origins in World War I, as a method of clearing the enemy trenches of soldiers at close-range. Fast-firing semi-automatic pistols fitted with a detachable stock pointed the way to the introduction of the first submachine gun (SMG). By the close of that war the Germans and Italians had produced the first submachine guns – the German weapon being a classic design.

### The Mauser pistol

Known as the "Military Model", the German 1895 Broomhandle Mauser pistol was never an official issue weapon, although it was popular with officers as a private-purchase sidearm. Although it had been made in 7.63mm with a special 9mm Mauser cartridge, by 1914 many had been converted to 9mm Parabellum (the most standard calibre). The standard model had a built-in ten-round magazine, fed by a clip from the top. A fully automatic type was also produced in limited numbers and used by German troops as a light machine pistol – a submachine gun by any other name.

**ABOVE** The Italian 9mm Glisenti Twin Villar Perosa. Though this unusual-looking weapon is a world away from modern submachine guns, it was in fact the world's first submachine gun. The Italians failed to see its potential at first and used it as a static light machine gun.

**ABOVE** A German Waffen-SS soldier takes aim with a private-purchase Mauser military pistol, converted from the original 7.63mm model to 9mm Parabellum. Fitted with a shoulder stock, this weapon could be fired very accurately by experienced shots, particularly against static targets.

### The first submachine guns

In 1915 Italy became the first country to adopt a submachine gun, known as either the "Villar Perosa", or the "Fiat" depending on its place of manufacture, or the "Revelli" after the designer Abiel Revelli. The original production had no stock, and two barrels with two 25-round box magazines and thumb-type triggers. Like all other early Italian submachine guns, it was chambered for 9mm Glisenti ammunition, basically a low-powered 9mm Parabellum cartridge. Although it was portable, it was largely used as a static machine gun. By 1918 Italian soldiers were re-equipped with a Beretta modification of the design and began to use the submachine gun in an assault role.

The German Bergmann MaschinenPistole 18 or MP18 was designed by Louis Schmeisser in 1917 and incorporated many of the features that would become standard in early submachine guns. The German army ordered 50,000 and around 10,000 had been delivered in time for the *Kaiserschlacht*, the 1918 offensive on the Western Front. After the war, stocks of the gun were taken over by the French Army which substituted a 20- or 32-round box magazine that loaded from the left. This feed mechanism was adopted when production recommenced in 1928 under licence in Belgium.

At the close of World War I the Beretta M1918 (or strictly the Beretta Moschetto Automatico 1918) was designed by the talented young engineer Tullio

**LEFT** The Soviet PPD-34/38 was produced at the Tula and Sestrorjetsk arsenals until 1940, when it was replaced by the simpler but well-made PPD-40.

**LEFT** The elegant Beretta Model 1918 was still in service with the Italian Army in World War II. A 25-round curved magazine fitted in the top of the receiver and it had a folding spike bayonet.

Marengoni, who used the Villar Perosa action, barrel, body and feed system for the cartridges. A new trigger and stock were added, with an ejection chute under the ejection slot. Finally, the bayonet catch and folding bayonet, two components from the Carcano military carbine, were added. It was issued to *Arditi* (assault troops) in the Italian army.

The PPD (Pistolet-Pulemyot Degtyarova) was developed by the Russian small arms designer Vassili A. Degtyarov in 1934 and adopted by the Red Army a year later. With a 25-round box magazine, it went into limited production with the designation PPD-34. Following modifications in 1938, it was produced until 1939 as the PPD-34/38 with a newly developed 71-round drum magazine. Although a new version was developed in 1940 with a two-part stock designed to accept a new pattern of 71-round drum magazine, by June 1941 it became clear that the PPD-40 was not suited to wartime mass production, and it was replaced by the more efficient and inexpensive PPSh-41.

The French 7.65mm Mitraillette MAS 38 submachine gun introduced in 1938 had evolved from the experimental MAS 35 and was an accurate short-range weapon machined from solid metal. It fired from a 32-round box magazine with a cyclic rate of between 600 and 700 rpm. Following the fall of France in 1940 the Germans kept production going at Manufacture d'Armes de St Etienne for their own use until 1944.

### Tullio Marengoni and Pietro Beretta

Firearms historians have described Tullio Marengoni as Europe's John Browning since his designs that began with a hammerless shotgun in the early 1900s continued to dominate every significant Beretta weapon for the next sixty years. Beretta and Marengoni had a unique working relationship, and would often work together all through the night. Marengoni came up with the concepts and Beretta engineered the working weapons from his designs. Their wide-ranging output included the monobloc breech for shotgun barrels, the classic Beretta over/under shotgun line, and the pistol design that would evolve into the official US military sidearm, the modern Model 92/M9. Marengoni remained a consultant for Beretta for several years after his official retirement in 1956.

**BELOW** The early 32-round "snail" magazine designed for the 9mm German MP18 submachine gun proved complex and prone to stoppages.

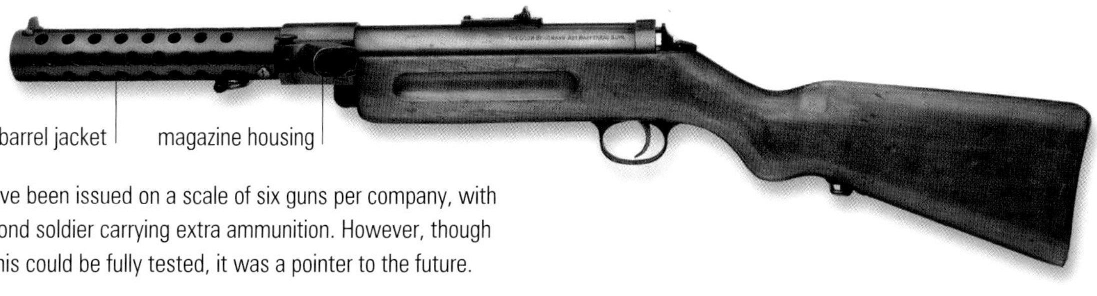


**RIGHT** The MP18 would have been issued on a scale of six guns per company, with gunners supported by a second soldier carrying extra ammunition. However, though World War I ended before this could be fully tested, it was a pointer to the future.

# The trench broom

The American M1928, the Thompson Model 1928 "Trench Broom" or "Tommy Gun", was the brainchild of John T. Thompson, who helped develop the M1903 Springfield rifle and the .45 M1911 pistol. Shortly after his retirement from the army in 1918, he began work on a handy, fast-firing weapon for use in attacks through field fortifications.

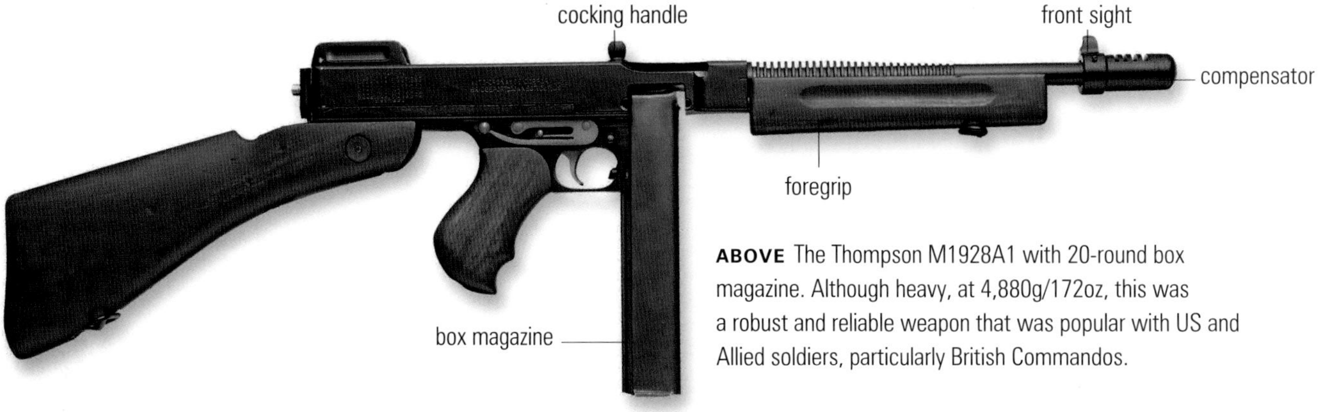


**ABOVE** The Thompson M1928A1 with 20-round box magazine. Although heavy, at 4,880g/172oz, this was a robust and reliable weapon that was popular with US and Allied soldiers, particularly British Commandos.

### The Thompson submachine gun

Drawing on experience of fighting on the Western Front, John T. Thompson recognized that the .45 bullet used in the M1911 pistol would transform a fully automatic weapon. Early in 1920, a prototype capable of firing 800 rpm was produced by Thompson's company, Auto-Ordnance.

Despite its performance in trials, neither the US Army nor the Marine Corps adopted the Thompson. Nevertheless, Thompson was able to sign a contract with Colt for 15,000 "Thompson Submachine Gun, Model of 1921".

**ABOVE** A French soldier, armed and equipped by the US Army, on guard in 1945 with his Thompson M1A1. Weighing 4,740g/167.2oz, this was the final simplified version of the submachine gun, with a fixed firing pin.

There were no further orders for submachine guns until the eve of the United States' entry into World War II. From 1942, the orders were huge. The reliability of the Thompson to outperform other submachine guns in adverse conditions such as dirt, mud and rain was one of its main assets. British Commandos retained their Thompsons after the Sten had become more widely available, and went ashore at D-Day in 1944 armed with them. The main drawbacks of the gun were weight, inaccuracy at ranges over 45m/50yd, and lack of penetrating power. However, as a close-range weapon it was devastating.

### The "Tommy Gun"

In 1940 the British Government rushed to purchase the Model 1928A1, Thompson Machine Carbine (TMC) or "Tommy Gun". Senior staff officers in the British army had referred to submachine guns disparagingly as "gangster weapons" because of their gangland reputation in Prohibition America, but the reservations of the British War Office were forgotten in the face of the threat of German invasion, and orders were placed for the Model 1928.

This gun saw service in North Africa and Italy. It weighed 4,800g/172oz was 857mm/33.75in long, had sights set out to 548m/1,800ft, and had a cyclic rate of 600 to 725 rpm with a 20- or 30-round box or a 50-round drum magazine. Most soldiers favoured the 20-round magazine that fitted into a pouch and made for easier movement in close country.

In 1942 the original Thompson M1928 had the cocking handle (which compresses the spring behind the bolt) on top of the receiver and utilized the Blish Lock system of operation. The Blish Lock system worked on a principle of static friction in a delayed-blowback breech lock. The gun was redesigned as the Thompson M1A1. The M1A1 used a simple blowback system of operation and the cocking handle was moved to the side. To cut manufacturing costs, the Cutts compensator (a device which alleviates the tendency of the muzzle to rise when firing on full automatic), the finned barrel, the fingered fore-grip, and the flip-up adjustable rear-sight were either simplified or eliminated. The M1A1 did not accept the drum magazine, which was abandoned for reasons including the fact that it was bulky and that the rounds rattled, a noise that could be fatal on night patrols. By the end of World War II, more than one million M1 and M1A1 submachine guns had been made.

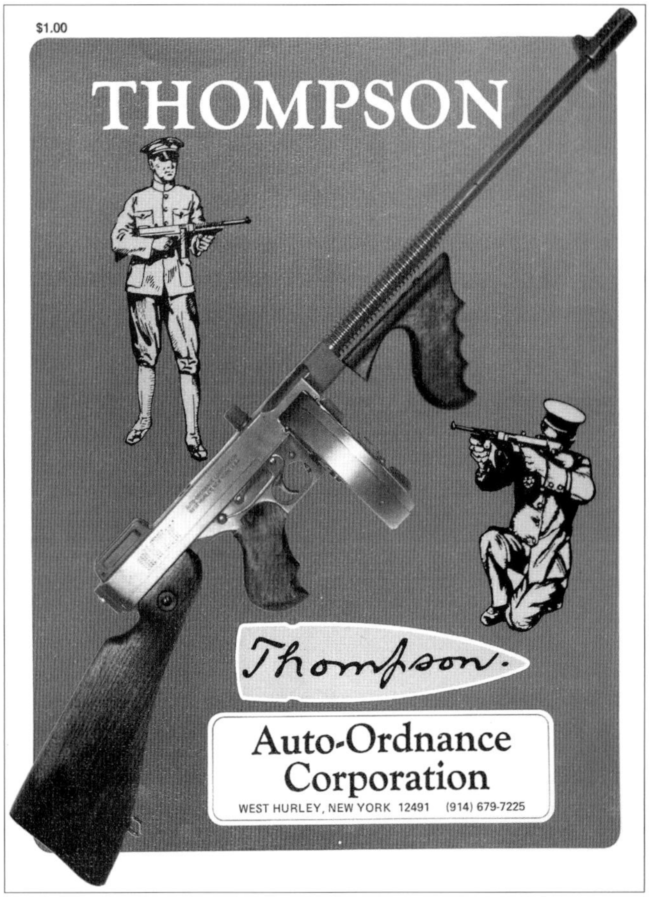


**RIGHT** A sales brochure for the Thompson submachine gun, published by the Auto-Ordnance Corporation. The "Tommy Gun" was used by police and gangsters in the 1920s and 1930s. This led the British War Office to describe them as gangster weapons and reject them in the 1930s.

## Gangster weapons

Compared with the thousands of Thompson submachine guns used properly by law-abiding Americans in the course of their duty, only a very small number of Thompsons were misused by Depression and Prohibition-era gangsters in the United States. Despite this, the weapon got a bad name in the late 1920s and 1930s.

The best-known front-page crime remains the notorious "St. Valentine's Day Massacre" of 1929 when henchmen of the gang-leader Al Capone, who had conveniently left town for Florida, shot down seven members of the "Bugs" Moran gang in a Chicago garage.

On a summer night in 1933, Oklahoma City oilman Charles Urschel was kidnapped from his home by gangster George Kelly. Kelly was armed with a Thompson submachine gun and this crime earned him the nickname "Machine Gun" Kelly.

"Public Enemy No.1" John Dillinger stole Thompsons from small-town police stations. Both the Dillinger–Nelson gang and Charles Arthur "Pretty Boy" Floyd customized their Thompsons, making them easier to conceal and fire one-handed. This was done by removing the butt and replacing the 50-round drum magazine with a 20-round box magazine.

Hollywood also played its part in giving the gun a bad reputation, with Jimmy Cagney and Edward G. Robinson playing Thompson-toting hard men in violent movies like *The Public Enemy* and *Little Caesar*.

**LEFT** John Dillinger, "Public Enemy No. 1", one of the American Prohibition-era gangsters who used the Thompson M1928 submachine gun with a 20-round box magazine.

# The 1930s: rearmament

When Adolf Hitler came to power in Germany in 1933, he introduced a vast programme of rearmament, in contravention of the Versailles Treaty of 1919. Some superb designs and concepts were developed in the late 1930s and early 1940s that have long outlasted the life of the Third Reich. The 9mm Walther Pistole 38 or P38 was designed to replace the P08 Luger and the compact PP and PPK pistols were introduced. In Italy Beretta produced the elegant Pistol Automatica Beretta Modello 1934/38 and the 8mm Mitra Beretta MAB38 submachine guns. However, the Browning 9mm High-Power pistol developed in the 1930s would be one of the most successful pistols of the period.

**ABOVE** The German wartime Walther P38 would return after 1945 as the lightweight Bundeswehr Model P1 pistol.

## The Walther pistole 38 (P38)

The German Walther P38 was safe, easy, and cheap to manufacture.The P38 has the distinctive feature of a positive safety catch that prevents accidental firing, even when cocked with a round in the breech. A pin indicator, which could be felt in the dark, showed if a round was loaded. The magazine held eight rounds that could be fired in 20 seconds with an effective range of 50m/164ft. Between 1939 and 1945 over one million P38s were made and it is widely acknowledged to have been the best military pistol of World War II.

**ABOVE** A British sergeant proudly displays the FN Browning 9mm High-Power pistol, captured during fighting in north-west Europe. The Brownings were popular with Allied and German soldiers because of their capacious double-stacked 13-round magazine.

## The Walther PPK

In 1928, before the Nazis came to power, Walther produced the Model PP or Polizei Pistole, a compact weapon with an eight-round magazine designed for police use. The PPK or Polizei Pistole Kriminal was only 150mm/5.91in long compared to the PP's 170mm/6.7in, and was intended for police working in plain clothes. During World War II it was the personal weapon of choice for senior officers in the German armed forces, and it remained in service after the war, later becoming famous as the weapon of Agent 007, Ian Fleming's fictional spy James Bond.

## Italian designs

In Italy another small-arms manufacturer with a worldwide reputation was producing new designs. The Pistol Automatica Beretta Modello 1934/38 was a handy blowback-operated weapon that weighed 616g/21.76oz. The finish was excellent and it became one of the most prized war trophies for the Allies.

The 8mm Mitra Beretta MAB38 submachine gun introduced in 1938 was based on the Villar Perosa. It had two triggers, one for semi-automatic and one for automatic fire. It fired from 10-, 20- or 40-round magazines that could be loaded by hand or by specific tools. The maximum range for the pistol-sized bullet (the same as the Beretta 34 pistol) was allegedly1,000m/3,281ft; in reality the effective range was around 100m/328ft.

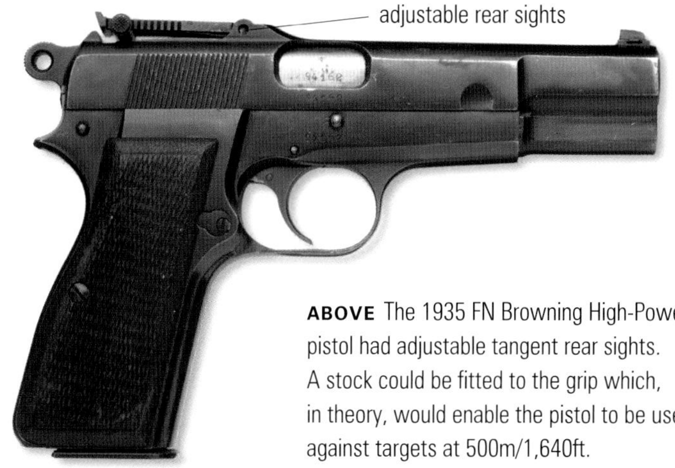


**ABOVE** The 1935 FN Browning High-Power pistol had adjustable tangent rear sights. A stock could be fitted to the grip which, in theory, would enable the pistol to be used against targets at 500m/1,640ft.

### The Browning high-power

In 1935 the Belgian firm of Fabrique National (FN) began production of the Browning 9mm GP or Grand Puissance (High-Power) pistol. They offered two versions: the standard with fixed sights and the "Adjustable Rearsight Model" with tangent rear sights, graduated up to 500m/1,640ft and a slot in the pistol grip to take a detachable wooden stock. The pistol had been designed a decade earlier by the weapons engineer John Moses Browning, and granted a US patent in February 1927 three months after his death. While Browning receives most of the credit for the gun, a great deal of refinement was done to the design by Dieudonne Saive. Without Saive's involvement, the gun would never have come to market in the form that it exists today. This superb weapon, with its double-stacked 13-round magazine, would be produced in Canada by Inglis for use by Allied troops, while the FN weapons were eagerly taken up by the Germans following the occupation of Belgium in 1940. Prior to 1939 the pistol had already been adopted as a service sidearm in Belgium, Denmark, Holland, Lithuania and Romania. In the late 20th century it remained in service in more than 55 countries and the improved 9mm Browning High-Power Mark 3 was still in production at FN.

**ABOVE** The 9mm Walther PPK, a compact automatic that was favoured as a sidearm by senior German officers in World War II.

**ABOVE** The compact Beretta M1934, one in a line of superb weapons designed by Tullio Maregoni for the Italian Beretta company. It fired a low-powered 9mm Short or .38 Auto round.

### 9mm Parabellum

This is a world standard for pistol and submachine gun ammunition used and manufactured throughout the world. The 9mm Parabellum cartridge was developed in 1902 by George Luger. "Parabellum" was taken from the ancient Latin saying *Si vis pacem, para bellum*, meaning "If you want peace, prepare for war".

The original cartridge used an 8g full metal or a semi-jacketed truncated-cone bullet. The jackets were nickel-plated steel, although later copper was used. The charge (0.35g) of smokeless powder gave a muzzle velocity of 310m/s (1,017ft/s).

The name "9mm Luger" was never an official designation but the Luger name was registered in 1923 as a marketing ploy by A.F. Stoeger, the American company who imported the ammunition in the years between the wars.

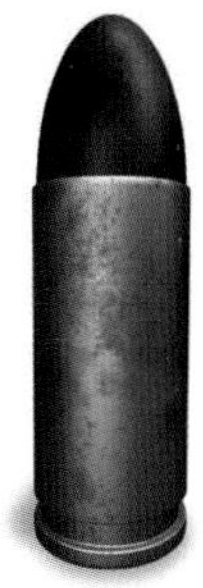

**RIGHT** The term Parabellum has been used in the naming of a number of cartridges. However, a Parabellum is most likely to refer to a 9mm cartridge.

# German submachine guns

The origins of the submachine gun in German service during World War II date back to 1916 when the Imperial German Army tasked the small-arms designer Hugo Schmeisser to produce a short-range rapid-fire weapon. It was ready for the 1918 offensive and was designated the Machine Pistol 18 or MP18. The first German submachine gun, the 9mm MP34/35, was designed by Bergmann. However, it was the MP38 and MP40 (the "Schmeisser") that would be seen as the classic German submachine gun of World War II.

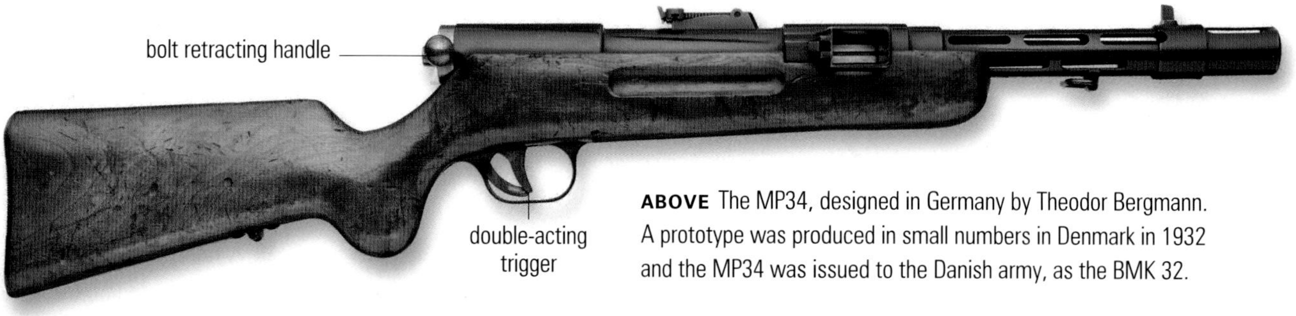


**ABOVE** The MP34, designed in Germany by Theodor Bergmann. A prototype was produced in small numbers in Denmark in 1932 and the MP34 was issued to the Danish army, as the BMK 32.

**ABOVE** A dramatic propaganda poster featuring a highly decorated German officer leading an assault armed with an MP38.

### The MP34/35

Production of the MP34/35 began in Germany in 1934. The bulk of the stock made by Junker & Ruh AG at Karlsruhe went to the Waffen-SS, the Nazi's fighting force. The trigger was unusual: a partial pull produced single shots, and automatic followed if it was pulled fully to the rear. Its most distinctive feature was that the magazine loaded from the right and, when fired on automatic, had a fearsome cyclic rate of 650 rpm.

### The Erma

The 9mm MP Erma (or EMP) was developed from an earlier Heinrich Vollmer design from the 1920s and was designed by Heinrich Vollmer and Berthold Giepel, both co-directors of Erma Werke. It remained in front line service until 1942. A silenced variant of the EMP was used to equip the Milice (the French security police who operated under German control) between 1940 and 1944. It had a lower muzzle velocity and rate of fire. The Erma submachine gun has unfairly become known by the name of "Schmeisser" after the senior designer at Haenel of Suhl. Haenel manufactured the weapon, and perhaps that is why Hugo Schmeisser has received the credit for the MP38, 38/40 and 40.

It was the first submachine gun to have a folding metal butt, which reduced its size from 833mm/32.8in to 630mm/24.8in and made it ideal for paratroops and vehicle crews. It had a distinctive lug called a "resting

**ABOVE** The MP38, first produced by the Erma Werke at Erfurt, included a folding metal butt and was also unusual in its use of plastic.

bar" below the muzzle so that it could be fired on automatic through weapons ports or over the side of vehicles with no danger of the vibration causing it to slip back inside. From the resting bar a metal fin called a "cooling strip" ran back to the receiver. The pistol grip and trigger combination drew on the US Thompson M1928 for inspiration – earlier submachine guns retained a carbine-style wooden stock. It was the first submachine gun to use plastic in the form of Bakelite in its construction.

The MP 38 went into production, and in the campaign in Poland in 1939 it soon emerged that the weapon had a dangerous fault. When the submachine gun was cocked the bolt could easily be knocked forward, accidentally causing it to fire. An improvised solution was a leather collar that fitted over the barrel with a strap that held the cocking handle. At the factory a simple safety catch was produced and these modified weapons were designated MP38/40.

### Cost cutting and fire power

The drive to cut production costs and speed manufacture led to the MP40. This weapon had many of the external features of the MP38/40. In the new weapon, machining was reduced to a minimum and steel pressings and welds used wherever possible. In Russia, German soldiers armed with the MP40 found themselves out-gunned by the Soviet PPSh-41 submachine gun with its 71-round magazine. To address this problem, late in 1943 Erma introduced the MP40/1. This consisted of a special housing which took two 30-round magazines fitted side by side. While this effectively produced a 60-round weapon, it also increased the weight to 5,402g/190.56oz.

By the end of World War II, some 1,047,000 MP40s had been manufactured. It is reported that an MP40 was the weapon that was used to kill the Italian fascist leader Benito Mussolini when Communist partisans captured him in 1945. After the war it was used by the French, and remained in service as the Maskin 9mm M40 with the Norwegian Army into the 1980s.

### "The Schmeisser"

The MP38 and MP40 submachine guns, known loosely by the Allies in World War II as the "Schmeisser", were issued to German Non-Commissioned Officers (NCOs) commanding MG34 and MG42 machine-gun crews. This ensured that if the gun crew was suddenly attacked by an enemy they had a weapon that could produce a high volume of short-range fire. Powerful as the machine gun was it could be difficult to handle in a confined space, unlike the handy submachine gun. The NCO was also issued with binoculars that allowed him to locate distant targets for the machine-gun crew.

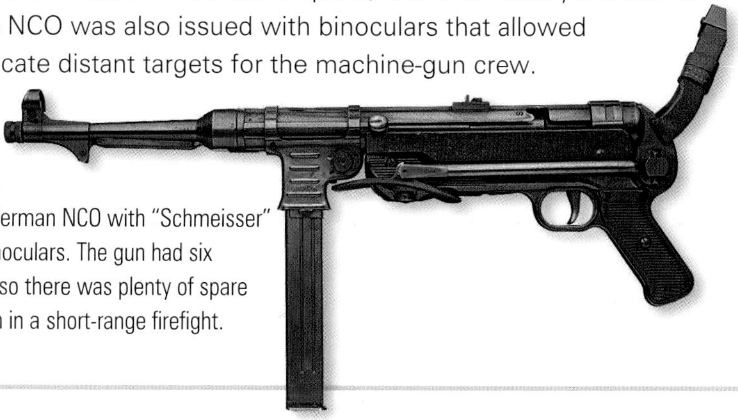

**RIGHT** A German NCO with "Schmeisser" gun and binoculars. The gun had six magazines so there was plenty of spare ammunition in a short-range firefight.

# Fast and cheap

During World War II some weapons were developed at short notice, while others were refined for faster, cheaper production. The definitive examples are the British Sten and the Soviet PPSh-41. The distinctive Owen gun was produced in Australia, and would serve from World War II until Vietnam, while the US developed the UD M42 or Marlin gun and the highly successful M3 "grease gun".

**ABOVE** The American .45 M3 or "grease gun", introduced in 1943, incorporated several innovative design features.

### The Owen gun

By 1939 in Australia, Evelyn Owen had developed his first automatic weapon, chambered for the .22 Long Rifle (LR) cartridge, and offered it to the Australian army, which rejected the curious-looking weapon. However, Owen persisted and by 1941 the Lysaghts Newcastle Works in New South Wales had produced several more prototypes in different calibres, including .45 ACP, 9mm Parabellum and even .38 Special revolver cartridges. The 9mm prototype weapon was tested successfully against the Thompson and Sten submachine guns. The Owen gun was adopted in 1942 and manufactured until 1945 in three basic versions: Mark 1-42, Mark 1-43 (or Mark 1 Wood Butt), and Mark 2. About 45,000 Owen submachine guns were made by Lysaghts, and these remained in service with Australian forces until the 1960s, through World War II, Korea and Vietnam. Although rather heavy, the robust, reliable and simple Owen gun was well liked by Australian soldiers.

### The Marlin gun

The American 9mm submachine gun that would be widely known as the Marlin gun, but had the official designation United Defense M42, was designed between 1941 and 1942 by Carl G. Swebilius, a small-arms designer working for the High Standard

**LEFT** An Australian soldier armed with an Owen Mark 1. The weapon was well-made and robust and the bolt was protected against mud and dirt. The vertical 33-round magazine ensured a reliable feed, combining gravity and a spring, that compared favourably with the Thompson.

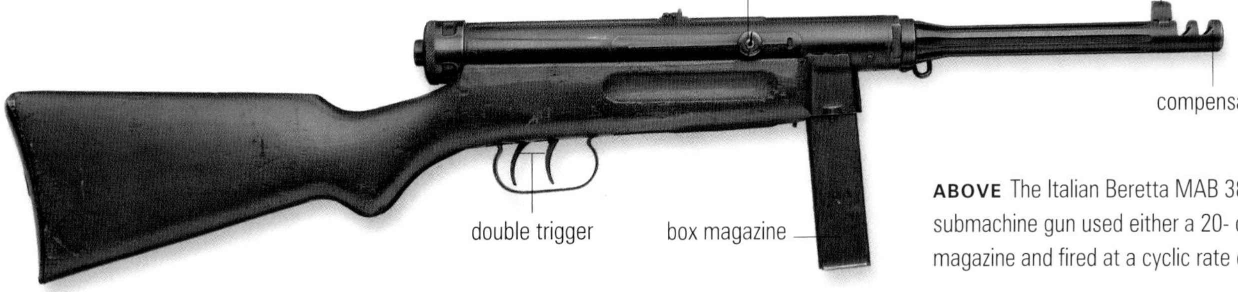


**ABOVE** The Italian Beretta MAB 38/42 submachine gun used either a 20- or 40-round magazine and fired at a cyclic rate of 550 rpm.

Manufacturing Company. The first UD M42 submachine guns were made by High Standard and Marlin to a Dutch order, and most were shipped to the Dutch East Indies just prior to the Japanese invasion. The remaining 15,000 guns made by the company were purchased by the US government and mostly used by Office of Strategic Services (OSS) operatives and supplied to Resistance groups, notably in Crete. The UD M42 was a somewhat complicated but well-made weapon that fired from a 20-round magazine. In an unusual development, twin reversed magazines were produced for quick reloading.

### The M3 "grease gun"

The American M3, a submachine gun produced in 1943 as a low-cost substitute for the Thompson, with several updated design features. Accessories were included, such as an oiler in the weapon's pistol grip and the ingenious wire stock that could be used as a screwdriver, a spanner to unscrew the barrel, a cleaning rod and a magazine filling tool. Though the M3 only fired on full automatic, the cyclic rate was notably low at 450 rounds per minute and the straight line of recoil thrust made it easier to control. An experienced soldier could fire single shots. Before firing, the ejection port cover had to be opened manually by the operator; this also functioned as the weapon's safety catch.

The exterior of the weapon was formed from two pressed-metal shells, welded together, while the barrel of the M3 was secured by a simple nut, and the bolt rode on two guide rods inside the receiver. This provided clearance between the bolt and receiver, preventing dirt from jamming the weapon, and making it a "soldier friendly" weapon in combat. Its main drawback was that the magazine had a tendency to jam or fall out of the housing if the magazine catch was accidentally depressed. Its unusual appearance earned it the nickname the "grease gun".

The M3 had a 30-round single position feed box magazine and fired the .45 ACP cartridge used in the M1911A1 pistol and Thompson submachine gun. It remained in service with the US Army in Korea, Vietnam and even with some units in the First Gulf War of 1990–91.

### MAB38

The Italian MAB38, known as the Moschetto Automatico, was manufactured in the Beretta factory at Brescia. Until 1943, it was only available to parachute units, Carabinieri and Polizia Africa Italiana. It became more widespread in the Armed Forces of the Republic of Salò, partisans and Italian units fighting under Allied command. A later version, the MAB 38/42, was lighter, shorter and had a higher rate of fire. It remained in service well into the 1970s with the Carabinieri and police.

**BELOW** The UD M42 submachine gun, also known as the Marlin Gun, had a double 20-round magazine and fired at a cyclic rate similar to the Thompson M1 and M1A1 of 700 rpm.

# The Sten gun

Following the fall of France and the evacuation at Dunkirk in 1940, the British faced the prospect of imminent invasion by a well-armed German Army, and urgently needed an inexpensive automatic weapon. The answer was a British submachine gun designed by Major R.V. Shepherd and H.J. Turpin at the Royal Small Arms Factory at Enfield. It was named the "S.T.EN" as a tribute to Shepherd's and Turpin's ingenuity and to the factory.

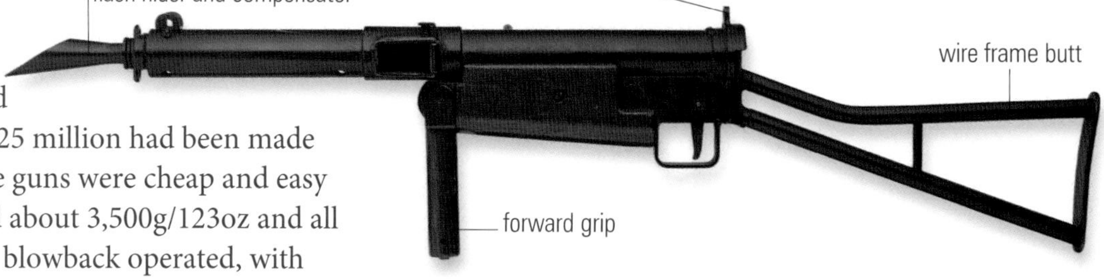


**ABOVE** The Sten Mark II entered service in the summer of 1941, but was not well received by soldiers on account of its rough and crudely made appearance.

### Powerfully simple

The Sten went into mass production and, by the end of the war, an estimated 3.25 million had been made in Britain and Canada. The guns were cheap and easy to make. The Sten weighed about 3,500g/123oz and all marks of the weapon were blowback operated, with a cyclic rate of 540 rpm and a muzzle velocity of 366m/s (1,201ft/s). Magazine capacity was 32 rounds, but since there were always feed problems this was normally kept down to 30. Between 1940 and 1945 the Sten was modified and improved, going through numerous marks.

**ABOVE** Home Guard weapons training for women in 1941. The gun in the foreground is a Sten Mark III and the other is a Mark I. The weapons are not cocked as the women are practising the basic techniques of holding and aiming.

### The development of the Sten

The Sten Mark I, which featured a flash hider (a device to reduce muzzle flash on firing), wooden furniture, and folding hand grip, was quickly replaced by the Sten Mark II, which saw widespread issue. The fact that the Mark II was compact and easy to take apart made it easy to hide, and it was a weapon of choice for many European Resistance groups. It was also very useful that the similarity of the magazine to the German MP40 meant that it could use captured German 9mm ammunition. However, as with the German MP40, jamming could sometimes be a problem. Easy to manufacture, it was a simply built weapon composed of 47 steel parts that were welded, riveted or pushed together. The bolt and barrel were the only machine-made components. Two million Sten Mark II weapons were manufactured.

One of the requirements in the original design of the Sten was that it could be made by manufacturers who were not specialist gunsmiths. This was exemplified by the Mark III, with its fixed barrel and all-in-one body and casing welded shut along the top. It was built by a firm of toy makers, Lines Brothers. The Sten Mark III was issued to troops in time for the Normandy landings in 1944. Surprisingly, although this was possibly the best Sten version of all, it was not produced in large numbers.

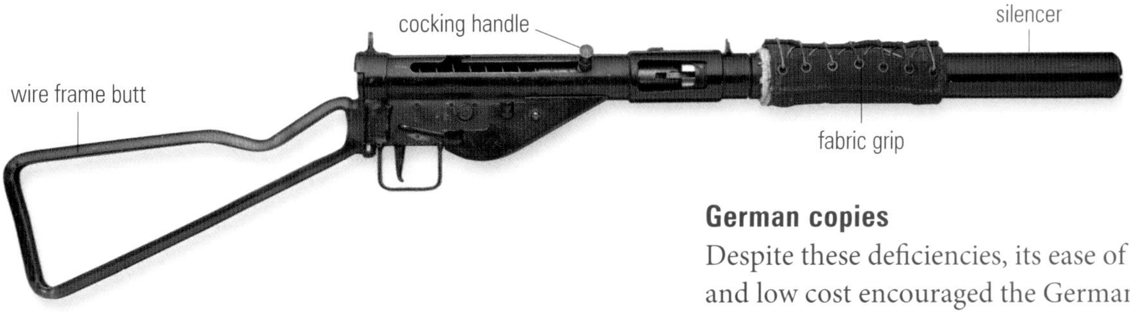


**ABOVE** The Sten Mark II (S) was introduced in 1943. It was popular with the Resistance and was designed to be fired on single shot. Although it was possible to fire it on automatic, the silencer was burned out when bullets were fired at 450 rpm.

Although the Sten was issued to vehicle crews, despatch riders, and those who had no need for a long-range weapon, it was principally issued to infantry battalions, especially platoon commanders, platoon sergeants, and section commanders. Although senior officers could carry a pistol as a personal weapon, many preferred the extra firepower of a Sten.

The Sten was not popular among troops because, besides jamming, it could be fired accidentally if the cocking handle snagged on clothing, or if it was dropped. This happened to Corporal Proctor of the Somerset Light Infantry during operations in Holland in 1944. A soldier slipped, dropped his Sten, and the weapon hit the ground and fired a single shot that hit Proctor in the groin. The platoon commander, Lt. Jary, condemned the weapon as "designed with little but cheap mass production in mind.... It had no locking device at the moment of firing and consequently, if the weapon was jolted sufficiently for the bolt to slide back and engage the stop round in the magazine, this would be fed into the breech and fired."

### Stens in action

The Sten first saw action at the disastrous raid at Dieppe in August 1942. In the weeks prior to the raid, Canadian soldiers had to constantly adjust and test their Stens to make sure they worked properly. The first raid, Operation *Jubilee*, was cancelled in July and the Stens were withdrawn. A day before the remounting of the raid, now called Operation *Rutter*, brand new Stens, still in their crates and packed in grease, were issued to some unimpressed soldiers.

### German copies

Despite these deficiencies, its ease of manufacture and low cost encouraged the Germans to copy it in 1944–45, producing weapons designated variously as the 9mm MaschinenPistole 3008, VolksmaschinenPistole, Gerät Potsdam and MaschinenPistole 749 (e). Having been so widely produced, the Sten had a lethal afterlife post-1945. The US Army technical manual *Unconventional Warfare Devices and Techniques* includes an example of a copy of the Mark II captured from the Viet Cong in 1964 during the war in Vietnam.

**ABOVE** Captain Brian Priday, second-in-command of 2nd Batallion of the Oxford and Bucks Light Infantry, armed with a Sten Mark V with fixed bayonet, Normandy 6 June 1944. Two key bridges had been captured across the river Orne and Orne Canal.

# Soviet firepower

**The weapon that would influence Soviet submachine-gun design and so eventually the war on the Eastern Front was the Suomi ("Finland") submachine gun. Used by the Finnish army in 1931 as the Suomi-KP Model 1931, it was produced by Finnish arms-designer Aimo Lachti between 1920–30. It would shape the design of the hugely successful Soviet PPSh-41 submachine gun.**

**ABOVE** The Finnish Suomi-KP M/31 submachine gun was an exceptionally well made weapon. It weighed 4.676kg/10.3lb because many of its components were made from solid metal. As a result it was very robust and would remain in service for many years.

### The Suomi

The Finnish Suomi-KP Model 1931 was also known simply as the KP-31, KP – *Konepistooli* or Automatic Pistol – and was manufactured in Finland by Tikkakoski Oy, licensed to Denmark, Sweden and Switzerland, and also widely exported. The Suomi was used very effectively during the Winter War of 1939–40 when the Soviet Union attacked Finland, and the experience of coming under fire from submachine guns with 71-round magazines had a profound impact on Soviet forces. Manufacture of the Suomi ceased in Finland in 1944, but it was used well into the 1990s when it was replaced in the Finnish army by assault rifles.

### The PPSh-41

Following the German invasion of the Soviet Union in 1941 when the Russians lost huge quantities of small arms and much of their engineering capability, there was an urgent demand for a light and simple weapon capable of a high volume of fire. The answer to this was the robust and very effective Pistolet-Pulemet Shpagina 1941g or PPSh-41 7.62mm submachine gun, designed by Georgii Shpagin. It was much cheaper and quicker to make than earlier Soviet submachine guns because there were no screws or bolts on it, and all metal parts were stamped or brazed. It weighed 3,500g/123oz and had a 71-round drum magazine based on the Suomi submachine gun, or a 35-round box magazine. It fired at 900 rpm, a rate of fire that in Korea would earn it the nickname the "burp gun".

During World War II Soviet soldiers knew their submachine gun affectionately as the *Pah-pah-shah*, or *Shpagin*. The gun used barrels taken from bolt-action Mosin Nagant M1891/30 rifles that were chromed to reduce corrosion and wear. Stripping was simple, as the receiver hinged open to reveal the bolt and spring.

**LEFT** A Finnish soldier in a trench on the Eastern Front, holding a Suomi with a 20-round magazine. The gun had a 318mm/12.5in barrel, which made it very accurate over longer ranges.

**ABOVE** The 7.62mm PPSh-41 submachine gun, one of the weapons that was mass produced in the USSR during World War II that armed Soviet tank-riding infantry fighting on the Eastern Front.

There was no selector lever (for single shots or automatic) on some of the late models, when the gun was capable of only automatic fire, and though this was high, a rudimentary compensator and muzzle brake helped to reduce muzzle climb (the upward movement of a gun as a result of recoil). The weapon had a few drawbacks: if dropped, it could accidentally discharge, reloading was difficult and the drums were prone to jamming, something which didn't occur with the box magazines.

About five million PPSh-41s had been made by 1945, and the Soviets adapted their infantry tactics to take full advantage of such huge numbers, often equipping complete units, notably "tank descent" infantry, with the submachine gun. The standard equipment load for a soldier seems to have been the one drum and five- or six-box magazines. Before magazines were introduced, it appears that soldiers would have been equipped with two drums. The short range of these weapons meant that these units had to close with their enemy in something of the style of a bayonet charge – a tactic that terrified the enemy on the Eastern Front. The Finns captured a little over 4,000 Soviet 7.62mm submachine guns during World War II. This was too small a number to justify retooling to make Soviet 7.62mm ammunition and posed an added logistic burden for Finnish front-line troops. However, the demand for more submachine guns remained high and, although Finnish army HQ explored the possibilities of modifying the gun to accept Finnish 9mm ammunition and Suomi magazines, production of this modified gun was never started.

### The MP717(r)

The Germans themselves were very impressed by the PPSh-41, and would use the guns as often as they captured them. Since the 7.62mm and 9mm Parabellum cartridges shared similar dimensions, only a 9mm barrel and a magazine housing adaptor was needed to convert the PPSh-41 to fire from MP38/40 32-round magazines. The Wehrmacht (the German armed forces) officially adopted the converted PPSh-41 as the MP717(r).

### The Leningrad gun

During the siege of Leningrad (1941–44), there were working munitions factories, but basic materials were in short supply. In these conditions A.I. Sudarev designed the PPS-42. It was soon improved and resulted in the Pistolet-Pulemet Sudareva 1943g or PPS-43 submachine gun, an all-metal weapon with a folding stock and a compact 35-round curved box magazine. This modern design remained in production after the war. The folding stock reduced the weapon's length and made it ideal for tank crews, paratroopers, and reconnaissance units. While the weapon had a slightly slower firing rate of 700 rpm, it more than made up for this with its lighter weight, small size and greater ease of manufacture. About 500,000 were made. Captured PPS-43s were used by the Germans, with the designation MP719(r).

**LEFT** The PPS-43 had a folding stock that reduced its length to a compact 622mm/24.48in, making it an ideal weapon for Armoured Fighting Vehicle (AFV) crews and paratroops.

# Submachine gun design advances

Following World War II many countries produced submachine guns for their armed forces and police. Many looked at the design features of wartime weapons, and with the leisure of peacetime production refined and improved on these combat-tested submachine guns. Some, like the Swedish Kulsprutpistole Model 45, French MAT-49 and Czech Model 61 Skorpion took on what could be called cult status. In Italy the 9mm Beretta Model 12 submachine gun proved to be a reliable weapon that enjoyed a long operational life.

**ABOVE** The Smith & Wesson Model 76, a licence-built version of the Swedish Carl Gustaf Model 45 9mm submachine gun. The US version was a popular weapon with the CIA in Vietnam in the 1960s and 1970s. It was also produced in Egypt by the Maadi Company as the Port Said.

### "The Swedish K"

The Kulsprutpistole Model 45 submachine gun was developed by Swedish state-owned Carl Gustaf Arms company in 1945 and was manufactured under licence in Indonesia, and in Egypt under the name of "Port Said", and sold to Ireland.

An almost exact copy of the Model 45 was also produced in the United States by the Smith & Wesson company in the early 1970s as the S&W Model 76. The Model 45 was not adopted by the US navy, army or police forces, but known colloquially as "the Swedish K" it did gain fame or notoriety when the Central Intelligence Agency (CIA) and special forces used it in South-east Asia during the Vietnam War. A silenced version was used in covert operations. The CIA and other agencies were able to buy these weapons without going through US military sources and men in civilian clothes seen in Vietnam carrying a Swedish K were easily recognizable as "spooks" (secret agents or spies).

The weapon had an excellent 36-round two-column magazine that was very reliable and has therefore been copied or type developed in Czechoslovakia (as it was then), Scandinavia and Germany. Uncomplicated and reliable overall, loading and maintainance are generally problem-free. It is easy to field strip and clean, and has a quick-change barrel. Partly due to the "in-line" design of the stock the Swedish K is a good shooting weapon: it is balanced, easy to handle and control for long bursts of fire. A compact gun, the rigid stock is folding and the cartridges push directly into the body, so the magazine does not need a loader.

### The MAT 49

The French state arms factory MAT (Manufacture Nationale d'Armes de Tulle) developed the MAT 49 submachine gun in the late 1940s. Adopted by the French army in 1949, the MAT 49 was widely used by the French army and police for nearly 30 years, and it also saw action in Indo-China and Algeria. It is a solid, well-made submachine gun with a magazine that hinges forward to clip under the muzzle when the weapon is not in use. The retractable wire butt can be slipped forward to reduce the length to a compact 460mm/18in. During the Vietnam War the Viet Cong produced a local copy of the MAT 49, chambered for Soviet 7.62mm ammunition.

### The Beretta Model PM 12 and PM 12 S

In 1959 the 9mm Beretta Model PM 12 submachine gun was developed by the venerable Italian small-arms manufacturer Pietro Beretta Spa. Designed by Domenico Salza, it went through a number of prototypes. The weapon was made from heavy sheet steel stampings spot-welded together to form the

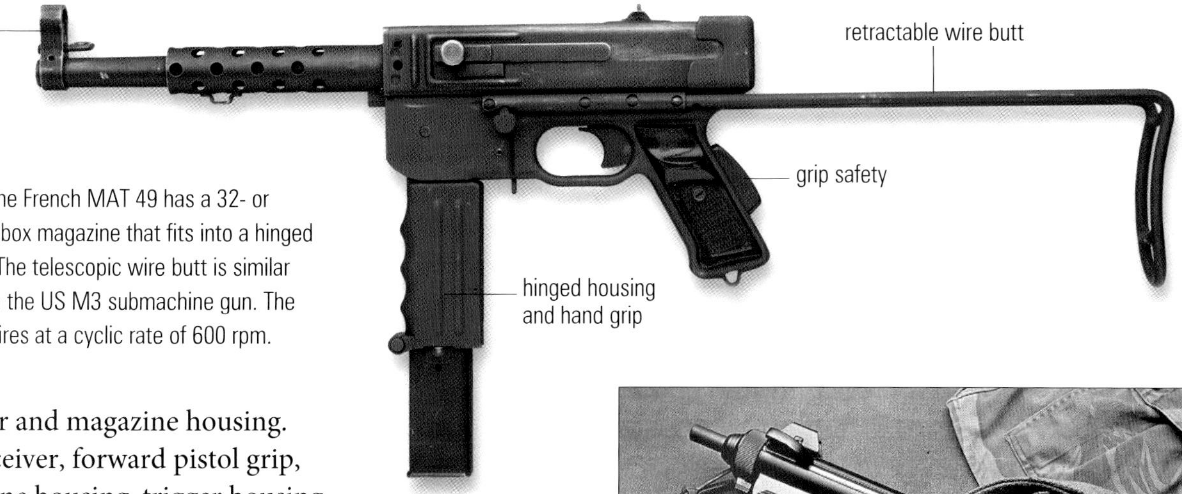


**RIGHT** The French MAT 49 has a 32- or 20-round box magazine that fits into a hinged housing. The telescopic wire butt is similar to that on the US M3 submachine gun. The MAT 49 fires at a cyclic rate of 600 rpm.

receiver and magazine housing. The receiver, forward pistol grip, magazine housing, trigger housing and pistol grip are all one unit. It has two safety catches. The Model 12 was adopted by the Italian army in 1961 and sold under licence to Brazil. It was also sold in Gabon, Libya, Nigeria, Saudi Arabia and Venezuela. The company followed the Model 12 with the Model PM 12 S. The Model PM 12 S included a number of modifications and improvements, among which was an epoxy-resin finish resistant to corrosion and wear. The Model PM 12 S had a safety catch that when applied blocked the grip safety and trigger. Both weapons had a cyclic rate of fire of 550 rpm. The Model PM 12 and the Model PM 12 S were designed for mass production but are compact and well made.

**ABOVE** Promotional literature from Beretta for the PM 12 S. The compact 9mm submachine gun has a 32-round detachable box magazine with options for a 20- or 40-round magazine. This model has a folding metal stock, but it is also available with a wooden butt stock.

## Skorpion's sting

The design philosophy behind the 7.65mm Model 61 Skorpion (Czech vz.61) was an almost futuristic concept in 1952. It was intended to replace the pistol, but could also be used as a close-combat assault weapon, as well as for personal defence. At 270mm/10.63in long with the butt folded, its small size makes it easy to conceal in a holster and can be used in confined spaces, such as cars or aircraft. Although it became popular with both police and security units in the 1960s, it was also used by terrorist groups.

The Skorpion has also been manufactured in Serbia as the Model 84, and police and security forces in Afghanistan, Angola, Egypt, Libya, Mozambique and Uganda have adopted it. The Skorpion was produced for export chambered for the 9mm Makarov cartridge and the Browning 9mm Short. The CZ91S is a semi-automatic version with very high "collector's" finish in black enamel. Today, the Skorpion lineup is still in use with the third generation known as the Skorpion EVO 3 A1.

**ABOVE** The Model 61 Skorpion was intended to be a dual-purpose weapon, combining the functions of pistol and submachine gun. Since it had a stock and can be held with two hands it was effective against targets that were beyond the range of a conventional pistol, and had greater firepower.

# Invention and innovation

In 1950, Uzi Gal, an engineer with Israel Military Industries (IMI), developed a very effective 9mm submachine gun, which would become known as the "Uzi". The British L2A3 9mm Sterling submachine gun entered service with the British Army in 1957 and would see action in the numerous campaigns fought from Borneo to the Falklands. The compact American MAC 10 and MAC 11 submachine guns have proved popular with undercover formations around the world.

**ABOVE** The Israeli 9mm Mini Uzi is a compact weapon that is ideal for close protection teams because it can be concealed inside a jacket. It can be fitted with a 20-, 25- or 32-round magazine.

### The Uzi

Since it entered service with the Israeli Army in 1951, the Uzi has been adopted by the police and armed forces of more than 90 countries, including Israel, Germany and Belgium. The more compact versions, the Mini and Micro Uzi, are used by many police, special operations and security units around the world, including the Israeli Sayeret and the US Secret Service.

The Uzi was based on the Czech M23 and 25 submachine guns, but with a completely different receiver (rectangular instead of round in cross-section) and other changes. It is a recoil-operated, select-fire submachine gun, firing from the open bolt (the bolt is the part of a firearm that blocks the rear of

**ABOVE** An officer "checks clear" to see that the breech is clear of rounds on the L2A3 Sterling submachine guns of a section of Gurkha soldiers during training in a Fighting In Built Up Area (FIBUA) complex in the 1980s.

### Uziel Gal (1923–2002)

Uziel "Uzi" Gal was born Gotthard Glass on 15 December 1923 in the town of Weimar in Germany. When Hitler came to power, the ten-year-old Glass moved with his school to England. In 1936, he moved to Kibbutz Yagur in what was then the British Mandate of Palestine. In Palestine he joined Palmach, the underground infantry arm of the Hagana, working as an armourer.

In 1948 Gal began work on the Uzi submachine gun shortly after Israel became a nation. In 1951 the submachine gun was adopted by the Israel Defence Force (IDF) and though Gal did not want the weapon to be named after him, his request was ignored. In 1958, for his work on the Uzi, Gal became the first person to receive the Israel Security Award, presented to him by Prime Minister David Ben-Gurion.

**RIGHT** The L2A3 9mm Sterling submachine gun entered service with the British Army in the 1950s. It was used around the world until the Gulf War.

the chamber while the powder burns). The bolt "sleeves" around the rear part of the barrel, reducing the overall length of the gun. The Uzi has a cyclic rate of fire of 600 rpm, while the Mini's rate is 1,500 to 1,900 and the Micro's is 1,200 to 1,400 rpm.

**BELOW** The Ingram MAC 10 is in service with the US navy and several Central American countries but, despite being excellent weapons, the .45 and 9mm MAC 10 and 11 have never been widely adopted.

### The Sterling submachine gun

The L2A3 9mm Sterling submachine gun entered service with the British Army in 1957 and soldiered on for almost 35 years. It would be used by officers, vehicle crews and radio operators in operations around the world until the Gulf War of 1990–91. It weighed 3,500g/123.46oz and was 690mm/27in long with its butt extended and 483mm/19in with it folded. The effective range was about 200m/654ft with a muzzle velocity of 390m/s (1,279ft/s) and cyclic rate of fire of 550 rpm. The standard magazine held 34 rounds, but was usually loaded with 28 to reduce pressure on the spring.

For covert operations stubby 10- and 15-round magazines, "stacked" for a quick change, were available. This arrangement proved efficient in use. Canada produced the Sterling submachine gun as the C1 and Spain as the C2.

### American genius

When weapons designer Gordon B. Ingram returned to the United States at the end of World War II he began working on submachine gun designs. In the late 1960s he came up with the tiny MAC 10 and MAC 11 submachine guns built at his Military Armament Company (hence the name MAC) at Powder Springs, Georgia. Also known as the Ingram, the versions of the MAC 10 and MAC 11 without stocks are respectively 267mm and 222mm/10.5in and 8.75in long. If the wire stock is extended, the guns are 548mm/21.5in and 460mm/18.11in long. These compact guns have a phenomenal rate of fire: the MAC 10 fires at 1,145 rpm, the 9mm MAC 10 at 1,090 rpm and the 9mm MAC 11 at 1,200 rpm. These small submachine guns are popular with security forces on covert operations since their external thread muzzle can be fitted with a MAC suppressor.

### The Colt M4 carbine

One American weapon that falls between a rifle and a submachine gun is the Colt M4 Carbine, the most compact of the Colt range of 5.56mm weapons. It features a four-position telescopic butt, a barrel length of 292mm/11.5in, and is designed for use wherever lightness, speed of action, mobility and close-quarters combat are required. It uses the same 30-round magazine as the M16 rifle. One veteran of the Vietnam War carried an M4 Carbine that had developed a reputation as a "jinxed" weapon since its previous users had been killed. Far from being jinxed, he said, it was a very handy weapon. It did, however, have a different signature when it was fired and consequently had attracted hostile fire when its former users had been caught in a firefight. As he explained, what had killed them was not the weapon, but their field craft and low-level tactics.

# Assault rifles to submachine guns

One of the most influential submachine guns of the post-war period was the Heckler & Koch MP5, but it was rivalled by the Soviet AKSU-74, a modified AK-74 assault rifle. In Chile, Fabricas y Maestranzas del Ejercito (FAMAE) produced a modular range of submachine guns under the designation SAF, and during the 1970s Russian Evgenij Dragunov designed the Kedr, a submachine gun that departed from the AK format.

**ABOVE** The Heckler & Koch MP5 mechanism is used in six different submachine guns including three silenced versions and the compact easy-to-conceal MP5K that is popular with counter-terrorist teams.

## The HK54

The West German Heckler & Koch MP5 submachine gun was first produced in the mid-1960s as the HK54. It was designated Machine Pistol 5, (MP5), when it was adopted by the West German government for use by its police and border guards. It was a lightweight, air-cooled, magazine-fed, select-fire weapon with delayed blowback operation. It could be shouldered or hand-fired in semi-automatic, with two- or three-round bursts, and sustained fire modes. It is a very accurate weapon that has a cyclic rate of fire of 800 rpm.

The modular design of the weapon consisted of six assembly groups and provided an unmatched degree of flexibility, as these groups can be exchanged with optional parts to create various styles of weapons for numerous operational requirements. The metal surfaces of the MP5 were phosphated and coated with a black lacquer finish that is highly resistant to salt-water corrosion and surface wear. The MP5 is made or has been made under licence in the United States, UK, Turkey, Pakistan, Mexico, Iran and Greece.

**ABOVE** The AKSU-74 has become notorious as a weapon favoured by terrorist and dissident groups in Afghanistan. Its compact length of 492mm/19.37in makes it an ideal weapon for such purposes as it fires powerful 5.45mm rounds from a 30-round magazine.

## The AKS-74U

Modified from the Russian 5.45mm AK-74 assault rifle, the AKS-74U was specifically designed for vehicle crews who needed a weapon with a much shorter barrel. The overall length of the submachine gun is only 492mm/19.37in with the metal stock folded, or 728mm/28.66in with extended stock. The AKS-74U has other advantages over the AK-74 assault rifle, as its loaded weight of 3,100g/109.34oz makes it significantly lighter and it also has a somewhat higher cyclic rate of fire at 650 to 735 rpm. The rear sight is a flip-type U-notch, while the front sight is a cylindrical post. At the end of the barrel, there is a device which operates as an expansion chamber to bleed off gases that could otherwise cause a violent recoil. It is also produced in Poland as the ONYX and in Serbia as the Zastava M85.

**ABOVE** The Spanish Star 9mm Model Z-84 submachine gun has a cyclic rate of 600 rpm. It is constructed using stampings and investment castings that helps to speed production and keep costs down.

### Compact Chilean

Fabricas y Maestranzas del Ejercito or FAMAE, the Chilean arms manufacturer, took the Swiss SIF 540 assault rifle that they were manufacturing under licence and developed it into the SAF and Mini-SAF submachine gun. The 9mm submachine gun comes in several forms: the standard with a fixed butt stock, standard with folding stock, silenced and Mini-SAF. They employ 20- or 30-round box magazines, and the 30-round is made from translucent plastic so a quick visual check can establish how much ammunition is available. The SAF submachine gun is in service with Chilean armed forces and police.

### Russian police weapons

In the early 1970s, Evgenij Dragunov, the designer of famous SVD sniper rifle, designed the Kedr submachine gun (then known as the PP-71). The project was shelved, but was revived in the early 1990s. The PP-71 was slightly modified and went into production in limited numbers, and was issued to Russian police units. New, more powerful ammunition was developed to replace the original 9mm Makarov ammunition. This new round, the PMM, while retaining the same dimensions, had a slightly lighter bullet and heavier charge, which increased its performance. In 1994 the Kedr was slightly strengthened to take this new ammunition, and the weapon was marketed as the submachine gun.

### The Spanish Z-84

Despite being compact and lightweight, the Spanish Z-84 is a submachine gun which was developed in the mid-1980s by Star Bonifacio Echeverria SA. It fires soft point and semi-jacketed bullets, as well as full metal jacket military ammunition, from 25- or 30-round magazines. Once it has been cocked the submachine gun has no external moving parts, which is one of the reasons that it has been adopted by special forces in the Spanish army and police units.

### Guns of the Special Air Service (SAS)

When six armed revolutionaries besieged the Iranian Embassy in London on 30 April 1979, Prime Minister Margaret Thatcher authorized the use of elite SAS counter-terrorist troops to neutralize them.

On 5 May, two SAS troopers clad in hooded black overalls were spotted outside the embassy as they positioned a frame charge against an upper-floor window. The large explosion that followed ten seconds later was a signal for the assault by teams at the front and rear, who moved nimbly across the balconies and through the smashed window.

The SAS weapon was the Heckler & Koch MP5, which they had encountered during joint training with the West German GSG9 counter-terrorist force, and which the SAS nicknamed the "Hockler".

**ABOVE** SAS troopers armed with Heckler & Koch MP5 submachine guns storm through the blasted windows at the front of the Iranian Embassy at Princes Gate, London, on 5 May, 1980.

# Silenced guns

In World War II Britain pioneered some silencer concepts, notably with the Sten Mark VI (S) which was the world's first silenced submachine gun when it was introduced in 1943. Britain also produced the hybrid De Lisle Silent Carbine for use by covert forces. After the war the British developed the L34A1 silenced Mark 5 Sterling submachine gun. The Chinese made two rather bulky silenced pistols in the 1960s: the Type 64 and Type 67.

ABOVE The Sten Mark VI (S) submachine gun was almost completely silent. It had a lower muzzle velocity compared with conventional Stens and lower cyclic rate of 450 rpm to reduce wear.

### Wartime innovations

The Sten Mark VI (S) submachine gun was intended for single shots only, though it could be fired on automatic in an emergency. With the silencer the weapon was 908mm/35.75in long, compared to the 762mm/30in of a standard weapon. It was also popular with Resistance groups, and German counter-intelligence officers were greatly impressed by captured weapons. Silenced weapons have been improved since 1945 so that the silencers have a longer life even if the gun is fired in bursts.

### De Lisle Carbine

The British De Lisle Silent Carbine is hard to pigeonhole – is it a bolt-action pistol or a pistol-calibre rifle? What it definitely is, is a silent weapon. To work effectively with a silencer a weapon has to generate a muzzle velocity below the speed of sound, around 330m/s (1,082.67ft/s) depending on altitude and air temperature. The De Lisle Carbine, developed for British Commandos and special forces in World War II, took a .303 Lee Enfield bolt-action rifle but chambered it for the standard .45 ACP from the Colt 1911 pistol. A massive silencer gave it a 210mm/8.25in barrel. The first examples used the standard Lee-Enfield wooden stock but a paratroop version with a folding stock was also produced. The signature or noise when the De Lisle Carbine was fired was a quiet "plop", a sound that would not arouse suspicion. However, although the carbine was reportedly accurate to over 300m/984.25ft, the velocity of around 260m/s (853ft/s), combined with a relatively light round-nosed bullet, produced a curved trajectory at long range, making accurate range estimation crucial.

### The L34A1 Mark V Silent Sterling

The British L34A1 Mark V Sterling was a silent version of the 9mm L2A3 Sterling. It weighed 4,300g/151.68oz, and was 864mm/34in long with the butt extended. It had an effective range of 152m/500ft, with a muzzle velocity of 292–310m/s (958–1,017ft/s). The basic

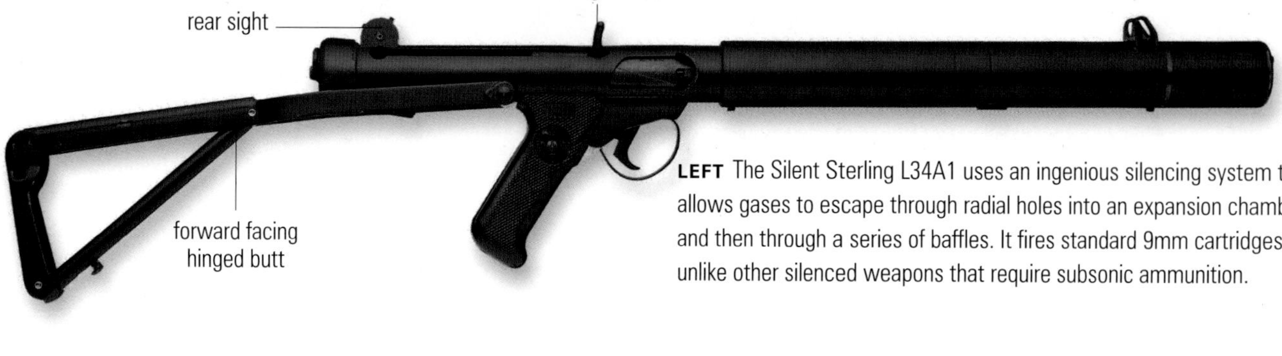


LEFT The Silent Sterling L34A1 uses an ingenious silencing system that allows gases to escape through radial holes into an expansion chamber and then through a series of baffles. It fires standard 9mm cartridges, unlike other silenced weapons that require subsonic ammunition.

**ABOVE** The De Lisle Carbine made by the Royal Small Arms Factory at Enfield, with a ten-round magazine. It was fitted with a .45 barrel forming part of a large, and very efficient silencer.

mechanism was the same as the Sterling but the Silent Sterling has a fixed silencer allied to a special barrel. In the barrel, 72 radial holes are drilled through allowing for the hot propellent gases that follow the bullet out of the muzzle to enter an "expansion chamber". Here these gases expand to dissipate some of their energy. The gases pass through a series of metal baffles, with a central hole to allow the passage of the bullet. The baffles deflect and slow the flow of gas emerging from the expansion chamber. By the time the gases emerge from the silencer, they are cooler, slower and silenced.

Compared to the standard Sterling the L34A1 Mark V appears clumsy and unbalanced. In fact, while it is not as compact, it handles well since the silencer is not intrinsically very heavy. However, it is recommended the silenced weapon should only be fired on single shots and automatic used only in an emergency. The standard Sterling submachine gun is not a noisy weapon when it is fired, but with the silencer fitted it is almost inaudible at 30m/100ft. Before the Heckler & Koch MP5 SD became more widely available on the world market, the L34A1 Mark 5 was very popular. Ironically, while it was used by British Special Forces, it was also bought by Argentina. The L34A1 Mark V was issued to the Special Forces who spearheaded the invasion of the Falkland Islands in 1982.

### Silent Sterling

There are few times when British Special Forces are on public view – and fewer still of the L34A1 Mark V Sterling. Ironically, the greatest exposure that the weapon received was on the morning of 2 April 1982 on news reports. It was slung from the shoulder of Sergeant I.M. Batista, the Argentine commando who escorted the Royal Marine naval party who had surrendered after their overnight defence of Government House in Port Stanley on the Falkland Islands. Batista's imperious manner and the glum Royal Marines with their hands raised in surrender did much to galvanize public opinion in Britain to back the despatch of a Task Force to the Falklands.

### Chinese silenced pistols

China had initially looked to the Soviet Union for weapons and copied these designs. However, in the Type 64 and its successor the Type 67, Chinese small arms designers came up with ingenious silenced weapons. The nine shot Type 67 and 64 pistols are built around an integral silencer. The Type 64 silencer is a light steel cylinder that contains steel mesh and several baffles that slow down and cool the gases from the muzzle blast. It could not fire standard ammunition. Instead it fires a relatively low-powered 7.65mm ammunition developed for the weapon that has a muzzle velocity of 241m/s (790ft/s). Though this helps to keep the sound down, the penalty is a short effective range of between 9–18 m /30–60ft. The pistol can also be fired manually using a lock system that prevents the semi-automatic action from operating.

The Type 67 silenced pistol is a further development of the Type 64 and has replaced the Type 64 in Chinese service. It provides the users with the same combat characteristics, but weighs 1,050kg/37.04oz in contrast to the 1,810g/63.85oz of the Type 64, and the shape of the silencer has been changed to make carrying easier.

**ABOVE** The Chinese Type 64 submachine gun combines a number of features associated with European weapons, including the Bren gun and the PPS-43. What also distinguishes the Type 64 is that it is not a modification but was designed as a silent weapon from the outset.

### Chinese submachine guns

Though the Chinese Type 64 was one of the first indigenously designed weapons it incorporated a number of features taken from European weapons. The bolt action comes from the Soviet PPS-43, the folding butt from the AKM and the trigger mechanism from the British Bren LMG. The silencer is integral to the SMG. It is said to be reasonably effective and to reduce any muzzle flash, and the use of the subsonic 7.62mm Type 64 round further reduces the firing signature. The gun can fire conventional 7.62mm TT ammunition but the higher velocity wears out the silencer. For a submachine gun, the Type 64 has a surprisingly high rate of fire at 1,315 rpm – however, it is a selective fire SMG and would probably be used for single shots.

The Type 85 produced by China North Industries Corporation (NORINCO) is a simplified and lighter version of the Type 64 that has been produced for the export market. The silencer is similar to that on the Type 64.

**ABOVE** A silenced MP5, part of the series SD1–6. The silencer requires no maintenance except rinsing in an oil-free cleaning agent.

It is most effective firing Type 64 ammunition with its heavy, subsonic bullet, but it can also fire standard 7.62mm ammunition, although there is an increased noise level. The Type 85 uses the same 30-round box magazines as the Type 64 submachine gun.

### Silenced German submachine guns

The German Heckler & Koch MP5 SD submachine gun series (SD1–SD6), introduced in 1974, was a superb weapon widely favoured by Western special forces. It had an integrated suppressor and a specially made barrel that has 30 2.5mm ports that reduce the muzzle velocity of its ammunition to subsonic and the the bullet crack and muzzle blast are much reduced. The result is that the MP5 SD series is almost inaudible at distances of more than 15m/49.21ft. Because of this remarkable sound reduction and the almost invisible muzzle flash, the gun has been selected by many police and military units around the world.

### Silent Soviet killers

The Soviet two-shot MSP pistol does not use a silencer, but instead has an ingenious type of ammunition, making it well suited to close-range assassination operations. The pistol was developed around 1972, intended as an easily concealed, short-range assassination weapon for the KGB, GRU, Spetznatz and other covert organizations. Because of its specially designed SP-3 silent ammunition, which encapsulates all powder gases within the cartridge case, the pistol does not require a silencer.

The MSP pistol is a two-barrel, non-automatic pistol. Two barrels are in an "over-under" configuration, and are tipped up at the rear for loading and unloading. The two cartridges come clipped together which makes reloading quicker. The trigger is single-action, with the manual safety catch just behind the trigger on the left side of the grip. The enclosed hammers are cocked manually using the cocking lever at the

## The sound of silence

No weapon is completely silent, and Heckler & Koch have the correct description when they describe the MP5 SD as *Schalldämpfer*, literally "sound dampened".

When a gun is fired there are actually two noises – the explosion of the cartridge and the high-velocity crack of the bullet if it breaks the sound barrier. In a firefight, timing the interval between "crack and thump" gives both an indication of range and also whether the rounds are being aimed at the listener. If there is a distinct delay between the crack and thump then the weapon is being fired at long range and consequently the shooting may not be very accurate. If, however, the sounds almost run together the marksman is nearby and this is the time to be worried. If all that is heard is the thump of the exploding cartridge the rounds are being fired in a different direction.

A suppressor, widely called a silencer, will reduce the speed of the bullet so that it is travelling below the speed of sound, thus removing the "crack" noise. The thump of the exploding cartridge can also be reduced so the sound is something like that of a pneumatic stapling gun or the rattle of machinery.

**RIGHT** A "night vision" view of a special forces operative clearing a room using a silent submachine gun, the MP5 SD, to dampen the sound in an enclosed area.

bottom of the trigger guard. Surprisingly, given that engagement ranges would probably be measured in a few feet, the pistol has small open sights.

Designed in the mid-to-late 1970s, the Soviet S-4 and S-4M pistols further developed the concept of the MSP, and were used in Afghanistan, as well as in many counter-terror operations closer to home. However, possibly because it was seen as a military weapon, the bigger S-4 pistol sacrificed ease of concealment for greater range and hitting power from the powerful silent PZ cartridges.

Adopted around 1983, the Soviet 7.62mm PSS Pistolet Spetsialnyj Samozaryadnyj or Special Self-loading Pistol is a sophisticated design that is a significant improvement on the MSP and S-4M silent pistols in performance and particularly firepower. It has a six-round box magazine and is much more compact and silent in action than conventional silenced pistols like the Soviet PB or Chinese Type 67. Currently, most elite Russian anti-terrorist teams use the PSS.

**RIGHT** The Russian PSS is a compact silent weapon that has a six-round magazine. The special SP-4 ammunition has an internal piston that encapsulates the propellent gases in the cartridge case. The breech block can also be locked closed to prevent the empty case being ejected to rattle to the ground, so ensuring complete silence.

# Specialist and personal defence

Some Personal Defence Weapons (PDWs) are almost novelty guns, while others, such as the classic Belgian FN P90 5.7mm, have a useful role as back-up weapons and are compact enough to be carried and concealed easily. The Personal Defence Weapon falls somewhere between a submachine gun and a handgun, and the Chinese and Soviet Union have both developed gun/knife combinations, an idea that actually dates back to the Frank Wesson dagger-pistol from the 1860s in the United States.

### Guns and knives

Introduced around 1994, the Chinese Firing Combat Knife falls outside the PDW category but merits description. Its blade is 40mm/1.58in long and it has four barrels chambered for .22 LR rounds built into the cylindrical handle. The barrels are positioned so that there are two on either side of the blade, with the muzzle at the base of the blade. By pressing a spring-loaded cap at the rear of the grip, the hilt cap is removed and rounds can be inserted into the chambers. The safety catch is a serrated ring in front of the handle. If it is rotated clockwise this locks the trigger, which doubles as a handguard. With the catch on, the combat knife can be used in knife mode. Twist the safety catch to the "off" position and the Combat Knife is ready to fire. The Firing Combat Knife has an effective range of 18m/60ft, although it is probably more useful at shorter ranges.

Although the Russian 7.62mm Scouting Knife fires only one round, this is a 7.62mm silent cartridge. Unlike the Chinese weapon, the muzzle of the Russian knife is in the hilt – so to fire it the knife is reversed and fired by pressing the trigger bar in the handle. A sliding safety catch prevents accidental firing. The effective range is 23m/75ft. The blade of the Scouting Knife is electrically insulated and is 152mm/6in long and 25mm/1in wide – substantial enough to cut heavy cables. A screwdriver is also incorporated.

### Small but deadly

The Heckler & Koch MP5K introduced in 1976 was a dumpy, short-barrelled version of the MP5 that had no shoulder stock and used a small 15-round magazine. It was adopted by German special forces, and police and military forces throughout the world. Perhaps the most famous users of the MP5 are the United States Secret Service, which protects the president, and the British SAS, who were famously photographed with the gun during Operation Nimrod in 1980, during the Iranian Embassy raid. In 1991 H&K in the United States produced a version with a special hinged shoulder stock that was renamed "MP5K-PDW," which could fire from 15- or 30-round magazines. Only 368mm/14.5in long with the butt folded, it became a much more stable weapon to fire from the shoulder or the hip once it was extended.

The Finnish 9mm Jati-Matic/GG-95 PDW has an unusual barrel location that allows the bolt to recoil up an inclined plane at an angle to the barrel and so reduce muzzle climb when fired on automatic. It has a select-fire trigger and a (rudimentary) folding foregrip. It fires from a 20- or 40-round box magazine and has a cyclic rate of 600 to 650 rpm. Although it is very compact, the fact that it fires 9mm ammunition puts it up against more proven systems like the Hecker & Koch MP5K-PDW. Despite this the Jati-Matic is manufactured under licence in China.

**ABOVE** Due to its compact size the MP5K has high mobility. However, it is not as popular as the PDW version of the MP5K which has a shoulder stock making control of the weapon much easier.

**ABOVE** Packed ready for transport, the SPP-1M Russian underwater pistol. It can be fired underwater, and on land when the diver has reached the shore, making it a truly amphibious weapon.

## Combat beneath the waves

The Russian Tsniitochmash organization produced the *Spetsialnyj Podvodnyj Pistolet* – the Special Underwater Pistol or SPP-1 – in the late 1960s for combat divers working in the Soviet navy. The SPP-1 is a four-barrelled, non-automatic weapon that fires 115mm/4.5in-long drag-stabilized darts that are lethal at 45m/147.5ft in the air and 15.5m/51ft under water. It is also lethal at greater depths than this, although at closer ranges. The sealed ammunition is loaded from the rear and the self-cocking mechanism fires one round with each pull of the trigger. The SPP-1 has been modified and upgraded as the SPP-1M and is still used by the Russian navy special forces.

## The definitive PDW

The Belgian P90 5.7mm PDW designed by Fabrique Nationale de Herstal (FN Herstal) entered service in 1994. It is a truly innovative weapon built around a new FN round that is a cross between a rifle and pistol bullet. PDWs are now required in service because existing pistol calibre cartridges are becoming increasingly ineffective at disabling troops equipped with body armour.

It is a lightweight and completely ambidextrous weapon with a compact, translucent 50-round magazine that runs horizontally across the top of the P90, and empty cases are ejected downwards, well away from the operator. Only the bolt and barrel are made of steel, the rest being from high-impact plastic material. It fires from a closed bolt, giving it outstanding accuracy and making it easy to keep on target. It has a cyclic rate of fire of 900 rpm and a combat range of 137m/450ft.

**BELOW** The FN P90 fires a new type of 5.7mm ammunition that uses dense plastic in place of conventional lead and can penetrate 48 layers of body armour, making it particularly lethal.

# Magnum force

Although the compact convenience and large magazines of automatic pistols seemed to spell the end of the revolver, the weapon still had its advocates after World War II and was much favoured by police. These guns include the .44 American Smith & Wesson Magnums, the .357 Colt Python and the .357 Ruger Blackhawk Magnum. The Russian 12.3mm Udar is a different type of revolver, but it still delivers a formidable punch.

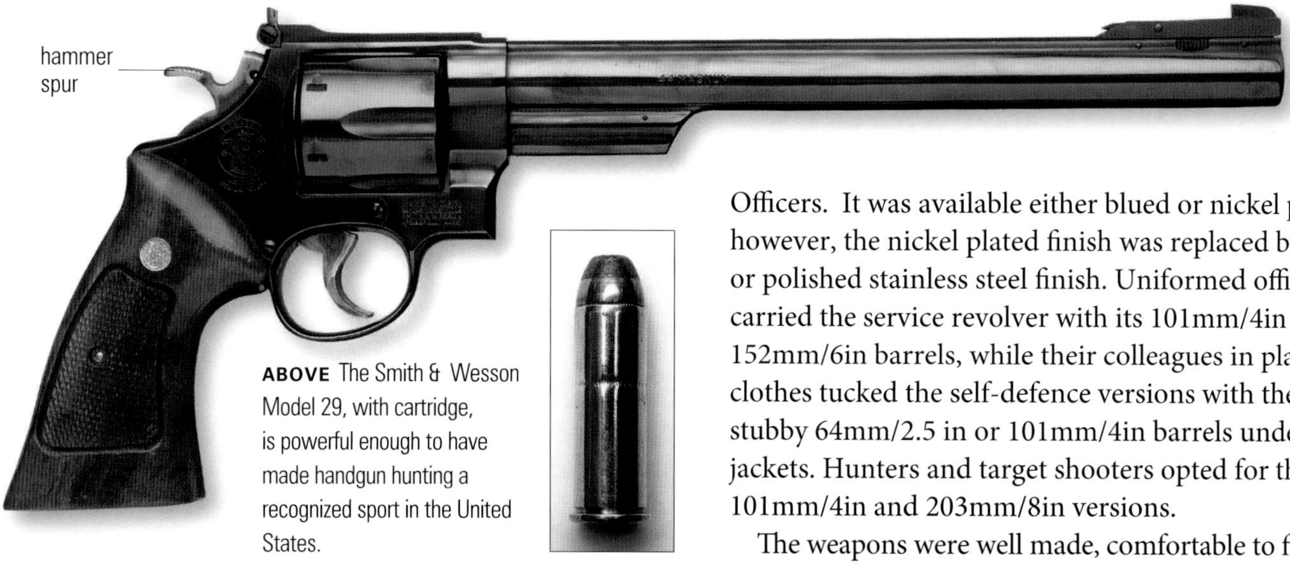


**ABOVE** The Smith & Wesson Model 29, with cartridge, is powerful enough to have made handgun hunting a recognized sport in the United States.

### Classic revolvers

One American handgun, the S&W Model 29, would become something of a film star in the 1970s. From 1955 to 1957 the big Smith & Wesson revolver was simply called "the .44 Magnum", but when in 1957 S&W standardized the model numbering of their products it became the S&W Model 29. Smith & Wesson .44 Magnum revolvers have heavyweight steel frames produced in blue or stainless-steel finishes. The blue and nickel models are called the Model 29, while the stainless-steel version is the Model 629. Versions such as the "629 Classic", "629 DX", "629 Classic Hunter" have specialized features such as interchangeable front sights, full lug barrels, and special grips. *Jane's Infantry Weapons* sums up the reputation of the .44 Magnum: "When the utmost power is required from a handgun, the Model 29 is the obvious answer, delivering upwards of 1600 J of muzzle energy with the longer barrels."

### The revolver revival

When it was introduced in 1955, the hand-made Colt Python .357 revolver immediately became one of the most popular personal weapons for US Law Officers. It was available either blued or nickel plated, however, the nickel plated finish was replaced by satin or polished stainless steel finish. Uniformed officers carried the service revolver with its 101mm/4in or 152mm/6in barrels, while their colleagues in plain clothes tucked the self-defence versions with their stubby 64mm/2.5 in or 101mm/4in barrels underneath jackets. Hunters and target shooters opted for the big 101mm/4in and 203mm/8in versions.

The weapons were well made, comfortable to fire and since they had originally been intended to be a big calibre target revolver – very accurate. The foresights were conventional with a red polymer dot insert, the rear sights adjustable for both windage and elevation and had a white edging. Production stopped in 1998 but Colt reintroduced many of the "Snake guns", beginning with the Cobra in 2017, King Cobra in 2019, the Python in 2020, and the Anaconda in 2021.

**ABOVE** The discharge of a Magnum revolver at a shooting range. The target is aimed at using an optical scope. Large-calibre weapons are best suited to target shooting and hunting.

ABOVE The Colt Python was originally made in a blued carbon-steel finish.

In 1955 the American gunmaker William Ruger, who had noted popular interest in single-action revolvers seen in Western films, produced a single-action gun that quickly became the flagship for all his single-action handguns – the .357 Blackhawk Magnum. This was followed by the .44 Magnum Blackhawk in 1956. Three years later the largest of the single action Rugers appeared, the Super Blackhawk, which had an all steel frame and could fire either .44 Magnum or .45 Colt ammunition. However, Ruger revolver designs were also innovative. The compact SP 101 is a stainless steel five shot weapon in various calibres and capable of handling powerful modern ammunition. In 1993 a double action pistol with a spurless hammer was introduced that was ideal for covert use as there was no risk of the spur snagging on clothing. It was available in 0.38 Special and 0.357 Magnum chambering.

## The Udar revolver

If a modern version of the film *Dirty Harry* were produced, the hero might choose the Russian 12.3mm Udar or "Blow". This compact weapon is a double-and single-action revolver designed to fire a range of special cartridges built around the 32-gauge hunting round, and has been developed for police and security forces. Clips are preloaded with different ammunition types that can be quickly replaced according to the tactical situation.

The armour-piercing round has a sub-calibre steel bullet that can penetrate a 5mm/0.2in steel plate at 45m/147.64ft, as well as conventional body armour. A plastic round is available for non-lethal operations, and a pyroliquid (coloured ink) bullet for training exercises and for marking offenders. The pistol fires conventional ball ammunition and a high-noise blank round. Empty cases are ejected simultaneously. Three filled reserve clips are carried in the box, together with the holster.

### "Do you feel lucky?"

Don Siegel's 1971 film *Dirty Harry* was considered sensational because of its overt violence. The duelling combatants, Clint Eastwood's unconventional cop and the pathological sadistic criminal, share traits of brutal violence and insanity.

When the film was being made, the .44 Model 29 Magnum was not in production, so strings had to be pulled to get a few made especially for the film. Eastwood spent time on the range prior to undertaking the role, so that he could properly replicate the .44's recoil when firing blank cartridges in the film. The blanks also had to be specially made, as the traditional Hollywood blanks would not fit the .44 chamber. In the film, Harry uses a light special load that gives better control because of its reduced

RIGHT Clint Eastwood in *Dirty Harry*. In the film he describes the S&W Model 29 as "The most powerful handgun in the world". This, together with "Do you feel lucky, punk?", are among the memorable lines uttered by the ruthless detective in the film.

# Post-war pistols

Pistol design expanded vastly after World War II in Europe, when the major users were police and the armed forces, with only a small number of private owners. In the United States, however, there was a large domestic market, too. Many designers took the best features of existing pistols, notably the German P38 and FN Browning 9mm High-Power and incorporated them into their pistols.

**ABOVE** The Czech 9mm CZ75 is a handy weapon that incorporates features like the safety from the P38 and the double stack magazine from the Browning HP.

### French service

The French 9mm MAS Model 1950 pistol was developed in the late 1940s by Manufacture d'Armes de Saint Etienne (MAS) in France, and manufactured by MAS and also by Manufacture d'Armes de Chatellerault (MAC) until 1970. The pistol was a development of the pre-war SACM Model 1935A pistol, designed by Swiss engineer Charles Petter. This recoil-operated, locked breech, semi-automatic pistol, uses a single-action trigger with slide-mounted safety. This locks the firing pin, which, by pressing the trigger with the safety engaged, enables the hammer to be lowered. The MAS Model 1950 has fixed sights and a single-stack nine-round magazine.

### Czech copies

Although the 9mm CZ75 pistol developed by the brothers Josef and Frantisek Koucky, seemed an ideal military pistol, it was only adopted by police forces. It would, however, prove to be a very influential design. It first appeared in 1975, with production beginning a year later. Obviously intended for the export market, it looked good, was comfortable to handle and shoot, and was quite accurate and reliable.

The CZ75 design had drawn on the best features of previous pistols such as the P38 and the Browning High Power, and in turn was widely copied and cloned. Israel's IMI produced the Jericho-941; in Italy Tanfoglio made the TZ75, TZ90 and T95; in Turkey Sarsilmaz manufactured the M2000; in Switzerland ITM the AT-88; while in China Norinco designed the NZ-75.

### Spanish designs

Two years after Llama-Gabilondo y Cia of Vitoria produced their 9mm M-82 pistol it was adopted by the Spanish Army. It has a 15-round magazine and is a recoil operated, locked breech pistol with a short recoiling barrel like the Walther P-38 or Beretta 92. To load with the safety "on", a magazine is inserted, the slide operated, a round is fed in, but the hammer drops in a safe condition. To fire, push the safety to "fire" and pull the trigger – this cocks and releases the hammer. For greater accuracy, the hammer can also be manually cocked for the first shot. With a steel frame and slide, the M82 is relatively heavy at 1,110g/39.15oz, but it is also strong; an alloy frame version weighs in at 875g/30.86oz.

**ABOVE** The Spanish Star Model 30M has a 15-round magazine and an ambidextrous safety catch. The trigger guard is shaped for a double-handed grip.

The 9mm Spanish Star Model 30M and 30 PK was developed and manufactured by Star Bonifacio Echeverria SA. It appeared in 1990 and is now in service with the Spanish army and police. An updated version of the earlier Star 28M, they are recoil-operated, locked-breech pistols, that use Browning-designed, linkless locking. Safety features include a magazine safety that prevents firing without a magazine, as well as a chamber loaded indicator.

### Safety and weapons handling

**ABOVE** The pistol is safe when the breech is empty of ammunition and the safety catch applied.

A firearm is a lethal tool that requires very little skill to use. To prevent accidents there are two simple safety rules. The first is to ensure that a weapon is unloaded. Remove the magazine while pointing the weapon in a safe direction. Then operate the action, which will eject a round that might be in the breech. Then, and only then, is the trigger pulled.

The weapon can then be "made safe" with the full magazine in place, but with the safety catch applied and no rounds in the breech. If it is unloaded, the magazine is removed and any rounds that may have been ejected are stowed back in the magazine, which is then put in a pocket or pouch.

If a weapon is handed from one user to another, he should, in British military parlance, "show clear", that it has been unloaded. A revolver is broken to show the empty cylinders, while the magazine is removed from an automatic weapon and the action pulled to the rear to show that the breech is empty. The second safety rule is never to point a weapon at anyone in fun.

In 1993 the Heckler & Koch Universal Self-loading Pistol (USP) – was marketed initially in 9mm and .40 S&W. With a modified Browning linkless locked-breech action with patented recoil reduction system, it is a very accurate pistol to fire since it is easy to recover the sight picture between shots. The USP has a moulded polymer frame with special grooves for the quick mounting of laser-aiming modules or tactical lights.

### Italian style on trial

Beretta 92 pistols first began production in 1976 and were based on the early Beretta model 1951. Developed by the Italian company Armi Pietro Beretta Spa, the Model 92 was adopted by the Italian army as well as being manufactured under licence in Egypt. It is a blowback operated, locked-breech semi-automatic pistol which has a vertically tilting locking block system and an external trigger bar on the right side of the frame similar to the Walther P38. It also has a double-action trigger with a frame-mounted safety. Aluminium alloy is used for the frame and steel for the slide. Although the original Beretta 92 is no longer being made, it has served as the basis for numerous modifications and improvements.

In 1985 the Beretta model 92F was submitted as the XM9 for US Army Pistol Trials. Improvements and modifications included a chromed barrel, a trigger guard designed for a double-handed grip, new grip panels and a trigger bar disconnect safety. There was considerable controversy in the United States when it was finally adopted as the 9mm M9 pistol. It is manufactured in Italy, and in the United States by Beretta United States.

**ABOVE** The Italian Beretta 92 was adopted by the US Army as the M9. It is available in several configurations, all of which have a Browning HP-style 15-round magazine.

# New guns, new materials

The attraction of new materials such as alloys and glass-reinforced plastic (GRP) in weapons construction is that they are lighter, sometimes stronger and do not rust or corrode. With a lower metallic content, they can be harder to detect by conventional security systems (found at airports for example), although some weapons developed using these new technologies have attracted controversy in the trade over materials and design.

## The Glock

Glock Gmbh of Austria had an established reputation for its combat knives and entrenching tools when its 9mm Glock 17 won at the Austrian army pistol trials. The gun was subsequently adopted in the early 1980s under the designation P-80 by Austrian police and military forces. Since then, the Glock 17 and its subsequent derivatives have become very popular firearms, being exported to more than 50 countries. Among the features that have attracted users are the small number of working parts (only 33 including the magazine), and the use of highly resistant polymer materials. The Glock was probably the first handgun to be made successfully using polymers.

Currently, Glocks are chambered for all major pistol calibres, and are available in full-size service models, semi-compact models, compact models for concealed/backup use, and in longslide competition models. The Glock Selective-Fire Submachine Pistol has fitted a fire selector and 19- or 33-round magazine to the basic pistol and produced a weapon with an awesome rate of fire of around 1,300 rpm. It is possible to obtain training versions, which fire non-lethal practice ammunition. To avoid confusion, the frame colour of "live" guns is red while guns that fire non-lethal ammunition are coloured blue.

**ABOVE** A Colt .357 Python revolver receives the hands-on treatment on the production line at the factory at Hartford, Connecticut, United States. The company introduced the pistol in 1955. While new guns and materials are introduced, older versions are still popular.

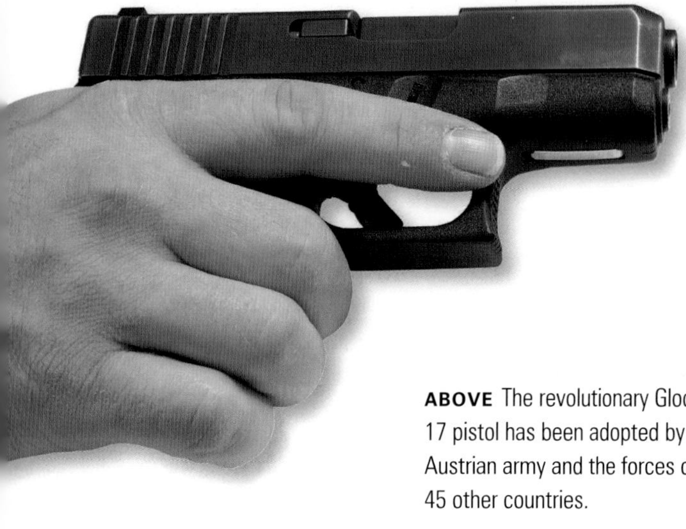

**ABOVE** The revolutionary Glock 17 pistol has been adopted by the Austrian army and the forces of 45 other countries.

## Special operations

The Heckler & Koch Mark 23 SOCOM pistol was developed to a requirement from the US Special Operations Command for a pistol of a calibre of no less than .45 with a 12-round magazine. The gun must have a service life of 30,000 rounds before major maintenance, and be capable of being fired when wet,

**ABOVE** The Heckler & Koch Mark 23 originated in 1991 when Heckler & Koch began development of a pistol for the US Special Operations Command (SOCOM). It finally passed all their rigorous tests and was issued by SOCOM in 1996.

dirty, icy or not maintained. A silencer and laser-aiming device were added to the specifications, which had to be instantly removable without tools and which would not adversely affect the accuracy of the gun upon refitting. Both Colt and Heckler & Koch entered the trials.

The H&K pistol had several parts (the slide and 12-round box magazine) made from polymers, and a mechanical recoil-suppression system that reduced recoil forces by 30 per cent. As well as the required flash and noise suppressor, it also had a laser-aiming module that could be attached to give an infrared or visual aiming spot. The H&K gun finally passed all the tests and became the .45 MK23 SOCOM offensive handgun and was issued in 1996.

### Police and civilian guns

The 9mm Vektor Compact pistol (CP1) manufactured by the DENEL Corporation of South Africa was another weapon built using a polymer frame and a stainless-steel barrel. Introduced during the late 1990s, it was intended as a concealed-carry weapon for police and civilian use. Magazines are double-stack and the Compact's 12-round magazine fits flush with the bottom of the grip, while the 13-round has extended finger rests at the bottom.

Weighing 720g/25.4oz with the 13-round magazine, the CP1 seemed a useful little handgun. However, controversy struck when the US gun enthusiast press published a recall notice in October 2000 warning that the loaded pistol could fire if bumped or dropped, and advised users not to load the gun under any circumstances.

### Hollow point or full metal jacket (FMJ)

The name "dum-dum" was used to describe a British military bullet that was developed at the Dum-Dum Arsenal, on the North-West Frontier of India in the late 1890s. It consisted of a jacketed .303 rifle bullet with the jacket nose open to expose its lead core. The aim was to improve the bullet's effectiveness by increasing its expansion upon impact; what this actually meant was terrible injuries to the victim. The phrase "dum-dum" was later expanded to include any soft-nosed or hollow-pointed bullet. The Hague Convention of 1899 outlawed the use of these bullets.

However, although soldiers are required to fire bullets that have a full metal jacket (FMJ), the police are not. While hollow-point rounds can make big holes when they hit human tissue, the rounds simply flatten if they hit a building, and will not ricochet off with the consequent chance of injuring innocent people in the vicinity.

**ABOVE** The hollow-point round causes extreme expansion or disintegration on impact.

### Controversy

In 1994 Smith & Wesson introduced the Sigma series of pistols with the Sigma 40F in .40 S&W, and this was followed by a 9mm version. S&W had taken ten years to develop the pistol, which was the first to be made using polymer for both the gun frame and slide. However, the Sigma pistol was so similar to a Glock, that some referred to the Sigma series as "Swocks", a play on words between S&W and Glock. Glock sued Smith & Wesson, and although Smith & Wesson were obliged to pay an undisclosed sum to Glock for breach of patents, they received the rights to continue production of the Sigma line, with some amendments.

# Modern handgun mechanisms

By the early years of the 20th century, the semi-automatic pistol and revolver had established themselves as viable weapons although the basic principles have not changed greatly since the 1930s. There are dozens of different operating methods for firearms, but the same basic principle applies to all: the firearm must be loaded, the hammer cocked for firing, and the firing pin must strike the primer of the cartridge for it to fire.

### Single-action mechanism

Single-action (SA) pistols have a single-action trigger mechanism. The hammer is cocked and the trigger fired to discharge a bullet. A semi-automatic pistol such as the Colt M1911 is an example of a pistol that must be cocked for the first shot, but after the first shot has been fired, it is cocked automatically. These types of pistols typically have a very light trigger pull, and are very accurate. The pistol mechanism is always partially cocked while being carried and during firing, but cannot discharge a cartridge before it is fired.

### Double-action mechanism

Traditional double-action (TDA) pistols have a mechanism that can be used in two ways. They can either be pre-cocked, like the single-action gun, or they can be fired with the gun uncocked. In this case, the gun has an additional mechanism added to the trigger that will cock the gun as the trigger is pulled. The hammer is released and the gun fired once the trigger is pulled far enough. For autoloading pistols, the self-loading mechanism will also recock the hammer after the first shot so that subsequent shots are fired single-action. Double-action-only (DAO) pistols do not use the motion of the slide to recock the hammer. Rather, both for the initial shot and all subsequent shots, the hammer is cocked by releasing the trigger.

### Firing a gun

When a single or semi-automatic pistol is fired the hammer is cocked to draw back the slide. Pulling the trigger then discharges the cartridge. This causes the slide to recoil backwards. As the slide recoils it opens the breech, ejecting the casing. At the same time the slide recocks the hammer for the next shot. The spring-loaded slide mechanism automatically returns to its position and a new cartridge is fed into the magazine.

### How the modern revolver works

A revolver has several firing chambers arranged in a circle in a cylindrical block. When the trigger of the revolver is pulled, the cartridge in the chamber is aligned with the barrel. At the same time the hammer is released and a compressed spring drives the hammer forward. The firing pin on the hammer extends through the body of the gun and hits the primer. The primer explodes, igniting the propellant. The propellant burns, releasing a large volume of gas, which drives the bullet down the barrel. The pressure of the gas also expands the cartridge case which has the effect of temporarily sealing the breech. At the same time the trigger is pulled, a mechanism attached to the trigger pushes on a ratchet to rotate the cylinder. This positions the next breech chamber in front of the gun barrel ready for firing.

**ABOVE** When the spent shells have been removed from the cylinder, individual cartridges can be placed in the chambers.

## How a semi-automatic pistol works

A semi-automatic pistol works by extracting and ejecting a fired cartridge automatically from a chamber, which then loads an unfired cartridge from a magazine into the chamber to be ready for the next trigger pull. This cycle uses the energy of the explosive discharge of each cartridge that is fired.

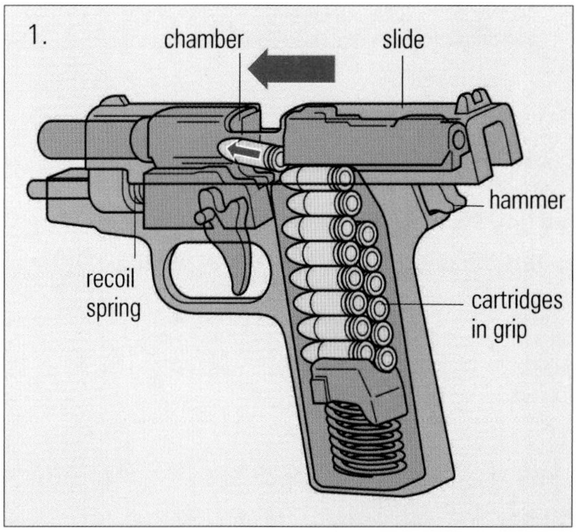


1. A magazine is loaded with 9mm cartridges, and then placed into the pistol's grip. The slide is pulled back. This cocks the hammer and is then released and is pushed forward by the recoil spring. The breech block feeds the first round of ammunition from the magazine into the barrel's chamber. The next round in the magazine is moved into position.

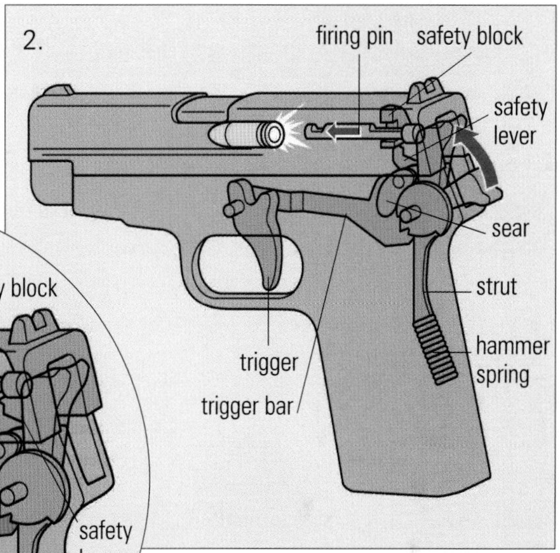


2. Now the pistol is loaded, the trigger is pulled. This draws the trigger bar forward. This pivots the safety lever, raising the firing pin safety block so the firing pin can move. Simultaneously, the trigger bar pulls the sear forwards, releasing the hammer. The main spring pushes the hammer forwards so that it strikes the back of the firing pin. This hits the cartridge and the primer causes the gun to fire.

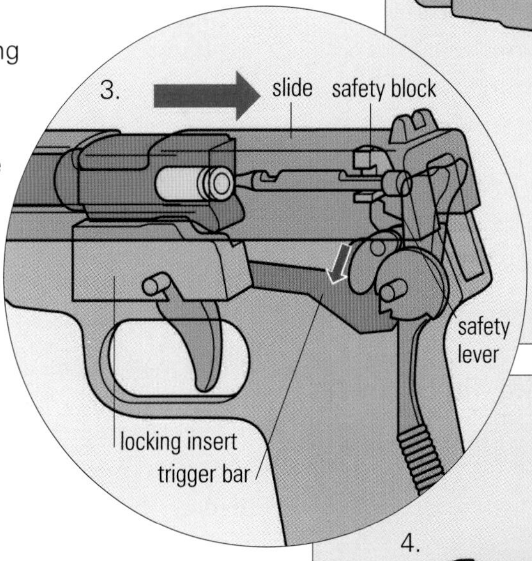


3. The force of driving the bullet out of the barrel also presses the empty cartridge case backwards as a result of recoil. The force also pushes the slide to the back. The firing pin safety block is activated by its separation from the safety lever. As it moves backwards the slide forces the trigger bar downwards and away from the safety lever. The slide also takes the barrel with it as it travels backward. The locking insert stops the backward motion and moves it down and away from the slide.

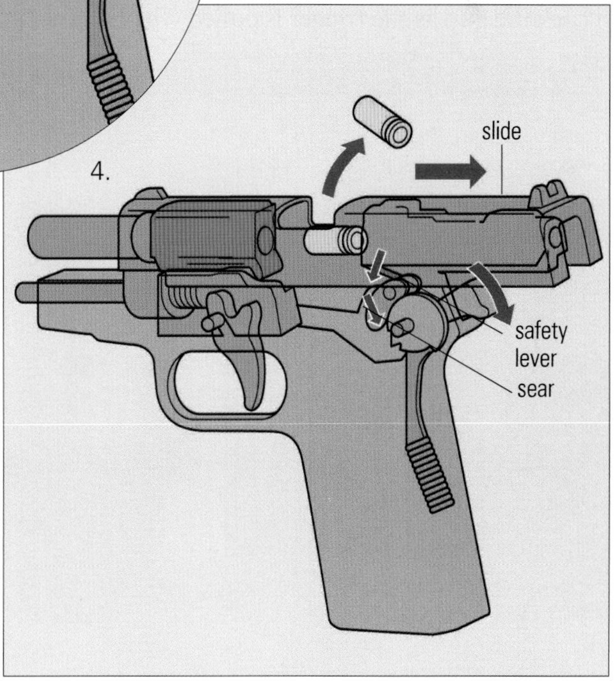


4. As the slide returns, the sear and safety lever go back to their starting points. The empty cartridge case is pushed upwards out of the ejection port. As the slide recoils to its stop, it cocks the hammer. The slide is pushed forward by the recoil spring, and the next round is fed into the chamber of the barrel as the slide locks up with the barrel again. The pistol can be fired again.

# The 21st century and the future

Non-lethal hand-held guns are now regarded as useful weapons, whereas 20 years ago a handgun was used simply to kill an assailant. Research continues into how to produce weapons that will stop an aggressive person without killing or severely injuring them. On a larger scale, riots present a different but related challenge. Arms manufacturers have produced a variety of solutions, from incapacitating gases that generate coughing and disorientation, but not lasting injury, to rubber bullets and anaesthetizing darts.

### CS gas and baton rounds

In 1928 two American scientists, Ben Carson and Roger Staughton, discovered 2-chlorobenzalmalononitrile, and the first two letters of the scientists' surnames were used to name the substance. This CS gas was developed and tested secretly at the British Chemical and Biological Warfare Establishment at Porton Down, Wiltshire, during the 1950s and 1960s. CS is actually a solid chemical and in order to deliver it to a human target it must be converted into a smoke or aerosol. In powder form it can be incorporated into riot-control munitions like baton rounds. The 12-gauge Ferret barricade round from Mace Security of the United States is designed to punch through barriers such as car windshields or wooden doors and scatter a quick-acting liquid irritant agent inside. However, unlike a baton round, the Ferret breaks up on impact with a barrier.

The British developed baton rounds in the late 1960s, when colonial police in Hong Kong used 51mm/2in wooden cylinders fired from large-bore weapons to disrupt riots. The aim was to replicate the effect of using a truncheon on demonstrators, without the police actually having to engage in hand-to-hand combat with the rioters.

The rounds were expected to fall a few feet short of rioters, to ricochet off the ground at about ankle height. However, the police found the wooden rounds often split, had unpredictable characteristics, and could prove lethal if fired at close range. When the "troubles" began in Northern Ireland in the 1970s, British troops were equipped with baton-round guns that fired tough rubber bullets, which were later replaced by PVC rounds. The use of baton rounds became increasingly controversial as injuries and deaths were linked to close-range hits.

**ABOVE** Police firing rubber bullets and tear gas as they struggle to stop supporters of Venezuelan President Hugo Chavez from clashing with opposition protesters, Caracas, 4 November 2002.

### Rubber bullets

The French company Manurhin, with a well-respected reputation for its small arms, devised the MR-35 Punch. This is a 35mm five-shot weapon that uses a small powder charge to fire a soft rubber ball. A hit will not kill, but it does deliver the sort of impact that you would feel if hit by a .38 Special bullet. Five balls can be fired from the MR-35 Punch in as many seconds and it can hit a 17cm$^2$ target at 7m (6in$^2$ at 20ft). Made largely from polymers, the MR-35 weighs only 1,500g/53oz loaded.

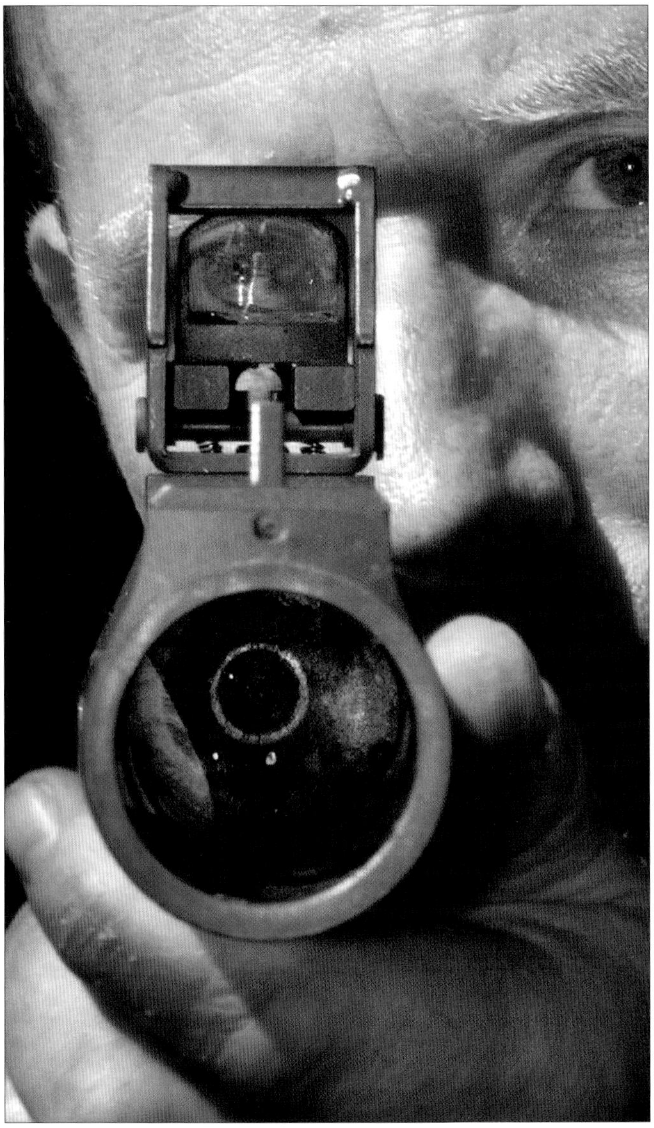

A similar concept is reflected in the American RB rubber ball series of 12-gauge cartridges. These contain nine small hard rubber balls that are designed to ricochet off the ground. Again, this firearm will knock down, wind and deter a hostile individual without causing fatal injury.

## The anaesthetic gun

The Chinese BBQ-901 anaesthetic gun system is a slightly sinister device for neutralizing an assailant and is probably derived from game conservancy dart rifles. It is a single-shot hand-held weapon that fires a projectile, that on impact, injects a liquid anaesthetic. Depending on the type of anaesthetic used, this will render the target unconscious in one to three minutes. The effects of the anaesthetic wear off in three to four minutes – which gives enough time for the subject to have been handcuffed.

## The grenade launcher

The South African MGL Mark 1 40mm grenade launcher is a six-shot shoulder or hip-fired revolver that fires baton rounds or tear gas cartridges. It has a minimum range of 30m/98ft and maximum of 400m/1,312ft. Like gun fighters in the Wild West, a skilled operator can fire six rounds in just three seconds.

**LEFT** A Metropolitan Police firearms officer with a L104AL baton gun. This weapon can be deployed at a distance no closer than 1 metre from a suspect. The L104AL fires a high-velocity plastic round.

## Knock down

One of the most effective non-lethal systems available to police and security services is the Taser, developed by Taser Inc. in the United States. The hand-held device fires two probes up to 5m/16ft carrying a lightweight wire. Once the probes have attached themselves to an assailant, an electrical signal is transmitted causing him to lose neuromuscular control. Once he has been knocked down, a series of pulses keeps him down and ensures that he cannot remove the probes. The Taser has become a device for controlling aggressive or dangerous individuals. Unlike a CS spray that must be directed at the face, or a handgun that has to be fired at a head or torso, the Taser works on whatever part of the body it hits.

**ABOVE** British police officers using a taser gun undertake specialist firearms training and are normally part of a first-response unit. Mandatory re-qualification takes place on a yearly basis.

RIGHT The Star Model 30M was produced in Spain during 1990 and issued to the Spanish Army, Navy, Marines and Air Force as well as to the Guardia Civil and the National Police.

BELOW The UK's Webley-Fosbery Model 1902 allowed for rapid and accurate shooting and was popular among target shooters. Although the Webley-Fosbery was never adopted as an official government sidearm, many were bought by British officers prior to and during World War I.

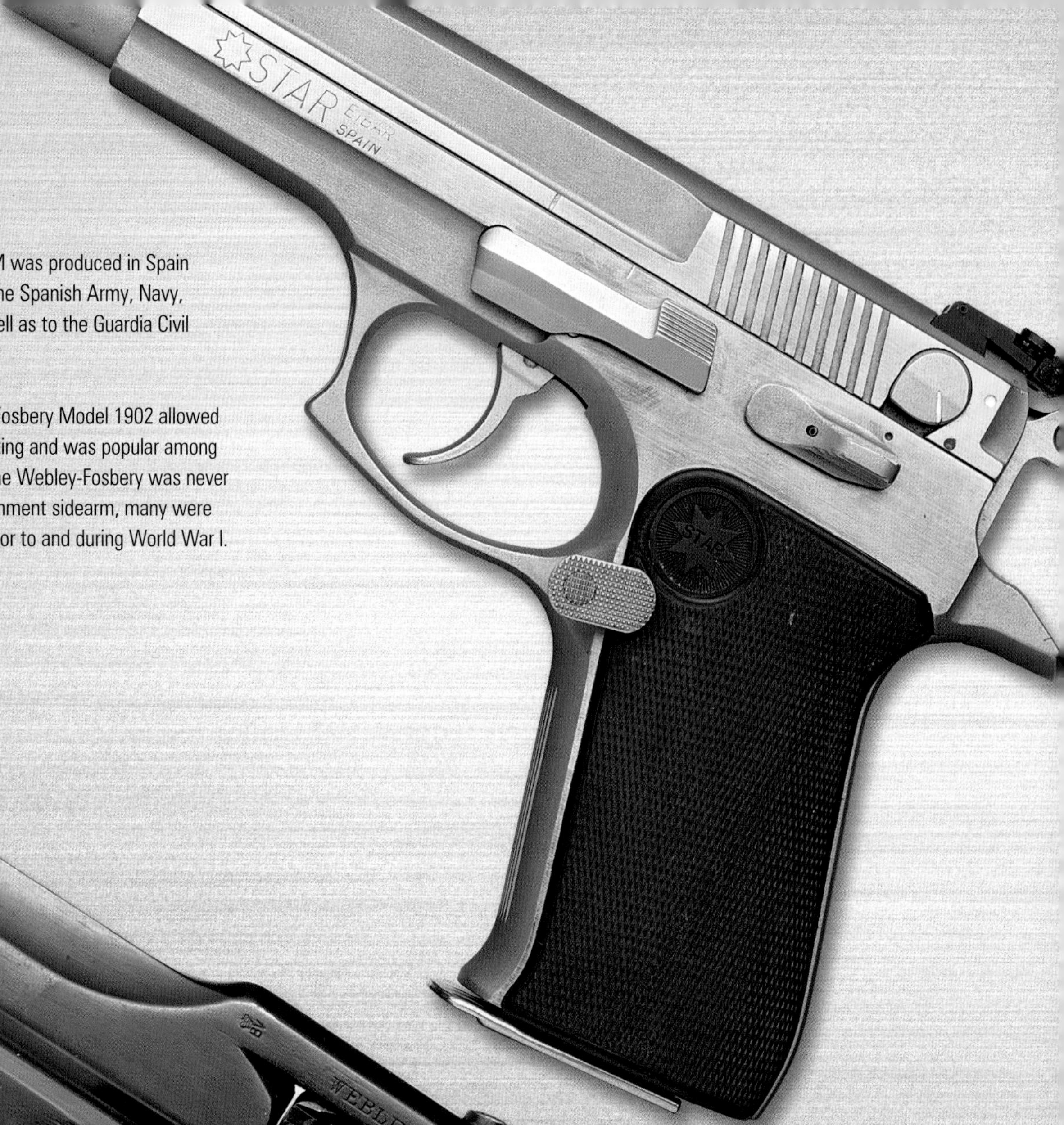

# A directory of pistols and revolvers from around the world

A variety of countries around the world produce and manufacture firearms. Some produce arms that are unique, while others produce or import versions of firearms from other countries under licence, sometimes with different fittings and specifications. This directory is a cross-section of selected countries of the world, west to east – and some of the firearms that are available in those countries and their main features. Within each country guns are organized alphabetically by manufacturer except where its historical development is shown more clearly chronologically or a company changes its name. Each firearm has a description and a specification that lists its vital measurements, including its calibre.

**KEY**

1 Canada
2 United States
3 Chile
4 Argentina
5 Brazil
6 Spain
7 UK
8 France
9 Belgium
10 Switzerland
11 Germany
12 Italy
13 Norway
14 Denmark
15 Austria
16 Czech Republic
17 Poland
18 Serbia
19 Hungary
20 Finland
21 Romania
22 Russia
23 Egypt
24 Turkey
25 Israel
26 Japan
27 China
28 South Korea

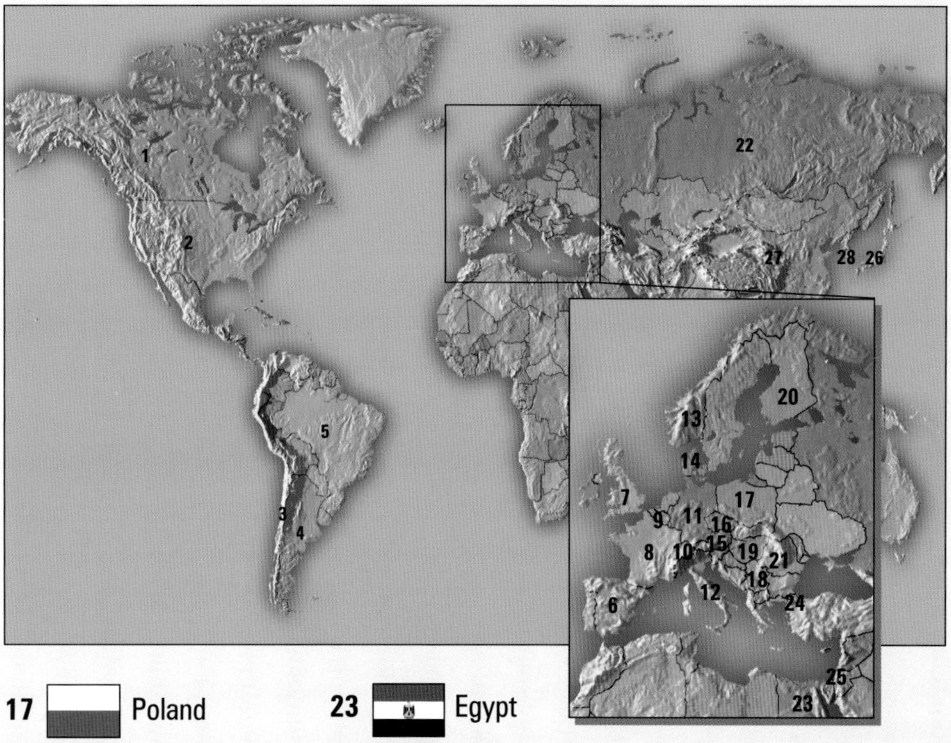

**ABOVE** The map indicates the countries of the world where pistols and revolvers are featured in this section.

**Note on specification boxes:** Traditionally guns developed in the United States have been given calibres in inches, while European countries have designated calibre in metric. Guns have retained this designation in this book. Calibre is given different names in different parts of the world – for example .380 ACP is called the 9mm Browning Short in Belgium, 9mm Corto in Italy, and 9mm Kurtz in Germany, and 9 x 17mm by many countries. Dimensions refer to the weapon shown, where illustrated. Weights and measurements are approximate.

# Canada

**Having previously relied largely on imports or copies of weapons from countries in Europe and the United States, Canada now has a small but highly reputable small-arms industry. The company Para-Ordnance, founded in 1985, has been credited with some of the most significant improvements on Browning's original M1911 design and since then has developed a wide range of pistols for the military, law enforcement, sports and competition markets. Para-Ordnance works in coordination with Colt Canada.**

## Browning M1935, John Inglis version

The M1935 was an improvement on the earlier and hugely successful M1911 pistol, first produced in Belgium in the early 20th century. The Browning M1935 was a semi-automatic 9mm pistol conceived by firearms inventor John Browning and produced in Belgium in 1935. It was the most advanced military pistol available. During World War II, John Inglis and Company in Ontario produced a Canadian version of the Browning M1935 for use by Allied Forces, including the British, Canadians and Greeks. The pistol was widely used by the British Special Air Service (SAS) as well as by the US Office of Strategic Services (OSS).

**SPECIFICATION**

**MANUFACTURER** John Inglis Ltd.
**CALIBRE** 9mm Parabellum
**MAGAZINE CAPACITY** 13
**ACTION** Recoil/single
**TOTAL LENGTH** 197mm/7.75in
**BARREL LENGTH** 118mm/4.65in
**WEIGHT UNLOADED** 920g/32.5oz

## Para-Ordnance P14-45

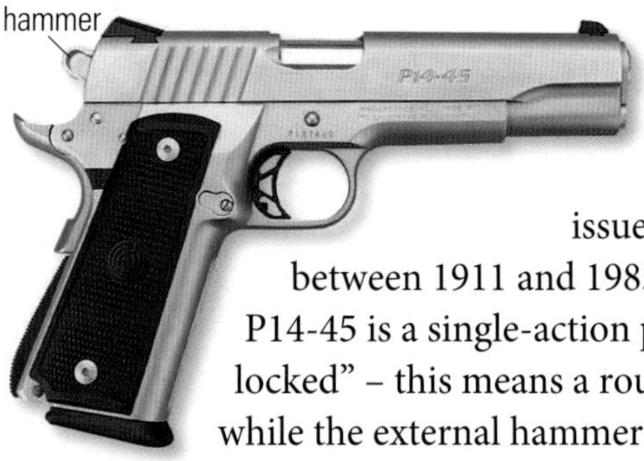


Introduced in 1990, this was the first pistol in the Para range – an updated version of the classic pistol, the M1911, which became the standard issue handgun used in the United States between 1911 and 1985. The .45 ACP (Automatic Colt Pistol) P14-45 is a single-action pistol that can be carried "cocked and locked" – this means a round can be carried in the chamber while the external hammer is checked and the thumb safety applied. Favoured by competition shooters, this is an effective combat weapon with a good reliability record.

**SPECIFICATION**

**MANUFACTURER** Para-Ordnance
**CALIBRE** .45 ACP
**MAGAZINE CAPACITY** 14
**ACTION** Recoil/single
**TOTAL LENGTH** 216mm/8.5in
**BARREL LENGTH** 127mm/5in
**WEIGHT UNLOADED** 1,334g/40oz

## Para-Ordnance Carry

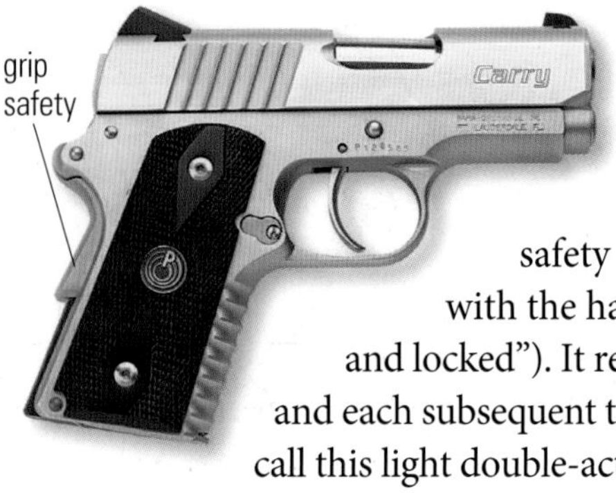


When this pistol was introduced in 1992, it was the world's smallest double-action-only (DAO) pistol in .45 ACP and the first in the Carry Option range. The safety system allows the pistol to be carried with the hammer down, ready for action ("cocked and locked"). It remains flush with the pistol when not firing and each subsequent trigger pull produces a smooth shot (Para call this light double-action or LDA). Before firing, the grip safety needs to be depressed before the gun can operate. Standard features of the Carry include night sights, which are used to acquire targets in poor light.

**SPECIFICATION**

**MANUFACTURER** Para-Ordnance
**CALIBRE** .45 ACP
**MAGAZINE CAPACITY** 6
**ACTION** Recoil/LDA
**TOTAL LENGTH** 165mm/6.5in
**BARREL LENGTH** 76mm/3in
**WEIGHT UNLOADED** 850g/30oz

## Para-Ordnance CCW (Concealed Carry Weapon)

**SPECIFICATION**

- **MANUFACTURER** Para-Ordnance
- **CALIBRE** .45 ACP
- **MAGAZINE CAPACITY** 7
- **ACTION** Recoil/LDA
- **TOTAL LENGTH** 196mm/7.7in
- **BARREL LENGTH** 108mm/4.25in
- **WEIGHT UNLOADED** 850g/30oz

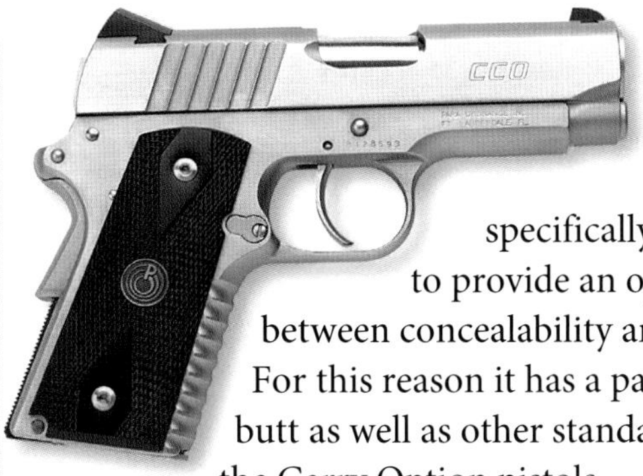

This Carry Option pistol, introduced in 2003, has been specifically developed to provide an optimum balance between concealability and ease of firing. For this reason it has a particularly short butt as well as other standard features of the Carry Option pistols.

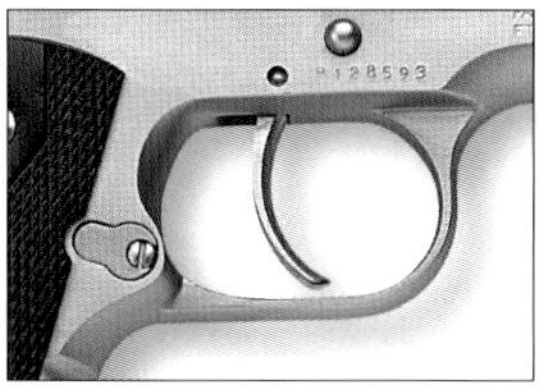

**ABOVE** Light double-action (LDA) Para triggers allowed a hammer-down carry for instant readiness, and a smooth trigger pull to keep the shot on target.

## Para-Ordnance Carry 12

The Carry 12, developed in 2004, is a high-capacity carry pistol. It is slim and compact enough to be easily concealed while providing a high level of firepower. The Carry 12 has all the standard features of the Carry range, with sophisticated night sights to help with targeting in poor light. It has a high-capacity magazine with 12 rounds of ammunition, while much of the recoil from firing the pistol is absorbed by its solid stainless-steel construction.

**SPECIFICATION**

- **MANUFACTURER** Para-Ordnance
- **CALIBRE** .45 ACP
- **MAGAZINE CAPACITY** 12
- **ACTION** Recoil/LDA
- **TOTAL LENGTH** 178mm/7in
- **BARREL LENGTH** 89mm/3.5in
- **WEIGHT UNLOADED** 963g/34oz

## Para-Ordnance 1911 SSP

**SPECIFICATION**

- **MANUFACTURER** Para-Ordnance
- **CALIBRE** .45 ACP
- **MAGAZINE CAPACITY** 7
- **ACTION** Recoil/single
- **TOTAL LENGTH** 216mm/8.5in
- **BARREL LENGTH** 127mm/5in
- **WEIGHT UNLOADED** 1,105g/39oz

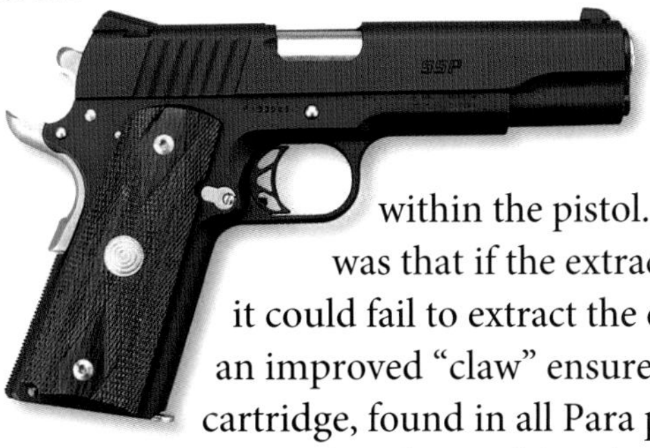

This pistol, introduced in 2004, was the first in the Para range to feature the new "power extraction" mechanism for extracting and feeding the cartridge within the pistol. One weakness of the original M1911 was that if the extractor did not maintain the proper tension, it could fail to extract the empty cartridge. A revised design and an improved "claw" ensures positive extraction and feeding of the cartridge, found in all Para pistols since 2004. The SSP also has an adjustable rear sight. The model includes extras such as competition triggers and hammers. It has a single-stack frame for cartridges.

## Para-Ordnance S12-45 Limited

**SPECIFICATION**

- **MANUFACTURER** Para-Ordnance
- **CALIBRE** .45 ACP
- **MAGAZINE CAPACITY** 10 or 12
- **ACTION** Recoil/single
- **TOTAL LENGTH** 180mm/7.1in
- **BARREL LENGTH** 89mm/3.5in
- **WEIGHT UNLOADED** 963g/34oz

Built for the accuracy of competition, this pistol developed in 2004 was designed to incorporate a high level of durability. It has a competition trigger that prevents backlash when shooting and ambidextrous safety features that allows the pistol to be well supported in use by both hands. It also includes an adjustable rear sight, which can be altered for windage and elevation. It is equipped with a 12-round magazine, and a 10-round magazine is also available.

## Para-Ordnance S14-45 Limited

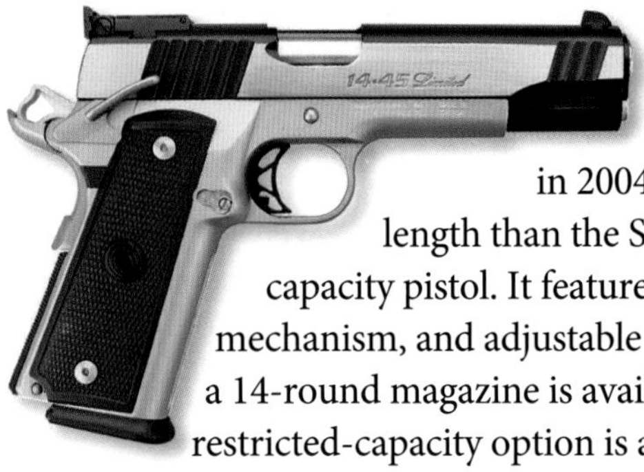

This single-action pistol, introduced in 2004, has a longer barrel length than the S12-45. This is a high-capacity pistol. It features the power extraction mechanism, and adjustable rear sight. While a 14-round magazine is available, a 10-round restricted-capacity option is also available.

**Chamber-loaded**
The Para-Ordnance range has a "chamber-loaded" indicator on top of the barrel that is visible through the ejection port.

| SPECIFICATION | |
|---|---|
| MANUFACTURER | Para-Ordnance |
| CALIBRE | .45 ACP |
| MAGAZINE CAPACITY | 10 or 14 |
| ACTION | Recoil/single |
| TOTAL LENGTH | 216mm/8.5in |
| BARREL LENGTH | 127mm/5in |
| WEIGHT UNLOADED | 1,134g/40oz |

## Para-Ordnance OPS (Operations)

This single-action pistol was introduced in 2004. It was designed for operations personnel in a support role who did not need to carry a full-size pistol. It features the power extraction mechanism for extracting and feeding the cartridge. Other standard features include a competition hammer, a match trigger and sophisticated sights. The grasping grooves on the front strap help to control recoil when firing.

| SPECIFICATION | |
|---|---|
| MANUFACTURER | Para-Ordnance |
| CALIBRE | .45 ACP |
| MAGAZINE CAPACITY | 7 |
| ACTION | Recoil/single |
| TOTAL LENGTH | 180mm/7.1in |
| BARREL LENGTH | 89mm/3.5in |
| WEIGHT UNLOADED | 907g/32oz |

## Para-Ordnance 1911 LTC (Lieutenant Colonel)

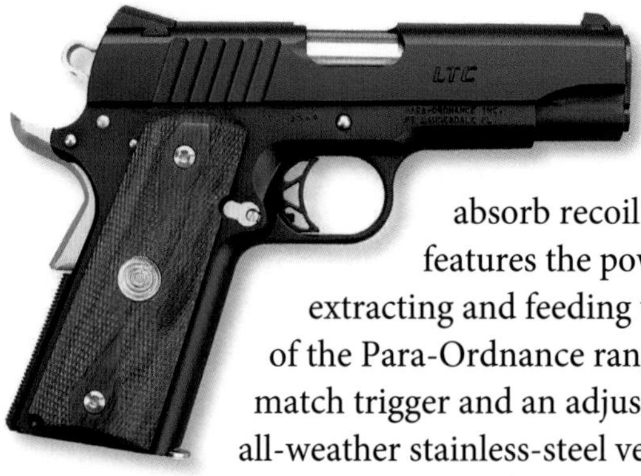


This pistol, introduced in 2004, is a full-size, single-action pistol. It has a steel frame which helps absorb recoil from firing the shot. The LTC features the power extraction mechanism for extracting and feeding the cartridge, which is a standard of the Para-Ordnance range. It has a competition hammer, match trigger and an adjustable rear sight. There is also an all-weather stainless-steel version of the same pistol.

| SPECIFICATION | |
|---|---|
| MANUFACTURER | Para-Ordnance |
| CALIBRE | .45 ACP |
| MAGAZINE CAPACITY | 7 |
| ACTION | Recoil/single |
| TOTAL LENGTH | 197mm/7.75in |
| BARREL LENGTH | 108mm/4.25in |
| WEIGHT UNLOADED | 992g/35oz |

## Para-Ordnance TAC-S

The TAC-S was introduced in 2004, based on an earlier model called the TAC-Four. Constructed from solid steel which helps absorb recoil from firing, it has the standard features of the Para range – an advanced DAO trigger system to aid accuracy, a power extraction mechanism for extracting and feeding the cartridge and sophisticated sights. Designed for marksmanship and competitive shooting, its durable green finish gives the TAC-S a military-style appearance and its comfortable size makes it a good choice for enthusiasts who wish to do a lot of shooting.

| SPECIFICATION | |
|---|---|
| MANUFACTURER | Para-Ordnance |
| CALIBRE | .45 ACP |
| MAGAZINE CAPACITY | 7 |
| ACTION | Recoil/LDA |
| TOTAL LENGTH | 184mm/7.25in |
| BARREL LENGTH | 108mm/4.25in |
| WEIGHT UNLOADED | 992g/35oz |

## Para-Ordnance Colonel

| SPECIFICATION | |
|---|---|
| MANUFACTURER | Para-Ordnance |
| CALIBRE | .45 ACP |
| MAGAZINE CAPACITY | 14 |
| ACTION | Recoil/LDA |
| TOTAL LENGTH | 197mm/7.75in |
| BARREL LENGTH | 108mm/4.25in |
| WEIGHT UNLOADED | 1,048g/37oz |

This high-capacity DAO pistol was introduced in 2004. It has a shortened slide and barrel and a lighter weight than other high-capacity models but still supplies 14 rounds of .45 ACP firepower. The pistol includes the standard power extraction mechanism for extracting and feeding the cartridge. The Colonel has sophisticated sights which can be adjusted for windage. The rear sight is rounded in order to prevent snagging when the pistol is drawn. The finish is black except for the non-reflective military-style olive surface for the frame and slide.

## Para-Ordnance Hi-Cap (High-Capacity)

| SPECIFICATION | |
|---|---|
| MANUFACTURER | Para-Ordnance |
| CALIBRE | .45 ACP |
| MAGAZINE CAPACITY | 14 |
| ACTION | Recoil/LDA |
| TOTAL LENGTH | 216mm/8.5in |
| BARREL LENGTH | 127mm/5in |
| WEIGHT UNLOADED | 1,134g/40oz |

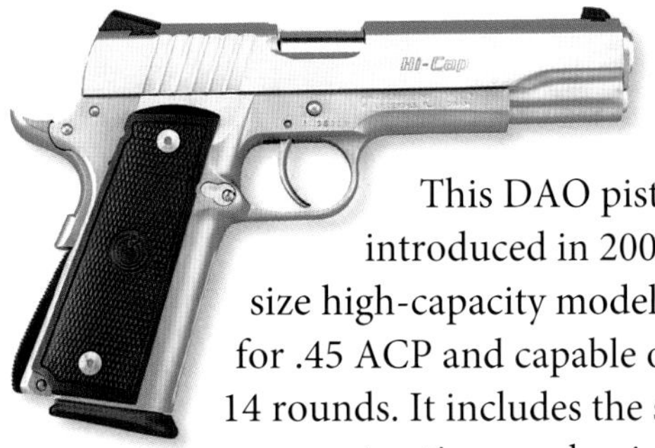

This DAO pistol was introduced in 2004 – a full-size high-capacity model chambered for .45 ACP and capable of delivering 14 rounds. It includes the standard power extraction mechanism for extracting and feeding the cartridge.

**Safety features**
The Para-Ordnance range has three vital safety features to accompany the trigger action: a thumb safety disengages the trigger, a grip safety locks the hammer assembly and an internal firing-pin block guards against the possibility of accidental discharge.

## Para-Ordnance Covert Black Hi-Cap 9

| SPECIFICATION | |
|---|---|
| MANUFACTURER | Para-Ordnance |
| CALIBRE | 9mm Parabellum |
| MAGAZINE CAPACITY | 18 |
| ACTION | Recoil/LDA |
| TOTAL LENGTH | 216mm/8.5in |
| BARREL LENGTH | 127mm/5in |
| WEIGHT UNLOADED | 1,134g/40oz |

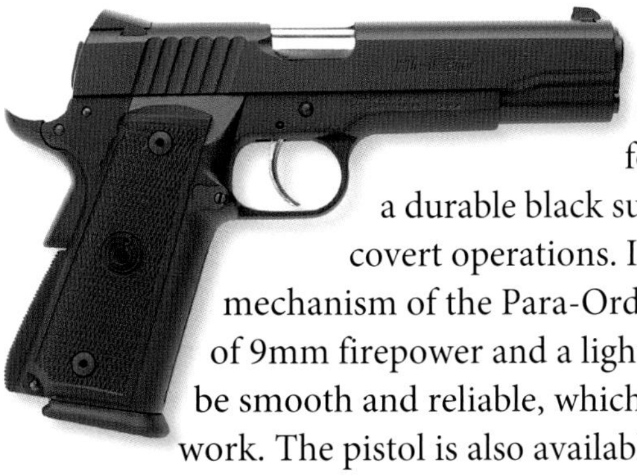

Para-Ordnance feature several high-capacity pistols that are chambered for the 9mm cartridge. Finished with a durable black surface, this DAO pistol is useful for covert operations. It has the standard power extraction mechanism of the Para-Ordnance range and includes 18 rounds of 9mm firepower and a light DAO trigger system. It is designed to be smooth and reliable, which is important when doing undercover work. The pistol is also available in a brushed stainless steel.

## Para-Ordnance Black Watch Companion

| SPECIFICATION | |
|---|---|
| MANUFACTURER | Para-Ordnance |
| CALIBRE | .45 ACP |
| MAGAZINE CAPACITY | 7 |
| ACTION | Recoil/LDA |
| TOTAL LENGTH | 180mm/7.1in |
| BARREL LENGTH | 89mm/3.5in |
| WEIGHT UNLOADED | 907g/32oz |

The Black Watch Companion is a slimline pistol that is also suitable for defence when undertaking covert operations. It incorporates the standard power extraction and light double-action trigger mechanism of the Para-Ordnance rang. It is designed to be smooth and reliable – essential when doing undercover work.

## Para-Ordnance Nite-Tac 9

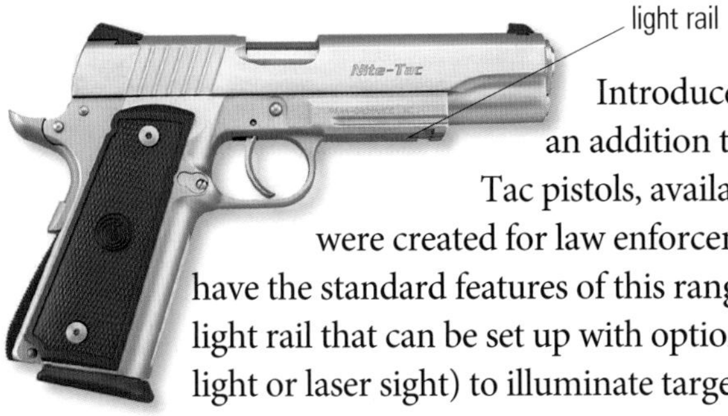


Introduced in 2005, the Nite-Tac 9 is an addition to the Para-Ordnance range of Nite-Tac pistols, available in .40 and .45 ACP calibre. They were created for law enforcement duty and defence. Nite-Tacs have the standard features of this range of pistols with the addition of a light rail that can be set up with optional light accessories (such as a mini light or laser sight) to illuminate targets when shooting.

**SPECIFICATION**

| | |
|---|---|
| **MANUFACTURER** | Para-Ordnance |
| **CALIBRE** | 9mm Parabellum |
| **MAGAZINE CAPACITY** | 18 |
| **ACTION** | Recoil/LDA |
| **TOTAL LENGTH** | 216mm/8.5in |
| **BARREL LENGTH** | 127mm/5in |
| **WEIGHT UNLOADED** | 1,134g/40oz |

## Para-Ordnance Warthog

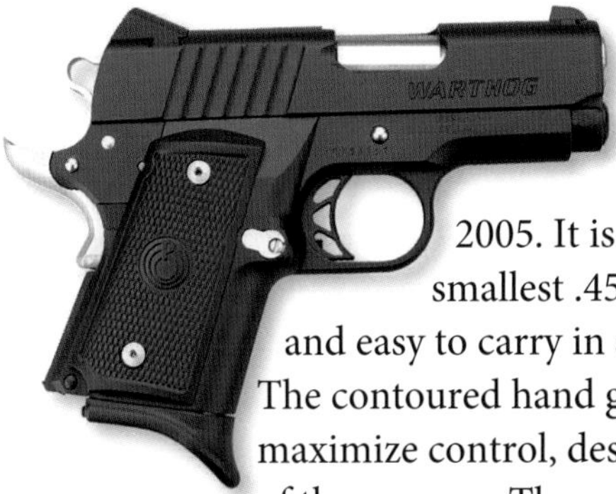

The single-action Warthog pistol was introduced in 2005. It is one of the world's smallest .45 ACP pistols, and easy to carry in any situation. The contoured hand grip is designed to maximize control, despite the small size of the weapon. The match-grade trigger is designed to prevent backlash. The receiver of the standard Warthog is made from alloy. This range of pistols incorporates the standard power extraction mechanism and safety mechanisms of the Para-Ordnance range.

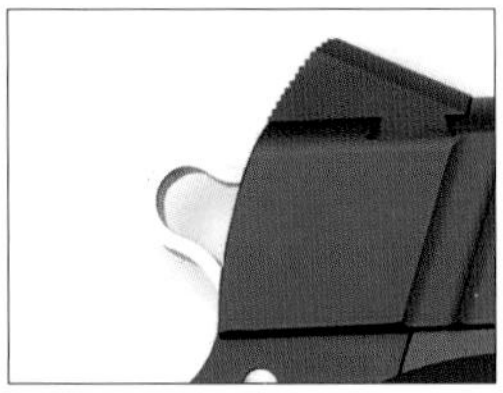

**ABOVE** There is a clean, crisp release of the skeletonized spur hammer on pressing the trigger. This allows for a precise shot when the shooter comes on target.

**SPECIFICATION**

| | |
|---|---|
| **MANUFACTURER** | Para-Ordnance |
| **CALIBRE** | .45 ACP |
| **MAGAZINE CAPACITY** | 10 |
| **ACTION** | Recoil/single |
| **TOTAL LENGTH** | 165mm/6.5in |
| **BARREL LENGTH** | 76mm/3in |
| **WEIGHT UNLOADED** | 680g/24oz |

**Stainless steel**

An all-weather stainless-steel version of this pistol is also available. The added weight reduces the level of recoil.

## Para-Ordnance Nite Hawg

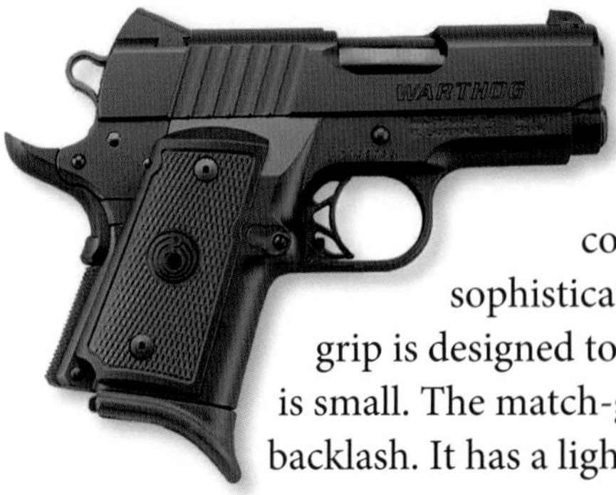

This single-action pistol, introduced in 2005, has similar features to the standard Warthog except that it has a non-reflective all-black finish for covert concealment. It is also fitted with sophisticated night sights. The contoured hand grip is designed to maximize control, although the weapon is small. The match-grade trigger is designed to eliminate backlash. It has a lightweight alloy frame.

**SPECIFICATION**

| | |
|---|---|
| **MANUFACTURER** | Para-Ordnance |
| **CALIBRE** | .45 ACP |
| **MAGAZINE CAPACITY** | 10 |
| **ACTION** | Recoil/single |
| **TOTAL LENGTH** | 165mm/6.5in |
| **BARREL LENGTH** | 76mm/3in |
| **WEIGHT UNLOADED** | 680g/24oz |

## Para-Ordnance Hawg 9

This high-capacity pistol is capable of carrying 12 rounds in a micro-compact frame. It is chambered for the popular 9mm Parabellum cartridge and was developed for those who do not need the stronger firepower of the .40 or .45 cartridges. The contoured hand grip is designed to maximize control, and the match-grade trigger reduces backlash. It has a lightweight alloy frame.

**SPECIFICATION**

| | |
|---|---|
| **MANUFACTURER** | Para-Ordnance |
| **CALIBRE** | 9mm Parabellum |
| **MAGAZINE CAPACITY** | 12 |
| **ACTION** | Recoil/single |
| **TOTAL LENGTH** | 165mm/6.5in |
| **BARREL LENGTH** | 76mm/3in |
| **WEIGHT UNLOADED** | 680g/24oz |

## Para-Ordnance Lite Hawg

| SPECIFICATION | |
|---|---|
| **MANUFACTURER** | Para-Ordnance |
| **CALIBRE** | .45 ACP |
| **MAGAZINE CAPACITY** | 10 or 12 |
| **ACTION** | Recoil/single |
| **TOTAL LENGTH** | 165mm/6.5in |
| **BARREL LENGTH** | 76mm/3in |
| **WEIGHT UNLOADED** | 893g/31.5oz |

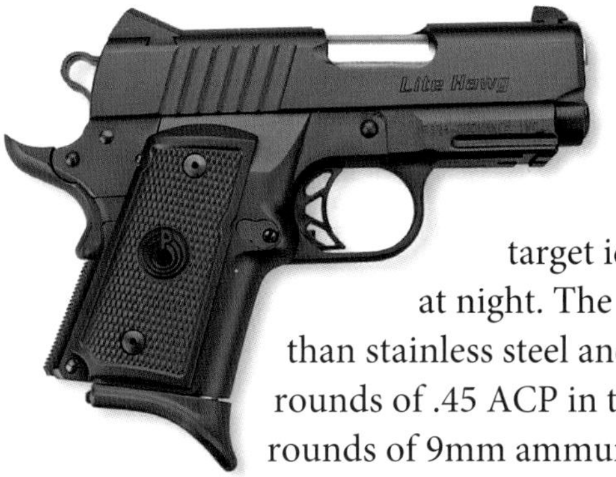


The Lite Hawg, introduced in 2006, is a single-action pistol. It has a light rail to attach accessories such as a mini light or laser sight in order to provide target identification in low light conditions or at night. The Lite Hawg is made of carbon steel rather than stainless steel and has a compact frame. It carries ten rounds of .45 ACP in the magazine but can also be used with 12 rounds of 9mm ammunition.

## Para-Ordnance Slim Hawg

| SPECIFICATION | |
|---|---|
| **MANUFACTURER** | Para-Ordnance |
| **CALIBRE** | .45 ACP |
| **MAGAZINE CAPACITY** | 6 |
| **ACTION** | Recoil/single |
| **TOTAL LENGTH** | 165mm/6.5in |
| **BARREL LENGTH** | 76mm/3in |
| **WEIGHT UNLOADED** | 850g/30oz |

The Slim Hawg, introduced in 2006, is a single-action pistol that is both light and slim, combined with the very small frame of the Warthog. It is made of stainless steel. It has grasping grooves to help control recoil and make every shot as accurate as possible (although this may not have featured on all shipped Slim Hawgs). The match-grade trigger is designed to eliminate backlash. The pistol is small enough to be easily concealed, light enough to carry for extended periods, very accurate for its small size and very reliable.

## Para-Ordnance Nite-Tac

| SPECIFICATION | |
|---|---|
| **MANUFACTURER** | Para-Ordnance |
| **CALIBRE** | .40 S&W |
| **MAGAZINE CAPACITY** | 16 |
| **ACTION** | Recoil/double |
| **TOTAL LENGTH** | 216mm/8.5in |
| **BARREL LENGTH** | 127mm/5in |
| **WEIGHT UNLOADED** | 1,134g/40oz |

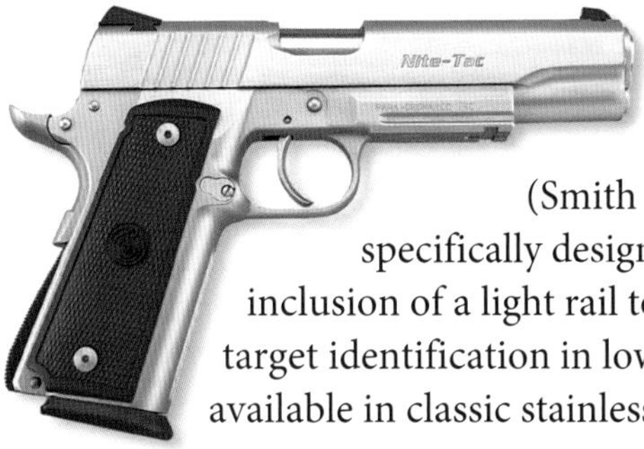


This pistol, introduced in 2006 is a modernized version of the P14-45, chambered for the popular .40 S&W (Smith & Wesson) cartridge. This pistol is specifically designed for night-time operations by the inclusion of a light rail to attach accessories in order to provide target identification in low light conditions and at night. It is available in classic stainless steel or black.

## Para-Ordnance Tac-Five

| SPECIFICATION | |
|---|---|
| **MANUFACTURER** | Para-Ordnance |
| **CALIBRE** | 9mm Parabellum |
| **MAGAZINE CAPACITY** | 18 |
| **ACTION** | Recoil/LDA |
| **TOTAL LENGTH** | 216mm/8.5in |
| **BARREL LENGTH** | 127mm/5in |
| **WEIGHT UNLOADED** | 1,063g/37.5oz |

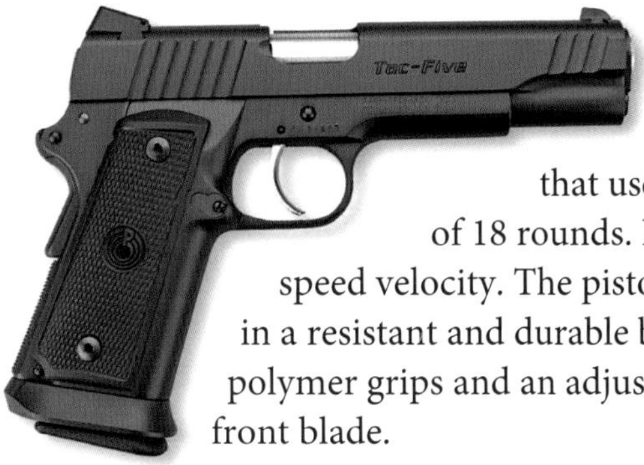


The Tac-Five, introduced in 2006, was designed to meet the needs of those "special operations" teams that used the 9mm cartridge, with a capacity of 18 rounds. Its barrel is designed to achieve high-speed velocity. The pistol is made of stainless steel covered in a resistant and durable black coating. Other features include polymer grips and an adjustable rear sight with a dovetailed front blade.

## Para-Ordnance SSP-SE (Special Edition) 1

This pistol, introduced in 2006, is a special-edition high-performance single-action pistol, chambered for the powerful .45 ACP cartridge. A full-size pistol, it includes features such as an ambidextrous safety, sophisticated sights with an adjustable rear sight. The special-edition pistols were limited production because the stocks were made of high-quality cocobolo wood. This is expensive and difficult to find – and is twice the density of walnut. Some Para-Ordnance models feature this stock with a double-diamond pattern for grip.

| SPECIFICATION | |
|---|---|
| MANUFACTURER | Para-Ordnance |
| CALIBRE | .45 ACP |
| MAGAZINE CAPACITY | 7 |
| ACTION | Recoil/single |
| TOTAL LENGTH | 216mm/8.5in |
| BARREL LENGTH | 127mm/5in |
| WEIGHT UNLOADED | 1,105g/39oz |

## Para-Ordnance Tac-Forty

Introduced in 2007, the new Para Tac-Forty is designed to meet the needs of those in law enforcement who use the .40 S&W cartridge. The barrel is a popular length for duty pistols and the light, double-action trigger system provides instant first-shot capability when security forces are on active duty in difficult circumstances or in poor weather conditions. This gives consistency to the shot. Made of rust-resistant stainless steel, the Tac-Forty has the standard feature of the Carry Option range, including an adjustable rear sight.

| SPECIFICATION | |
|---|---|
| MANUFACTURER | Para-Ordnance |
| CALIBRE | .40 S&W |
| MAGAZINE CAPACITY | 15 |
| ACTION | Recoil/single |
| TOTAL LENGTH | 196mm/7.7in |
| BARREL LENGTH | 108mm/4.25in |
| WEIGHT UNLOADED | 1,020g/36oz |

## Para-Ordnance Carry (GAP)

The Carry and the Companion Carry Option (CCO) were chambered for the .45 GAP (Glock Automatic Pistol) cartridge introduced in 2007. Modern technology has made it possible to achieve the ballistics of the .45 ACP in a cartridge that has the shorter overall length of a round of 9mm ammunition. Using the shorter cartridge means that the grip of the pistol does not need to be increased in size to accommodate it. The shooter can keep grip on a smaller pistol without having to give up any of the power of the .45 ACP cartridge. A better grip translates into greater accuracy and control for the shooter.

| SPECIFICATION | |
|---|---|
| MANUFACTURER | Para-Ordnance |
| CALIBRE | .45 GAP |
| MAGAZINE CAPACITY | 6 |
| ACTION | Recoil/LDA |
| TOTAL LENGTH | 163mm/6.4in |
| BARREL LENGTH | 76mm/3in |
| WEIGHT UNLOADED | 822g/29oz |

## Sig C22

The Sig C22 is the designation given to Canada's newest military pistol. Based on the company's P320 design, it is a full-size modular pistol with ambidextrous controls that has interchangeable grip frames to fit soldiers of different sizes and builds. A minimum of 7,000 units are being purchased for the Canadian Army, with the potential for 9,500 more for the Royal Canadian Air Force, Royal Canadian Navy, and the Military Police.

| SPECIFICATION | |
|---|---|
| MANUFACTURER | SIG SAUER |
| CALIBRE | .9mm Parabellum |
| MAGAZINE CAPACITY | 17 |
| ACTION | Short recoil/single |
| TOTAL LENGTH | 203mm/8in |
| BARREL LENGTH | 119mm/4.7in |
| WEIGHT UNLOADED | 836g/2.5oz |

# United States

**Perhaps like no other country in the world, small-arms manufacture in the United States is bound up with its history and identity. The invention of the revolver by Samuel Colt, and the succession of designs by Colt, Smith & Wesson, Remington and other manufacturers, played a key part in the establishment of European settlers in the Native American territories, the independence of Texas in 1836, the Mexican War (1846–48) and the American Civil War (1861–65). Another American, John Moses Browning, was to design the definitive pistol of modern times, the M1911. The right to carry a firearm as an aspect of personal freedom has remained deeply ingrained in the American psyche.**

## Colt Paterson

**SPECIFICATION**

- **MANUFACTURER** Colt Patent Arms Manufacturing Co.
- **CALIBRE** .36
- **CYLINDER** 5
- **ACTION** Percussion/single
- **TOTAL LENGTH** 292mm/11.5in
- **BARREL LENGTH** 190mm/7.5in
- **WEIGHT UNLOADED** 1,134g/40oz

The Colt Paterson was an iconic revolver, not only in the history of the percussion revolver and the Colt firearms manufacturing company but also in the history of Texas and the Wild West. This handgun with a revolving cylinder and .36 calibre lead ball was invented by Samuel Colt in 1831. It was patented in 1836 and manufactured until 1842. As manufacturing took place at Paterson in New Jersey, this was the name given to one of these early types. The .36 Paterson was used not only by the Texas Navy but also by mounted Texas Rangers. In both scenarios, it proved to be remarkably successful.

## Colt Walker

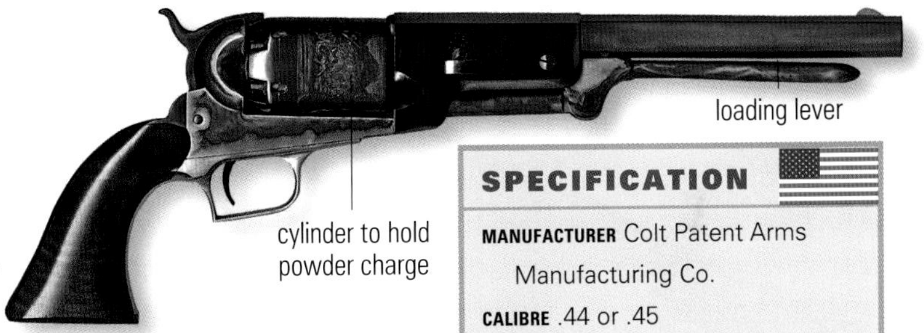


This revolver, produced in 1847, was officially designated a pistol because the Army Ordnance Department had never come across a revolver before. The Colt Walker revolver was named after a hero of the Mexican War, Captain Samuel Hamilton Walker, who was instrumental in ensuring that Colt secured an official US Government contract, so avoiding the company's bankruptcy. The Walker was a development of the existing Paterson design that had already seen success on the US western frontier. It was reputed to have firepower similar to that of a rifle and that made US cavalrymen formidable opponents. It could take up to 50 grains of powder and a .44 or .45 calibre lead ball.

**SPECIFICATION**

- **MANUFACTURER** Colt Patent Arms Manufacturing Co.
- **CALIBRE** .44 or .45
- **CYLINDER** 6
- **ACTION** Percussion/single
- **TOTAL LENGTH** 400mm/15.75in
- **BARREL LENGTH** 229mm/9in
- **WEIGHT UNLOADED** 2,040g/72oz

## Colt Dragoon M1848

**SPECIFICATION**

- **MANUFACTURER** Colt Firearms Co.
- **CALIBRE** .44
- **CYLINDER** 6
- **ACTION** Percussion/single
- **TOTAL LENGTH** 355mm/14in
- **BARREL LENGTH** 190mm/7.5in
- **WEIGHT UNLOADED** 1,871g/66oz

The Colt Dragoon was slightly smaller than the Colt Walker. Designed for use in the Mexican War, the Walker had proved effective but also heavy and sometimes prone to accidental explosion. The Dragoon had a shorter cylinder, shorter barrel and an improved loading lever. Changes were made to the metal used in manufacture. It was produced from 1848 to 1863. The Dragoon became a popular weapon in the 1850s and continued the upward spiral in Colt's fortunes. It was produced in three models and the US Government ordered over 8,000 of them.

## Colt Single Action Navy 1851

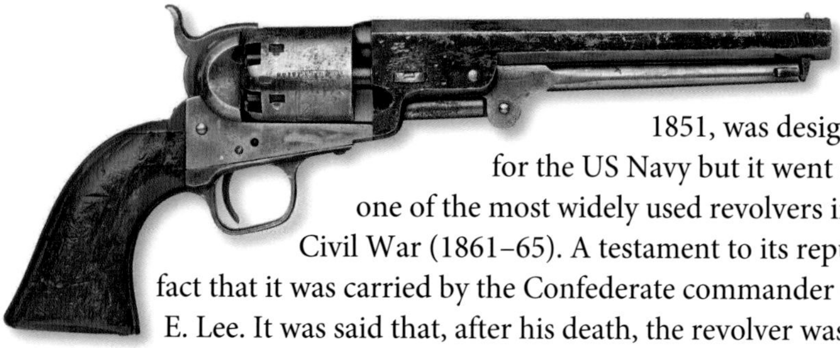

This revolver, produced in 1851, was designed specifically for the US Navy but it went on to become one of the most widely used revolvers in the American Civil War (1861–65). A testament to its reputation was the fact that it was carried by the Confederate commander General Robert E. Lee. It was said that, after his death, the revolver was successfully fired, despite having been loaded seven years earlier. The 1851 Colt Navy revolver was in use for many years after the Civil War in the hands of such men as "Wild Bill" Hickock and "Buffalo Bill" Cody. With over a quarter of a million manufactured between 1851 and 1873, it was one of the most popular and long-lived revolvers in the Wild West.

**SPECIFICATION**

**MANUFACTURER** Colt Firearms Co.
**CALIBRE** .36
**CYLINDER** 6
**ACTION** Percussion/single
**TOTAL LENGTH** 305mm/12in
**BARREL LENGTH** 190mm/7.5in
**WEIGHT UNLOADED** 907g/32oz

**British forces copies**
Thousands of the Colt Navy Model were produced for the British forces in the Crimea War.

## Colt New Army Model 1860

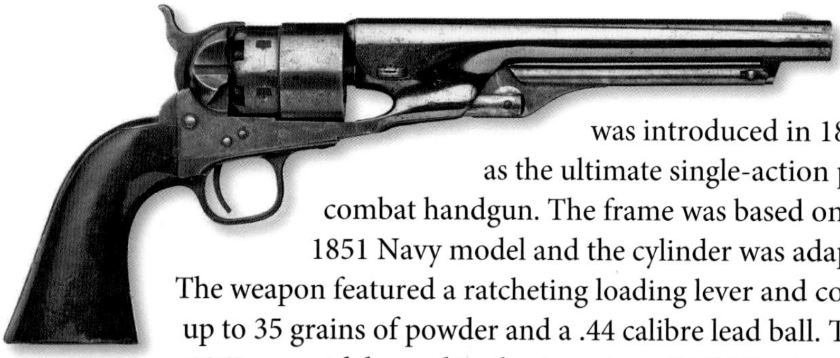

This revolver was introduced in 1860 by Colt as the ultimate single-action percussion combat handgun. The frame was based on the Colt 1851 Navy model and the cylinder was adapted to fit. The weapon featured a ratcheting loading lever and could take up to 35 grains of powder and a .44 calibre lead ball. The Colt 1860 was widely used in the American Civil War by officers, cavalrymen and artillerymen. It had a fine, streamlined profile and quickly won favour with the military. Some variants were supplied with a detachable rifle stock which was said to improve accuracy. Over 200,000 1860 Army revolvers were produced between 1860 and 1873. The first 1,000 Army revolvers were equipped with seven-inch barrels, but they quickly gave way to the eight-inch barrel the Army preferred, and the style of the cylinder was also updated.

**SPECIFICATION**

**MANUFACTURER** Colt Firearms Co.
**CALIBRE** .44
**CYLINDER** 6
**ACTION** Percussion/single
**TOTAL LENGTH** 356mm/12.5in
**BARREL LENGTH** 203mm/8in
**WEIGHT UNLOADED** 1,077g/38oz

**Colt copies**
This revolver was so popular with Confederate armies that they went on to produce southern-made copies of the weapon.

## Colt Richards-Mason 1860 cartridge conversion

This revolver was a conversion carried out first by an employee of Colt, Charles Richards, in 1871. He was awarded a patent for converting Colt percussion models to breech-loading cartridge revolvers. Another colleague, William Mason, was awarded a patent for an improvement to the original Richards patent in 1872. The 1860 revolver was converted, along with the 1851 Navy model. The conversion entailed cutting off the cap-and-ball cylinders at the back and installing a conversion ring that would accept cartridges. The Richards-Mason conversions gave a new lease of life to some of the classic Colt revolvers and had the effect of improving their efficiency and safety, obviating the dangers of the old ball-and-powder system which could sometimes result in the simultaneous explosion of all six cylinders.

**SPECIFICATION**

**MANUFACTURER** Colt Firearms Co.
**CALIBRE** .44
**CYLINDER** 6
**ACTION** Percussion/single
**TOTAL LENGTH** 356mm/14in
**BARREL LENGTH** 203mm/8in
**WEIGHT UNLOADED** 1,134g/40oz

## Colt Single Action Army

This was one of the most famous revolvers of the American Wild West. Designed for the US Cavalry, it was first produced in 1873 and was often known as the "Colt 45". The Single Action Army (SAA) used .45 Long Colt cartridges (which were not the same as the .45 ACP cartridge commonly used in semi-automatic pistols). This revolver had no conventional safety so in theory a round could be discharged if the hammer was to receive a hard blow. As a precaution, one chamber was often left empty while the revolver was being carried in order to avoid accidental discharge. The revolver was loaded by opening a gate on the right behind the cylinder. This had disadvantages in terms of speed and ease of loading but it meant that the frame was rigid and strong, with no break points to reveal the full cylinder, as on other weapons. Various Colt SAA models were built from 1873 to 1940, and again from 1976 in a variety of calibres and barrel lengths. Famous names given to variants of the SAA include the Peacemaker. The Single Action Army has been copied by numerous makers both in America and in Europe including Aldo Uberti in Italy, and United States Firearms Mfg. Co. in Hartford, Connecticut.

**SPECIFICATION**

**MANUFACTURER** Colt Firearms Co.
**CALIBRE** .45 Long Colt
**CYLINDER** 6
**ACTION** Single
**TOTAL LENGTH** 260mm/10.25in
**BARREL LENGTH** 121mm/4.75in
**WEIGHT UNLOADED** 1,077g/38oz

**Original value**
Among the most valuable to the collector are original, good condition, first generation Single Action Army revolvers (produced before 1940).

## Colt M1877 Lightning

**SPECIFICATION**

**MANUFACTURER** Colt Firearms Co.
**CALIBRE** .38 Colt. .41 Colt
**CYLINDER** 6
**ACTION** Double
**TOTAL LENGTH** 228mm/9in
**BARREL LENGTH** 114.3mm/4.5in
**WEIGHT UNLOADED** 652g/23oz

This was Colt's first production double-action revolver, with the mechanism designed by inventor William Mason. It was produced from 1877 to 1909. The Lightning is known to have been used in some famous gunfights in the Wild West. It was still early days for the double-action system and the M1877 Lightning had some problems in this respect with fragile mechanisms and complicated actions, so was not reliable. One explanation may be that users, familiar with single-action pistols, attempted to cock and fire the pistol in the old way, which may have damaged the mechanism. Few surviving examples of the revolver are said to work smoothly. Remaining revolvers that saw action are often in poor condition because the original finish was thin and has worn away.

## Colt M1878 Double Action Army

**SPECIFICATION**

**MANUFACTURER** Colt Firearms Co.
**CALIBRE** .45 Colt
**CYLINDER** 6
**ACTION** Double
**TOTAL LENGTH** 250mm/9.85in
**BARREL LENGTH** 121mm/4.75in
**WEIGHT UNLOADED** 1,020g/36oz

The Double Action Army revolver was a development of the New Model Double Action, itself based on the Single Action Army revolver. The Army version was much more robust than the New Model and it found favour with the US Army who purchased 4,500 in 1902. It was available in a variety of barrel lengths. The M1878 was used in action on America's frontier and throughout the world until production ceased in 1905. There proved to be some problems, however, with the mainspring which meant the Army did not repeat their order.

## Colt New Army and Navy Model

The model of 1889 was a significant leap forward by Colt. Before this, all Colt revolvers had fixed cylinders, loaded one chamber at a time. Colt introduced the "swing-out" cylinder. It was an immediate success. The cylinder swung out on a crane which was connected to a pin that entered a recess in the centre of a rotating ratchet at the rear of the cylinder, and was locked back in position with a latch. The Navy Department ordered over 5,000 of these revolvers, followed by the Army three years later, and there were strong civilian sales. Some of the most ornate finishes produced by Colt appeared on the 1889s. The revolver was very solidly built. However, one problem was that the trigger did not always return to its original position after firing, due to a weak spring.

**SPECIFICATION**

**MANUFACTURER** Colt Firearms Co.
**CALIBRE** .38 Colt, .41 Colt
**CYLINDER** 6
**ACTION** Double
**TOTAL LENGTH** 292mm/11.5in
**BARREL LENGTH** 152mm/6in
**WEIGHT UNLOADED** 940g/33.16oz

## Colt New Service

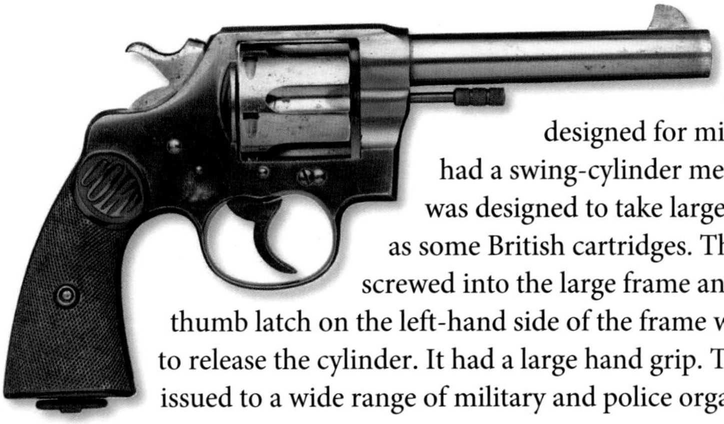

This revolver of 1898 was designed for military use. It had a swing-cylinder mechanism and was designed to take large calibres, as well as some British cartridges. The barrel was screwed into the large frame and there was a thumb latch on the left-hand side of the frame which was used to release the cylinder. It had a large hand grip. This revolver was issued to a wide range of military and police organizations.

**SPECIFICATION**

**MANUFACTURER** Colt Firearms Co.
**CALIBRE** .45 Colt, .44 Special, .38-40
**CYLINDER** 6
**ACTION** Double
**TOTAL LENGTH** 275mm/10.83in
**BARREL LENGTH** 140mm/5.50in
**WEIGHT UNLOADED** 1,162g/41oz

## Colt Model 1900

This was a semi-automatic, self-loading pistol which was developed from designs made by Browning in the 1890s. The Model 1900 was a key development in the history of pistol design as it heralded the introduction of John Browning's invention, a method of returning a weapon to position, loaded and ready to fire on each time the trigger was pulled. This mechanism was to be copied in just about every effective pistol from then on and was certainly key to the continued development and success of Browning's own pistol designs that were to result in the famous M1911.

**SPECIFICATION**

**MANUFACTURER** Colt Firearms Co.
**CALIBRE** .38 ACP
**MAGAZINE CAPACITY** 7
**ACTION** Recoil/single
**TOTAL LENGTH** 228.6mm/9in
**BARREL LENGTH** 152mm/6in
**WEIGHT UNLOADED** 992g/35oz

## Colt Model 1903 Pocket Hammer

This semi-automatic pistol was a derivative of the Colt Model 1900. It was developed from a sporting model introduced in 1902 but had a shorter barrel and slide. The 1903 model did not prove to be very successful and only a few models were produced, partly because it fell between categories as it was neither a pocket nor a full-size model.

**SPECIFICATION**

**MANUFACTURER** Colt/FN, Herstal
**CALIBRE** .38 ACP
**MAGAZINE CAPACITY** 7 or 8
**ACTION** Recoil/single
**TOTAL LENGTH** 205mm/7in
**BARREL LENGTH** 127mm/5in
**WEIGHT UNLOADED** 930g/24oz

**SPECIFICATION**

**MANUFACTURER** Colt Firearms Co.
**CALIBRE** .45 ACP
**MAGAZINE CAPACITY** 7
**ACTION** Recoil/single
**TOTAL LENGTH** 203mm/8in
**BARREL LENGTH** 127mm/5in
**WEIGHT UNLOADED** 921g/32.5oz

## Colt Model 1905

The Model 1905 was a single-action semi-automatic pistol, an adapted version of the earlier autoloading model including Browning's method of returning a weapon to position, loaded and ready to fire each time the trigger was pulled. It also included modifications suggested by the US authorities, making a crucial model in the development process that was to result in the world's longest-serving and most famous pistol, the M1911. Over 6,000 pistols were produced and sold between 1905 and 1911.

**SPECIFICATION**

**MANUFACTURER** Colt Firearms Co.
**CALIBRE** .32 S&W, .38 Colt New Police
**CYLINDER** 6
**ACTION** Double
**TOTAL LENGTH** 216mm/8.5in
**BARREL LENGTH** 102mm/4in
**WEIGHT UNLOADED** 565g/20oz

## Colt Police Positive

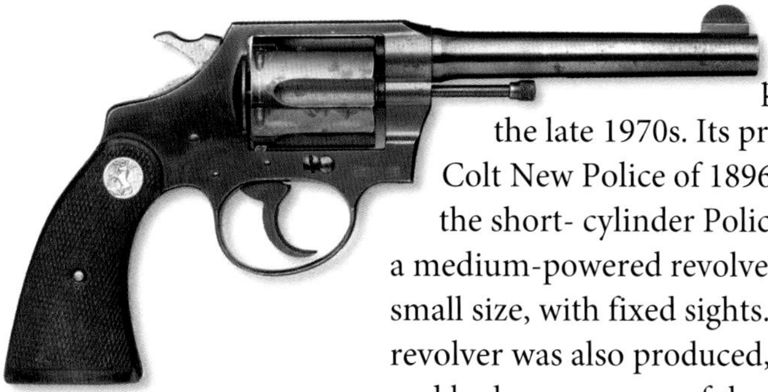

This revolver was produced from 1908 until the late 1970s. Its predecessors included the Colt New Police of 1896, the Pocket Positive and the short- cylinder Police Positive of 1905. It was a medium-powered revolver of light weight and a small size, with fixed sights. A Police Positive Special revolver was also produced, which was slightly heavier and had a more powerful cartridge.

## Colt Model 1911A1 and Government Model

**SPECIFICATION**

**MANUFACTURER** Colt/Various
**CALIBRE** .45 ACP, .38 Super
**MAGAZINE CAPACITY** 7
**ACTION** Recoil/single
**TOTAL LENGTH** 216mm/8.5in
**BARREL LENGTH** 127mm/5in
**WEIGHT UNLOADED** 1,130g/39.86oz

This is simply the most successful semi-automatic pistol of all time. Designed by John Moses Browning and initially produced by Colt, it was adopted by the US Army in March 1911, and was still in service in 1985. At least 2.7 million units were issued by the US Government to various parts of their armed forces during that period. The M1911 was single-action, with short-recoil operation. On recoil, the barrel dipped downwards, disengaging from the inner surface of the slide. Once the breech had re-chambered a round, the rear of the barrel moved back to its normal operating position.

## Beretta M9

Adopted in 1985, the Beretta M9 unseated the Colt 1911 from its unprecedented 75-year run as the US military's official sidearm. The pistol offered multiple improvements over the 1911, including a higher magazine capacity and double or single action operation. Critics of the gun cited its magazine capacity as a detriment because it meant using a smaller calibre – 9mm– over the more traditional .45 ACP.

**SPECIFICATION**

**MANUFACTURER** Beretta Holding
**CALIBRE** 9mm Parabellum
**MAGAZINE CAPACITY** 15
**ACTION** Short recoil/double or single
**TOTAL LENGTH** 216mm/8.5in
**BARREL LENGTH** 125mm/4.9in
**WEIGHT UNLOADED** 944g/33.3oz

## Colt Model 1917

This revolver was a variant of the New Service model that had been introduced in 1898. It was a swing-cylinder design of substantial size. The 1917 model was designed with the US Army in mind, at a time when it was short of pistols. The revolver had a shortened cylinder and used the .45 ACP rimless cartridge which was loaded by means of two half-moon spring clips, holding three cartridges each. The weapon featured a positive hammer lock and a pivoted firing pin. It remained in production until after World War II.

**SPECIFICATION**

**MANUFACTURER** Colt Firearms Co.
**CALIBRE** .45 ACP
**CYLINDER** 6
**ACTION** Double
**TOTAL LENGTH** 275mm/10.83in
**BARREL LENGTH** 140mm/5.5in
**WEIGHT UNLOADED** 1,162g/41oz

## Colt Commando Special

The .38 revolver had been the standard US forces sidearm prior to the introduction of the M1911 semi-automatic pistol. The Colt Commando revolver was a development of the Official Police revolver for the military, which in turn evolved from the Army Special of 1908. The Commando was largely issued to security personnel and factory guards, though some were ordered by the undercover organization, Office of Secret Services (OSS). Only about 1,800 Commandos went to the US Navy, although there had been requests for the revolver, Colt was not always able to keep up with demand. However, about 45,000 Colt Commandos were produced in 1945 alone.

**SPECIFICATION**

**MANUFACTURER** Colt Firearms Co.
**CALIBRE** .38 Special
**CYLINDER** 6
**ACTION** Double
**TOTAL LENGTH** 285mm/11.22in
**BARREL LENGTH** 152mm/6in
**WEIGHT UNLOADED** 1,030g/36.3oz

## Colt Python

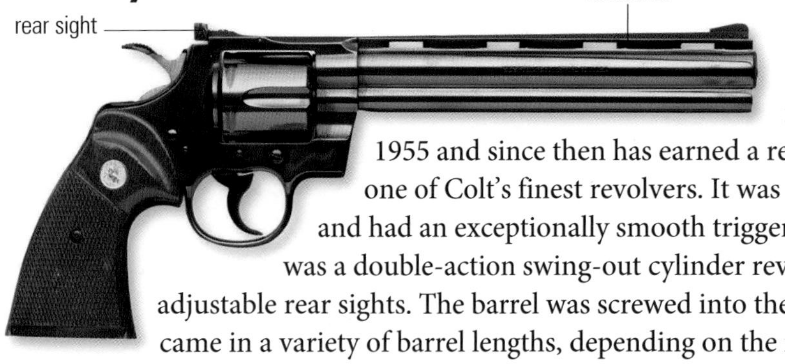


This revolver was first introduced in 1955 and since then has earned a reputation as one of Colt's finest revolvers. It was solidly made and had an exceptionally smooth trigger action. It was a double-action swing-out cylinder revolver with adjustable rear sights. The barrel was screwed into the frame and came in a variety of barrel lengths, depending on the intended use. It was distinguished by a vented upper rib (to expel gases from the cartridge) and it also had a full-length bottom rib with extractor rod.

**SPECIFICATION**

**MANUFACTURER** Colt Firearms Co.
**CALIBRE** .357 Magnum
**CYLINDER** 6
**ACTION** Double
**TOTAL LENGTH** 343mm/13.5in
**BARREL LENGTH** 203mm/8in
**WEIGHT UNLOADED** 1,360g/48oz

## Colt Anaconda

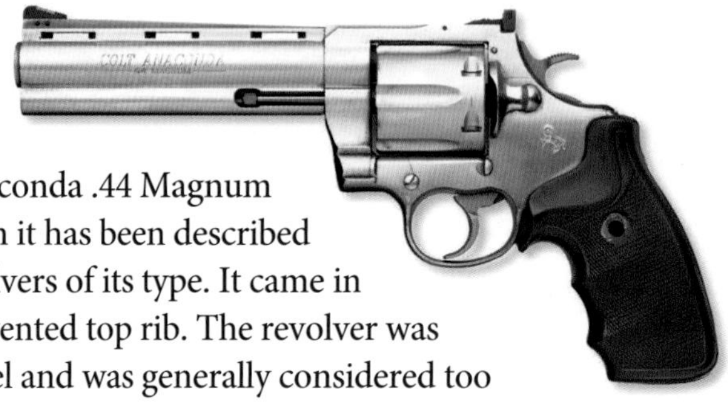

Similar in design to the .357 Colt Python, but chambered for a more powerful round, the Anaconda .44 Magnum first appeared in 1990. Since then it has been described as one of the most accurate revolvers of its type. It came in various lengths of barrel with a vented top rib. The revolver was manufactured from stainless steel and was generally considered too unwieldy for regular police and military use, though it may have been used when extra firepower was required. Otherwise it was used for sport and hunting.

**SPECIFICATION**

**MANUFACTURER** Colt Firearms Co.
**CALIBRE** .44 Magnum
**CYLINDER** 6
**ACTION** Double
**TOTAL LENGTH** 330mm/13in
**BARREL LENGTH** 152mm/6in
**WEIGHT UNLOADED** 1,700g/52oz

## Glock 19M

**SPECIFICATION**

**MANUFACTURER** Glock Inc.
**CALIBRE** 9mm Parabellum
**MAGAZINE CAPACITY** 15
**ACTION** Short recoil/double – Safe Action (SA)
**TOTAL LENGTH** 187mm/7.3in
**BARREL LENGTH** 102mm/4in
**WEIGHT UNLOADED** 623g/22oz

Developed for use by the US FBI in 2016, the 19M is essentially the forerunner to all current Gen5 Glocks, as it is equipped with now-standard features including a straight front grip area, flared magwell, nDLC finish, as well as the Glock Marksman Barrel. Beyond this, Ameriglo Agent night sights, an extended ambidextrous slide stop lever and a unique rounded "FBI" magazine catch were added to meet FBI standards. Functionally, it is the same as all previous Glock 19 pistols.

## Remington Army Model 1858

**SPECIFICATION**

**MANUFACTURER** Remington
**CALIBRE** .44
**CYLINDER** 6
**ACTION** Percussion/single
**TOTAL LENGTH** 342mm/13.5in
**BARREL LENGTH** 203mm/8in
**WEIGHT UNLOADED** 1,106.7g/39oz

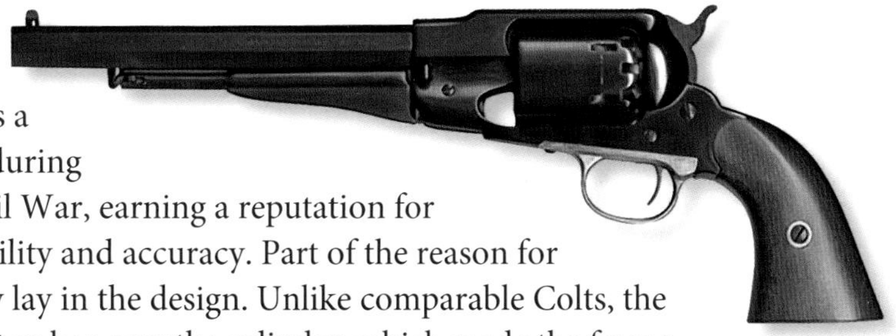

The Remington model of 1858 was a popular revolver during the American Civil War, earning a reputation for ruggedness, reliability and accuracy. Part of the reason for its high popularity lay in the design. Unlike comparable Colts, the Remington had a top bar over the cylinder, which made the frame more rigid and may have had a positive influence on accuracy. A Navy .36 calibre was also available.

## Remington New Model Army 1875

**SPECIFICATION**

**MANUFACTURER** Remington
**CALIBRE** .44 Remington, .45 Colt
**CYLINDER** 6
**ACTION** Percussion/single
**TOTAL LENGTH** 305mm/12in
**BARREL LENGTH** 305mm/7.5in
**WEIGHT UNLOADED** 1,220g/43oz

The Remington 1875 was manufactured for the US Army from 1875 to 1889. It was solidly built, with the Remington trademark top bar that gave added strength to the frame. The revolver had a brass trigger guard and a wooden hand grip. Over 25,000 New Model Army revolvers were produced by Remington. They were high-quality, very strong and accurate revolvers. Although widely appreciated, the Remington 1875 could not compete with the Single Action Army model, and the company was soon bought out.

## Savage 1907

**SPECIFICATION**

**MANUFACTURER** Savage Arms
**CALIBRE** .32 ACP, .380 ACP
**MAGAZINE CAPACITY** 10 or 9
**ACTION** Delayed blowback/single
**TOTAL LENGTH** 168mm/6.62in
**BARREL LENGTH** 90mm/3.5in
**WEIGHT UNLOADED** 652.04g/23oz

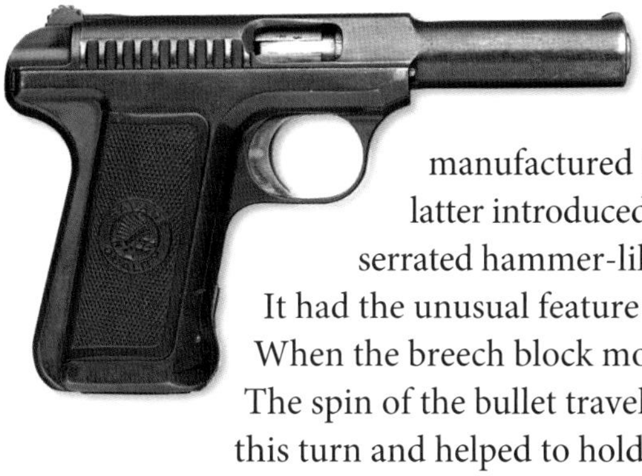

This pistol was invented by Major Searles (formerly of Springfield Armouries) and was manufactured in both .32 and .380 calibre, the latter introduced in 1913. The pistol featured a serrated hammer-like device at the rear of the slide. It had the unusual feature of a locking action for the barrel. When the breech block moved backwards, the barrel turned. The spin of the bullet travelling through the barrel resisted this turn and helped to hold the breech locked. Another selling feature of the pistol was its large magazine capacity: the .32 could hold ten rounds and the .380 nine rounds.

## Sig M17

| SPECIFICATION | |
|---|---|
| MANUFACTURER | SIG SAUER |
| CALIBRE | 9mm Parabellum |
| CYLINDER | 17 or21 |
| ACTION | Short recoil/single |
| TOTAL LENGTH | 203mm/8in |
| BARREL LENGTH | 119mm/4.7in |
| WEIGHT UNLOADED | 833g/29.6oz |

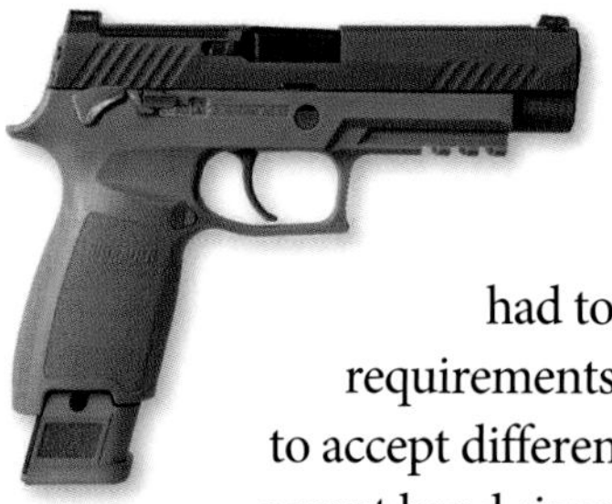

Competing against 11 other companies, the Sig M17 won the contract for the US Army's Modular Handgun System (MHS), replacing the Beretta M9. To be a contender, companies had to submit designs that met the Army's MHS requirements. This included: suppressor compatibility, ability to accept different magazine sizes, modular grips, a grip that would accept hand sizes from the 5th to 95th percentile, ability to mount lasers and lights on a Picatinny rail, and ability to accept different slide/ barrel combinations. The first few thousand guns were delivered with matching coyote tan controls, but they were recalled and replaced by black controls.

## Sig M18

| SPECIFICATION | |
|---|---|
| MANUFACTURER | SIG SAUER |
| CALIBRE | 9mm Parabellum |
| CYLINDER | 17 |
| ACTION | Short recoil/single |
| TOTAL LENGTH | 183mm/7.2in |
| BARREL LENGTH | 99mm/3.9in |
| WEIGHT UNLOADED | 797g/28.1oz |

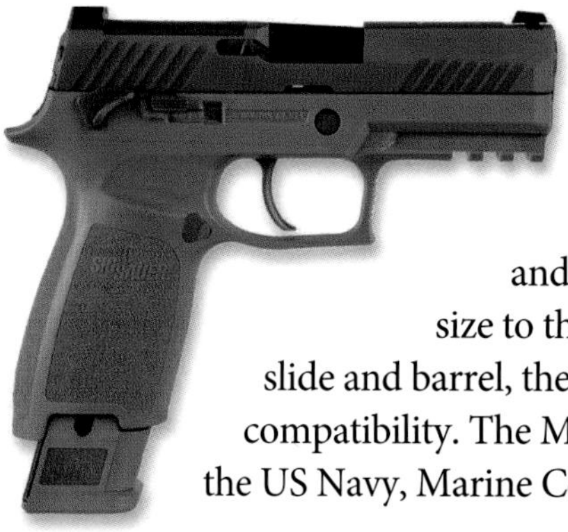

The Sig M18 is the "little brother" to the Sig M17. It uses the same size frame but has a compact size slide and a shorter barrel. This makes it similar in size to the Sig P320 Carry pistol. Other than the slide and barrel, the two guns are the same in terms of MHS compatibility. The M18 was selected as the sidearm of choice for the US Navy, Marine Corps, and Air Force.

## Smith & Wesson Model 1

| SPECIFICATION | |
|---|---|
| MANUFACTURER | Smith & Wesson Inc. |
| CALIBRE | .22 Rimfire |
| CYLINDER | 6 |
| ACTION | Single |
| TOTAL LENGTH | 171mm/6.75in |
| BARREL LENGTH | 81mm/3.18in |
| WEIGHT UNLOADED | 284g/10oz |

Although Colt was making American history with its early revolver designs, Smith & Wesson had a large claim to fame as well. The Model 1 was in many respects a leap into the future. Horace Smith and Daniel B. Wesson, all too aware of the time-consuming nature of the traditional ball and powder designs, devised a revolver that would take a self-contained metallic cartridge. Their first design was patented as the Model 1, First Issue Revolver in 1857. It was the first revolver to combine using a .22 Rimfire cartridge and a bored-through cylinder. The revolver was in high demand because of its easily-loaded rimfire cartridge and was highly significant in the history of firearms.

## Smith & Wesson Model 2

| SPECIFICATION | |
|---|---|
| MANUFACTURER | Smith & Wesson Inc. |
| CALIBRE | .32 Rimfire |
| CYLINDER | 6 |
| ACTION | Single |
| TOTAL LENGTH | 254mm/10in |
| BARREL LENGTH | 127mm/5in |
| WEIGHT UNLOADED | 595g/21oz |

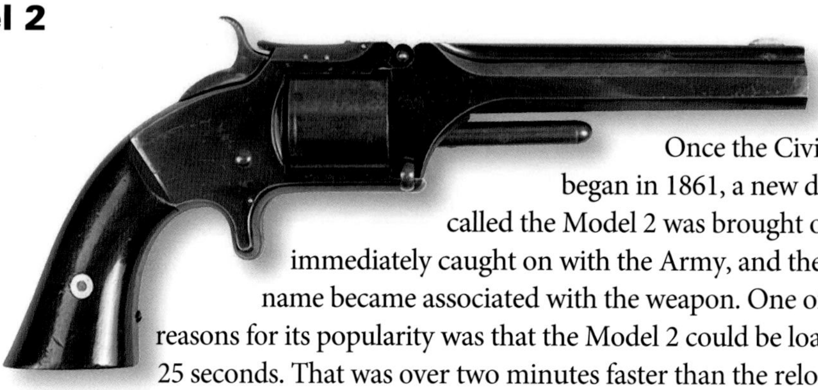

Once the Civil War began in 1861, a new design called the Model 2 was brought out. This immediately caught on with the Army, and the Army name became associated with the weapon. One of the reasons for its popularity was that the Model 2 could be loaded in just 25 seconds. That was over two minutes faster than the reload time for comparable weapons available at the time, and in battle could have meant the difference between life and death.

## Smith & Wesson Model 3

This revolver was first produced in the 1870s and was an immediate success. Smith & Wesson had devised a top-break design, whereby when the revolver was broken open the barrel tipped downwards. At the same time, an ejector system ejected spent cases from all six cylinders simultaneously. This made reloading much quicker. About 2,000 Smith & Wesson Model 3s were issued to the Army and many more were bought by individuals. The weapon was also used in engagements with Native Americans. A variant of the Model 3 was adopted by the Russian military and made in large quantities.

**SPECIFICATION**

**MANUFACTURER** Smith & Wesson Inc.
**CALIBRE** .44 S&W American, .44 S&W
**CYLINDER** 6
**ACTION** Single
**TOTAL LENGTH** 305mm/12in
**BARREL LENGTH** 165mm/6.5in
**WEIGHT UNLOADED** 1,134g/40oz

## Smith & Wesson New Century

**SPECIFICATION**

**MANUFACTURER** Smith & Wesson Inc.
**CALIBRE** .44 Special, .455 Eley
**CYLINDER** 6
**ACTION** Double
**TOTAL LENGTH** 300mm/11.75in
**BARREL LENGTH** 165mm/6.5in
**WEIGHT UNLOADED** 1,079g/37.9oz

This revolver is often regarded as a high point in revolver design. It had a triple-lock system: a side-swing cylinder which was anchored by an additional latch in the front of the frame to make for positive alignment. For the first time the ejector rod was enclosed in a shroud under the barrel. The revolver was precisely engineered and manufactured throughout, which made it a reliable weapon to use in the heat of battle. The .455 Eley model was made for the British Army and over 5,000 were delivered.

## Smith & Wesson Hand Ejector 2nd Model

**SPECIFICATION**

**MANUFACTURER** Smith & Wesson Inc.
**CALIBRE** .44 Special, .45 ACP, .455 Eley
**CYLINDER** 5
**ACTION** Double
**TOTAL LENGTH** 300mm/11.75in
**BARREL LENGTH** 165mm/6.5in
**WEIGHT UNLOADED** 1,079g/37.9oz

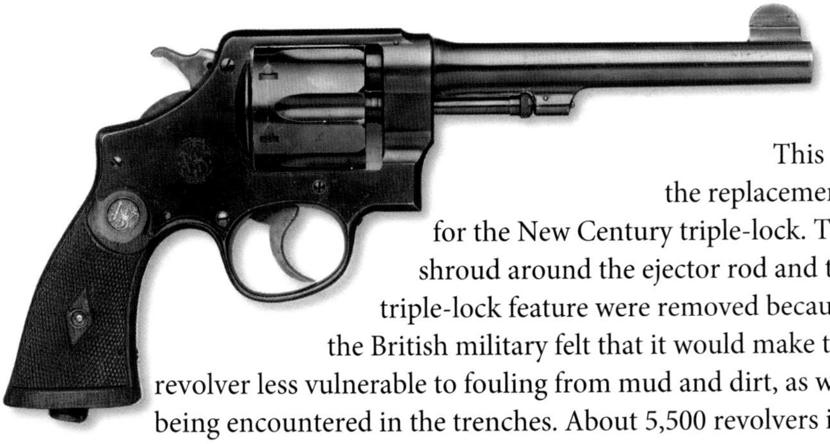

This was the replacement for the New Century triple-lock. The shroud around the ejector rod and the triple-lock feature were removed because the British military felt that it would make the revolver less vulnerable to fouling from mud and dirt, as was being encountered in the trenches. About 5,500 revolvers in .455 Eley were supplied to the British during World War I. A .45 ACP version of this revolver was used by the US military as the M1917.

## Smith & Wesson Model 36

**SPECIFICATION**

**MANUFACTURER** Smith & Wesson Inc.
**CALIBRE** .38 Special, .357 Magnum
**CYLINDER** 5
**ACTION** Double
**TOTAL LENGTH** 216mm/8.5in
**BARREL LENGTH** 102mm/4in
**WEIGHT UNLOADED** 566g/20oz

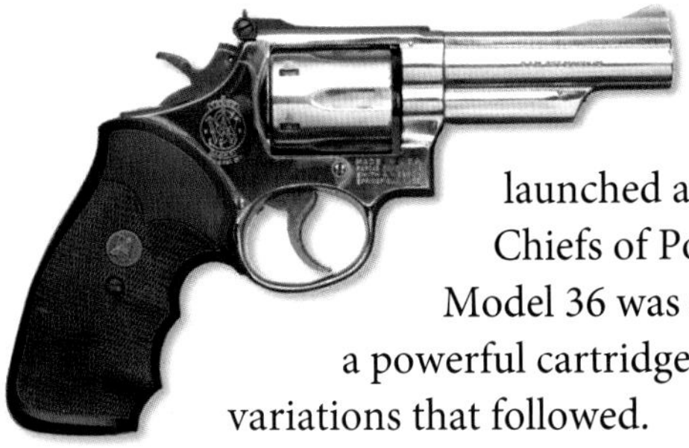

This revolver, originally designated the Model 388, was also described as the "Chief's Special", as it was launched at the International Association of Chiefs of Police (IACP) conference in 1950. The Model 36 was a small-frame revolver that could take a powerful cartridge. It became the basis of many different variations that followed.

## Smith & Wesson Model 39

**SPECIFICATION**

**MANUFACTURER** Smith & Wesson Inc.
**CALIBRE** 9mm Parabellum
**MAGAZINE CAPACITY** 8
**ACTION** Recoil/double
**TOTAL LENGTH** 190mm/7.5in
**BARREL LENGTH** 102mm/4in
**WEIGHT UNLOADED** 780g/27.52oz

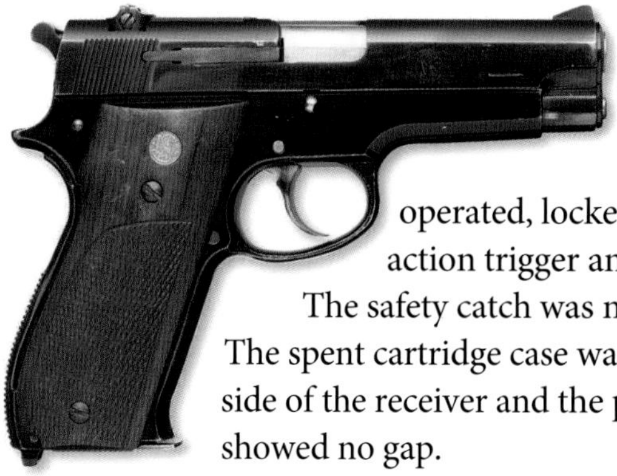

This was the first double-action pistol to be produced in the United States, in 1955. It was a recoil-operated, locked-breech pistol with a double-action trigger and a Browning-style locking system. The safety catch was mounted on the side of the receiver. The spent cartridge case was ejected from a gap on the right side of the receiver and the profile of the pistol from the left showed no gap.

## Smith & Wesson Model 29

**SPECIFICATION**

**MANUFACTURER** Smith & Wesson Inc.
**CALIBRE** .44 Magnum
**CYLINDER** 6
**ACTION** Double
**TOTAL LENGTH** 357mm/14in
**BARREL LENGTH** 210mm/8.27in
**WEIGHT UNLOADED** 1,374g/48.5oz

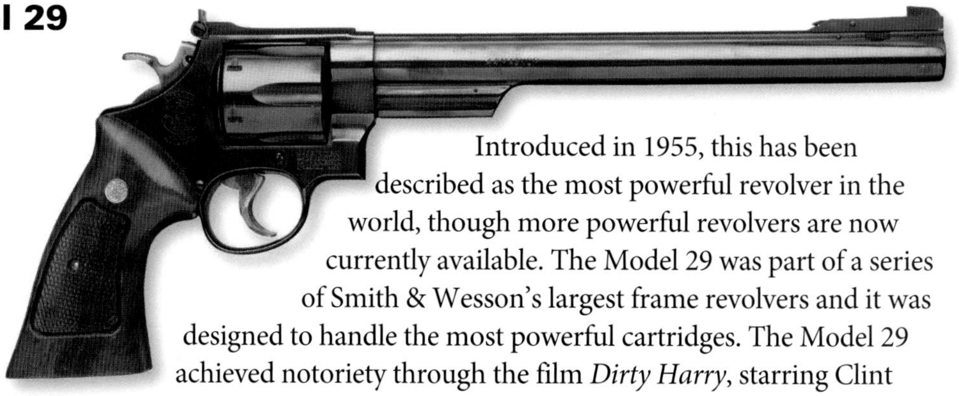

Introduced in 1955, this has been described as the most powerful revolver in the world, though more powerful revolvers are now currently available. The Model 29 was part of a series of Smith & Wesson's largest frame revolvers and it was designed to handle the most powerful cartridges. The Model 29 achieved notoriety through the film *Dirty Harry*, starring Clint Eastwood. A modern version, the 629, is currently in production.

## Smith & Wesson Model 19

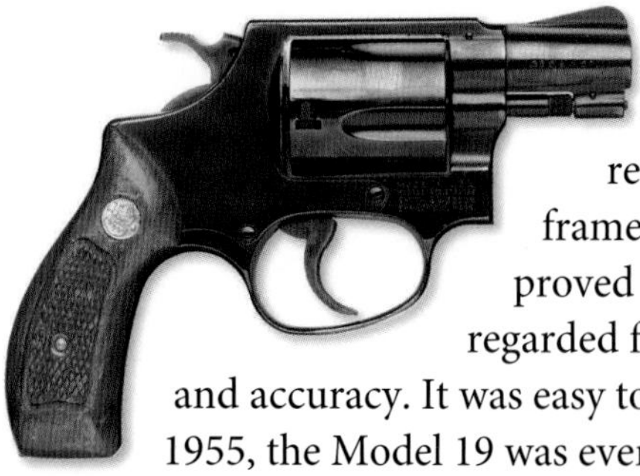

There were two calibres of the Model 19 produced, the .38 Special and the .357 Magnum revolver. The Model 19 had a medium frame and adjustable sights. This revolver proved to be an instant success and was highly regarded for its power as well as its good balance and accuracy. It was easy to carry and handled well. Introduced in 1955, the Model 19 was eventually replaced by the Model 66.

**SPECIFICATION**

**MANUFACTURER** Smith & Wesson Inc.
**CALIBRE** .38 Special, .357 Magnum
**CYLINDER** 6
**ACTION** Double
**TOTAL LENGTH** 203mm/8in
**BARREL LENGTH** 64mm/2.5in
**WEIGHT UNLOADED** 865g/30.5oz

## Smith & Wesson Model 10

The Smith & Wesson Military & Police revolver was a mainstay in holsters for decades. During World War II, the guns were known as Victory models with V-prefix serial numbers. They were also issued in great numbers to England under the Lend-Lease Act. In 1957, the name was changed to the Model 10, but the six-shot capacity revolver has remained essentially unchanged since its introduction in the early 1900s.

**SPECIFICATION**

**MANUFACTURER** Smith & Wesson Inc.
**CALIBRE** .38 Special
**MAGAZINE CAPACITY** 6
**ACTION** Double
**TOTAL LENGTH** 254mm/10in
**BARREL LENGTH** 102mm/4in
**WEIGHT UNLOADED** 865g/30.5oz

## Smith & Wesson Model 15

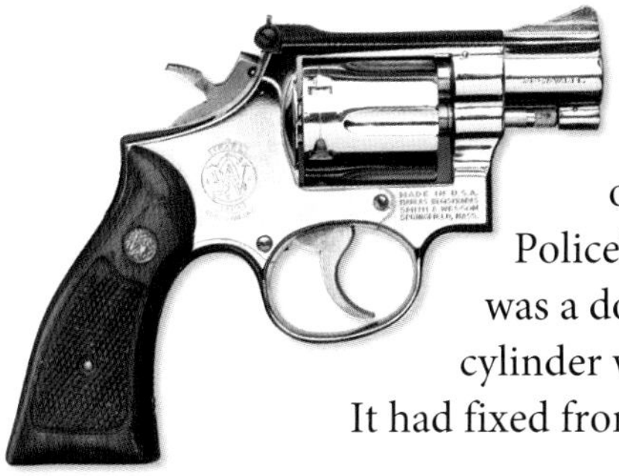

Introduced in 1957, the Model 15 revolver was a combat weapon. As part of the Smith & Wesson "Military and Police" series, this was a successful product. It was a double-action revolver with a swing-out cylinder with a dual-locked six-chamber cylinder. It had fixed front and rear sights.

**SPECIFICATION**

**MANUFACTURER** Smith & Wesson Inc.
**CALIBRE** .38 Special
**CYLINDER** 6
**ACTION** Double
**TOTAL LENGTH** 203mm/8in
**BARREL LENGTH** 51mm/2in
**WEIGHT UNLOADED** 1,020g/36oz

## Smith & Wesson Model 59

**SPECIFICATION**

**MANUFACTURER** Smith & Wesson Inc.
**CALIBRE** 9mm Parabellum
**MAGAZINE CAPACITY** 8
**ACTION** Recoil/double
**TOTAL LENGTH** 192mm/7.55in
**BARREL LENGTH** 102mm/4in
**WEIGHT UNLOADED** 840g/30oz

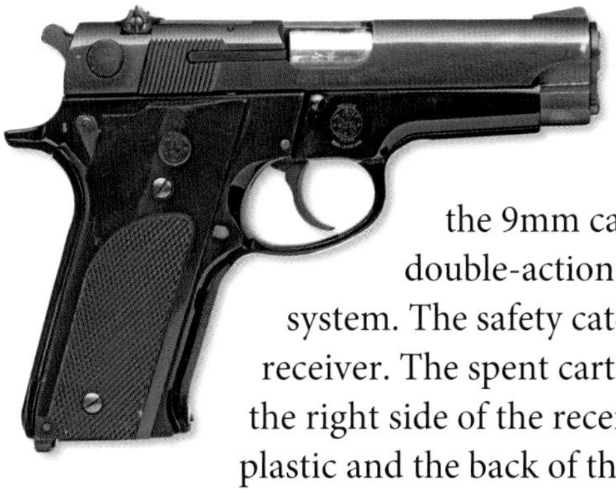

The Model 59, introduced in 1971, was a development of the Model 39 and the first high-capacity double-action pistol for the 9mm cartridge. It was recoil operated with a double-action trigger and Browning-style locking system. The safety catch was mounted on the side of the receiver. The spent cartridge case was ejected from a gap on the right side of the receiver. The hand-grip furniture was plastic and the back of the hand grip had a straight edge, as opposed to the curved back on the Model 39.

**SPECIFICATION**

**MANUFACTURER** Smith & Wesson Inc.
**CALIBRE** .357 Magnum, .38 Special
**CYLINDER** 6
**ACTION** Double
**TOTAL LENGTH** 292mm/11.5in
**BARREL LENGTH** 152mm/6in
**WEIGHT UNLOADED** 1,250g/44oz

## Smith & Wesson 686

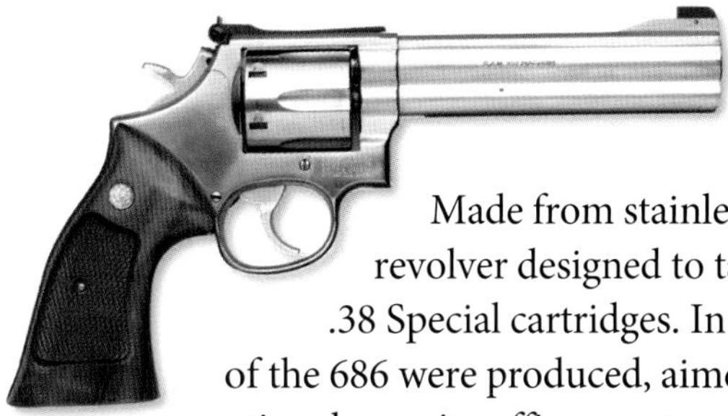

This revolver was introduced by Smith & Wesson in 1981 and it had a considerable impact. Made from stainless steel, it was a double-action revolver designed to take .357 Magnum cartridges and .38 Special cartridges. In due course a number of variations of the 686 were produced, aimed at specialized users, such as national security officers or target shooters. Smith & Wesson had intended this revolver to be light enough for extended carry by uniformed officers while providing considerable firepower.

**SPECIFICATION**

**MANUFACTURER** Smith & Wesson Inc.
**CALIBRE** .44 Special
**MAGAZINE CAPACITY** 6
**ACTION** Double
**TOTAL LENGTH** 197mm/7.8in
**BARREL LENGTH** 76mm/3in
**WEIGHT UNLOADED** 1,134g/40oz

## Smith & Wesson 624 ("Horton Special")

The Lew Horton Special was introduced in 1985. It was based on popular earlier models of S&W revolvers and was chambered for a .44 Special cartridge. The weapon became known as the "Horton Special" because it was put in production following the order of a Massachusetts gun distributor, Lew Horton. It had a solid frame with a cylinder that swung out to the left, a chrome-plated finish and a "birdshead"-shaped grip. The revolver is considered to be technologically outdated because of its low-pressure calibre.

## Smith & Wesson Model 581

**SPECIFICATION**

| | |
|---|---|
| MANUFACTURER | Smith & Wesson Inc. |
| CALIBRE | .357 Magnum |
| CYLINDER | 6 |
| ACTION | Double |
| TOTAL LENGTH | 216mm/8.5in |
| BARREL LENGTH | 102mm/4in |
| WEIGHT UNLOADED | 1,134g/40oz |

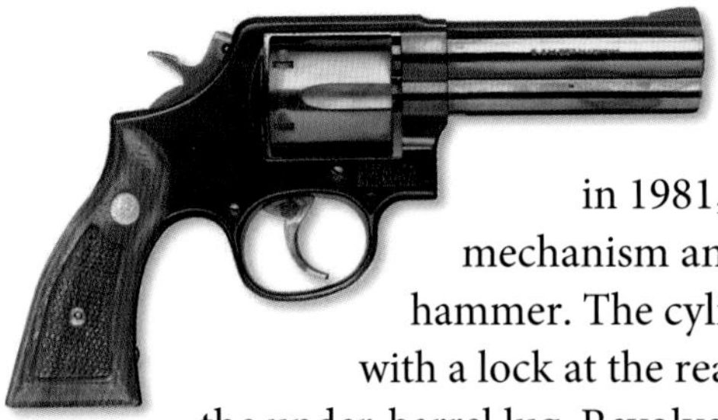

This was part of a lightweight series of Smith & Wesson revolvers and made from carbon steel. Introduced in 1981, it had a double-action trigger mechanism and the firing pin mounted on the hammer. The cylinder was double-locked to the frame with a lock at the rear of the cylinder and another on the under-barrel lug. Revolvers in this series proved popular with police forces and other security services as they were easy to carry and conceal

## Smith & Wesson 645

**SPECIFICATION**

| | |
|---|---|
| MANUFACTURER | Smith & Wesson Inc. |
| CALIBRE | .45 ACP |
| MAGAZINE CAPACITY | 8 |
| ACTION | Recoil/double |
| TOTAL LENGTH | 225mm/10in |
| BARREL LENGTH | 127mm/5in |
| WEIGHT UNLOADED | 1,247g/44oz |

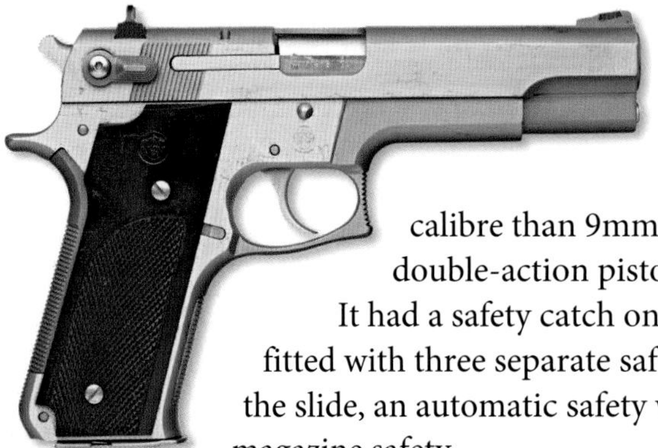

Introduced in 1985, the 645 was designed for the US civil market with a more powerful calibre than 9mm Parabellum. This was a double-action pistol based on a Browning design. It had a safety catch on the rear of the slide. It was fitted with three separate safeties: a safety catch mounted on the slide, an automatic safety which held the firing pin, and a magazine safety.

## Starr Model Army Revolver 1858

**SPECIFICATION**

| | |
|---|---|
| MANUFACTURER | Starr |
| CALIBRE | .44 |
| CYLINDER | 6 |
| ACTION | Percussion/double |
| TOTAL LENGTH | 296mm/11.67in |
| BARREL LENGTH | 152mm/6in |
| WEIGHT UNLOADED | 1,360g/48oz |

This pistol, designed by Ebenezer Townsend Starr, was issued to the US Army during the American Civil War and was also used by individuals on the Western Frontier. The Starr Model Army Revolver was an innovative double-action design, as for the first time, a revolver could be fired without having first to be manually cocked. This was achieved in two stages. First, the pull on the trigger would rotate the cylinder and cock the hammer. Second, the trigger pressed on an actuator at the back of the trigger guard that fired the weapon. The Starr also had a hinged frame and the cylinder could be changed for ease of reloading. It was, however, more prone to breaking than single-action revolvers.

## Ruger Mark I

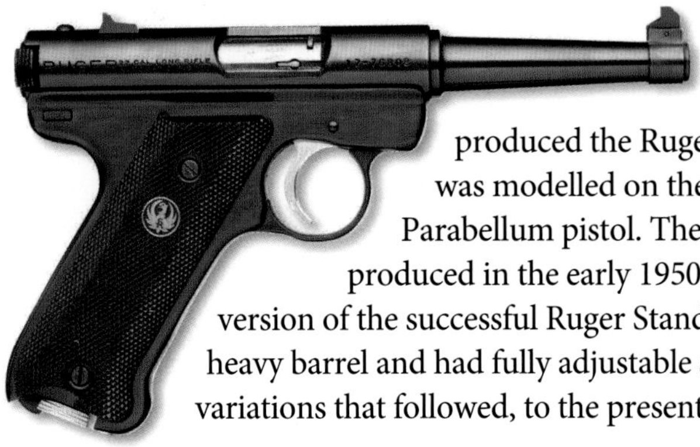

In 1949 the Ruger company based in Southport, Connecticut, produced the Ruger Standard pistol. This pistol was modelled on the iconic German Luger/ Parabellum pistol. The Mark I version was first produced in the early 1950s and was a target-shooting version of the successful Ruger Standard. It was fitted with a heavy barrel and had fully adjustable sights. The models and variations that followed, to the present day, were very successful.

**SPECIFICATION**

| | |
|---|---|
| MANUFACTURER | Sturm, Ruger & Co. Inc. |
| CALIBRE | .22 Long Rifle |
| MAGAZINE CAPACITY | 9 |
| ACTION | Blowback/single |
| TOTAL LENGTH | 276mm/10.87in |
| BARREL LENGTH | 175mm/6.89in |
| WEIGHT UNLOADED | 1,190g/42oz |

## Ruger Security Six

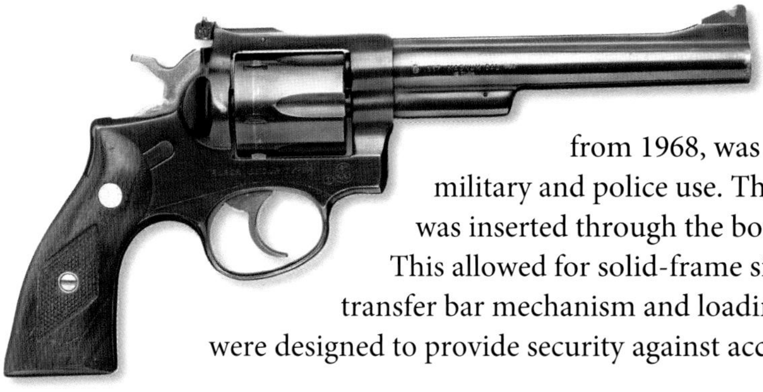

This revolver, in production from 1968, was designed for military and police use. The lock mechanism was inserted through the bottom of the frame. This allowed for solid-frame sidewalls. The Ruger transfer bar mechanism and loading-gate interlock were designed to provide security against accidental discharge.

**SPECIFICATION**

**MANUFACTURER** Sturm, Ruger & Co. Inc.
**CALIBRE** .357 Magnum
**CYLINDER** 6
**ACTION** Double
**TOTAL LENGTH** 235mm/9.25in
**BARREL LENGTH** 102mm/4in
**WEIGHT UNLOADED** 950g/33.5oz

## Ruger Police Service Six

**SPECIFICATION**

**MANUFACTURER** Sturm, Ruger & Co. Inc.
**CALIBRE** .357 Magnum
**CYLINDER** 6
**ACTION** Double
**TOTAL LENGTH** 254mm/10in
**BARREL LENGTH** 102mm/4in
**WEIGHT UNLOADED** 950g/33.5oz

This revolver was based on the Security Six. It had slightly modified grips and a sighting groove in the backstrap (instead of a separate rear sight). This modification was intended to provide adequate sights for quick combat firing at short range but also to avoid catching the sight on a holster or clothing as it was drawn. The Service Six was a successful handgun, strongly built and reliable. It was widely used by US police forces. The manufacture of the Service Six was discontinued in the late 1980s. Another police revolver, the Ruger Speed Six, with a shorter barrel was also available until replaced by the Ruger GP-100.

## Ruger Redhawk

**SPECIFICATION**

**MANUFACTURER** Sturm, Ruger & Co. Inc.
**CALIBRE** .44 Magnum, .45 Long Colt
**CYLINDER** 6
**ACTION** Double
**TOTAL LENGTH** 330mm/13in
**BARREL LENGTH** 190mm/7.5in
**WEIGHT UNLOADED** 1,502g/53oz

The Ruger Redhawk was first introduced in 1979 and was one of the most powerful handguns in the world. It was based on previous Ruger models, with square butt grip, adjustable sights and two barrel lengths. The Redhawk was a conventional double-action revolver with a triple-locking cylinder, locked into the frame at the front, rear and bottom, and a mechanism that made for a lighter trigger pull than earlier models. It also had a one-piece frame, rather than a removable sideplate, which gave it better strength.

## Ruger GP-100

**SPECIFICATION**

**MANUFACTURER** Sturm, Ruger & Co. Inc
**CALIBRE** .357 Magnum, .38 Special
**CYLINDER** 6
**ACTION** Double
**TOTAL LENGTH** 248mm/9.75in
**BARREL LENGTH** 102mm/4in
**WEIGHT UNLOADED** 1,200g/42oz

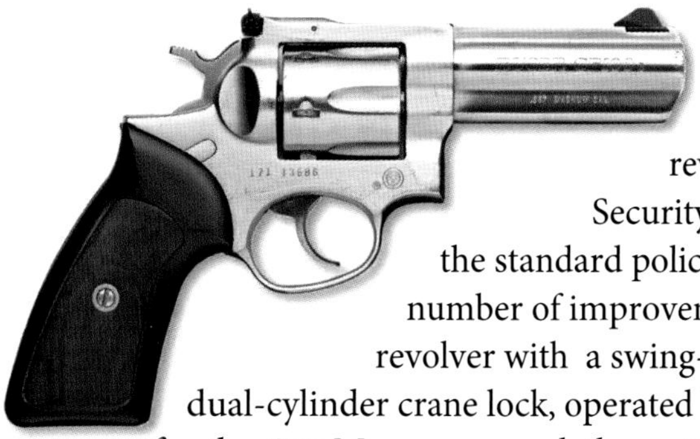

The GP-100, introduced in 1986, was a medium-sized revolver that replaced the Security Six and Police Service Six as the standard police revolver. It incorporated a number of improvements. It was a double-action revolver with a swing-out cylinder and fitted with a dual-cylinder crane lock, operated by a pushbutton. Chambered for the .357 Magnum round, the series was also available in .38 Special. The trigger mechanism was easily removable for maintenance. There was an option for either adjustable or fixed rear sights.

## Ruger P89

The Ruger P-series began with the Ruger 85 in the mid-1980s as a series of personal defence weapons. The Ruger P89 was first produced in 1987. It was a conventional full size double-action pistol with a locked breech. It had several stainless-steel components, including a stainless-steel barrel and hammer. The safety catch was on the left above the hand grip. The trigger guard was wide enough to accommodate a gloved hand.

| SPECIFICATION | |
|---|---|
| **MANUFACTURER** | Sturm, Ruger & Co. Inc. |
| **CALIBRE** | 9mm Parabellum |
| **MAGAZINE CAPACITY** | 10 or 15 |
| **ACTION** | Short recoil/double |
| **TOTAL LENGTH** | 200mm/7.87in |
| **BARREL LENGTH** | 114mm/4.49in |
| **WEIGHT UNLOADED** | 907g/33.5oz |

## Ruger Super Redhawk

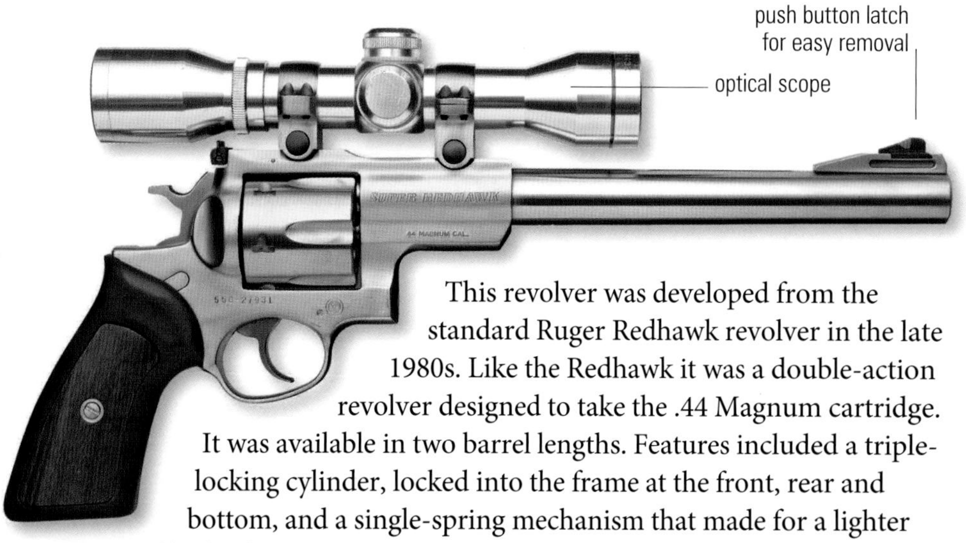


This revolver was developed from the standard Ruger Redhawk revolver in the late 1980s. Like the Redhawk it was a double-action revolver designed to take the .44 Magnum cartridge. It was available in two barrel lengths. Features included a triple-locking cylinder, locked into the frame at the front, rear and bottom, and a single-spring mechanism that made for a lighter trigger pull. The frame on the Super Redhawk was extended so that an optical scope could be fitted. The Super Redhawk also featured a cushioned hand grip. The stainless-steel finish was available with a low glare option that was corrosion resistant. The Ruger Super Redhawk was more than capable of carrying more powerful cartridges and within a few years it was chambered for new cartridges such as the .480 Ruger.

| SPECIFICATION | |
|---|---|
| **MANUFACTURER** | Sturm, Ruger & Co. Inc. |
| **CALIBRE** | .44 Magnum |
| **CYLINDER** | 6 |
| **ACTION** | Double |
| **TOTAL LENGTH** | 343mm/13.5in |
| **BARREL LENGTH** | 190mm/7.5in |
| **WEIGHT UNLOADED** | 1,474g/52oz |

**Redhawk models**
Sturm, Ruger & Co.'s double-action Redhawk models are based on the first double-action revolvers, such as the Security Six, Police Six and Speed Six, manufactured between 1972 and 1988.

## Ruger SP101

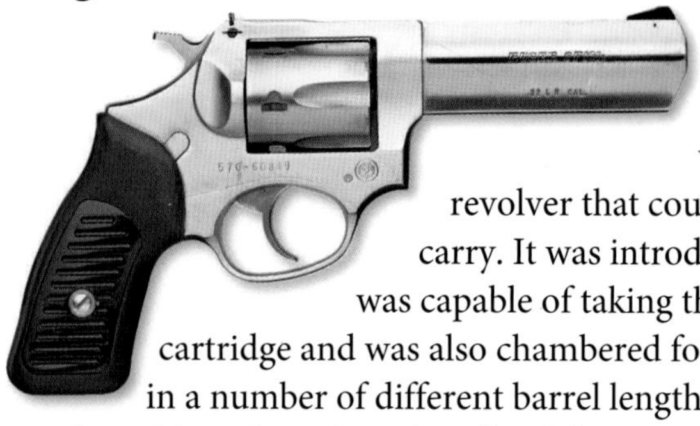

This small-frame revolver was introduced as a compact revolver that could be used for concealed carry. It was introduced in the late 1980s and was capable of taking the powerful .357 Magnum cartridge and was also chambered for other rounds. It was available in a number of different barrel lengths and options for fixed or adjustable sights. The sidewalls of the revolver were solid and integral to the rest of the frame. It had a triple-locking cylinder: this was locked into the frame at the front, rear and bottom in order to ensure positive alignment, and it had a forward latch mechanism to open it.

| SPECIFICATION | |
|---|---|
| **MANUFACTURER** | Sturm, Ruger & Co. Inc. |
| **CALIBRE** | .22 Long Rifle, .38 Special, 9mm Parabellum, .357 Magnum |
| **CYLINDER** | 5 |
| **ACTION** | Double |
| **TOTAL LENGTH** | 181mm/7.12in |
| **BARREL LENGTH** | 57mm/2.25in |
| **WEIGHT UNLOADED** | 694.56g/24.5oz |

## Ruger P90

| SPECIFICATION | |
|---|---|
| **MANUFACTURER** | Sturm, Ruger & Co. Inc. |
| **CALIBRE** | .45 ACP |
| **MAGAZINE CAPACITY** | 8 |
| **ACTION** | Recoil/double and DAO |
| **TOTAL LENGTH** | 200mm/7.75in |
| **BARREL LENGTH** | 114mm/4.5in |
| **WEIGHT UNLOADED** | 963g/34oz |

The Ruger P90, introduced in the early 1990s, had typical characteristics of this series of pistols, including a rugged build and overall durability. It was also capable of firing a high-pressure round. The P90 featured a firing pin block safety which was only disengaged once the trigger was fully depressed. The frame was manufactured from aluminium alloy, and other parts from stainless steel. It was designed to be easily disassembled. The P90 was found to be a very accurate and reliable pistol, though somewhat cumbersome compared to some other weapons of its calibre and/or power.

## Ruger P94

| SPECIFICATION | |
|---|---|
| **MANUFACTURER** | Sturm, Ruger & Co. Inc. |
| **CALIBRE** | 9mm Parabellum |
| **MAGAZINE CAPACITY** | 10 |
| **ACTION** | Recoil/double and DAO |
| **TOTAL LENGTH** | 190mm/7.5in |
| **BARREL LENGTH** | 108mm/4.25in |
| **WEIGHT UNLOADED** | 930g/27oz |

This pistol featured a hard-coated, aircraft-quality aluminium frame, a rugged steel slide and polycarbonate grip panels. It was fitted with a manual ambidextrous safety that, when engaged, prevented firing unless the lever was returned to the "fire" position. It has been developed by Ruger to reduce the impact of recoil when firing. The pistol has been fitted with high-visibility front and rear sights. Pistols in this series were designed to be easily maintained and could be field stripped into five major subassemblies for cleaning, without the need for special tools.

## Ruger P95

| SPECIFICATION | |
|---|---|
| **MANUFACTURER** | Sturm, Ruger & Co. Inc. |
| **CALIBRE** | 9mm Parabellum |
| **MAGAZINE CAPACITY** | 10 |
| **ACTION** | Recoil/double and DAO |
| **TOTAL LENGTH** | 184mm/7.25in |
| **BARREL LENGTH** | 99mm/3.9in |
| **WEIGHT UNLOADED** | 765g/27oz |

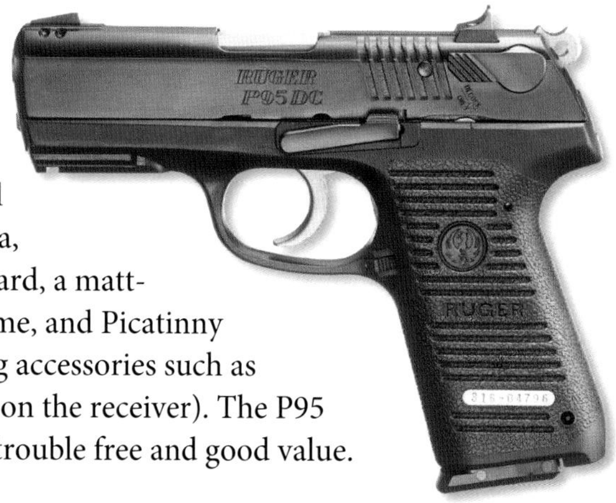


The P95 from the mid-1990s built upon the success of the earlier pistols in the P-series. The newest versions of the pistol had a non-slip, textured grip area, a contoured, rounded trigger guard, a matt-finished reinforced-polymer frame, and Picatinny rail (a bracket used for mounting accessories such as sights and lights, placed directly on the receiver). The P95 has a good reputation for being trouble free and good value.

## Ruger 22/45 Mark III bull barrel

| SPECIFICATION | |
|---|---|
| **MANUFACTURER** | Sturm, Ruger & Co. Inc. |
| **CALIBRE** | .22 Long Rifle |
| **MAGAZINE CAPACITY** | 10 |
| **ACTION** | Recoil/double and DAO |
| **TOTAL LENGTH** | 203mm/8in |
| **BARREL LENGTH** | 102mm/4in |
| **WEIGHT UNLOADED** | 878.84g/31oz |

This pistol was designed to provide the feel of a 1911 pistol. It was fitted with both front and rear sights. It had a molded polymer grip frame with a serrated front strap and chequered grip panel area. A cylindrical bolt construction ensured better accuracy than other moving-slide designs. An internal lock maintained the safety in the "safe" position. The pistol was fitted with a magazine disconnect to prevent accidental discharge when the magazine had been removed. A bull barrel is an unusually thick walled barrel that adds weight to the muzzle of the pistol and reduces recoil.

## Ruger P345

| SPECIFICATION | |
|---|---|
| MANUFACTURER | Sturm, Ruger & Co. Inc. |
| CALIBRE | .45 ACP |
| MAGAZINE CAPACITY | 8 |
| ACTION | Recoil/double and DAO |
| TOTAL LENGTH | 190mm/7.5in |
| BARREL LENGTH | 108mm/4.25in |
| WEIGHT UNLOADED | 822g/29oz |

The P345 pistol has been available since 2002. As with all of the P-series, this is a double-action, recoil-operated semi-automatic pistol. Its slim profile, smooth edges and rounded contours make it a useful pistol for concealed carry. The combination of stopping power and controlled penetration make the .45 ACP practical for police use. It has a dovetailed, three-dot sight system for faster, more precise targeting, and a slim contoured slide and frame.

## Taurus PT92 B-17

The PT92 (or Model 92) was first developed in the early 1980s. It is based on the Italian Beretta 92, with which it shares a large number of features – both are recoil operated with a locked-breech system. Like the Beretta it also has a double-action trigger and an ambidextrous frame-mounted manual safety with three positions (which can also be used as a de-cocking lever). This means the weapon can be carried "cocked and locked" The compact version of this model was introduced in 1991.

| SPECIFICATION | |
|---|---|
| MANUFACTURER | Taurus Int. MFG, Inc. |
| CALIBRE | 9mm Parabellum |
| MAGAZINE CAPACITY | 17 |
| ACTION | Recoil/double or single |
| TOTAL LENGTH | 216mm/8.5in |
| BARREL LENGTH | 127mm/5in |
| WEIGHT UNLOADED | 964g/34oz |

## Taurus PT99 SS

The PT99 (or Model 99) was developed in 1982. Like the PT92, the design is based on the Beretta 92, with which it shares a large number of features. It has a double-action trigger and an ambidextrous frame-mounted manual safety with three positions (which can also be used as a de-cocking lever). This means the weapon can be carried in "cocked-and-locked" mode. The PT99 has many similar features to the PT92 except that the rear sights are micrometer-click adjustable making target acquisition more accurate. The PT99 has been extensively tested and widely used. It has proved to be reasonably reliable.

| SPECIFICATION | |
|---|---|
| MANUFACTURER | Taurus Int. MFG, Inc. |
| CALIBRE | 9mm |
| MAGAZINE CAPACITY | 17 |
| ACTION | Short recoil/double |
| TOTAL LENGTH | 216mm/8.5in |
| BARREL LENGTH | 127mm/5in |
| WEIGHT UNLOADED | 964g/34oz |

## Taurus PT100 SS11

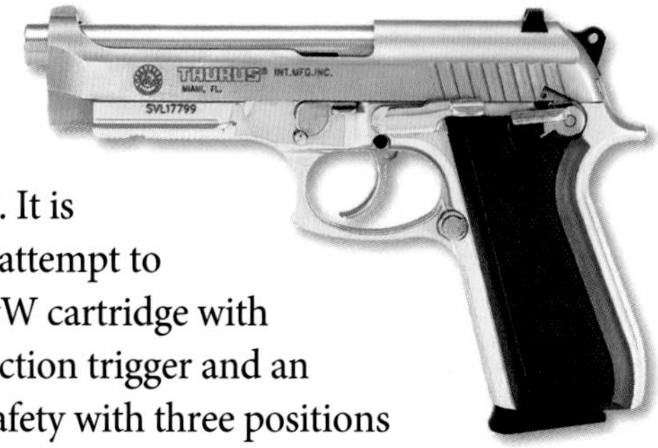

The PT100 (or Model 100), introduced in 1991, was also based on the Beretta 92. It is chambered for the larger cartridge in an attempt to capitalize on the popularity of the .40 S&W cartridge with US police departments. It has a double-action trigger and an ambidextrous frame-mounted manual safety with three positions (which can also be used as a de-cocking lever). This means the weapon can be carried in "cocked-and-locked" mode. It has a fixed two-dot rear sight and fixed one-dot front sight.

| SPECIFICATION | |
|---|---|
| MANUFACTURER | Taurus Int. MFG, Inc. |
| CALIBRE | .40 S&W |
| MAGAZINE CAPACITY | 11 |
| ACTION | Recoil/double |
| TOTAL LENGTH | 216mm/8.5in |
| BARREL LENGTH | 127mm/5in |
| WEIGHT UNLOADED | 964g/34oz |

## Taurus PT22 BGR

Introduced in 1992, the PT22 (or Model 22) is a small frame pistol easily concealed in a handbag or about the person. The barrel is hinged at the muzzle end so that it is easy to unload and also easy to carry out inspection and maintenance. The design of the gun was based on that of the Beretta M21. The pistol incorporates a magazine safety which prevents a round being fired if there is no magazine inserted.

**SPECIFICATION**

| | |
|---|---|
| **MANUFACTURER** | Taurus Int. MFG, Inc. |
| **CALIBRE** | .22 Long Rifle |
| **MAGAZINE CAPACITY** | 8 |
| **ACTION** | Blowback/DAO |
| **TOTAL LENGTH** | 133mm/5.25in |
| **BARREL LENGTH** | 65mm/2.56in |
| **WEIGHT UNLOADED** | 349g/12.3oz |

## Taurus PT25 N

**SPECIFICATION**

| | |
|---|---|
| **MANUFACTURER** | Taurus Int. MFG, Inc. |
| **CALIBRE** | .25 ACP |
| **MAGAZINE CAPACITY** | 9 |
| **ACTION** | Blowback/DAO |
| **TOTAL LENGTH** | 133mm/5.25in |
| **BARREL LENGTH** | 70mm/2.75in |
| **WEIGHT UNLOADED** | 349g/12.3oz |

Produced as a small but powerful pistol for self-defence, the PT25 (or Model 25) is virtually the same as the PT22. The main difference between them is that the PT25 takes the .25 ACP cartridge. Like the PT22, it is designed to be easily concealed, and has the tip-up barrel feature. The PT25 has a DAO trigger system and a manual safety.

**Brazil and the USA**
Forjas Taurus was originally a small-arms manufacturer based in Port Alegre, Brazil. An affiliated company was set up in Miami, Florida, in 1982 and today, Taurus produces weapons in both Brazil and the United States.

## Taurus PT908

**SPECIFICATION**

| | |
|---|---|
| **MANUFACTURER** | Taurus Int. MFG, Inc. |
| **CALIBRE** | 9mm Parabellum, .357 SIG |
| **MAGAZINE CAPACITY** | 10 |
| **ACTION** | Recoil/double |
| **TOTAL LENGTH** | 178mm/7in |
| **BARREL LENGTH** | 95mm/3.75in |
| **WEIGHT UNLOADED** | 770g/27.2oz |

Introduced in 1993, the medium-sized PT908 is a modification of the PT92 and was designed for US combat duties. It is sturdy, reliable and easy to conceal. It has a double-action trigger and a three-point ambidextrous frame-mounted manual safety. The pistol is also available in .357 SIG. Despite a good performance, the PT908 ceased to be manufactured after 1997.

## Taurus PT945 B

**SPECIFICATION**

| | |
|---|---|
| **MANUFACTURER** | Taurus Int. MFG, Inc. |
| **CALIBRE** | .45 ACP |
| **MAGAZINE CAPACITY** | 8 |
| **ACTION** | Recoil/double and single |
| **TOTAL LENGTH** | 190mm/7.5in |
| **BARREL LENGTH** | 108mm/4.25in |
| **WEIGHT UNLOADED** | 836g/29.5oz |

The PT945 B is a medium-framed steel and alloy pistol with chequered rubber grips. It is chambered for the .45 ACP cartridge. It is fitted with a manual safety and de-cocker, a firing-pin block automatic safety and a chamber-loaded indicator. The ambidextrous three-position safety allows the pistol to be carried "cocked and locked". The PT945 is a sturdy pistol, well suited as a duty gun and powerful, while being relatively easy to shoot.

## Taurus Millennium PRO PT145 SSP

The lightweight polymer frame with chequered polymer grips makes this pistol a useful weapon for law enforcement. It is also aimed at the personal safety market in some countries. It is a compact-size pistol that has been produced to a high standard. It carries three safety features which consist of a manual safety lever, trigger-block mechanism and a firing-pin block.

**SPECIFICATION**

**MANUFACTURER** Taurus Int. MFG, Inc.
**CALIBRE** .45 ACP
**MAGAZINE CAPACITY** 10
**ACTION** Recoil/double and single
**TOTAL LENGTH** 158mm/6.2in
**BARREL LENGTH** 83mm/3.25in
**WEIGHT UNLOADED** 629g/22.2oz

## Taurus Millennium Model PT111 B

The Millennium Model PT111B l is constructed from both polymer and steel and is ergonomically designed for optimum grip. Its lightweight frame makes it a useful weapon for law enforcement. It is also intended as a concealed carry defensive weapon for civilians. Like the other pistols in the range, it is a locked breech pistol that uses modified Browning-type locking, with single lug on the barrel which engages the ejection port in the slide. Similarly, the pistol is DAO and fitted with a manual safety as well as a firing-pin block safety.

**SPECIFICATION**

**MANUFACTURER** Taurus Int. MFG, Inc.
**CALIBRE** 9mm Parabellum
**MAGAZINE CAPACITY** 10
**ACTION** Recoil/DAO
**TOTAL LENGTH** 158mm/6.2in
**BARREL LENGTH** 83mm/3.25in
**WEIGHT UNLOADED** 530g/18.7oz

## Taurus Millennium PRO PT140 SSP

The Millennium Pro PT140 SSP is a compact polymer frame pistol. Its modern design and materials offers good ergonomics and strong performance. The magazine is relatively high capacity, carrying 10 rounds in a double magazine. This DAO pistol is lightweight and easy to handle, which makes it suitable for both law enforcement and the personal defence market. The PT140 carries three safety features including a manual safety lever, trigger-block mechanism and a firing-pin block. Like the other Millennium pistols, the Taurus PT140 SSP is known for good reliability and reasonable firepower, despite its relatively compact size.

**SPECIFICATION**

**MANUFACTURER** Taurus Int. MFG, Inc.
**CALIBRE** .40 S&W
**MAGAZINE CAPACITY** 10
**ACTION** Recoil/DAO
**TOTAL LENGTH** 159mm/6.25in
**BARREL LENGTH** 83mm/3.25in
**WEIGHT UNLOADED** 530g/18.7oz

## Taurus PT24/7 40BP

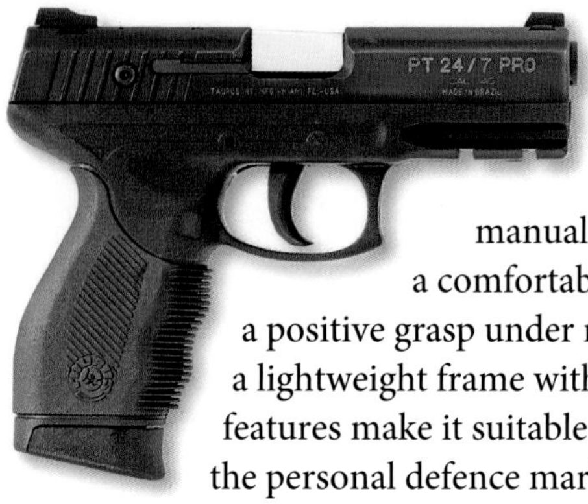


The PT24/7 is a large polymer- and steel-framed pistol with advanced ergonomics. It also includes features such as a chamber-loaded indicator, manual safety, internal trigger safety, and a comfortable moulded rubber grip offering a positive grasp under recoil. The pistol is DAO. It has a lightweight frame with integral accessory rail system. Its features make it suitable for use in law enforcement and for the personal defence market.

**SPECIFICATION**

**MANUFACTURER** Taurus Int. MFG, Inc.
**CALIBRE** .40 S&W
**MAGAZINE CAPACITY** 15
**ACTION** Recoil/DAO
**TOTAL LENGTH** 181mm/7.12in
**BARREL LENGTH** 102mm/4in
**WEIGHT UNLOADED** 771g/27.2oz

## Taurus 65 SS4

| SPECIFICATION | |
|---|---|
| MANUFACTURER | Taurus Int. MFG, Inc. |
| CALIBRE | .357 Magnum |
| CYLINDER | 6 |
| ACTION | Double and single |
| TOTAL LENGTH | 268mm/10.5in |
| BARREL LENGTH | 102mm/4in |
| WEIGHT | 1,077g/38oz |

The Taurus 65 SS4 (or Model 65) is made of steel with a rubber grip, and has a medium frame. It was designed largely for use by security personnel. It holds six rounds of the powerful Magnum load. The transfer bar mechanism prevents the hammer from striking the firing pin unless the trigger is pulled fully to the rear.

## Taurus 444 SS6 Raging Bull

| SPECIFICATION | |
|---|---|
| MANUFACTURER | Taurus Int. MFG, Inc. |
| CALIBRE | .44 Magnum |
| CYLINDER | 6 |
| ACTION | Double and single |
| TOTAL LENGTH | 305mm/12in |
| BARREL LENGTH | 165mm/6.5in |
| WEIGHT UNLOADED | 1,502g/53oz |

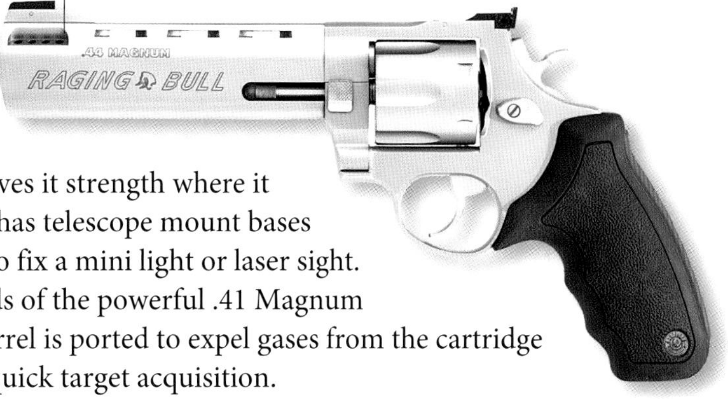


The 444 SS6 Raging Bull features a double-lockup cylinder which gives it strength where it is needed. It also has telescope mount bases along the barrel to fix a mini light or laser sight. It holds six rounds of the powerful .41 Magnum cartridge. The barrel is ported to expel gases from the cartridge and to allow for quick target acquisition.

## Taurus 44 Tracker 4SS

| SPECIFICATION | |
|---|---|
| MANUFACTURER | Taurus Int. MFG, Inc. |
| CALIBRE | .44 Magnum |
| CYLINDER | 5 |
| ACTION | Double and single |
| TOTAL LENGTH | 228mm/9in |
| BARREL LENGTH | 102mm/4in |
| WEIGHT UNLOADED | 964g/34oz |

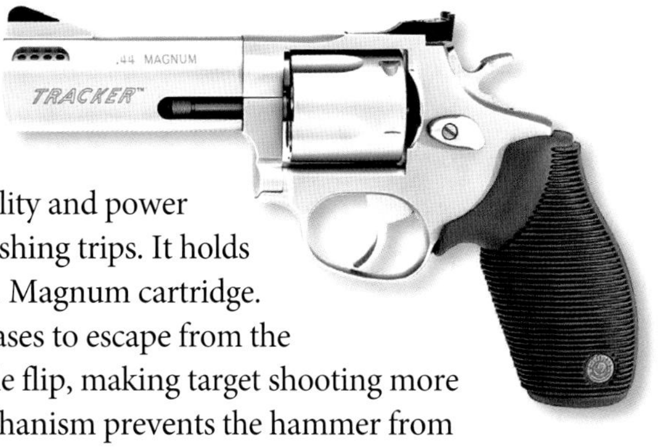


This 44 Tracker 4SS is designed to give the best combination of weight, durability and power for protection on hunting or fishing trips. It holds five rounds of the powerful .41 Magnum cartridge. The barrel is ported to allow gases to escape from the cartridge and so control muzzle flip, making target shooting more accurate. The transfer bar mechanism prevents the hammer from striking the firing pin unless the trigger is pulled fully to the rear.

## Taurus 444 Multi-4 Ultra-Lite

| SPECIFICATION | |
|---|---|
| MANUFACTURER | Taurus Int. MFG, Inc. |
| CALIBRE | .44 Magnum |
| CYLINDER | 6 |
| ACTION | Double and single |
| TOTAL LENGTH | 249mm/9.8in |
| BARREL LENGTH | 102mm/4in |
| WEIGHT UNLOADED | 802g/28.3oz |

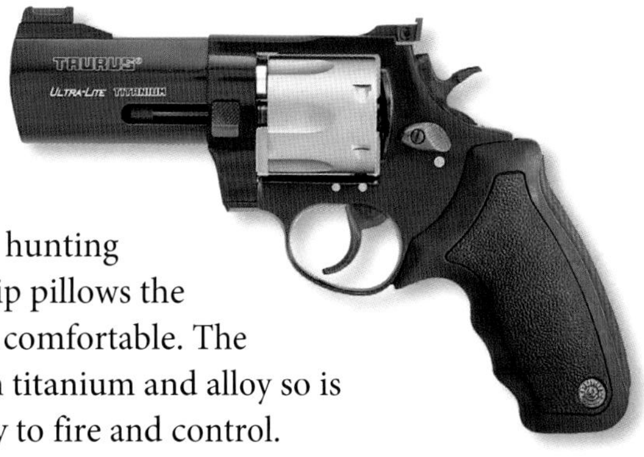


The 444 Multi-4 Ultra-Lite revolver was designed around the Raging Bull frame and has a powerful .44 Magnum cartridge. It was produced for hunting trips. The cushioned insert grip pillows the recoil, making shooting more comfortable. The revolver is made entirely from titanium and alloy so is exceptionally lightweight, easy to fire and control.

## Taurus 605 B2

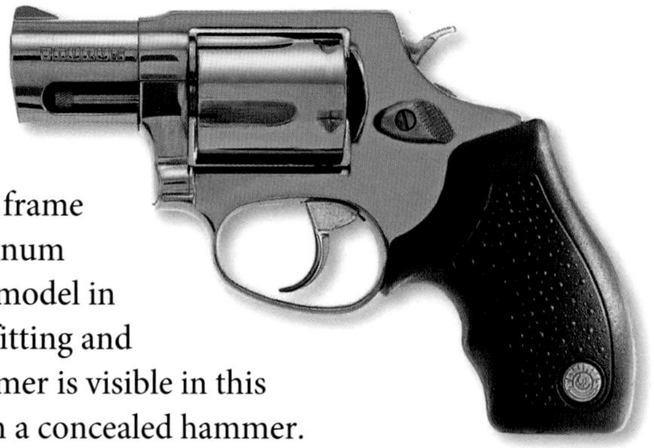

This concealable revolver is made of steel and is designed primarily for personal defence. For a small frame it fires the powerful .357 Magnum load. It is a very finely tuned model in terms of design, fabrication, fitting and performance. While the hammer is visible in this model, it is also available with a concealed hammer.

**SPECIFICATION**

**MANUFACTURER** Taurus Int. MFG, Inc.
**CALIBRE** .357 Magnum
**CYLINDER** 5
**ACTION** Double and single
**TOTAL LENGTH** 165mm/6.5in
**BARREL LENGTH** 51mm/2in
**WEIGHT UNLOADED** 680g/24oz

## Taurus 607

Introduced in 1995, this weapon was the first ever standard-production revolver to have a seven-round cylinder. The longest barrel length is 165mm/6.5in, with a full-length underlug, adjustable sights, and a vent rib on top. The long-barrel model comes with an integral compensator (a device to reduce recoil). Immediately, the US manufacturer Smith & Wesson produced their own seven-round revolver by issuing a variant of their popular Model 686 revolver as the Model 686 Plus. Within a year the 607 was eclipsed by the Taurus Model 608 which featured an eight-round cylinder.

**SPECIFICATION**

**MANUFACTURER** Taurus Int. MFG, Inc.
**CALIBRE** .357 Magnum
**CYLINDER** 7
**ACTION** Double and single
**TOTAL LENGTH** 301mm/11.87in
**BARREL LENGTH** 165mm/6.5in
**WEIGHT UNLOADED** 1,418g/52oz

## Taurus 608 SS6

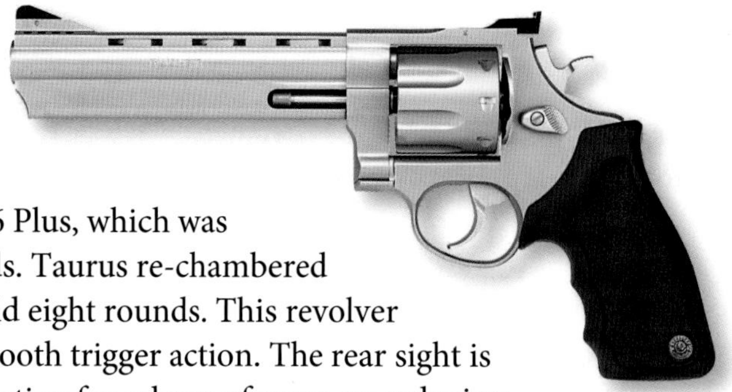

The Taurus 608 SS6 was produced in 1997 in response to Smith & Wesson's .357 Model 686 Plus, which was chambered for seven rounds. Taurus re-chambered their large-frame 607 to hold eight rounds. This revolver was designed to achieve smooth trigger action. The rear sight is adjustable. It has factory porting for release of gases, so reducing recoil. The Model 608 SS6 is available in three different barrel lengths. Scope mount bases are available to match the finish for the larger models.

**SPECIFICATION**

**MANUFACTURER** Taurus Int. MFG, Inc.
**CALIBRE** .357 Magnum
**CYLINDER** 8
**ACTION** Double and single
**TOTAL LENGTH** 295mm/11.62in
**BARREL LENGTH** 165mm/6.5in
**WEIGHT UNLOADED** 1,446g/51oz

## Taurus 650 SS2 "CIA" hammerless

This revolver was designed primarily as a backup weapon for law enforcement or for concealed carry and personal protection. It has a small, lightweight, steel construction with a rubber grip. Despite its diminutive size, it is chambered for five rounds of the .357 Magnum cartridge and is also available chambered for the .35 Special cartridge as the Model 850.

**SPECIFICATION**

**MANUFACTURER** Taurus Int. MFG, Inc.
**CALIBRE** .357 Magnum, .35 Special
**CYLINDER** 5
**ACTION** DAO
**TOTAL LENGTH** 165mm/6.5in
**BARREL LENGTH** 51mm/2in
**WEIGHT UNLOADED** 678g/23.9oz

## Taurus Model 651 SS2 Protector

**SPECIFICATION**

**MANUFACTURER** Taurus Int. MFG, Inc.
**CALIBRE** .357 Magnum, .38 Special
**CYLINDER** 5
**ACTION** Double and single
**TOTAL LENGTH** 165mm/6.5in
**BARREL LENGTH** 51mm/2in
**WEIGHT UNLOADED** 709g/25oz

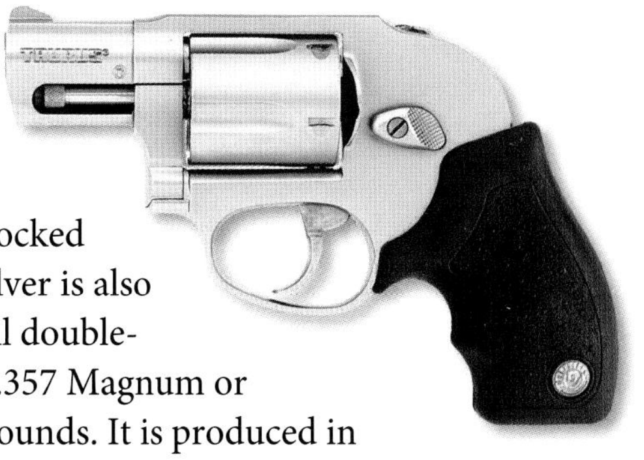

The Taurus Protector is a small revolver designed particularly for personal protection. The revolver features a hammer that is hidden and can be manually cocked or de-cocked in single-action operation. The revolver is also designed to function smoothly in full double-action. The Protector is available in .357 Magnum or .38 Special, both versions hold five rounds. It is produced in both matt stainless steel and titanium.

## Taurus 817S SUL

**SPECIFICATION**

**MANUFACTURER** Taurus Int. MFG, Inc.
**CALIBRE** .38 Special
**CYLINDER** 7
**ACTION** Double and single
**TOTAL LENGTH** 165mm/6.5in
**BARREL LENGTH** 51mm/2in
**WEIGHT UNLOADED** 595g/21oz

This revolver is unusual in providing an extra round in the cylinder, chambered for seven shots. The soft rubber grip and low-profile sights are provided to make the revolver more comfortable to use and easy to draw. It is ultra- light making it suitable for either law enforcement or personal defence.

## Taurus Model 851 B2 "CIA" Protector

**SPECIFICATION**

**MANUFACTURER** Taurus Int. MFG, Inc.
**CALIBRE** .38 Special, .357 Magnum
**CYLINDER** 5
**ACTION** Double and single
**TOTAL LENGTH** 165mm/6.5in
**BARREL LENGTH** 51mm/2in
**WEIGHT UNLOADED** 595g/21oz

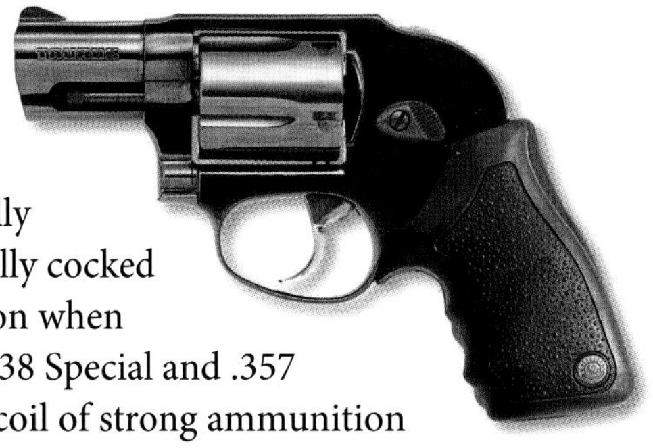

This small, ultra-light stainless steel or all-titanium model was designed for the home defence market. It is a double-action revolver that has a fully shrouded hammer that can be manually cocked or de-cocked in single-action operation when needed. The Protector is available in .38 Special and .357 Magnum holding five rounds. The recoil of strong ammunition is cushioned to a certain extent by the rubber grip.

## Taurus 905 SS2

**SPECIFICATION**

**MANUFACTURER** Taurus Int. MFG, Inc.
**CALIBRE** 9mm Parabellum, .45 ACP
**CYLINDER** 5
**ACTION** Double and single
**TOTAL LENGTH** 165mm/6.5in
**BARREL LENGTH** 51mm/2in
**WEIGHT UNLOADED** 630g/22.2oz

Designed for law enforcement professionals at close range, this is a small-frame, lightweight revolver with rubber grips chambered for five rounds of the popular 9mm cartridge (and is also available for the .45 ACP round). The idea is that should users wish to carry both a revolver and a pistol then they need to carry and use just one calibre of ammunition.

## Taurus/Rossi 351 02

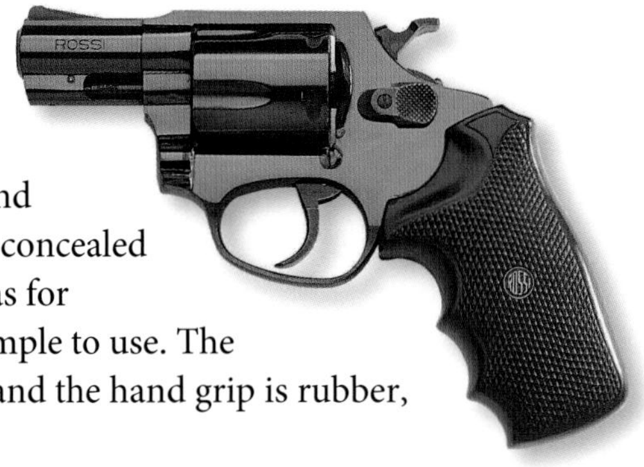

The small-frame Rossi 351 02 revolver is chambered for the .38 Special cartridge. With five rounds and a 2-inch/51-mm barrel, it is ideal for concealed carriage in undercover work as well as for personal defence. It is reliable and simple to use. The Rossi 351 02 is finished in blue steel and the hand grip is rubber, contoured for optimum finger grip.

**SPECIFICATION**

**MANUFACTURER** Taurus Int. MFG, Inc.
**CALIBRE** .38 Special
**CYLINDER** 5
**ACTION** Double and single
**TOTAL LENGTH** 165mm/6.5in
**BARREL LENGTH** 51mm/2in
**WEIGHT UNLOADED** 680g/24oz

## Taurus/Rossi R461 02

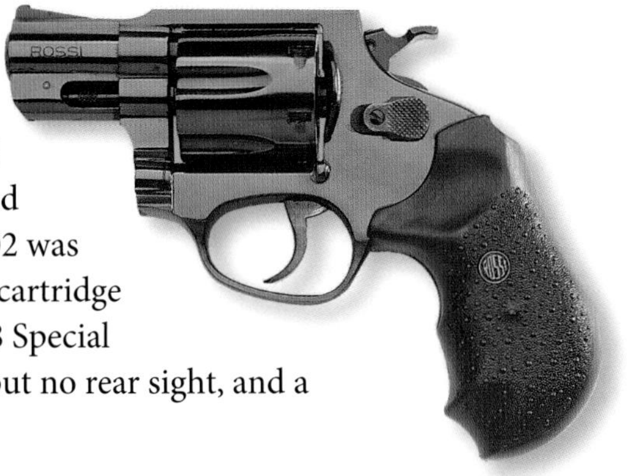

The .357 Magnum round is widely regarded as an ideal round for use in revolvers that are created for self-defence. The Rossi R461 02 was built to handle the .357 Magnum cartridge and it can also fire the popular .38 Special rounds. It has a fixed front sight but no rear sight, and a contoured rubber grip.

**SPECIFICATION**

**MANUFACTURER** Taurus Int. MFG, Inc.
**CALIBRE** .357 Magnum, .38 Special
**CYLINDER** 6
**ACTION** Double
**TOTAL LENGTH** 165mm/6.5in
**BARREL LENGTH** 50.8mm/2in
**WEIGHT UNLOADED** 737.09g/26oz

## Taurus/Rossi 851 04

**SPECIFICATION**

**MANUFACTURER** Taurus Int. MFG, Inc.
**CALIBRE** .38 Special
**CYLINDER** 6
**ACTION** Double and single
**TOTAL LENGTH** 216mm/8.5in
**BARREL LENGTH** 102mm/4in
**WEIGHT UNLOADED** 908g/32oz

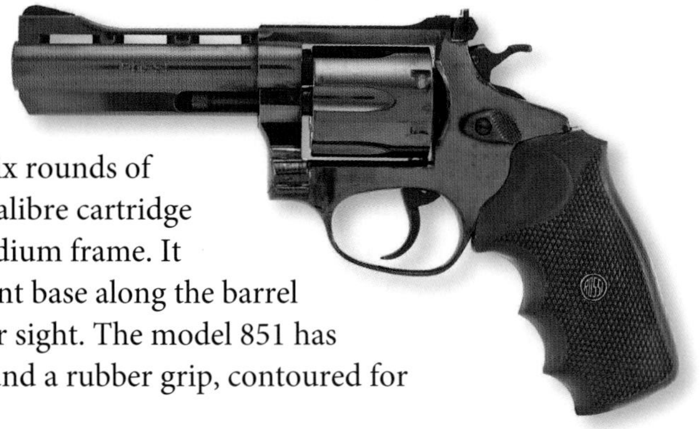

The Rossi 851 04 was designed for service and duty use. It carries six rounds of the popular .38 Special calibre cartridge in an easy-to-handle medium frame. It also has a telescope mount base along the barrel to fix a mini light or laser sight. The model 851 has an adjustable rear sight and a rubber grip, contoured for optimum finger grip.

## Taurus/Rossi 971 04

**SPECIFICATION**

**MANUFACTURER** Taurus Int. MFG, Inc.
**CALIBRE** .357 Magnum, .38 Special
**CYLINDER** 6
**ACTION** Double
**TOTAL LENGTH** 216mm/8.5in
**BARREL LENGTH** 102mm/4in
**WEIGHT UNLOADED** 907.18g/32oz

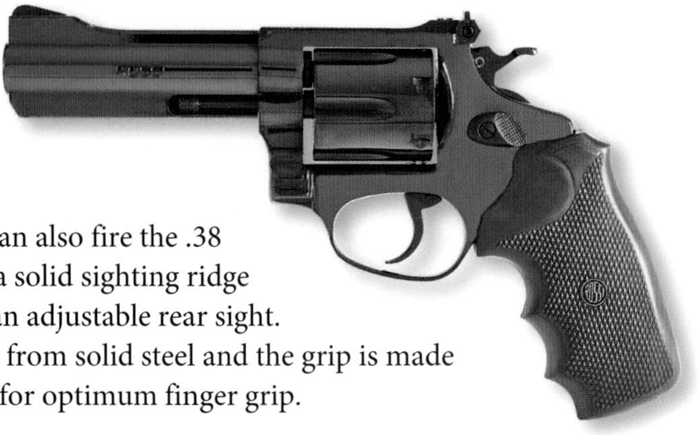

The model 971 04 is a double-action .357 Magnum revolver with a steel barrel. The revolver can also fire the .38 Special round. It has a solid sighting ridge along the barrel and an adjustable rear sight. This revolver is made from solid steel and the grip is made of contoured rubber, for optimum finger grip.

## Taurus/Rossi R972 06

**SPECIFICATION**

**MANUFACTURER** Taurus Int. MFG, Inc.
**CALIBRE** .357 Magnum, .38 Special
**CYLINDER** 6
**ACTION** Double
**TOTAL LENGTH** 268mm/10.5in
**BARREL LENGTH** 152mm/6in
**WEIGHT UNLOADED** 992g/35oz

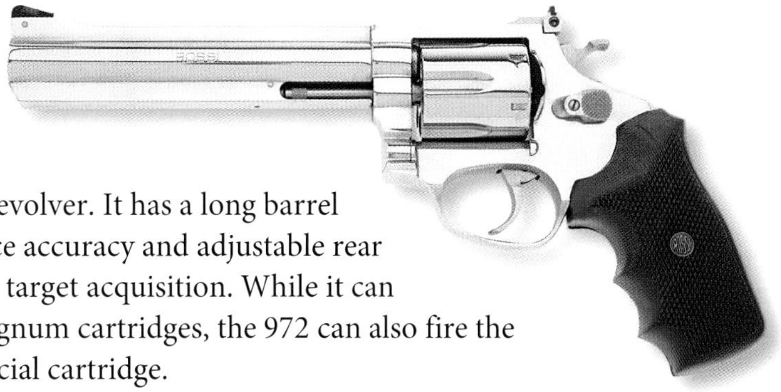

The Rossi R972 06 is a double-action, stainless steel .357 Magnum revolver. It has a long barrel for long-distance accuracy and adjustable rear sights for better target acquisition. While it can handle .357 Magnum cartridges, the 972 can also fire the popular .38 Special cartridge.

# Chile

**Chilean small-arms manufacture is centred round the firm of FAMAE (Las Fábricas y Maestranzas del Ejército), which was founded in 1811 and is said to be the oldest company of its type in South America. Small-arms production is largely focused on assault rifles (in association with Swiss Arms, known as SIG, the oldest manufacturer of arms in Switzerland) and submachine guns, which are developed by FAMAE.**

## FAMAE Volcano-F

The prototype of this pistol was announced in 2020 as the Vulcano, but upon entering actual production, the name was changed to Volcano-F. Motivation for developing this pistol was driven by a need for sidearms among Chilean law enforcement, armed forces, and other security personnel. Made with a steel slide and barrel, weight is kept to a minimum by using a polymer frame. FAMAE lists one of the gun's biggest features as its redesigned centre of gravity, which makes it easier to shoot and reacquire the sight picture for follow-up shots.

**SPECIFICATION**

**MANUFACTURER** Las Fábricas y Maestranzas del Ejército (FAMAE)
**CALIBRE** 9mm Parabellum
**MAGAZINE CAPACITY** 16
**ACTION** Short recoil/double or single
**TOTAL LENGTH** 211mm/8.3in
**BARREL LENGTH** 113mm/4.4in
**WEIGHT UNLOADED** 1,175g/41.4oz

## Steyr Hahn Model 1911

**SPECIFICATION**

**MANUFACTURER** Ostereichische Waffenfabriks-Gesellschaft Steyr
**CALIBRE** 9mm Steyr
**MAGAZINE CAPACITY** 8
**ACTION** Recoil/single
**TOTAL LENGTH** 216mm/8.5in
**BARREL LENGTH** 128mm/5.04in
**WEIGHT UNLOADED** 1,134g/40oz

This was a Chilean version of a famous pistol designed by Bohemian Karel Krnka and developed in Austria for military use. It was adopted by Austro-Hungarian forces towards the end of World War I, and exports to countries such as Chile were an important part of the production run. The pistol achieved a high reputation for robustness and reliability. On recoil, the barrel turned about 20 degrees and was then brought to a halt by lugs, while the rest of the slide continued rearward. The magazine was integral to the butt and was loaded with a charger. The Chilean versions had the coat of arms on the left of the slide and the words "Ejército de Chile" on the right, above the grip.

# Argentina

**In Argentina the firm of Ballester-Molina dates back to 1929 when two Spaniards, Arturo Ballester and Eugenio Molina, set up an engineering firm to provide parts for Hispano-Suiza cars. In due course they were commissioned by the Argentine Army to produce small arms. In the early to mid-1960s the firearms company Bersa began production and it still remains in business today.**

## Bersa Model 64

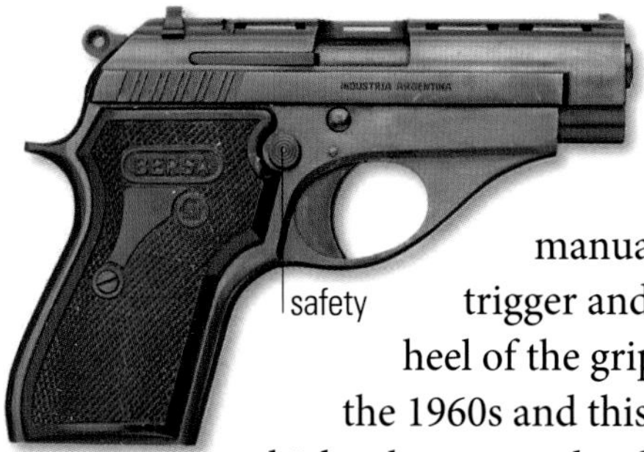


Bersa's earliest pistols were simple, blowback-operated single-action designs chambered for the .22 Long Rifle cartridge. A trigger-blocking manual safety was placed just behind the trigger and a magazine catch was located near the heel of the grip. The Bersa model line has run since the 1960s and this pistol was one of the basic designs from which others were developed for the first generation of pistols.

**SPECIFICATION**

**MANUFACTURER** Bersa S.A.
**CALIBRE** .22 Long Rifle
**MAGAZINE CAPACITY** 7
**ACTION** Blowback/single
**TOTAL LENGTH** 168mm/6.63in
**BARREL LENGTH** 90mm/3.54in
**WEIGHT UNLOADED** 794g/28oz

## Bersa Model 62

This pistol was based on the Bersa 64, the first of the Bersa model line. The Bersa 62 was a blowback-operated single-action pocket pistol, fired by a hammer. The Model 62 had a longer barrel than the Model 64, so the front sight was positioned farther down the barrel, enabling the pistol to be used for target shooting. Like the Model 64 it was also chambered for the .22 Long Rifle round. It was manufactured between 1962 and 1968. Bersa's first generation of pistols were produced until the end of the 1970s, when modifications were made for the next generation.

**The guide rod**
A separate recoil spring guide rod is inserted under the barrel. Guide rods are said to improve reliability and moderate recoil.

**SPECIFICATION**

**MANUFACTURER** Bersa S.A.
**CALIBRE** .22 Long Rifle
**MAGAZINE CAPACITY** 10
**ACTION** Blowback/single
**TOTAL LENGTH** 229mm/9in
**BARREL LENGTH** 152mm/6in
**WEIGHT UNLOADED** 695g/24.5oz

## Bersa Model 97

Produced between 1978 and 1982, the single-action Model 97 represented a second-generation model and Bersa's first pistol in .380 ACP. Like previous Bersa models, it was a blowback-operated single-action pistol. Unlike previous models it did not have a recoil spring guide, as the barrel itself was used for this purpose. A slide-mounted hammer-blocking safety and a magazine disconnect safety were added as new features. A dedicated barrel pin was used as the trigger pin, freeing up the slide catch. The pistol featured windage-adjustable rear sights. After four years of production, the Model 97 was replaced in 1983 by the Model 383.

**SPECIFICATION**

**MANUFACTURER** Bersa S.A.
**CALIBRE** .380 ACP
**MAGAZINE CAPACITY** 7
**ACTION** Blowback/single
**TOTAL LENGTH** 168mm/6.63in
**BARREL LENGTH** 90mm/3.54in
**WEIGHT UNLOADED** Not known

## Bersa Model 383

| SPECIFICATION | |
|---|---|
| **MANUFACTURER** | Bersa S.A. |
| **CALIBRE** | .380 ACP |
| **MAGAZINE** | 7 |
| **ACTION** | Blowback/single |
| **TOTAL LENGTH** | 168mm/6.63in |
| **BARREL LENGTH** | 90mm/3.54in |
| **WEIGHT UNLOADED** | 680g/24oz |

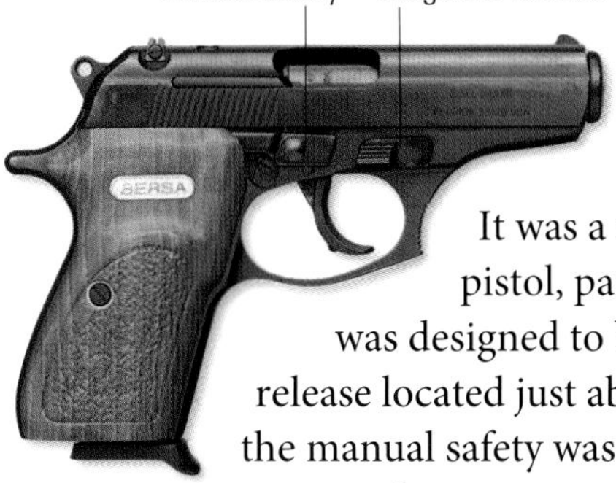


The Model 383 succeeded the Model 97 and was produced from 1983 to 1985. It was a compact, single-action blowback-operated pistol, part of the third generation. The Model 383 was designed to be easily concealed. It had a large magazine release located just above the hand grip on the right side, and the manual safety was above and to the rear of this. It also had a recurved trigger-guard with a finger rest. The double-action version of the 383 (called the 383A) was produced between 1986 and 1988 with various modifications of the fourth generation of Bersa pistols. The Model 383A was produced in polished blue or nickel with walnut grips.

## Bersa Model 90

| SPECIFICATION | |
|---|---|
| **MANUFACTURER** | Bersa S.A. |
| **CALIBRE** | 9mm Parabellum |
| **MAGAZINE** | 15 |
| **ACTION** | Blowback/double |
| **TOTAL LENGTH** | Not known |
| **BARREL LENGTH** | Not known |
| **WEIGHT UNLOADED** | 695g/24.5oz |

The Model 90 was part of the range of Bersa models from the early 1990s and was chambered for the 9mm Parabellum cartridge. The fifth generation of Bersa pistols was similar to previous models, but used new materials. The external slide catch was removed (although later reinstated on the Model 90). Instead of a slide catch, the pistol used an internal mechanism which allowed it to be released from slide-lock using the slide. High-capacity magazines were introduced. However, when legislation was introduced in the United States in 1994 to reduce magazine capacity, Bersa designs were modified.

## Bersa Thunder 9

| SPECIFICATION | |
|---|---|
| **MANUFACTURER** | Bersa S.A. |
| **CALIBRE** | 9mm Parabellum |
| **MAGAZINE** | 17 |
| **ACTION** | Recoil/double |
| **TOTAL LENGTH** | 192mm/7.56in |
| **BARREL LENGTH** | 110mm/4in |
| **WEIGHT UNLOADED** | 870g/30oz |

This semi-automatic pistol was available from 1994. It had a substantial trigger guard that was designed to accommodate a gloved finger. The rear sight was dovetailed and the front sight was incorporated in the slide. The pistol was fitted with a firing-pin safety. The Thunder 9 was imported into the United States only after the lifting of the ban on high-capacity magazines in 2004. Bersa Thunder 9 pistols are standard issue pistols for the Argentine Federal Police and the Buenos Aires Province Police.

## Bersa Thunder 380

| SPECIFICATION | |
|---|---|
| **MANUFACTURER** | Bersa S.A. |
| **CALIBRE** | .380 ACP |
| **MAGAZINE** | 7 or 9 |
| **ACTION** | Blowback/double |
| **TOTAL LENGTH** | 168mm/6.63in |
| **BARREL LENGTH** | 90mm/3.54in |
| **WEIGHT UNLOADED** | 567g/19.75oz |

This small, lightweight semi-automatic pistol was introduced in 1995. Intended primarily for civilian use, the weapon was also used by a variety of security and military forces. It had a safety switch mounted on the slide and a magazine safety that prevented the weapon firing if a magazine was not inserted. It was not possible to carry the pistol "cocked and locked". It also featured a trigger lock, operated by a key. Although the .380 ACP cartridge was comparatively weak, the light and convenient setup of this weapon made it a convenient pistol to carry. In the United States, the Thunder 380 was known as the Firestorm 380. It was a popular model with a long production run.

## Bersa Thunder 45 Ultra-Compact

This pistol was produced from 2002 and designed for concealed carriage by civilians as well as for law enforcement and military personnel. It was a compact double-action pistol with a locked breech. Much attention has been paid to ergonomics. The safety catch was ambidextrous, as was the slide-release lever. The magazine release could be mounted on either side of the hand grip. The trigger could be locked with a key. Some versions had a rail attachment for a laser or light below the barrel.

**SPECIFICATION**

**MANUFACTURER** Bersa S.A.
**CALIBRE** .45 ACP
**MAGAZINE CAPACITY** 7
**ACTION** Recoil/double
**TOTAL LENGTH** 173mm/6.81in
**BARREL LENGTH** 92mm/3.62in
**WEIGHT UNLOADED** 780g/27.5oz

## Ballester-Molina

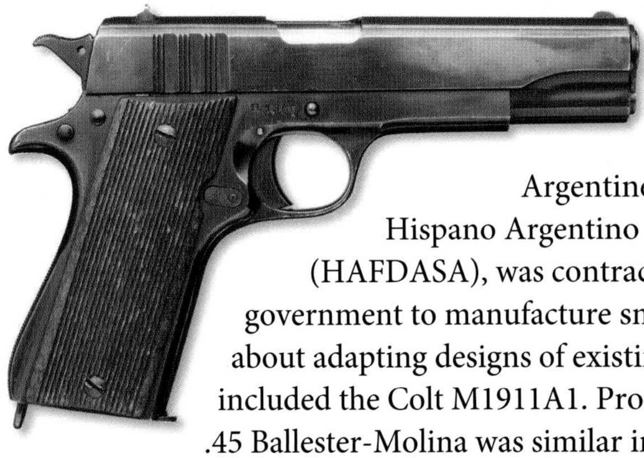

This pistol was originally made by a Spanish automotive company, Hispano-Suiza. The Argentine section of the company, Hispano Argentino de Automóviles S.A. (HAFDASA), was contracted by the Argentine government to manufacture small arms. The company set about adapting designs of existing weapons, one of which included the Colt M1911A1. Produced in the late 1930s, the .45 Ballester-Molina was similar in appearance to the Colt. However, there were a number of significant differences between the two weapons, including the design of the hammer strut, safety lock, firing-pin stop and mainspring housing. The success of the modified design was such that the pistol was adopted by the Argentine Police and Army and was also ordered by the British for use by members of the Special Operations Executive (SOE).

**The Hafdasa**
This pistol is sometimes known as the "Hafdasa" from the initials of the manufacturer (Hispano Argentino Fábrica de Automóviles S.A.).

**SPECIFICATION**

**MANUFACTURER** Hispano Argentino Fábrica de Automóviles S.A.
**CALIBRE** .45 ACP
**MAGAZINE CAPACITY** 7
**ACTION** Recoil/single
**TOTAL LENGTH** 216mm/8.5in
**BARREL LENGTH** 127mm/5in
**WEIGHT UNLOADED** 1,077g/38oz

## Modelo 1905

The Mannlicher 1905 pistol was originally made in Austria. It was known in Europe as the M1901 and was purchased by the Argentine Army in 1905. It was a semi-automatic pistol and had an unusually elegant appearance, with a gentle curve from the hand grip up over the trigger-guard area. The Modelo 1905 had an open-topped slide and the barrel was screwed into the breech. The slide was a short breech-block section behind the barrel and incorporated both the extractor and the firing pin. The pistol had a delayed blowback mechanism. The magazine was integral to the butt and was loaded via a charger through the action mechanism. This pistol remained popular and in use in South America long after it had been discontinued in Europe.

**SPECIFICATION**

**MANUFACTURER** Osterreichische Waffenfabriks Gesellschaft
**CALIBRE** 7.63mm Mannlicher
**MAGAZINE CAPACITY** 8
**ACTION** Blowback/single
**TOTAL LENGTH** 246mm/9.69in
**BARREL LENGTH** 160mm/6.3in
**WEIGHT UNLOADED** 910g/32oz

# Brazil

**Small-arms manufacture in Brazil is largely centred around Industria de Material Bélico (IMBEL), which is government-owned and has close links with the Ministry of Defence and the Army. It was established in 1975 and brought together a number of ammunition factories in Brazil.**

## IMBEL M973

**SPECIFICATION**

**MANUFACTURER** Indústria de Material Bélico do Brasil (IMBEL)
**CALIBRE** 9mm Parabellum, .45 ACP
**MAGAZINE CAPACITY** 9
**ACTION** Short recoil/single
**TOTAL LENGTH** 216mm/8.5in
**BARREL LENGTH** 128mm/5.04in
**WEIGHT UNLOADED** 1,010g/35.6oz

First produced in 1973, this pistol was a 9mm version of the Colt M1911A1. It was chambered in .45 ACP as the standard IMBEL. It was standard issue to the Brazilian Army and has also been widely exported. It was a semi-automatic pistol, based on the short-recoil system. The Colt M1911 was the longest-serving service weapon in the world. Like many others throughout the world, the Brazilian security forces chose a classic design as their weapon of choice due to its rugged design, robustness and reliability. The only drawback for its future service is the development of modern body armour that is resistant even to the 9mm Parabellum round.

## IMBEL MD1

**SPECIFICATION**

**MANUFACTURER** Indústria de Material Bélico do Brasil (IMBEL)
**CALIBRE** .45 ACP, 9mm Parabellum
**MAGAZINE CAPACITY** 13 or 17
**ACTION** Short recoil/single
**TOTAL LENGTH** 216mm/8.5in
**BARREL LENGTH** 128mm/5.04in
**WEIGHT UNLOADED** 1,060g/37.4oz

The MD1 was developed as a high-capacity version of the M973, which itself was a close copy of the American Colt M1911A1. Except for its magazine, trigger, grips and magazine-catch assembly, almost all of the rest of its parts were interchangeable with the M975 pistol in the same chambering. The MD1 was most commonly made in .45 ACP with a 13-round magazine and in 9mm with a 17-round magazine. The MD1 entered production in 1989.

**SPECIFICATION**

**MANUFACTURER** Indústria de Material Bélico do Brasil (IMBEL)
**CALIBRE** .45 ACP, 9mm Parabellum
**MAGAZINE CAPACITY** 13 or 17
**ACTION** Short recoil/single
**TOTAL LENGTH** 216mm/8.5in
**BARREL LENGTH** 128mm/5.04in
**WEIGHT UNLOADED** 1,060g/37.4oz

## IMBEL MD2

This was a compact version of the high capacity MD1 in .45 ACP and 9mm Parabellum. Because of its flat design, the original Colt M1911A1-based models were surprisingly easy to carry concealed and this reduced-size model was even more so. This made it a good choice for police, military and civilian concealed carry.

**Colt .45-based models**
Brazil has a number of models based on the Colt .45, available in .45, .40 and 9mm calibres, for use by military and police (M1911A1, M973, IMBEL and variants), and .38 calibre for civilian use.

# Spain

**Spain produced a wide variety of pistols and revolvers throughout the 20th century, mostly centred on the firms of Astra-Unceta y Cia. S.A. and Star Bonifacio Echeverría S.A. Although these were primarily designed to meet the requirements of the Spanish armed forces, the police and the Guardia Civil, a number of designs were also exported as far afield as China. Both of these companies went out of business in the late 1990s, but a new firm, Astra, was formed, which produces a range of firearms.**

## Star Military Model

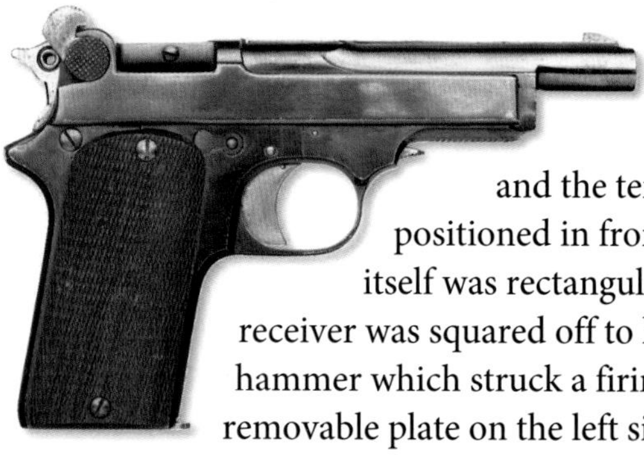

This pistol was based on the style of the Mannlicher pistols and the ten-round magazine would be positioned in front of the trigger guard. The bolt itself was rectangular and the top rear part of the receiver was squared off to house it. There was an external hammer which struck a firing pin in the bolt. It had a removable plate on the left side and a separate barrel return spring. Although its history was not well documented, the Military Model was produced before World War I. It was a well-made pistol that was exported in large numbers. It was also issued to Spanish security forces.

| SPECIFICATION | |
|---|---|
| MANUFACTURER | Star Bonifacio Echeverría S.A. |
| CALIBRE | 7.65mm (.32 ACP) |
| MAGAZINE CAPACITY | 10 |
| ACTION | Recoil/single |
| TOTAL LENGTH | 312mm/12.3in |
| BARREL LENGTH | 160mm/6.3in |
| WEIGHT UNLOADED | 646g/23oz |

## Star Model 1920

The Model 1920 was produced solely for the Guardia Civil, the Spanish police. This was the first Star pistol designed in the style of the Colt M1911. The 1920 model was made in at least four variants, produced between 1920 and 1921. Although it had the general outline of the Colt and was locked via a Browning-style tipping barrel and link system, there were other changes. The safety was an all-new rotating lever, but it was mounted high at the extreme rear of the slide. These changes indicated that it was not simply copied from the Colt-Browning, but was a new design in its own right. Subsequent models continued to be produced to meet the needs of the Guardia Civil, known as the "military model".

| SPECIFICATION | |
|---|---|
| MANUFACTURER | Star Bonifacio Echeverría S.A. |
| CALIBRE | 9mm Largo |
| MAGAZINE CAPACITY | 8 |
| ACTION | Recoil/single |
| TOTAL LENGTH | 200mm/7.87in |
| BARREL LENGTH | 122mm/4.8in |
| WEIGHT UNLOADED | 1,100g/38.8oz |

## Star Model 1921

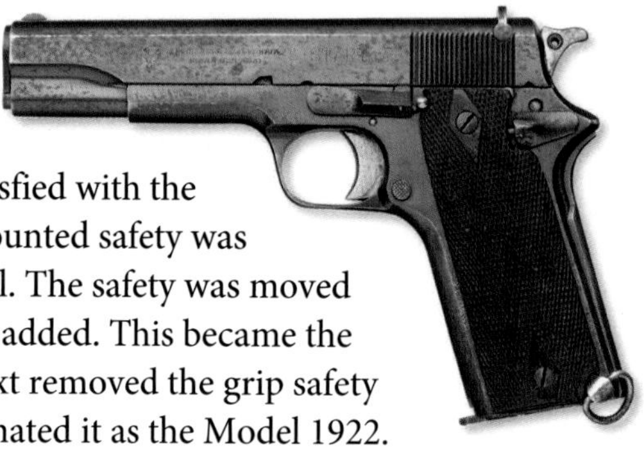

Shortly after adopting the 1920 pistol, the Guardia Civil decided that they were not completely satisfied with the design. They felt that the slide-mounted safety was not appropriate for a service pistol. The safety was moved to the frame and a grip safety was added. This became the Star Modelo Militar 1921. Star next removed the grip safety from the Model 1921 and redesignated it as the Model 1922.

| SPECIFICATION | |
|---|---|
| MANUFACTURER | Star Bonifacio Echeverría S.A. |
| CALIBRE | 9mm Largo |
| MAGAZINE CAPACITY | 8 |
| ACTION | Recoil/single |
| TOTAL LENGTH | 200mm/7.87in |
| BARREL LENGTH | 122mm/4.8in |
| WEIGHT UNLOADED | 1,100g/38.8oz |

## Star Model B

**SPECIFICATION**

**MANUFACTURER** Star Bonifacio Echeverría S.A.
**CALIBRE** 9mm Parabellum
**MAGAZINE CAPACITY** 9
**ACTION** Recoil/single
**TOTAL LENGTH** 215mm/8.46in
**BARREL LENGTH** 122mm/4.8in
**WEIGHT UNLOADED** 1,085g/38.27oz

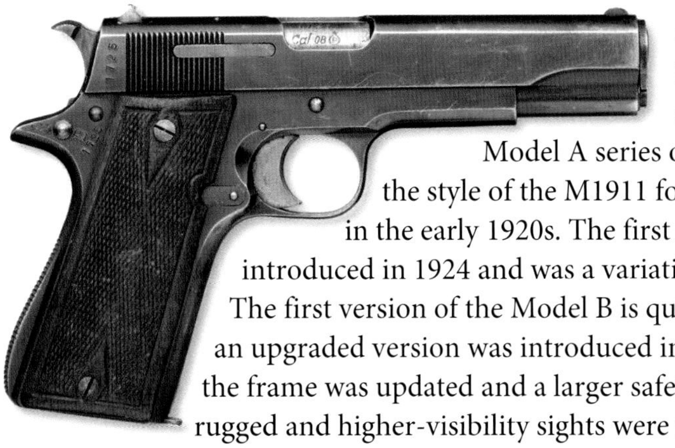

Star's Model B series was a continuation of the Model A series of pistols designed in the style of the M1911 for the Guardia Civil in the early 1920s. The first Model B pistol was introduced in 1924 and was a variation of the Model A. The first version of the Model B is quite rare today and an upgraded version was introduced in 1931. The style of the frame was updated and a larger safety as well as more rugged and higher-visibility sights were fitted. This model was to remain in service until 1983. Some specially designated Model B pistols were issued to German forces during World War II.

## Star Model D

**SPECIFICATION**

**MANUFACTURER** Star Bonifacio Echeverría S.A.
**CALIBRE** 9mm Corto (.380 ACP)
**MAGAZINE CAPACITY** 6
**ACTION** Blowback/single
**TOTAL LENGTH** 145mm/5.7in
**BARREL LENGTH** 80mm/3.15in
**WEIGHT UNLOADED** 420g/14.28oz

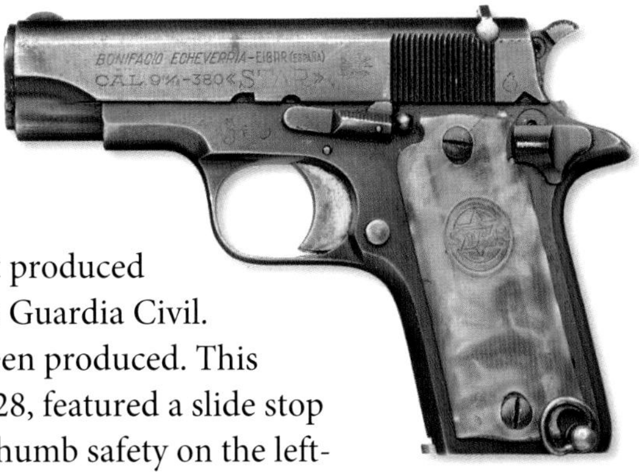

The Model D series was designed both as a weapon for personal self-defence and also as a concealable weapon for security forces. It was first produced in the 1920s and issued to the Guardia Civil. A number of variants have been produced. This version of the pistol, from 1928, featured a slide stop over the trigger and it had a thumb safety on the left-hand side of the receiver. One version of the pistol was produced in collaboration with Colt in the United States, but the partnership did not last very long and few pistols were produced.

## Star Model E

**SPECIFICATION**

**MANUFACTURER** Star Bonifacio Echeverría S.A.
**CALIBRE** 6.35mm (.25 ACP)
**MAGAZINE CAPACITY** Not known
**ACTION** Blowback/single
**TOTAL LENGTH** 102mm/4in
**BARREL LENGTH** 51mm/2in
**WEIGHT UNLOADED** Not known

**Starlite**
A series of pistols, known as Starlite, were produced in the 1990s and have similar features to the Model E series.

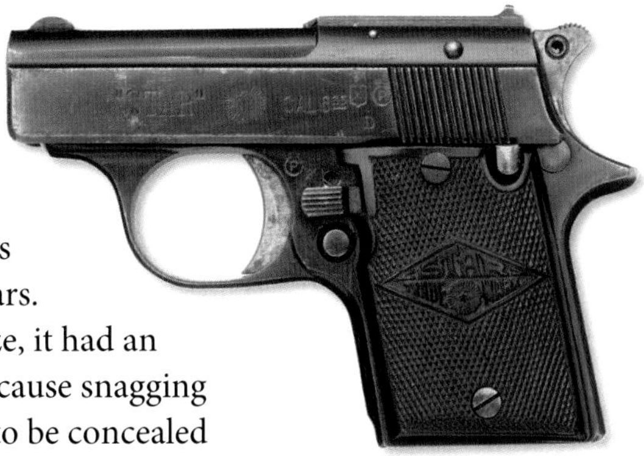

Pistols in the Star Model E series were the smallest of the Star "vest pocket" pistols. This subcompact pistol was first introduced in 1925 and was in production for nearly ten years. Unusually for a pistol of this size, it had an external hammer, which could cause snagging problems for a pistol designed to be concealed around the body. The slide was designed so that it did not fully hide the barrel (which keeps the weight down). A safety catch was positioned just behind the trigger guard. It had quite basic round-section front sights. The magazine release catch was also positioned behind the trigger guard, which was also very unusual for a pistol of this size. The Model E series was produced until the mid-1930s.

## Star Model F

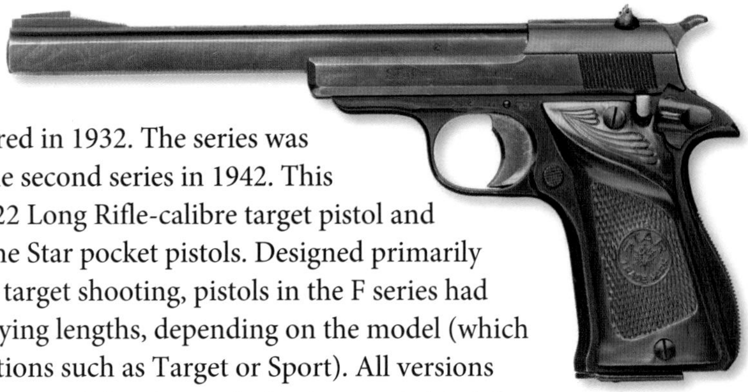

The first Model F series of Star pistols appeared in 1932. The series was updated to the second series in 1942. This pistol was a .22 Long Rifle-calibre target pistol and a variant of the Star pocket pistols. Designed primarily for sport and target shooting, pistols in the F series had barrels of varying lengths, depending on the model (which include variations such as Target or Sport). All versions had adjustable rear sights. Instead of being just behind the trigger, the second Model F series had more conventional safeties, situated behind the gripframe, just behind the hammer pin.

**SPECIFICATION**

**MANUFACTURER** Star Bonifacio Echeverría S.A.
**CALIBRE** .22 Long Rifle
**MAGAZINE CAPACITY** 10
**ACTION** Blowback/single
**TOTAL LENGTH** 255mm/10.04in
**BARREL LENGTH** 180mm/7in
**WEIGHT UNLOADED** 895g/32oz

**The end of an era**
In 1983, when Star stopped producing the classic series, the whole of the model F series went out of production.

## Star Model CO

The Model CO series of pistols were small, "vest pocket" pistols produced between 1930 and the mid-1950s. In 1956 they were replaced with the Model CU series, which were manufactured up until the early 1970s. The CO and the CU were produced as single-action pistols with a fixed barrel. The layout of the Model CO was very typical of small pocket pistols. The magazine release was positioned on the left side behind the trigger guard instead of on the butt, and the safety was a small lever behind the trigger. Although numerous small changes were made to bring the Model CU up to date, the main change was to incorporate a conventional thumb safety. The gripframe was lengthened and slightly widened at the bottom and the magazine release was enlarged. The Model CK was introduced in 1973 and was in production for about ten years.

**SPECIFICATION**

**MANUFACTURER** Star Bonifacio Echeverría S.A.
**CALIBRE** .25 ACP
**MAGAZINE CAPACITY** 7
**ACTION** Blowback/single
**TOTAL LENGTH** 122mm/4.8in
**BARREL LENGTH** 60mm/2.36in
**WEIGHT UNLOADED** 420g/14.8oz

**Model COE**
The model COE ("engraved") was manufactured from mother of pearl.

## Star Model BM

This pistol was first introduced in 1972 and was a variant of the earlier Star B series, produced from 1924. It had a manual safety but it did not have a grip safety. The Model BM was a reasonably compact firearm made of steel which lended itself well to concealed carriage. Over 200,000 Star Model BM pistols were produced between 1972 and 1992 and many were exported to countries including the United States. Other models were also produced, such as the BKS, produced slightly earlier than the BM, and the BKM. Both were alloy framed and generally have not remained in as good condition as the Model BMs.

**SPECIFICATION**

**MANUFACTURER** Star Bonifacio Echeverría S.A.
**CALIBRE** 9mm Parabellum
**MAGAZINE CAPACITY** 8
**ACTION** Recoil/single
**TOTAL LENGTH** 182mm/7.17in
**BARREL LENGTH** 99mm/3.9in
**WEIGHT UNLOADED** 965g/34oz

**A popular choice**
Despite being rather heavy, the Model BM is a relatively popular handgun as it is reasonably inexpensive to purchase.

## Star Model PD Compact

| SPECIFICATION | |
|---|---|
| **MANUFACTURER** Star Bonifacio Echeverría S.A. | |
| **CALIBRE** .45 ACP | |
| **MAGAZINE CAPACITY** 6 | |
| **ACTION** Recoil/single | |
| **TOTAL LENGTH** 180mm/7.6in | |
| **BARREL LENGTH** 100mm/3.94in | |
| **WEIGHT UNLOADED** 710g/25oz | |

The Model P series was started in the 1920s and a number of variants have since been produced. This included the Model PKM in 1974, on which the Model PD is based. The Model PD was produced between 1975 and today. It was designed to be easily carried and concealed while providing considerable power. The pistol had a locking system similar to a Browning design but with only one interlocking lug between barrel and slide. An internal plastic buffer had been added to reduce the effects of recoil. The frame was of light alloy and the rear sight was adjustable. The pistol had a manual safety but no grip safety.

## Star Firestar M43

| SPECIFICATION | |
|---|---|
| **MANUFACTURER** Star Bonifacio Echeverría S.A. | |
| **CALIBRE** 9mm Parabellum | |
| **MAGAZINE CAPACITY** 7 | |
| **ACTION** Recoil/single | |
| **TOTAL LENGTH** 165mm/6.5in | |
| **BARREL LENGTH** 86mm/3.4in | |
| **WEIGHT UNLOADED** 855g/30.2oz | |

The Firestar series was a group of small, compact pistols designed for concealed carry. The M43 had a short-barrel recoil and Browning-style locking. It was fitted with an automatic firing-pin safety and a magazine disconnect safety. It also had a frame-mounted ambidextrous safety lever. The pistol could be carried "cocked and locked". It was, however, quite heavy being manufactured from solid steel. There were two other pistols in the Firestar series – the M40 and the M45 – which were double-action pistols with a similar frame-mounted ambidextrous safety that also allowed for "cocked-and-locked" carry. The M40 was chambered for the .40 S&W cartridge and the M45 for the .45 ACP cartridge, and both carried six rounds.

## Star Model 30M

| SPECIFICATION | |
|---|---|
| **MANUFACTURER** Star Bonifacio Echeverría S.A. | |
| **CALIBRE** 9mm Parabellum | |
| **MAGAZINE CAPACITY** 15 | |
| **ACTION** Recoil/double | |
| **TOTAL LENGTH** 205mm/8.1in | |
| **BARREL LENGTH** 119mm/4.69in | |
| **WEIGHT UNLOADED** 1,140g/40.21oz | |

**Use in the services**
The Model 30M was issued to the Navy, Marines and Air Force as well as to the Guardia Civil and the national police.

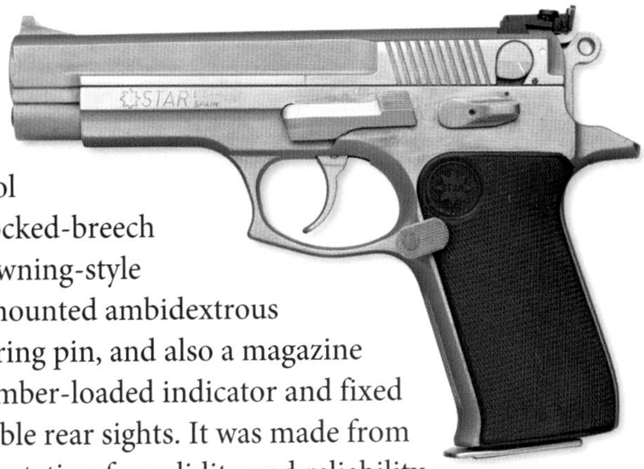

The Star Model 30M was the main pistol in a series beginning with the Model 28. This pistol was a recoil-operated locked-breech pistol that featured Browning-style locking. It had a slide-mounted ambidextrous safety that locked the firing pin, and also a magazine safety. It also had a chamber-loaded indicator and fixed front sights and adjustable rear sights. It was made from solid steel and had a reputation for solidity and reliability. The Star Model 30M was produced in 1990. The Model 31 was an updated version of the 30M and incorporated a number of both external and internal modifications, for example to the safety lever and to the extractor mechanism.

## Campo-Giro Model 1913

This pistol was a development of a design first conceived by Venancio Lopez de Ceballos y Aguirre, a retired Lieutenant-Colonel and Count of Conde del Campo Giro. The first demonstration model was produced in Oviedo in 1903. In 1910, 25 prototypes were completed and in 1912 the pistol was adopted as the 9mm Campo-Giro pistol, known as the Model 1913 and issued to the Army. Various modifications had been made to the design and it was revised again in 1921. The pistol had some design failings and in due course it was thoroughly revised and renamed the Astra 400.

| SPECIFICATION | |
|---|---|
| **MANUFACTURER** | Esperanza y Unceta |
| **CALIBRE** | 9mm Largo |
| **MAGAZINE CAPACITY** | 8 |
| **ACTION** | Blowback/single |
| **TOTAL LENGTH** | 237mm/9.33in |
| **BARREL LENGTH** | 165mm/6.5in |
| **WEIGHT UNLOADED** | 950g/33.5oz |

## Astra Model 400

In 1920 the Campo-Giro Model 1913 was phased out as the Army issue model. The Astra 400, an improved version of this pistol, was selected to replace it. The Astra 400 was produced between 1921 and 1950. It was an adaptable pistol that could fire the powerful 9mm Largo cartridge as well as a variety of other 9mm cartridges, which made it unique. It had a safety catch on the left just behind the trigger guard. The Astra 400 was used by both sides in the Spanish Civil War (1936–39) and by German forces in World War II.

| SPECIFICATION | |
|---|---|
| **MANUFACTURER** | Esperanza y Unceta |
| **CALIBRE** | 9mm Largo |
| **MAGAZINE CAPACITY** | 8 |
| **ACTION** | Blowback/single |
| **TOTAL LENGTH** | 225mm/8.86in |
| **BARREL LENGTH** | 150mm/5.91in |
| **WEIGHT UNLOADED** | 1,140g/40.21oz |

## Astra Model 300

This pistol was essentially a smaller version of the Astra 400 and was produced in 1922. It had the same tubular slide which also acted as a breech block, and it had three lugs on the barrel. It was fitted with a grip safety and had an internal hammer. The Astra 300 was largely issued to security guards in Spain, and large numbers were also purchased by the German armed forces.

| SPECIFICATION | |
|---|---|
| **MANUFACTURER** | Esperanza y Unceta |
| **CALIBRE** | 7.65mm (.32 ACP) |
| **MAGAZINE CAPACITY** | 8 |
| **ACTION** | Blowback/single |
| **TOTAL LENGTH** | 162mm/6.38in |
| **BARREL LENGTH** | 102mm/4in |
| **WEIGHT UNLOADED** | 623.69g/22oz |

## Astra Model 600

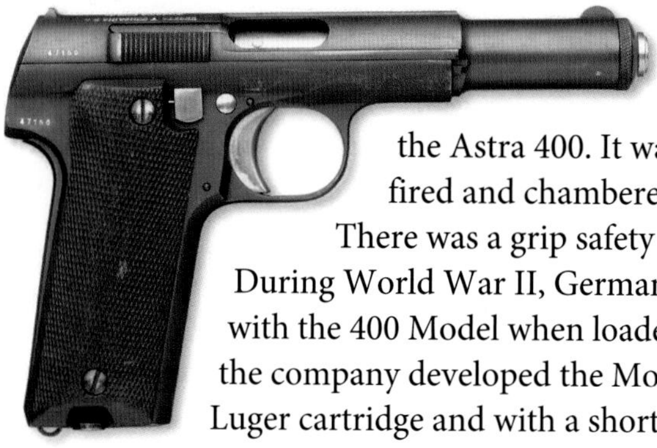

This pistol first appeared in 1943. It was a more compact version of the Astra 400. It was blowback operated, hammer-fired and chambered for the 9mm Luger cartridge. There was a grip safety at the back of the hand grip. During World War II, German troops encountered problems with the 400 Model when loaded with 9mm ammunition, so the company developed the Model 600 chambered for the 9mm Luger cartridge and with a shorter barrel and slide.

| SPECIFICATION | |
|---|---|
| **MANUFACTURER** | Astra-Unceta y Cia S.A. |
| **CALIBRE** | 9mm Luger |
| **MAGAZINE CAPACITY** | 8 |
| **ACTION** | Blowback/single |
| **TOTAL LENGTH** | 205mm/8.1in |
| **BARREL LENGTH** | 133mm/5.25in |
| **WEIGHT UNLOADED** | 905g/31.92oz |

## Astra Model 900

**SPECIFICATION**

- **MANUFACTURER** Astra-Unceta y Cia S.A.
- **CALIBRE** 7.63mm
- **MAGAZINE CAPACITY** 10
- **ACTION** Recoil/single
- **TOTAL LENGTH** 310mm/12.1in
- **BARREL LENGTH** 160mm/6.3in
- **WEIGHT UNLOADED** 1,360g/48oz

This pistol was first introduced in 1927 and was said to have been inspired by the model 1896 "Broomhandle". It had a separate barrel-return spring that lay in a frame below the chamber. The bolt lock was pinned to the barrel extension and engaged the bolt via a spring-loaded bar. Both bolt and barrel recoil together and the bolt cocked the hammer. On its movement back into position, the bolt chambered a new round. The Astra Model 900 was issued to Spanish internal forces such as the Guardia Civil and it had some success abroad.

## Astra 2000 (Cub)

**SPECIFICATION**

- **MANUFACTURER** Astra-Unceta y Cia S.A.
- **CALIBRE** 6.35mm (.25 ACP)
- **MAGAZINE CAPACITY** 6
- **ACTION** Blowback/single
- **TOTAL LENGTH** 112mm/4.41in
- **BARREL LENGTH** 57mm/2.24in
- **WEIGHT UNLOADED** 354g/12.5oz

This pistol was a development of the Astra Model 200, a small-calibre pistol first introduced in 1920 that remained in service for about 70 years. The Astra 2000 was made after World War II and was sturdy and reliable. It had an external hammer and, unlike the Model 200, it had no grip safety.

## Astra Model 4000

**SPECIFICATION**

- **MANUFACTURER** Astra-Unceta y Cia S.A.
- **CALIBRE** 7.65mm (.32 ACP)
- **MAGAZINE CAPACITY** 7
- **ACTION** Blowback/single
- **TOTAL LENGTH** 164mm/6.46in
- **BARREL LENGTH** 99mm/3.9in
- **WEIGHT UNLOADED** 646g/22.79oz

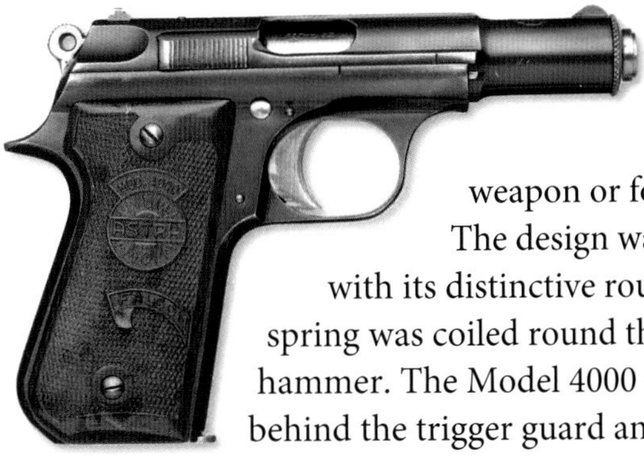

This pistol was introduced after World War II and was designed primarily as a personal defence weapon or for use in the second line of defence. The design was rooted in the Campo-Giro 1913, with its distinctive round barrel and receiver. The return spring was coiled round the barrel and the pistol had a visible hammer. The Model 4000 was fitted with a manual safety behind the trigger guard and also had a magazine safety.

## Llama Model 8

**SPECIFICATION**

- **MANUFACTURER** Llama-Gabilondo y Cia S.A.
- **CALIBRE** 9mm
- **MAGAZINE CAPACITY** 15
- **ACTION** Recoil/single
- **TOTAL LENGTH** 209mm/8.23in
- **BARREL LENGTH** 114mm/4.5in
- **WEIGHT UNLOADED** 875g/30.86oz

This pistol was first produced in 1986 and issued to the Spanish armed forces. It had a similar system to the German Walther P38, whereby breech locking was performed by a dropping block. The barrel remained fixed and the safety catch was mounted on the slide. The pistol was loaded with the safety in the "safe" position, the magazine was then inserted and the slide drawn back to feed a round into the chamber. Once the safety was moved to "fire", the movement on the trigger cocked and released the hammer. Subsequent shots were fired in single-action mode.

# United Kingdom

**Small-arms manufacture in the UK in the late 19th and early 20th centuries was centred largely around the independent firm of Webley, later Webley & Scott, and the British Government's Royal Small Arms Factory at Enfield. Webley started producing weapons for the British Army from 1887 and continued to supply a variety of revolvers through the hey-day of the Empire. Between World War I and World War II, production moved to Enfield, which created some friction over what Webley claimed as their own designs. The Enfield No. 2 revolver, based on the Webley Mark VI, remained the standard British service sidearm until the advent of the Browning High-Power automatic pistol.**

## Lancaster Oval Bore

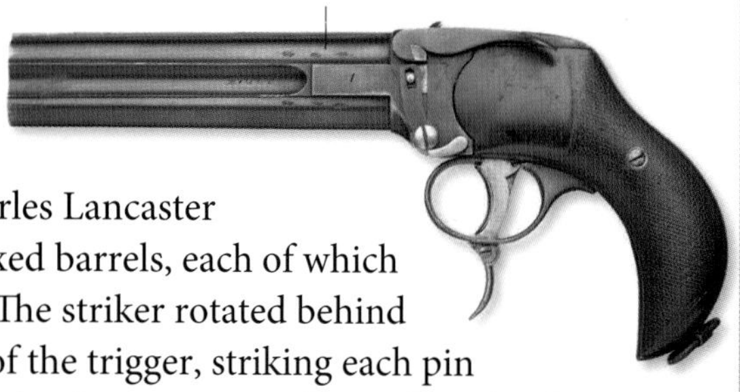


This pistol was designed and produced by London barrel-maker Charles Lancaster in the 1870s. It had four fixed barrels, each of which had a firing pin behind it. The striker rotated behind the firing pin at each pull of the trigger, striking each pin in turn. The pistol could be broken open on a hinge for reloading.

**SPECIFICATION**

**MANUFACTURER** Charles Lancaster
**CALIBRE** .455 Webley
**MAGAZINE CAPACITY** 4
**ACTION** Double
**TOTAL LENGTH** 248mm/9.75in
**BARREL LENGTH** 152mm/6in
**WEIGHT UNLOADED** 1,247g/44oz

## Webley RIC (Royal Irish Constabulary) 1872

James Webley set up a business making revolvers in Birmingham in the 1830s. Webley's first official contract was for the Royal Irish Constabulary (RIC), which was adopted by police and military forces throughout Europe. The 1872 model was a civilian version of this revolver. It was a solid-frame revolver and the cylinder was loaded through a gate on the left-hand side. An ejector rod was positioned underneath the barrel. The revolver was designed to be easily concealed and had a short barrel. The .450 Webley built a reputation for reliability, in both its service and commercial models.

**SPECIFICATION**

**MANUFACTURER** P. Webley & Sons
**CALIBRE** .450 Eley
**CYLINDER** 6
**ACTION** Double-action only (DAO)
**TOTAL LENGTH** 203mm/8in
**BARREL LENGTH** 82mm/3.23in
**WEIGHT UNLOADED** 700g/24.7oz

## Enfield Mark II

**SPECIFICATION**

**MANUFACTURER** Royal Small Arms Factory, Enfield
**CALIBRE** .476 Eley
**CYLINDER** 6
**ACTION** Double
**TOTAL LENGTH** 805mm/12in
**BARREL LENGTH** 152mm/6in
**WEIGHT UNLOADED** 1,150g/40.6oz

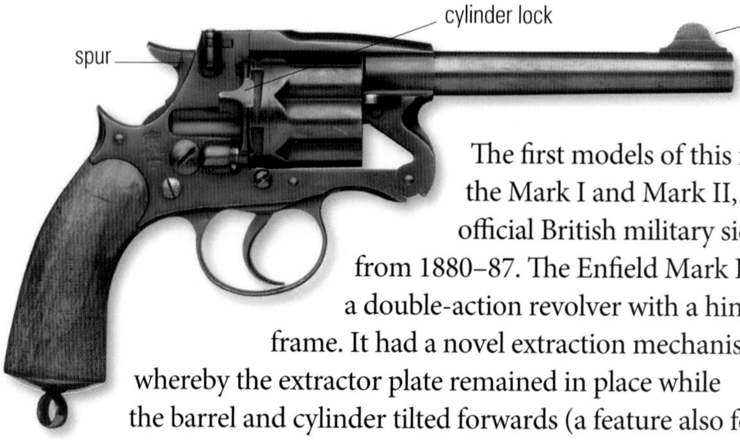


The first models of this revolver, the Mark I and Mark II, were official British military sidearms from 1880–87. The Enfield Mark II was a double-action revolver with a hinged frame. It had a novel extraction mechanism whereby the extractor plate remained in place while the barrel and cylinder tilted forwards (a feature also found on Webleys). A rounded front sight and a cylinder lock prevented movement of the cylinder when the revolver was in its holster.

## Webley Mark I

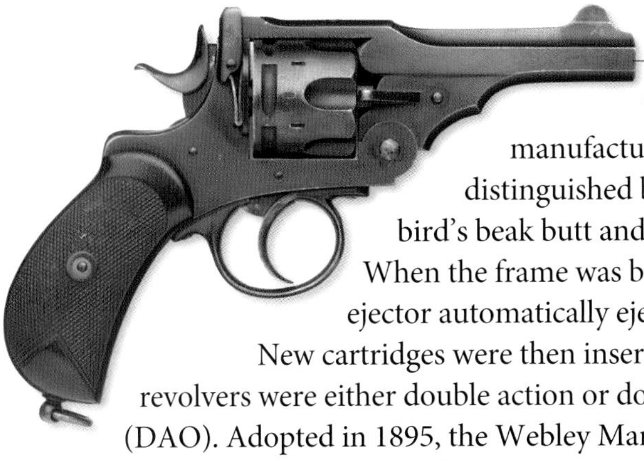


This revolver, first manufactured in 1887, could be distinguished by its hinged frame, bird's beak butt and four-inch barrel. When the frame was broken open, the ejector automatically ejected the empty cases. New cartridges were then inserted by hand. Webley revolvers were either double action or double-action only (DAO). Adopted in 1895, the Webley Mark II was almost the same as the Mark I, but with hammer and grip modifications.

**SPECIFICATION**

**MANUFACTURER** P. Webley & Sons
**CALIBRE** .455 Webley
**CYLINDER** 6
**ACTION** Selective double
**TOTAL LENGTH** 260mm/10.23in
**BARREL LENGTH** 102mm/4in
**WEIGHT UNLOADED** 995g/36oz

## Webley Mark III

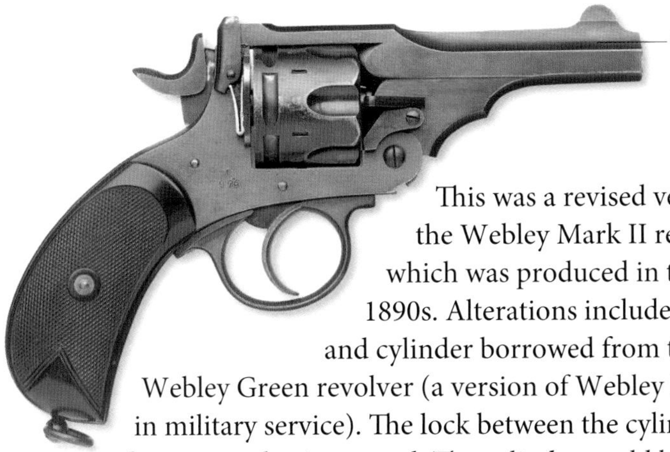


This was a revised version of the Webley Mark II revolver which was produced in the mid-1890s. Alterations included a barrel and cylinder borrowed from the 1892 Webley Green revolver (a version of Webley Mark I used in military service). The lock between the cylinder and the frame was also improved. The cylinder could be removed for maintenance. The introduction of Mark IV (1899), known as the "Boar War" model, and Mark V (1913) made further small improvements in design and materials including changes to accept smokeless (cordite) ammunition.

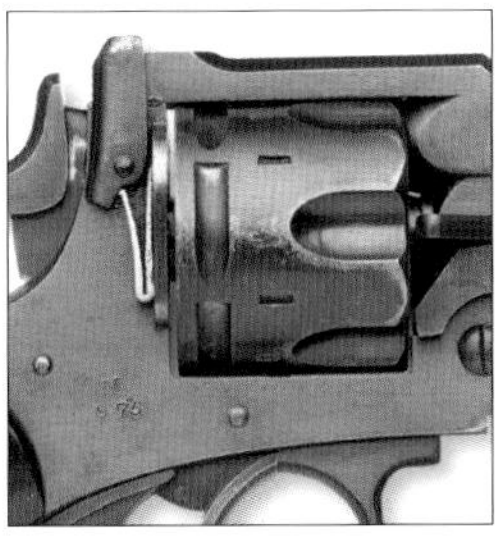

**LEFT** The Mark III was an updated edition of Mark I with an an improved cylinder-to-frame lock.

**SPECIFICATION**

**MANUFACTURER** P. Webley & Sons
**CALIBRE** .455 Webley
**CYLINDER** 6
**ACTION** Selective double
**TOTAL LENGTH** 260mm/10.23in
**BARREL LENGTH** 102mm/4in
**WEIGHT UNLOADED** 995g/36oz

## Webley Mark VI

**SPECIFICATION**

**MANUFACTURER** P. Webley & Sons
**CALIBRE** .455 Webley
**CYLINDER** 6
**ACTION** Selective double
**TOTAL LENGTH** 286mm/11.25in
**BARREL LENGTH** 152mm/6in
**WEIGHT UNLOADED** 1,075g/37.9oz

This version of the Webley was first produced in 1915 and remained in service through to World War II. In many respects, it was similar to the Webley Mark V, first produced in 1913. The Mark VI was a top-breaking revolver, opened by a pivoting lever on the side of the receiver. The hand grip was altered from a bird's beak design to a squared style. This revolver was issued to the British and Commonwealth forces. It was used throughout World War I and stood up well to the mud and dirt in the trenches. A short bayonet was also designed and proved useful, although it was never officially adopted. The Webley Mark VI was considered the ultimate Webley until the arrival of the Enfield No. 2 Mark I in the 1930s. The Mark VI was manufactured until 1921 but became obsolete during the next decade.

## Webley-Fosbery Model 1901

The Webley-Fosbery was designed by Lieutenant-Colonel George Vincent Fosbery, VC, and was based on patents from 1896. It was produced by the Webley & Scott company from 1901 to 1915. The revolver was a mixture of ideas between Webley and Fosbery and it incorporated ideas that had appeared in the semi-automatic pistol, particularly making use of the recoil energy to both turn the cylinder and recock the weapon. During this movement a stud on the frame was engaged in the grooves on the cylinder; the movement caused the cylinder to be rotated during each stroke. The turning of the cylinder was completed by the return movement of the barrel unit, operated by a spring, and a new round was aligned for firing. The recoil action had the effect of absorbing recoil and therefore improving accuracy. The revolver was reliable, but proved expensive to produce.

**SPECIFICATION**

**MANUFACTURER** Webley & Scott Revolver Arms Co.
**CALIBRE** .455
**CYLINDER** 6
**ACTION** Recoil/single
**TOTAL LENGTH** 267mm/10.5in
**BARREL LENGTH** 152mm/6in (various available)
**WEIGHT UNLOADED** 1,155g/40.8oz

## Webley-Fosbery Model 1902

This was a revised version of the Webley-Fosbery 1901. The Webley-Fosbery models had quickly proved popular among target-shooters. The trigger mechanism did not rotate, which meant that the cylinder shots were smooth and consistent. This allowed rapid and accurate shooting. The Webley-Fosbery was never adopted as an official government sidearm, although many were privately purchased by British officers before and during World War I. However, production of the model ceased during this time.

**SPECIFICATION**

**MANUFACTURER** Webley & Scott Revolver Arms Co.
**CALIBRE** .38 ACP
**CYLINDER** 8
**ACTION** Single
**TOTAL LENGTH** 267mm/10.5in
**BARREL LENGTH** 152mm/6in
**WEIGHT UNLOADED** 1,065g/37.6oz

## Webley & Scott 1905/1906

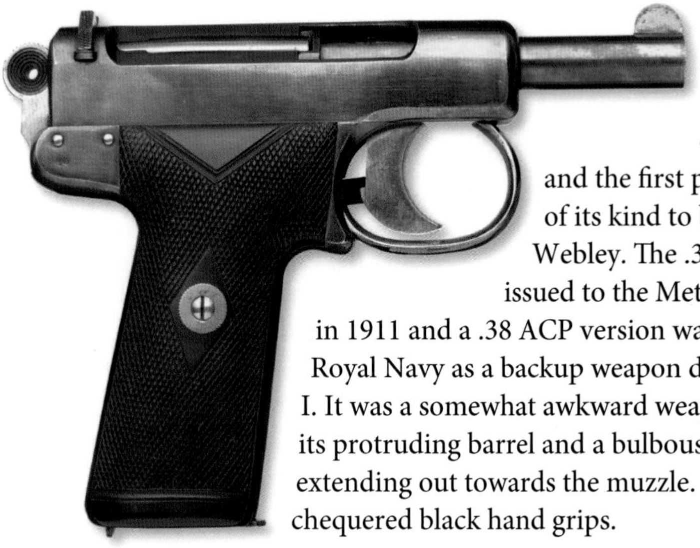

This was a blowback-operated pistol and the first production model of its kind to be offered by Webley. The .32 ACP pistol was issued to the Metropolitan Police in 1911 and a .38 ACP version was issued to the Royal Navy as a backup weapon during World War I. It was a somewhat awkward weapon to use, with its protruding barrel and a bulbous trigger guard extending out towards the muzzle. It had distinctive chequered black hand grips.

**SPECIFICATION**

**MANUFACTURER** Webley & Scott Revolver Arms Co.
**CALIBRE** .32 ACP
**MAGAZINE CAPACITY** 8
**ACTION** Blowback/single
**TOTAL LENGTH** 159mm/6.25in
**BARREL LENGTH** 89mm/3.5in
**WEIGHT UNLOADED** 565g/20oz

## Webley & Scott Mark I

| SPECIFICATION | |
|---|---|
| MANUFACTURER | Webley & Scott Revolver Arms Co. |
| CALIBRE | .455 Webley Auto |
| MAGAZINE CAPACITY | 7 |
| ACTION | Recoil/single |
| TOTAL LENGTH | 216mm/8.5in |
| BARREL LENGTH | 127mm/5in |
| WEIGHT UNLOADED | 1,110g/39.2oz |

This was a recoil-operated automatic pistol produced in the early 20th century. It was fitted with a safety system that could hold the hammer at full cock. It could be fitted with a shoulder stock for greater control when aiming and firing. The pistol was issued to members of the Royal Flying Corps, the theory being that pilots would occasionally have the opportunity to fire at their opponents with a handgun. It was also issued to the Royal Horse Artillery, although it was said that the mechanism was prone to jamming in dirty conditions, which made it an impractical weapon for combat duties.

## Webley & Scott Mark IV

| SPECIFICATION | |
|---|---|
| MANUFACTURER | Webley & Scott Revolver Arms Co. |
| CALIBRE | .38/200 (.38 S&W) |
| CYLINDER | 6 |
| ACTION | Double |
| TOTAL LENGTH | 257mm/10.12in |
| BARREL LENGTH | 152mm/6in |
| WEIGHT UNLOADED | 735g/26oz |

This revolver was a British double-action military revolver first designed in 1923. The revolver used the same extraction system as the Webley .455 service revolvers, and this was produced as a scaled-down version of these models. The Webley .38 Mark IV was produced until 1945 and was in service with the British Army from 1929 to 1956 becoming obsolete in the 1960s. The demands of manufacturing guns for World War II were too great for the three factories making the Enfield revolver and the army bought supplies of the Mark IV from Webley & Scott.

## Enfield No. 2 Mark I

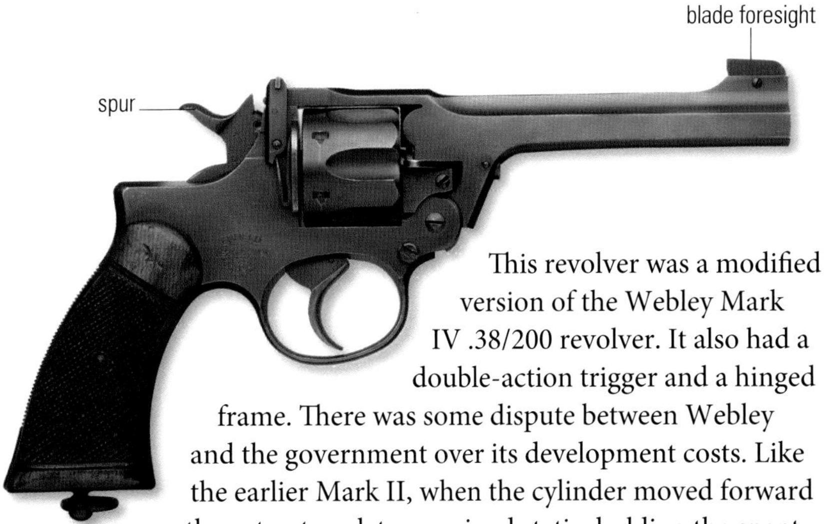


| SPECIFICATION | |
|---|---|
| MANUFACTURER | Royal Small Arms Factory, Enfield |
| CALIBRE | .38/200 (.38 S&W) |
| CYLINDER | 6 |
| ACTION | Double-action only (DAO) |
| TOTAL LENGTH | 260mm/10.23in |
| BARREL LENGTH | 127mm/5in |
| WEIGHT UNLOADED | 780g/27.5oz |

**Modified Webley**
The vast majority of Mark I revolvers were modified to Mark I*. They reverted to a spurless hammer to make them more serviceable in action.

This revolver was a modified version of the Webley Mark IV .38/200 revolver. It also had a double-action trigger and a hinged frame. There was some dispute between Webley and the government over its development costs. Like the earlier Mark II, when the cylinder moved forward the extractor plate remained static, holding the spent cartridges. The hammer spur was removed to prevent it catching on the controls or cables inside armoured fighting vehicles in versions called Mark I* (1938). The .38 Enfield No. 2 Mark I was in service from 1932 and large numbers were sent to Free French Forces during World War II. The Mark I** version appeared between 1942 and 1945.

# France

**The French small-arms industry has a long and distinguished history. Development and production have taken place across a number of state factories, including Manufacture d'Armes de St Etienne (MAS), Manufacture d'Armes de Bayonne (MAB), Manufacture des Machines du Haut-Rhin (Manurhin). The French police were issued with the Manurhin MR-93 from 1993.**

## Automatique Française

This pistol, first produced before 1914, was based on a Mannlicher design and had a slide with arms that lay alongside the barrel. At the front the arms joined and held the return spring. The barrel was mostly exposed. The pistol had an unusual appearance, with a deep butt, which was fitted with a heavily stylized grip. The hand grip included a grip safety and there was a magazine release button at the base. The manufacturer, the Société Française d'Armes Automatiques de Saint Etienne, went out of business before the end of World War I.

**SPECIFICATION**

**MANUFACTURER** Société Française d'Armes Automatiques de Saint Etienne
**CALIBRE** 6.35mm (.25 ACP)
**MAGAZINE CAPACITY** 6
**ACTION** Blowback/single
**TOTAL LENGTH** 120mm/4.72in
**BARREL LENGTH** 60mm/2.36in
**WEIGHT UNLOADED** 315g/11.1oz

## MAB D

The company Manufacture d'Armes de Bayonne brought into production in 1933 a pistol based on the Browning 1910. This was a blowback-operated pistol with a recoil spring set around the barrel. It had a single-action trigger. After the occupation of France by the Germans in 1939, some MAB Ds were issued in considerable numbers to German forces. The German-issue pistols were marked "Pistole MAB Kaliber 7.65 m". The MAB D had been designed primarily for police use but it was regarded as a robust and accurate weapon that could be used for relatively short-range defence in military operations.

**SPECIFICATION**

**MANUFACTURER** Manufacture d'Armes de Bayonne (MAB)
**CALIBRE** 7.65mm (.32 ACP)
**MAGAZINE CAPACITY** 9
**ACTION** Blowback/single
**TOTAL LENGTH** 176mm/6.9in
**BARREL LENGTH** 103mm/4.06in
**WEIGHT UNLOADED** 725g/25.57oz

## SACM M1935A

The development of the M1935A followed a protracted series of trials by the French authorities, begun in 1922, to find a replacement for the obsolete weapons then in service. Pistol trials held in 1933 yielded no satisfactory candidates. The process was repeated in 1935 with four contenders, out of which the SACM pistol was selected. The M1935 was essentially a modified Browning Colt M1911. It featured a removable unit comprising the hammer, hammer spring, ejector and sear. A safety catch was also added on the side as well as a magazine safety. One factor that limited distribution of this weapon outside France was the unique 7.65mm Long French cartridge, which was not compatible with weapons manufactured outside France.

**SPECIFICATION**

**MANUFACTURER** Société Alsacienne de Construction Mécanique (SACM)
**CALIBRE** 7.65mm Long French
**MAGAZINE CAPACITY** 8
**ACTION** Short recoil/single
**TOTAL LENGTH** 189mm/7.45in
**BARREL LENGTH** 109mm/4.29in
**WEIGHT UNLOADED** 730g/25.75oz

## MAC M1935S

**SPECIFICATION**

**MANUFACTURER** Manufacture d'Armes de Châtellerault (MAC)
**CALIBRE** 7.65mm French Long
**MAGAZINE CAPACITY** 8
**ACTION** Short recoil/single
**TOTAL LENGTH** 189mm/7.45in
**BARREL LENGTH** 109mm/4.29in
**WEIGHT UNLOADED** 730g/25.75oz

Following the introduction of the M1935A, demand from the French military was such that SACM was unable to meet it on its own. The military therefore ordered one of the unsuccessful contenders in the competition, Manufacture d'Armes de Châtellerault (MAC), to produce its pistol, designated the M1935S. In this version the locking system on the barrel was changed. The visible difference was that the butt was straight and the muzzle slightly protruded. By 1938, the M1935S was the primary production model, although SACM continued to manufacture the M1935A. Although 10,000 of the M1935S were ordered, with production starting in February 1939, France was overtaken by invasion before anything like this number could be produced. Only about 1,400 came off the production line and none was manufactured during the Occupation (1940 to 1944).

## Unique Kriegsmodell

**SPECIFICATION**

**MANUFACTURER** Manufacture d'Armes des Pyrénées d'Hendaye
**CALIBRE** 7.65mm (.32 ACP)
**MAGAZINE CAPACITY** 10
**ACTION** Blowback/single
**TOTAL LENGTH** 150mm/5.91in
**BARREL LENGTH** 80mm/3.15in
**WEIGHT UNLOADED** 652g/23oz

**Kriegsmodell 17**
Developed by the Germans, the Kriegsmodell 17 had the addition of a hammer and a curved grip frame.

This pistol was a single-action blowback-operated pistol which was manufactured in Hendaye during the German Occupation in World War II. It was modified by the Germans and the replacement was known as the Kriegsmodell 17, and over 25,000 were produced before France was liberated in 1944. The slide did not have positive locking and neither did it stay to the rear once the last cartridge had been fired. The pistol featured a safety catch on the left side of the frame which doubled as a means for dismantling the weapon. A magazine safety prevented the pistol from being fired unless a magazine was inserted. The magazine release catch was located at the back of the frame.

## MAC M1950

**SPECIFICATION**

**MANUFACTURER** Manufacture d'Armes de St Etienne (MAS) & Châtellerault (MAC)
**CALIBRE** 9mm Parabellum
**MAGAZINE CAPACITY** 9
**ACTION** Short recoil/single
**TOTAL LENGTH** 195mm/7.67in
**BARREL LENGTH** 112mm/4.41in
**WEIGHT UNLOADED** 860g/30.34oz

In 1946 the French Army General Staff called for a new pistol to replace all current in-service pistols, partly in order to rationalize the various calibres. After a series of tests, the pistol submitted by Manufacture d'Armes de Saint Etienne (MAS) was adopted. This pistol was a development of the M1935S, with a short-recoil operation. The new pistol retained the cross-bolt safety as well as the magazine safety of the M1935S. The hammer could be lowered when the pistol was set to "safe" as the safety prevented the hammer from striking the firing pin. Although the pistol was originally designed by Manufacture d'Armes de Saint Etienne (MAS), much of the initial production run came from Manufacture d'Armes de Châtellerault (MAC). From 1961, however, production reverted to MAS.

## MAB PA-15

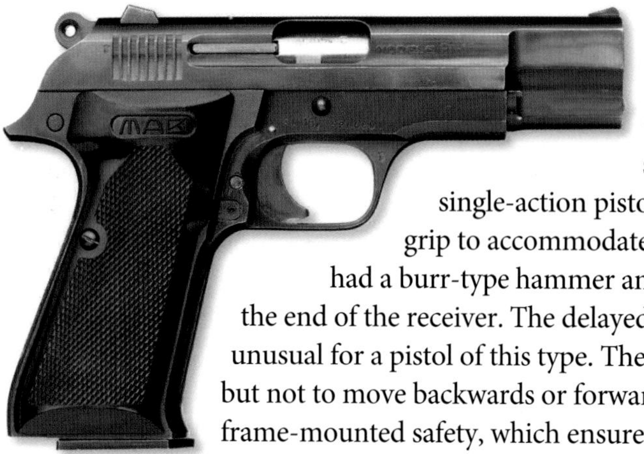

This pistol was a French attempt at the 9mm Parabellum market that was moderately successful. It was a single-action pistol and had a bulky hand grip to accommodate the wider magazine. It had a burr-type hammer and a prominent spur at the end of the receiver. The delayed blowback action was unusual for a pistol of this type. The barrel was able to rotate but not to move backwards or forwards. The PA-15 had a frame-mounted safety, which ensured the gun could not be fired when the magazine was removed. The MAB PA-15 was introduced in 1952 and bought for some sections of the French Army and the Finnish Border Police. It went out of production in the late 1980s.

**SPECIFICATION**

**MANUFACTURER** Manufacture d'Armes de Bayonne (MAB)
**CALIBRE** 9mm Parabellum
**MAGAZINE CAPACITY** 15
**ACTION** Delayed blowback/single
**TOTAL LENGTH** 203mm/8in
**BARREL LENGTH** 114mm/4.5in
**WEIGHT UNLOADED** 1,090g/38.45oz

**No competition**
Because of its single action the PA-15 was not able to be a potential competitor to the Czech CZ75.

## Manurhin MR73

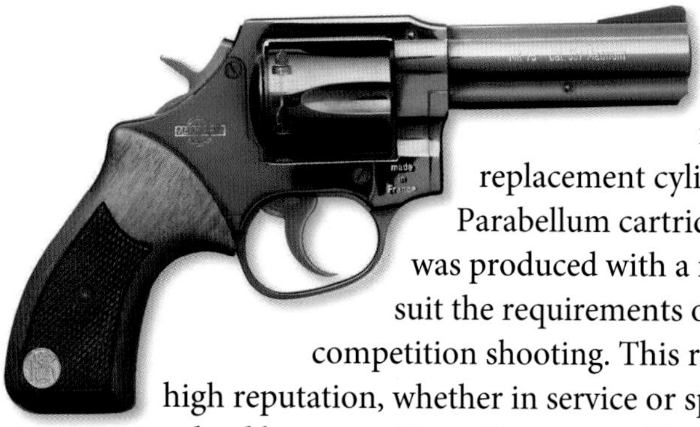

This was an adaptable, compact double-action revolver, which could fire two types of round, a replacement cylinder being fitted for the Parabellum cartridge. Developed in 1973, it was produced with a range of barrel lengths, to suit the requirements of either military, police or competition shooting. This revolver soon achieved a high reputation, whether in service or sporting use, being equally valued by competition shooters and by elite military and police units. The action was regarded as one of the smoothest and lightest available and the construction was of high quality. The cold-hammering production process of the barrel, for instance, was said to produce longer wear as well as improving precision.

**Special operations**
This revolver was issued not only to the French Police but also to elite units that undertook special operations.

**SPECIFICATION**

**MANUFACTURER** Manufacture des Machines du Haut-Rhin (Manurhin)
**CALIBRE** .357 Magnum, 9mm Parabellum
**CYLINDER** 6
**ACTION** Double
**TOTAL LENGTH** 195mm/7.67in
**BARREL LENGTH** 64mm/2.5in
**WEIGHT UNLOADED** 1,090g/38.45oz

## MAS GI

This pistol was essentially the same as the Beretta M92, which used a short recoil operating system. Produced in the 1970s it had a double-action trigger system, and a short recoil system. This system used a falling locking block which was driven down to disengage the slide from the barrel and arrest the barrel as it moved backwards. Unlike the Italian Beretta M92, it did not have a manual safety using a decking lever instead. The magazine release was located at the bottom of the hand grip. A controversial issue for the MAS GI was the material used in the manufacture of the slide. For the MAS GI, this included a mineral called tellurium, which was hard though brittle and prone to cracking and breaking.

**SPECIFICATION**

**MANUFACTURER** Manufacture d'Armes de Saint Etienne
**CALIBRE** 9mm Parabellum
**MAGAZINE CAPACITY** 10, 15 or 17
**ACTION** Short recoil/single or double
**TOTAL LENGTH** 217mm/8.54in
**BARREL LENGTH** 125mm/4.92in
**WEIGHT UNLOADED** 945g/32.63oz

# Belgium

**The Belgian small-arms industry is centred on the Fabrique Nationale de Herstal, otherwise known as FN Herstal, which was originally set up in 1889 to manufacture Mauser rifles. Through a highly profitable association with the American arms-designer John Moses Browning, FN Herstal went on to produce some of the most famous and long-lasting pistols of all time, including the FN Browning High-Power, designed in the first decade of the 20th century. Versions of that pistol are still current issue to various armed forces throughout the world, including Great Britain, in the first quarter of the 21st century.**

## Pieper Bayard 1908

**SPECIFICATION**

**MANUFACTURER** Anciens Établissements Pieper (AEP), Herstal
**CALIBRE** 7.65mm (.32 ACP)
**MAGAZINE CAPACITY** 6
**ACTION** Blowback/single
**TOTAL LENGTH** 125mm/4.92in
**BARREL LENGTH** 57mm/2.25in
**WEIGHT UNLOADED** 481.94g/17oz

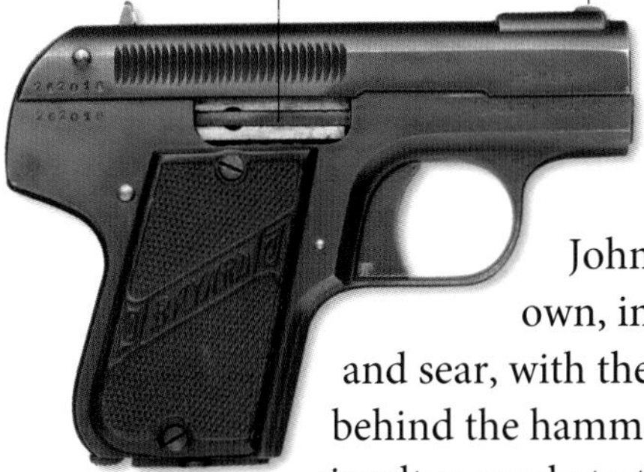


This compact pistol was designed by Bernard Clarus of the Anciens Établissements Pieper (AEP) company and was based on a system developed by John Browning. Clarus introduced ideas of his own, including a novel design for the hammer and sear, with the sear being suspended in the slide behind the hammer. The slide, hammer and sear moved simultaneously to the rear during recoil and the recoil energy was absorbed by ramps and a leaf spring. There were several variations of the 1908 pistol but the size remained identical for different calibres.

## Pieper Bayard 1923

**SPECIFICATION**

**MANUFACTURER** Anciens Établissements Pieper (AEP), Herstal
**CALIBRE** 7.65mm (.32 ACP)
**MAGAZINE CAPACITY** 6
**ACTION** Blowback/single
**TOTAL LENGTH** 149mm/5.88in
**BARREL LENGTH** 85mm/3.35in
**WEIGHT UNLOADED** 340.2g/12oz

This pistol was also designed by Bernard Clarus and was similar in design to the Browning 1910. The innovative Clarus design for the hammer and sear, with the sear being suspended in the slide behind the hammer, remained. AEP is recognized for the manufacture of Bayard pistols and their manufacture continued throughout the 1930s. It only ceased with the German invasion of Belgium in 1940, in the initial stages of World War II.

## Clement 1907

This pistol was designed by Liège gunsmith Charles Clement and was a development of his earlier highly original designs that comprised a fixed barrel and mobile bolt. As the bolt recoiled, it was restrained by a return spring via an extension. The return spring was housed above the bolt. The magazine was a detachable box carrying six rounds. The pistol was also chambered for the 6.35mm cartridge.

**SPECIFICATION**

**MANUFACTURER** Charles Ph. Clement
**CALIBRE** 7.65mm (.32 ACP), 6.35mm
**MAGAZINE CAPACITY** 6
**ACTION** Blowback/single
**TOTAL LENGTH** 150mm/5.91in
**BARREL LENGTH** 75mm/2.95in
**WEIGHT UNLOADED** 584g/20.6oz

## FN Browning M1900

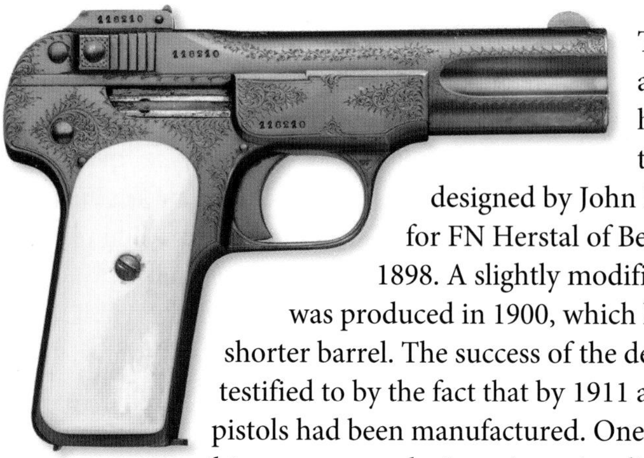

This was a single-action handgun that was designed by John Browning for FN Herstal of Belgium in 1898. A slightly modified version was produced in 1900, which had a slightly shorter barrel. The success of the design was testified to by the fact that by 1911 at least 700,000 pistols had been manufactured. One reason for this success was the ingenious simplicity of the design which reduced the number of parts to be manufactured and assembled. A feature of the pistol was a recoil spring located above the barrel and connected to the breech block by a lever.

**Model names**
This model is known by several names, including the FN M1900, FN Mle.1900 Browning M1900 and Browning No.1.

**SPECIFICATION**

**MANUFACTURER** FN Herstal
**CALIBRE** 7.65mm (.32 ACP)
**MAGAZINE CAPACITY** 7
**ACTION** Blowback/single
**TOTAL LENGTH** 170mm/6.75in
**BARREL LENGTH** 102mm/4in
**WEIGHT UNLOADED** 620g/21.87oz

## FN Browning M1903

This was an improvement on the design of the M1900 and it was manufactured not only by FN Herstal but also by Colt in the United States and by Husqvarna Vapenfabriks of Sweden. The pistol had a simple blowback mechanism and its comparatively long barrel contributed to a high level of accuracy. It had a safety catch on the left-hand side above the pistol grip. This model was produced in large numbers and became standard issue for various armed forces, including those of the United States, Belgium and Sweden.

**SPECIFICATION**

**MANUFACTURER** FN Herstal
**CALIBRE** 9mm Browning Long
**MAGAZINE CAPACITY** 7
**ACTION** Blowback/single
**TOTAL LENGTH** 203mm/8in
**BARREL LENGTH** 127mm/5in
**WEIGHT UNLOADED** 910g/32oz

## FN Browning M1910

This pistol was a development of both the M1900 and M1903 versions. A classic design, it was to continue in almost uninterrupted production until 1983. In this model the recoil spring was mounted round the barrel, which gave the weapon a different appearance to its two predecessors. In addition to the safety catch on the left side of the frame, the M1910 also had a grip safety at the back of the grip. Comparatively lightweight and relatively small, the M1910 was often used as a personal weapon and was also issued by several armed forces around the world.

**SPECIFICATION**

**MANUFACTURER** FN Herstal
**CALIBRE** 7.65mm (.32 ACP), 9mm Browning Short (.380 ACP)
**MAGAZINE CAPACITY** 7
**ACTION** Blowback/single
**TOTAL LENGTH** 152mm/6in
**BARREL LENGTH** 89mm/3.5in
**WEIGHT UNLOADED** 600g/21oz

**Assassination**
An FN M1910 was used by Gavrilo Princip to assassinate Archduke Franz Ferdinand of Austria in Sarajevo on 28 June 1914.

## FN Browning M1922

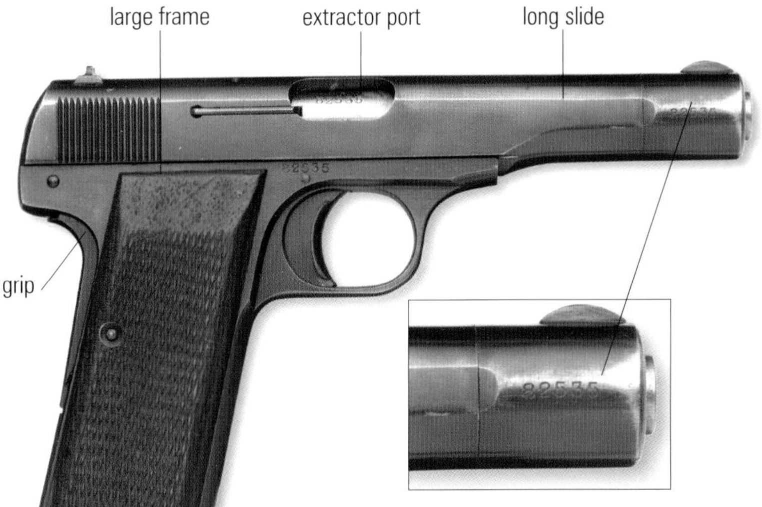


**ABOVE** The M1922 had a long slide and barrel. The jointed bayonet extension to the slide is about 20mm/1in long, spring activated and removable.

**SPECIFICATION**

**MANUFACTURER** FN Herstal
**CALIBRE** 7.65mm (.32 ACP), 9mm Browning Short (.380 ACP)
**MAGAZINE CAPACITY** 9
**ACTION** Blowback/single
**TOTAL LENGTH** 178mm/7.01in
**BARREL LENGTH** 114mm/5in
**WEIGHT UNLOADED** 730g/25.75oz

The M1922 pistol was a development of the 1910 model. For the M1922, the barrel was lengthened in order to improve accuracy and velocity. The frame size was increased and the slide lengthened. The lengthening of the slide was achieved by attaching a removable extension or nose piece. The M1922 was used widely by European military and police forces, including the Greek, Turkish, Dutch, French and Yugoslav armies. Between the two World Wars these pistols became very popular across Europe as police, military and self-defence guns. Production continued throughout World War II (where several hundred thousand were made for the Germans during their occupation of Belgium). The exceptionally long production run of this successful design lasted until 1983. In the United States both the M1910 and M1922 were imported as the Browning 380 pistol, chambered in .380 ACP. After 1971, these guns had adjustable target-type sights and bigger grips to meet US gun laws.

**Grip safety**
The grip safety of these models was primarily introduced to prevent accidental discharge – such as to prevent the gun from being fired if accidentally dropped.

## FN Browning Baby

**SPECIFICATION**

**MANUFACTURER** FN Herstal
**CALIBRE** 6.35mm (.25 ACP)
**MAGAZINE CAPACITY** 6
**ACTION** Blowback/single
**TOTAL LENGTH** 103mm/4.06in
**BARREL LENGTH** 54mm/2.13in
**WEIGHT UNLOADED** 275g/9.70oz

**Early Browning Baby**
An early version of the Browning Baby was produced in 1905, but this pistol was not manufactured officially until 1932.

This pistol was first officially produced in 1932 and was largely based on the compact 1906 model. It could be identified by its squared-off appearance, due to the fact that the frame was the same length as the slide. Its sights were fixed. Early models could also be easily identified by the name "Baby" engraved on both sides of the hand grip at the base. This version did not have a grip safety, though it had a manual safety lever under the grip. The pistol was normally used two-handed due to a very strong recoil. It was first imported into the United States in 1954.

## FN Browning High-Power M1935 (Grand Puissance 35)

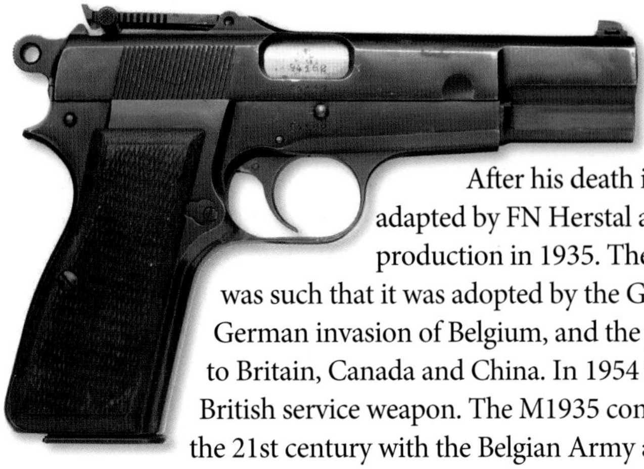

The M1935 9mm pistol was the last model to be designed by John Browning. After his death in 1926, the design was adapted by FN Herstal and only came into production in 1935. The success of the pistol was such that it was adopted by the German Army after the German invasion of Belgium, and the pistol also found its way to Britain, Canada and China. In 1954 it became the official British service weapon. The M1935 continued in service in the 21st century with the Belgian Army and Police, the British Army, and with other law enforcement agencies. It is the second-longest-serving service pistol after the Colt 1911, also designed by Browning. Plans are underway to replace it in the UK because the 9mm Parabellum round is no longer effective against the latest body armour technology.

**SPECIFICATION**

**MANUFACTURER** FN Herstal
**CALIBRE** 9mm Parabellum
**MAGAZINE CAPACITY** 13
**ACTION** Recoil/single
**TOTAL LENGTH** 197mm/7.75in
**BARREL LENGTH** 118mm/4.64in
**WEIGHT UNLOADED** 990g/34.92oz

**Today's High-Powers**
Despite its age, and the many copies and modified versions that have been produced, original Browning High-Powers are still manufactured.

## FN Browning Mark II

This is an adaptation of the Browning High-Power, one of the classic pistol designs of all time. Although it was essentially an improvement on the previous model, with a new grip and an ambidextrous safety catch, the Mark II did not go far enough in its revisions to enable it to be competitive against modern pistol designs that were coming into the market. It fell between two stools – the classic High-Power and a requirement for a truly revised version. The production run was relatively short – from about 1980 to 1987.

**SPECIFICATION**

**MANUFACTURER** FN Herstal
**CALIBRE** 9mm Parabellum
**MAGAZINE CAPACITY** 13
**ACTION** Short recoil/single
**TOTAL LENGTH** 200mm/7.87in
**BARREL LENGTH** 118mm/4.64in
**WEIGHT UNLOADED** 930g/28oz

## FN Browning Mark III

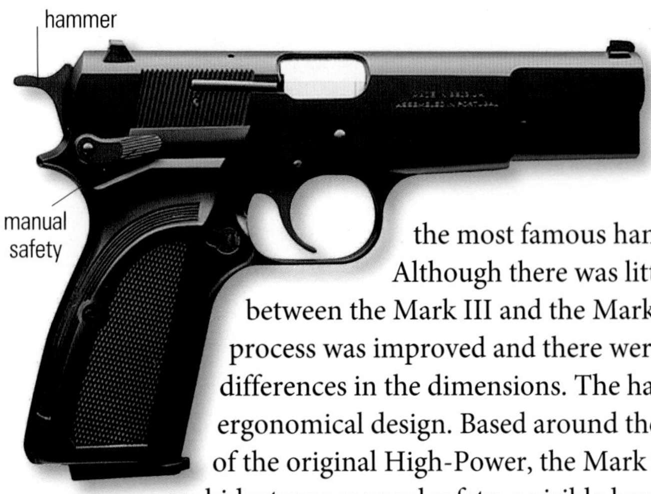


The improvements that resulted in the Browning Mark III in the 1990s finally did justice to what is arguably the most famous handgun in the world. Although there was little obvious difference between the Mark III and the Mark II, the manufacturing process was improved and there were small but significant differences in the dimensions. The hand grips had a better ergonomical design. Based around the design principles of the original High-Power, the Mark III featured a large, ambidextrous manual safety, a visible hammer, a half-cock notch that prevented the weapon firing if the hammer accidentally slipped, a firing-pin safety and a magazine safety that disengaged the trigger when the magazine was removed. Sight improvement made for quick aiming.

**SPECIFICATION**

**MANUFACTURER** FN Herstal
**CALIBRE** 9mm Parabellum
**MAGAZINE CAPACITY** 13
**ACTION** Short recoil/single
**TOTAL LENGTH** 197mm/7.75in
**BARREL LENGTH** 118mm/4.64in
**WEIGHT UNLOADED** 990g/34.92oz

**Modern techniques**
FN Herstal combined computer technology with a classic design to produce a weapon that was very competitive.

## FN BDA 380

| SPECIFICATION |
| --- |
| **MANUFACTURER** FN Herstal/Italy |
| **CALIBRE** .380 ACP |
| **MAGAZINE CAPACITY** |
| **ACTION** Blowback/double |
| **TOTAL LENGTH** 173mm/6.81in |
| **BARREL LENGTH** 50mm/1.97in |
| **WEIGHT UNLOADED** 640g/22.58oz |

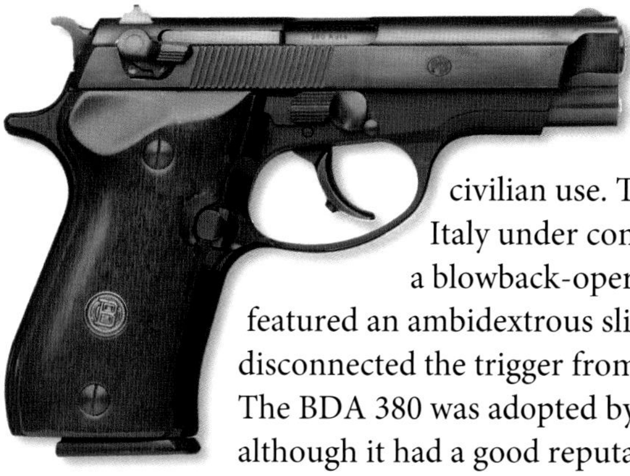

This pistol was first produced in the early 1980s and was designed for law enforcement as well as civilian use. The pistol was manufactured in Italy under contract from FN Herstal. It was a blowback-operated double-action pistol and featured an ambidextrous slide-mounted safety switch that disconnected the trigger from the hammer when engaged. The BDA 380 was adopted by the Belgian police force and, although it had a good reputation, production ceased in 1997.

## FN BDA (Browning Double Action)

| SPECIFICATION |
| --- |
| **MANUFACTURER** FN Herstal |
| **CALIBRE** 9mm Parabellum |
| **MAGAZINE CAPACITY** 15 |
| **ACTION** Short recoil/double |
| **TOTAL LENGTH** 200mm/7.87in |
| **BARREL LENGTH** 118mm/4.65in |
| **WEIGHT UNLOADED** 875g/30.86oz |

This pistol, produced in the 1990s, was derived from the FN High-Power and its essential mechanics were the same. The main differences were a double-action trigger and a hammer de-cocking lever which replaced the safety catch. The de-cocking lever was on both sides of the frame and could be operated by either hand. The magazine release could be fitted for either left- or right-hand use. The most obvious difference in the BDA was the extended trigger guard. A further development of this weapon was the BDA0, developed for law enforcement duties. The trigger was modified to reduce the likelihood of involuntary discharge.

## FN Browning High-Power

| SPECIFICATION |
| --- |
| **MANUFACTURER** FN Herstal |
| **CALIBRE** .40 S&W |
| **MAGAZINE CAPACITY** 10 |
| **ACTION** Recoil/single |
| **TOTAL LENGTH** 197mm/7.75in |
| **BARREL LENGTH** 118mm/4.64in |
| **WEIGHT UNLOADED** 885g/31.32oz |

The .40 High-Power was produced for the civilian market. It had a redesigned and strengthened slide in order to accommodate the more powerful cartridge and the magazine capacity was reduced to ten rounds. Only High-Powers specifically built for these rounds could be used to fire them. Like the other Brownings, the .40 pistol was recoil operated with a locked breech. It had linkless barrel-to-slide locking, a mechanism invented by John Browning. The trigger was single-action, with an external hammer.

## FN Five-SeveN

This pistol was developed in the 1990s to cope with modern battlefield conditions and, with the 5.7mm cartridge, was able to penetrate most of the latest battlefield armour. The pistol was extremely light due to the use of modern synthetic materials in its construction. It had a very low recoil, thus increasing the accuracy of follow-up shots. The high-capacity magazine carried 20 rounds. The Five-SeveN was designed to be fully safe through the use of a double-action firing mechanism. The pistol had been designed to have an extremely smooth exterior, with very few protrusions. It could be fitted with accessories, including a laser target designator and tactical light.

| SPECIFICATION |
| --- |
| **MANUFACTURER** FN Herstal |
| **CALIBRE** 5.7mm FN |
| **MAGAZINE CAPACITY** 20 |
| **ACTION** Delayed blowback/double |
| **TOTAL LENGTH** 208mm/8.23in |
| **BARREL LENGTH** 123mm/4.84in |
| **WEIGHT UNLOADED** 620g/21.87oz |

### FN Browning PRO-9

This pistol, otherwise known as the FNP-9, was designed for law enforcement. It had a polymer frame that was 30 per cent lighter than a steel-frame pistol. It could be set in either single-action or double/single-action mode, the first for quick reaction and the second for greater safety and requiring a more deliberate pull on the trigger. The hammer housing was removable for maintenance or replacement. The hammer was visible in its cocked modes and there was also a red indicator under the extractor to indicate a chambered round. Interchangeable back straps could be fitted to the hand grip to allow for different hand sizes.

**SPECIFICATION**

**MANUFACTURER** FN Herstal
**CALIBRE** 9mm Parabellum
**MAGAZINE CAPACITY** 15
**ACTION** Short recoil/single and double/single
**TOTAL LENGTH** 180mm/7.1in
**BARREL LENGTH** 102mm/4in
**WEIGHT UNLOADED** 709g/25oz

## Switzerland

**With their worldwide reputation for exceptional manufacturing quality, especially with regard to mechanisms with small moving parts and fine tolerances, it is no surprise that the Swiss also produce high-quality handguns. Schweizerische Industrie Gesellschaft (SIG), partnered with J.P. Sauer & Sohn of Germany, continue to manufacture pistols that are used by elite and other armed forces as well as a wide range of police and security units throughout the world.**

### SIG-Sauer P220 (Pistole/Model 75)

This pistol was developed specifically for the Swiss Army and was adopted in 1975 as the Pistole 75. It was a locked-breech, short-recoil pistol based on principles devised by John Browning. The pistol was also adapted by the armed forces of both the United States and Japan. It featured the SIG-Sauer four-point safety system of de-cocking lever, patented automatic firing-pin safety block, safety intercept notch, and trigger bar disconnector. The P220 was produced in a number of variants, including the "Carry" version and the "Combat" version.

**SPECIFICATION**

**MANUFACTURER** SIG Arms/ J.P. Sauer & Sohn GmbH.
**CALIBRE** 9mm Parabellum and .45 ACP
**MAGAZINE CAPACITY** 9
**ACTION** Short recoil/double
**TOTAL LENGTH** 198mm/7.8in
**BARREL LENGTH** 112mm/4.41in
**WEIGHT UNLOADED** 830g/29.3oz

### SIG-Sauer P225

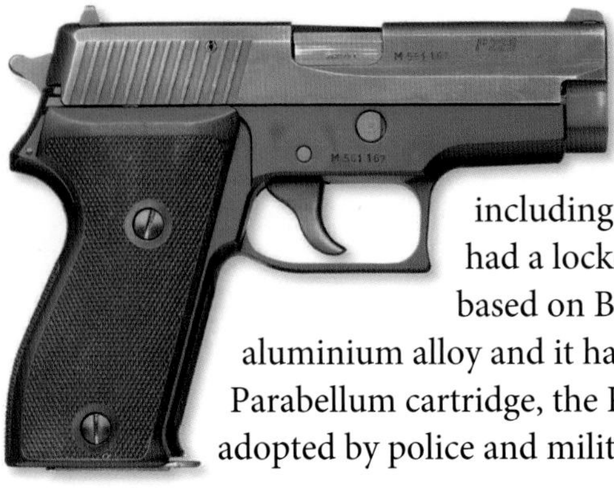

The P225 was first produced in the late 1970s and was essentially a smaller and lighter version of the P220 with the same features, including the four-point safety system. It had a locked-breech system with short recoil based on Browning principles. The frame was aluminium alloy and it had a steel slide. Fitted with the 9mm Parabellum cartridge, the P225 proved to be successful and was adopted by police and military forces throughout Europe.

**SPECIFICATION**

**MANUFACTURER** SIG Arms/ J.P. Sauer & Sohn GmbH.
**CALIBRE** 9mm Parabellum
**MAGAZINE CAPACITY** 8
**ACTION** Short recoil/double
**TOTAL LENGTH** 180mm/7.1in
**BARREL LENGTH** 98mm/3.86in
**WEIGHT UNLOADED** 740g/26.1oz

## SIG-Sauer P230

**SPECIFICATION**

**MANUFACTURER** SIG Arms/ J.P. Sauer & Sohn GmbH.
**CALIBRE** .380 ACP, .32 ACP
**MAGAZINE CAPACITY** 7 or 8
**ACTION** Blowback/double or single or DAO
**TOTAL LENGTH** 168mm/6.63in
**BARREL LENGTH** 92mm/3.62in
**WEIGHT UNLOADED** 460g/16.2oz

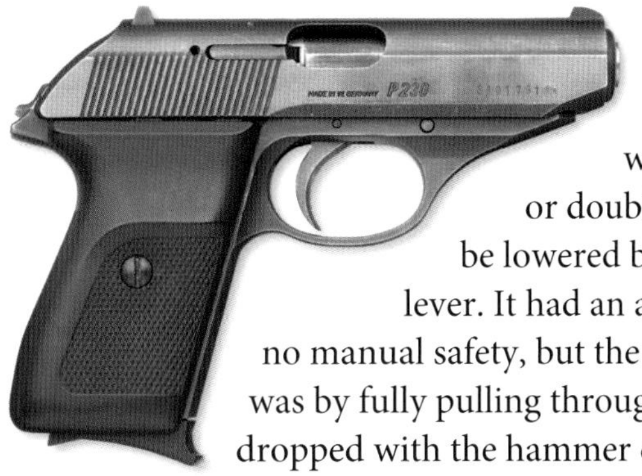

Introduced in the 1970s, the P230 was a blowback-operated pistol which could be used in either single or double-action modes. The hammer could be lowered by depressing the hammer de-cocking lever. It had an automatic firing-pin lock. There was no manual safety, but the only way the pistol could be fired was by fully pulling through the trigger. The pistol could be dropped with the hammer cocked and the pistol would not fire. The SIG-Sauer P230 achieved a reputation for reliability and good build quality. It was also available in .32 ACP (8-round magazine).

## SIG-Sauer P226

**SPECIFICATION**

**MANUFACTURER** SIG Arms/ J.P. Sauer & Sohn GmbH.
**CALIBRE** 9mm Parabellum
**MAGAZINE CAPACITY** 15
**ACTION** Short recoil/single or double
**TOTAL LENGTH** 196mm/7.7in
**BARREL LENGTH** 112mm/4.41in
**WEIGHT UNLOADED** 964g/34oz

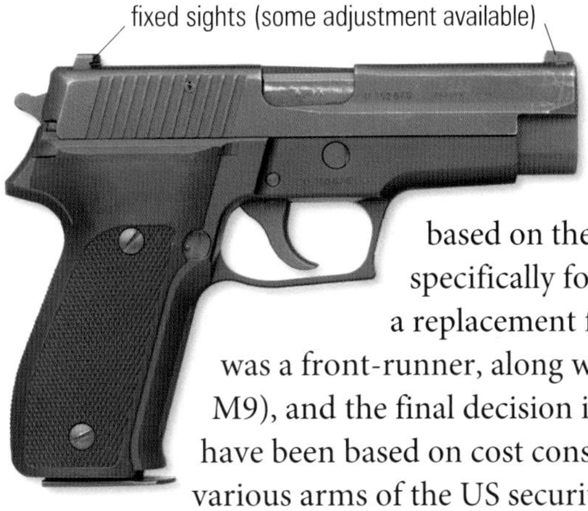


The P226, introduced in the early 1980s, was one of the most successful designs to be based on the P220. The pistol was developed specifically for the US Army trials set up to find a replacement for the Colt M1911A1. The P226 was a front-runner, along with the Beretta 92F (US designation M9), and the final decision in favour of the Beretta was said to have been based on cost considerations. The P226 was issued to various arms of the US security forces and military, including the US Navy SEALs (Air, Sea and Land), as well as to special operations teams in other countries, including the British SAS (Special Air Service).

## SIG-Sauer P228

**SPECIFICATION**

**MANUFACTURER** SIG Arms/ J.P. Sauer & Sohn GmbH.
**CALIBRE** 9mm Parabellum
**MAGAZINE CAPACITY** 13
**ACTION** Blowback/double, single or DAO
**TOTAL LENGTH** 180mm/7.1in
**BARREL LENGTH** 98mm/3.8in
**WEIGHT UNLOADED** 825g/29.1oz

**US imports**
SIG Arms was established in 1985 to import and distribute SIG firearms into the States.

The P228, introduced in the late 1980s, was a more compact version of the P226. It was a blowback-operated, locked-breech pistol with a linkless locking system based on Browning principles. It also featured the four-point SIG-Sauer safety system. The frame was constructed from aluminium alloy. While the Beretta 92F had been favoured over the P226 on cost grounds at the US Army trials, in the 1980s the more compact P228 (US designation M11) was selected as the sidearm of choice for aircrew and any other personnel who required a more compact pistol than the M9. While .40 calibre pistols became popular in the United States, many intelligence agencies still use the 9mm Parabellum P228 as a weapon of choice. One of its advantages is that recoil is near-negligible with the P228. The 9mm Parabellum round is more easily controlled than the .40 or .45 ACP rounds.

## Sig-Sauer P229

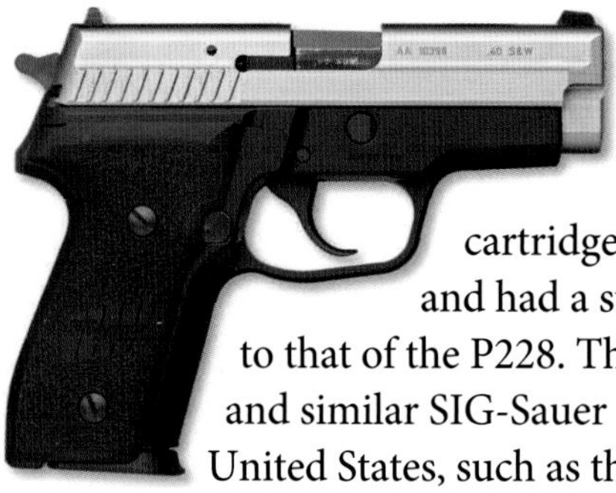

This pistol, introduced in the early 1990s, was almost identical to the P228 but was developed with law-enforcement officers in mind, chambered for the .40 S&W cartridge. It was fitted with high-contrast sights and had a stainless-steel slide with a different design to that of the P228. There was a high level of use for this pistol and similar SIG-Sauer types by top-level security agencies in the United States, such as the FBI (Federal Bureau of Investigation) and DEA (Drug Enforcement Administration).

**SPECIFICATION**

**MANUFACTURER** SIG Arms/ J.P. Sauer & Sohn GmbH.
**CALIBRE** .40 S&W
**MAGAZINE CAPACITY** 12
**ACTION** Short recoil/double or single or DAO
**TOTAL LENGTH** 180mm/7.1in
**BARREL LENGTH** 98mm/3.86in
**WEIGHT UNLOADED** 865g/30.51oz

## SIG-Sauer P232

This was the smallest and lightest pistol in the SIG-Sauer range, and was developed in the late 1990s. Featuring a fixed-barrel blowback action, the P232 was designed to be a reliable back-up pistol. It was well balanced and its smooth shape and rounded, snag-free edges were designed to make it easy to deploy quickly for personal protection. The compact size allows the pistol to be easily concealed whether in a discreet holster, handbag or on the ankle. The hand grip was ergonomically designed to allow for a secure hold. The P232 was said to be a widely used off-duty gun carried by federal agents and law enforcement professionals.

**SPECIFICATION**

**MANUFACTURER** SIG Arms/ J.P. Sauer & Sohn GmbH.
**CALIBRE** .380 ACP
**MAGAZINE CAPACITY** 7
**ACTION** Blowback/double or single
**TOTAL LENGTH** 168mm/6.63in
**BARREL LENGTH** 92mm/3.62in
**WEIGHT UNLOADED** 499g/17.6oz

## SIG-Sauer P239

The P239 was similar in design and concept to the P228 but it was a more compact version. It was designed for ease of concealment, perhaps in undercover operations, and could be used as a secondary weapon for emergencies. The frame was aluminium alloy while the slide was solid steel. The P239 was a recoil-operated, locked-breech weapon and incorporated the linkless locking system based on Browning's ideas. Chambered for the 9mm Parabellum cartridge, it was also available in larger calibres. The P239 has become quite popular in the United States as a concealed carry pistol.

**SPECIFICATION**

**MANUFACTURER** SIG Arms/ J.P. Sauer & Sohn GmbH.
**CALIBRE** 9mm Parabellum
**MAGAZINE CAPACITY** 8
**ACTION** Recoil/double or single or DAO
**TOTAL LENGTH** 167mm/6.6in
**BARREL LENGTH** 92mm/3.62in
**WEIGHT UNLOADED** 775g/27.34oz

## SIG-Pro SP2022

This pistol was designed to provide optimum safety, reliability and accuracy and to resist corrosion. The trigger guard had a serrated finger rest for better control when firing. It was fitted with a chamber-loaded indicator that provided both visual and tactile control of the gun status. A variety of trigger sizes and systems, grips, floor plates and calibre options have been devised to accommodate individual requirements. In 2003, the largest European post-war order for law-enforcement service pistols was awarded to Swiss Arms, formerly SIG-Sauer (acquired by German investors in 2000). The SP2022 is the standard service and law-enforcement weapon in France.

**SPECIFICATION**

**MANUFACTURER** Swiss Arms/ J.P. Sauer & Sohn GmbH.
**CALIBRE** 9mm Parabellum
**MAGAZINE CAPACITY** 15
**ACTION** Short recoil/double or DAO
**TOTAL LENGTH** 187mm/7.36in
**BARREL LENGTH** 99mm/3.9in
**WEIGHT UNLOADED** 760g/26.8oz

# Germany

**From the late 19th to the early 21st century, the most significant developments in Germany have been in pistols, as opposed to revolvers. German design ingenuity, backed up by high-quality manufacturing, has resulted in such key designs as the 9mm Luger by George Luger (inspired by earlier designs) and the 7.65mm Walther PP of 1929. Firms such as Carl Walther and Heckler & Koch continue to uphold this reputation today with innovative and highly successful designs.**

## Bergmann Model 1896

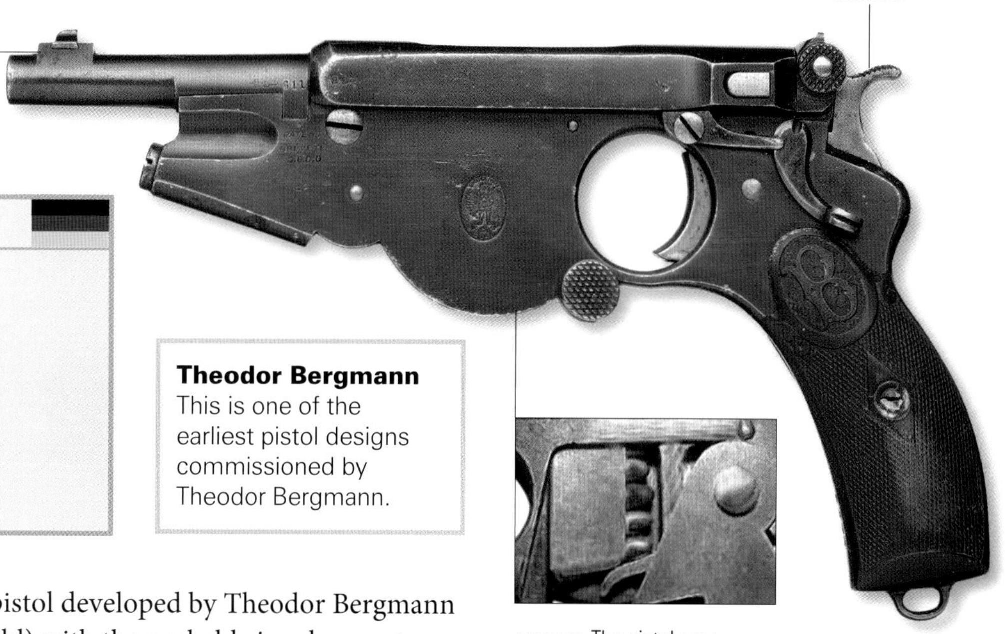


**SPECIFICATION**

**MANUFACTURER** V.C. Schilling, Suhl
**CALIBRE** 5mm Bergmann
**MAGAZINE CAPACITY** 5
**ACTION** Blowback/single
**TOTAL LENGTH** 175mm/6.89in
**BARREL LENGTH** 80mm/3.15in
**WEIGHT UNLOADED** 470g/16.6oz

**Theodor Bergmann**
This is one of the earliest pistol designs commissioned by Theodor Bergmann.

**ABOVE** The pistol was loaded from the right side by opening the casing by the trigger-guard. A magazine clip was placed inside and the cover shut. A lifter spring pushes up the round one by one and, when empty, the clip was removed downwards.

This was a blowback-operated pistol developed by Theodor Bergmann (the founder of Bergmann in Suhl) with the probable involvement of Louis Schmeisser, a technical designer, who often played a role in realizing Bergmann-inspired designs. The 1894 model was unusual in having a folding trigger and no extractor. The empty case was simply ejected when it hit a protrusion, though this system did not always work. This rather hit-and-miss approach did not prove to be a success and the 1894 version was soon replaced with the 1896. Although the first 1896 had the same extraction system, this was soon replaced with a conventional extractor. The Bergmann 1896 never gained any real popularity as the Mauser models were found to be more effective.

**SPECIFICATION**

**MANUFACTURER** Anciens Établissements Pieper (AEP)
**CALIBRE** 9mm Bergmann-Bayard (9mm Largo)
**MAGAZINE CAPACITY** 6
**ACTION** Recoil/single
**TOTAL LENGTH** 250mm/9.84in
**BARREL LENGTH** 102mm/4in
**WEIGHT UNLOADED** 1,015g/35.8oz

## Bergmann-Bayard 1908

This pistol incorporated the design patented by Bergmann for a gun with a vertically moving locking piece which locked the breech block. The bolt extracted and ejected the spent cartridge casing and cocked the hammer on the recoil strike. It then pulled a round from the magazine and chambered it on the return. The Bergmann-Bayard was supplied to the Danish, Belgian and Spanish armed forces, where it was designated the Modelo 1908. This was the start of a long history of servicing the Spanish military and police.

## Luger 1900

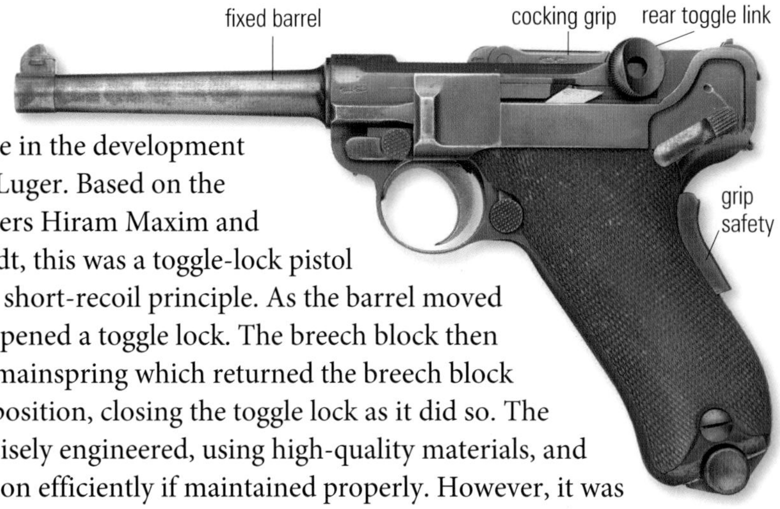


This pistol was an important stage in the development of the famous Luger. Based on the ideas of designers Hiram Maxim and Hugo Borchardt, this was a toggle-lock pistol operating on a short-recoil principle. As the barrel moved to the rear, it opened a toggle lock. The breech block then compressed a mainspring which returned the breech block to its original position, closing the toggle lock as it did so. The pistol was precisely engineered, using high-quality materials, and it would function efficiently if maintained properly. However, it was very sensitive to dirt and this could be a problem in combat conditions. The 1900 had a grip safety in the rear of the butt as well as a manual safety on the left-hand side of the frame. The 1900 was issued to the Swiss Army.

**SPECIFICATION**

**MANUFACTURER** Deutsche Waffen und Munitions Fabrik (DWM)
**CALIBRE** 7.65mm Luger
**MAGAZINE CAPACITY** 8
**ACTION** Short recoil/single
**TOTAL LENGTH** 211mm/8.31in
**BARREL LENGTH** 122mm/4.8in
**WEIGHT UNLOADED** 840g/29.6oz

**Luger accuracy**
A feature of the Luger is that the barrel remains aligned or fixed with the frame axis, said to improve accuracy.

## Luger P08

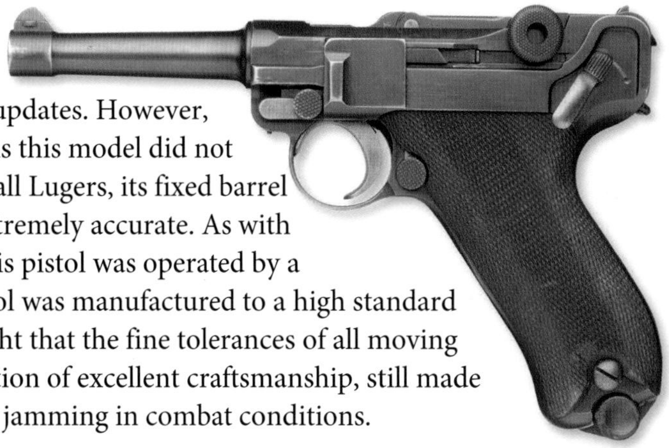

The 9mm P08 model followed several Luger updates. However, unlike the earlier models this model did not have a grip safety. Like all Lugers, its fixed barrel meant the pistol was extremely accurate. As with the previous models, this pistol was operated by a toggle action. Each pistol was manufactured to a high standard but it is generally thought that the fine tolerances of all moving parts, though an indication of excellent craftsmanship, still made the pistol susceptible to jamming in combat conditions.

**SPECIFICATION**

**MANUFACTURER** DWM
**CALIBRE** 9mm Parabellum
**MAGAZINE CAPACITY** 8
**ACTION** Short recoil/single
**TOTAL LENGTH** 223mm/88.78in
**BARREL LENGTH** 102mm/4in
**WEIGHT UNLOADED** 850g/30oz

## HK4

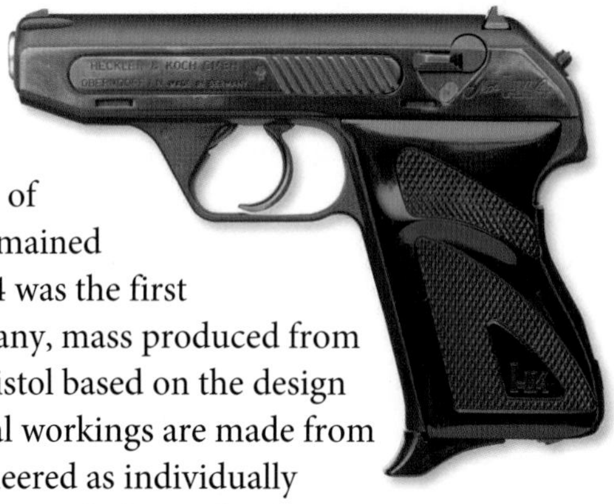

Heckler & Koch grew up out of the ashes of the Mauser firm, which had been damaged and closed down as part of reparations after World War II (and remained closed for a number of years). The HK4 was the first pistol to be manufactured by the company, mass produced from the late 1960s. It was a double-action pistol based on the design of the Mauser HSc of 1937. The internal workings are made from stamped steel but are as precisely engineered as individually machined parts. The frame was made from a lightweight alloy. A variety of calibres were available in addition to the .380 with 7 rounds. The calibre could be altered by changing the barrel and the magazine, and different barrels could be purchased with the weapon. The pistol was issued to German customs police and was produced until the mid-1980s as the P11.

**SPECIFICATION**

**MANUFACTURER** Heckler & Koch GmbH.
**CALIBRE** .380 ACP, 7.65mm (.32 ACP), 6.35mm (.25 ACP), .22 Long Rifle
**MAGAZINE CAPACITY** 7 (.380 ACP) or 8
**ACTION** Blowback/double
**TOTAL LENGTH** 157mm/6.18in
**BARREL LENGTH** 85mm/3.35in
**WEIGHT UNLOADED** 480g/16.9oz

**Alex Seidel**
The HK4 was devised by Alex Seidel, a co-founder of Heckler & Koch and former employee of the Mauser company.

## HK P9

**SPECIFICATION**

**MANUFACTURER** Heckler & Koch GmbH.
**CALIBRE** 9mm Parabellum, .45 ACP
**MAGAZINE CAPACITY** 9
**ACTION** Delayed blowback/double (P9), single (P9S)
**TOTAL LENGTH** 192mm/7.56in
**BARREL LENGTH** 102mm/4in
**WEIGHT UNLOADED** 880g/31oz

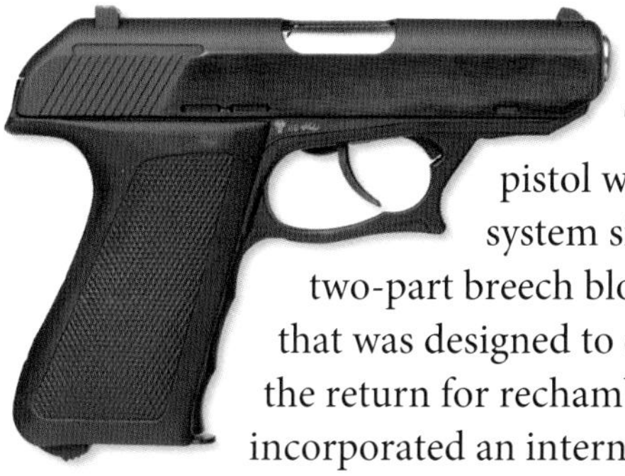

The HKP9 was a delayed-blowback pistol with a roller-locked breech-block inertia system similar to that used on the G3 rifle. A two-part breech block incorporated a roller mechanism that was designed to create inertia in recoil and to enable the return for rechambering the next round. The HKP9 incorporated an internal hammer and there was a de-cocking lever on the left-hand side of the receiver. The HKP9S (a sporting version of the P9) had a double-action lock and a polygonal rifled barrel. Despite its sophisticated design, the HKP9 did not sell large quantities.

## HK VP70

**SPECIFICATION**

**MANUFACTURER** Heckler & Koch GmbH.
**CALIBRE** 9mm Parabellum
**MAGAZINE CAPACITY** 18
**ACTION** Short recoil/double
**TOTAL LENGTH** 204mm/8in
**BARREL LENGTH** 116mm/4.6in
**WEIGHT UNLOADED** 820g/28.9oz

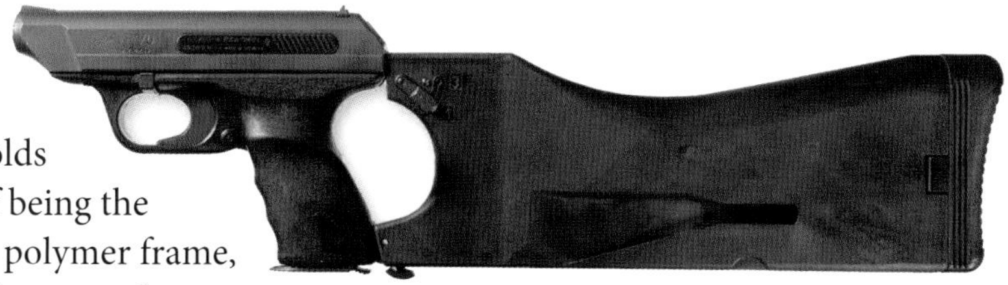

The HK VP70 holds the distinction of being the first pistol with a polymer frame, predating Glock by more than a decade. Nomenclature for the HK VP70 is very straightforward. The VP stands for Volkspistole, or People's Pistol, and the 70 is for 1970, which is the year it was introduced. Capable of being fired in semi-auto or three-round-burst, the pistol has a rate of fire of 2,200 rounds per minute. An included holster is designed to attach to the grip and act as a stock when the gun is being used.

## HK P11

**SPECIFICATION**

**MANUFACTURER** Heckler & Koch GmbH.
**CALIBRE** 7.62x36mm dart
**BARRELS** 5
**ACTION** Electric ignition
**TOTAL LENGTH** 200mm/7.9in
**WEIGHT UNLOADED** 1,200g/42oz

Designed for underwater use, the P11 fires darts instead of bullets. This allows shots fired from the gun to be more accurate and have a greater range of approximately 10 to 15 metres. If fired above water, the range is approximately 30 metres. The darts are fired electronically by means of a battery pack in the grip, and once all five darts have been shot, the gun's five-barrel unit has to be sent back to Heckler & Koch in order to be reloaded.

## HK P7

**SPECIFICATION**

**MANUFACTURER** Heckler & Koch GmbH.
**CALIBRE** 9mm Parabellum
**MAGAZINE CAPACITY** 8
**ACTION** Delayed blowback/single
**TOTAL LENGTH** 171mm/6.75in
**BARREL LENGTH** 105mm/4.13in
**WEIGHT UNLOADED** 780g/27.5oz

The first version of the HKP7, the PSP (Police Self-loading Pistol), was produced between 1976 and 1979. The HKP7 was primarily designed for use by police forces but it was also entered for trials with the US Army to replace the Colt M1911A1. It was a single-action pistol with a grip safety on the front of the hand grip. This had to be squeezed before the weapon could be cocked. The blowback system was gas delayed, in other words the gases from the exploded cartridge were released into a cylinder and slow down the recoil. The HKP7 was one of the most accurate 9mm service pistols available.

## HK MK23 (SOCOM pistol)

| SPECIFICATION | |
|---|---|
| **MANUFACTURER** | Heckler & Koch GmbH. |
| **CALIBRE** | .45 ACP |
| **MAGAZINE CAPACITY** | 12 |
| **ACTION** | Short recoil/double and single |
| **TOTAL LENGTH** | 245mm/9.65in |
| **BARREL LENGTH** | 149mm/5.87in |
| **WEIGHT UNLOADED** | 1,097g/38.72oz |

**Special operations**
This pistol was developed for special units such as the US Navy SEALs and Green Berets.

This was a short-recoil operated, locked-breech pistol, which originated in 1991 when Heckler & Koch began development for the US Special Operations Command (SOCOM), and finally passed all the tests and was issued by SOCOM in 1996. The barrel locked into the slide with a single lug. It had a one-piece machined steel slide and a frame-mounted de-cocking lever and a separate ambidextrous lever. The pistol could be carried "cocked and locked" when the safety was applied. The extractor doubled as a chamber-loaded indicator. The pistol was fitted with an oversize trigger guard so that it could be fired with gloves. It was also fitted with grooves for mounting accessories such as a laser pointer.

## HK USP (Universal Self-loading Pistol)

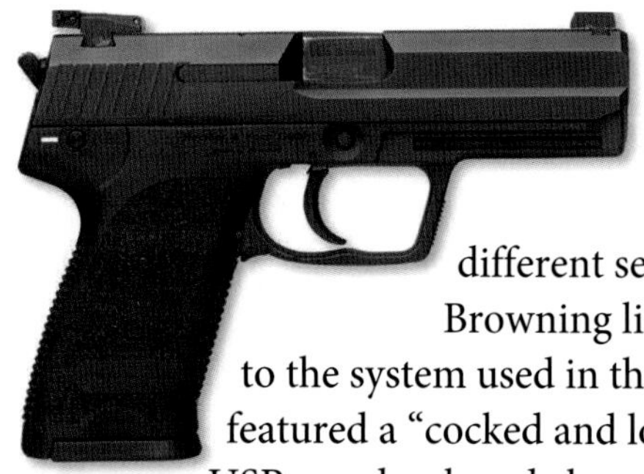

This USP was introduced in the early 1990s as a modular concept, adaptable to the requirements of different security forces. The pistols incorporated a Browning linkless locked- breech action, similar to the system used in the Browning High-Power. It also featured a "cocked and locked" system for safe carriage. The USP was developed alongside the MK23 for US Special Operations Command (SOCOM). The pistol that won the US contract had a longer slide than the USP and special mountings for a laser-aiming module (LAM). The barrel was also extended so that a suppressor could be screwed on.

| SPECIFICATION | |
|---|---|
| **MANUFACTURER** | Heckler & Koch GmbH. |
| **CALIBRE** | 9mm Parabellum, .40 S&W, .45 ACP |
| **MAGAZINE CAPACITY** | 13 |
| **ACTION** | Recoil/double or single |
| **TOTAL LENGTH** | 194mm/7.64in |
| **BARREL LENGTH** | 108mm/4.25in |
| **WEIGHT UNLOADED** | 830g/29.3oz |

## HK P8

This was a recoil-operated pistol chambered for the 9mm NATO cartridge. It had a locked breech and tilting barrel introduced in 1994, and was a modified version of the standard USP. It was introduced to replace the Walther P1 that had been in service with the German armed forces for 35 years. The hand grip was made of glass-fibre reinforced polymer with corrosion-proof metal inserts. The pistol had a safety lever on the left for safety and de-cocking function. There was an integrated support rail so that scopes could be attached. The P8 included the mechanical recoil reduction system, which meant the handgun absorbed some of the recoil, reducing the amount felt by the user.

| SPECIFICATION | |
|---|---|
| **MANUFACTURER** | Heckler & Koch GmbH. |
| **CALIBRE** | 9mm Parabellum |
| **MAGAZINE CAPACITY** | 15 |
| **ACTION** | Recoil/double and single |
| **TOTAL LENGTH** | 194mm/7.64in |
| **BARREL LENGTH** | 108mm/4.25in |
| **WEIGHT UNLOADED** | 780g/27.51oz |

**Standard sidearm**
The P8 is the standard sidearm of the *Bundeswehr* (German armed forces).

## HK P10

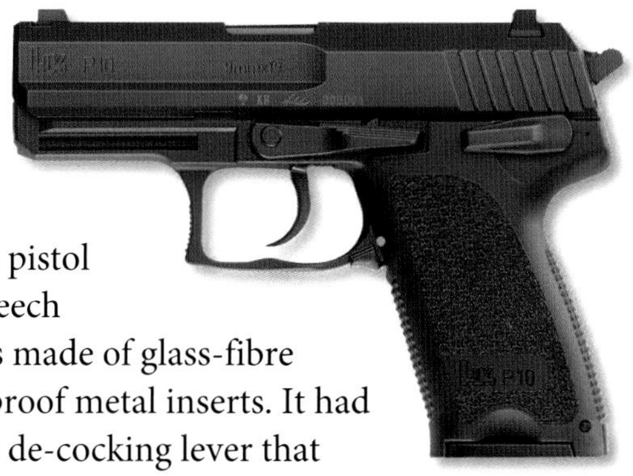

The P10 was a USP Compact with a spurred hammer, and the firing control mechanism of the P8. It was chambered for the 9mm Parabellum cartridge. This pistol was recoil operated with a locked breech and tilting barrel. The hand grip was made of glass-fibre reinforced polymer with corrosion proof metal inserts. It had a single/double-action trigger with a de-cocking lever that could be positioned either on the left or the right of the pistol. There was an integrated support rail to which a scope or other device could be fitted. It had an open square notch rear sight with contrast points. This was the first pistol to meet and be certified to the requirements of the Technical Guidelines on pistols of the German Police Staff College. It has also been issued to a number of police forces outside Germany.

**SPECIFICATION**

**MANUFACTURER** Heckler & Koch GmbH.
**CALIBRE** 9mm Parabellum
**MAGAZINE CAPACITY** 13
**ACTION** Recoil/double or single
**TOTAL LENGTH** 173mm/6.81in
**BARREL LENGTH** 91mm/3.58in
**WEIGHT UNLOADED** 648g/22.86oz

**Police forces**
The Heckler & Koch HKP10 combines some of the best attributes of both the P8 and the USP in order to meet the stringent requirements of police forces.

## HK USP Tactical

**SPECIFICATION**

**MANUFACTURER** Heckler & Koch GmbH.
**CALIBRE** .45 ACP, 9mm Parabellum
**MAGAZINE CAPACITY** 13
**ACTION** Short recoil/double or single
**TOTAL LENGTH** 219mm/8.64in
**BARREL LENGTH** 129mm/5in
**WEIGHT UNLOADED** 862g/30.4oz

The USP .45 ACP Tactical met the requirements of the US military but in a smaller model. The differences between a Tactical and a standard USP included the adjustable sights, a threaded and extended barrel for a suppressor (silencer) and a match trigger. It also had an adjustable micrometer sight. The Tactical was soon issued by SOCOM (Special Operations Command) and became the preferred choice of the special operations units. The USP Tactical has undergone testing in extreme conditions. It was available in .45 ACP and 9mm Parabellum as USPSD.

## HK USP Expert

**SPECIFICATION**

**MANUFACTURER** Heckler & Koch GmbH.
**CALIBRE** 9mm Parabellum, .40 S&W, .45 ACP
**MAGAZINE CAPACITY** 10
**ACTION** Short recoil/double or single
**TOTAL LENGTH** 221mm/8.74in
**BARREL LENGTH** 132mm/5.2in
**WEIGHT UNLOADED** 1,043g/36.8oz

Introduced in 1998, this version incorporated most of the features of the Tactical with all the design advantages of a target-shooting pistol, focusing on extreme precision. It could be used by security forces as a highly accurate weapon, or as a competition pistol. It had an elongated steel slide and was recoil operated with a locked breech and tilting barrel. The hand grip and magazine were manufactured from glass-like polymer with metal inserts. In addition to 9mm Parabellum, the USP Expert was available in .40 S&W and .45 ACP. In order to convert from one calibre to another, the slide, barrel, recoil spring, guide rod and magazine could be changed.

## HK P2000

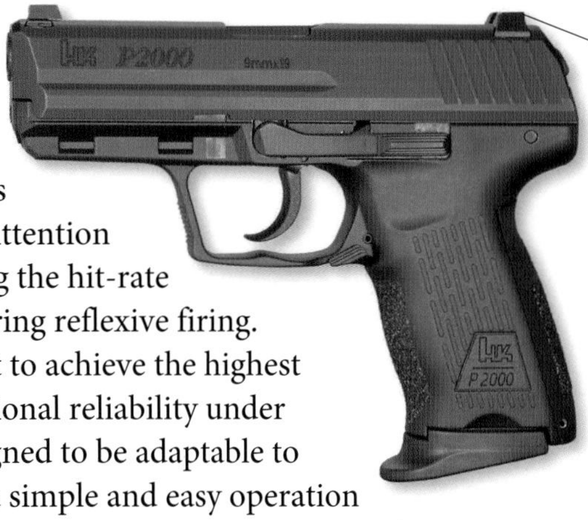

The design brief for this pistol was that it should offer a high level of safety for police and special units undertaking operations. Attention was also paid to improving the hit-rate capabilities of the user during reflexive firing. The manufacturers set out to achieve the highest possible safety and operational reliability under all conditions. It was designed to be adaptable to individual users and had a simple and easy operation by both right- and left-handed shooters. Due to its modular design, the HKP2000 could be fitted to the individual needs of the shooter. The requirements of the user could be met due to a variety of trigger and de-cocking systems. The HKP2000 had a safety trigger with concealed cocking piece in the hammer and centrally arranged de-cocking lever for firing in either single or double action mode. The P2000 V1 also had a safety trigger with concealed cocking piece in the hammer, with a constant trigger pull from the first shot to the last, without de-cocking.

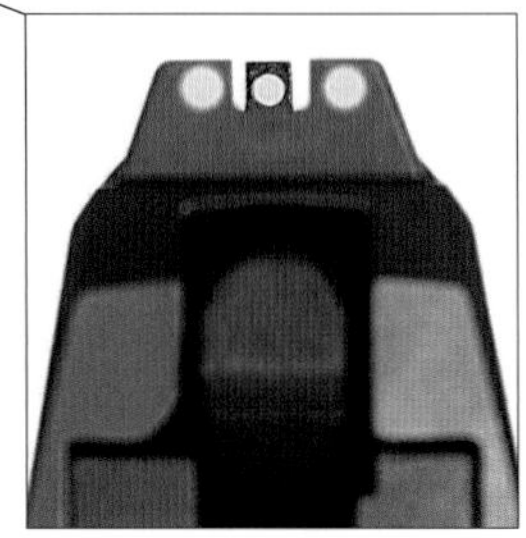

**LEFT** The HKP2000 has a square notch rear sight. The long glowing contrast points allow accurate shooting in poor lighting conditions.

**SPECIFICATION**

**MANUFACTURER** Heckler & Koch GmbH.
**CALIBRE** 9mm Parabellum
**MAGAZINE CAPACITY** 13 or 16
**ACTION** Recoil/single and double
**TOTAL LENGTH** 173mm/6.81in
**BARREL LENGTH** 93mm/3.66in
**WEIGHT UNLOADED** 620g/21.87oz

## HK P30

This pistol was designed primarily for police forces and it incorporated a high level of safety as well as being quick to deploy. The open square notch rear sight with long glow contrast points was designed to allow fast and accurate target acquisition in all light conditions. The pistol was said to have a good weight balance and the hand grip was made of high-grade fibre-reinforced polymer. The grip was ergonomically moulded in order to maximize accuracy during reflexive firing. The grip also incorporated an ambidextrous magazine release and captive slide release. There was automatic hammer and firing pin safety. It was also fitted with a chamber-loaded indicator. The P30 featured a modular trigger and de-cocking system capable of being individually tailored to various requirements. It had a safety trigger with a concealed cocking piece in the hammer with spur. There was a central de-cocking latch, with a constant double-action trigger pull, without operation of the de-cocking latch, and defined let-off point.

**LEFT** Magazine removal is equally easy for right- and left-handed shooters. It can be operated by the thumb/index finger of either hand.

**HP3000/HP30**
The HP30 is a refinement of the HKP2000 pistol and was to be known as the HKP3000. It is a state-of-the-art design with highly moulded hand grips.

**SPECIFICATION**

**MANUFACTURER** Heckler & Koch GmbH.
**CALIBRE** 9mm Parabellum or .40 S&W
**MAGAZINE CAPACITY** 15 (9mm) or 13 (.40 S&W)
**ACTION** Short recoil/double or single
**TOTAL LENGTH** 181mm/7.1in
**BARREL LENGTH** 98mm/3.9in
**WEIGHT UNLOADED** 647g/22.8oz

## Korth Combat

| SPECIFICATION | |
|---|---|
| **MANUFACTURER** Korth | |
| **CALIBRE** .357 Magnum, .38 Special | |
| **CYLINDER** 6 | |
| **ACTION** Double or single | |
| **TOTAL LENGTH** 168mm/6.63in | |
| **BARREL LENGTH** 75mm/3in | |
| **WEIGHT UNLOADED** 936g/33oz | |

The Korth Combat revolver was in many respects a Rolls-Royce of revolvers. No expense was spared in its design, development and manufacture. It was a precision-engineered weapon manufactured using very high-quality steel and with a walnut hand grip to finish it off. Its owners were those prepared to pay for this level of excellence. It was a six-shot double-action revolver with a single-action option. The trigger had a telescoped, coil-type mainspring. The cylinder could be released and, if necessary, exchanged to change calibres. It had a full-length ejector rod shroud. The sights were adjustable. The Korth was usually chambered in .357 Magnum or .38 Special, with optional 9mm cylinders and a variety of barrels.

## Borchardt 1893

| SPECIFICATION | |
|---|---|
| **MANUFACTURER** Ludwig Loewe & Co. | |
| **CALIBRE** 7.63mm Borchardt | |
| **MAGAZINE CAPACITY** 8 | |
| **ACTION** Recoil/single | |
| **TOTAL LENGTH** 279mm/10.98in | |
| **BARREL LENGTH** 165mm/6.5in | |
| **WEIGHT UNLOADED** 1,160g/40.9oz | |

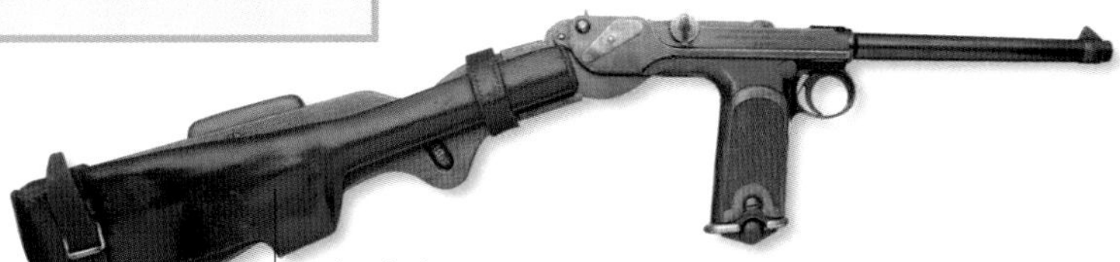


**ABOVE** The original pistol would have been supplied with a leather holster for storage, integrated with the shoulder stock.

This extraordinary looking pistol was designed by firearms inventor and engineer Hugo Borchardt and manufactured by Ludwig Loewe. Part of the reason for the pistol's strange appearance was the toggle lock and clock-style return spring housed in the rear overhang. The magazine was inserted into the hand grip, which was at the centre of the weapon. Despite the bizarre appearance, the pistol was technically accomplished and regarded with some respect by connoisseurs. It could not compete, however, with more modern and utilitarian designs.

## Mauser Model 1878

| SPECIFICATION | |
|---|---|
| **MANUFACTURER** Gebr. Mauser & Co. | |
| **CALIBRE** 9mm Mauser | |
| **CYLINDER** 6 | |
| **ACTION** Double | |
| **TOTAL LENGTH** 270mm/10.63in | |
| **BARREL LENGTH** 136mm/5.35in | |
| **WEIGHT UNLOADED** 750g/26.5oz | |

This is sometimes known as the "zig zag" revolver due to the method for moving the cylinder onwards. The cylinder was grooved in a zig zag pattern and a stud followed the groove and moved the cylinder round. Once the movement was completed, the stud acted as a brake on the cylinder. The M1878 also had an unusual way of opening. The revolver broke open and pivoted from a position just forward of the base of the cylinder and was locked by a ring catch in front of the trigger guard. These innovative design ideas were not considered entirely practical by the German High Command and sales were limited.

## Mauser Model 1896 ("Broomhandle")

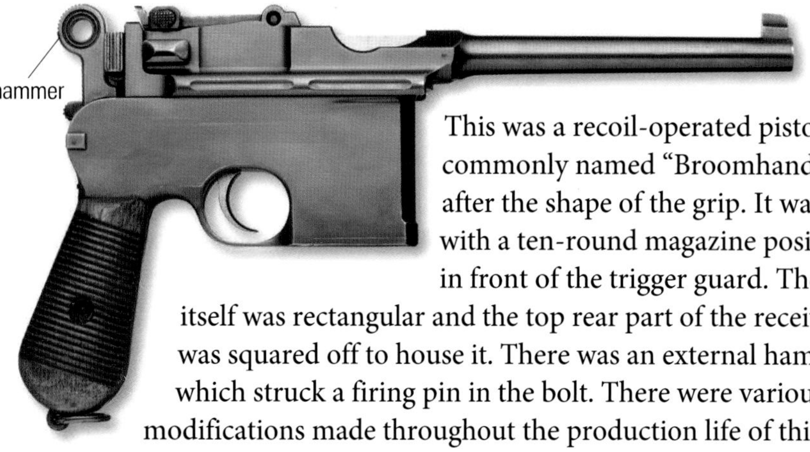


This was a recoil-operated pistol, commonly named "Broomhandle" after the shape of the grip. It was fitted with a ten-round magazine positioned in front of the trigger guard. The bolt itself was rectangular and the top rear part of the receiver was squared off to house it. There was an external hammer which struck a firing pin in the bolt. There were various modifications made throughout the production life of this pistol and about a million were manufactured between 1896 and 1936.

**SPECIFICATION**

**MANUFACTURER** Waffenfabrik Mauser AG.
**CALIBRE** 7.63mm Mauser
**MAGAZINE CAPACITY** 10
**ACTION** Recoil/single
**TOTAL LENGTH** 295mm/11.62in
**BARREL LENGTH** 140mm/5.51in
**WEIGHT UNLOADED** 1,045g/36.9oz

**Mauser records**
All records from the Mauser plant were destroyed in 1945.

## Mauser Model 1914

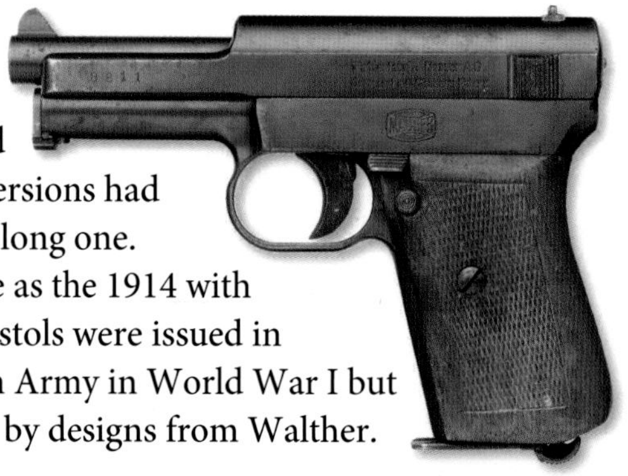

This was a blowback-operated pistol which was striker-fired. It had a fixed barrel and an open-top slide. Early versions had a short extractor and later versions a long one. The 1934 version was much the same as the 1914 with a revised hand grip. These Mauser pistols were issued in considerable numbers to the German Army in World War I but eventually they would be superseded by designs from Walther.

**SPECIFICATION**

**MANUFACTURER** Waffenfabrik Mauser AG.
**CALIBRE** 7.65mm (.32 ACP)
**MAGAZINE CAPACITY** 8
**ACTION** Blowback/single
**TOTAL LENGTH** 153mm/6.02in
**BARREL LENGTH** 87mm/3.43in
**WEIGHT UNLOADED** 600g/21oz

## Mauser HSc

The Mauser HSc (Self-cocking Hammer pistol, model C) was a blowback-operated pistol with a fixed barrel, from 1937. The hand grip shape provided optimum hold. The pistol was designed primarily for military use and saw service in the German Luftwaffe.

**SPECIFICATION**

**MANUFACTURER** Waffenfabrik Mauser AG.
**CALIBRE** 7.65mm (.32 ACP)
**MAGAZINE CAPACITY** 8
**ACTION** Blowback/double
**TOTAL LENGTH** 162mm/6.38in
**BARREL LENGTH** 86mm/3.39in
**WEIGHT UNLOADED** 640g/22.6oz

## Dreyse 1907

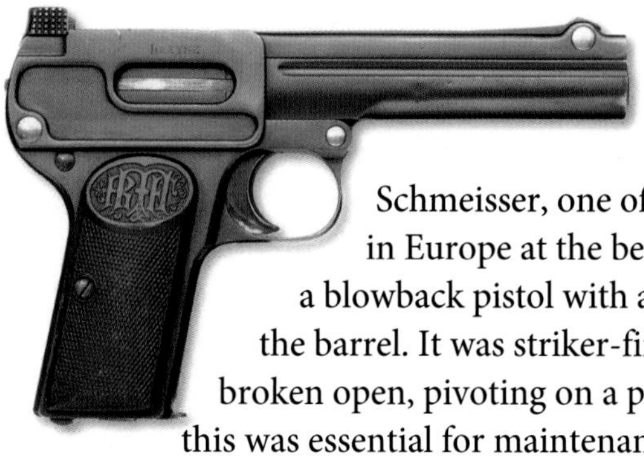

This pistol was designed by Louis Schmeisser, one of the best-known technical designers in Europe at the beginning of the 20th century. It was a blowback pistol with a breech block that surrounded the barrel. It was striker-fired. The frame and slide could be broken open, pivoting on a pin in front of the trigger guard, and this was essential for maintenance. The Dreyse 1907 proved to be quite a popular pistol and it was issued to some German police forces.

**SPECIFICATION**

**MANUFACTURER** Rheinische Metallwaaren und Maschinefabrik
**CALIBRE** 7.65mm (.32 ACP)
**MAGAZINE CAPACITY** 7
**ACTION** Blowback/single
**TOTAL LENGTH** 160mm/6.3in
**BARREL LENGTH** 93mm/3.66in
**WEIGHT UNLOADED** 710g/25oz

## Sauer Model 13

**SPECIFICATION**

**MANUFACTURER** J.P. Sauer & Sohn GmbH.
**CALIBRE** 7.65mm (.32 ACP)
**MAGAZINE CAPACITY** 7
**ACTION** Blowback/double and single
**TOTAL LENGTH** 144mm/5.67in
**BARREL LENGTH** 75mm/2.95in
**WEIGHT UNLOADED** 570g/20.1oz

This was a blowback pistol with a fixed barrel and a tubular slide. The breech block was retained in the slide by a screw-cap at the back. It had a safety catch just behind the trigger guard. The pistol was a successful design and quickly caught on. Due to its compact size it was often favoured by military officers as a personal defence weapon and it was also issued more widely to police and military forces. The magazine was inserted in the butt.

## Sauer Model 38

**SPECIFICATION**

**MANUFACTURER** J.P. Sauer & Sohn GmbH.
**CALIBRE** 7.65mm (.32 ACP)
**MAGAZINE CAPACITY** 8
**ACTION** Blowback/single and double
**TOTAL LENGTH** 171mm/6.73in
**BARREL LENGTH** 84mm/3.31in
**WEIGHT UNLOADED** 720g/25.4oz

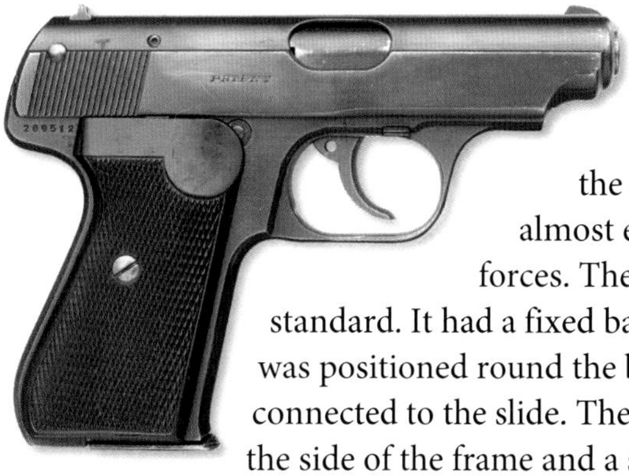

This blowback-operated pistol was based on earlier models and became available near the end of 1939. It was produced almost entirely for the German armed forces. The pistol was produced to a high standard. It had a fixed barrel and the recoil spring was positioned round the barrel. The breech block was connected to the slide. There was a decocking lever on the side of the frame and a safety catch which locked the hammer. The pistol also featured a magazine safety, whereby the pistol would not function unless the magazine was loaded.

## Schwarzlose 1908

**SPECIFICATION**

**MANUFACTURER** A.W. Schwarzlose GmbH.
**CALIBRE** 7.65mm (.32 ACP)
**MAGAZINE CAPACITY** 6
**ACTION** Blow forward/single
**TOTAL LENGTH** 143mm/5.63in
**BARREL LENGTH** 121mm/4.76in
**WEIGHT UNLOADED** 532.69g/18.79oz

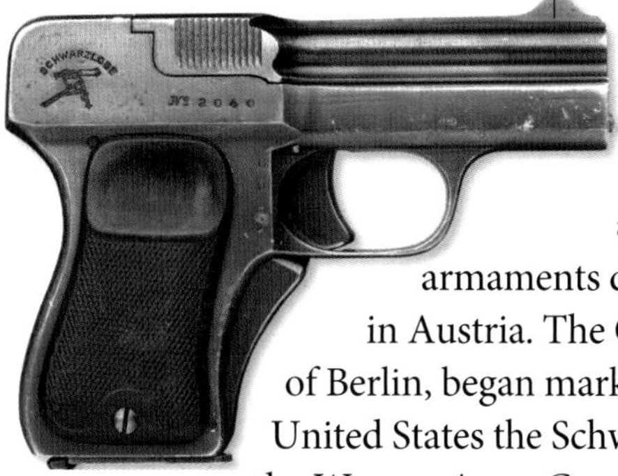


This pocket pistol was a blow forward-operated service pistol as devised by Ferdinand Ritter von Mannlicher, a German-born engineer and small-armaments designer who worked for most of his life in Austria. The German company, A.W. Schwarzlose of Berlin, began marketing the 1908 pistol in 1909. In the United States the Schwarzlose was imported and assembled by the Warner Arms Company of Brooklyn, New York, until the model stopped being manufactured in 1911. The Schwarzlose was not an altogether successful design – the pistol was prone to jam and it was uncomfortable for the shooter to use. The grip safety was on the front of the grip frame and was squeezed before firing. Alternatively the grip safety could be locked with a push button. As it was made for only a short time, the Schwarzlose 1908 was a relatively rare model.

**Mannlicher**
Although Mannlicher's design for pistols were relatively successful, his greater success was with his bolt-action rifles.

## Walther Model 4

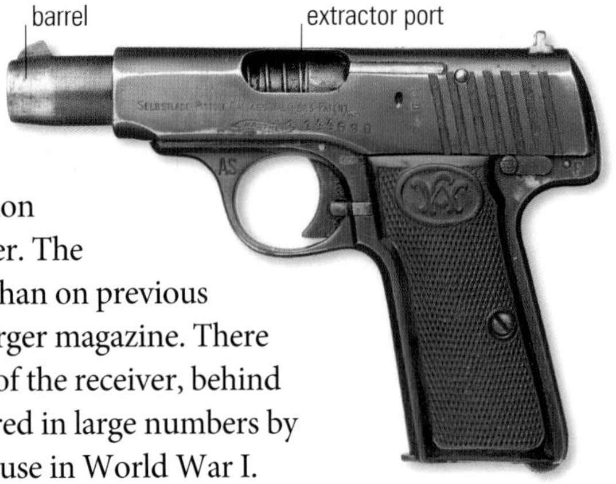


This was a striker-fired blowback-operated pistol with a fixed barrel. It had a full-length slide with an extraction port on its left and an internal hammer. The hand grip on the Model 4 was larger than on previous models in order to accommodate a larger magazine. There was a manual safety catch in the rear of the receiver, behind the hand grip. The Model 4 was ordered in large numbers by the German Army and saw extensive use in World War I.

**SPECIFICATION**

**MANUFACTURER** Carl Walther GmbH. Waffenfabrik
**CALIBRE** 7.65mm (.32 ACP)
**MAGAZINE CAPACITY** 8
**ACTION** Blowback/single
**TOTAL LENGTH** 152mm/6in
**BARREL LENGTH** 85mm/3.35in
**WEIGHT UNLOADED** 550g/19.4oz

## Walther PP

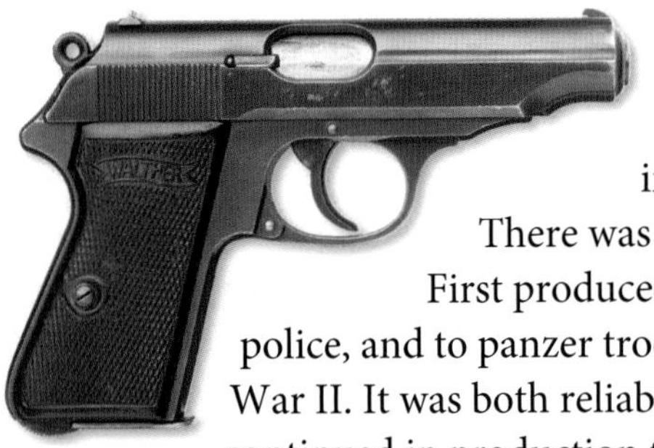

This pistol set a new standard in double-action design. It had a double-action lock and an external hammer, and a signal pin indicated whether the chamber was loaded. There was a safety catch on the side of the receiver. First produced in 1929, the PP was issued to German police, and to panzer troops and the Luftwaffe during World War II. It was both reliable and easily concealed. The Walther PP continued in production to the end of the 20th century and was purchased by security forces and individuals in many countries.

**SPECIFICATION**

**MANUFACTURER** Carl Walther GmbH. Waffenfabrik
**CALIBRE** 7.65mm (.32 ACP), .380 ACP
**MAGAZINE CAPACITY** 8
**ACTION** Blowback/double
**TOTAL LENGTH** 160mm/6.7in
**BARREL LENGTH** 98mm/3.86in
**WEIGHT UNLOADED** 695g/24.5oz

## Walther PPK

The Walther PPK was first produced in 1931. It was a more compact version of the Walther PP and it was designed to be easily concealed and carried. The internal workings of the PPK were the same as those of the PP. Apart from the different dimensions, the only real external design alteration was the hand grip. Otherwise the PPK had the same smooth lines as the PP, which was to make it one of the most iconic of pistol designs. A PPK is thought to have been carried by Adolf Hitler. It was also made famous by Ian Fleming's character James Bond in *Dr No*, who later updated to the P99.

**SPECIFICATION**

**MANUFACTURER** Carl Walther GmbH. Waffenfabrik
**CALIBRE** 7.65mm (.32 ACP), .380 ACP
**MAGAZINE CAPACITY** 8
**ACTION** Blowback/double
**TOTAL LENGTH** 154mm/6.06in
**BARREL LENGTH** 84mm/3.31in
**WEIGHT UNLOADED** 580g/20.5oz

## Walther P38

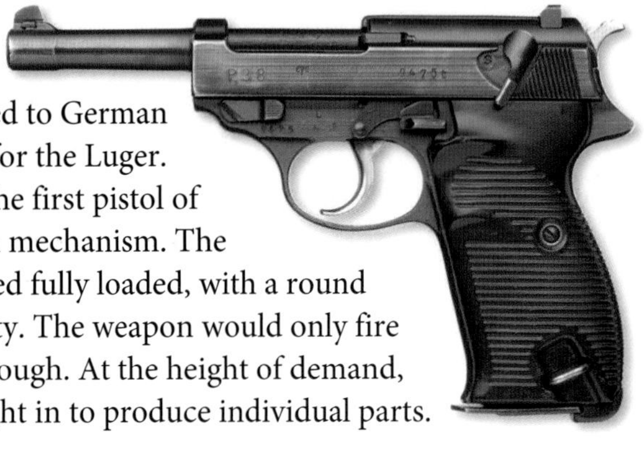

This short-recoil pistol was issued to German forces in 1938 as a replacement for the Luger. It had a locked breech and was the first pistol of this type to have a double-action mechanism. The weapon could therefore be carried fully loaded, with a round chambered, in considerable safety. The weapon would only fire if the trigger was fully pulled through. At the height of demand, other manufacturers were brought in to produce individual parts.

**SPECIFICATION**

**MANUFACTURER** Carl Walther GmbH. Waffenfabrik
**CALIBRE** 9mm Parabellum
**MAGAZINE CAPACITY** 8
**ACTION** Short recoil/double
**TOTAL LENGTH** 213mm/8.38in
**BARREL LENGTH** 127mm/5in
**WEIGHT UNLOADED** 960g/33.86oz

## Walther P5

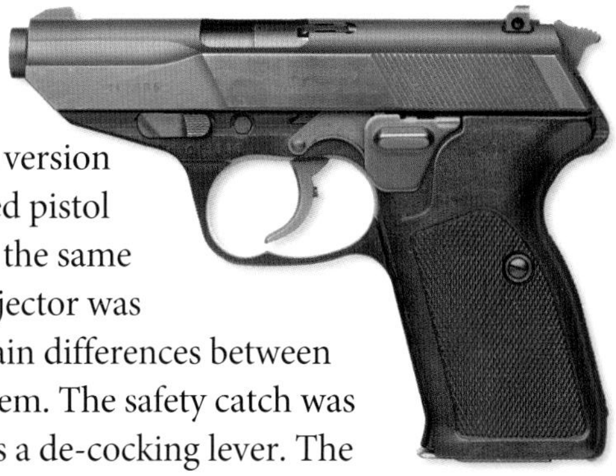

| SPECIFICATION | |
|---|---|
| MANUFACTURER | Carl Walther GmbH. Waffenfabrik |
| CALIBRE | 9mm Parabellum |
| MAGAZINE CAPACITY | 8 |
| ACTION | Short recoil/double or single |
| TOTAL LENGTH | 180mm/7.1in |
| BARREL LENGTH | 90mm/3.54in |
| WEIGHT UNLOADED | 795g/28oz |

Developed in 1979, the P5 was a revised version of the classic P38. It was a recoil-operated pistol with a double-action trigger system and the same breech-locking system as the P38. The ejector was moved to the left of the receiver. The main differences between the P5 and the P38 are in the safety system. The safety catch was moved left side of the frame and used as a de-cocking lever. The weapon would not be fired by a fall of the external hammer unless the trigger had been pulled. The pistol was issued widely to the German Police.

## Walther P88

| SPECIFICATION | |
|---|---|
| MANUFACTURER | Carl Walther GmbH. Waffenfabrik/Sportwaffen |
| CALIBRE | 9mm Parabellum |
| MAGAZINE CAPACITY | 15 |
| ACTION | Recoil/double |
| TOTAL LENGTH | 187mm/7.36in |
| BARREL LENGTH | 102mm/4in |
| WEIGHT UNLOADED | 900g/31.7oz |

First produced in 1988, it continued in production until 1996. It was a highly regarded recoil-operated, locked-breech pistol. Instead of a locking wedge, it used a variation of the Browning cam system. With this system the barrel block lug locked into an ejection port in the slide. It also featured an ambidextrous frame-mounted de-cocking lever. It was fully ambidextrous, with magazine release and de-cocking lever on both sides of the frame. The P88 was designed for both military and law-enforcement use.

## Walther P99

| SPECIFICATION | |
|---|---|
| MANUFACTURER | Carl Walther GmbH. Sportwaffen |
| CALIBRE | 9mm Parabellum |
| MAGAZINE CAPACITY | 16 |
| ACTION | Recoil/double or single |
| TOTAL LENGTH | 180mm/7.1in |
| BARREL LENGTH | 102mm/4in |
| WEIGHT UNLOADED | 630g/22.22oz |

This pistol was produced in 1996. The main aim was to develop a new, modern-style police and self-defence pistol. The P99 used an internal striker rather than an external hammer, and had a chamber-loaded indicator on the right side of the slide. There was a quick-action trigger system in which the striker was partially pre-cocked. Then, when the trigger was pulled, the striker was fully cocked and released, firing the pistol. It also featured four internal safeties, a de-cocking button and adjustable sights. There was an ambidextrous magazine release incorporated into the trigger guard.

## Walther P22

| SPECIFICATION | |
|---|---|
| MANUFACTURER | Carl Walther GmbH. Sportwaffen |
| CALIBRE | .22 Long Rifle |
| MAGAZINE CAPACITY | 10 |
| ACTION | Blowback/double and single |
| TOTAL LENGTH | 160mm/6.3in |
| BARREL LENGTH | 86mm/3.4in |
| WEIGHT UNLOADED | 430g/15.17oz |

Although this was a compact pistol, it was said to retain all of the features of a full-sized version. The P22 could be adapted to several different equipment configurations. The compact design and light weight have been achieved by the use of a polymer frame. It featured ambidextrous controls for both left- and right-handed shooters. There was an integrated trigger lock, chamber-loaded indicator, as well as a magazine disconnect, hammer safety and firing-pin safety. The fixed barrel was said to improve accuracy. The rear sight was adjustable for windage and elevation while the front sight was interchangeable.

# Italy

**Italian gun manufacturers, including Beretta and Bernadelli, have long and distinguished histories going back to the 16th and 18th centuries. As such, they form part of the history of gunmaking, and they are also renowned manufacturers of both traditional and modern firearms. Beretta won the contract to replace the longest-serving pistol in history, the Colt M1911, with the Beretta 92F (designated the M9 in the US). The contract was updated in 2005 for Beretta to produce the M9A1.**

## Benelli MP90S

Benelli is a long-established Italian firm of gunmakers who have specialized in producing target pistols. The MP90S was produced in the 1980s. It was operated by delayed blowback and had a fully adjustable, single-action trigger release and a square-section sight. The sight line was extremely close to the barrel axis. This minimized movement caused by wrist torsion, which in turn allowed for better control of the pistol for target shooting. The sights were fixed and adjustable for windage and elevation.

**SPECIFICATION**

**MANUFACTURER** Benelli Armi SpA.
**CALIBRE** .32 S&W Wadcutter
**MAGAZINE CAPACITY** 5
**ACTION** Delayed blowback/single
**TOTAL LENGTH** 218mm/8.58in
**BARREL LENGTH** 110mm/4.33in
**WEIGHT UNLOADED** 1,180g/41.62oz

## Beretta Model 1915

This was a historic design for Beretta, as it was their first ever pistol. Beretta designed a simple blowback pistol, fired by a concealed hammer. Although most were chambered for either .32 or .38 ACP, a few were chambered to fire the 9mm Glisenti cartridge. During World War I there was increased demand for firearms. The Model 1915 was produced in large numbers during these years, while other manufacturers such as Carl Walther were on standby to fill the gap in arms production. The Model 1915 was produced between 1915 and 1945 and was later used for the military and the police.

**SPECIFICATION**

**MANUFACTURER** Pietro Beretta SpA.
**CALIBRE** .32 ACP, .38 ACP, 9mm Glisenti
**MAGAZINE CAPACITY** 7
**ACTION** Blowback/single
**TOTAL LENGTH** 149mm/5.87in
**BARREL LENGTH** 83mm/3.25in
**WEIGHT UNLOADED** 570g/20.1oz

## Beretta Model 1915/19

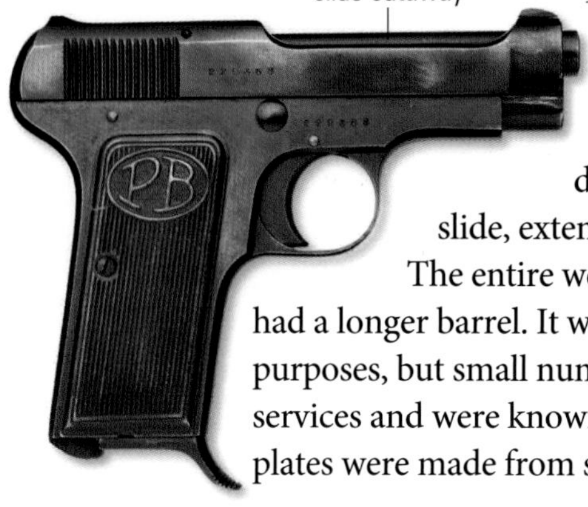


This pistol was an improved version of the Model 1915. It had a revised ejection port and a smaller safety catch than the earlier model. This design also had a larger cutaway in the slide, extending halfway towards the rear sight. The entire weapon was also slightly shorter, yet had a longer barrel. It was not produced primarily for military purposes, but small numbers were manufactured for the services and were known as the Model 1922. The hand grip plates were made from sheet metal instead of the usual wood.

**SPECIFICATION**

**MANUFACTURER** Pietro Beretta SpA.
**CALIBRE** .32 ACP
**MAGAZINE CAPACITY** 7
**ACTION** Blowback/single
**TOTAL LENGTH** 145mm/5.7in
**BARREL LENGTH** 85mm/3.35in
**WEIGHT UNLOADED** 670g/23.63oz

## Beretta Model 1923

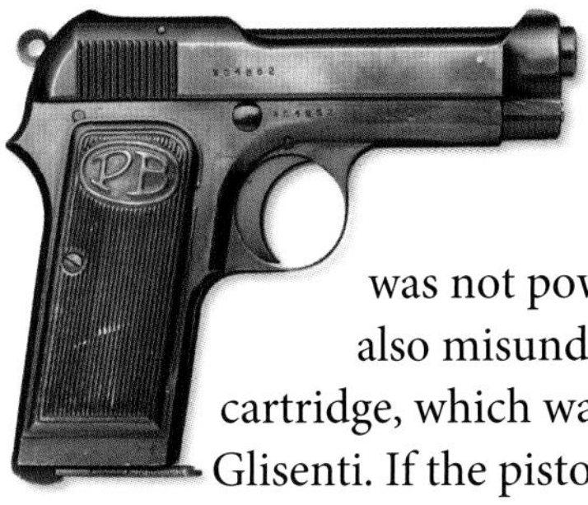

The Model 1923 pistol was designed to consolidate the improvements of the 1915/19 model and to take the 9mm Glisenti round. However, the Model 1923 Glisenti cartridge was not powerful enough to be fully effective. There were also misunderstandings over use of the 9mm Parabellum cartridge, which was a much more powerful round than the Glisenti. If the pistol was loaded and fired with this ammunition, it could damage the pistol as it was not designed to handle this round. Only about 10,000 of these pistols were produced.

**SPECIFICATION**

- **MANUFACTURER** Pietro Beretta SpA.
- **CALIBRE** 9mm Glisenti
- **MAGAZINE CAPACITY** 7
- **ACTION** Blowback/single
- **TOTAL LENGTH** 177mm/6.96in
- **BARREL LENGTH** 87mm/3.43in
- **WEIGHT UNLOADED** 800g/28.22oz

## Beretta Model 1931

**SPECIFICATION**

- **MANUFACTURER** Pietro Beretta SpA.
- **CALIBRE** 7.65mm (.32 ACP)
- **MAGAZINE CAPACITY** 7
- **ACTION** Blowback/single
- **TOTAL LENGTH** 177mm/6.96in
- **BARREL LENGTH** 87mm/3.43in
- **WEIGHT UNLOADED** 800g/28.22oz

This weapon was an adaptation of the Model 1923 and a precursor of the Model 1934. The main difference between this pistol and the Model 1923 was that it was chambered for the .32 ACP round, rather than the 9mm Glisenti round and so did not have its associated problems with its cartridges. The Model 1931 was issued to the Italian Navy and could be instantly recognized by the Regia Marina emblem on the hand grip.

## Beretta Model 1934

**SPECIFICATION**

- **MANUFACTURER** Pietro Beretta SpA.
- **CALIBRE** 9mm Corto (.380 ACP)
- **MAGAZINE CAPACITY** 7
- **ACTION** Blowback/single
- **TOTAL LENGTH** 152mm/6in
- **BARREL LENGTH** 94mm/3.7in
- **WEIGHT UNLOADED** 660g/23.28oz

This blowback-operated pistol was first introduced in 1936. It was essentially an improved version of the 1915/19 pistol. Although it was chambered for the 9mm round, it used a short Corto cartridge to keep the pressure within safe limits. The only real drawback with the Model 1934 was that the round was underpowered. The pistol was designed for the Italian armed forces and many were issued to officers. The Model 1934 proved to be a reliable weapon, partly due to its rugged manufacture and relatively few parts.

## Beretta Model 1951

**SPECIFICATION**

- **MANUFACTURER** Pietro Beretta SpA.
- **CALIBRE** 9mm Parabellum
- **MAGAZINE CAPACITY** 8
- **ACTION** Short recoil/single
- **TOTAL LENGTH** 203mm/8in
- **BARREL LENGTH** 115mm/4.53in
- **WEIGHT UNLOADED** 890g/31oz

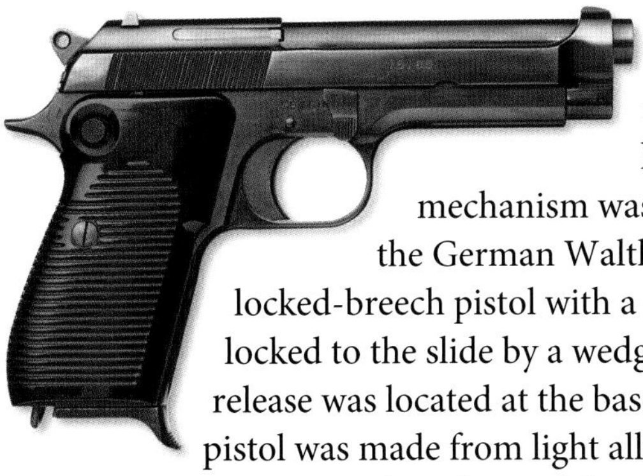

This pistol went into production in 1953 and was made under licence in Egypt for many years. Its mechanism was based on a system designed for the German Walther P38. It was a recoil-operated, locked-breech pistol with a short recoiling barrel, which was locked to the slide by a wedge under the barrel. The magazine release was located at the base of the hand grip. The original pistol was made from light alloy, but was soon found not to be sturdy enough and a steel frame was developed.

## Beretta Model 76

This was a blowback-operated single-action pistol. The frame, slide and barrel were made from heavy steel. The pistol had a safety lever on the left-hand side of the frame. Although this was designed as a target pistol, its rugged and angular appearance meant that it could easily be mistaken for a full combat pistol.

| SPECIFICATION | |
|---|---|
| **MANUFACTURER** | Pietro Beretta SpA. |
| **CALIBRE** | .22 Long Rifle |
| **MAGAZINE** | 10 |
| **ACTION** | Blowback/single |
| **TOTAL LENGTH** | 233mm/9.17in |
| **BARREL LENGTH** | 150mm/5.91in |
| **WEIGHT UNLOADED** | 930g/32.8oz |

## Beretta Model 81

This pistol first went into production in 1976. It was a blowback-operated weapon. It had an ambidextrous safety catch on the frame. The sights were fixed. The pistol took a 12-round magazine. It had a reversible magazine release button and could be fitted with an optional magazine safety. The frame was made from a light alloy, and the slide from steel. The hand grips were wood or plastic. The M81 formed the basis of several later models, such as the Model 82, Model 84 and Model 85.

| SPECIFICATION | |
|---|---|
| **MANUFACTURER** | Pietro Beretta SpA. |
| **CALIBRE** | .32 ACP |
| **MAGAZINE** | 12 |
| **ACTION** | Blowback/single or double |
| **TOTAL LENGTH** | 172mm/6.77in |
| **BARREL LENGTH** | 97mm/3.82in |
| **WEIGHT UNLOADED** | 670g/21.54oz |

## Beretta Model 84

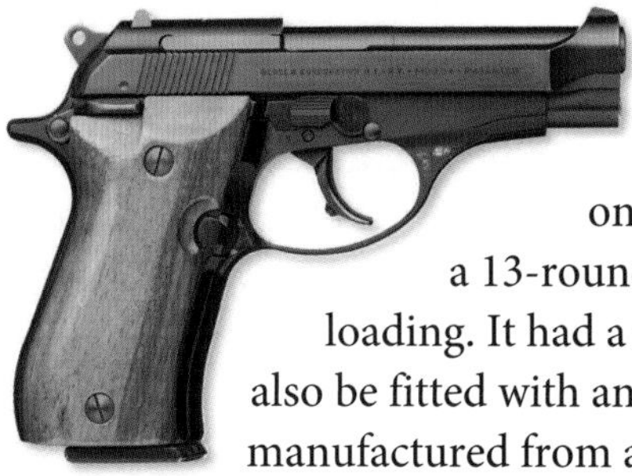

This was a blowback-operated, hammer-fired weapon produced from 1976 to 1995. It had an ambidextrous safety catch on the frame and fixed sights. The pistol took a 13-round magazine which was designed for staggered loading. It had a reversible magazine-release button. It could also be fitted with an optional magazine safety. The frame was manufactured from a light alloy and the slide from steel.

| SPECIFICATION | |
|---|---|
| **MANUFACTURER** | Pietro Beretta SpA. |
| **CALIBRE** | .380 ACP |
| **MAGAZINE** | 13 |
| **ACTION** | Blowback/single or double |
| **TOTAL LENGTH** | 172mm/6.77in |
| **BARREL LENGTH** | 97mm/3.82in |
| **WEIGHT UNLOADED** | 660g/21.22oz |

## Beretta Model 89

| SPECIFICATION | |
|---|---|
| **MANUFACTURER** | Pietro Beretta SpA. |
| **CALIBRE** | .22 Long Rifle |
| **MAGAZINE** | 8 |
| **ACTION** | Blowback/single |
| **TOTAL LENGTH** | 240mm/9.45in |
| **BARREL LENGTH** | 152mm/5.98in |
| **WEIGHT UNLOADED** | 1,160g/40.92oz |

This was a simple blowback-operated pistol, manufactured specifically for target practice. It had a heavy barrel mounted on a mixed alloy frame. The pistol was fitted with an external hammer, an ambidextrous safety catch and a magazine safety device. It had fully adjustable rear sights and a front sight that could be changed. The trigger pull was finely set. As a target pistol, the Model 89 did not have a safety hammer de-cocking device. This meant the hammer did not have been pulled back first if there was a round in the chamber.

## Beretta Model 92

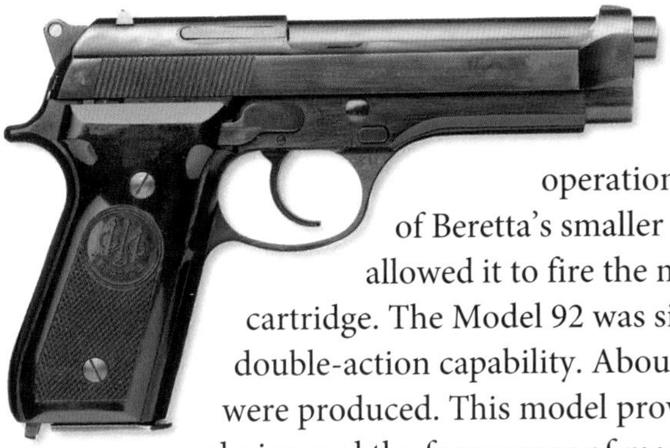

**SPECIFICATION**

**MANUFACTURER** Pietro Beretta SpA.
**CALIBRE** 9mm Parabellum
**MAGAZINE** 15 (10 civilian)
**ACTION** Short recoil/single and double
**TOTAL LENGTH** 217mm/8.54in
**BARREL LENGTH** 125mm/4.92in
**WEIGHT UNLOADED** 950g/33.51oz

This pistol was first manufactured in 1976. It used a short-recoil system of operation instead of the blowback system of Beretta's smaller designs. This reduced recoil and allowed it to fire the more powerful 9mm Parabellum cartridge. The Model 92 was single-action pistol with a double-action capability. About 5,000 Beretta Model 92 pistols were produced. This model proved to be a highly successful design and the forerunner of many successful variants.

## Beretta Model 92SB Compact

**SPECIFICATION**

**MANUFACTURER** Pietro Beretta SpA.
**CALIBRE** 9mm Parabellum
**MAGAZINE** 13
**ACTION** Short recoil/single or double
**TOTAL LENGTH** 211mm/8.31in
**BARREL LENGTH** 119mm/4.69in
**WEIGHT UNLOADED** 915g/32.28oz

The full-size Beretta 92SB was introduced in 1981, a development of the base Beretta Model 92. The Model 92 had been modified by adding a slide-mounted combined safety and de-cocking lever and replacing the frame-mounted manual thumb safety. The Model 92SB won the approval of the US armed forces during trials which resulted in formal issue by the US Government. The Model 92SB Compact was also produced from 1981, and had a shorter barrel and slide. It was chambered for 13 rounds rather than the 15 of the Model 92SB.

**SPECIFICATION**

**MANUFACTURER** Pietro Beretta SpA.
**CALIBRE** 9mm Parabellum
**MAGAZINE** 15 (10 civilian)
**ACTION** Short recoil/single or double
**TOTAL LENGTH** 211mm/8.31in
**BARREL LENGTH** 119mm/4.69in
**WEIGHT UNLOADED** 915g/32.28oz

## Beretta Model 92F

The Model 92F was a slightly modified version of the Beretta 92SB. It was first called the Model 92SB-F and the minor modifications of the "F" version were later included in the standard issue pistol as it evolved during US trials. It operated on the short-recoil, delayed-block system. The Model 92F was designed to have parts that were interchangeable with all Model 92 variants, to ease maintenance. It also had a redesigned trigger guard, a chromed barrel inside and a renewed finish on the outside. At least 500,000 were produced.

## Beretta Model 92FS

The Model 92FS was introduced in the late 1980s as a further modification of the Model 92. Improvements included an ambidextrous manual safety that also functioned as a de-cocking lever. There was a chamber-loaded indicator that was visible and could be felt to the touch, and a firing-pin block that secured the firing pin. It also had a rotating firing-pin striker. These modifications were designed to prevent over-travel of the slide, which could be dangerous to the user if the slide failed.

**SPECIFICATION**

**MANUFACTURER** Pietro Beretta SpA.
**CALIBRE** 9mm Parabellum
**MAGAZINE** 15
**ACTION** Short recoil/single or double
**TOTAL LENGTH** 211mm/8.31in
**BARREL LENGTH** 119mm/4.69in
**WEIGHT UNLOADED** 915g/32.28oz

## Beretta Model 93R

| SPECIFICATION | |
|---|---|
| MANUFACTURER | Pietro Beretta SpA. |
| CALIBRE | 9mm Parabellum |
| MAGAZINE | 20 |
| ACTION | Short recoil/single/rapid burst |
| TOTAL LENGTH | 240mm/9.45in |
| BARREL LENGTH | 156mm/6.16in |
| WEIGHT UNLOADED | 1,120g/39.51oz |

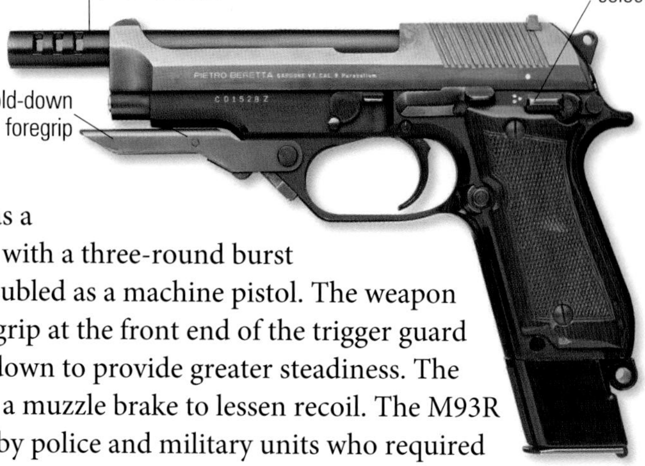


This model, produced in 1986, was similar to the Model 92, produced a decade earlier. It was a selective-fire weapon with a three-round burst facility. As such, it doubled as a machine pistol. The weapon was fitted with a foregrip at the front end of the trigger guard that could be folded down to provide greater steadiness. The barrel was fitted with a muzzle brake to lessen recoil. The M93R was designed for use by police and military units who required a highly concealable weapon with a rapid-burst facility.

## Beretta Model 8000 Cougar

This pistol was first produced in 1994 to meet a requirement for a more compact pistol than the full-size Model 92F (US M9). The weapon was intended for police duties, personal defence and covert operations. It was a recoil-operated, locked-breech pistol with a rotating barrel locking system. The pistol had an ambidextrous safety de-cocking lever, a rotating firing-pin striker, an automatic firing-pin block and a chamber-loaded indicator. The trigger guard was designed for double-handed use.

| SPECIFICATION | |
|---|---|
| MANUFACTURER | Pietro Beretta SpA. |
| CALIBRE | 9mm Parabellum |
| MAGAZINE CAPACITY | 13 |
| ACTION | Short recoil/single |
| TOTAL LENGTH | 180mm/7.1in |
| BARREL LENGTH | 92mm/3.62in |
| WEIGHT UNLOADED | 800g/28.2oz |

## Beretta 9000S

This was the most compact pistol in the Beretta range, launched in 2000. Its lightness in weight was partly achieved through the use of glass-reinforced fibre (GRP) materials and polymers. The hand grips were made from a soft polymer and provide a high level of grip. The 9000S featured a patented locking system that incorporated a tilting barrel and open slide. The pistol developed in two versions. The version "F" was both single and double action, with a manual safety lever that also worked as de-cocker. The version "D" was a double-action only (DAO) pistol, without manual safety, and did not have a de-cocking feature.

| SPECIFICATION | |
|---|---|
| MANUFACTURER | Pietro Beretta SpA. |
| CALIBRE | 9mm Parabellum |
| MAGAZINE CAPACITY | 12 |
| ACTION | Recoil/single or double |
| TOTAL LENGTH | 168mm/6.63in |
| BARREL LENGTH | 88mm/3.46in |
| WEIGHT UNLOADED | 755g/26.63oz |

## Bernadelli Model 60

This pistol was introduced in 1959 and manufactured during the late 1950s and 1960s. It was a blowback-operated pistol with twin return springs to decrease the effect of recoil on the user. It had a locked-breech system and was made of steel throughout. The barrel was forged together with the frame and the pistol could be dismantled by releasing a spring catch, after which the slide could be removed. The pistol was available in three calibres, .22 LR, 7.65mm (.32 ACP) and .380 ACP.

| SPECIFICATION | |
|---|---|
| MANUFACTURER | Vincenzo Bernadelli SpA. |
| CALIBRE | .22 Long Rifle, 7.65mm, .380 ACP |
| MAGAZINE CAPACITY | 8 |
| ACTION | Blowback/single |
| TOTAL LENGTH | 165mm/6.5in |
| BARREL LENGTH | 90mm/3.54in |
| WEIGHT UNLOADED | 685g/24.2oz |

## Bernardelli P6

**SPECIFICATION**

**MANUFACTURER** Vincenzo Bernadelli SpA.
**CALIBRE** .22 Long Rifle, 7.65mm (.32 ACP), .380 ACP
**MAGAZINE** 10, 8 and 7
**ACTION** Blowback/double
**TOTAL LENGTH** 168mm/6.63in
**BARREL LENGTH** 89mm/3.5in
**WEIGHT UNLOADED** 505g/17.8oz

This pistol was designed to be a light and easy-to-carry pocket and defence pistol with external hammer and lightweight alloy frame. It was similar in style to the German Walther PP. The Bernardelli P6 was available in versions that chamber .22 Long Rifle, 7.65mm and .380 ACP rounds with a magazine capacity of 10, 8 and 7 rounds respectively. It could be fitted with either plastic or walnut hand grips designed to absorb and distribute recoil between the wooden or plastic components. The pistol featured a chamber-loaded indicator and adjustable rear sights.

## Bernardelli P8 Compact

**SPECIFICATION**

**MANUFACTURER** Vincenzo Bernadelli SpA.
**CALIBRE** .22 Long Rifle, 7.65mm, .380 ACP
**MAGAZINE** 10
**ACTION** Blowback/double
**TOTAL LENGTH** 168mm/6.63in
**BARREL LENGTH** 89mm/3.5in
**WEIGHT UNLOADED** 507g/17.88oz

This was a lightweight, compact pistol designed for home defence and backup. The hand grip was fitted with plastic target grips. It had manual thumb, half-cock, magazine and auto-locking firing-pin safeties as well as a loaded-chamber indicator and click-adjustable rear sight.

**Safety mechanisms**
The P6 and P8 Compact were largely identical, with the P8 adding safety mechanisms to comply with arms regulations in some countries.

## Bernardelli P90

**SPECIFICATION**

**MANUFACTURER** Vincenzo Bernadelli SpA.
**CALIBRE** .22 Long Rifle, 7.65mm, .380 ACP
**MAGAZINE** 10 and 7
**ACTION** Blowback/double
**TOTAL LENGTH** 228mm/9in (full size)
**BARREL LENGTH** 152mm/6in
**WEIGHT UNLOADED** 693g/24.5oz

This pistol was designed as a precision shooting pistol for both sport shooting and police and military use. In many ways similar to the P6, the P90 was manufactured with three different barrel lengths with a choice of three different calibres, .22 Long Rifle, 7.65mm (.32 ACP) and .380 ACP. The P90 frame was lightweight and the pistol had a fixed barrel outside the muzzle with a front sight screwed on to the end of the barrel. The rear sight was adjustable. The hand grip was ergonomically designed for ease of use and had either plastic or walnut grips.

## Bernadelli Model P0-18

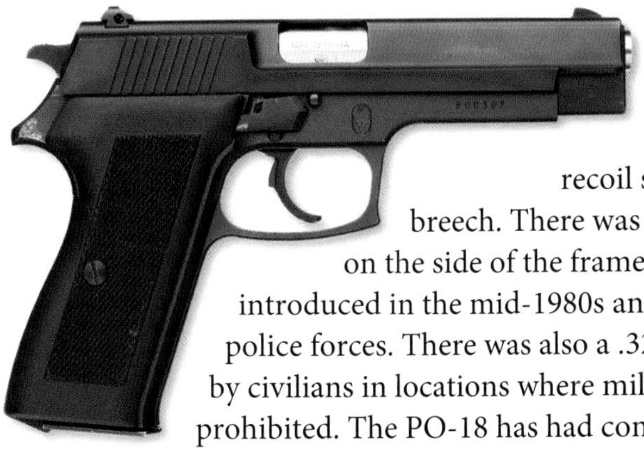

Introduced in 1984, this was a selective double-action pistol with a Browning-style short-recoil system and a locking breech. There was a safety catch mounted on the side of the frame. The P0-18 was first introduced in the mid-1980s and was bought by some police forces. There was also a .32 ACP version for use by civilians in locations where military calibres were prohibited. The PO-18 has had considerable commercial success. A compact model is also available and variations of this were chambered for both rounds of ammunition.

**SPECIFICATION**

**MANUFACTURER** Vincenzo Bernadelli SpA.
**CALIBRE** 9mm Parabellum, 7.65mm (.32 ACP)
**MAGAZINE** 16
**ACTION** Short recoil/double
**TOTAL LENGTH** 213mm/8.38in
**BARREL LENGTH** 122mm/4.8in
**WEIGHT UNLOADED** 1,010g/35.6oz

## Bernardelli POne

Successor to the P0-18, this double-action pistol was designed to achieve accuracy, stability, shooting speed and reliability. Produced in the 1980s, it was intended for use by law enforcement and military professionals as well as for personal defence or sport shooting. The pistol had a forged steel frame, slide and barrel, and it was designed to be durable, light and reliable. The hand grip was slim and was fitted with plastic or walnut grips. Full-length slide rails were designed to achieve both stability and accuracy.

| SPECIFICATION | |
|---|---|
| MANUFACTURER | Vincenzo Bernadelli SpA. |
| CALIBRE | 9mm Parabellum |
| MAGAZINE | 15 |
| ACTION | Blowback/double |
| TOTAL LENGTH | 212mm/8.35in |
| BARREL LENGTH | 122mm/4.8in |
| WEIGHT UNLOADED | 971g/34.25oz |

## Glisenti Model 1910

This pistol was derived from a design by the Italian inventor Bethel Abiel Revelli. He assigned the patent to the manufacturers, Glisenti. After further development, the design was first accepted by the Italian Army as a 7.65mm pistol. In due course, the Italian Army requested a 9mm pistol and, having passed it on to another manufacturer, it was adapted to become the Glisenti Model 1910. The pistol was used in World War I and was also used by Italian forces during World War II.

| SPECIFICATION | |
|---|---|
| MANUFACTURER | Metallurgica Brescia gia Tempini; Societa Siderurgica Glisenti |
| CALIBRE | 9mm Glisenti |
| MAGAZINE CAPACITY | 7 |
| ACTION | Short recoil/single |
| TOTAL LENGTH | 207mm/8.15in |
| BARREL LENGTH | 100mm/3.94in |
| WEIGHT UNLOADED | 820g/29oz |

## Tanfoglio TA90

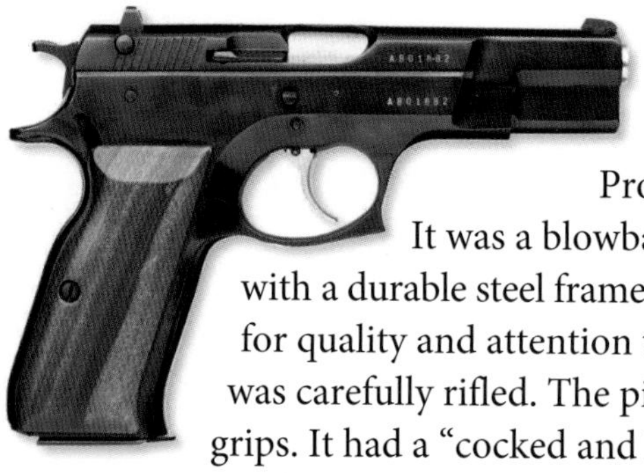

The TA-90 was inspired by the design of the Czech CZ75 pistol. Production of the TA90 started in 1984. It was a blowback-operated, locked-breech pistol with a durable steel frame. The pistol had a good reputation for quality and attention to detail. The barrel, for example, was carefully rifled. The pistol had fixed sights and rubber grips. It had a "cocked and locked" safety mounted on the frame as well as an automatic firing-pin safety. The pistol was bought commercially and had also been issued to some security forces.

| SPECIFICATION | |
|---|---|
| MANUFACTURER | Fratelli Tanfoglio SNC. |
| CALIBRE | 9mm Parabellum |
| MAGAZINE | 15 |
| ACTION | Short recoil/double |
| TOTAL LENGTH | 202mm/7.96in |
| BARREL LENGTH | 120mm/4.72in |
| WEIGHT UNLOADED | 1,015g/36oz |

## Tanfoglio Standard

Production of the Standard started in the mid-1980s. It was designed as a blowback-operated, locked breech self-defence pistol based on features of the Browning High-Power. It featured a hammer-drop ambidextrous safety, a de-cocking system located on the slide, a double-action trigger, a standard reversible magazine catch, a standard hammer, rubber hand grips, three-dot sights and a compact magazine with a high capacity. A compact version was also available as a pocket-sized model.

| SPECIFICATION | |
|---|---|
| MANUFACTURER | Fratelli Tanfoglio SNC. |
| CALIBRE | 9mm Parabellum, .40 S&W, .45 ACP |
| MAGAZINE CAPACITY | 16, 12, 10 |
| ACTION | Blowback/double |
| TOTAL LENGTH | 210mm/8.27in |
| BARREL LENGTH | 113mm/4.45in |
| WEIGHT UNLOADED | 1,150g/40.57oz |

## Tanfoglio Combat

**SPECIFICATION**

**MANUFACTURER** Fratelli Tanfoglio SNC.
**CALIBRE** 9mm Parabellum
**MAGAZINE CAPACITY** 16, 12, 10
**ACTION** Blowback/double
**TOTAL LENGTH** 210mm/8.27in
**BARREL LENGTH** 113mm/4.45in
**WEIGHT UNLOADED** 1,150g/40.57oz

Production of this pistol started in the mid-1980s and it was the basic model for the Tanfoglio combat range of pistols. It was designed primarily for self-defence and sport shooting. It could be carried "cocked and locked" and it also had an automatic firing-pin safety, a double-action trigger, standard reversible magazine catch, standard hammer, rubber hand grips, three-dot sights and a standard magazine. The Combat was available in blued, chromed or duotone finish.

**SPECIFICATION**

**MANUFACTURER** Fratelli Tanfoglio SNC.
**CALIBRE** .22 Long Rifle, .32 ACP, .380 ACP
**MAGAZINE CAPACITY** 7
**ACTION** Blowback/single
**TOTAL LENGTH** 160mm/6.3in
**BARREL LENGTH** 83mm/3.25in
**WEIGHT UNLOADED** 700g/24.69oz

## Tanfoglio GT22

This was a blowback-operated pistol developed in 1992. It had an external hammer and an open-top slide. A target-shooting version of this pistol was also developed. It had a longer barrel and featured an adjustable rear sight. The magazine featured a finger rest at the base to improve the user's grip.

**Tanfoglio**
Tanfoglio models G22 and G27/GT28 were available worldwide from 1992. Some models are not available in the USA.

## Tanfoglio GT27 and GT28

**SPECIFICATION**

**MANUFACTURER** Fratelli Tanfoglio SNC.
**CALIBRE** .25 ACP (GT27), 8mm (GT28)
**MAGAZINE CAPACITY** 6
**ACTION** Blowback/single
**TOTAL LENGTH** 120mm/4.72in
**BARREL LENGTH** 63mm/2.48in
**WEIGHT UNLOADED** 350g/12.35oz

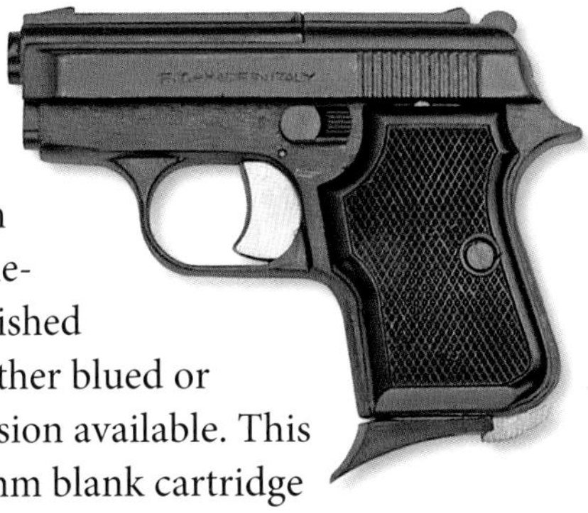

Production of the GT27 was started by Tanfoglio in 1992. This was a super-compact self-defence pistol with fixed barrel and single-action trigger, available in only .25 ACP. It had a trigger safety, a single-column magazine. The hand grips were finished in wood or plastic and it was available in either blued or chromed finish. There was also a GT28 version available. This was a signal pistol, chambered to fire an 8mm blank cartridge (containing an explosive charge but no bullet).

## Tanfoglio Professional Defence

**SPECIFICATION**

**MANUFACTURER** Fratelli Tanfoglio SNC.
**CALIBRE** 9mm Parabellum, .40 S&W, .45 ACP
**MAGAZINE CAPACITY** 16, 12, 10
**ACTION** Blowback/double
**TOTAL LENGTH** 210mm/8.27in
**BARREL LENGTH** 133mm/5.25in
**WEIGHT UNLOADED** 1,150g/40.57oz

This was a pistol specially made for professional use by special operations and law enforcement agencies. Production of the pistol started in 1994. The Professional Defence had a stainless-steel frame with a rounded trigger guard, and stainless-steel compact slide. There were chequered straps on both the front and rear of the hand grip and rubber side grips. The double-action trigger was an extended beavertail design. The pistol had a dovetail front night sight on the slide and carried a standard magazine. The barrel had a compensator to reduce recoil. It was available in a variety of chamberings including 9mm Parabellum.

## Tanfoglio Carry

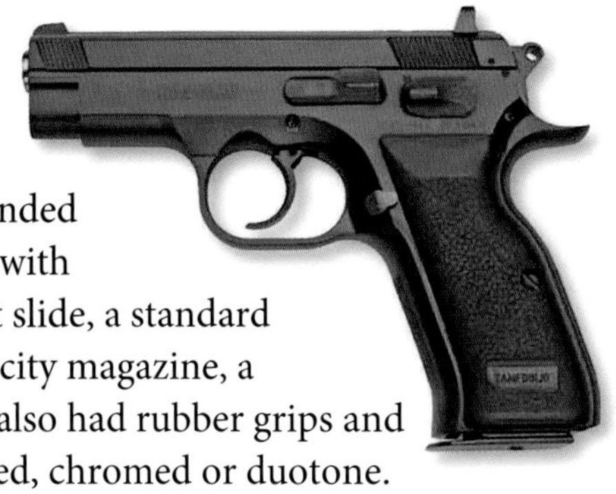

This self-defence pistol was designed as a carry pistol for special operations and law enforcement agencies. Production started in 1994. Its frame had a large rounded trigger guard suitable for a gloved hand, with a double-action trigger. It had a compact slide, a standard reversible magazine catch and high-capacity magazine, a standard safety and hammer. The pistol also had rubber grips and three-dot sights. It was available in a blued, chromed or duotone.

**SPECIFICATION**

**MANUFACTURER** Fratelli Tanfoglio SNC.
**CALIBRE** 9mm Parabellum, .40 S&W, .45 ACP
**MAGAZINE CAPACITY** 16, 12, 10
**ACTION** Blowback/double
**TOTAL LENGTH** 185mm/7.28in
**BARREL LENGTH** 93mm/3.66in
**WEIGHT UNLOADED** 1,100g/38.8oz

## Tanfoglio Force

This pistol, introduced in 1996, was designed primarily for personal defence and in particular for use by the police. The Force had a light polymer frame for ease of carriage and a high-capacity magazine. The pistol could be carried "cocked and locked". Features included a double-action trigger, standard reversible magazine catch, standard hammer and three-dot sights.

**Tanfoglio**
This Italian company is based in the Gardone valley in Brescia. Firearms have been produced at Tanfoglio for over 500 years.

**SPECIFICATION**

**MANUFACTURER** Fratelli Tanfoglio SNC.
**CALIBRE** 9mm Parabellum, .40 S&W, .45 ACP
**MAGAZINE CAPACITY** 16, 12, 10
**ACTION** Blowback/double
**TOTAL LENGTH** 210mm/8.27in
**BARREL LENGTH** 113mm/4.45in
**WEIGHT UNLOADED** 850g/29.98oz

## Tanfoglio Force Compact

This was a pocket-size version of the Force model, produced in 1996. It had a shorter barrel and a shorter grip. It was designed to be easily carried by police on duty or as a personal-defence weapon. It also featured a high-capacity magazine. It had a "cocked and locked" safety on the frame with an automatic firing-pin safety, double-action trigger, standard reversible magazine catch, standard hammer, three-dot sights and a compact magazine.

**SPECIFICATION**

**MANUFACTURER** Fratelli Tanfoglio SNC.
**CALIBRE** 9mm Parabellum, .40 S&W, .45 ACP
**MAGAZINE CAPACITY** 13, 10, 8
**ACTION** Blowback/double
**TOTAL LENGTH** 195mm/7.67in
**BARREL LENGTH** 93mm/3.66in
**WEIGHT UNLOADED** 750g/26.45oz

## Tanfoglio Stock

This pistol was designed for either self-defence or target shooting. It was known as the Stock in Europe and the Witness in the United States, where it is sold by European American Armory Corporation (EAA). Among its features it had a custom reversible magazine catch and extended safety. It had a steel frame and slide and specially designed polygonal barrel and was available in several calibres.

**Witness brand**
In the USA the brand is known as "EAA Witness". This includes a variety of individual models that can be customized with optional features.

**SPECIFICATION**

**MANUFACTURER** Fratelli Tanfoglio SNC.
**CALIBRE** 9mm Parabellum, .40 S&W, .45 ACP
**MAGAZINE CAPACITY** 16, 12, 10
**ACTION** Blowback/double
**TOTAL LENGTH** 210mm/8.27in
**BARREL LENGTH** 113mm/4.45in
**WEIGHT UNLOADED** 1,150g/40.57oz

# Norway

**Norway does not have a tradition of designing and manufacturing pistols and revolvers, and weapons in this category issued to its armed forces were mainly imported. Some, however, such as the US Colt and the Russian Nagant (originally Belgian), were manufactured under licence in Norwegian factories.**

**SPECIFICATION**

**MANUFACTURER** Kongsberg Arsenal
**CALIBRE** .45 ACP
**MAGAZINE** 7
**ACTION** Short recoil/single
**TOTAL LENGTH** 216mm/8.5in
**BARREL LENGTH** 127mm/5in
**WEIGHT UNLOADED** 1,130g/39.86oz

## Colt 1914

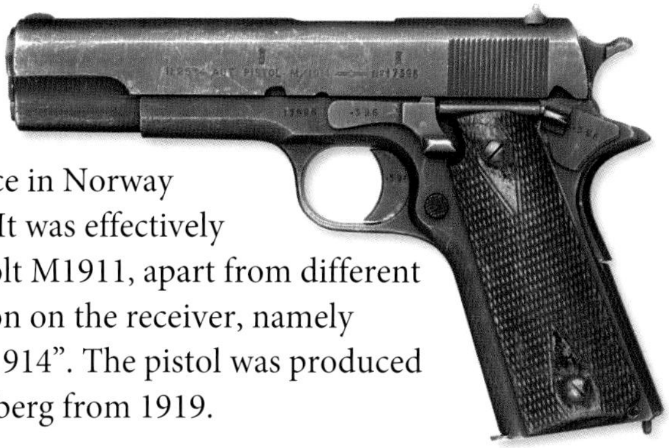

This pistol was manufactured under licence in Norway at the Kongsberg Arsenal. It was effectively the same weapon as the Colt M1911, apart from different markings, and identification on the receiver, namely "11.25mm Aut. Pistol. M/1914". The pistol was produced in large numbers at Kongsberg from 1919.

**SPECIFICATION**

**MANUFACTURER** Manufacture d'Armes Nagant Freres/Tula Arsenal
**CALIBRE** 7.5mm Nagant
**CYLINDER** 7
**ACTION** Single or double action
**TOTAL LENGTH** 229mm/9.06in
**BARREL LENGTH** 110mm/4.35in
**WEIGHT UNLOADED** 790g/27.87oz

## Nagant Model 1893

This revolver was one of many versions of the Russian Nagant revolver and many were imported, though some may have been assembled in Norway. It was replaced by the .45 ACP Colt Model of 1911.

**Use in Europe**
The Nagant was provided for the military in Sweden, Denmark, Belgium and Luxembourg.

# Denmark

**Danish pistol and revolver design, production and manufacture have included both entirely home-grown developments and adaptations of foreign designs. Some of these designs, such as the Schouboe of 1907, were innovative, but unfortunately ingenious designs such as these did not always find a ready market.**

**SPECIFICATION**

**MANUFACTURER** Anciens Établissements Pieper (AEP)
**CALIBRE** 9mm Bergmann-Bayard
**MAGAZINE** 6
**ACTION** Recoil/single
**TOTAL LENGTH** 250mm/9.84in
**BARREL LENGTH** 102mm/4in
**WEIGHT UNLOADED** 1,015g/35.8oz

## Bergmann-Bayard Model 1910

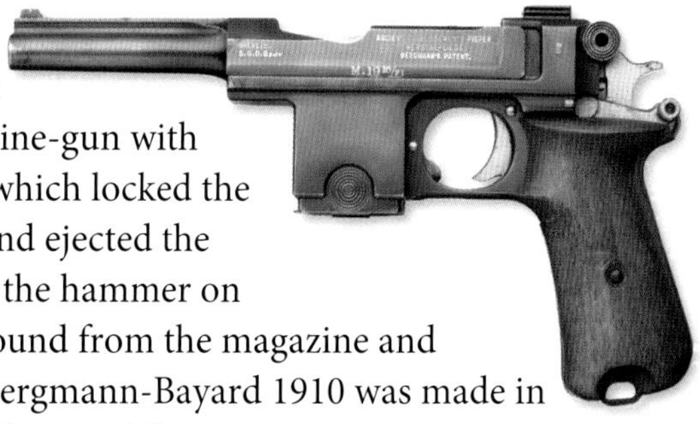

This pistol incorporated the design patented by Bergmann for a machine-gun with a vertically moving locking piece which locked the breech block. The bolt extracted and ejected the spent cartridge casing and cocked the hammer on the recoil strike. It then pulled a round from the magazine and chambered it on the return. The Bergmann-Bayard 1910 was made in Belgium and supplied to the Danish armed forces.

### Schouboe M1907

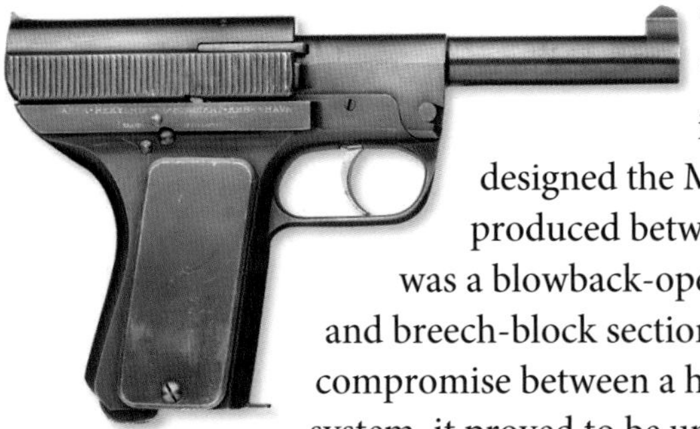

This pistol was designed by Jens Torring Schouboe, an officer in the Danish Army who also designed the Madsen submachine gun. It was produced between 1907 and 1917. The M1907 was a blowback-operated pistol with a short slide and breech-block section at the rear. In order to achieve a compromise between a heavy-calibre round and blowback system, it proved to be unsuccessful. Schouboe used an extremely light bullet to minimize recoil. The problem with this was that the bullet proved to be too light to be accurate.

**SPECIFICATION**

**MANUFACTURER** Dansk Rekylriffel Syndikat AS
**CALIBRE** 11.35mm Schouboe
**MAGAZINE CAPACITY** 6
**ACTION** Blowback/single
**TOTAL LENGTH** 203mm/8in
**BARREL LENGTH** 130mm/5.12in
**WEIGHT UNLOADED** 690g/24.3oz

## Austria

**Austria has a tradition of producing world-class small arms that continue to be used by armed forces throughout the world. Ferdinand Ritter von Mannlicher was one of the most famous armaments designers of all time and lends his name to the current firm of Steyr-Mannlicher. Another leading small arms producer in Austria is Glock, which was founded in 1963.**

### Glock 17

This was the first Glock handgun, introduced in 1983. It was innovative both for its pure polymer frame and for the "Safe Action" safety system – a semi-double-action trigger system along with a striker instead of a hammer and firing pin which allowed for several trigger pulls. Glock pistols had three independent and automatic safeties – trigger safety, firing-pin safety and drop safety – which sequentially disengaged when the trigger was pulled and which re-engaged as the pistol fired and the trigger returned to its forward position. Glock pistols are said to have about half the number of components as comparable handguns. The Glock 17 had only 33 parts and could be disassembled and reassembled with one tool.

**SPECIFICATION**

**MANUFACTURER** Glock GmbH.
**CALIBRE** 9mm Parabellum
**MAGAZINE CAPACITY** 17
**ACTION** Recoil/double – Safe Action (SA)
**TOTAL LENGTH** 186mm/7.32in
**BARREL LENGTH** 114mm/44in
**WEIGHT UNLOADED** 625g/22oz

### Glock 18

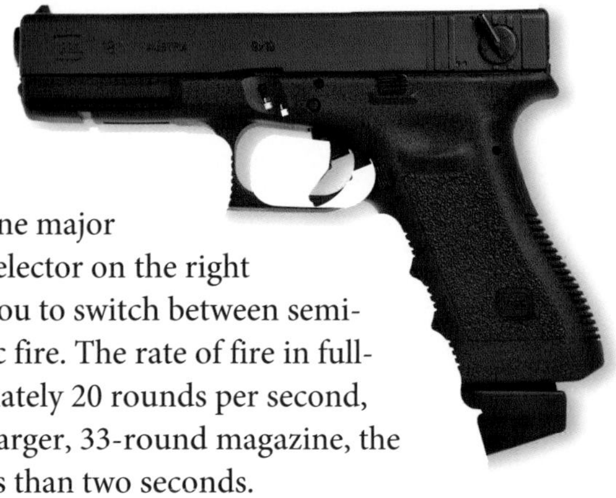

Released in 1987 with the same specifications as the Glock 17, the Glock 18 has one major difference. An external fire selector on the right rear side of the slide allows you to switch between semi-automatic and full-automatic fire. The rate of fire in full-automatic mode is approximately 20 rounds per second, meaning that even with the larger, 33-round magazine, the gun can be shot empty in less than two seconds.

**SPECIFICATION**

**MANUFACTURER** Glock GmbH.
**CALIBRE** 9mm Parabellum
**MAGAZINE CAPACITY** 19 or 33
**ACTION** Short recoil/double or full-automatic – Safe Action (SA)
**TOTAL LENGTH** 204mm/8in
**BARREL LENGTH** 114mm/4.4in
**WEIGHT UNLOADED** 625g/22oz

## Glock 19

Developed in 1988, the Glock 19 was essentially the same as the Glock 17 but of reduced size, designed for ease of concealment. Compared with the original Glock 17, the Glock 19 had a slide and grip that were slightly shorter. The advantage of the Glock 19 was the magazine capacity of 15 for 9mm Parabellum calibre rounds, which was more common in larger pistols. The Glock 19 is used for law enforcement and self-defence.

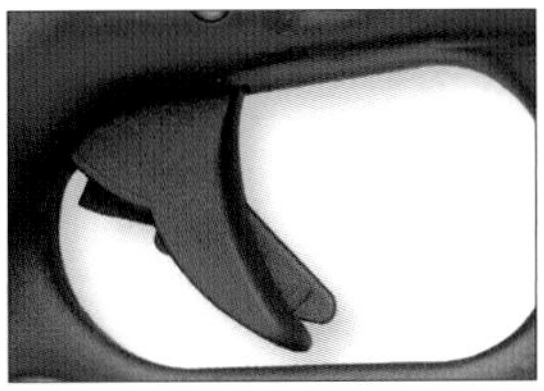

**ABOVE** Glocks have a small lever set in the face of the trigger locking it until the pistol is properly engaged.

**SPECIFICATION**

**MANUFACTURER** Glock GmbH.
**CALIBRE** 9mm Parabellum
**MAGAZINE CAPACITY** 15
**ACTION** Recoil/double (SA)
**TOTAL LENGTH** 174mm/6.85in
**BARREL LENGTH** 102mm/4in
**WEIGHT UNLOADED** 595g/20.99oz

## Glock 20

**SPECIFICATION**

**MANUFACTURER** Glock Ges.mbH
**CALIBRE** 10mm Auto
**MAGAZINE CAPACITY** 15
**ACTION** Recoil/double (SA)
**TOTAL LENGTH** 193mm/7.59in
**BARREL LENGTH** 117mm/4.61in
**WEIGHT UNLOADED** 785g/27.68oz

This pistol, produced in 1990, was similar in most respects to the Glock 17, but was both longer and wider in dimensions and had a significantly increased calibre. The slide and barrel of the Glock 20 was heavier than the lighter 9mm Parabellum pistols such as the Glock 17. The pistol was carried by some police departments. It provided the same accuracy and power as a Magnum hunting revolver.

## Glock 21

**SPECIFICATION**

**MANUFACTURER** Glock Ges.mbH
**CALIBRE** .45 ACP
**MAGAZINE CAPACITY** 13
**ACTION** Recoil/double (SA)
**TOTAL LENGTH** 193mm/7.59in
**BARREL LENGTH** 117mm/4.61in
**WEIGHT UNLOADED** 745g/26.28oz

This was a large-frame Glock, produced in 1990. It was based on the Glock 20 and fired the .45 ACP cartridge. It had a modified Glock 20 frame, slide and magazine, but these difference were quite minor. This pistol was designed to fulfil the requirement for a personal defence handgun and was also used for law enforcement. Because of its frame size, its grip was too large for many people, but well suited for those with bigger hands.

## Glock 22

**SPECIFICATION**

**MANUFACTURER** Glock Ges.mbH
**CALIBRE** .40 S&W
**MAGAZINE CAPACITY** 15
**ACTION** Recoil/double (SA)
**TOTAL LENGTH** 186mm/7.32in
**BARREL LENGTH** 114mm/4.59in
**WEIGHT UNLOADED** 650g/22.92oz

This pistol, produced in 1990, was distinguished by the novel .40 S&W-calibre cartridge and was popular for self-defence and law-enforcement. Otherwise it was essentially the same as the Glock 17, apart from its modified slide, frame, barrel size and magazine. In 2006, the Glock 22 was the most popular sidearm in use in the United States. It was used by law enforcement agencies, the military, security personnel and also by private citizens.

## Glock 23

This pistol was essentially the same as the Glock 19 in size, with modified slide, frame and .40 S&W cartridge, with the size reduced for ease of concealment. In the United States many police patrol officers carry full-size Glock 22s, while detectives, officers and supporting staff carry the slightly smaller Glock 23. This pistol had the benefit of being the size of a 9mm pistol while having the ballistics of the bigger cartridge.

**SPECIFICATION**

**MANUFACTURER** Glock GmbH.
**CALIBRE** .40 S&W
**MAGAZINE CAPACITY** 13
**ACTION** Recoil/double (SA)
**TOTAL LENGTH** 174mm/6.85in
**BARREL LENGTH** 102mm/4.02in
**WEIGHT UNLOADED** 600g/21.16oz

## Glock 24

This pistol had a composite alloy frame and a long slide. It was designed primarily for use in competitive shooting. Essentially the Glock 24 was the same as a variant of the Glock 17, but chambered for the bigger .40 S&W cartridge. The Glock 24 was discontinued in the late 1990s but special orders for components and pistols could still be made.

**SPECIFICATION**

**MANUFACTURER** Glock GmbH.
**CALIBRE** .40 S&W
**MAGAZINE CAPACITY** 10, 15, 29
**ACTION** Recoil/double (SA)
**TOTAL LENGTH** 225mm/8.86in
**BARREL LENGTH** 153mm/6.02in
**WEIGHT UNLOADED** 757g/26.7oz

## Glock 25

Introduced in 1995, the Glock 25 was marketed for countries that do not allow standard military calibres for private use. Although the Glock 25 was the same size as the more powerful Glock 19, it had the more compact .380 chambering. The Glock 25 was a blowback pistol with no barrel lock-up as this is not required with the .380 ACP round.

**The .380 ACP cartridge**
This was a rimless, straight-sided cartridge that was designed by John Browning. It was specifically designed for pistols that did not have a barrel lock-up mechanism and therefore had a low breech pressure.

**SPECIFICATION**

**MANUFACTURER** Glock GmbH.
**CALIBRE** .380 ACP
**MAGAZINE CAPACITY** 15
**ACTION** Blowback/double (SA)
**TOTAL LENGTH** 174mm/6.85in
**BARREL LENGTH** 102mm/4.02in
**WEIGHT UNLOADED** 570g/20.11oz

## Glocks 26, 27 and 28

The Glock 26 and Glock 27 were introduced in 1996. They shared the same exterior dimensions and were smaller Glock pistols, though retained many of features of the larger Glocks. They were small enough to fit in the palm of the hand and could be easily concealed in a jacket pocket or an ankle holster. The Glock 28, introduced a year later, was a blowback-operated system designed for use in countries that did not allow standard military calibres for private use, and was slightly lighter in unloaded weight than the Glock 26 and Glock 27.

**SPECIFICATION**

**MANUFACTURER** Glock GmbH.
**CALIBRE** 9mm Parabellum (G26), .40 S&W (G27) and .380 ACP (G28)
**MAGAZINE CAPACITY** 9 to 33
**ACTION** Blowback/double (SA)
**TOTAL LENGTH** 160mm/6.3in
**BARREL LENGTH** 88mm/3.46in
**WEIGHT UNLOADED** 560g/19.75oz (G26/27), 529g/18.66oz (G28)

## Glocks 29 and 30

**SPECIFICATION**

**MANUFACTURER** Glock GmbH.
**CALIBRE** 10mm (G29), .45 ACP (G30)
**MAGAZINE CAPACITY** 9 to 15
**ACTION** Recoil/double action
**TOTAL LENGTH** 172mm/6.77in
**BARREL LENGTH** 96mm/3.78in
**WEIGHT UNLOADED** 700g/24.69oz (G29), 680g/23.99oz (G30)

The Glock 29 and 30 were subcompact pistols, although they were only slightly smaller than the Glock 19. They retained plenty of power for their size and were very popular for self-defence in the United States. The Glock 30 was identical to the Glock 29, except for a different calibre, and slightly lighter unloaded weight.

**10mm calibre**
The Glock 29 used 10mm calibre ammunition that was comparatively powerful, especially for a subcompact pistol. These pistols featured a double recoil spring that absorbed the recoil energy.

## Glock 31

**SPECIFICATION**

**MANUFACTURER** Glock GmbH.
**CALIBRE** .357 SIG
**MAGAZINE CAPACITY** 15, 17
**ACTION** Recoil/double (SA)
**TOTAL LENGTH** 186mm/7.32in
**BARREL LENGTH** 114mm/5in
**WEIGHT UNLOADED** 660g/23.28oz

With the growing popularity of the new .357 SIG calibre, Glock decided to develop a new pistol in this calibre. The Glock 31 was almost identical to the Glock 22 in appearance. It had a modified slide, frame, larger barrel and magazine. It also had a magazine capacity of 15 rounds and was chambered for the .357 SIG cartridge, which was preferred by many shooters. This pistol was designed primarily for law enforcement duties. It was not as comfortable to shoot as the Glock 22 as it had a sharper recoil.

## Glock 32

**SPECIFICATION**

**MANUFACTURER** Glock GmbH.
**CALIBRE** .357 SIG
**MAGAZINE CAPACITY** 13, 15, 17
**ACTION** Recoil/double (SA)
**TOTAL LENGTH** 174mm/6.85in
**BARREL LENGTH** 102mm/4in
**WEIGHT UNLOADED** 610g/21.52oz

The Glock 32 was a compact Glock, almost identical to the Glock 19 and the Glock 23. They were identical in barrel length and external dimensions. The Glock 32 was slightly heavier in unloaded weight, which may have been due to a wider barrel width, used a .357 cartridge and used a modified slide and frame. It was designed for law enforcement duties. The Glock 32 could be converted to .40 S&W.

**Wear resistant**
Glock pistols are treated with Tenifer in the final stage of hardening to improve corrosion and wear resistance. The process involves what is known as carbonitriding, whereby the metal absorbs both carbon and nitrogen.

## Glocks 33, 34 and 35

Introduced in 1997, this pistol was a subcompact version and about the same size as the Glock 26 and Glock 27, and the smallest Glock available in .357 chambering. It had a magazine with a capacity of 9 rounds, with a legal limit of 10 rounds, which could be acquired through a magazine extension kit. More innovations were made in the same year by developing the International Practical Shooting Federation (IPSF)-sized Glock 34 in 9mm Parabellum and the Glock 35 in .40 ACP.

**SPECIFICATION**

**MANUFACTURER** Glock GmbH.
**CALIBRE** .357 SIG (G33), 9mm Parabellum (G34), .40 ACP (G35)
**MAGAZINE CAPACITY** 9 to 33
**ACTION** Recoil/double (SA)
**TOTAL LENGTH** 160mm/6.3in
**BARREL LENGTH** 88mm/3.46in
**WEIGHT UNLOADED** 560g/19.75oz

## Glock 36

Introduced in 1999, this pistol was distinguished from the others in the Glock family by its slimline design, for ease of concealment. It was flatter than the other Glocks so had a more comfortable hold on the trigger. It had a single stack (rather than a double stack) magazine. It was a popular model for personal defence, providing a potency of firepower with ease of handling.

**SPECIFICATION**

**MANUFACTURER** Glock GmbH.
**CALIBRE** .45 ACP
**MAGAZINE CAPACITY** 6
**ACTION** Recoil/double (SA)
**TOTAL LENGTH** 172mm/6.77in
**BARREL LENGTH** 96mm/3.78in
**WEIGHT UNLOADED** 570g/20.1oz

## Glock 37

The G37 first appeared in 2003 and in most respects was similar to the Glock 17, but it had a wider slide and a 10-round magazine. It was designed for law enforcement and self-defence use. Its larger calibre offered improved single-shot stopping power, while avoiding the larger frame-size problems of the Glock 21. The new .45 GAP round added to its appeal.

**GAP/ACP**

The .45 GAP (Glock Automatic Pistol) is a round specifically devised by Glock. It is slightly shorter than the .45 ACP round designed by John Browning and it is said to have comparable performance.

**SPECIFICATION**

**MANUFACTURER** Glock GmbH.
**CALIBRE** .45 GAP
**MAGAZINE CAPACITY** 10
**ACTION** Recoil/double (SA)
**TOTAL LENGTH** 186mm/7.32in
**BARREL LENGTH** 114mm/4.5in
**WEIGHT UNLOADED** 735g/25.92oz

## Glock 38

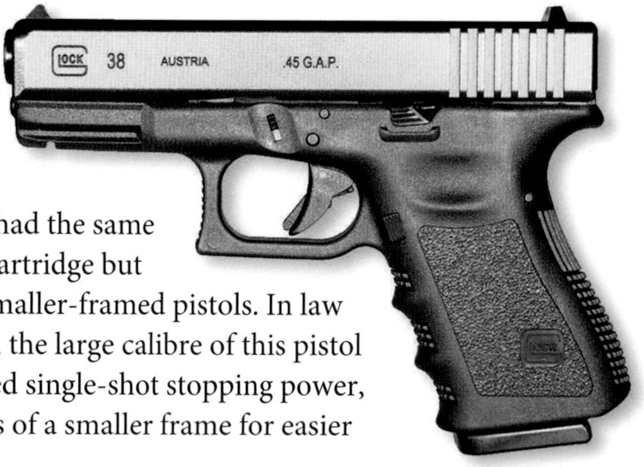


This pistol was first produced in 2005 and featured the .45 GAP cartridge. Designed by Glock, the .45 GAP cartridge had the same performance as the .45 ACP cartridge but was short enough to fit into smaller-framed pistols. In law enforcement and self-defence, the large calibre of this pistol was intended to offer improved single-shot stopping power, while maintaining the benefits of a smaller frame for easier concealed carry.

**SPECIFICATION**

**MANUFACTURER** Glock GmbH.
**CALIBRE** .45 GAP
**MAGAZINE CAPACITY** 8, 10
**ACTION** Recoil/double (SA)
**TOTAL LENGTH** 174mm/6.85in
**BARREL LENGTH** 102mm/4in
**WEIGHT UNLOADED** 685g/24.16oz

## Glock 39

The Glock 39 was released in 2005. Like the Glock 37 it used the .45 GAP cartridge. The Glock 39 had the same frame size as the Glock 26 (in 9mm) and the Glock 27 (.40 S&W). It was one of the lightest of all Glock pistols when unloaded, which made it ideal for self-defence by a concealed weapons carrier. It was designed for law enforcement and self-defence use. Its large calibre offered considerable single-shot stopping power, while the smaller frame made it easier for concealed carry.

**SPECIFICATION**

**MANUFACTURER** Glock GmbH.
**CALIBRE** .45 GAP
**MAGAZINE CAPACITY** 6, 8, 10
**ACTION** Recoil/double (SA)
**TOTAL LENGTH** 160mm/6.3in
**BARREL LENGTH** 88mm/3.46in
**WEIGHT UNLOADED** 548g/19.33oz

## Mannlicher M1900

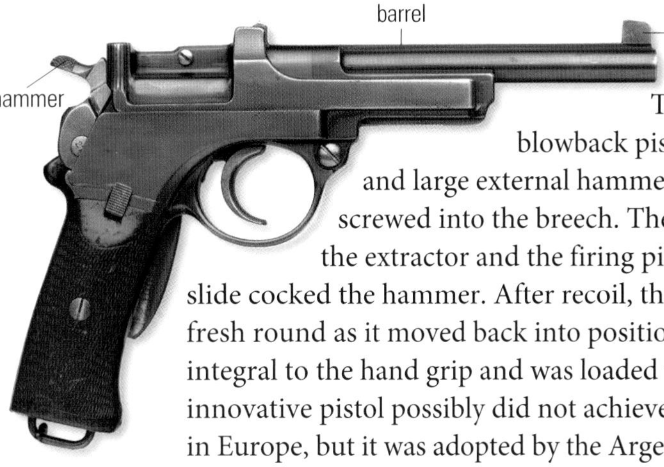


| SPECIFICATION | |
|---|---|
| **MANUFACTURER** | Osterreichische Waffenfabrik Steyr |
| **CALIBRE** | 7.63mm Mannlicher |
| **MAGAZINE CAPACITY** | 8 |
| **ACTION** | Delayed blowback/single |
| **TOTAL LENGTH** | 246mm/9.69in |
| **BARREL LENGTH** | 160mm/6.3in |
| **WEIGHT UNLOADED** | 910g/32.1oz |

This was a delayed-blowback pistol with a heavy spring and large external hammer. The barrel was screwed into the breech. The slide included the extractor and the firing pin. As it moved back, the slide cocked the hammer. After recoil, the slide re-chambered a fresh round as it moved back into position. The magazine was integral to the hand grip and was loaded with a charger. This innovative pistol possibly did not achieve the success it deserved in Europe, but it was adopted by the Argentine armed forces as the Modelo 1905 and produced in considerable numbers.

## Roth-Steyr M1907

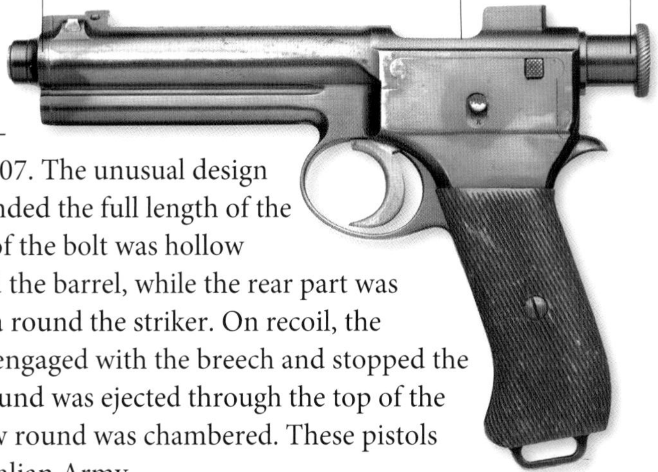


| SPECIFICATION | |
|---|---|
| **MANUFACTURER** | Osterreichische Waffenfabrik Steyr |
| **CALIBRE** | 8mm Steyr |
| **MAGAZINE CAPACITY** | 10 |
| **ACTION** | Recoil/single |
| **TOTAL LENGTH** | 233mm/9.17in |
| **BARREL LENGTH** | 131mm/5.16in |
| **WEIGHT UNLOADED** | 1,030g/36.3oz |

This pistol, developed by George Roth, was first issued to the Austro-Hungarian Cavalry in 1907. The unusual design included a bolt that extended the full length of the receiver. The front part of the bolt was hollow and this part surrounded the barrel, while the rear part was solid, apart from the area round the striker. On recoil, the barrel rotated until lugs engaged with the breech and stopped the movement. The spent round was ejected through the top of the receiver casing and a new round was chambered. These pistols were also issued to the Italian Army.

## Steyr Hahn M1911/M1912

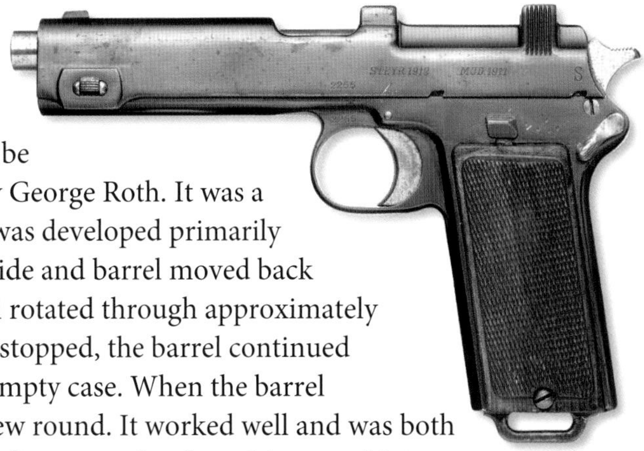

| SPECIFICATION | |
|---|---|
| **MANUFACTURER** | Osterreichische Waffenfabriks-Gesellschaft |
| **CALIBRE** | 9mm Steyr |
| **MAGAZINE CAPACITY** | 8 |
| **ACTION** | Recoil/single |
| **TOTAL LENGTH** | 216mm/8.5in |
| **BARREL LENGTH** | 128mm/5.04in |
| **WEIGHT UNLOADED** | 1,020g/35.98oz |

**Steyr Hahn**
"Hahn" is a German word that means hammer. The hammer on this pistol is clumsy but workable.

The M1911 was designed by firearms designer Karel Krnka, and was believed to be based on an earlier work by George Roth. It was a recoil-operated pistol that was developed primarily for military use. Both the slide and barrel moved back during recoil and the barrel rotated through approximately 20 degrees. When the slide stopped, the barrel continued backwards, extracting the empty case. When the barrel returned, it chambered a new round. It worked well and was both a notable mechanism and a fine example of precision machining. The M1911 had a fixed blade front sight, while the M1912, produced a year later, was identical except for a dovetailed front sight. Numbers of these weapons were taken over by the German Army after the annexation of Austria by Germany in 1938. The Germans standardized many of these weapons to 9mm Parabellum (named P-08) at the Mauser firm.

## Rast & Gasser M1898

This was an eight-chamber revolver first made by Rast & Gasser of Vienna in the 1870s. The M1898 was used widely by Austrians in World War I, and many were in the hands of Italians in World War II.

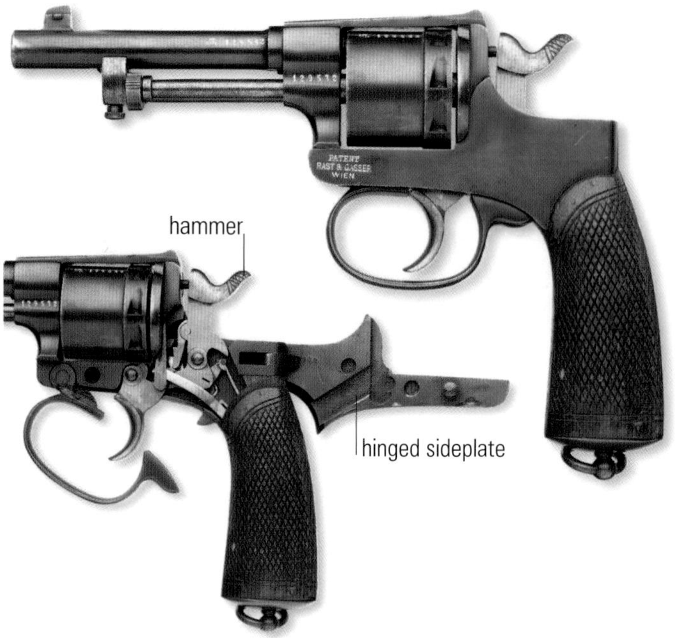


**RIGHT** The M1898 had a hinged sideplate that could be opened to allow access to the internal workings of the revolver. When the gun was opened the trigger was disconnected from the hammer.

**SPECIFICATION**

**MANUFACTURER** Rast & Gasser
**CALIBRE** 8mm Rast & Gasser
**CYLINDERS** 8
**ACTION** Single/double
**TOTAL LENGTH** 220mm/8.66in
**BARREL LENGTH** 116mm/4.57in
**WEIGHT UNLOADED** 1,077g/38oz

## Steyr Mannlicher M1894

The first version of this pistol was produced in 1894 in Switzerland by the Austrian firm Mannlicher and several years of development followed. The pistol was a departure in pistol design as it used a concept known as "blow forward" whereby the barrel was moved forward against a spring positioned around the barrel to extract the empty cartridge and to strip off a new cartridge. The hammer was manually cocked by the user. Rounds were loaded via a clip into the receiver and the cartridges could then be pressed into the magazine.

**SPECIFICATION**

**MANUFACTURER** Schweizerische Industrie-Gesellschaft (SIG)
**CALIBRE** 6.5mm Mannlicher
**MAGAZINE CAPACITY** 5
**ACTION** Blow forward/single
**TOTAL LENGTH** 215mm/8.46in
**BARREL LENGTH** 165mm/6.5in
**WEIGHT UNLOADED** 850g/30oz

## Steyr GB (Gas Break)

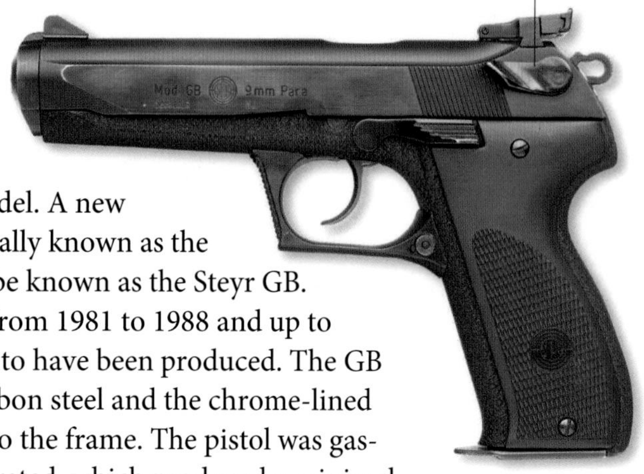


In the early 1970s, Austria decided to replace the standard army issue P38 pistol and the Browning High-Power with a new model. A new pistol was developed, originally known as the P1-18, which later came to be known as the Steyr GB. Production for the GB ran from 1981 to 1988 and up to 20,000 pistols were thought to have been produced. The GB was manufactured from carbon steel and the chrome-lined barrel was attached solidly to the frame. The pistol was gas-retarded and blowback-operated, which produced a minimal amount of recoil. It was fitted with a double-action trigger and included a slide-mounted de-cocking lever.

**SPECIFICATION**

**MANUFACTURER** Steyr Mannlicher AG & Co. KG.
**CALIBRE** 9mm Parabellum
**MAGAZINE CAPACITY** 18
**ACTION** Blowback/double
**TOTAL LENGTH** 216mm/8.5in
**BARREL LENGTH** 136mm/5.35in
**WEIGHT UNLOADED** 845g/29.81oz

**Barnitzke**
The GB uses a gas-delayed blowback action developed by a German engineer and known as the Barnitzke system.

## Steyr SPP (Special Purpose Pistol)

**SPECIFICATION**

**MANUFACTURER** Steyr Mannlicher AG & Co. KG.
**CALIBRE** 9mm Parabellum
**MAGAZINE CAPACITY** 15 or 30
**ACTION** Delayed blowback/single
**TOTAL LENGTH** 282mm/11.1in
**BARREL LENGTH** 130mm/5.12in
**WEIGHT UNLOADED** 1,300g/45.86oz

The 9mm Steyr SPP, developed in 1993, was a civilian semi-automatic version of the Steyr TMP (Tactical Machine Pistol), categorized as a submachine gun. The Steyr SPP used the same frame and receiver as the TMP. It allowed for a two-handed hold, with one hand on the grip and the other on a spur at the front of the pistol. The SPP was supplied with a 15-round magazine, but 30-round magazines were also available. It had a delayed-blowback operating system, and a locked-breech design with rotating barrel. This design provided more accuracy during rapid fire than simple blowback pistols.

## Steyr M40

**SPECIFICATION**

**MANUFACTURER** Steyr Mannlicher AG & Co. KG.
**CALIBRE** .40 S&W
**MAGAZINE CAPACITY** 12
**ACTION** Short recoil/double
**TOTAL LENGTH** 180mm/7.1in
**BARREL LENGTH** 102mm/4in
**WEIGHT UNLOADED** 794g/28oz

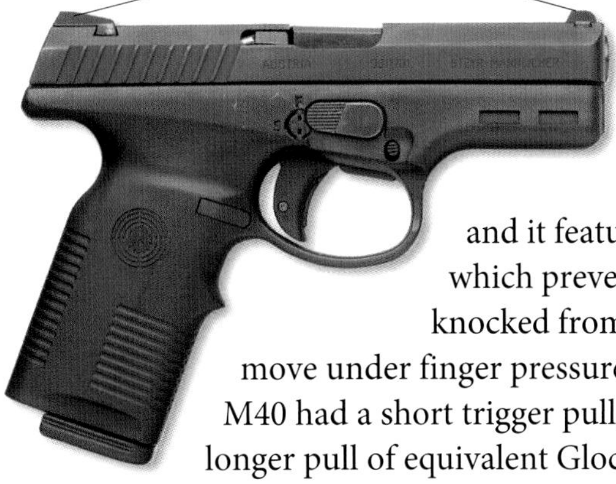


The Steyr M40 was the first Steyr "M" series pistol to be launched, in 1999. The pistol was said to feed rounds efficiently and it featured a safety catch on the trigger which prevented the trigger releasing if it was knocked from the side. The trigger would only move under finger pressure pulling directly backwards. The M40 had a short trigger pull, which some users preferred to the longer pull of equivalent Glock pistols. The pistol was fitted with triangular or trapezoid sights.

## Steyr M9

**SPECIFICATION**

**MANUFACTURER** Steyr Mannlicher AG & Co. KG.
**CALIBRE** 9mm Parabellum
**MAGAZINE CAPACITY** 14
**ACTION** Short recoil/single
**TOTAL LENGTH** 180mm/7.1in
**BARREL LENGTH** 102mm/4in
**WEIGHT UNLOADED** 794g/28oz

**Variations**
Since the M9 pistol came on to the market a number of variations have also been introduced, including the M40, M357 and smaller models called the S9, S40 and S357.

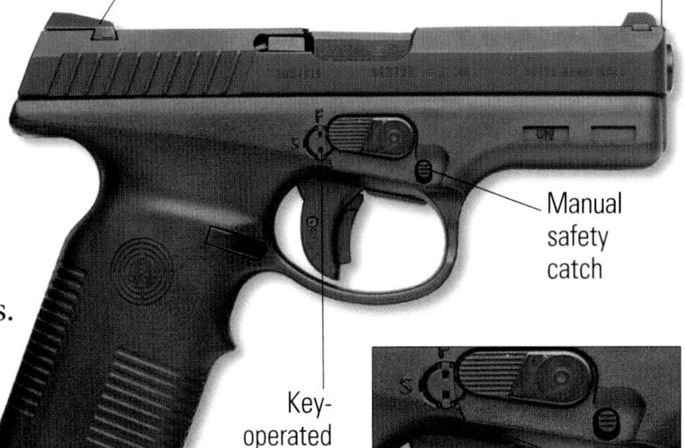


This pistol, launched in 1999, featured a number of innovations and was manufactured using advanced polymer synthetics, typical of the Steyr brand. The M9 pistol was the result of careful development by Steyr in order to match the highly successful Glock pistols. It had the first integrated limited-access key-lock safety for use when the gun was cocked – and also featured triangular or trapezoid sights, designed for rapid target acquisition. The pistol also had a chamber-loaded indicator that could be both seen and touched. The pistol was developed mainly for law enforcement duties, although some earlier models were thought to have too light a trigger; the trigger resistance was increased in later models.

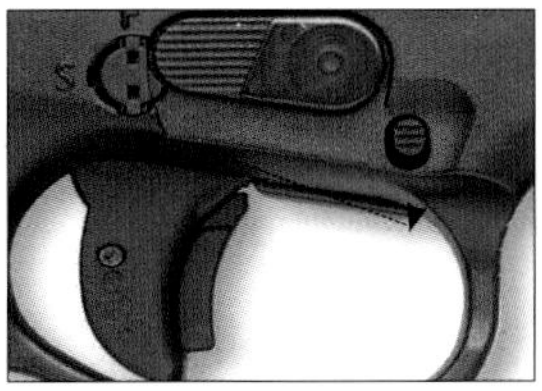

**ABOVE** The manual safety can be used when the gun is cocked. It is activated by pulling down one of the little catches on either side of the gun just above the front of the trigger guard.

# Sweden

**With regard to the specific manufacture of pistols and revolvers, Sweden has relied almost exclusively on imports or weapons manufactured in Sweden under licence. Until 1943, a copy of the Browning 1903 was the standard service weapon, after which a copy of the Finnish Lahti pistol was brought in.**

## Nagant 1887

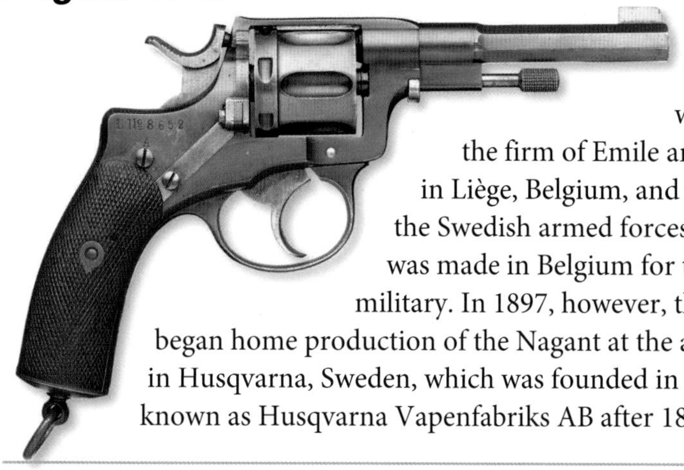

This revolver was designed by the firm of Emile and Leon Nagant in Liège, Belgium, and was selected by the Swedish armed forces. At first it was made in Belgium for the Swedish military. In 1897, however, the Swedish began home production of the Nagant at the arms factory in Husqvarna, Sweden, which was founded in 1689 and was known as Husqvarna Vapenfabriks AB after 1867.

**SPECIFICATION**

- **MANUFACTURER** E & L Nagant, Liège/ Husqvarna Vapenfabriks AB.
- **CALIBRE** 7.5mm Nagant
- **CYLINDER** 6
- **ACTION** Double
- **TOTAL LENGTH** 235mm/9.25in
- **BARREL LENGTH** 114mm/4.5in
- **WEIGHT UNLOADED** 770g/27.2oz

## Browning 1907

This pistol was a Swedish version of the Browning 1903 pistol, manufactured under licence by Husqvarna Vapenfabriks. It had a simple blowback mechanism. Its comparatively long barrel contributed to a high level of accuracy. It had a safety catch on the left-hand side above the pistol grip. The 1907 model was produced in large numbers and became standard issue for various armed forces.

**SPECIFICATION**

- **MANUFACTURER** Husqvarna Vapenfabriks AB.
- **CALIBRE** 9mm Browning Long
- **MAGAZINE CAPACITY** 7
- **ACTION** Blowback/single
- **TOTAL LENGTH** 203mm/8in
- **BARREL LENGTH** 127mm/5in
- **WEIGHT UNLOADED** 910g/32oz

## Lahti Husqvarna Model 40

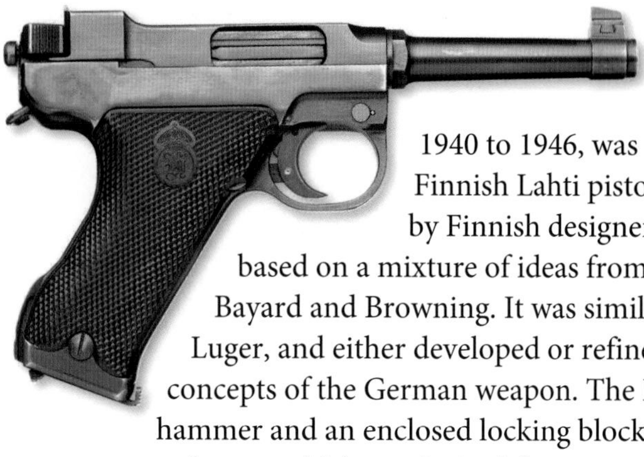

The Husqvarna Model 40, manufactured from 1940 to 1946, was a Swedish copy of the Finnish Lahti pistol. This had been designed by Finnish designer Aimo Lahti and was based on a mixture of ideas from the Luger, Bergmann-Bayard and Browning. It was similar in appearance to the Luger, and either developed or refined some of the design concepts of the German weapon. The Lahti had an internal hammer and an enclosed locking block. It also featured an accelerator which maximized the energy from the recoiling barrel.

**SPECIFICATION**

- **MANUFACTURER** Husqvarna Vapenfabriks AB.
- **CALIBRE** 9mm Parabellum
- **MAGAZINE CAPACITY** 8
- **ACTION** Short recoil/single
- **TOTAL LENGTH** 240mm/9.45in
- **BARREL LENGTH** 120mm/4.72in
- **WEIGHT UNLOADED** 1,250g/44oz

# Czech Republic

**The Czech Republic has a tradition of quality arms manufacturing, centred around the Skoda works. The largest producer of small arms is the firm of Česká Zbrojovka. Founded in 1936, the firm has established an excellent reputation for well-designed and rugged sidearms. One pistol in its line-up, the CZ75B, is said to be the most widely issued pistol to military and police forces around the world.**

## Česká Zbrojovka CZ22

**SPECIFICATION**

**MANUFACTURER** Česká Zbrojovka
**CALIBRE** 9mm Vzor 22
**MAGAZINE CAPACITY** 8
**ACTION** Short recoil/single
**TOTAL LENGTH** 152mm/5.98in
**BARREL LENGTH** 91mm/3.58in
**WEIGHT UNLOADED** 700g/24.69oz

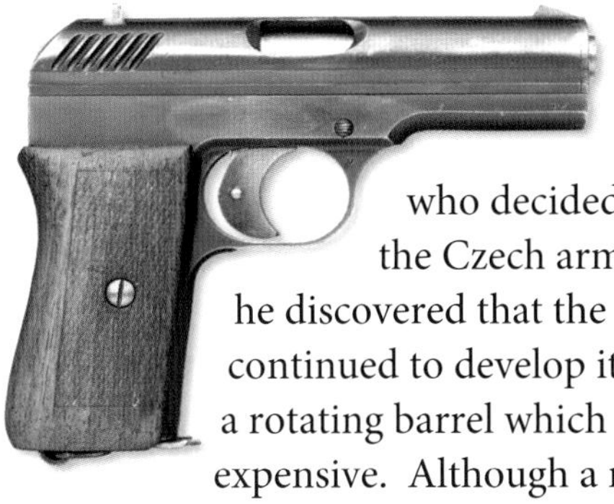

This pistol was initially developed by Josef Nickel for German arms company Mauser, who decided not to take it up. When Nickel moved to the Czech arms factory at Brno to deliver new machinery, he discovered that the Czechs were seeking a pistol and he continued to develop it there. The design was complex, involving a rotating barrel which locked the breech, and the pistol was expensive. Although a new version was introduced in 1922, only about 35,000 of the type were produced before production ceased in 1926. Unfortunately the 9mm Vzor 22 cartridge was not widely used.

## Česká Zbrojovka CZ24

**SPECIFICATION**

**MANUFACTURER** Česká Zbrojovka
**CALIBRE** 7.65mm (.32 ACP)
**MAGAZINE CAPACITY** 8
**ACTION** Short recoil/single
**TOTAL LENGTH** 152mm/5.98in
**BARREL LENGTH** 91mm/3.58in
**WEIGHT UNLOADED** 700g/24.69oz

The CZ24 pistol was a development of the CZ22 and finally achieved what the CZ22 had not in 1925: acceptance by the Czech Army. Although there were some minor visible differences between the CZ24 and its predecessor, such as a magazine safety, the crucial change was the adoption of the more popular 7.65mm (.32 ACP) cartridge. Production began in June 1926 in a new factory and by 1937 some 190,000 had been delivered. However, the complicated mechanism was expensive and inefficient to produce. This would be resolved to some extent in the CZ27.

## Česká Zbrojovka CZ27

**SPECIFICATION**

**MANUFACTURER** Česká Zbrojovka
**CALIBRE** 7.65mm (.32 ACP)
**MAGAZINE CAPACITY** 8
**ACTION** Blowback/single
**TOTAL LENGTH** 158mm/6.2in
**BARREL LENGTH** 100mm/3.94in
**WEIGHT UNLOADED** 700g/24.69oz

Despite the relative success of the CZ24, its complex design meant that the development of a simplified version was just a matter of time. Designer Frantishek Myshka took on the task before 1939 and came up with the CZ27, that was outwardly similar to the CZ24 but radically different under the surface. The CZ27 had a conventional blowback mechanism and used the reduced calibre 7.65mm round. It was easier and cheaper to produce than the CZ24. The CZ27 was adopted by the German Army when it occupied Czechoslovakia and renamed it the Pistole 2727(t).

## Česká Zbrojovka CZ50

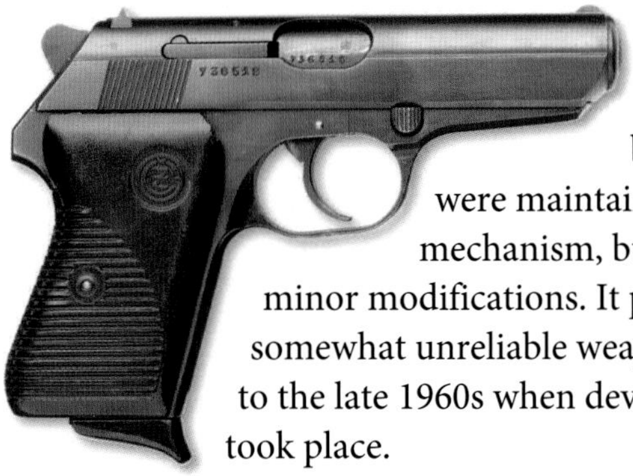

The Czech Ministry of the Interior ordered a new pistol based on the Walther PP in the late 1940s. The basic mechanics of the Walther PP were maintained, including the double-action mechanism, but otherwise there were a number of minor modifications. It proved to be an undistinguished and somewhat unreliable weapon. The CZ50 was produced through to the late 1960s when development of a replacement, the CZ70, took place.

**SPECIFICATION**

**MANUFACTURER** Česká Zbrojovka
**CALIBRE** 7.65mm, .32 ACP
**MAGAZINE CAPACITY** 8
**ACTION** Blowback/double
**TOTAL LENGTH** 167mm/6.6in
**BARREL LENGTH** 94mm/3.7in
**WEIGHT UNLOADED** 660g/23.28oz

## Česká Zbrojovka CZ52

This pistol was first produced in 1952. It was single-action with a recoil mechanism which involved the barrel and slide being interlocked by two rollers, upon which they recoiled together. The rollers then moved together again which released the slide. Once the barrel stopped moving, the slide continued rearwards to eject an empty case and strip off a new round. The pistol featured a three-position manual safety and could be carried "cocked and locked".

**SPECIFICATION**

**MANUFACTURER** Česká Zbrojovka
**CALIBRE** 7.62mm Tokarev
**MAGAZINE CAPACITY** 8
**ACTION** Short recoil/single
**TOTAL LENGTH** 209mm/8.23in
**BARREL LENGTH** 120mm/4.72in
**WEIGHT UNLOADED** 950g/33.51oz

## Česká Zbrojovka CZ70

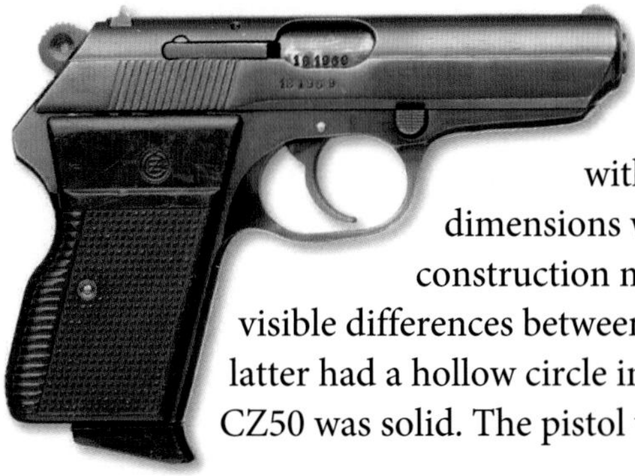

The CZ70 was developed in order to remedy the problems that had emerged in the CZ50, mostly with regard to reliability. The internal dimensions were modified and some of the construction materials were changed. One of the visible differences between the CZ50 and the CZ70 was that the latter had a hollow circle in the hammer, while the hammer of the CZ50 was solid. The pistol was manufactured from 1970 to 1984.

**SPECIFICATION**

**MANUFACTURER** Česká Zbrojovka
**CALIBRE** .32 ACP
**MAGAZINE CAPACITY** 8
**ACTION** Blowback/double
**TOTAL LENGTH** 167mm/6.6in
**BARREL LENGTH** 94mm/3.7in
**WEIGHT UNLOADED** 660g/23.28oz

## Česká Zbrojovka CZ75

Introduced in 1975, this pistol soon became an established favourite among many armed forces around the world. The CZ75 was a pistol that used the locked-breech principle. It was recoil-operated and chambered for the 9mm Parabellum cartridge. It had a double-action trigger system, with the safety catch on the left side of the frame, locking the hammer linkage. It was similar to the Browning High-Power.

**SPECIFICATION**

**MANUFACTURER** Česká Zbrojovka
**CALIBRE** 9mm Parabellum
**MAGAZINE CAPACITY** 8
**ACTION** Short recoil/double
**TOTAL LENGTH** 203mm/8in
**BARREL LENGTH** 120mm/4.7in
**WEIGHT UNLOADED** 1,000g/35.27oz

## Česká Zbrojovka CZ83

**SPECIFICATION**

- **MANUFACTURER** Česká Zbrojovka
- **CALIBRE** .45 Makarov and .380 ACP
- **MAGAZINE CAPACITY** 15
- **ACTION** Blowback/double or single
- **TOTAL LENGTH** 173mm/6.81in
- **BARREL LENGTH** 96mm/3.78in
- **WEIGHT UNLOADED** 650g/22.93oz

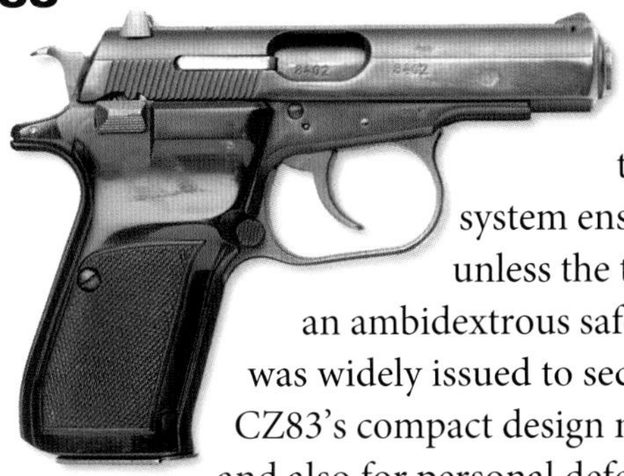

The CZ83, developed in 1983, was a blowback pistol with a double-action trigger mechanism. An automatic safety system ensured that the hammer would not operate unless the trigger was fully pressed. There was also an ambidextrous safety catch and a magazine safety. The CZ83 was widely issued to security forces in former Czechoslovakia. The CZ83's compact design meant that it was useful for undercover duties and also for personal defence. The ergonomics, calibre and light weight lend themselves to an easy-to-operate weapon.

## Česká Zbrojovka CZ85

**SPECIFICATION**

- **MANUFACTURER** Česká Zbrojovka
- **CALIBRE** 9mm Parabellum
- **MAGAZINE CAPACITY** 16
- **ACTION** Short recoil/double
- **TOTAL LENGTH** 206mm/8.11in
- **BARREL LENGTH** 120mm/4.72in
- **WEIGHT UNLOADED** 1,000g/35.27oz

This pistol was derived from the successful CZ75 and was made from the mid-1980s. The pistol featured a firing-pin safety to enhance the drop-safety advantages of this firearm. It also had an ambidextrous manual safety lever and slide stop. The pistol was designed for maximum comfort in either hand, with a well-proportioned rubber-lined hand grip. It had a three-dot illuminated sight system and in the Combat version of this pistol, the rear sights are adjustable.

## Česká Zbrojovka CZ92

**SPECIFICATION**

- **MANUFACTURER** Česká Zbrojovka
- **CALIBRE** .25 ACP
- **MAGAZINE CAPACITY** 8
- **ACTION** Short recoil/DAO
- **TOTAL LENGTH** 126mm/4.94in
- **BARREL LENGTH** 64mm/2.52in
- **WEIGHT UNLOADED** 309g/10.9oz

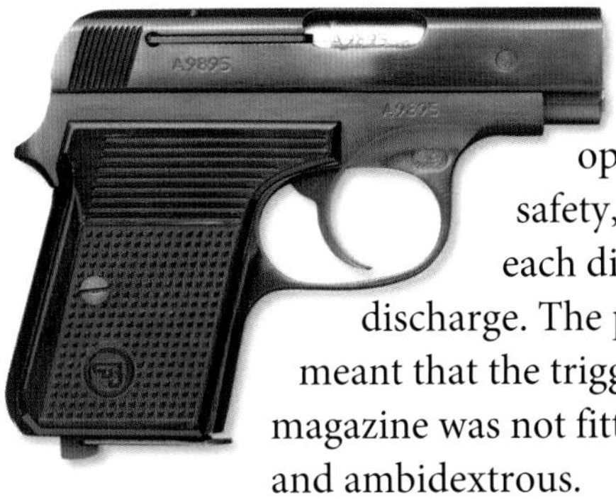

This was a subcompact handgun designed for maximum ease of concealment, either for personal defence or for covert operations. Although it did not have a manual safety, the hammer returned to its position after each discharge as a protection against unintentional discharge. The pistol also had a magazine safety, which meant that the trigger mechanism would not operate if a magazine was not fitted. The pistol was ergonomically designed and ambidextrous.

## Česká Zbrojovka CZ97

First introduced in 1997, this was a more powerful version of the CZ75 and is described as one of the best combat handguns of the 20th century. The construction was all steel and the barrel was hammer forged. It also featured a chamber-loaded indicator and an ergonomic grip. The gun used the locked-breech principle and was double action. The slide remained locked open when the last magazine from the cartridge had been fired. The pistol also incorporated a firing-pin safety to prevent accidental discharge when it was dropped. The weapon was said to be well balanced and to have a high level of accuracy. It had a long service life and was both rugged and reliable.

**SPECIFICATION**

- **MANUFACTURER** Česká Zbrojovka
- **CALIBRE** .45 ACP
- **MAGAZINE CAPACITY** 10
- **ACTION** Short recoil/double
- **TOTAL LENGTH** 212mm/8.35in
- **BARREL LENGTH** 123mm/4.84in
- **WEIGHT UNLOADED** 1,150g/40.57oz

## Česká Zbrojovka CZ100

This pistol was developed to incorporate modern synthetic materials that significantly reduced its overall weight. It had a double- action-only (DAO) trigger mechanism with a firing-pin safety. The slide remained locked open when the last cartridge was fired. The design concept included the potential for firing the weapon effectively with gloved hands and it could be fired with either hand. Without a manual safety, the pistol could be deployed at short notice.

**SPECIFICATION**

**MANUFACTURER** Česká Zbrojovka
**CALIBRE** 9mm Parabellum
**MAGAZINE CAPACITY** 13
**ACTION** Short recoil/DAO
**TOTAL LENGTH** 180mm/7.1in
**BARREL LENGTH** 98mm/3.86in
**WEIGHT UNLOADED** 665g/23.46oz

## Česká Zbrojovka CZ P-10 C

**SPECIFICATION**

**MANUFACTURER** Česká Zbrojovka
**CALIBRE** 9mm Parabellum or .40 S&W
**MAGAZINE CAPACITY** 15 (9mm) or 12 (.40 S&W)
**ACTION** Short recoil/single
**TOTAL LENGTH** 190mm/7.3in
**BARREL LENGTH** 102mm/4.02in
**WEIGHT UNLOADED** 740g/26oz

The Czech Army signed a contract with CZ in 2020 to supply, among other items, more than 21,000 CZ P-10 pistols over a five-year period. Development began in 2014 and production of the pistol began in earnest in 2017. Designed to compete directly with the Glock 19, the P-10 C is similar in size. The P-10 C is striker-fired and has a firing pin block, but it does not have a magazine disconnect, allowing it to still fire without a magazine. In addition to being used by the Czechs, around 2,000 of the pistols have also been sent to various Polish outfits for testing.

# Poland

**Poland produced a high-quality pistol known as the Radom before World War II. It was an ingenious design and proved popular with its users. Manufacture of the Radom was taken over by the Germans after the invasion of Poland. Subsequent production of pistols in Poland was based around designs such as the Soviet Makarov. More recent designs have been produced by the Polish firm Zaklady Metalowe.**

## Radom or VIS Model 1935

This pistol was designed by Wilniewczyc and Skrzypinski, and manufactured from 1935 to 1939. It had an external similarity to the Browning M1911. It also used a Browning-derived linkless breech-lock mechanism. The pistol was not fitted with a manual safety but it did have a grip safety located on the back of the hand grip. The pistol was issued to the German Army during the occupation of Poland and it earned a reputation for both quality and efficiency in use.

**SPECIFICATION**

**MANUFACTURER** Fabryka Broni Radom
**CALIBRE** 9mm Parabellum
**MAGAZINE CAPACITY** 8
**ACTION** Short recoil/single
**TOTAL LENGTH** 205mm/8.1in
**BARREL LENGTH** 115mm/4.53in
**WEIGHT UNLOADED** 1,025g/36.16oz

## M48

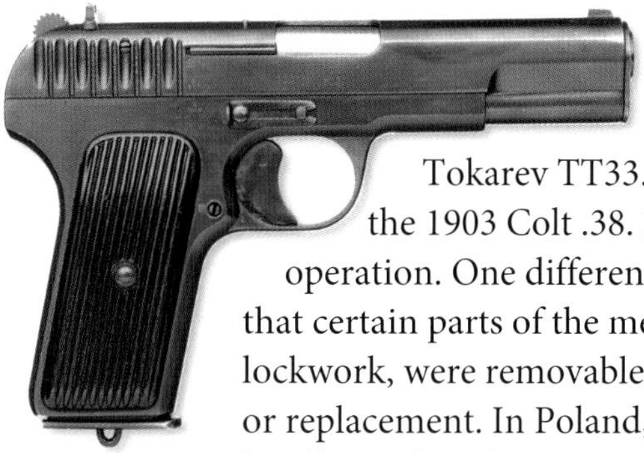

**SPECIFICATION**

**MANUFACTURER** Fabryka Broni Radom
**CALIBRE** 7.62mm Tokarev
**MAGAZINE CAPACITY** 8
**ACTION** Recoil/single
**TOTAL LENGTH** 193mm/7.59in
**BARREL LENGTH** 116mm/4.57in
**WEIGHT UNLOADED** 830g/29.28oz

This pistol, produced in 1930, was a Polish version of the Russian Tokarev TT33. The design was influenced by the 1903 Colt .38. It had a single action with recoil operation. One difference from the Browning design was that certain parts of the mechanism, including the hammer and lockwork, were removable, which made for ease of maintenance or replacement. In Poland, Hungary and the former Yugoslavia, locally produced TT33s were all known as the M48.

## P64

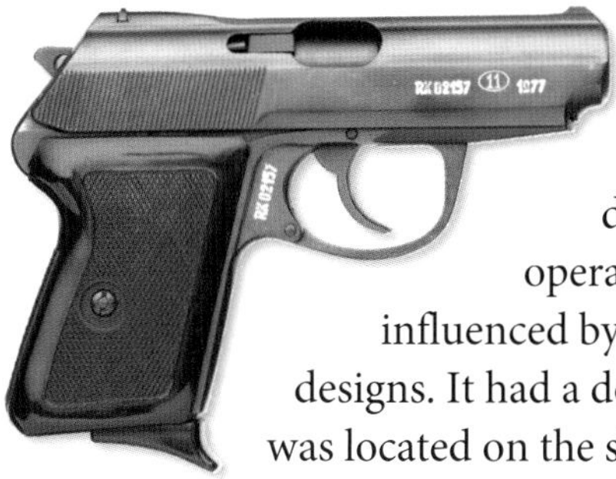

**SPECIFICATION**

**MANUFACTURER** State Arsenals
**CALIBRE** 9mm Makarov
**MAGAZINE CAPACITY** 6
**ACTION** Blowback/single or double
**TOTAL LENGTH** 155mm/6.1in
**BARREL LENGTH** 84mm/3.31in
**WEIGHT UNLOADED** 636g/22.43oz

This pistol was a replacement for the Pistolet TT, which in turn was based on the Tokarev TT33 pistol. The P64 was developed in the late 1950s. It was a blowback-operated pistol which appeared to have been influenced by both the Makarov and the Walther PP pistol designs. It had a double-action mechanism and the safety catch was located on the slide. It could also be fired in single-action mode and this involved pulling back the external hammer.

## P83

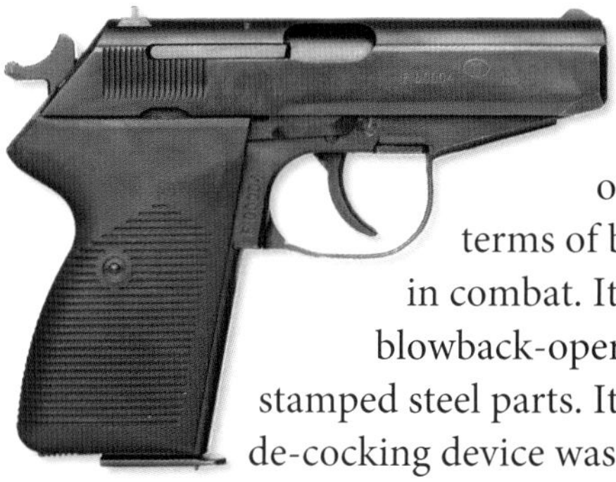

The P83 featured various improvements over the previous P64 service pistol in terms of both manufacturing cost and effectiveness in combat. It also had a larger magazine. This was a blowback-operated pistol manufactured largely from stamped steel parts. It had a double-action trigger and a safety/de-cocking device was mounted on the slide. Unlike the P64, the magazine release catch was located at the bottom of the plastic hand grip. It had fixed sights, with the rear sight dovetailed into the slide.

**SPECIFICATION**

**MANUFACTURER** State Arsenals
**CALIBRE** 9mm Makarov
**MAGAZINE CAPACITY** 8
**ACTION** Blowback/single or double
**TOTAL LENGTH** 165mm/6.5in
**BARREL LENGTH** 90mm/3.54in
**WEIGHT UNLOADED** 730g/25.75oz

## VIS 100

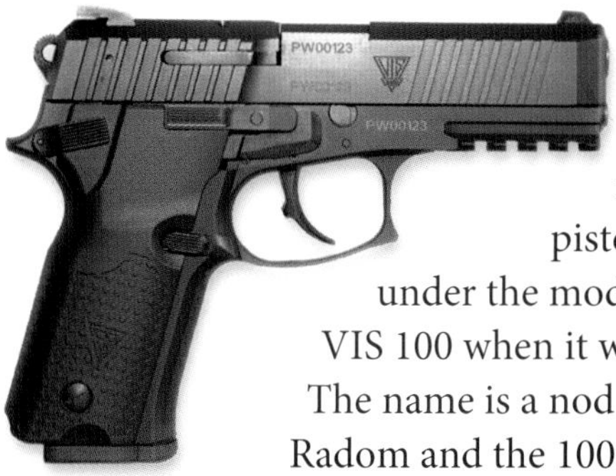

Work on this pistol began in 2009 as a replacement for the earlier P64 and P83 pistols. At the time, development was done under the model name PR-15 Ragun, but was renamed VIS 100 when it was adopted by the Polish military in 2018. The name is a nod to the WWII-era Vis pistol made by Radom and the 100th anniversary of Polish independence. The frame is an aluminum alloy with steel inserts to accommodate the Tenifer-coated steel slide.

**SPECIFICATION**

**MANUFACTURER** Fabryka Broni Radom
**CALIBRE** 9mm Parabellum
**MAGAZINE CAPACITY** 15
**ACTION** Short recoil/double or single
**TOTAL LENGTH** 197mm/7.8in
**BARREL LENGTH** 110mm/4.3in
**WEIGHT UNLOADED** 695g/24.5oz

# Serbia

**Since before World War II, small-arms production in the former Yugoslavia has been based at the firm of Zavodi Crvena Zastava (meaning "Red Flag"). It is located 138 km (86 miles) south-east of Belgrade and still produces a wide range of both civilian and military small arms, based on Russian or German designs.**

## Zastava M57 and M57 Lux

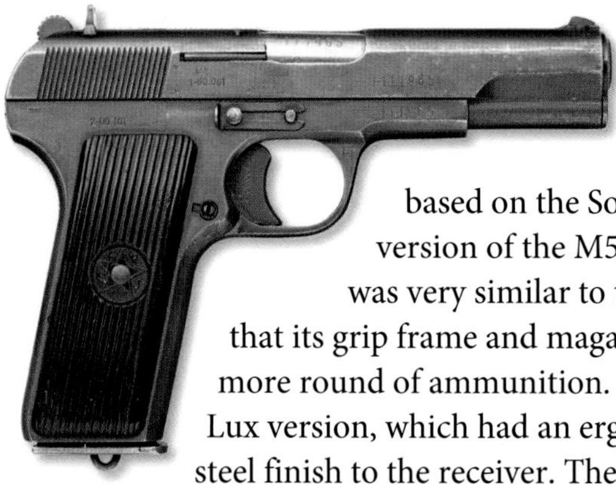

This pistol, introduced in 1957, had a short-recoil barrel and a locked breech. The design was based on the Soviet Tokarev TT33. The basic version of the M57 had an old-fashioned look which was very similar to the original Russian pistol, except that its grip frame and magazine were longer and it held one more round of ammunition. Zastava also produced the M57 Lux version, which had an ergonomic hand grip and a stainless-steel finish to the receiver. The M57 was primarily designed as a personal defence weapon and was easy to handle and maintain.

**SPECIFICATION**

**MANUFACTURER** Zastava Arms Co.
**CALIBRE** 7.62mm Tokarev
**MAGAZINE CAPACITY** 9
**ACTION** Short recoil/single
**TOTAL LENGTH** 200mm/7.87in
**BARREL LENGTH** 116mm/4.57in
**WEIGHT UNLOADED** 850g/29.98oz

## Zastava M70 and M70A

Like the M57, the M70 had a short-recoil barrel and a locked breech. The design was also based on the Tokarev TT33, and its operation was based on the Browning swing-link system. The M70, and improved version the M70A, were very similar to the M57. The main difference is that they were chambered for the 9mm Parabellum cartridge and had improved rifling in the barrel. The change of calibre made the pistol slightly easier and more comfortable to handle and more attractive for export.

**SPECIFICATION**

**MANUFACTURER** Zastava Arms Co.
**CALIBRE** 9mm Parabellum
**MAGAZINE CAPACITY** 9
**ACTION** Short recoil/single
**TOTAL LENGTH** 200mm/7.87in
**BARREL LENGTH** 116mm/4.57in
**WEIGHT UNLOADED** 850g/29.98oz

## Zastava M70 and M70(k) Pocket Pistol

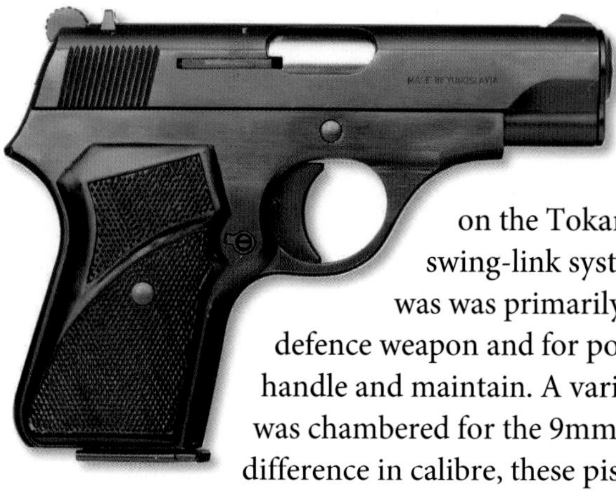

Like the M57, this pistol had a short recoil barrel and a locked breech, but chambered for .32 ACP. The design was also based on the Tokarev TT33, and the Browning swing-link system. The M70 Pocket Pistol was was primarily designed as a personal defence weapon and for police use, and was easy to handle and maintain. A variant, known as the M70(k) was chambered for the 9mm cartridge. Apart from the difference in calibre, these pistols were otherwise the same.

**SPECIFICATION**

**MANUFACTURER** Zastava Arms Co.
**CALIBRE** .32 ACP
**MAGAZINE CAPACITY** 9
**ACTION** Short recoil/single
**TOTAL LENGTH** 200mm/7.87in
**BARREL LENGTH** 94mm/3.7in
**WEIGHT UNLOADED** 740g/26.1oz

**Police and military use**
For many years this pistol was used by the Yugoslavian Police and military officers. They are still sold worldwide.

## Zastava M83/84

**SPECIFICATION**

**MANUFACTURER** Zastava Arms Co.
**CALIBRE** .357 Magnum, .38 Special
**CYLINDER** 6
**ACTION** Double
**TOTAL LENGTH** 254mm/10in
**BARREL LENGTH** 64mm/2.52in
**WEIGHT UNLOADED** 900g/31.75oz

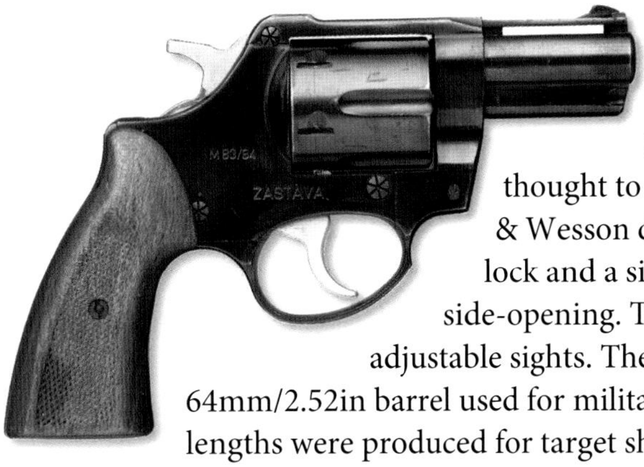


This revolver was first introduced in 1983 and was thought to have been based on a Smith & Wesson design. It had a double-action lock and a six-cylinder chamber with a side-opening. There was an option for fitting adjustable sights. The standard version had a 64mm/2.52in barrel used for military and police. Other barrel lengths were produced for target shooting and for personal use.

## Zastava CZ99

The design is thought to be influenced by the SIG-Sauer P220. It was a double-action, locked-breech semi-automatic pistol with a forged-steel barrel. It had an ambidextrous safety lever and de-cocking lever, the latter positioned underneath the grip on the left. The pistol also had a chamber-loaded indicator and an indicator to show when there are only three rounds left in the magazine. The pistol was ergonomically designed and had a visible hammer. There is also a .40 S&W version and a compact version (CZ99G Compact). The Zastava CZ999 was the most recent addition to the Zastava range.

**SPECIFICATION**

**MANUFACTURER** Zastava Arms Co.
**CALIBRE** 9mm Parabellum, .40 S&W
**MAGAZINE CAPACITY** 10 (9mm Parabellum) or 15 (.40 S&W)
**ACTION** Short recoil/double
**TOTAL LENGTH** 198mm/7.8in
**BARREL LENGTH** 108mm/4.25in
**WEIGHT UNLOADED** 920g/32.45oz

# Hungary

**The Hungarian Army's requirements in the early 20th century were satisfied by Rudolf Frommer, George Roth and Karel Krnka designs. The Frommer Stop pistol was unusual for having a long-recoil system.**

**This design tradition is continued by the company known today as FÉGArmy Arms Manufacturing Ltd, in Budapest. It specializes in precision engineering, mostly for arms manufacturing.**

## CZ P07 NATO

**SPECIFICATION**

**MANUFACTURER** Česká Zbrojovka
**CALIBRE** 9mm Parabellum
**MAGAZINE** 15
**ACTION** Short recoil/double or single
**TOTAL LENGTH** 182.8mm/7.2in
**BARREL LENGTH** 92.25mm/3.75in
**WEIGHT UNLOADED** 785g/27.7oz

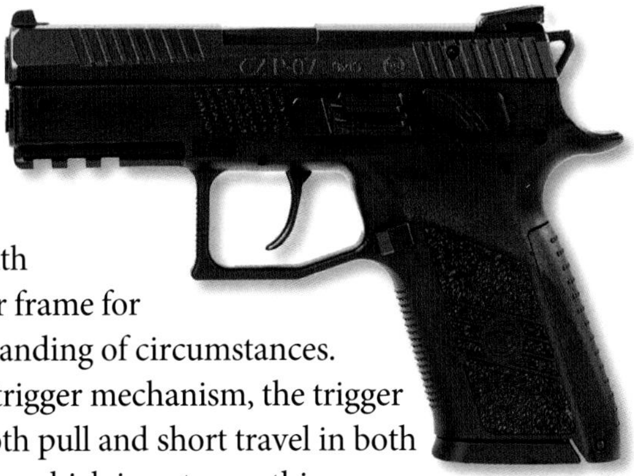

Designed for concealed carry by armed forces, the P-07 NATO has a similar slide-in-frame design that is found on the CZ 75 pistols. It is made with a fibreglass-reinforced polymer frame for durability under the most demanding of circumstances. Equipped with CZ's OMEGA trigger mechanism, the trigger is known for having very smooth pull and short travel in both single and double action modes, which is not something you always find in double action. Ambidextrous controls, including the ability to switch between safety and decocker, as well as reverse the magazine release, allow for ease of use by all shooters.

## Frommer M1910

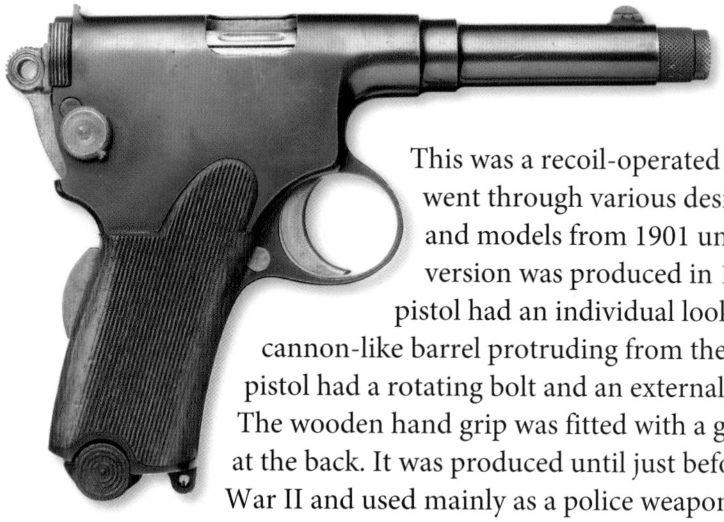

**SPECIFICATION**

**MANUFACTURER** Fegyver es Gepgyar Reszvenytarsasag (FÉG)
**CALIBRE** .32 ACP
**MAGAZINE** 8
**ACTION** Recoil/single
**TOTAL LENGTH** 186mm/7.32in
**BARREL LENGTH** 100mm/3.94in
**WEIGHT UNLOADED** 635g/22.4oz

This was a recoil-operated pistol that went through various design phases and models from 1901 until the final version was produced in 1910. The pistol had an individual look, with a long cannon-like barrel protruding from the frame. The pistol had a rotating bolt and an external hammer. The wooden hand grip was fitted with a grip safety at the back. It was produced until just before World War II and used mainly as a police weapon.

## Frommer Stop 1912

This pistol was an unusual design as it operated on the long-recoil system. The Frommer Stop 1912 was developed by Rudolf Frommer and was issued to the Austro-Hungarian Army and Police. When the pistol was fired, the bolt and the barrel lock recoiled together. Two recoil springs were compressed, one for the barrel and one for the bolt. The bolt was temporarily held by a catch while the barrel-recoil spring pushed the barrel back to its original position. The barrel released the catch and the bolt was also returned to position by its spring. As they returned, the barrel stripped out the empty case while the bolt chambered the next round. The bolt rotated to lock the breech.

**SPECIFICATION**

**MANUFACTURER** Fegyver es Gepgyar Reszvenytarsasag (FÉG)
**CALIBRE** 7.65mm Frommer, .380 ACP
**MAGAZINE** 7
**ACTION** Long recoil/single
**TOTAL LENGTH** 186mm/7.32in
**BARREL LENGTH** 100mm/3.94in
**WEIGHT UNLOADED** 635g/22.4oz

## Frommer Baby 1912

The Frommer Stop and Frommer Baby were patented in 1912. Most of the early guns produced were the Frommer Baby, in both 7.65mm (similar to but not intechangeable with .32 ACP) and .380 ACP calibres. The Frommer Baby was produced in small quantities at first, probably because the Fegyver es Gepgyar factory in Budapest was also producing the Roth Steyr pistol for service between 1911 and 1914. The Frommer Baby was mainly produced for the civilian market in .32 ACP, but a small number was produced for the Hungarian Air Force. It is thought that the Frommer Baby and Frommer Stop were made until the end of the 1920s.

**SPECIFICATION**

**MANUFACTURER** Fegyver es Gepgyar Reszvenytarsasag (FÉG)
**CALIBRE** 7.65mm Frommer, .380 ACP
**MAGAZINE** 5 or 6
**ACTION** Recoil/single
**TOTAL LENGTH** 122mm/4.8in
**BARREL LENGTH** 58mm/2.3in
**WEIGHT UNLOADED** 500g/17.6oz

**Rudolph Frommer**
This Hungarian designer was born in Budapest in 1868. During his lifetime he registered over 100 patents for pistols and machine guns.

## Frommer Model 1937

**SPECIFICATION**

**MANUFACTURER** Femaru es Szerszamgepgyar NV
**CALIBRE** 7.65mm Frommer
**MAGAZINE** 7
**ACTION** Blowback/single
**TOTAL LENGTH** 182mm/7.17in
**BARREL LENGTH** 110mm/4.33in
**WEIGHT UNLOADED** 770g/27.2oz

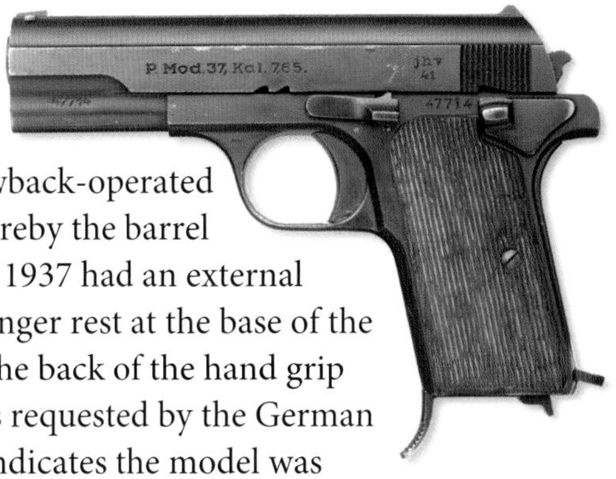

This pistol was a development of an earlier model from 1929. It was a blowback-operated pistol with a Browning operation whereby the barrel was retained in the frame. The Model 1937 had an external hammer and there was an extended finger rest at the base of the hand grip. There was a grip safety at the back of the hand grip and the model had a manual safety, as requested by the German Luftwaffe. The marking on the slide indicates the model was part of a contract between the Hungarians and the German government.

## Tokarev Tokagypt/48M

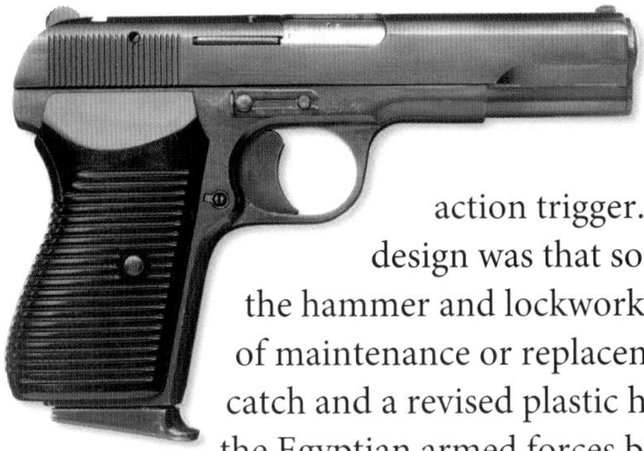

This pistol was an adapted version of the Tokarev TT33. The design was influenced by the .38 Colt from 1903. It was recoil operated with a single-action trigger. One difference from the Browning design was that some parts of the mechanism, including the hammer and lockwork, were removable, which made for ease of maintenance or replacement. The Tokagypt had a new safety catch and a revised plastic hand grip. The pistol was designed for the Egyptian armed forces but many ended up on the open market.

**SPECIFICATION**

**MANUFACTURER** Femaru es Szerszamgepgyar NV
**CALIBRE** 9mm Parabellum
**MAGAZINE CAPACITY** 7
**ACTION** Recoil/single
**TOTAL LENGTH** 192mm/7.56in
**BARREL LENGTH** 115mm/4.53in
**WEIGHT UNLOADED** 910g/32.1oz

## FÉG PA-63 and AP9

**SPECIFICATION**

**MANUFACTURER** FÉG
**CALIBRE** 9mm Makarov (PA-63), .32 ACP, .380 ACP (AP9)
**MAGAZINE** 8
**ACTION** Blowback/double
**TOTAL LENGTH** 170mm/6.7in
**BARREL LENGTH** 98mm/3.86in
**WEIGHT UNLOADED** 695g/24.5oz

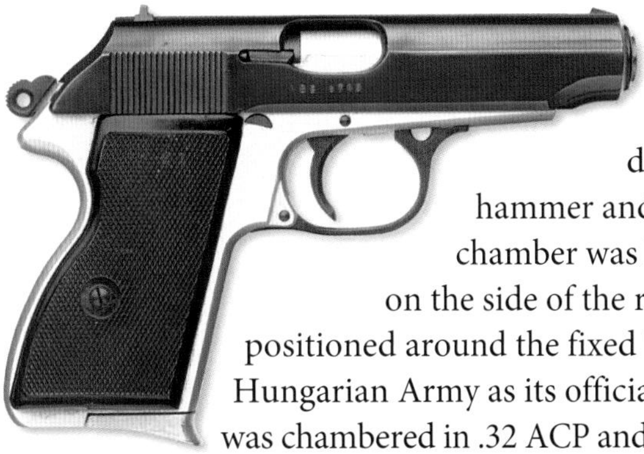

This pistol was based on the famous Walther PP. It had a double-action lock, and an external hammer and signal pin indicated whether the chamber was loaded. There was a safety catch on the side of the receiver. The return spring was positioned around the fixed barrel. The PA-63 was issued to the Hungarian Army as its official pistol. A civilian version, the AP9, was chambered in .32 ACP and .380 ACP. It had an aluminium frame and had all the same operating features as the PA-63.

## FÉG P9M

This was FÉG's primary single-action service pistol. The P9M is a short recoil operated, locked breech-pistol. This is a near-exact copy of the FN Belgium M1935 Browning High-Power pistol in its standard version and had all the features of that pistol. The only difference is that the frame-mounted safety lever is longer than the original GP-35 safety lever. The frame and slide are made from carbon steel. The P9M was not used in Hungary as the pistols were intended for export, but may be used as service pistols in other Eastern European countries.

**SPECIFICATION**

**MANUFACTURER** FÉG
**CALIBRE** 9mm Parabellum
**MAGAZINE** 13
**ACTION** Short recoil/single
**TOTAL LENGTH** 198mm/7.8in
**BARREL LENGTH** 118mm/4.64in
**WEIGHT UNLOADED** 910g/32.1oz

## FÉG P9R

The P9R was FÉG's primary double-action service pistol produced in the early 1990s. This pistol had a steel frame and a double-action firing mechanism with an external hammer. It had a slide-mounted rotating safety that de-cocked the hammer and allowed a round to be chambered with the safety engaged. If carried with the hammer down and the safety off the first shot could be fired double action or the hammer could be manually cocked first. The front sight was permanently fixed to the slide, while the rear sight was dovetailed. In Europe the FÉG P9R was known as the Mauser 90DA, as it was distributed through Mauser. The 90DA was almost identical to the Mauser 90SA except for the double action, larger trigger guard and a safety/de-cocking lever.

**SPECIFICATION**

**MANUFACTURER** FÉG
**CALIBRE** 9mm Parabellum
**MAGAZINE** 10 or 14
**ACTION** Short recoil/double
**TOTAL LENGTH** 203mm/8in
**BARREL LENGTH** 118mm/4.64in
**WEIGHT UNLOADED** 1,000g/35.27oz

# Romania

**Romania produced the Austrian Steyr Hahn M12 under licence and has produced other weapons particularly for Soviet countries. It has been increasing its arms exports in recent years. It exports semi-automatic weapons to the main civilian markets for firearms, Switzerland and the USA.**

## Steyr Hahn M12

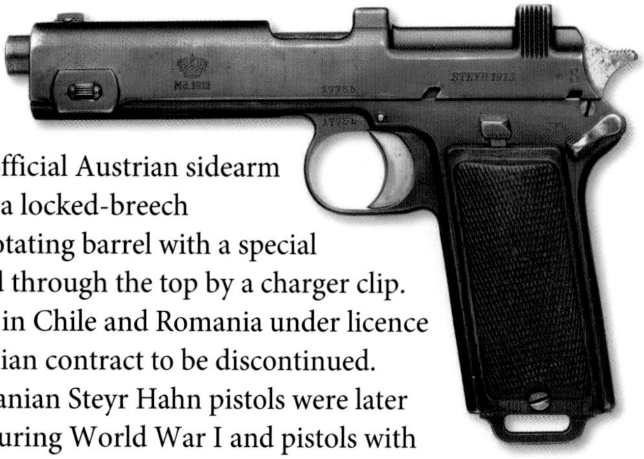

This pistol was adopted by the Austro-Hungarian Army in 1912 and was the official Austrian sidearm during World War I. It had a locked-breech mechanism operated by a rotating barrel with a special 9mm Steyr cartridge, loaded through the top by a charger clip. The pistol was also adopted in Chile and Romania under licence until war caused the Romanian contract to be discontinued. A large number of the Romanian Steyr Hahn pistols were later captured by the Austrians during World War I and pistols with both Romanian parts and Austrian proof marks were common at the time. During World War II many Romanian and Austrian pistols were captured by Germans and converted to 9mm Parabellum.

**SPECIFICATION**

**MANUFACTURER** Osterreichische Waffenfabriks-Gesellschaft
**CALIBRE** 9mm Steyr
**MAGAZINE CAPACITY** 8
**ACTION** Recoil/single
**TOTAL LENGTH** 216mm/8.5in
**BARREL LENGTH** 128mm/5.1in
**WEIGHT UNLOADED** 990g/34.92oz

## Cugir Pistol md. 2000

A modernized version of the Pistol md. 1995, the Pistol md. 2000 still borrows heavily from the Jericho 941 pistol, which is itself based on the CZ 75. Despite borrowing from arms designs in both the Czech Republic and Israel, this pistol is made completely in Romania. In 2021, a newer model known as the Pandurul was proposed, but the design has yet to be finalized and it remains to be seen if it will replace the Pistol md. 2000.

**SPECIFICATION**

**MANUFACTURER** ROMARM Cugir
**CALIBRE** 9mm Parabellum
**MAGAZINE CAPACITY** 15
**ACTION** Short recoil/double or single
**TOTAL LENGTH** 206mm/8.1in
**BARREL LENGTH** 112mm/4.4in
**WEIGHT UNLOADED** 900g/32oz

# Finland

**Although Finland has produced relatively few individual pistol and revolver designs, some of them have been outstanding. Some of the most successful, including the Lahti L35, were designed by the famous Finnish master-armourer and self-taught weapons designer, Aimo Johannes Lahti.**

## Ahlberg

**SPECIFICATION**

**MANUFACTURER** Ahlberg
**CALIBRE** 7.65mm (.32 ACP)
**MAGAZINE CAPACITY** 7
**ACTION** Blowback/single
**TOTAL LENGTH** 167mm/6.6in
**BARREL LENGTH** 95mm/3.75in
**WEIGHT UNLOADED** 623.68g/22oz

This was an extremely rare pistol of which only about 1,000 examples are known to have been made. This model was similar to the Browning M1910 developed for FN in Belgium, but with a longer barrel. Like the 1910 model, the recoil spring was mounted round the barrel, giving the weapon its distinctive shape and appearance.

## Lahti L35

**SPECIFICATION**

**MANUFACTURER** Valtion Kivaaritehdas (VKT), Jyvastalyla/Valmet Oy Tourula Factories
**CALIBRE** 9mm Parabellum
**MAGAZINE CAPACITY** 8
**ACTION** Short recoil/single
**TOTAL LENGTH** 245mm/9.68in
**BARREL LENGTH** 120mm/4.72in
**WEIGHT UNLOADED** 1,220g/43oz

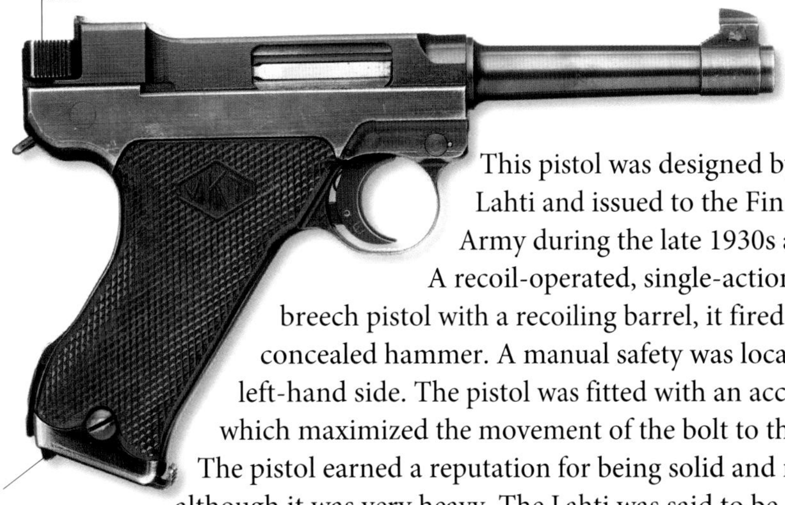


**Disassembly**
The Lahti could only be disassembled or stripped for cleaning or repairs by an armourer with access to the correct tools.

This pistol was designed by Aimo Lahti and issued to the Finnish Army during the late 1930s and 1940s. A recoil-operated, single-action, locked-breech pistol with a recoiling barrel, it fired with a concealed hammer. A manual safety was located on the left-hand side. The pistol was fitted with an accelerator which maximized the movement of the bolt to the rear. The pistol earned a reputation for being solid and reliable, although it was very heavy. The Lahti was said to be exceptionally well sealed against the intrusion of dirt and reliable in freezing conditions. However, the use of submachine ammunition (often used by Finnish troops) could cause the slide to crack and many new slides were produced in the 1950s as replacements. The complexity of the design meant that it could not be easily maintained in the field, but was reliable enough to make this situation unusual. The production of the Lahti started in 1936 and over half of the 9,000 pistols produced were issued to the Finnish armed forces. After World War II, the pistols was produced more commercially and also sold abroad. However, after several revisions it was clear that the pistol was too costly and complicated to continue production. Replacement parts for the L35 were manufactured until the 1970s. In 1985, Valmet Oy Tourula Factories made a 50-year commemoration series of L35 pistols. This was the last production series of the pistol.

# Russia

**Russia and the Soviet Union have produced a wide variety of arms over the 19th and 20th century and competitive designs continue to be produced. In the 1920s the Tokarev TT33 was one of the mainstays, while the the 9mm Makarov was introduced in the 1950s and issued to both Soviet and Warsaw Pact forces. A number of more recent designs have been developed for police, security services and military use.**

## Nagant Revolver M1895

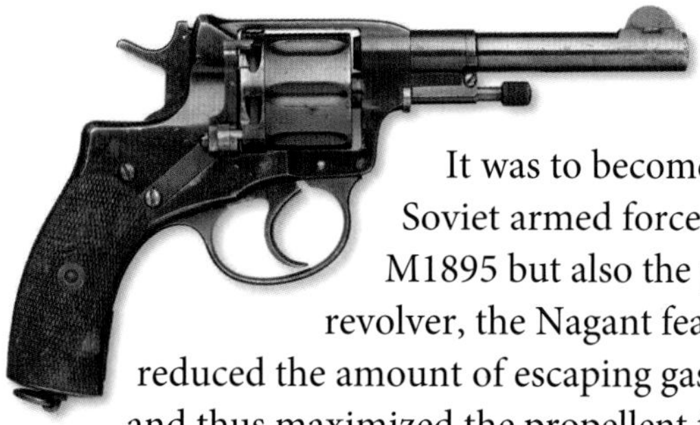

This revolver was developed in Belgium by Leon Nagant in 1894. It was to become most identified, however, with the Soviet armed forces who bought not only the Nagant M1895 but also the production rights. Unusually for a revolver, the Nagant featured a gas-sealed cylinder which reduced the amount of escaping gas to which many revolvers are prone and thus maximized the propellent force on the round. This mechanism required a uniquely designed round in order to work properly. The Nagant had a solid frame and loading was accomplished via a loading gate on the right side of the frame. It was produced in both single-action and double-action models.

**SPECIFICATION**

**MANUFACTURER** L. Nagant & Co., Liège/Imperial Russian Arms Factory, Tula
**CALIBRE** 7.62mm Nagant
**CYLINDER** 7
**ACTION** Double and single
**TOTAL LENGTH** 229mm/9.33in
**BARREL LENGTH** 110mm/4.33in
**WEIGHT UNLOADED** 790g/27.87oz

## Korovin TK (Tula Korovin)

The Korovin TK was the first semi-automatic pistol produced in the Soviet Union. It was designed by Sergey Korovin in 1926 and, due to its relatively small size, was used both commercially and by military officers as a personal defence weapon. It was a blowback, single-action pistol fired by a striker. It was fitted with a manual safety above the trigger guard and it had fixed sights.

**SPECIFICATION**

**MANUFACTURER** Soviet Tula Arms Factory
**CALIBRE** .25 ACP
**MAGAZINE** 8
**ACTION** Blowback/single
**TOTAL LENGTH** 127mm/5in
**BARREL LENGTH** 688mm/27.09in
**WEIGHT UNLOADED** 423g/14.9oz

## Tokarev TT30

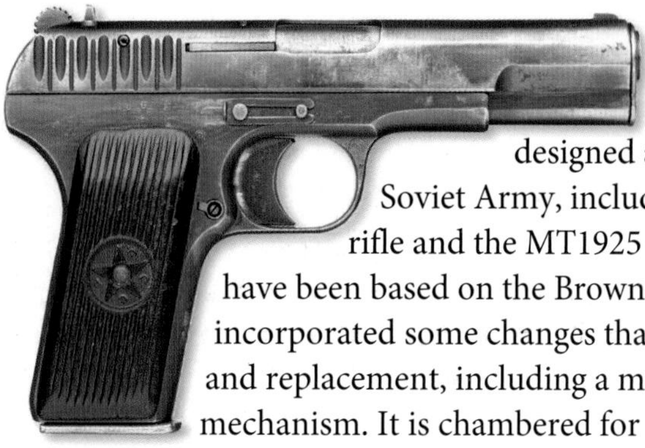

This pistol was designed by Fedor V. Tokarev, who also designed a range of weapons for the Soviet Army, including the SVT-1938 automatic rifle and the MT1925 pistol. The TT30 appears to have been based on the Browning Colt M1911, though it incorporated some changes that made for ease of manufacture and replacement, including a modular hammer and lockwork mechanism. It is chambered for the 7.62mm Tokarev cartridge, which is similar to the 7.63mm Mauser round. A modified version, the TT33, was to entirely replace the TT30.

**SPECIFICATION**

**MANUFACTURER** Soviet Tula Arms Factory
**CALIBRE** 7.62mm Tokarev
**MAGAZINE CAPACITY** 8
**ACTION** Short recoil/single
**TOTAL LENGTH** 193mm/7.59in
**BARREL LENGTH** 116mm/4.57in
**WEIGHT UNLOADED** 830g/29.28oz

## Tokarev TT33

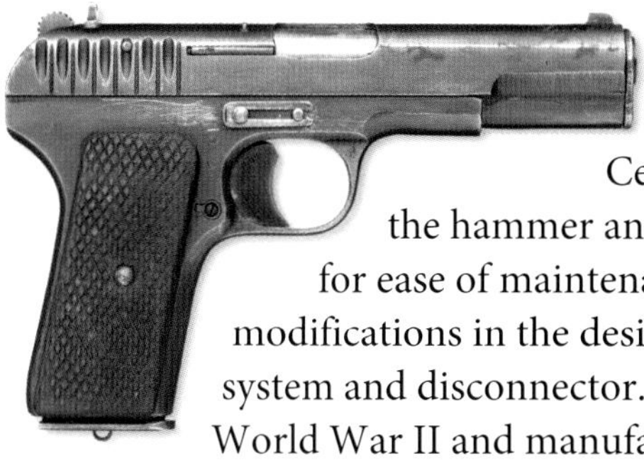

Adopted in 1933, this pistol was a development of the Tokarev TT30. Certain parts of the mechanism, including the hammer and lockwork, were removable, which made for ease of maintenance or replacement. The TT33 had slight modifications in the design of the barrel and also a new locking system and disconnector. Large numbers were produced during World War II and manufacturing continued until the 1950s.

**SPECIFICATION**

**MANUFACTURER** Soviet Tula Arsenal
**CALIBRE** 7.62mm Tokarev
**MAGAZINE CAPACITY** 8
**ACTION** Short recoil/single
**TOTAL LENGTH** 193mm/7.59in
**BARREL LENGTH** 116mm/4.57in
**WEIGHT UNLOADED** 830g/29.28oz

## Pistolet Makarova (PM)

**SPECIFICATION**

**MANUFACTURER** Izhevsk Mechanical Plant (IZHMECH)
**CALIBRE** 9mm Makarov
**MAGAZINE CAPACITY** 8
**ACTION** Recoil/double and single
**TOTAL LENGTH** 160mm/6.3in
**BARREL LENGTH** 91mm/3.58in
**WEIGHT UNLOADED** 663g/23.39oz

This pistol was designed at the end of the 1940s by Nikolai Fyodorovich Makarov and it became standard issue to Soviet armed forces. It was developed as a replacement for the Tokarev TT33. It had a blowback operation, although it was based around a new 9mm round devised by Makarov, which was incompatible with NATO firearms. The weapon had a free firing pin and was designed to have very few parts. It was a double-action, single-action (DA/SA) pistol. The first shot was fired with the hammer down after loosening the safety catch and required a long, heavy trigger pull. All shots after the first were single shots with a light trigger pull.

## Makarov PM silenced

**SPECIFICATION**

**MANUFACTURER** IZHMECH
**CALIBRE** 9mm Makarova
**MAGAZINE CAPACITY** 8
**ACTION** Short recoil/double and single
**TOTAL LENGTH** 160mm/6.3in
**BARREL LENGTH** 91mm/3.58in
**WEIGHT UNLOADED** 663g/23.39oz

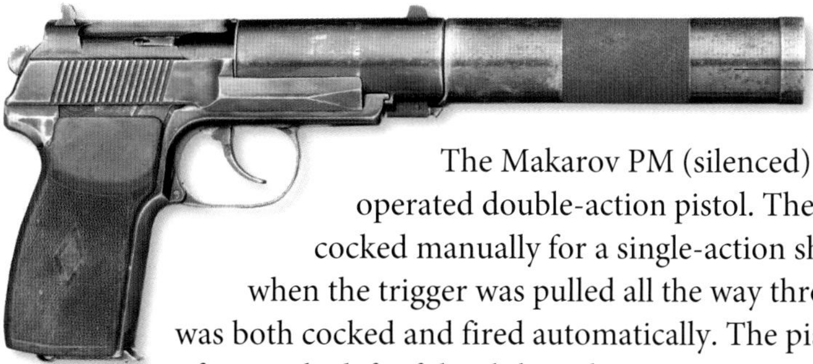


The Makarov PM (silenced) was a blowback-operated double-action pistol. The hammer could be cocked manually for a single-action shot. Alternatively, when the trigger was pulled all the way through, the pistol was both cocked and fired automatically. The pistol had a manual safety on the left of the slide and a magazine catch at the base of the hand grip. This silenced version of the Makarov was designed for undercover work and stealth operations.

## Baikal-442 pistol

This pistol was a modified version of the Makarov PMM, designed for the export market: it could take both the Russian 9mm Makarov cartridge and the 9mm Luger cartridge and an 8, 10 or 12-round magazine. Like the Makarov PMM, the Baikal had a delayed- blowback system.

**IZMECH**
Two large arsenals in Izhevsk in Russia are better known as IZHMASH and IZHMECH. IZHMASH was founded in 1807, while IZHMECH was founded as a separate production facility in 1942, known for its Makarov and Stechkin pistols, and owned the "Baikal" trademark.

**SPECIFICATION**

**MANUFACTURER** IZHMECH
**CALIBRE** 9mm Makarov or Luger
**MAGAZINE CAPACITY** 8 or 12
**ACTION** Delayed blowback/double
**TOTAL LENGTH** 161mm/6.34in
**BARREL LENGTH** 94mm/3.7in
**WEIGHT UNLOADED** 730g/25.75oz

## Stechkin

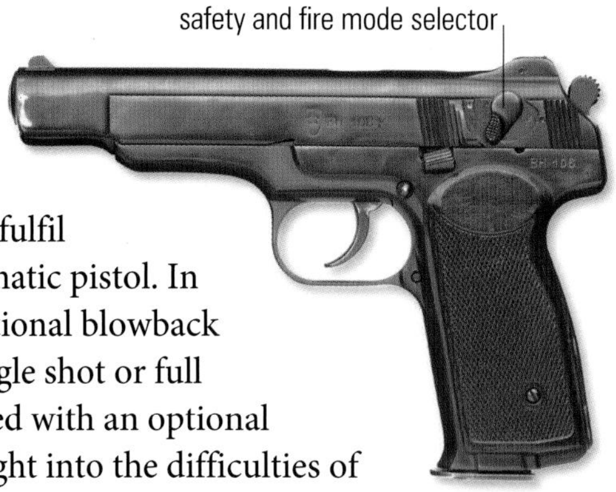


This weapon was designed by Igor Stechkin in Tula after World War II to fulfil the requirement for a large, semi-automatic pistol. In production from 1951, it had a conventional blowback operation and could be set to either single shot or full automatic fire. The weapon was supplied with an optional shoulder stock, which provided an insight into the difficulties of weapon control when firing in full automatic mode. Due to the fact that it was difficult to categorize, the Stechkin was withdrawn from Russian service.

| SPECIFICATION | |
|---|---|
| **MANUFACTURER** | State Arsenals |
| **CALIBRE** | 9mm Makarov |
| **MAGAZINE CAPACITY** | 20 |
| **ACTION** | Blowback/double |
| **TOTAL LENGTH** | 225mm/8.86in |
| **BARREL LENGTH** | 127mm/5in |
| **WEIGHT UNLOADED** | 1,030g/36.33oz |

## Stechkin silenced

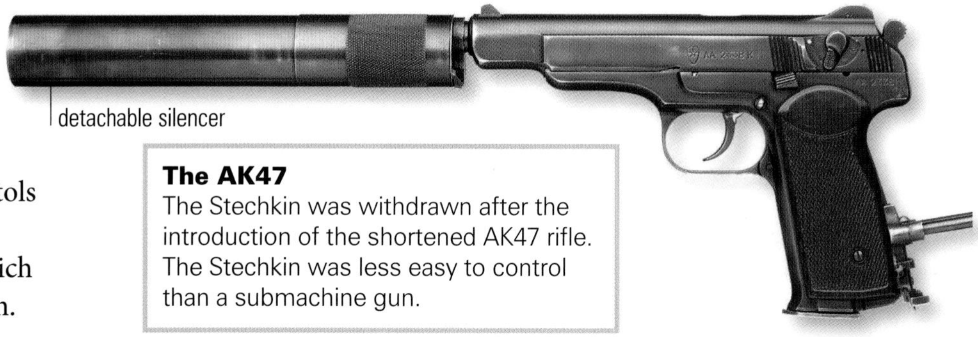


This was a silenced version of the somewhat unsuccessful Stechkin pistol. During the 1970s, some of the Stechkin pistols were modified and issued with quickly detachable silencers which reduced the crack of the weapon.

**The AK47**
The Stechkin was withdrawn after the introduction of the shortened AK47 rifle. The Stechkin was less easy to control than a submachine gun.

## Margolin MT

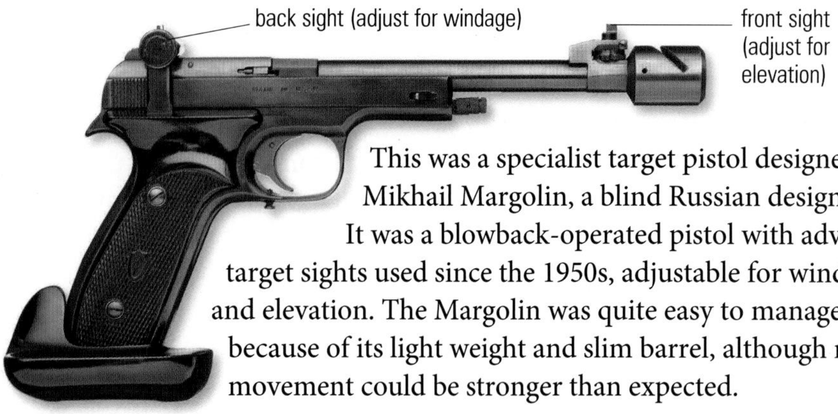


This was a specialist target pistol designed by Mikhail Margolin, a blind Russian designer. It was a blowback-operated pistol with advanced target sights used since the 1950s, adjustable for windage and elevation. The Margolin was quite easy to manage because of its light weight and slim barrel, although recoil movement could be stronger than expected.

| SPECIFICATION | |
|---|---|
| **MANUFACTURER** | IZHMECH |
| **CALIBRE** | .22 Long Rifle |
| **MAGAZINE CAPACITY** | 6 |
| **ACTION** | Blowback/single |
| **TOTAL LENGTH** | 310mm/12.2in |
| **BARREL LENGTH** | 160mm/6.3in |
| **WEIGHT UNLOADED** | 1,180g/41.6oz |

## PSM (small self-loading pistol)

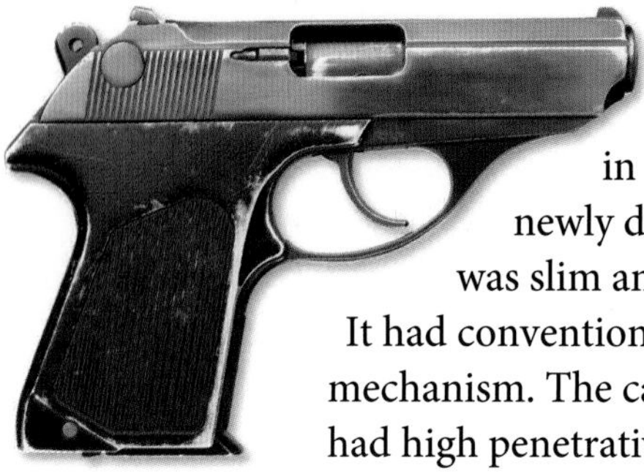

This pistol became standard issue to police and security forces in Russia in the 1970s. It was designed around the newly developed small bore 5.45mm cartridge and was slim and compact and could be easily concealed. It had conventional recoil operation with a double-action mechanism. The cartridge was of relatively low power but it had high penetrative qualities. The safety catch was positioned to the rear of the slide.

| SPECIFICATION | |
|---|---|
| **MANUFACTURER** | IZHMECH |
| **CALIBRE** | 5.45mm PSM |
| **MAGAZINE CAPACITY** | 8 |
| **ACTION** | Recoil/double |
| **TOTAL LENGTH** | 155mm/6.1in |
| **BARREL LENGTH** | 85mm/3.35in |
| **WEIGHT UNLOADED** | 460g/16.2oz |

## MP-443

**SPECIFICATION**

**MANUFACTURER** TsNIITochMash
**CALIBRE** 9mm Parabellum
**MAGAZINE CAPACITY** 18
**ACTION** Blowback/double
**TOTAL LENGTH** 205mm/8.1in
**BARREL LENGTH** 132mm/5.2in
**WEIGHT UNLOADED** 900g/31.75oz

This was a self-loading pistol with a floating barrel, firing from a closed bolt. It had a conventional blowback action. The weapon was designed for a high level of penetration and was said to be effective against fragmentation vests at 50m/164ft or against steel plate at 30m/98ft. The military index "6P35" was given to all the handguns which were submitted at the "Grach" (meaning "rook") trials which took place in the 1990s, aimed at replacing military pistols. This pistol, initially known as the 6P35 or as MP-443 "Grach", is now officially adopted by the Russian Government for the military and for law enforcement.

## "Udar" revolver

**SPECIFICATION**

**MANUFACTURER** TsNIITochMash
**CALIBRE** 12.3mm/pyroliquid/noise
**CYLINDER** 5
**ACTION** Double
**TOTAL LENGTH** 210mm/8.27in
**BARREL LENGTH** 56mm/2.2in
**WEIGHT UNLOADED** 950g/33.51oz

This revolver was developed as a specialist weapon for police and special forces and it was designed as a defensive weapon to achieve a variety of tasks that might be encountered in a crowd-control emergency or other crisis. The weapon was supplied with a number of alternative cartridges, some of which were entirely different to a standard round. It took a 12.3mm cartridge with a plastic bullet; a pyroliquid cartridge; or a noise cartridge. These cartridges enabled the weapon user to deal with threats with different levels of deterrent. It was unlikely that this revolver could do very much physical harm when fired.

## PSS (silent self-loading pistol)

**SPECIFICATION**

**MANUFACTURER** TsNIITochMash
**CALIBRE** 7.62mm special, noiseless cartridge
**CYLINDER CAPACITY** 6
**ACTION** Blowback/double
**TOTAL LENGTH** 165mm/6.5in
**BARREL LENGTH** 60mm/2.36in
**WEIGHT UNLOADED** 700g/24.7oz

This small pistol was devised for covert use by special forces and was sometimes known as the "Vul". In production from 1995, it was designed to be silent and to deliver a high-impact round that would penetrate a steel helmet at 25m/82ft. The pistol automatically reloaded after each shot. It was equipped with a safety catch to prevent accidental firing. The pistol was not fitted with a silencer; instead the silencing effect was derived from the design of the cartridge.

## SR1M

Originally known as the Gyurza (Russian for "blunt-nosed viper"), the pistol remains the same but is now known as the SR1M. Slide to barrel locking is accomplished in the same way as a Walther P38 or a Beretta 92. While it lacks a traditional manual safety lever, it does have a grip safety similar to what is found on 1911-style pistols and a trigger safety similar to those found on Glock pistols.

**SPECIFICATION**

**MANUFACTURER** TsNIITochMash
**CALIBRE** 9x21mm Gyurza
**CYLINDER CAPACITY** 18
**ACTION** Short recoil/double or single
**TOTAL LENGTH** 195mm/7.7in
**BARREL LENGTH** 112.5mm/4.42in
**WEIGHT UNLOADED** 950g/33.5oz

# Egypt

**The Egyptian defence industry is spread across a number of engineering factories which together contribute to making Egypt one of the primary arms producers in the Arab world. The Helwan pistol was a licenced version of a Beretta design. It is named after the local industrial area in which it was produced.**

## Helwan

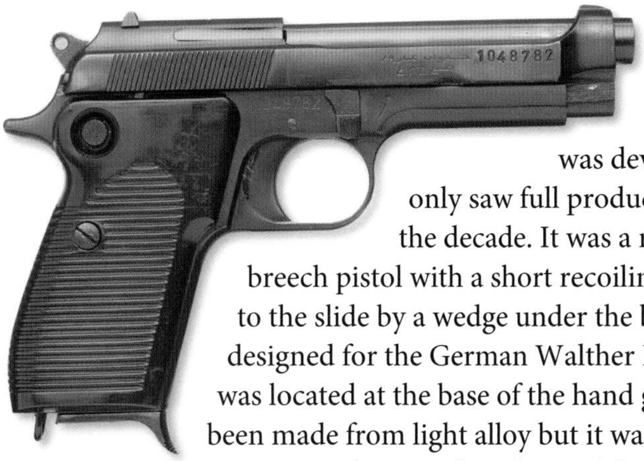

The Egyptian Helwan was a licence-built version of the Beretta M1951, which was developed in the 1950s, and only saw full production towards the end of the decade. It was a recoil-operated, locked-breech pistol with a short recoiling barrel, which was locked to the slide by a wedge under the barrel. This was a system designed for the German Walther P38. The magazine release was located at the base of the hand grip. The original pistol had been made from light alloy but it was soon discovered that this was not sturdy enough and a steel frame was then developed. The M1951 pistol was taken into service with the Italian armed forces and it was also adopted by both Israel and Egypt.

**SPECIFICATION**

**MANUFACTURER** Local Egyptian manufacturer
**CALIBRE** 9mm Parabellum
**MAGAZINE CAPACITY** 8
**ACTION** Recoil/single
**TOTAL LENGTH** 203mm/8in
**BARREL LENGTH** 115mm/4.53in
**WEIGHT UNLOADED** 890g/31.41oz

# Turkey

**Turkey was the first country to adopt and issue a pistol from another country. They purchased over a thousand German Mauser M1896 pistols in 1896. Turkey then adopted the Belgian FN Browning M1903 pistol before World War I. Turkey manufactured a copy of the famous Walther PP pistol, which was known as the Kirikkale, although minor alterations were made to suit Turkish production methods.**

## Kirikkale MKE

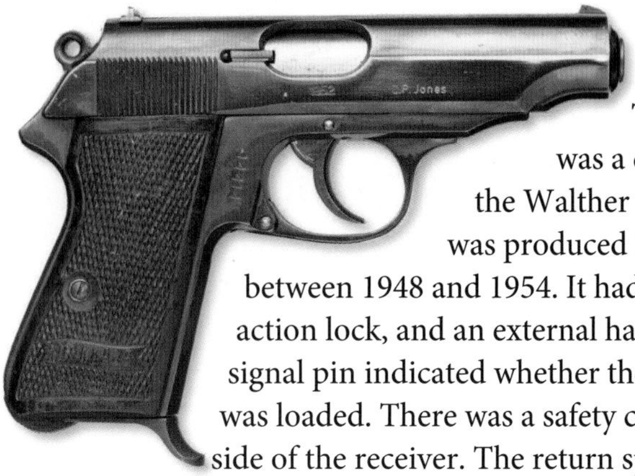

This pistol was a copy of the Walther PP and it was produced in Turkey between 1948 and 1954. It had a double-action lock, and an external hammer and signal pin indicated whether the chamber was loaded. There was a safety catch on the side of the receiver. The return spring was positioned around the fixed barrel.

**ABOVE** The double-action trigger was a feature of the Walther PP and its clones. The pistol was considered easy to handle and control.

**SPECIFICATION**

**MANUFACTURER** Local Turkish manufacturer
**CALIBRE** .380 ACP, .32 ACP
**MAGAZINE** 8
**ACTION** Blowback/double
**TOTAL LENGTH** 170mm/6.7in
**BARREL LENGTH** 98mm/3.86in
**WEIGHT UNLOADED** 695g/24.5oz

## Yavuz 16

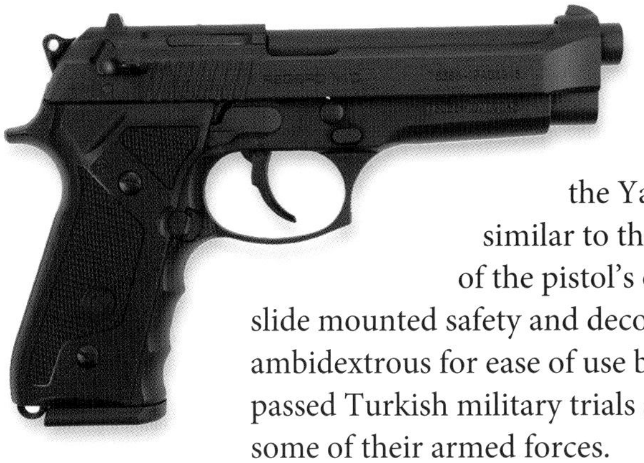

Utilizing a vertically-tilting locking piece similar to the one found on the Walther P38, the Yavuz 16 uses an open-top slide similar to the Beretta 92, from which much of the pistol's overall design borrows heavily. A slide mounted safety and decocker lever, like the Beretta 92 is ambidextrous for ease of use by all shooters. The Yavuz 16 has passed Turkish military trials and is currently being used by some of their armed forces.

**SPECIFICATION**

**MANUFACTURER** Girsan
**CALIBRE** 9mm Parabellum
**MAGAZINE** 15
**ACTION** Short recoil/double or single
**TOTAL LENGTH** 217mm/8.5in
**BARREL LENGTH** 125mm/4.9in
**WEIGHT UNLOADED** 850g/29.9oz

# Israel

**Israeli small-arms production is most famous for the Uzi submachine gun. The smallest of these can arguably be categorized as a pistol, though some might say this is stretching a point. Otherwise Israeli Military Industries developed the Desert Eagle, a Magnum Pistol which has earned some fame for its sheer size and power. KSN Industries and Ta'as Israel Industries also have products in the pistols category.**

## Jericho 941

**SPECIFICATION**

**MANUFACTURER** Israel Weapon Industries
**CALIBRE** 9mm Parabellum
**MAGAZINE** 16
**ACTION** Short recoil/double or single
**TOTAL LENGTH** 208mm/8.2in
**BARREL LENGTH** 111mm/4.4in
**WEIGHT UNLOADED** 1,043g/636.80z

In use by a variety of Israeli police and security forces, the design of the Jericho 941 is popular the world over and has been exported under various names for use by at least a half dozen foreign countries. Nicknamed the "Baby Eagle" because of its similar appearance to that of the Desert Eagle, the guns are internally completely different. The Jericho 941 is modelled after the CZ75, with myriad sub-models available in different calibres and configurations, but the full-size 9mm version is currently in use by the Israeli Security Forces.

## Desert Eagle

**SPECIFICATION**

**MANUFACTURER** Magnum Research Inc/ Israel Military Industries (IMI)
**CALIBRE** .44 Magnum, .357 Magnum, .50 Action Express
**MAGAZINE** 9
**ACTION** Gas recoil/single
**TOTAL LENGTH** 260mm/10.3in
**BARREL LENGTH** 152mm/6in
**WEIGHT UNLOADED** 1,715g/62oz

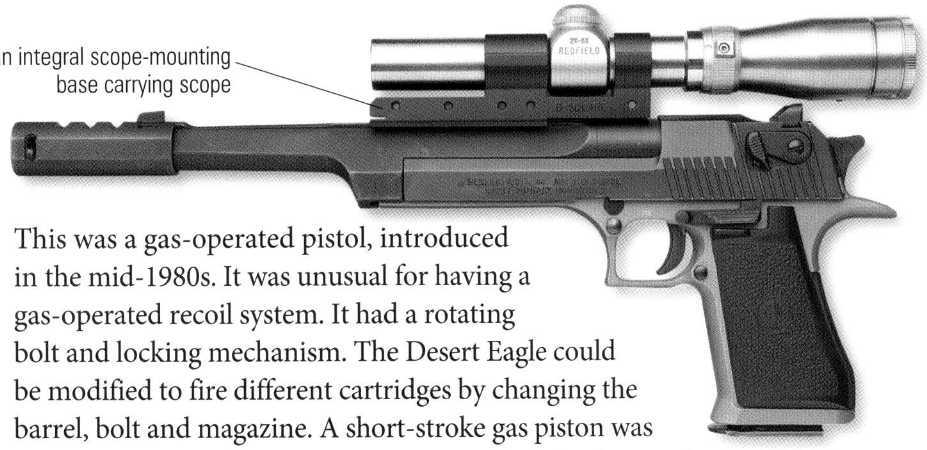


This was a gas-operated pistol, introduced in the mid-1980s. It was unusual for having a gas-operated recoil system. It had a rotating bolt and locking mechanism. The Desert Eagle could be modified to fire different cartridges by changing the barrel, bolt and magazine. A short-stroke gas piston was located below the barrel towards the muzzle end. The pistol had a single-action trigger, an exposed hammer and an ambidextrous safety.

# Japan

**Early 20th century Japanese pistols and revolvers were centred on the designs of Colonel Kijiro Nambu. Not all of these were world-class – and some were bedevilled by poor manufacture. In the post-World War II era, Japan was to prove itself a world leader in the quality of its manufacturing processes but it was also a nation dedicated to putting the past behind it and the development of small arms was definitely not a priority.**

## Nambu Baby

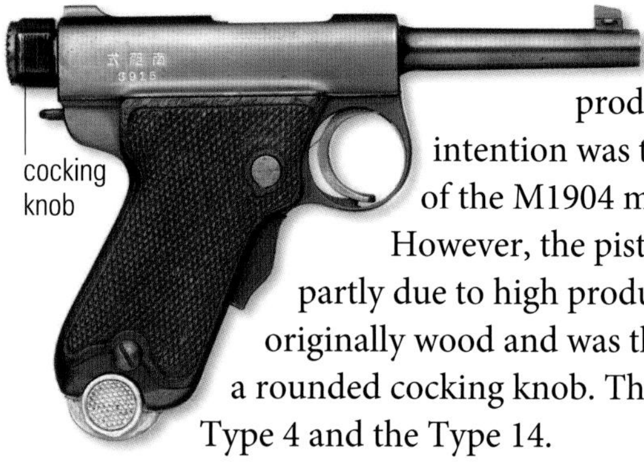


This pistol was a smaller-size version of the Nambu Model 1904, and was produced in the early 20th century. The intention was to overcome some of the criticisms of the M1904 mainly regarding size and weight. However, the pistol did not prove to be a great success, partly due to high production costs. The magazine base was originally wood and was then changed to aluminium, and it had a rounded cocking knob. The 1904 pistol had two variations, the Type 4 and the Type 14.

| SPECIFICATION | |
|---|---|
| MANUFACTURER | Koishikawa Arsenal |
| CALIBRE | 7mm Nambu |
| CYLINDER | 7 |
| ACTION | Short recoil/single |
| TOTAL LENGTH | 171mm/6.75in |
| BARREL LENGTH | 83mm/3.25in |
| WEIGHT UNLOADED | 650g/22.93oz |

## Nambu Type 14

| SPECIFICATION | |
|---|---|
| MANUFACTURER | Nagoya Arsenal |
| CALIBRE | 8mm Nambu |
| CYLINDER | 8 |
| ACTION | Short recoil/single |
| TOTAL LENGTH | 227mm/8.9in |
| BARREL LENGTH | 121mm/4.76in |
| WEIGHT UNLOADED | 900g/31.75oz |

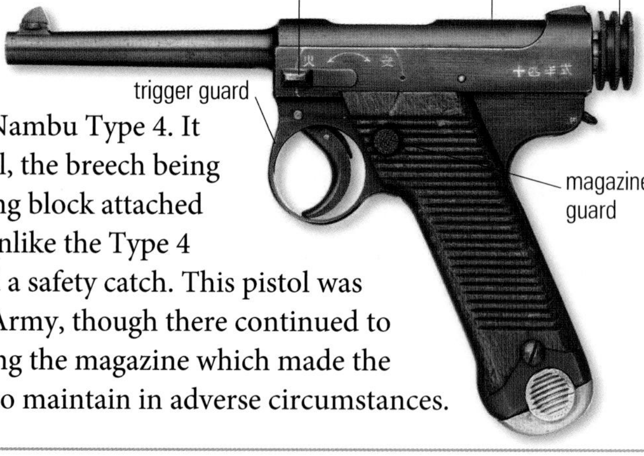


The Nambu Type 14 was essentially an improved version of the Nambu Type 4. It was a locked-breech pistol, the breech being locked by a floating locking block attached to the barrel extension. Unlike the Type 4 Model, the pistol featured a safety catch. This pistol was adopted by the Japanese Army, though there continued to be problems with removing the magazine which made the Type 14 a tricky weapon to maintain in adverse circumstances.

## Nambu Type 94

| SPECIFICATION | |
|---|---|
| MANUFACTURER | Nagoya Rifle Mfg Co. |
| CALIBRE | 8mm |
| CYLINDER | 6 |
| ACTION | Short recoil/single |
| TOTAL LENGTH | 183mm/7.2in |
| BARREL LENGTH | 96mm/3.78in |
| WEIGHT UNLOADED | 765g/26.98oz |

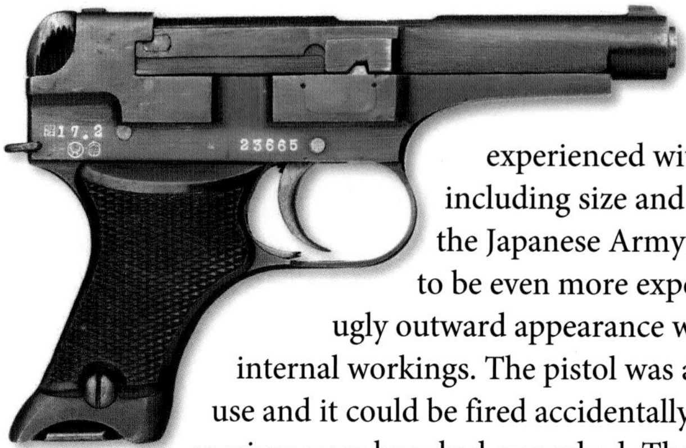

This was a totally revised pistol, designed by Nambu to try to overcome the problems experienced with some of the previous designs, including size and weight. After design input from the Japanese Army, however, the pistol turned out to be even more expensive than its predecessor. The ugly outward appearance was an accurate reflection of the internal workings. The pistol was awkward and inefficient to use and it could be fired accidentally if a sear on the side of the receiver were knocked or pushed. The design seemed to show scant regard for the convenience or safety of the user.

## HK SFP9

**SPECIFICATION**

**MANUFACTURER** Heckler & Koch GmbH.
**CALIBRE** 9mm Parabellum
**CYLINDER** 15, 17 or 20
**ACTION** Short recoil/single
**TOTAL LENGTH** 186mm/7.3in
**BARREL LENGTH** 104mm/4in
**WEIGHT UNLOADED** 708g/25oz

Japan's Ministry of Defense announced in 2019 that the HK SFP9 would be adopted by the Japanese Self Defence Forces, which already uses HK's USP pistols for special forces. This is a milestone for both HK and Japan, as it is the first time that the SFP9 (also known as the VP9) has been adopted by a national military. HK succeeded over Beretta and Glock in the Japanese MoD trials, which placed an emphasis on accuracy first and speed second. A customizable grip was also a big selling point, with swappable side panels and back straps to fit a variety of hand sizes.

# China

**The Chinese small-arms industry is centred on the state-owned China North Industries Corporation (Norinco). This company produces a number of small arms, though currently the production is focused largely on automatic rifles, submachine guns and heavy machine guns.**

## Makarov Type 59

**SPECIFICATION**

**MANUFACTURER** China North Industries Corp.
**CALIBRE** 9mm Makarov
**MAGAZINE CAPACITY** 8
**ACTION** Blowback/double or single
**TOTAL LENGTH** 162mm/6.38in
**BARREL LENGTH** 94mm/3.7in
**WEIGHT UNLOADED** 730g/25.75oz

This appeared to be a copy of the Russian Makarov pistol, though there were differences in both size and weight. The Makarov was in turn similar to the German Walther PP. The Type 59 was a double-action pistol with blowback operation. It had a manual safety on the left-hand side. The magazine was inserted into the hand grip and the first round was chambered by drawing back the slide and releasing it. The pistol could be fired in single-action mode by cocking the hammer with the thumb or by double-action, which involved pulling the trigger all the way through to cock and release the hammer.

## QSZ-92

The QSZ-92 was a state-of-the-art pistol that had been adopted by the Chinese People's Liberation Army. It was a short recoil-operated, locked-breech pistol with a polymer frame. It incorporated a rotating barrel system which unlocked the slide during recoil. The pistol was fitted with an accessory rail which could accept either laser sights or lighting systems. The pistol was available in two versions, one the more common 9mm Parabellum cartridge and one for the Chinese type 5.8mm bottle-necked cartridge. Development of the pistol was thought to have started in 1994.

**SPECIFICATION**

**MANUFACTURER** Norinco
**CALIBRE** 9mm Parabellum
**MAGAZINE CAPACITY** 15
**ACTION** Short recoil/double
**TOTAL LENGTH** 190mm/7.5in
**BARREL LENGTH** 111mm/4.37in
**WEIGHT UNLOADED** 760g/26.8oz

## Tokarev Type 51

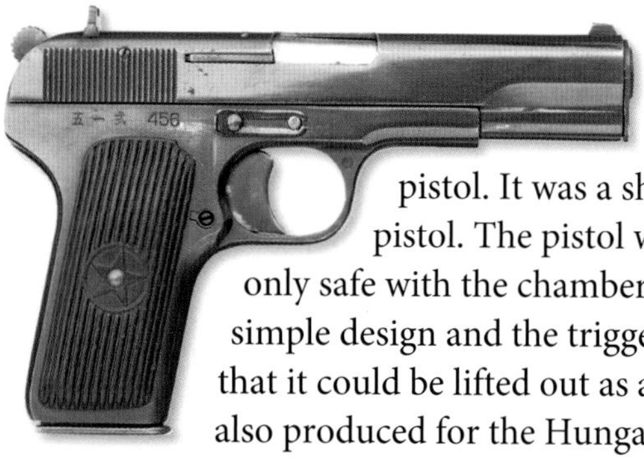

The Chinese Type 51 was a copy of the Russian Tokarev TT33. It became the standard Chinese Army pistol. It was a short recoil-operated, locked-breech pistol. The pistol was not fitted with a safety and was only safe with the chamber empty. The Type 51 was a rugged and simple design and the trigger system was designed in such a way that it could be lifted out as a complete unit. Similar pistols were also produced for the Hungarian armed forces.

**SPECIFICATION**

**MANUFACTURER** State Arsenals
**CALIBRE** 7.62mm Tokarev
**MAGAZINE CAPACITY** 8
**ACTION** Short recoil/single
**TOTAL LENGTH** 196mm/7.7in
**BARREL LENGTH** 116mm/4.57in
**WEIGHT UNLOADED** 830g/29.28oz

## Norinco Tokarev Type 54

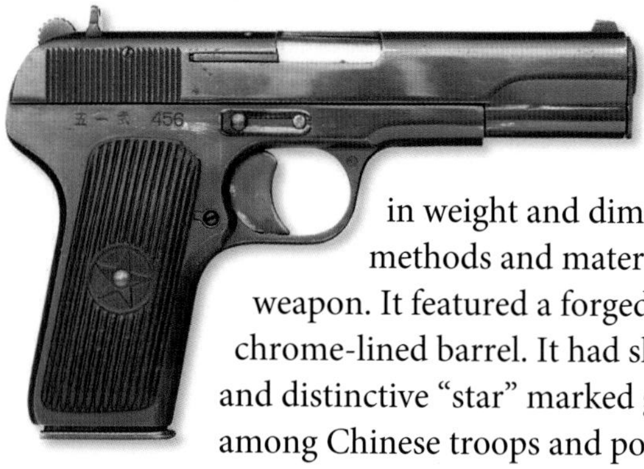

The Norinco Type 54 was also copied from the Russian Tokarev TT33 with some minor differences in weight and dimensions due to manufacturing methods and materials used; it was otherwise the same weapon. It featured a forged steel frame and slide, and a chrome-lined barrel. It had slide serrations for improved grip, and distinctive "star" marked grip panels. This pistol was common among Chinese troops and police forces.

**SPECIFICATION**

**MANUFACTURER** Norinco
**CALIBRE** 7.62mm Tokarev
**MAGAZINE CAPACITY** 8
**ACTION** Short recoil/single
**TOTAL LENGTH** 196mm/7.7in
**BARREL LENGTH** 116mm/4.57in
**WEIGHT UNLOADED** 900g/31.75oz

## Norinco Tokarev Type 213

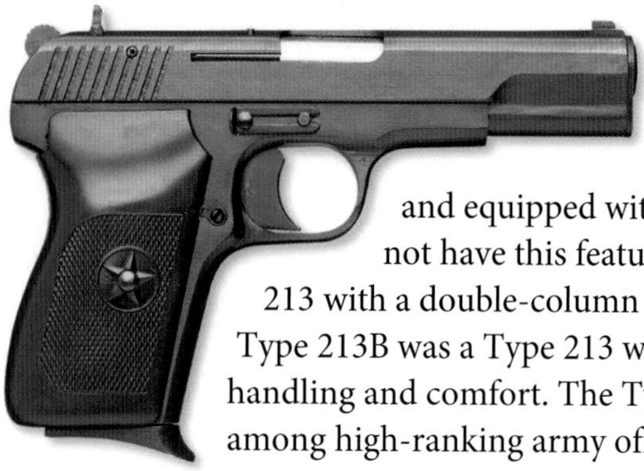

The Norinco Tokarev Type 213 was a Type 54 chambered for 9mm Parabellum ammunition and equipped with a manual safety (the Type 54 did not have this feature). The Type 213A was a Type 213 with a double-column magazine and a wider grip. The Type 213B was a Type 213 with moulded rubber grips for easier handling and comfort. The Type 213 pistol was found mainly among high-ranking army officers.

**SPECIFICATION**

**MANUFACTURER** Norinco
**CALIBRE** 9mm Parabellum
**MAGAZINE CAPACITY** 8
**ACTION** Short recoil/single
**TOTAL LENGTH** 195mm/7.67in
**BARREL LENGTH** 115mm/4.53in
**WEIGHT UNLOADED** 830g/29.28oz

## Type 64 Silent Pistol

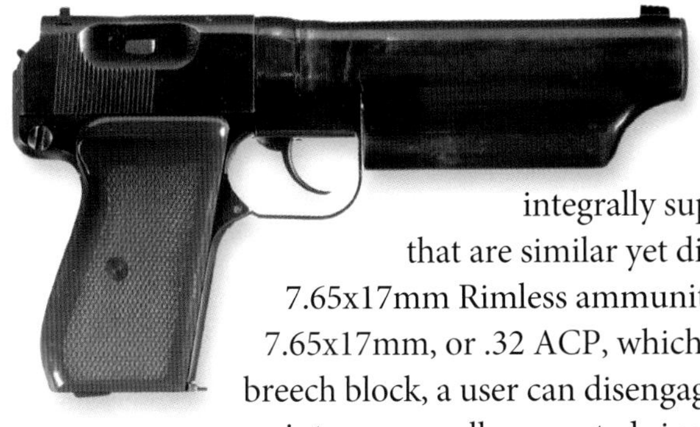

Not to be confused with the similarly named Type 64, the Type 64 Silent Pistol has an integrally suppressed barrel. Keeping with things that are similar yet different, the Type 64 Silent Pistol uses 7.65x17mm Rimless ammunition, which is not the same as 7.65x17mm, or .32 ACP, which is semi-rimmed. A toggle on the breech block, a user can disengage the blowback action and turn the gun into a manually-operated single-shot pistol. The benefit of this is to reduce sound even more by preventing the gun from cycling. The barrel is a two-stage suppressor, with traditional baffles in line with the bore and a second chamber below the barrel that doubles as an expansion chamber in one part and a mesh baffle system in the other part.

**SPECIFICATION**

**MANUFACTURER** China North Industries Corp.
**CALIBRE** 7.65x17mm Rimless
**MAGAZINE CAPACITY** 9
**ACTION** Blowback
**TOTAL LENGTH** 220mm/8.6in
**BARREL LENGTH** 95mm/3.7in
**WEIGHT UNLOADED** 95g/3.7oz

## QSW-06

The QSW-06 nomenclature stands for Suppressed Pistol – 2006. In pinyin, it means "minimal noise handgun." Based on the QSZ-92, the QSW-06 is externally visually similar, but internally it functions differently because of the suppressor. The main difference being the QSW-06 does not have a rotating barrel lock. It was the winning design after reviewing two different handgun models and 15 different suppressor models, and is chambered in 5.8x21mm DCV05, which is a Chinese-designed armour-piercing cartridge for handguns and submachine guns.

**SPECIFICATION**

**MANUFACTURER** China North Industries Corp.
**CALIBRE** 5.8x21mm DCV05
**MAGAZINE CAPACITY** 20
**ACTION** Short recoil/double or single
**TOTAL LENGTH WITH SUPPRESSOR** 373mm/14.6in
**TOTAL LENGTH WITHOUT SUPPRESSOR** 195mm/7.6in
**BARREL LENGTH** 120mm/4.7in
**WEIGHT UNLOADED WITH SUPPRESSOR** 1,050g/37oz

# South Korea

**After liberation from Japan in 1945, South Korea depended heavily on the United States for military weapons. Early South Korean arms designs were reverse-engineered from US weapons. Now in the 21st century, South Korea has developed a thriving arms industry and is one of the leading countries in defence exports.**

## Daewoo K5

Introduced in 1989, the K5 features a steel slide and an aluminum alloy frame. Capable of firing in double or single action, it has a unique trigger design that is known as Fast Action, Triple Action, or Double Action Plus. This allows the hammer to be decocked while still compressing the mainspring. By doing so, trigger travel is still long like normal double action, but the pull weight is reduced to that of single action. This pistol is most frequently carried by commissioned officers in the South Korean military.

**SPECIFICATION**

**MANUFACTURER** Daewoo Telecom Ltd.
**CALIBRE** 9mm
**MAGAZINE** 13 or 15
**ACTION** Short recoil/double or single
**TOTAL LENGTH** 178mm/7in
**BARREL LENGTH** 104.1mm/4.1in
**WEIGHT UNLOADED** 734g/25.90z

**KEY**

1 Canada
2 United States
3 Mexico
4 Chile
5 Argentina
6 Brazil
7 Portugal
8 Spain
9 UK
10 France
11 Switzerland
12 Germany
13 Italy
14 Denmark
15 Austria
16 Sweden
17 Czech Republic
18 Poland
19 Croatia
20 South Africa
21 Finland
22 Romania
23 Russia
24 Egypt
25 Israel
26 China
27 Australia
28 South Korea
29 Japan

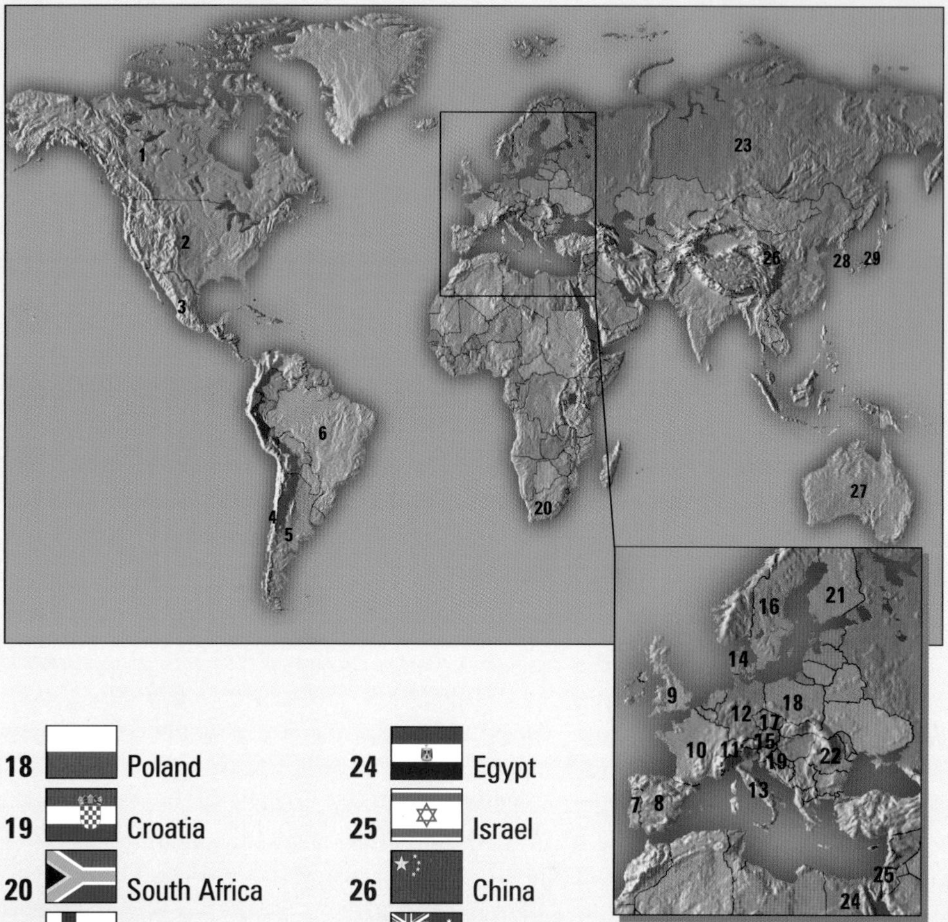


**ABOVE** The map indicates the countries of the world where submachine guns are featured in this section.

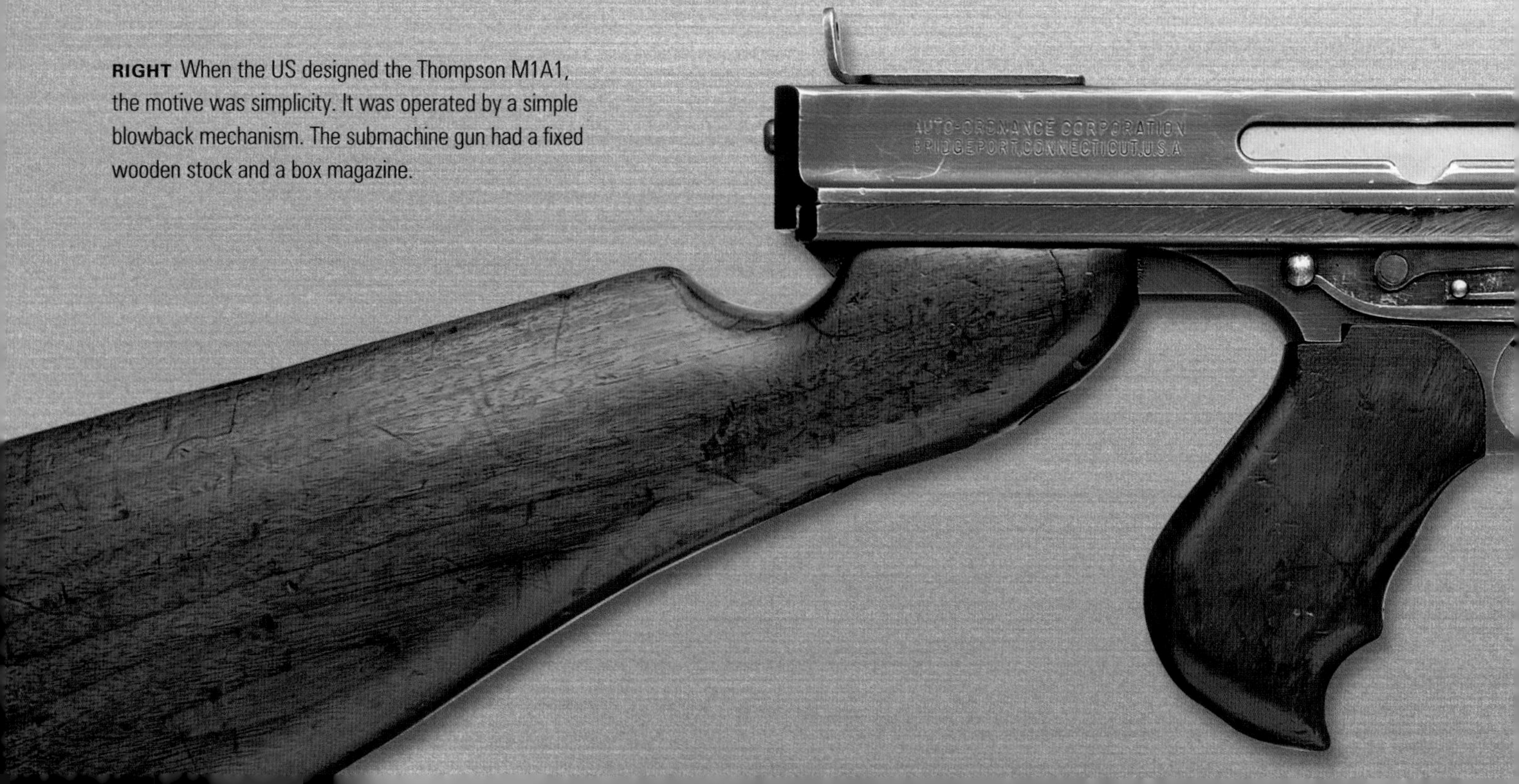


**RIGHT** When the US designed the Thompson M1A1, the motive was simplicity. It was operated by a simple blowback mechanism. The submachine gun had a fixed wooden stock and a box magazine.

# A directory of submachine guns from around the world

Submachine guns are manufactured in many parts of the world. Some manufacturers produce unique firearms, while others produce or import versions of arms from other countries under licence. Taking a cross-section of selected countries of the world, west to east, this directory aims to feature a broad selection of the firearms that are available in those countries and detail their main features. Within each country's entry submachine guns are organized alphabetically by manufacturer except where its historical development is shown more clearly chronologically or a company changes its name. Each firearm has a description and a specification that lists its vital measurements, including its calibre.

**BELOW** The rugged-looking MAT-49 was developed in France during the late 1940s.

**ABOVE** Israel's Uzi submachine gun is an extremely efficient weapon of its type.

# Canada

**Canada does not have a tradition of designing weapons in the submachine gun category, and those that have been used in the past have been derived from other parts of the world. The Canadian military has used the Thompson, the Sten and the MP5 and produced a version of the C1.**

## C1 SMG

The C1 was a Canadian version of the ubiquitous L2A1 Sterling submachine gun. As the Sterling L2A1 was a reliable weapon with a good performance record, there was not much requirement for change. The small changes that were made included a reduction in magazine capacity (from 34 rounds), which also involved a change to the feed mechanism. The C1 was a blowback-operated weapon with selective fire and a folding butt. It was used by the Canadian military in the 1950s.

**SPECIFICATION**

**MANUFACTURER** Canadian Arsenals Ltd.
**CALIBRE** 9mm Parabellum
**MAGAZINE CAPACITY** 30 or 10
**ACTION** Blowback
**TOTAL LENGTH (STOCK EXTENDED)** 686mm/27in
**TOTAL LENGTH (STOCK RETRACTED)** 493mm/19.41in
**BARREL LENGTH** 198mm/7.8in
**WEIGHT UNLOADED** 2,950g/104oz

# United States

**The most famous submachine gun produced in the United States was the Thompson submachine gun. It has iconic status among submachine guns and this gun is probably the most easily identified model ever produced, later replaced by the more workman-like M3A1 "grease gun". Today, Smith & Wesson and Ruger produce submachine guns, and weapons are manufactured for American forces and for export.**

## American 180

The American 180 (AM180) was imported from Austria by American Arms International (AAI) in 1972 before being manufactured domestically. The original design was by US designer Richard Casull, who devised a series of small-calibre rifles. It was a conventional blowback-operated submachine gun fired from an open bolt in either full automatic or single-shot mode. After AAI went out of business in 1986, the Illinois Arms Company (Ilarco) produced the weapon with some modifications, such as reducing the magazine capacity from 177 rounds to 165. It was fitted with an extremely high-capacity magazine, not unlike those fitted to fighter aircraft. The magazine was unusual because it was in a flat pan of layered ammunition. The .22 Long Rifle cartridge gave the user the advantages of low recoil, good accuracy and a high rate of fire. It was used mainly by police departments for riot-control duties. The gun had a high standard of manufacture, with solid machined steel parts, and a solid wooden stock and forehand grip.

**SPECIFICATION**

**MANUFACTURER** American Arms International/Illinois Arms Co.
**CALIBRE** .22 Long Rifle
**MAGAZINE CAPACITY** 177 or 165
**ACTION** Blowback
**TOTAL LENGTH** 900mm/35.43in
**BARREL LENGTH** 470mm/18.5in
**WEIGHT UNLOADED** 2,600g/91.7oz

## Thompson M1921

**SPECIFICATION**

**MANUFACTURER** Auto-Ordnance Corp.
**CALIBRE** .45 ACP
**MAGAZINE CAPACITY** 18, 20 or 30 box; 50 or 100 drum
**ACTION** Delayed blowback
**TOTAL LENGTH** 857mm/33.74in
**BARREL LENGTH** 267mm/10.51in
**WEIGHT UNLOADED** 4,690g/165oz

This weapon was developed by John Thompson, the founder of the Auto- Ordnance Corporation. It had a delayed-blowback mechanism fed from a round box or round drum magazine. The 1921 version was developed from the 1920 version (which in turn followed the 1918 and 1919 models). Although it was the first production model, the M1921 was not adopted by any of the US armed services. The M1921 proved to be the defining model in terms of appearance for the Thompson submachine gun, losing the barrel jacket that had been a feature of earlier models. It had a forward hand grip and a detachable buttstock.

## Thompson M1928A1

**SPECIFICATION**

**MANUFACTURER** Auto-Ordnance Corp./ Savage Arms Corp./Colts Patents Firearms Corp.
**CALIBRE** .45 ACP
**MAGAZINE CAPACITY** 18, 20 or 30 box; 50 or 100 drum
**ACTION** Delayed blowback
**TOTAL LENGTH** 857mm/33.74in
**BARREL LENGTH** 267mm/10.51in
**WEIGHT UNLOADED** 4,880g/172oz

This version of the Thompson submachine gun was the same in many respects as the M1921 version. However, it was under the M1928 designation that the weapon achieved its first major orders by the US armed forces, especially the US Navy and US Marine Corps. It was also ordered by Britain and France in considerable numbers. With the start of World War II in 1939, these commissions saved the manufacturer from bankruptcy. The A1 version had some minor modifications. This variant entered mass production before the attack on Pearl Harbor in December 1941, and replaced stocks of the M1928. Only two factories supplied M1928A1 Thompson submachine guns during the early years of World War II. It was used mainly in the Pacific by the US military.

## Thompson M1A1

**SPECIFICATION**

**MANUFACTURER** Auto-Ordnance Corp./ Savage Arms Corp.
**CALIBRE** .45 ACP
**MAGAZINE CAPACITY** 20 or 30
**ACTION** Blowback
**TOTAL LENGTH** 813mm/32in
**BARREL LENGTH** 266mm/10.47in
**WEIGHT UNLOADED** 4,820g/170oz

In 1942 the Thompson M1928 was redesigned and called the Thompson M1A1. The design motive behind the M1A1 was simplicity. The earlier Thompsons all incorporated the "Blish" mechanism, which relied on friction to delay the opening of the breech. This mechanism was complex, of questionable value and time-consuming, and therefore expensive to produce. The M1A1 incorporated a simple blowback mechanism which helped to radically reduce production time. The cocking handle was moved to the side. It also came with a fixed stock and simplified sights. The trademark drum magazine was replaced with a simpler stick magazine. The M1A1 was differentiated from the M1 by the design of the firing pin.

## Calico M961A

First produced in the 1990s, Calico weapons were unique in their design features. They had large magazine capacities with a helical magazine on the top of the receiver. The spent cases were ejected down through the ejection chute at the front of the trigger guard. The M961A was a compact version of the previously produced M960A. The M961A was a selective-fire weapon, firing either single shots or fully automatic. It was distinguished from the M960A by a shorter barrel.

**SPECIFICATION**

**MANUFACTURER** Calico, Oregon
**CALIBRE** 9mm Parabellum
**MAGAZINE CAPACITY** 50 or 100
**ACTION** Delayed blowback
**TOTAL LENGTH (STOCK EXTENDED)** 835mm/32.87in
**TOTAL LENGTH (STOCK RETRACTED)** 647mm/25.47in
**BARREL LENGTH** 330mm/12.99in
**WEIGHT UNLOADED** 2,170g/76.54oz

## Colt Model 635

This weapon was based on the design of the M16A2/A4 rifle and was first produced in 1987. It had a closed-bolt mechanism and relatively low recoil, which improved accuracy. The weapon had a sliding, heavy-duty buttstock. The major working parts were the same as on the M16 rifle, making it easy for troops to cross between the two weapons. Due to its compact size, it was relatively easy to conceal and it was well suited to operations in environments with restricted space, such as vehicles, ships and buildings. It was adopted by the US armed forces and various law enforcement agencies, and has also been exported around the world.

**SPECIFICATION**

**MANUFACTURER** Colt Firearms
**CALIBRE** 9mm Parabellum
**MAGAZINE CAPACITY** 20 or 32
**ACTION** Blowback
**TOTAL LENGTH (STOCK EXTENDED)** 730mm/28.74in
**TOTAL LENGTH (STOCK RETRACTED)** 650mm/25.59in
**BARREL LENGTH** 260mm/10.23in
**WEIGHT UNLOADED** 2,610g/92oz

## M3

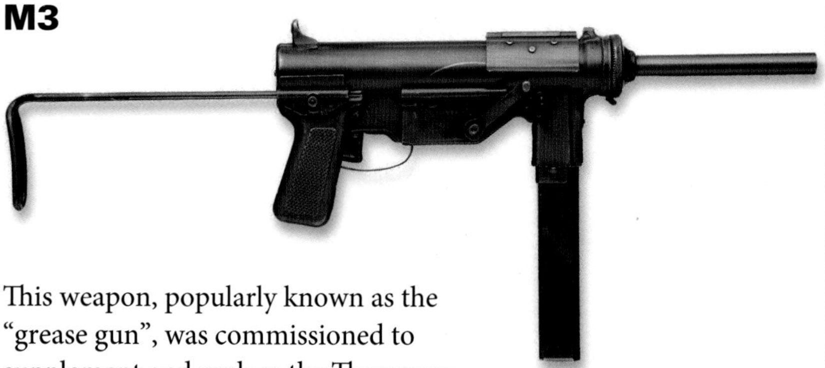

This weapon, popularly known as the "grease gun", was commissioned to supplement and replace the Thompson submachine gun that had been the mainstay of US forces. Although an efficient weapon, the Thompson was expensive and inefficient to produce. The M3 was first produced in December 1942 and it was manufactured from stampings rather than machining operations. It had a comparatively low rate of fire and moderate recoil but it proved to be somewhat unreliable. The bolt-retracting handle was awkward to operate and the magazine had a tendency to jam. A later version, the M3A1, had a modified bolt-retracting system. The weapon had a retractable butt. It was deployed throughout the Korean War, in Vietnam and in the first Gulf War.

**SPECIFICATION**

**MANUFACTURER** Guide Lamp Division, General Motors Corp.
**CALIBRE** .45 ACP
**MAGAZINE CAPACITY** 30
**ACTION** Blowback
**TOTAL LENGTH (STOCK EXTENDED)** 757mm/29.8in
**TOTAL LENGTH (STOCK RETRACTED)** 579mm/22.8in
**BARREL LENGTH** 203mm/8in
**WEIGHT UNLOADED** 3,668g/129oz

### M3A1

An improved version of the M3, the M3A1, was developed during the 1940s to correct some of M3's weaknesses, including a complete redesign of the bolt-retracting mechanism. By the end of World War II the M3A1 became the standard submachine gun of the US military.

## Hyde-Inland M2

**SPECIFICATION**

**MANUFACTURER** Marlin Firearms
**CALIBRE** .45 ACP
**MAGAZINE CAPACITY** 20 or 30
**ACTION** Blowback
**TOTAL LENGTH** 812mm/32in
**BARREL LENGTH** 304mm/12in
**WEIGHT UNLOADED** 4,195g/148oz

Designed by George Hyde and sent to General Motors' Inland Manufacturing to create the prototype, the M2 was actually produced by Marlin because Inland shifted their focus to the M1 Carbine. The M2 was intended to be a substitute for the Thompson M1 submachine gun but it wasn't able to meet performance standards during military tests. Marlin's contract for 164,450 guns was cancelled after just 400 were made because the design was supplanted by the M3 "Grease Gun", which was much simpler and less expensive to make.

## Reising Model 50

**SPECIFICATION**

**MANUFACTURER** Harrington and Richardson
**CALIBRE** .45 ACP
**MAGAZINE CAPACITY** 12 or 20
**ACTION** Delayed blowback
**TOTAL LENGTH** 959mm/37.76in
**BARREL LENGTH** 279mm/10.98in
**WEIGHT UNLOADED** 3,100g/109oz

**Drawbacks of the Reising**
Although the Reising was well-designed and manufactured, it was quite a complex weapon and fine tolerances made it liable to jam. Large-scale production ceased in 1945.

The Reising Model 50 was designed in the 1940s by Eugene Reising (a US designer who had previously worked with John Browning) and entered service with the US armed forces, primarily the US Navy. The Model 50 was brought in to supplement supplies of the Thompson submachine gun, which was proving costly and time-consuming to manufacture. Unlike most other submachine guns it had a closed-bolt mechanism. It proved accurate and reliable in trials. However, perhaps due to the intricacy of the design, it was unreliable in combat conditions and it rapidly became unpopular with servicemen. In the later stages of World War II the weapon was largely issued to personnel in non-combat roles.

## Reising Model 55

wire folding stock

**SPECIFICATION**

**MANUFACTURER** Harrington and Richardson
**CALIBRE** .45 ACP
**MAGAZINE CAPACITY** 12 or 20
**ACTION** Delayed blowback
**TOTAL LENGTH (STOCK EXTENDED)** 787mm/31in
**TOTAL LENGTH (STOCK RETRACTED)** 570mm/22.44in
**BARREL LENGTH** 279mm/10.98in
**WEIGHT UNLOADED** 2,889g/101.92oz

This was an adapted version of the Reising Model 50 which could be identified immediately by the use of a wire stock in place of the wooden stock of the Model 50. Since the wooden furniture under the receiver was retained, the M55 had a somewhat unbalanced appearance and the wire stock did not prove strong enough to provide a secure firing platform. The rest of the weapon remained the same as its predecessor and retained all of its problems. Like the Reising M50, the M55 could only be operated effectively in a clean, non-combat environment. The gun was withdrawn from frontline service in 1943.

## UD M42

This weapon was designed for the High Standard Manufacturing Company in the United States and produced in 1942. It was also manufactured by Marlin. It was a conventional blowback-operated weapon, firing from an open bolt, while an independent hammer engaged the firing pin. The slide handle acted independently of the bolt. The M42 was ordered by Dutch forces in the East Indies and was also issued to some OSS (Office of Strategic Services) forces, but it could never challenge the Thompson submachine gun in popularity.

**SPECIFICATION**

**MANUFACTURER** High Standard Mfg. Co./Marlin Firearms Co.
**CALIBRE** 9mm Parabellum
**MAGAZINE CAPACITY** 20
**ACTION** Blowback
**TOTAL LENGTH** 820mm/32.28in
**BARREL LENGTH** 279mm/10.98in
**WEIGHT UNLOADED** 4,110g/144.96oz

## Interdynamic USA KG9

This automatic pistol originated in Sweden as the TEC-9. It was devised as an inexpensive weapon manufactured largely from polymers. However, due to relative lack of interest from potential customers, a subsidiary company, Interdynamic USA (later renamed Intratec), was set up in the United States. The weapon was redesignated the KG9. Initially it had an open-bolt mechanism but the US authorities ruled that it should only be produced in closed-bolt form due to the ease with which earlier versions could be converted to full automatic. The KG9 was intended for use by special forces and has consistent and reasonable power for a small-barrelled gun.

**SPECIFICATION**

**MANUFACTURER** Intratec
**CALIBRE** 9mm
**MAGAZINE CAPACITY** 10, 20, 32, 36 or 50
**ACTION** Blowback
**TOTAL LENGTH** 241mm/9.49in
**BARREL LENGTH** 76mm/3in
**WEIGHT UNLOADED** 1,230g/43oz

**Intratec USA**
Intratec was an arms company based in Miami, Florida until it went out of business in 2001. Intratec's most famous firearm was the TEC-9.

## Intratec DC9

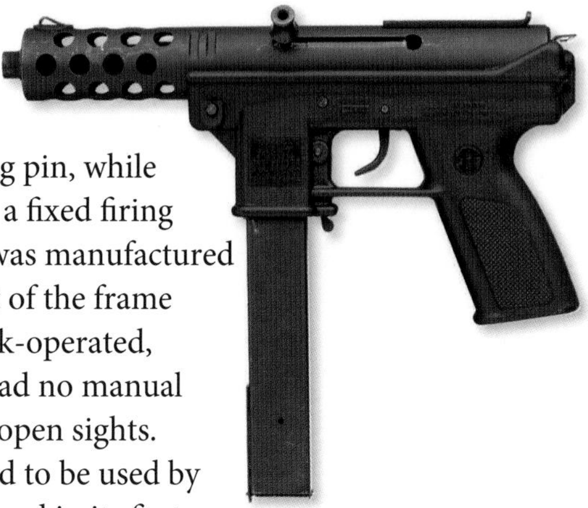

The Intratec DC9 differs in some ways from the Intratec KG9: the DC9 had a closed bolt and separate firing pin, while the KG9 had an open bolt and a fixed firing pin. The receiver on the DC9 was manufactured from steel while the lower part of the frame was polymer. It was a blowback-operated, semi-automatic weapon and had no manual safety. It was fitted with fixed, open sights. Like the KG9, the DC9 was said to be used by criminal gangs, and it was banned in its first production form in the United States.

**SPECIFICATION**

**MANUFACTURER** Intratec
**CALIBRE** 9mm Parabellum
**MAGAZINE CAPACITY** 10, 20, 32, 36 or 50
**ACTION** Blowback
**TOTAL LENGTH** 241mm/9.49in
**BARREL LENGTH** 76mm/3in
**WEIGHT UNLOADED** 1,230g/43oz

**Barrel extension**
The DC9 could be fitted with a screw-on barrel extension, designed to provide better balance or to make the weapon look more powerful.

**SPECIFICATION**

**MANUFACTURER** Police Ordnance Co.
**CALIBRE** 9mm Parabellum
**MAGAZINE CAPACITY** 30
**ACTION** Blowback
**TOTAL LENGTH** 762mm/30in
**BARREL LENGTH** 228mm/9in
**WEIGHT UNLOADED** 3,290g/116oz

## Ingram Model 6

This weapon was similar in appearance to the Thompson submachine gun and was first produced in the early 1950s. It was one of the first weapons to use a two-stage trigger whereby initial pressure would produce single shots and sustained pressure would produce automatic fire. Considerable thought went into manufacturing the weapon as cheaply and efficiently as possible. In the event, however, there was not enough of a market for the weapon in either the United States or Europe.

## Smith & Wesson Model 76

**SPECIFICATION**

**MANUFACTURER** Smith & Wesson Inc.
**CALIBRE** 9mm Parabellum
**MAGAZINE CAPACITY** 36 or 50
**ACTION** Blowback
**TOTAL LENGTH (STOCK EXTENDED)** 806mm/31.73in
**TOTAL LENGTH (STOCK RETRACTED)** 552mm/21.73in
**BARREL LENGTH** 203mm/8in
**WEIGHT UNLOADED** 3,430g/121oz

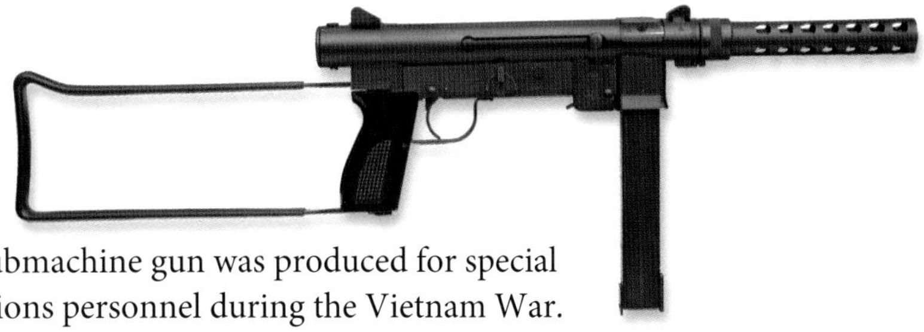

This submachine gun was produced for special operations personnel during the Vietnam War. The design was based on the Swedish Gustaf M45, which had previously been issued to US forces. Supplies of the Gustaf are said to have been limited because of political opposition within Sweden to the Vietnam War. About 6,000 weapons were produced between 1968 and 1974.

**SPECIFICATION**

**MANUFACTURER** Sturm, Ruger & Co. Inc.
**CALIBRE** 9mm Parabellum
**MAGAZINE CAPACITY** 32
**ACTION** Blowback
**TOTAL LENGTH (STOCK EXTENDED)** 556mm/21.89in
**TOTAL LENGTH (STOCK RETRACTED)** 376mm/14.8in
**BARREL LENGTH** 173mm/6.81in
**WEIGHT UNLOADED** 2,700g/95oz

## Ruger MP-9

This weapon, originally known as the Gal-Tech, was produced in the 1980s and was the result of an attempt by the Ruger Company to improve the Uzi submachine gun. It was a compact, blowback-operated weapon that fired from a closed bolt. It had a fire-selector for single or automatic fire. The trigger guard was placed forward of the second hand grip. The magazine was inserted into the pistol grip at the centre of the weapon, which provided a good balance. It had a folding buttstock which fitted neatly against the back of the receiver and the rear hand grip when folded.

## Ingram MAC 10

**SPECIFICATION**

**MANUFACTURER** Various
**CALIBRE** 9mm Parabellum, .45 ACP
**MAGAZINE CAPACITY** 30
**ACTION** Blowback
**TOTAL LENGTH (STOCK EXTENDED)** 548mm/21.6in
**TOTAL LENGTH (STOCK RETRACTED)** 269mm/10.59in
**BARREL LENGTH** 146mm/5.75in
**WEIGHT UNLOADED** 2,840g/100oz

This weapon was designed by Gordon B. Ingram in the 1960s and set new standards for compact submachine gun design. It was short and made from rugged steel pressings and incorporated a wrap-around bolt with the firing pin placed well back in order to envelop the breech. The cocking handle could be locked by rotating it. On the right of the trigger guard there was a safety catch. The weapon featured a telescopic stock. Although it did not achieve general-issue status, the Mac 10 was used by special forces units in various parts of the world.

# Mexico

**Small-arms manufacture in Mexico goes back to the Mexican Revolution, and the firm of Mendoza began producing arms in 1911. Due to restrictions imposed by the Mexican Government in the 1970s, Mendoza has branched out into other areas, but still retains the impressive HM-3 submachine gun in its catalogue.**

## Mendoza HM-3

This was a lightweight, blowback-operated weapon of all-steel construction, produced in the 1990s. The magazine slid into the pistol grip which incorporated a grip safety. The HM-3 had a selector on the right-hand side of the weapon and the stock could either be folded or unfolded. The HM-3 has achieved a good reputation for its quality of construction and over 6,000 have been produced for the Mexican armed forces. The weapon can be dismantled and put back together again without the use of tools. It had an indicator to show when a round had been chambered. The manufacturers claimed the weapon was well balanced and that it achieved a high level of accuracy.

**SPECIFICATION**

**MANUFACTURER** Productos Mendoza S.A.
**CALIBRE** 9mm Parabellum
**MAGAZINE CAPACITY** 32
**ACTION** Blowback/selective fire
**TOTAL LENGTH (STOCK EXTENDED)** 635mm/25in
**TOTAL LENGTH (STOCK RETRACTED)** 395mm/15.55in
**BARREL LENGTH** 255mm/10.04in
**WEIGHT UNLOADED** 2,690g/94.89oz

# Chile

**FAMAE (Las Fábricas y Maestranzas del Ejército), the oldest manufacturer of firearms in South America, produces a range of submachine guns and assault rifles. The submachine guns are original designs and the assault rifles are made under licence from the Swiss firm SIG.**

## FAMAE SAF

FAMAE is the Chilean Government small-arms factory. The FAMAE SAF was a development of the SIG 540 rifle. The SIG 540 rifle was produced under licence in Chile in the 1980s. The FAMAE SAF was produced in 1996. In general, the design was a shortened version of the SIG 540 rifle, but the rifle's rotating bolt had been replaced with a simple blowback bolt. The submachine gun had a closed-bolt mechanism with a hammer and floating-pin firing mechanism. The upper and lower parts of the receiver could be separated by removal of two pins, allowing access to the internal mechanism. A safety selector switch allowed the operator to select safe, single shot or three-round burst or fully automatic mode. The weapon was available with either folding or fixed stocks. Translucent magazines could be clipped together for speed of interchange. This gun has been issued not only to the Chilean security forces but more widely in South America. There is also a Mini-SAF available that has a forward hand grip, a much shorter barrel and no shoulder stock. It can use the standard 30-round magazine but has a special 20-round magazine that makes it more compact.

**SPECIFICATION**

**MANUFACTURER** Las Fábricas y Maestranzas del Ejército (FAMAE)
**CALIBRE** 9mm Parabellum
**MAGAZINE CAPACITY** 20 or 30
**ACTION** Blowback/closed bolt/selective fire
**TOTAL LENGTH (STOCK EXTENDED)** 640mm/25in
**TOTAL LENGTH (STOCK RETRACTED)** 410mm/16.14in
**BARREL LENGTH** 200mm/7.87in
**WEIGHT UNLOADED** 2,700g/95oz

**FAMAE variations**

The FAMAE submachine guns come in four versions: the SAF Standard, for police and special forces; the Mini SAF, for security personnel and VIP work; the silenced SAF, for special units; and the MT-40, primarily designed for the police.

# Argentina

**Argentina produced some original submachine-gun designs as well as some derived from other makes. In the first category was the Halcón, a design which proved to be easy to manufacture and to maintain, and in the second the PAM, PA and FMK – designs loosely based on the US M3A1.**

## Halcón ML43

**SPECIFICATION**

**MANUFACTURER** Fábrica de Armas de Halcón
**CALIBRE** 9mm Parabellum
**MAGAZINE CAPACITY** 17 or 30
**ACTION** Blowback
**TOTAL LENGTH** 848mm/33.39in
**BARREL LENGTH** 292mm/11.5in
**WEIGHT UNLOADED** 4,080g/143.9oz

Developed in the early 1940s, this gun was issued to the Argentine Gendarmería Nacional (GNA) which is primarily a frontier guard force but it was also issued for other roles. This was a blowback-operated weapon with a simple design concept that made it easy to manufacture. Its mechanism also kept it fairly light for its intended purpose. The 1946 model was known as the Modelo Aeronáutica and was issued to the Argentine Air Force. In 1949 a new version was brought out in 9mm Parabellum. This version had a curved magazine and was issued to the Army.

## Halcón ML63

**SPECIFICATION**

**MANUFACTURER** Fábrica de Armas de Halcón
**CALIBRE** 9mm Parabellum
**MAGAZINE CAPACITY** 42
**ACTION** Blowback
**TOTAL LENGTH** 848mm/33.39in
**BARREL LENGTH** 292mm/11.5in
**WEIGHT UNLOADED** 4,380g/154.10oz

An updated version of the Halcón design, simplified in a way that reduced the manufacturing costs of producing the model. It had two triggers which could shoot the weapon in automatic form or a single shots. However, its heavier weight has made the weapon difficult to handle for the functions that it was designed for – such as by air force personnel and for operations by armed forces on the ground.

## PAM1/PAM2

**SPECIFICATION**

**MANUFACTURER** Fábrica de Armas de Halcón
**CALIBRE** 9mm Parabellum
**MAGAZINE CAPACITY** 17 or 30
**ACTION** Blowback
**TOTAL LENGTH (STOCK EXTENDED)** 725mm/28.54in
**TOTAL LENGTH (STOCK RETRACTED)** 535mm/21.06in
**BARREL LENGTH** 200mm/7.87in
**WEIGHT UNLOADED** 2,990g/105.47oz

The PAM1 and 2 submachine guns were directly inspired by the successful US M3A1 "grease gun". The M3A1 was blowback operated and fully automatic. It had a retractable stock, made from steel wire, which could double as a cleaning rod and it also had a magazine loading tool. The PAM1 and PAM2 were slightly shorter and were issued widely to the Argentine Army and Police from 1950 to the mid-1960s.

## PA-3DM

This weapon was a development of the PAM1 and appeared in two models: one with a fixed butt and the other with a sliding butt. The barrel could be released by unscrewing a cap at the end of the gun body. The magazine slid into the pistol grip, which incorporated a grip safety. There was a cocking handle on the left of the receiver. The wrap-around bolt was a design influence from the Israeli Uzi submachine gun. The PA-3DM was manufactured up to 1978 and about 15,000 were made. This weapon is no longer in active service in Argentina, but may still be found among paramilitary groups and police.

**SPECIFICATION**

**MANUFACTURER** Fábrica Militar de Armas Portátiles "Domingo Matheu", Rosario
**CALIBRE** 9mm Parabellum
**MAGAZINE CAPACITY** .25
**ACTION** Blowback
**TOTAL LENGTH** 523mm/20.59in
**BARREL LENGTH** 290mm/11.42in
**WEIGHT UNLOADED** 3,400g/120oz

## FMK-3 Model 2

This machine gun was a development of the PA-3DM and has become the new standard Argentine submachine gun. It was mostly produced with the sliding stock reminiscent of the US M3A1 "grease gun", although the fixed-stock version is occasionally seen. Like its predecessor, the FMK-3 was blowback operated. The magazine slid into the pistol grip, which incorporated an automatic safety. On the left side, above the pistol grip, there was a manual safety selector. The front and back sights could be flipped up when required.

**SPECIFICATION**

**MANUFACTURER** Fábrica Militar de Armas Portátiles "Domingo Matheu", Rosario
**CALIBRE** 9mm Parabellum
**MAGAZINE** .25
**ACTION** Blowback
**TOTAL LENGTH (STOCK EXTENDED)** 693mm/27.3in
**TOTAL LENGTH (STOCK RETRACTED)** 523mm/20.5in
**BARREL LENGTH** 290mm/11.42in
**WEIGHT UNLOADED** 3,170g/112oz

# Brazil

**Brazilian industry has developed a wide range of submachine guns over the years, one of which was an adaptation of the Danish Madsen. The company Indústria de Material Bélico do Brasil (IMBEL) developed a couple of submachine gun types, and another was developed and produced by Mekanika Indústria e Comércio Lda, known as the Uru Mekanika.**

## INA MB50

The Madsen submachine gun had been developed by Madsen in Denmark after World War II. One of its most notable characteristics was that it could be opened in two halves, pivoting on a hinge at the rear. The barrel, bolt, return spring and trigger unit could all be accessed easily once the gun was opened. The weapon was manufactured under licence in Brazil as the INA MB50, initially in .45 ACP and later in 9mm Parabellum. A muzzle compensator was added to improve performance and in general the weapon was easy to control. The revised weapon was issued to the Brazilian Army and Police.

**SPECIFICATION**

**MANUFACTURER** Indústria de Material Bélico do Brasil (IMBEL)
**CALIBRE** .45 ACP, 9mm Parabellum
**MAGAZINE** 30
**ACTION** Blowback
**TOTAL LENGTH (STOCK EXTENDED)** 800mm/31.5in
**TOTAL LENGTH (STOCK RETRACTED)** 530mm/20.87in
**BARREL LENGTH** 200mm/7.87in
**WEIGHT UNLOADED** 3,170g/112oz

## Uru Mekanika

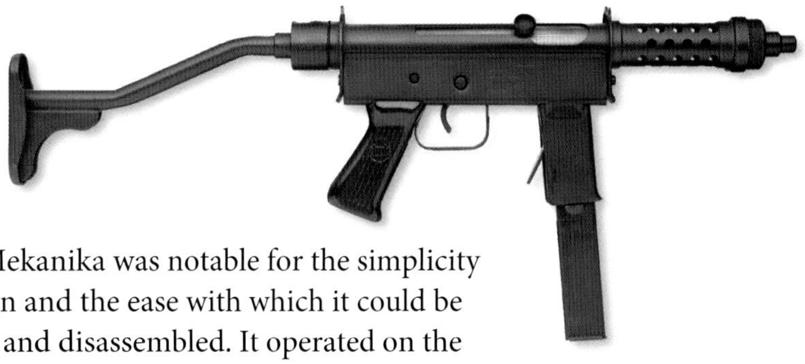

**SPECIFICATION**

**MANUFACTURER** Mekanika Indústria e Comércio Lda.
**CALIBRE** 9mm Parabellum
**MAGAZINE** 30
**ACTION** Blowback
**TOTAL LENGTH (STOCK EXTENDED)** 670mm/26.38in
**TOTAL LENGTH (STOCK RETRACTED)** 425mm/16.73in
**BARREL LENGTH** 175mm/6.89in
**WEIGHT UNLOADED** 2,580g/91oz

The Uru Mekanika was notable for the simplicity of its design and the ease with which it could be assembled and disassembled. It operated on the blowback principle and included a plastic rear grip, trigger guard and a metal forward grip into which the magazine was inserted. On the left-hand side there was a fire selector with settings for safe, semi-automatic and automatic modes. The Uru went into production in the late 1970s. Since then large numbers have been delivered to the Brazilian security forces. Sales have also been achieved elsewhere in South America as well as in Africa and the Middle East. The Brazilian company Bilbao bought the rights from Mekanika in 1988. In 1997 Mekanika Indústria e Comércio re-acquired the rights to the Uru Mekanika.

# Portugal

**Portugal did not produce any submachine guns of its own until 1948. With its ongoing colonial commitments that carried on into the early 1970s, Portugal developed some highly serviceable submachine guns, some of which were based on previous designs and others which were innovative.**

## FBP M948

**SPECIFICATION**

**MANUFACTURER** Fábrica Militar de Braço de Prata
**CALIBRE** 9mm Parabellum
**MAGAZINE CAPACITY** 32
**ACTION** Blowback
**TOTAL LENGTH (STOCK EXTENDED)** 812mm/32in
**TOTAL LENGTH (STOCK RETRACTED)** 635mm/25in
**BARREL LENGTH** 250mm/9.84in
**WEIGHT UNLOADED** 3,740g/122.4oz

The design for this weapon is said to be derived from both the German MP-40 and the American M3. The MP-40 inspired the design of the internal workings, such as the bolt, return spring and telescopic guide, and the M3 inspired the design of the receiver and general exterior appearance. The wire stock was also based on the M3 design. Produced in 1948, this weapon was manufactured largely from steel pressings and it was issued widely to Portuguese forces, also finding its way into the hands of various guerrilla groups in Portuguese colonial Africa.

## FBP M976

**SPECIFICATION**

**MANUFACTURER** Indústrias Nacionais de Defesa
**CALIBRE** 9mm Parabellum
**MAGAZINE CAPACITY** 32 or 36
**ACTION** Blowback
**TOTAL LENGTH (STOCK EXTENDED)** 850mm/33.45in
**TOTAL LENGTH (STOCK RETRACTED)** 657mm/25.87in
**BARREL LENGTH** 250mm/9.84in
**WEIGHT UNLOADED** 3,120g/110oz

The M976 was a development of the M948 submachine gun and continued the emphasis on ease of manufacture through the use of stamped-steel parts. As the M948 had questionable accuracy, efforts were made to improve this in the M976 through the use of a cold-forged steel barrel and a perforated barrel jacket. The trigger mechanism was designed as one unit, which can be removed for maintenance or replacement. There was a safety selector as well as a grip safety. The weapon was mostly issued to Portuguese colonial forces.

## INDEP Lusa

The INDEP Lusa was an all-new design which replaced the M976. It was possibly influenced by the Italian Franchi submachine gun. Much more compact than its predecessors, the INDEP incorporated an overhanging bolt and a double-cylinder receiver. The clever design included a space for the sliding buttstock to slide between the two curves on the receiver. There was a fire selector above the trigger on the left-hand side. The front magazine housing also acted as the forward hand grip. A1 and A2 versions were produced, one with a removable barrel and the other with a perforated barrel cover.

**SPECIFICATION**

**MANUFACTURER** Fábrica Militar de Braço de Prata
**CALIBRE** 9mm Parabellum
**MAGAZINE CAPACITY** 30
**ACTION** Blowback
**TOTAL LENGTH (STOCK EXTENDED)** 600mm/23.6in
**TOTAL LENGTH (STOCK RETRACTED)** 445mm/17in
**BARREL LENGTH** 160mm/6.3in
**WEIGHT UNLOADED** 2,500g/88.18oz

# Spain

**Spanish production of submachine guns ranges from somewhat rudimentary designs urgently produced at the time of the Spanish Civil War (1936–39), adaptations of the German MP40, to original and successful weapons like the Z84 produced by Star Bonifacio Echeverría.**

## Astra Model 901

The Model 901 was the first of three Astra machine pistols which were copies of a design made by Peter Paul Mauser in 1885. Manufacturers such as Unceta y Cia. (known today as Astra), located in the city of Eibar (Gipuzkoa province) copied this design and made improvements. The Model 901 was a development of the Model 900 and could be set to automatic fire. It had a 10-round magazine. The Model 902 differed only in being able to take a 20-round magazine. The Model 903 could take either a 10-round or a 20-round magazine and was also fitted with a fire selector for single or automatic fire. Some versions could be fitted with a stock.

**SPECIFICATION**

**MANUFACTURER** Unceta y Cia.
**CALIBRE** 7.63mm Mauser
**MAGAZINE CAPACITY** 10 or 20
**ACTION** Blowback
**TOTAL LENGTH** 312mm/12.28in
**BARREL LENGTH** 140mm/5.51in
**WEIGHT UNLOADED** 1,250g/49.21oz

## Labora

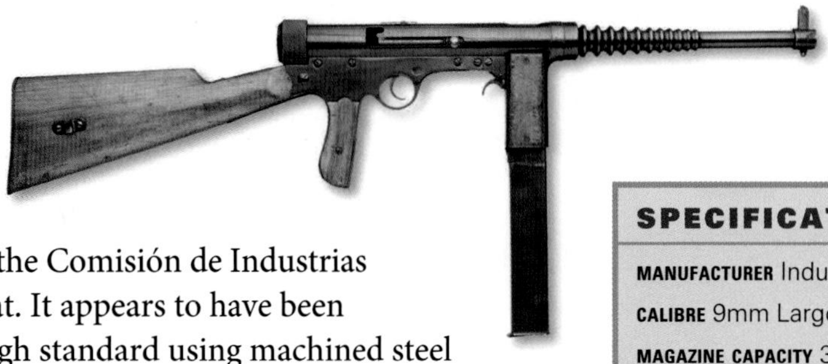

There is some uncertainty over the initial development of this weapon, although it was probably initiated by the Comisión de Industrias de Guerra de la Generalitat. It appears to have been manufactured to a very high standard using machined steel parts as opposed to steel stampings. The magazine was inserted into the forward hand grip and the cocking handle was located on the right of the receiver. Despite its effectiveness, the weapon does not appear to have been used extensively in the Spanish Civil War (1936–39) and few examples remain.

**SPECIFICATION**

**MANUFACTURER** Industrio de Guerra de Cataluña
**CALIBRE** 9mm Largo
**MAGAZINE CAPACITY** 36
**ACTION** Blowback
**TOTAL LENGTH** 806mm/31.75in
**BARREL LENGTH** 260mm/10.3in
**WEIGHT UNLOADED** 4,250g/149.9oz

## Largo Star S135

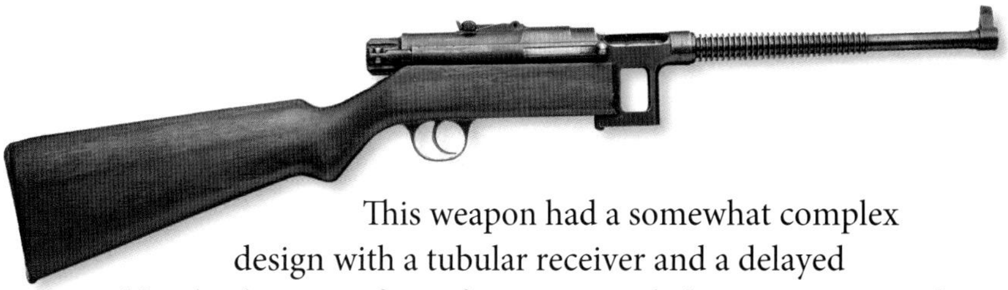

**SPECIFICATION**

**MANUFACTURER** Star Bonifacio Echeverría S.A.
**CALIBRE** 9mm Largo
**MAGAZINE CAPACITY** 10, 30 or 40
**ACTION** Delayed blowback
**TOTAL LENGTH** 900mm/35.45in
**BARREL LENGTH** 269mm/10.59in
**WEIGHT UNLOADED** 3,740g/131.9oz

This weapon had a somewhat complex design with a tubular receiver and a delayed blowback system firing from an open bolt. It was equipped with two multi-position selectors that had to be co-ordinated in order to achieve single-shot or automatic fire. This unnecessary complexity was to ruin the weapon's chances of being selected for major production contracts and it was rejected by both the British and the Americans. It saw limited service in the Spanish Civil War. It had a conventional full wooden stock.

## Largo Star Z45

**SPECIFICATION**

**MANUFACTURER** Star Bonifacio Echeverría S.A.
**CALIBRE** 9mm Largo
**MAGAZINE CAPACITY** 10 or 30
**ACTION** Blowback
**TOTAL LENGTH (STOCK EXTENDED)** 840mm/33.1in
**TOTAL LENGTH (STOCK RETRACTED)** 580mm/22.83in
**BARREL LENGTH** 192mm/7.56in
**WEIGHT UNLOADED** 3,870g/136.5oz

**Tried and tested**
In 1942 Star received blueprints and plans for the MP40 through a German engineer working at the plant. As it was based on a proven design, the Z45 could hardly fail.

The Z45, which was introduced in 1945, appeared in a number of forms, some of which had full wooden stocks, some with pistol grips and a wooden piece under the receiver, and some in full metal with folding metal stocks. It was based on the German MP40 and, with its proven design, was adopted by the Spanish armed forces as well as by some other countries. One difference with the MP40 was that the Z45 had a two-mode trigger which could fire single shots, or automatic fire with finger pressure. It also incorporated a barrel-change feature, whereby the barrel and compensator could be removed together by twisting. By simply changing the barrel another calibre of cartridge could be used.

## CETME C2

**SPECIFICATION**

**MANUFACTURER** CETME
**CALIBRE** 9x23mm Largo or 9mm Parabellum
**MAGAZINE CAPACITY** 30 or10
**ACTION** Blowback
**TOTAL LENGTH (STOCK EXTENDED)** 500mm/19.6in
**TOTAL LENGTH (STOCK RETRACTED)** 720mm/28.3in
**BARREL LENGTH** 212mm/8.3in
**WEIGHT UNLOADED** 2,693g/93.1oz

The CETME C2 is visually similar to the British Sterling L2A3 submachine gun, even down to the crackle paint finish, but the two guns do not share any parts compatibility. The gun fires from an open bolt and was originally chambered in 9 x 23mm Largo, but later versions were chambered in 9mm Parabellum in an attempt to make the gun more appealing on the export market. The C2 has a helical bolt with a floating firing pin and the bolt is not linked to the charging handle, meaning that it does not reciprocate like the handle on the Sterling.

## STAR Model Z70

This weapon was a development of the Z62 and it came about due to problems with the trigger mechanism of the Z62. Designed in 1971, it had a conventional trigger mechanism that was installed with a selector on the left of the receiver for single-shot or automatic fire. Otherwise, it is a blowback-operated weapon with a folding buttstock. It is constructed from metal pressings and plastics.

**SPECIFICATION**

**MANUFACTURER** Star Bonifacio Echeverría S.A.
**CALIBRE** 9mm Parabellum
**MAGAZINE CAPACITY** 20, 30 or 40
**ACTION** Blowback
**TOTAL LENGTH (STOCK EXTENDED)** 700mm/27.56in
**TOTAL LENGTH (STOCK RETRACTED)** 450mm/17.72in
**BARREL LENGTH** 200mm/7.87in
**WEIGHT UNLOADED** 2,870g/101.24oz

## STAR Model Z84

The Z84 was an all-new weapon designed to be easy and efficient to manufacture. It was blowback operated with an open-bolt system and it had a wrap-around breech block, allowing maximum barrel length without extending the exterior length of the weapon. The pistol grip was located centrally below the receiver and also acts as the magazine housing. Due to the central location of the pistol grip, the weapon was well balanced. On the left of the receiver there was a fire selector for single or automatic fire. There was a separate safety catch within the trigger guard. The Z84 entered service with Spanish forces in 1985. It has also been sold to other forces.

**SPECIFICATION**

**MANUFACTURER** Star Bonifacio Echeverría S.A.
**CALIBRE** 9mm Parabellum
**MAGAZINE CAPACITY** 25 or 30
**ACTION** Blowback
**TOTAL LENGTH (STOCK EXTENDED)** 615mm/24.21in
**TOTAL LENGTH (STOCK RETRACTED)** 410mm/16.14in
**BARREL LENGTH** 410mm/16.4in
**WEIGHT UNLOADED** 3,000g/105.8oz

## Bergmann MP28 copy

The German MP28 was a development of the MP18 and manufactured between 1928 and 1938. It was widely produced in Germany and was used in the Spanish Civil War, on both sides of the conflict, by Nationalists and Republicans alike. Copies were produced in Spanish factories. The success of the weapon in the Spanish Civil War is said to have influenced the German high command in encouraging further developments of the design.

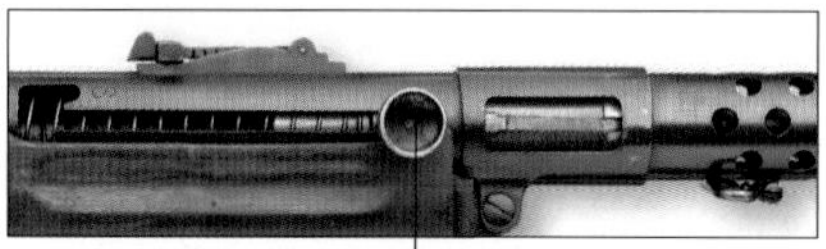

**ABOVE** The Spanish copies of the Bergmann MP28 are distinguishable by the large retracting handle that does not appear on the German model.

**SPECIFICATION**

**MANUFACTURER** Various
**CALIBRE** 9mm Largo
**MAGAZINE CAPACITY** 32
**ACTION** Blowback
**TOTAL LENGTH** 812mm/31.97in
**BARREL LENGTH** 196mm/7.7in
**WEIGHT UNLOADED** 4,190g/147.8oz

# United Kingdom

**British submachine-gun design began with a copy of the German MP28. Later, Messrs Shepherd and Turpin of the Royal Small Arms Factory at Enfield came up with what was to prove to be the British submachine gun of World War II and the immediate post-war era: the Sten, which remained in service until the 1960s.**

## BSA Thompson M1926 and M1929

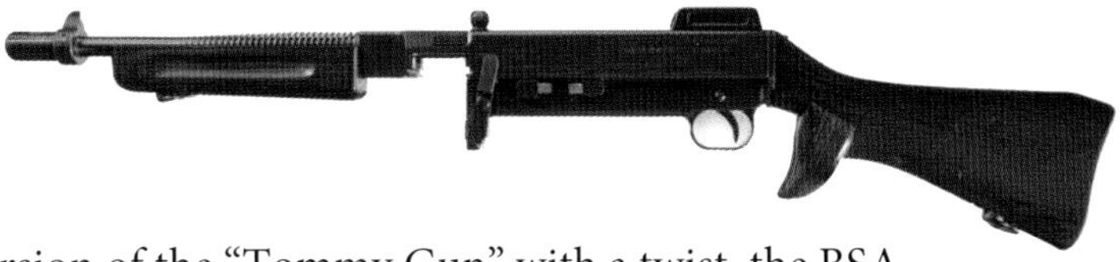

**SPECIFICATION**

**MANUFACTURER** Birmingham Small Arms Co.
**CALIBRE** 9mm Parabellum (both), 9x20mm Browning Long, 7.63 Mauser (M1926); 9x23mm Bergmann, .45 ACP (M1929)
**MAGAZINE CAPACITY** 20
**ACTION** Blowback
**TOTAL LENGTH** 813mm/32in
**BARREL LENGTH** 304mm/12in
**WEIGHT UNLOADED** 3,997g/141oz

A licensed version of the "Tommy Gun" with a twist, the BSA Thompson M1926 uses the same Thompson firing mechanism and Blish lock, but it isn't chambered for the .45 ACP. Visually, the gun differs from the traditional Thompson with a redesigned lower receiver, smaller forearm, an unprotected rear sight, and more traditionally-styled rifle buttstock. Rate of fire was a fast 1,200 rounds per minute.

The redesigned M1929 featured a ribbed barrel with a Cutts compensator and protective wings on the rear sight. The gun was offered in a variety of calibres in an attempt to spark interest in foreign sales, but the idea fell flat rather quickly and production never began in earnest.

## Sten Mark I

**SPECIFICATION**

**MANUFACTURER** Birmingham Small Arms Co./ Royal Ordnance Factory
**CALIBRE** 9mm Parabellum
**MAGAZINE CAPACITY** 32
**ACTION** Blowback
**TOTAL LENGTH** 895mm/35.25in
**BARREL LENGTH** 196mm/7.7in
**WEIGHT UNLOADED** 3,260g/115oz

The Sten gun was named after its designers, Major-General Reginald Sheperd and Harold Turpin and the location Enfield, where the Royal Small Arms Factory was located, hence S.T.EN. The Sten gun was a quick solution to Britain's desperate need for a submachine gun after British troops were rescued at Dunkirk in France in 1940. The Sten prototype was first put forward in 1941. The Sten gun's rudimentary design proved to be ideal for use by resistance fighters who required a simple, rugged weapon that was easy to assemble, maintain and conceal. A Sten Mark II version was produced between 1942 and 1944 in large numbers.

## Silent Sten Mark II (S)

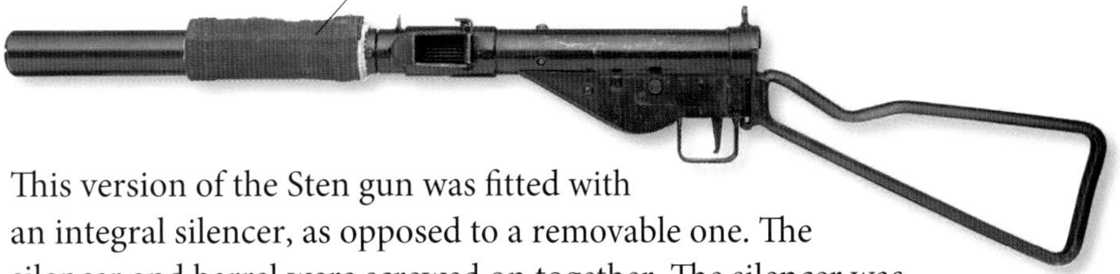


**SPECIFICATION**

**MANUFACTURER** Birmingham Small Arms Co./ Royal Ordnance Factory
**CALIBRE** 9mm Parabellum
**MAGAZINE CAPACITY** 32
**ACTION** Blowback
**TOTAL LENGTH** 908mm/35.75in
**BARREL LENGTH** 89mm/3.5in
**WEIGHT UNLOADED** 3,520g/124oz

This version of the Sten gun was fitted with an integral silencer, as opposed to a removable one. The silencer and barrel were screwed on together. The silencer was formed of a series of baffles which had the effect of slowing down the gases so that they emerged from the end of the muzzle without making a noise. The baffles proved to be sensitive to wear and later the Mark II (S) was used almost exclusively in single-shot mode.

## Sten Mark III

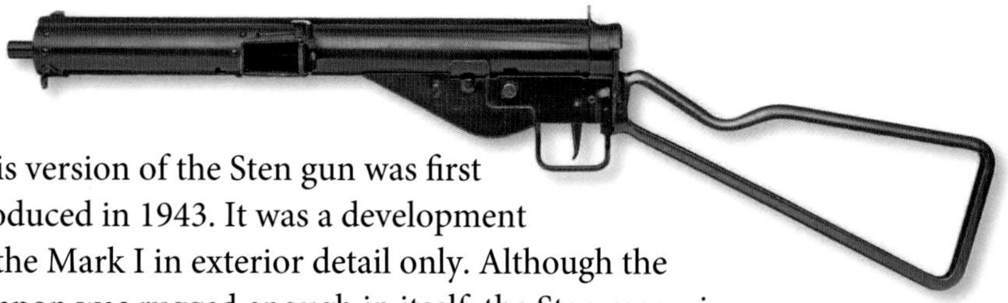

This version of the Sten gun was first produced in 1943. It was a development of the Mark I in exterior detail only. Although the weapon was rugged enough in itself, the Sten magazine was apt to jam. It had a fixed barrel and tubular buttstock but would accept all types of stock made for the Sten.

**SPECIFICATION**

**MANUFACTURER** Birmingham Small Arms Co./ Royal Ordnance Factory
**CALIBRE** 9mm Parabellum
**MAGAZINE CAPACITY** 32
**ACTION** Blowback
**TOTAL LENGTH** 762mm/30in
**BARREL LENGTH** 196mm/7.7in
**WEIGHT UNLOADED** 3,180g/112oz

## Sten Mark V

This gun was introduced in 1944 and saw service until well into the 1950s. It was essentially the same as the Mark II but with a more elaborate stock and hand grip. It was issued to the British Parachute Regiment and was famously used in the ill-fated World War II Arnhem campaign on the Dutch/German border in 1944.

**SPECIFICATION**

**MANUFACTURER** Birmingham Small Arms Co./ Royal Ordnance Factory
**CALIBRE** 9mm Parabellum
**MAGAZINE CAPACITY** 32
**ACTION** Blowback
**TOTAL LENGTH** 762mm/30in
**BARREL LENGTH** 196mm/7.7in
**WEIGHT UNLOADED** 3,860g/136oz

## Silent Sten Mark VI

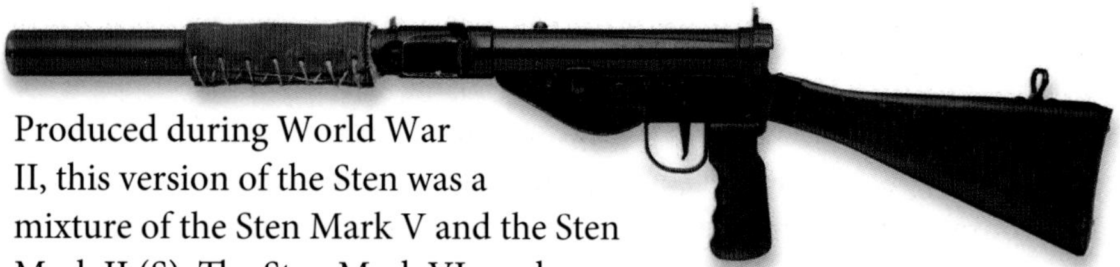

Produced during World War II, this version of the Sten was a mixture of the Sten Mark V and the Sten Mark II (S). The Sten Mark VI can be distinguished by a wooden butt, as opposed to the folding metal butt of other versions, and a pistol grip behind the trigger guard. The silencer was a different design from that of the Mark II (S).

**SPECIFICATION**

**MANUFACTURER** Birmingham Small Arms Co./ Royal Ordnance Factory
**CALIBRE** 9mm Parabellum
**MAGAZINE CAPACITY** 32
**ACTION** Blowback
**TOTAL LENGTH (SILENCED)** 908mm/35.8in
**BARREL LENGTH** 196mm/7.7in
**WEIGHT UNLOADED** 4,450g/157oz

## Lanchester

The Lanchester was named after George Lanchester who developed the weapon as a direct copy of the German MP28 with some essential modifications. In 1940, after the evacuation of British troops at Dunkirk, there was little time to design a new submachine gun from scratch and therefore this adaptation of an existing design seemed to be a sensible way round the problem. The Lanchester proved to be a well-made weapon with a solid wooden stock, brass fittings and high-quality working parts. In use from 1941 to 1960, the Lanchester saw service in the Royal Navy and Royal Air Force, both during and after World War II.

**SPECIFICATION**

**MANUFACTURER** Sterling Armament Co.
**CALIBRE** 9mm Parabellum
**MAGAZINE CAPACITY** 50
**ACTION** Blowback
**TOTAL LENGTH** 85mm/33.5in
**BARREL LENGTH** 203mm/8in
**WEIGHT UNLOADED** 4,340g/153oz

## Sterling L2A3

**SPECIFICATION**

**MANUFACTURER** Sterling Armament Co./ Royal Ordnance Factory, Fazakeley
**CALIBRE** 9mm Parabellum
**MAGAZINE CAPACITY** 34
**ACTION** Blowback
**TOTAL LENGTH (STOCK EXTENDED)** 690mm/27.16in
**TOTAL LENGTH (STOCK RETRACTED)** 483mm/19in
**BARREL LENGTH** 198mm/7.8in
**WEIGHT UNLOADED** 2,720g/95.95oz

This version of the Sterling submachine gun first appeared in 1956 and proved to be the last version to be produced by Sterling/Royal Ordnance and issued to the British Army. The magazine was inserted into the left side of the receiver and there was a selector lever above the trigger which was used to select rapid fire, single shots or safe mode. There were also versions of the L2A3 which fired single shots only. The weapon had a successful sales record, being sold to about 90 countries around the world, including Canada, Ghana, India, Libya, Malaysia, Nigeria, Tunisia and some Arabian Gulf states. The Sterling L2A3 was replaced from 1988 by the SA80 assault rifle.

## Sterling L2

**SPECIFICATION**

**MANUFACTURER** Sterling Armament Co./ Royal Ordnance Factory, Fazakeley
**CALIBRE** 9mm Parabellum
**MAGAZINE CAPACITY** 34
**ACTION** Blowback
**TOTAL LENGTH (STOCK EXTENDED)** 690mm/27.16in
**TOTAL LENGTH (STOCK RETRACTED)** 483mm/19in
**BARREL LENGTH** 198mm/7.8in
**WEIGHT UNLOADED** 2,720g/95.95oz

The Sterling L2 was the official designation for what was originally known as the Patchett gun. This design was one of a few under consideration by the British Government, including the Sten, a BSA design and an Australian contender. The Sterling L2 prototype was introduced in the 1960s. The weapon was blowback operated and the action incorporated a steel spring that caught the bolt on recoil. The bolt incorporated ribs that were designed to clear any dirt out of the casing. The weapon was manufactured from steel and plastic and its basically simple mechanism left little to go wrong.

## Sterling L34A1

**SPECIFICATION**

**MANUFACTURER** Sterling Armament Co./ Royal Ordnance Factory, Fazakeley
**CALIBRE** 9mm Parabellum
**MAGAZINE CAPACITY** 34
**ACTION** Blowback
**TOTAL LENGTH (STOCK EXTENDED)** 864mm/34in
**TOTAL LENGTH (STOCK RETRACTED)** 660mm/26in
**BARREL LENGTH** 198mm/7.8in
**WEIGHT UNLOADED** 3,600g/126.97oz

In production from 1966 to 1985, this weapon was the silenced version of the Sterling L2A3 submachine gun. Its design was based on the Silent Sten as a guide, but the technology was improved. The barrel was perforated in order to allow gases to escape into a diffuser. Movement of the gases was controlled through a system of metal wrappings and spirals that ensured that the gas emerging from the end of the silencer was travelling at a reduced rate. Apart from the silencer, the basic mechanics of the L34A1 were the same as those of the L2A3.

# France

**A variety of submachine guns have been produced in France over the years by Manufacture d'Armes de St Etienne (MAS), Manufacture d'Armes de Tulle (MAT) and Groupement Industriel des Armements Terrestres (GIAT). Latterly, submachine guns issued to French forces have been replaced by the FAMAS assault rifle.**

## Hotchkiss "Universal"

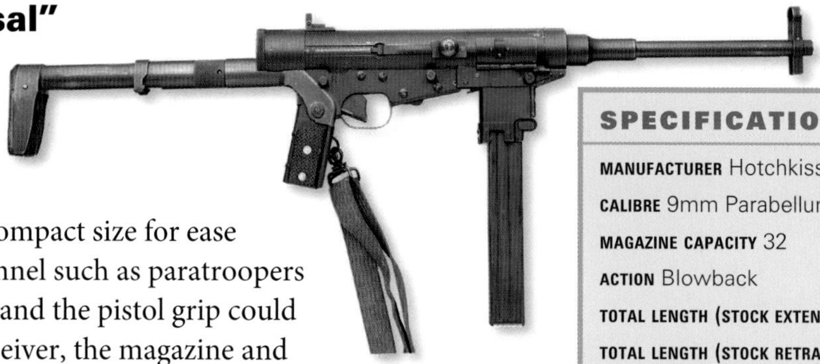

This submachine gun was first produced shortly after the end of World War II. It was designed to fold into a compact size for ease of carriage by military personnel such as paratroopers or other units. Both the butt and the pistol grip could be folded underneath the receiver, the magazine and its housing underneath the barrel, and the barrel itself could be telescoped into the receiver. Despite these convenient design features, it was over-complicated and was not sold in large numbers.

**SPECIFICATION**

**MANUFACTURER** Hotchkiss et Cie.
**CALIBRE** 9mm Parabellum
**MAGAZINE CAPACITY** 32
**ACTION** Blowback
**TOTAL LENGTH (STOCK EXTENDED)** 776mm/30.6in
**TOTAL LENGTH (STOCK RETRACTED)** 538mm/21.2in
**BARREL LENGTH** 270mm/10.63in
**WEIGHT UNLOADED** 3,400g/120oz

## MAS 38

This model was produced just before the start of World War II and could be recognized by its curved appearance. This was due to the fact that the receiver and butt sloped away from the axis of the barrel. A tube ran into the butt to allow room for the bolt to travel on recoil. Instead of a conventional safety catch, the bolt could be locked by pushing the trigger forward. Uniquely for this kind of weapon, it had a buffered sear to prevent wear. Production of the MAS 38 was taken over by the Germans after the invasion of France in 1940 and some weapons were issued to the German army.

**SPECIFICATION**

**MANUFACTURER** Manufacture d'Armes de St Etienne (MAS)
**CALIBRE** 7.65mm French Long
**MAGAZINE CAPACITY** 32
**ACTION** Blowback
**TOTAL LENGTH (STOCK EXTENDED)** 623mm/24.5in
**BARREL LENGTH** 224mm/8.8in
**WEIGHT UNLOADED** 2,870g/101oz

## MAT 49

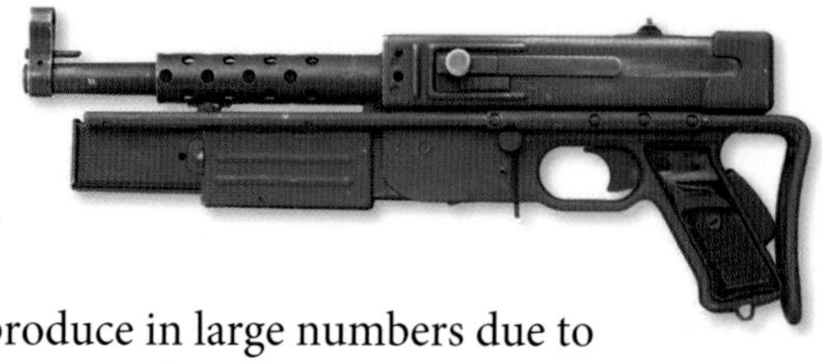

The MAT 49 was developed in the late 1940s. It had a rugged design which was possible to produce in large numbers due to an efficient machine-stamping process. The weapon was blowback operated and had a novel system whereby the magazine housing could be locked flat against the barrel, which also prevented the weapon being fired. The magazine housing doubled as a forward hand grip and, when the magazine was in the firing position, the weapon was also protected by a grip safety. It had flip-up sights and was provided with a sliding wire stock that could be locked at different lengths.

**SPECIFICATION**

**MANUFACTURER** Manufacture d'Armes de Tulle (MAT)
**CALIBRE** 9mm Parabellum
**MAGAZINE CAPACITY** 32
**ACTION** Blowback
**TOTAL LENGTH (STOCK EXTENDED)** 720mm/28in
**TOTAL LENGTH (STOCK RETRACTED)** 460mm/18in
**BARREL LENGTH** 228mm/9in
**WEIGHT UNLOADED** 3,630g/128oz

## Gevarm D4

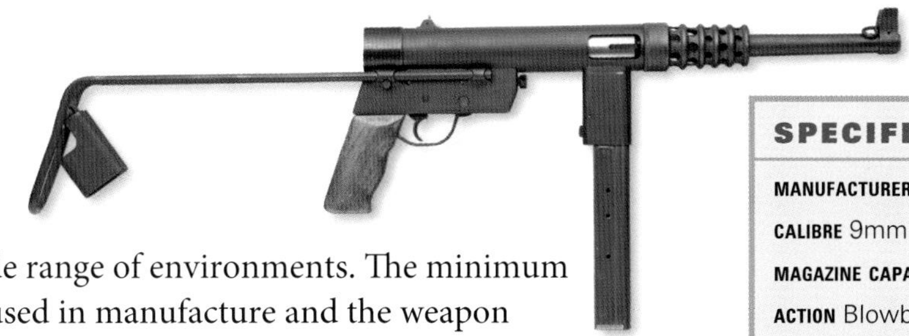

The Gevarm was developed as a rugged, easy-to-use weapon that would provide reliable service in a wide range of environments. The minimum number of parts were used in manufacture and the weapon is said to continue to function well in the dirty and dusty conditions encountered by combat infantry. The weapon could be set to automatic or single-shot fire via a lever on the left of the trigger block. The Gevarm was fitted with a retractable wire stock.

**SPECIFICATION**

**MANUFACTURER** Société Gevarm et Gevelot
**CALIBRE** 9mm Parabellum
**MAGAZINE CAPACITY** 32
**ACTION** Blowback
**TOTAL LENGTH** 500mm/19.69in
**BARREL LENGTH** 220mm/8.66in
**WEIGHT UNLOADED** 3,200g/112.9oz

# Belgium

**In 1945 Belgium produced a successful submachine gun designed by a retired Belgian army officer, Colonel Vigneron. With its exceptionally long barrel, the Vigneron could not be in greater contrast to the foreshortened FN Herstal P90, which was designed as a reserve weapon for non-frontline personnel.**

## Vigneron M2

**SPECIFICATION**

**MANUFACTURER** Société Anonyme Précision Liégeoise, Herstal
**CALIBRE** 9mm Parabellum
**MAGAZINE** 32
**ACTION** Blowback
**TOTAL LENGTH (STOCK EXTENDED)** 886mm/34.9in
**TOTAL LENGTH (STOCK RETRACTED)** 706mm/27.8in
**BARREL LENGTH** 305mm/12in
**WEIGHT UNLOADED** 3,290g/116oz

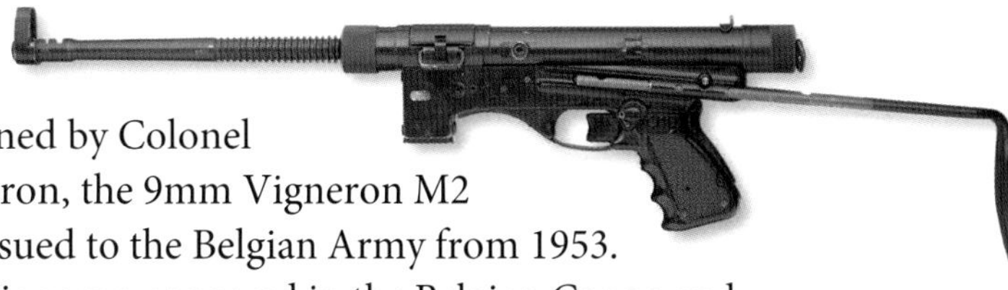

Designed by Colonel Vigneron, the 9mm Vigneron M2 was issued to the Belgian Army from 1953. The Vigneron appeared in the Belgian Congo and was also issued by the Portuguese Army for operations in Angola and Mozambique. The Vigneron was a blowback-operated weapon with a telescopic steel stock. The pistol grip had an integrated safety and it also incorporated a three-position safety catch which could select full safety, single fire and automatic fire. The weapon also incorporated a variable-pressure trigger that could produce either single shots or automatic fire.

## FN P90 Personal Weapon

**SPECIFICATION**

**MANUFACTURER** FN Herstal
**CALIBRE** 5.7mm FN
**MAGAZINE** 50
**ACTION** Blowback
**TOTAL LENGTH** 500mm/19.69in
**BARREL LENGTH** 150mm/5.91in
**WEIGHT UNLOADED** 1,400g/49.40oz

The P90 was developed in the late 1980s. It was an unusual design with the trigger well forward along the receiver and close to the barrel muzzle. The stock was integrated with the rear portion of the receiver. Designed as a personal defence weapon, it could also be used by special forces and law-enforcement units in close combat. The FN90 had a smooth design to minimize the chances of snagging. The magazine sat over the front portion of the barrel. There was a rail on the top designed to take sights and side rails will take tactical lights and lasers. There was a cocking handle on each side of the weapon, contributing to its ambidextrous qualities.

# Switzerland

**Switzerland has produced some successful submachine-gun designs, although some have proved too complicated for easy manufacture. In a market full of simpler serviceable weapons, Swiss designs such as the SIG MP310 did not achieve the recognition they deserved. As a result companies such as SIG focused their design and development on such armaments as pistols and assault rifles.**

## MP43/44

When the invasion of Switzerland by Germany seemed likely in the early 1940s, the Swiss Army was issued with the Furrer MP41/44 developed at Waffenfabrik in Bern. It soon became apparent that the M41/44 could not be produced fast enough to satisfy demand and the Swiss Army procured a tried and tested weapon to replace it. A licence was obtained from Suomi of Finland to reproduce their 1931 Suomi submachine gun almost identically, with just minor modifications known as the MP43/44. It proved to be a success and remained in service through to the 1960s.

**SPECIFICATION**

**MANUFACTURER** Hispano-Suiza SA., Genf
**CALIBRE** 9mm Parabellum
**MAGAZINE CAPACITY** 50
**ACTION** Blowback
**TOTAL LENGTH** 890mm/33.9in
**BARREL LENGTH** 315mm/12.4in
**WEIGHT UNLOADED** 4,760g/167.9oz

## Rexim "Favor" Mk 4

This weapon was developed in the 1950s by Swiss small arms company Rexim in Geneva. The Rexim was a conventional blowback-operated weapon with a somewhat complex firing mechanism incorporating an independent hammer. As with other complex designs, the weapon was not accepted by major armed forces. The parent company eventually went out of business in 1957.

**SPECIFICATION**

**MANUFACTURER** Rexim SA., Geneva
**CALIBRE** 9mm Parabellum
**MAGAZINE CAPACITY** 32
**ACTION** Blowback
**TOTAL LENGTH (STOCK EXTENDED)** 873mm/34.37in
**TOTAL LENGTH (STOCK RETRACTED)** 617mm/24.3in
**BARREL LENGTH** 340mm/13.38in
**WEIGHT UNLOADED** 4,670g/164.7oz

## B&T MP9

Based on the Steyr TMP, B&T purchased the rights to make the MP9 from Steyr in 2001. The MP9 differs from the TMP in that it has a folding stock and integrated picatinny rail. Equipped with three safeties – an ambidextrous manual safety, trigger safety, and drop safety – the MP9 has a rate of fire of 900 rounds per minute. The gun first saw military service in 2004 and is now in use by six different countries.

**SPECIFICATION**

**MANUFACTURER** B&T AG
**CALIBRE** 9mm Parabellum
**MAGAZINE CAPACITY** 15, 20, 25 and 30
**ACTION** Short recoil
**TOTAL LENGTH (STOCK EXTENDED)** 520mm/20.5in
**TOTAL LENGTH (STOCK RETRACTED)** 302mm/11.9n
**BARREL LENGTH** 129mm/5.1in
**WEIGHT UNLOADED** 1,397g/49.3oz

## B&T APC9 PRO

The APC9 PRO was designed with ease of use and modularity in mind. It features Magpul M-LOK accessory slots, and M4 compatible pistol grip, a folding stock, as well as a folding charging handle. Utilizing a proprietary hydraulic buffer system, more than half of its parts are compatible with other firearms in B&T's APC lineup. It can accept B&T, Glock, and SIG P320 magazines as well as being able to swap to a .40S&W lower. A tri-lug barrel allows for easy on-and-off of a suppressor.

**SPECIFICATION**

**MANUFACTURER** B&T AG
**CALIBRE** 9mm Parabellum
**MAGAZINE CAPACITY** 20
**ACTION** Blowback
**TOTAL LENGTH (STOCK EXTENDED)** 604.5mm/23.8in
**TOTAL LENGTH (STOCK RETRACTED)** 375mm/14.8in
**BARREL LENGTH** 172mm/6.8in
**WEIGHT UNLOADED** 2,798g/98.7oz

# Germany

**In 1916, German designers and manufacturers created the first true submachine gun, the 9mm MP18. Almost a century later they are producing some of the most widely used and respected submachine guns, with weapons such as the Heckler & Koch MP5 and the HK UMP40 (Universal Machine Pistol).**

## Bergmann MP18/I

**SPECIFICATION**

**MANUFACTURER** Theodor Bergmann Waffenfabrik
**CALIBRE** 9mm Parabellum
**MAGAZINE CAPACITY** 32
**ACTION** Blowback
**TOTAL LENGTH** 812mm/31.97in
**BARREL LENGTH** 196mm/7.75in
**WEIGHT UNLOADED** 4,190g/81.13oz

This weapon, devised by Hugo Schmeisser (son of Louis Schmeisser) had a strong influence on the design and development of the submachine gun. Arguably the first true submachine gun, the MP18/I was developed at Spandau (a district of Berlin) and featured a revolutionary blowback mechanism. Construction of the weapon was to the highest standards and the inherent simplicity of the design contributed to a high level of reliability. The weapon was fed from a snail-drum magazine and was set to constant automatic mode. Later versions would be designed to fire single shots as well.

## Bergmann MP28/II

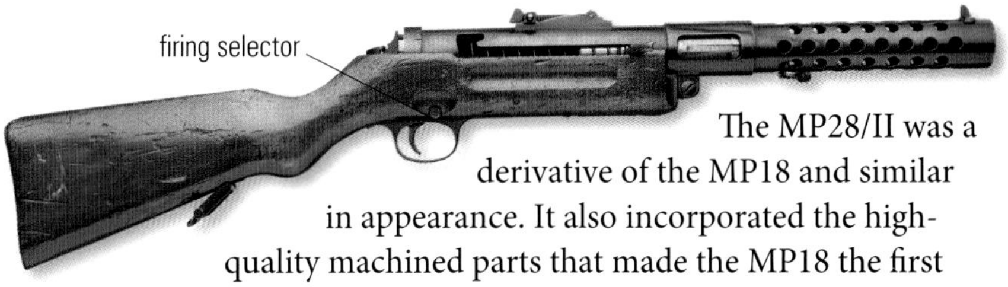


**SPECIFICATION**

**MANUFACTURER** C.G. Haenel Waffenfabrik
**CALIBRE** 9mm Parabellum
**MAGAZINE CAPACITY** 20, 32 or 50
**ACTION** Blowback
**TOTAL LENGTH** 812mm/31.97in
**BARREL LENGTH** 196mm/7.75in
**WEIGHT UNLOADED** 3,970g/140oz

The MP28/II was a derivative of the MP18 and similar in appearance. It also incorporated the high-quality machined parts that made the MP18 the first truly successful submachine gun. A fire selector was added for single shots or automatic fire and it was also fitted with a box magazine to replace the snail-drum used in the MP18. The fire selector was a cross-bolt, push-button device. When pushed from the right-hand side two Ds, denoting *Dauerfeuer* or duration firing, were shown on the left of the selector. When pushed the other way, two Es, denoting *Einzelfeuer* or single-shot firing, were shown. The MP28 also had a larger-diameter operating spring than the MP18.

## Bergmann MP34/I and MP35/I

This design was developed from the Bergmann MP28 and was personally designed by Bergmann, as opposed to Schmeisser. It had a different bolt-handle design to the MP28 which was located at the rear of the receiver, as opposed to on the side. It also featured a double-action trigger that could fire either single shots or automatic fire, depending on the amount of pressure placed on the trigger. It was produced in both long and short versions. The MP35/I had minor modifications.

**SPECIFICATION**

**MANUFACTURER** Carl Walther GmbH. Waffenfabrik/Junker & Ruth AG
**CALIBRE** 9mm Parabellum
**MAGAZINE CAPACITY** 24 or 32
**ACTION** Blowback
**TOTAL LENGTH** 840mm/33.1in
**BARREL LENGTH** 196mm/7.75in
**WEIGHT UNLOADED** 4,050g/142.86oz

## Vollmer Erma Machine Pistol (EMP)

This weapon was developed by Henrich Vollmer (the chief designer at Erma in Erfurt) and was in production for most of the 1930s. It was issued to German forces and saw widespread use until about 1942, when it was replaced by the MP40. It had conventional blowback operation. It was easily identified by its full wooden stock and forward wooden hand grip.

**SPECIFICATION**

**MANUFACTURER** Erfurter Maschinenfabrik Berthold Geipel GmbH. (Erma Werke)
**CALIBRE** 9mm Parabellum
**MAGAZINE CAPACITY** 25 or 32
**ACTION** Blowback
**TOTAL LENGTH** 902mm/35.5in
**BARREL LENGTH** 254mm/10in
**WEIGHT UNLOADED** 4,400g/155.2oz

## MP38

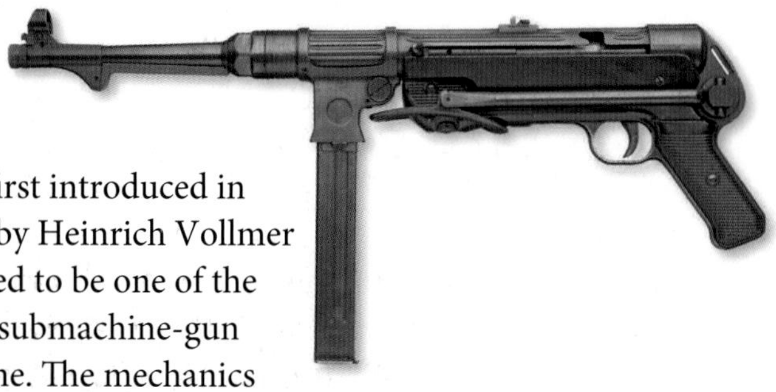

The MP38 was first introduced in 1938. Designed by Heinrich Vollmer at Erma, it proved to be one of the most successful submachine-gun designs of all time. The mechanics of the weapon were unremarkable – it was a simple blowback design. However, its overall appearance, with a folding metal stock and no wooden fittings, helped to define the new generation of submachine guns. The manufacturing processes of the MP38 were, however, inefficient and its magazine had a tendency to jam.

**SPECIFICATION**

**MANUFACTURER** Erfurter Maschinenfabrik Berthold Geipel GmbH. (Erma Werke)
**CALIBRE** 9mm Parabellum
**MAGAZINE CAPACITY** 32
**ACTION** Blowback
**TOTAL LENGTH (STOCK EXTENDED)** 832mm/32.75in
**TOTAL LENGTH (STOCK RETRACTED)** 630mm/24.75in
**BARREL LENGTH** 247mm/9.75in
**WEIGHT UNLOADED** 4,140g/146oz

## MP40

The MP40 was a revised version of the MP38 which made substantial use of pressed-steel parts. It could therefore be produced in much greater numbers than the MP38. It became the definitive submachine gun of the German Army during World War II. The rate of fire and recoil of the weapon were lower than contemporary submachine guns, making it very manageable. It also had an improved safety device. The weapon had a folding metal stock and incorporated plastic furniture instead of wood, which was advanced for its day.

**SPECIFICATION**

**MANUFACTURER** Erfurter Maschinenfabrik Berthold Geipel GmbH. (Erma Werke)/Various
**CALIBRE** 9mm Parabellum
**MAGAZINE CAPACITY** 32
**ACTION** Blowback
**TOTAL LENGTH (STOCK EXTENDED)** 833mm/32.80in
**TOTAL LENGTH (STOCK RETRACTED)** 630mm/24.8in
**BARREL LENGTH** 251mm/9.9in
**WEIGHT UNLOADED** 3,970g/140oz

**"The Schmeisser"**
The MP40 was often called the Schmeisser by the Allies, after weapons designer Hugo Schmeisser. However, he did not design the weapon, but only the magazines for the MP40, which bear his name.

## HK MP5A3

**SPECIFICATION**

**MANUFACTURER** Heckler & Koch GmbH.
**CALIBRE** 9mm Parabellum
**MAGAZINE CAPACITY** 15 or 30
**ACTION** Delayed blowback
**TOTAL LENGTH (STOCK EXTENDED)** 660mm/26in
**TOTAL LENGTH (STOCK RETRACTED)** 490mm/19.3in
**BARREL LENGTH** 225mm/8.85in
**WEIGHT UNLOADED** 2,550g/88.18oz

The Heckler & Koch MP5 was first introduced in 1966 and was immediately issued to West German police and border-guard units. Developed from the G3 rifle, the MP5 had a roller-delayed blowback mechanism. It fired from a closed bolt, which lended itself to both accuracy and efficiency of operation. Different variants of the weapon are produced: the MP5A2 had a rigid plastic butt while the MP5A3 had a telescopic metal stock. The MP5 was used by the world's elite forces.

## HK MP53

**SPECIFICATION**

**MANUFACTURER** Heckler & Koch GmbH.
**CALIBRE** 5.56mm
**MAGAZINE CAPACITY** 25
**ACTION** Delayed blowback
**TOTAL LENGTH (STOCK EXTENDED)** 755mm/29.72in
**TOTAL LENGTH (STOCK RETRACTED)** 563mm/22.17in
**BARREL LENGTH** 211mm/8.31in
**WEIGHT UNLOADED** 3,050g/107.56oz

Produced from 1975 onwards, this weapon could be used as a submachine gun, or an assault rifle. It had the same roller mechanism that typified the Heckler & Koch submachine-gun range. The HK33 rifle was also unusual because it worked by a delayed blowback mechanism. Similar in appearance to the HK33K rifle, the MP53 was shorter and could be fitted with a fixed or a telescoping butt. A switch could be used to select single shots, automatic fire or full safety.

## HK MP5K

**SPECIFICATION**

- **MANUFACTURER** Heckler & Koch GmbH.
- **CALIBRE** 9mm Parabellum
- **MAGAZINE CAPACITY** 15/30
- **ACTION** Delayed blowback
- **TOTAL LENGTH** 325mm/12.80in
- **BARREL LENGTH** 115mm/4.53in
- **WEIGHT UNLOADED** 2,100g/74oz

Introduced in 1976, the MP5K was essentially the same weapon as the standard MP5. The major difference was its more compact size, with a smaller barrel and magazine (the K stands for *kurz* in German, which means "short"). This version was not fitted with a stock and instead had an additional forward grip, plus a guard to prevent fingers from sliding over the muzzle. It was easily concealed but its size meant that it had a limited range of fire.

## HK MP7

This weapon was developed to meet new requirements for a personal defence weapon, as broadly laid down by NATO. It was produced from 2001 onwards and designed for close combat as well as for mid-range personal defence. In view of advances in body armour technology, a new calibre of high-penetration round was formulated. The round was unique to the weapon, reducing recoil and increasing accuracy and penetration, The light weight of the MP7 was achieved through the use of polymers in its construction.

**SPECIFICATION**

- **MANUFACTURER** Heckler & Koch GmbH.
- **CALIBRE** 4.6mm H&K
- **MAGAZINE CAPACITY** 20 or 40
- **ACTION** Gas
- **TOTAL LENGTH (BUTT EXTENDED)** 640mm/25.2in
- **TOTAL LENGTH (BUTT RETRACTED)** 420mm/16.4in
- **BARREL LENGTH** 180mm/7.09in
- **WEIGHT UNLOADED** 1,800g/63.49oz

## HK UMP40

The HK UMP (Universal Machine Pistol) was developed in the 1990s as a replacement for the HKMP5 and was available from 2002. Constructed largely of polymers, it was lighter than the MP5. It was produced in three different versions, according to calibre (.40 S&W, .45 ACP and 9mm Parabellum). To allow for the range of calibres it had a reduced rate of fire, but a longer range than comparable weapons. The UMP had a side-folding buttstock. It could be fitted with optional extras, such as flashlights, optical sights or laser sights.

**SPECIFICATION**

- **MANUFACTURER** Heckler & Koch GmbH.
- **CALIBRE** .40 S&W, .45 ACP, 9mm Parabellum
- **MAGAZINE CAPACITY** 30
- **ACTION** Recoil
- **TOTAL LENGTH (STOCK EXTENDED)** 600mm/27.17in
- **TOTAL LENGTH (STOCK RETRACTED)** 450mm/17.72in
- **BARREL LENGTH** 200mm/7.87in
- **WEIGHT UNLOADED** 2,100g/74oz

## Walther MPK

The MPK was first produced in 1963 and was deployed by police and some naval units until production ceased in 1987. The MPK was a conventional blowback weapon. The stock could be folded away and used as a forward hand grip. The MPK had a selector for single shots, automatic fire or full safety. There was a cocking handle on the right of the receiver, which could be locked into the bolt if necessary to clear stoppages.

**SPECIFICATION**

- **MANUFACTURER** Carl Walther, Ulm, Donau
- **CALIBRE** 9mm Parabellum
- **MAGAZINE CAPACITY** 32
- **ACTION** Blowback
- **TOTAL LENGTH (STOCK EXTENDED)** 653mm/25.71in
- **TOTAL LENGTH (STOCK RETRACTED)** 368mm/14.5in
- **BARREL LENGTH** 171mm/6.7in
- **WEIGHT UNLOADED** 2,800g/98.77oz

# Italy

**After the production of the famous Villar Perosa (OVP) in the 1920s, much of the manufacture of Italian submachine guns was undertaken by Beretta. More recently, some attempts have been made by smaller firms to enter the submachine-gun market, one of the most successful of which was the Spectre.**

## Beretta Model 1918

**SPECIFICATION**

**MANUFACTURER** Pietro Beretta SpA.
**CALIBRE** 9mm Glisenti
**MAGAZINE CAPACITY** 25
**ACTION** Delayed blowback
**TOTAL LENGTH** 850mm/33.5in
**BARREL LENGTH** 305mm/12in
**WEIGHT UNLOADED** 3,260g/115oz

This submachine gun went into service with the Italian armed forces. It was based on the Villar Perosa (OVP) mechanisms as no other submachine gun designs existed at that time. The receiver and barrel were the same as the Villar Perosa and a wooden stock was added. Some versions of the Model 1918 had two triggers, one for single shots and the other for automatic fire. The design proved to be successful and some examples of the Beretta Model 1918 were still in use during World War II.

## Beretta Model 1938A

**SPECIFICATION**

**MANUFACTURER** Pietro Beretta SpA.
**CALIBRE** 9mm Parabellum
**MAGAZINE CAPACITY** 10, 20, 30 or 40
**ACTION** Blowback
**TOTAL LENGTH** 953mm/37.5in
**BARREL LENGTH** 318mm/12.5in
**WEIGHT UNLOADED** 4,190g/147.78oz

This proved to be a successful design and one that was derived from a semi-automatic carbine produced in 1935.

The weapon had a conventional blowback mechanism and a double-trigger arrangement whereby one could be used for firing single shots and the other for automatic fire.There were various versions, with slight modifications in designand manufacture. The Model 1938A was issued to Italian and German forces and saw extensive service. Further adaptations were made to produce the Model 38/42, Model 38/44 and Model 38/49 and the Beretta 5.

## Beretta Model 1938/42 and 1938/44

**SPECIFICATION**

**MANUFACTURER** Pietro Beretta SpA.
**CALIBRE** 9mm Parabellum
**MAGAZINE CAPACITY** 20 or 40
**ACTION** Blowback
**TOTAL LENGTH** 800mm/31.5in
**BARREL LENGTH** 216mm/8.5in
**WEIGHT UNLOADED** 3,260g/115oz

The 1938/42 weapon was a modified version of the Model 1938A and had a shorter barrel. The wooden stock was less extensive and finished short of the magazine. Like the Model 1938A, the Model 1938/42 proved to be a highly successful design which was ordered in large numbers by the German Army as well as by the Romanian Army.

The 1938/44 was a simplified version of the Beretta Model 1938/42 and was designed for ease of production at the end of World War II. In the internal mechanism, the bolt was reduced in length from 180mm/7.1in to 150mm/5.91in. The 38/44 was issued to the German Army and was designated the MP739.

## Beretta Model 5

The Beretta Model 5, introduced in 1957, was mainly a series improvement on the Beretta Model 1938/49 (a modified version of the Model 1938/44). A new safety system was designed and fitted, which comprised a grip safety that had to be depressed to allow the weapon to fire. This device was located in the wooden furniture on the side of the receiver and it was operated by the forward hand. The spring-loaded catch freed the bolt when it was depressed. It was produced until 1959.

| SPECIFICATION | |
|---|---|
| **MANUFACTURER** | Pietro Beretta SpA. |
| **CALIBRE** | 9mm Parabellum |
| **MAGAZINE CAPACITY** | 20 or 40 |
| **ACTION** | Blowback |
| **TOTAL LENGTH** | 800mm/31.5in |
| **BARREL LENGTH** | 216mm/8.5in |
| **WEIGHT UNLOADED** | 3,260g/115oz |

## Beretta Model 12S

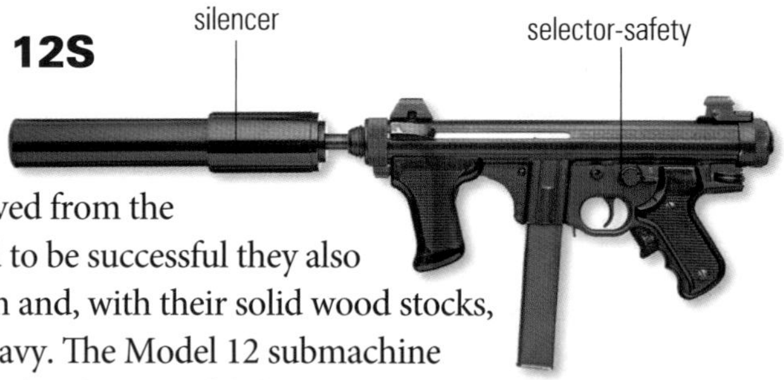


Although the submachine guns derived from the Model 1938/44 proved to be successful they also became dated in design and, with their solid wood stocks, were comparatively heavy. The Model 12 submachine gun proved to be a novel and successful design. The Model 12 was adopted by the Italian Army in 1979 and was also sold widely in Africa and South America. In 1983 a revised model was introduced, designated the 12S.

| SPECIFICATION | |
|---|---|
| **MANUFACTURER** | Fabbrica D'Armi P. Beretta SpA. |
| **CALIBRE** | 9mm Parabellum |
| **MAGAZINE CAPACITY** | 32 |
| **ACTION** | Blowback |
| **TOTAL LENGTH** | 418mm/16.47in |
| **BARREL LENGTH** | 200mm/7.87in |
| **WEIGHT UNLOADED** | 3,000g/105.80oz |

## Beretta PMX

Introduced in 2017, the Beretta PMX designed to replace the aging M12, which had been in production since 1959. Operating from a closed bolt, the PMX has a rate of fire of 900 rounds per minute. It was selected in 2018 for use by Italy's Carabinieri with more than 5,000 PMXs currently in use. In 2022, it was chosen for the Saudi Royal Guard Regiment and in 2023 for use by the Elite Forces of Malaysia.

| SPECIFICATION | |
|---|---|
| **MANUFACTURER** | Pietro Beretta SpA. |
| **CALIBRE** | 9mm Parabellum |
| **MAGAZINE CAPACITY** | 30 |
| **ACTION** | Blowback |
| **TOTAL LENGTH (STOCK EXTENDED)** | 640mm/25.2in |
| **TOTAL LENGTH (STOCK RETRACTED)** | 418mm/16.5in |
| **BARREL LENGTH** | 175mm/6.9in |
| **WEIGHT UNLOADED** | 2,358g/83.2oz |

## Beretta Mx4 Storm

Designed with military and law enforcement in mind, the Mx4 Storm is capable of fully automatic fire at a rate of 1,000 rounds per minute. In the interest of compatibility with Beretta's handguns, the Mx4 Storm is available in two different models: one that accepts Beretta 92/96 magazines and one that accepts Beretta Px4 magazines. This means that it can be used with magazines that hold fewer rounds as is common with handguns, but it is most commonly used with 30-round magazines. The firearm has been adopted by various military units in Italy, India, Libya, Russia, and Venezuela.

| SPECIFICATION | |
|---|---|
| **MANUFACTURER** | Pietro Beretta SpA. |
| **CALIBRE** | 9mm Parabellum |
| **MAGAZINE CAPACITY** | 30 |
| **ACTION** | Blowback |
| **TOTAL LENGTH** | 647mm/25.4in |
| **BARREL LENGTH** | 312mm/12.2in |
| **WEIGHT UNLOADED** | 2,477g/87.4oz |

## FNAB Model 1943

This rare weapon was developed and produced during World War II in small numbers. Unusually, it went against the trend of the time, which was to produce inexpensive and easily assembled weapons. It was a finely engineered product with high manufacturing quality.

**SPECIFICATION**

**MANUFACTURER** Fabbrica Nazionale d'Armi
**CALIBRE** 9mm Parabellum
**MAGAZINE CAPACITY** 20 or 40
**ACTION** Delayed blowback
**TOTAL LENGTH (STOCK EXTENDED)** 790mm/31.10in
**TOTAL LENGTH (STOCK RETRACTED)** 527mm/20.75in
**BARREL LENGTH** 198mm/7.79in
**WEIGHT UNLOADED** 3,250g/114.64oz

## Franchi LF57

The Franchi LF57 was produced from 1957 to 1980. It was manufactured from pressed steel. Like many compact weapons of this type, it had a telescoping bolt, though the bolt was positioned above the barrel rather than around it. It had a simple folding metal stock and it was also fitted with a pressure safety in the pistol grip which had to be pressed before the weapon would fire. The Franchi LF57 was issued to the Italian Navy but otherwise did not achieve major orders.

**SPECIFICATION**

**MANUFACTURER** Luigi Franchi SpA.
**CALIBRE** 9mm Parabellum
**MAGAZINE CAPACITY** 20/40
**ACTION** Blowback
**TOTAL LENGTH (STOCK EXTENDED)** 688mm/27in
**TOTAL LENGTH (STOCK RETRACTED)** 419mm/16.5in
**BARREL LENGTH** 203mm/8in
**WEIGHT UNLOADED** 3,170g/111.81oz

## TZ45

Developed at the end of World War II, the TZ45 was a basic design and had low manufacturing costs. It had a retracting metal stock and was equipped with a grip safety. Although some of these weapons were exported, it failed to impress in terms of either quality or performance and it was soon discontinued in Italy.

**SPECIFICATION**

**MANUFACTURER** Giandoso
**CALIBRE** 9mm Parabellum
**MAGAZINE CAPACITY** 40
**ACTION** Blowback
**TOTAL LENGTH (STOCK EXTENDED)** 850mm/33.46in
**TOTAL LENGTH (STOCK RETRACTED)** 545mm/21.45in
**BARREL LENGTH** 230mm/9.05in
**WEIGHT UNLOADED** 3,260g/114.99oz

## SPECTRE M-4

Introduced in 1984, this weapon had a closed-bolt system and a double action trigger that incorporated a de-cocking lever. A pull on the trigger cocked the hammer and a round was chambered. In this mode it could still be carried safely. The magazine had a four-column design which allowed a greater number of rounds in a reduced-length magazine. The Spectre was the only submachine gun on the market to have a double-action system in the mid-1980s.

**SPECIFICATION**

**MANUFACTURER** SITES SpA.
**CALIBRE** 9mm Parabellum
**MAGAZINE CAPACITY** 30 or 50
**ACTION** Blowback
**TOTAL LENGTH (STOCK RETRACTED)** 350mm/13.78in
**BARREL LENGTH** 130mm/5.1in
**WEIGHT UNLOADED** 2,900g/102.29oz

## Socimi Type 821

The Socimi (named after the manufacturer Societa Construzioni Industriali Milano) was said to be influenced by the Israeli Uzi submachine gun. Introduced in 1984, it had a rectangular steel receiver, and a pistol grip protruded from the centre of the weapon giving it good balance. The magazine was inserted into the base of the pistol grip. The pistol grip was covered in plastic furniture, as was the forward underpart of the receiver where the front hand would grip. It had a retracting stock that pivoted from the base of the receiver. A pressure safety was located at the back of the pistol grip, which needed to be pressed before the weapon was fired. The Socimi was produced for about five years until the late 1980s.

**SPECIFICATION**

**MANUFACTURER** Societa Construzioni Industriali Milano SpA.
**CALIBRE** 9mm Parabellum
**MAGAZINE CAPACITY** 32
**ACTION** Blowback
**TOTAL LENGTH (STOCK EXTENDED)** 600mm/23.6in
**TOTAL LENGTH (STOCK RETRACTED)** 400mm/15.7in
**BARREL LENGTH** 200mm/78.4in
**WEIGHT UNLOADED** 2,450g/86.42oz

## Twin Villar Perosa

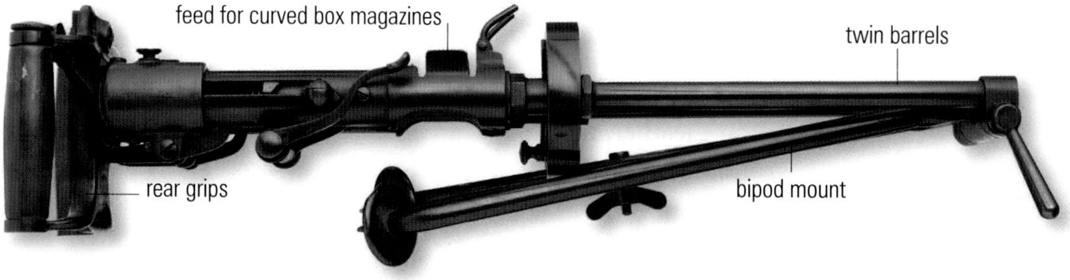


This somewhat strange-looking weapon is not instantly recognizable as a submachine gun. Early versions were produced between 1915–17 and so the earliest model was designated as "the first submachine gun". It was also known as the "Fiat" (when manufactured from Revelli factories in Italy). It came with a bipod (or tripod) mount for ground use and a shield which could be used in fixed positions or on the move. The Villar Perosa had double barrels and also double magazines firing 9mm cartridges and a delayed-blowback mechanism. Although it was an original design, the Villar Perosa was somewhat clumsy as a personal weapon and poor tactical handling meant that it soon gave way to more conventional designs.

**SPECIFICATION**

**MANUFACTURER** Various (in Italy and Canada)/ Oficina di Villar Perosa
**CALIBRE** 9mm Glisenti
**MAGAZINE CAPACITY** 25
**ACTION** Delayed blowback
**TOTAL LENGTH** 953mm/37.5in
**BARREL LENGTH** 318mm/12.5in
**WEIGHT UNLOADED** 4,190g/147.8oz

## Villar Perosa (OVP)

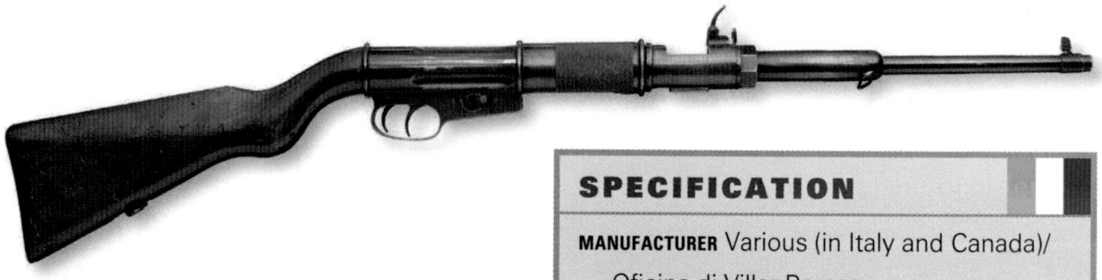

This weapon, unlike its predecessor, the twin Villar Perosa, was an entirely conventional design with a wooden stock and single, extended barrel. It was developed after World War I and introduced in the early 1920s. The weapon was directly derived from the Twin Villar Perosa, being based round a single barrel of the older weapon. The cocking mechanism was adapted so that it could be operated when firing from the shoulder. The trigger setup incorporated two triggers: the front one was used for automatic fire and the rear for single shots. The OVP was used during World War II.

**SPECIFICATION**

**MANUFACTURER** Various (in Italy and Canada)/ Oficina di Villar Perosa
**CALIBRE** 9mm Glisenti
**MAGAZINE CAPACITY** 25
**ACTION** Delayed blowback
**TOTAL LENGTH** 776mm/35.5in
**BARREL LENGTH** 280mm/11in
**WEIGHT UNLOADED** 3,670g/129.45oz

# Denmark

**Danish submachine-gun design and manufacture has been largely centred on the Madsen M45 and M46 models. The first model did not prove to be successful due to its complexity, but the second was an original design that caught the imagination, especially because of the novel way of opening the side of the weapon so that the internal workings were visible. The Madsen M50 and M53 were developments of this gun.**

## Madsen M46

**SPECIFICATION**

**MANUFACTURER** Dansk Industri Syndikat, Madsen
**CALIBRE** 9mm Parabellum
**MAGAZINE CAPACITY** 32
**ACTION** Blowback
**TOTAL LENGTH (STOCK EXTENDED)** 780mm/30.71in
**TOTAL LENGTH (STOCK RETRACTED)** 550mm/21.65in
**BARREL LENGTH** 200mm/7.87in
**WEIGHT UNLOADED** 3,150g/111.11oz

The first Madsen model to be produced at the end of World War I was the M45, but it had little commercial success. The M46, introduced a year later (designated the P16), was far more successful. It was made of two sheet-steel frames, hinged at the rear. The frame could open to allow access for cleaning, maintenance or replacement. It was blowback operated and had an open-bolt mechanism. It had a folding stock, partly covered with leather, which folded to the right. It also had a grip safety to the rear of the magazine holder. The weapon proved successful in South America.

## Madsen M53

**SPECIFICATION**

**MANUFACTURER** Dansk Industri Syndikat, Madsen
**CALIBRE** 9mm Parabellum
**MAGAZINE CAPACITY** 32
**ACTION** Blowback
**TOTAL LENGTH (STOCK EXTENDED)** 800mm/31.5in
**TOTAL LENGTH (STOCK RETRACTED)** 530mm/20.87in
**BARREL LENGTH** 200mm/7.8in
**WEIGHT UNLOADED** 3,200g/112oz

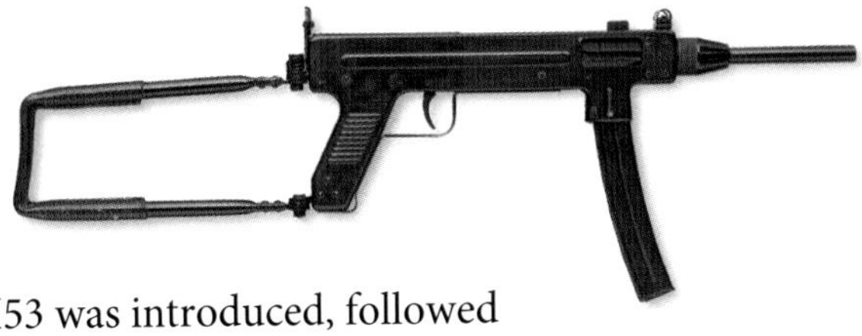

The M50 (designated the P56) was a slightly modified version of the M46. In 1953, the M53 was introduced, followed very shortly after by the Mark II, in a variety of models. As with all Madsens the frame was sheet-steel, hinged at the rear and fired from the open-bolt position. The Mark II had a fire-selector lever above the left-side rear pistol grip and wood or heat-insulating pistol grips (to prevent oveheating by the sun). The stock folded to the right. Apart from the curved frame of the magazine, the M53 and the Mark II were almost identical to the M46 and M50.

## M49 Hovea

**SPECIFICATION**

**MANUFACTURER** Haerens Vabenarsenalet
**CALIBRE** 9mm Parabellum
**MAGAZINE CAPACITY** 36
**ACTION** Blowback
**TOTAL LENGTH (STOCK EXTENDED)** 810mm/31.9in
**TOTAL LENGTH (STOCK RETRACTED)** 550mm/21.65in
**BARREL LENGTH** 216mm/8.5in
**WEIGHT UNLOADED** 3,500g/123.45oz

Originally designed in Sweden in the mid-1940s, it was a blowback-operated automatic weapon with a cylindrical receiver. It had a folding metal stock and a wooden hand grip behind the trigger guard. It was similar to the Carl Gustaf, and in trials for the Swedish armed forces the Carl Gustaf model won the contract. The Hovea won a competition held by the Danish armed forces and it was then produced under licence in Denmark.

# Austria

**In Steyr Mannlicher GmbH, Austria has one of the world's leading small-arms manufacturers, providing leading-edge designs to armed forces throughout the world. The Steyr Aug Para submachine gun, developed from the Steyr Aug rifle, is just one example in this impressive line up.**

## Steyr MPi 69

Introduced in 1969, the Steyr MPi 69 was a simplified version of the world-renowned Uzi submachine gun. It was issued to a number of security forces around the world but has since been replaced by the Steyr Aug. It was a blowback-operated selective-fire weapon with a wrap-around bolt. The weapon fired either single shots or automatic fire depending on the pressure exerted on the trigger. The safety catch located above the trigger had three positions. The magazine was inserted into the vertical pistol hand grip. The stock could be folded. The receiver fitted into a plastic hand grip. The sling strap could be attached to the cocking handle. The MPi 81 was an updated version with a higher rate of fire and a conventional cocking handle.

| SPECIFICATION | |
|---|---|
| MANUFACTURER | Steyr Mannlicher GmbH. |
| CALIBRE | 9mm Parabellum |
| MAGAZINE | 25 or 32 |
| ACTION | Blowback |
| TOTAL LENGTH (STOCK EXTENDED) | 670mm/26.38in |
| TOTAL LENGTH (STOCK RETRACTED) | 465mm/18.3in |
| BARREL LENGTH | 260mm/10.24in |
| WEIGHT UNLOADED | 2,930g/103.35oz |

## Steyr Aug Para

The Steyr Aug family of weapons was first introduced in the 1970s. The Para was a submachine gun version of the Aug assault rifle, the main difference being a new 9mm barrel, a closed-bolt firing system and a magazine adaptor. The length produced a higher muzzle energy as well as greater accuracy. The weapon had a blowback operating system and the bolt was one-piece, whereas the rifle had a bolt and a carrier system. The barrel was threaded and could accept a range of silencers. The rifle could be turned into a submachine gun by the use of a conversion kit.

| SPECIFICATION | |
|---|---|
| MANUFACTURER | Steyr-Mannlicher GmbH. |
| CALIBRE | 9mm Parabellum |
| MAGAZINE | 25 |
| ACTION | Blowback |
| TOTAL LENGTH | 665mm/26.18in |
| BARREL LENGTH | 420mm/16.54in |
| WEIGHT UNLOADED | 3,700g/130.51oz |

## Steyr TMP (Tactical Machine Pistol)

The design brief for the Steyr TMP was for an easy-to-handle weapon with significant firepower and a pistol-type grip. It was manufactured in 1993 from composite materials and had a very smooth, moulded design to minimize snagging. It had a delayed-blowback, closed-bolt system and a rotating barrel. The trigger was automatically selective and adjusted from single shots to automatic fire according to pressure. The mode could also be controlled with the safety catch. The Steyr TMP was designed to take a silencer as well as a variety of sights.

| SPECIFICATION | |
|---|---|
| MANUFACTURER | Steyr-Mannlicher GmbH. |
| CALIBRE | 9mm Parabellum |
| MAGAZINE | 15, 20 or 25 |
| ACTION | Delayed blowback |
| TOTAL LENGTH | 270mm/10.6in |
| BARREL LENGTH | 150mm/5.9in |
| WEIGHT UNLOADED | 1,400g/49.39oz |

# Sweden

**Although Sweden has only produced one submachine gun of its own design, it has become a classic. The Carl Gustaf M45 was used by the US Army during the Vietnam War and, when supplies ran out, the US produced their own copy. The Egyptians copied it in two homemade versions. The M45 was rugged, simple, effective and, almost as important, it had the right look.**

## Carl Gustaf M45

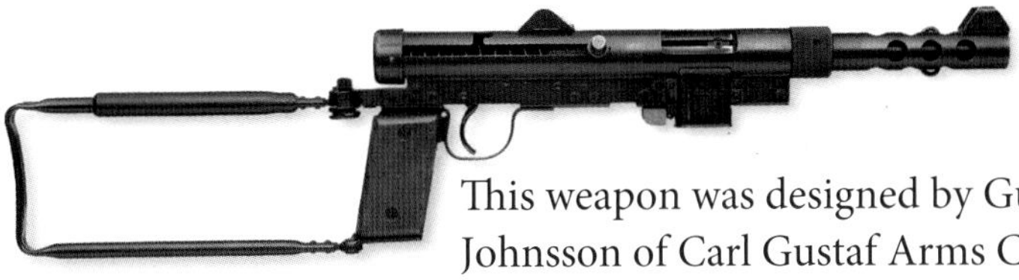

**SPECIFICATION**

**MANUFACTURER** Carl Gustaf Arms Co.
**CALIBRE** 9mm Parabellum
**MAGAZINE CAPACITY** 36 or 50
**ACTION** Blowback
**TOTAL LENGTH (STOCK EXTENDED)** 806mm/31.7in
**TOTAL LENGTH (STOCK RETRACTED)** 552mm/21.7in
**BARREL LENGTH** 203mm/7.99in
**WEIGHT UNLOADED** 3,430g/121oz

This weapon was designed by Gunnar Johnsson of Carl Gustaf Arms Company. He is said to have been inspired by the German Bergmann MP35 used widely during World War II. The M45 was issued to the Swedish Army after 1945. It was also later issued to US special forces and was used in service in Vietnam. It was a blowback-operated weapon firing from an open bolt. Due to the comparatively low rate of fire and small amount of recoil, the M45 was relatively easy to handle. Early versions did not have a magazine support, but this was rectified in later versions. The design of the magazine itself was widely acclaimed.

## Suomi/Husqvarna M37-39

**SPECIFICATION**

**MANUFACTURER** Husqvarna Vapenfabriks AB
**CALIBRE** 9mm Parabellum
**MAGAZINE CAPACITY** 36 box or 71 drum
**ACTION** Blowback
**TOTAL LENGTH** 831mm/32.7in
**BARREL LENGTH** 249mm/9.8in
**WEIGHT UNLOADED** 2,900g/102oz

A licenced model of the Finnish Suomi M31 was made by the Husqvarna factory in Sweden, where it was designated the M37-39. Sweden also exported their version to other countries, including their neighbours, Norway and Denmark, and countries farther afield such as Indonesia and Egypt. The main design differences between the Suomi M/31 and the Husqvarna M37-39 were the stock, the barrel and the sights.

## Hovea prototype

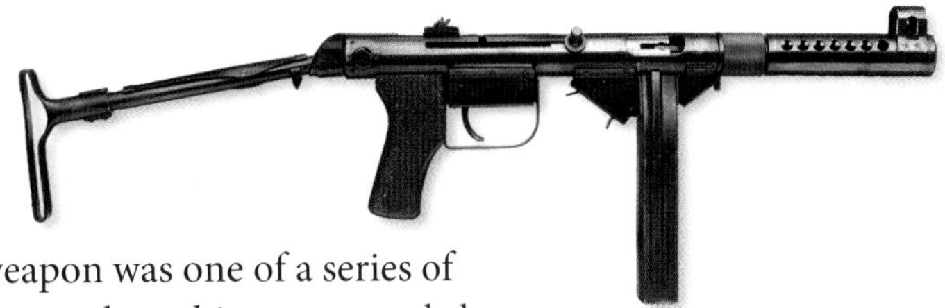

**SPECIFICATION**

**MANUFACTURER** Husqvarna Vapenfabriks AB
**CALIBRE** 9mm Parabellum
**MAGAZINE CAPACITY** 71 drum
**ACTION** Blowback
**TOTAL LENGTH (STOCK EXTENDED)** 845mm/33.27in
**TOTAL LENGTH (STOCK RETRACTED)** 590mm/21.65in
**BARREL LENGTH** 212mm/8.46in
**WEIGHT UNLOADED** 3,000g/105.82oz

This weapon was one of a series of prototype submachine guns made by Husqvarna for the submachine-gun trials held during late 1944 and 1945. This was a blowback-operated automatic weapon with a cylindrical receiver similar to that of the Sten. It had a folding metal stock and a wooden hand grip behind the trigger guard. The design lost out to the Carl Gustaf, which was a similar design, in Swedish military trials. The rights of manufacture were sold to Denmark.

# Czech Republic

**Czech industry has produced a variety of highly regarded armaments over the years and most of these have been manufactured by Ceskoslovenská Zbrojovka (sister company to Ceská Zbrojovka). Pioneering designs include the CZ23–26 series of submachine guns, with their wraparound bolts.**

## ZK 383

The standard ZK 383 was developed in the 1930s and was used by the Czech forces in World War II. The weapon was a heavy submachine gun that is sometimes described as a light automatic rifle and it is heavy enough to be deployed as a squad submachine gun. Characteristics that are more typical of a heavy submachine gun include a bipod and an interchangeable barrel. There were variations on the design, including the ZK 383H and ZK 383P. The ZK 383 was issued to German troops and to the Bulgarian Army, and also appeared in parts of South America.

| SPECIFICATION | |
|---|---|
| MANUFACTURER | Ceskoslovenská Zbrojovka |
| CALIBRE | 9mm Parabellum |
| MAGAZINE CAPACITY | 30 |
| ACTION | Blowback |
| TOTAL LENGTH | 902mm/35.5in |
| BARREL LENGTH | 325mm/12.8in |
| WEIGHT UNLOADED | 4,250g/150oz |

## CZSA 25

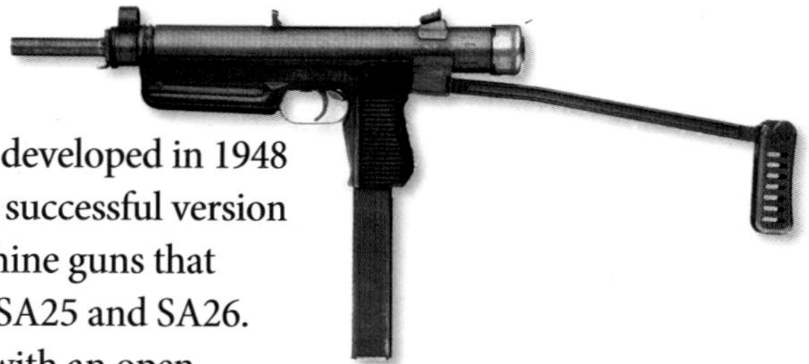

This submachine gun was developed in 1948 and was possibly the most successful version among a series of submachine guns that included the SA23, SA24, SA25 and SA26. The action was blowback with an open-bolt system that wraps around the rear end of the barrel – one of the first designs to incorporate this system. There is a fire-selection system in the trigger, whereby the gun will fire single shots or automatic fire according to finger pressure. The magazine was inserted in the hand grip, which helped to balance the weapon. The earlier versions, CZ 23 and CZ 24, were distinguished by a wooden stock, whereas the CZ 25 had a metal stock.

| SPECIFICATION | |
|---|---|
| MANUFACTURER | Ceskoslovenská Zbrojovka |
| CALIBRE | 9mm Parabellum |
| MAGAZINE CAPACITY | 24 or 40 |
| ACTION | Blowback |
| TOTAL LENGTH (STOCK EXTENDED) | 686mm/27in |
| TOTAL LENGTH (STOCK RETRACTED) | 445mm/17.5in |
| BARREL LENGTH | 284mm/11.2in |
| WEIGHT UNLOADED | 3,817g/134.39oz |

## Skorpion M61

The Skorpion submachine gun had a somewhat iconic design that has appeared in different versions with different calibres. Most notable were the vz.61 and vz.62, in both .32 ACP and 9mm calibre. It is characterized by small dimensions and light weight. It has been deployed successfully by specialist paramilitary and police units who have to operate in confined spaces, such as buildings, aircraft and other vehicles. The weapon had a retractable shoulder stock and it could be carried in a holster if necessary. The pressure-sensitive trigger allowed for the firing of single shots or automatic fire.

| SPECIFICATION | |
|---|---|
| MANUFACTURER | Ceskoslovenská Zbrojovka |
| CALIBRE | .32 ACP, 9mm Parabellum |
| MAGAZINE CAPACITY | 10 or 20 |
| ACTION | Blowback |
| TOTAL LENGTH (STOCK EXTENDED) | 517mm/20.35in |
| TOTAL LENGTH (STOCK RETRACTED) | 270mm/10.63in |
| BARREL LENGTH | 113mm/4.45in |
| WEIGHT UNLOADED | 1,440g/50.79oz |

# Poland

**Apart from the PM-63 submachine gun developed in Poland in the 1960s, the Polish armed forces relied largely on a copy of the classic Soviet PPS-43 submachine gun in the immediate post-war years. In the 1980s the PM-84 and PM-98 were developed as replacements for the PM-63.**

## Sudaev PPS-43

| SPECIFICATION | |
|---|---|
| MANUFACTURER | State Arsenals |
| CALIBRE | 7.62mm Tokarev |
| MAGAZINE CAPACITY | 35 |
| ACTION | Blowback |
| TOTAL LENGTH (STOCK EXTENDED) | 808mm/32.25in |
| TOTAL LENGTH (STOCK RETRACTED) | 606mm/24.25in |
| BARREL LENGTH | 269mm/10.75in |
| WEIGHT UNLOADED | 5,625g/198.42oz |

This weapon was designed by Soviet engineer Aleksei Sudaev in 1942 and it proved to be one of the most effective submachine guns used by the Russians in World War II. It was based on the PPSh-41 and PPSh-42 designed by Georgii Shpagin but was less expensive to produce. The PPS-43 was a modified and standardized version of the PPS-42. It had a blowback operation, firing from an open bolt, and it was set to permanent automatic fire. The folding stock made it a handy weapon for paratroop units and tank crews. The Polish armed forces were issued with copies after 1945.

## PM-63 (Pistolet Maszynowy wz.63)

| SPECIFICATION | |
|---|---|
| MANUFACTURER | State Arsenals |
| CALIBRE | 9mm Makarov |
| MAGAZINE CAPACITY | 15 or 25 |
| ACTION | Blowback |
| TOTAL LENGTH (STOCK EXTENDED) | 583mm/22.95in |
| TOTAL LENGTH (STOCK RETRACTED) | 333mm/13.11in |
| BARREL LENGTH | 152mm/5.98in |
| WEIGHT UNLOADED | 1,800g/63.49oz |

This weapon was designed by Peter Wilniewczyc in 1963 and was issued to the Polish armed forces in 1965. It was a blowback-operated weapon with an open-bolt mechanism. For single shots, the weapon was cocked by pulling back the slide until it locked. After the firing action, the slide returned to the cocked position, ready for the next round to be fired. A more firm pressure on the trigger enabled automatic fire. Otherwise, the PM-63 was designed in much the same way as a pistol. It could be fired single-handedly, like a pistol, with varying degrees of accuracy, or the shoulder stock could be used to improve control.

## PM-84P

| SPECIFICATION | |
|---|---|
| MANUFACTURER | State Arsenals (Radom) |
| CALIBRE | 9mm Makarov |
| MAGAZINE CAPACITY | 15 or 25 |
| ACTION | Blowback |
| TOTAL LENGTH (STOCK EXTENDED) | 575mm/22.64in |
| TOTAL LENGTH (STOCK RETRACTED) | 375mm/14.76in |
| BARREL LENGTH | 185mm/7.28in |
| WEIGHT UNLOADED | 2,170g/76.54oz |

The PM-84 (sometimes called the "Glauberyt") was developed in the early 1980s as a replacement for the PM-63. The weapon had a higher proportion of stamped parts over its predecessor as technology had improved. It was a conventional blowback design, fired from an open bolt. The weapon could be cocked from either side of the receiver and there was a fire selector and safety switch above the hand grip. A further development of the weapon in the 1990s was the PM-98. The new model could also be fitted with a laser-pointer or flashlight.

# Croatia

**A number of submachine guns have been produced in Croatia over the years, including the Agram 2000, the Sokacz, said to be influenced by the Russian PPSh-41 (and often built by local machine shops) and the Ero, which was a version of the Israeli Uzi submachine gun with minor differences.**

## Ero

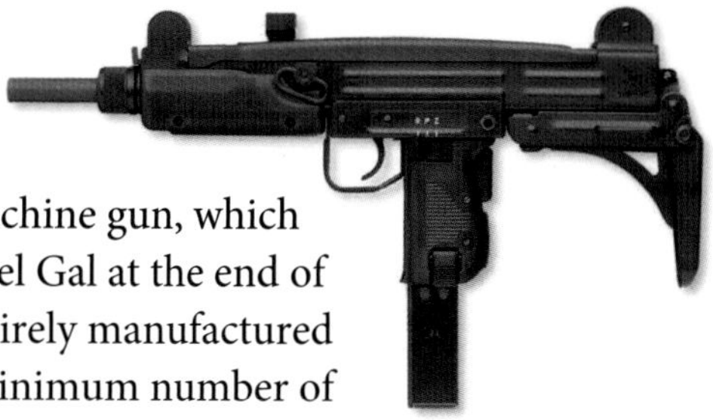

The Ero was a 1994 Croatian version of the Israeli Uzi submachine gun, which was first designed by Major Uziel Gal at the end of the 1940s. The Ero is almost entirely manufactured from stamped steel and has a minimum number of parts. The magazine is inserted into the hand grip, which is placed at the centre of the weapon. This makes for optimum balance and also makes it easier to reload in dark conditions. Other than differences in weight and size, the main difference between the Ero and the Uzi is the grip safety at the top of the pistol grip.

**SPECIFICATION**

**MANUFACTURER** Local Croatian manufacturer
**CALIBRE** 9mm Parabellum
**MAGAZINE CAPACITY** 32
**ACTION** Blowback
**TOTAL LENGTH (STOCK EXTENDED)** 650mm/25.59in
**TOTAL LENGTH (STOCK RETRACTED)** 470mm/18.5in
**BARREL LENGTH** 260mm/10.24in
**WEIGHT UNLOADED** 3,730g/131.57oz

## Sokacz

The Sokacz was effectively a copy of Soviet Georgii Shpagin's PPSh-41. It was produced in the mid-1990s entirely from stamped metal parts, which were relatively cheap and easy to produce. The receiver was hinged and could be opened easily for maintenance of the internal working parts. The weapon had a very high rate of fire, making it a formidable tool. It had a built-in compensator to reduce muzzle lift while firing. Designed originally for internal security forces, the weapon began to be used throughout Europe after the break-up of Yugoslavia.

**SPECIFICATION**

**MANUFACTURER** Local Croatian manufacturer
**CALIBRE** 9mm Parabellum
**MAGAZINE CAPACITY** 32 or 40
**ACTION** Blowback
**TOTAL LENGTH (STOCK EXTENDED)** 880mm/34.65in
**TOTAL LENGTH (STOCK RETRACTED)** 605mm/23.82in
**BARREL LENGTH** 300mm/11.81in
**WEIGHT UNLOADED** 3,580g/126.28oz

## Agram 2000

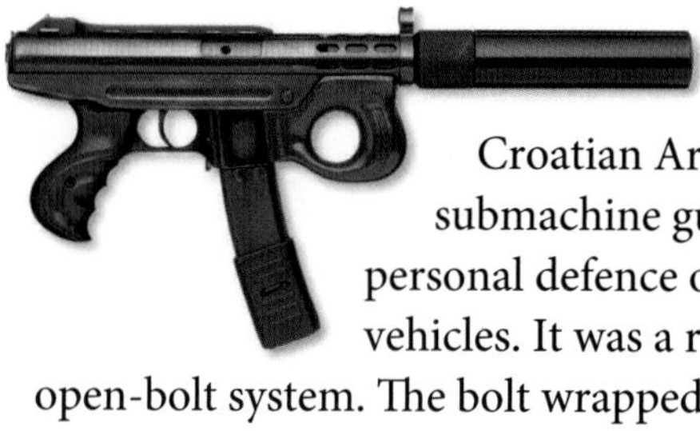

The Agram was developed for the Croatian Army from the Italian Beretta PM12-S submachine gun. It was primarily intended for personal defence or for use by troops in armoured vehicles. It was a recoil-operated weapon with an open-bolt system. The bolt wrapped round the rear of the barrel so as to reduce the overall length. There was an automatic safety incorporated in the grip and a three-position safety and fire selector. A modified 2002 version of the Agram was also available, designed without the foregrip.

**SPECIFICATION**

**MANUFACTURER** Local Croatian manufacturer
**CALIBRE** 9mm Parabellum
**MAGAZINE CAPACITY** 22, 32 or 40
**ACTION** Recoil
**TOTAL LENGTH** 482mm/18.98in
**BARREL LENGTH** 200mm/7.87in (various)
**WEIGHT UNLOADED** 1,800g/63.49oz

# South Africa

**The BXP submachine gun is produced by Vektor, part of the large Denel corporation, which produces a wide range of armaments. It was designed in the 1980s when international sanctions against South Africa led to a shortage of arms. It was similar to the US Ingram MAC 10 submachine gun.**

**SPECIFICATION**

**MANUFACTURER** Vektor
**CALIBRE** 9mm Parabellum
**MAGAZINE CAPACITY** 22 or 32
**ACTION** Blowback
**TOTAL LENGTH (STOCK EXTENDED)** 607mm/23.9in
**TOTAL LENGTH (STOCK RETRACTED)** 387mm/15.2in
**BARREL LENGTH** 208mm/8.2in
**WEIGHT UNLOADED** 2,500g/88.18oz

## BXP

Developed in the mid-1980s, this was a compact design with a conventional blowback mechanism firing from an open bolt. It was small enough and well-balanced enough to be fired like a pistol with one hand. The bolt overlapped the rear end of the barrel, which contributed to the compact size and provided better balance. The cocking handle was located on the top of the receiver and there were fire-selector and safety levers on both sides of the receiver. The weapon had a folding shoulder stock and, when folded, the buttstock could be used as a front hand grip.

# Finland

**Finland produced one of the most famous and reliable submachine guns before World War II, the Suomi Model 31. It was extremely well made and proved to be highly effective in the Finnish defence of their country against Soviet invasion forces. The Suomi was adopted by Denmark, Sweden and Switzerland.**

**SPECIFICATION**

**MANUFACTURER** Tampereen Asepaja Oy
**CALIBRE** 9mm Parabellum
**MAGAZINE CAPACITY** 20 or 40
**ACTION** Blowback
**TOTAL LENGTH** 400mm/15.74in
**BARREL LENGTH** 249mm/9.8in
**WEIGHT UNLOADED** 1,650g/58oz

## Jati-Matic

The Jati-Matic was introduced in the 1980s. It was a blowback-operated weapon with a select-fire mechanism. There was an upward incline at the rear which had the effect of braking the bolt on recoil. The rear hand grip could be positioned higher than on standard designs. It had a pressure-selective trigger which could fire either single shots or automatic. A forward handle acted as a safety when locked and also doubled as a cocking handle. A new model, the GG-95, was introduced in 1995.

## Suomi Model 1931

Designed during the 1920s, the Suomi was still being used in the 1980s. Part of the reason for its longevity was the quality of its manufacture. The bolt was similar to that of a rifle and the drum magazine was similar to that of the Thompson submachine gun. The Suomi played a major role for the Finnish Army in fighting between Finland and the Soviet Union in 1940. It was exported widely, with manufacturing licences granted to Denmark, Sweden and Switzerland.

**SPECIFICATION**

**MANUFACTURER** Tikkakoski Oy
**CALIBRE** 9mm Parabellum
**MAGAZINE CAPACITY** 20, 36, 40, 50 or 70
**ACTION** Blowback
**TOTAL LENGTH** 870mm/34.25in
**BARREL LENGTH** 314mm/12.36in
**WEIGHT UNLOADED** 4,600g/162.26oz

### M44

This weapon was essentially a copy of the Soviet PPS-43 submachine gun. Considerable numbers were manufactured in Finland in 1944 and it was the standard submachine gun of the Finnish Army. In the 1950s production was restarted in Spain, when the manager of the Tikkakoski Arsenal moved to Oviedo. The Model 1944 could take either a Carl Gustaf box magazine or a Thompson-style drum magazine.

**SPECIFICATION**

**MANUFACTURER** Tikkakoski Oy
**CALIBRE** 9mm Parabellum
**MAGAZINE CAPACITY** 36 box or 71 drum
**ACTION** Blowback
**TOTAL LENGTH (STOCK EXTENDED)** 831mm/32.71in
**TOTAL LENGTH (STOCK RETRACTED)** 622mm/24.49in
**BARREL LENGTH** 249mm/9.8in
**WEIGHT UNLOADED** 2,900g/102oz

## Romania

**In 1941 the Cugir Arsenal, based in the Transylvanian part of Romania, produced a submachine-gun design known as the Orita. It was quite similar in general appearance to the German MP41, but was a sturdier weapon. It had a limited production but was used extensively by Romanians in Soviet territory.**

### Orita M41

This weapon was designed by Leopold Jaska and was manufactured to a high standard using machined parts. It normally had a solid wooden butt. It had a blowback operation and bolt mechanism similar to the one used in the Thompson submachine gun. The cocking handle was located on the left of the receiver and the fire selector on the right of the receiver, for either single shots or automatic fire. The weapon was used by pro-German Romanian forces in the invasion of Russia.

**SPECIFICATION**

**MANUFACTURER** Cugir Arsenal
**CALIBRE** 9mm Parabellum
**MAGAZINE CAPACITY** 25 or 32
**ACTION** Blowback
**TOTAL LENGTH** 894mm/35.2in
**BARREL LENGTH** 287mm/11.3in
**WEIGHT UNLOADED** 3,460g/122oz

## Russia

**The Soviets had few doubts about the effectiveness of submachine guns when the Finnish Suomi was used against them to devastating effect in 1940. During the Siege of Leningrad (1941–44), the war industry produced the rugged PPS-43. More recently produced models were adaptations of the AKS-74 rifle.**

### Makarov Bizon

This submachine gun was designed by a team that included Victor Kalashnikov and Alexei Dragunov, and introduced in 1995. The design is said to have been influenced by the US Calico submachine gun, especially the helical magazine, located under the receiver on the Bizon. The weapon fired from a closed bolt. Many of the working parts were similar to those found on Kalashnikov rifles. The heavy-duty buttstock folded to the side when not in use.

**SPECIFICATION**

**MANUFACTURER** Izhevsk Mechanical Plant (IZHMECH)
**CALIBRE** 9mm Makarov
**MAGAZINE CAPACITY** 64 **ACTION** Blowback
**TOTAL LENGTH** 660mm/25.98in
**BARREL LENGTH** 425mm/16.7in
**WEIGHT UNLOADED** 2,470g/87oz

## PPD 1934/38

**SPECIFICATION**

**MANUFACTURER** State Arsenals
**CALIBRE** 7.62mm Tokarev
**MAGAZINE CAPACITY** 25 box or 71 drum
**ACTION** Blowback
**TOTAL LENGTH** 779mm/30.6in
**BARREL LENGTH** 269mm/10.75in
**WEIGHT UNLOADED** 3,730g/131.57oz

This submachine gun was designed by Russian arms-designer Vasily Degtyarev and produced in 1934. He was influenced by the German Bergmann MP28 and the Finnish Suomi Model 31. It was manufactured to a high standard using machined steel parts, and the inside of the barrel was chromium plated. The weapon was fitted with a drum magazine, located underneath the receiver. First introduced in 1935, the weapon proved to be too complex to produce in great numbers and it saw only limited service in World War II.

## PPD 1940

**SPECIFICATION**

**MANUFACTURER** State Arsenals
**CALIBRE** 7.62mm Tokarev
**MAGAZINE CAPACITY** 71
**ACTION** Blowback
**TOTAL LENGTH** 790mm/31in
**BARREL LENGTH** 260mm/10.5in
**WEIGHT UNLOADED** 3,630g/128oz

The PPD 1940 was a modification of the PPD 1934/38 and was designed for greater ease of manufacture. It retained the high-quality levels of the PPD 1934/38 and was also a better weapon. It became the standard Soviet service issue in 1940. However, despite the efforts to simplify the manufacturing process, the weapon could still not be produced in sufficient numbers to satisfy the requirements of the Soviet Union on a war footing, and it was not long before an alternative was sought.

## PPSh-41

**SPECIFICATION**

**MANUFACTURER** State Arsenals
**CALIBRE** 7.62mm Tokarev
**MAGAZINE CAPACITY** 35 box or 71 drum
**ACTION** Blowback
**TOTAL LENGTH** 838mm/33in
**BARREL LENGTH** 266mm/10.5in
**WEIGHT UNLOADED** 3,640g/128.4oz

This weapon answered the requirement of the Soviet Union for a reliable and effective submachine gun that could also be produced in large numbers. Designed by Russian engineer Georgii Shpagin, the PPSh-41 was produced entirely from stamped metal parts, which were relatively cheap and easy to produce. The receiver was hinged and could be opened easily for maintenance of the internal working parts. The weapon had a very high rate of fire, making it a formidable tool in the hands of large numbers of troops.

## PPS-43

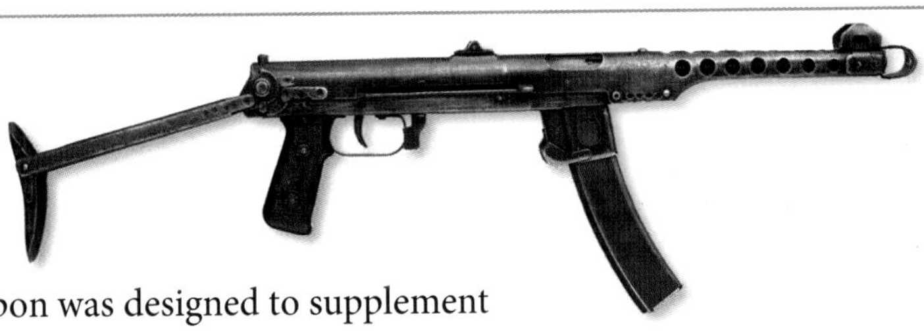

**SPECIFICATION**

**MANUFACTURER** State Arsenals
**CALIBRE** 7.62mm Tokarev
**MAGAZINE CAPACITY** 35
**ACTION** Blowback
**TOTAL LENGTH (STOCK EXTENDED)** 808mm/32.251in
**TOTAL LENGTH (STOCK RETRACTED)** 606mm/24.25in
**BARREL LENGTH** 254mm/10in
**WEIGHT UNLOADED** 5,625g/198.41oz

This weapon was designed to supplement existing supplies of weapons during the Siege of Leningrad. Designed by Russian engineer Aleksei Sudaev and based on earlier models such as the PPSh-41, it proved to be one of the most effective submachine guns of World War II. One major difference was that it had a folding stock, which made it a handy weapon for paratroop units and tank crews. The PPS-43 had blowback operation, firing from an open bolt, and it was set to permanent automatic fire.

## AKS-74U

This gun was developed from the AK-74 rifle, used by the Soviet Union in place of submachine guns. It had a short barrel and gas tube. The receiver has been altered so that it is hinged at the top. There is an expansion chamber on the top of the receiver which was designed to release the gas pressure. The internal mechanism remained identical to the AK-74 rifle. The stock folded round and could be locked into the side of the receiver. The plastic magazine was strengthened. Developed in the 1970s, the weapon is said to have been first used in Afghanistan in 1983.

**SPECIFICATION**

**MANUFACTURER** State Arsenals
**CALIBRE** 5.45mm
**MAGAZINE CAPACITY** 30
**ACTION** Gas
**TOTAL LENGTH (STOCK EXTENDED)** 675mm/26.6in
**TOTAL LENGTH (STOCK RETRACTED)** 420mm/16.5in
**BARREL LENGTH** 200mm/7.87in
**WEIGHT UNLOADED** 2,710g/95.6oz

## SR-2 Veresk

**SPECIFICATION**

**MANUFACTURER** TsNIITochMash
**CALIBRE** 9x21mm Gyurza
**MAGAZINE CAPACITY** 20 or 30
**ACTION** Gas-operated rotating bolt
**TOTAL LENGTH (STOCK EXTENDED)** 603mm/23.7in
**TOTAL LENGTH (STOCK RETRACTED)** 367mm/14.4in
**BARREL LENGTH** 174mm/6.9in
**WEIGHT UNLOADED** 1,587g/56

Russia's Federal Security Service urged development of the SR-2 Veresk in the mid-1990s, with a production gun emerging in 1999. Unlike most submachine guns that use blowback operation, this one has a gas-operated rotating bolt that is normally found on larger assault rifles. The gun bears visual similarity to the Uzi, with its magazine being inserted into the pistol grip. It also borrows the same safety/selector lever as the ones found on AKs. The 9x21mm Gyurza round was chosen for its ability to penetrate Class II body armour and thin-skinned vehicles at distances up to 200 metres.

## PP-19 Vityaz

The PP-19 Vityaz was introduced in 2004 and is based on the larger AK-74 and, as a result, shares some parts interchangeably. Since the gun operates as a straight blowback design, the internals were adjusted accordingly to eliminate the need for the gas system found on the AK-74. It bears standard AK front and rear sights, but also has a Picatinny rail for other sight attachment. The rate of fire is 800 rounds per minute.

**SPECIFICATION**

**MANUFACTURER** Izhmash
**CALIBRE** 9mm Parabellum
**MAGAZINE CAPACITY** 30
**ACTION** Blowback
**TOTAL LENGTH (STOCK EXTENDED)** 705mm/27.75in
**TOTAL LENGTH (STOCK RETRACTED)** 480mm/18.8in
**BARREL LENGTH** 237mm/9.4in
**WEIGHT UNLOADED** 2,891g/102oz

## PP-2000

Designed for close-quarters combat, the PP-2000 was intended for use by special operations soldiers and police riot control. It was adopted by Russian police in 2008. When loaded with 7N21 or 7N31 9mm ammunition, the gun has similar armour-piercing capabilities as the FN PS90 and the HK MP7. A spare 44-round magazine can be stored on the rear of the gun, acting as a stock. The charging handle is located on the top of the receiver and folds down out of the way of the front sight when not in use.

**SPECIFICATION**

**MANUFACTURER** KBP Instrument Design Bureau
**CALIBRE** 9mm Parabellum
**MAGAZINE CAPACITY** 20 or 44
**ACTION** Blowback
**TOTAL LENGTH (STOCK EXTENDED)** 555mm/21.8in
**TOTAL LENGTH (STOCK RETRACTED)** 340mm/23.3in
**BARREL LENGTH** 182mm/7.2in
**WEIGHT UNLOADED** 1,397g/49.3oz

# Israel

**There is only one word for submachine gun in Israel: that word is Uzi. The same name is instantly recognizable around the world. By using a wraparound bolt, the gun was very compact and easily concealed for covert operations. An even smaller variety, the Mini-Uzi, was also produced, as well as a Micro-Uzi, which is sometimes categorized as a pistol.**

## Uzi

| SPECIFICATION |
|---|
| **MANUFACTURER** Ta'as Israel Industries Ltd. |
| **CALIBRE** 9mm Parabellum |
| **MAGAZINE CAPACITY** 25 or 32 |
| **ACTION** Blowback |
| **TOTAL LENGTH (STOCK EXTENDED)** 650mm/25.59in |
| **TOTAL LENGTH (STOCK RETRACTED)** 470mm/18.5in |
| **BARREL LENGTH** 260mm/10.2in |
| **WEIGHT UNLOADED** 3,500g/123oz metal stock |

The Uzi submachine gun, introduced in the 1950s, has become a byword for efficient weapons of this type. It was designed by Major Uziel Gal at the end of the 1940s, influenced by Czech designs. The design was simple and effective, being made up of steel pressings, spot-welded and riveted together. It was a blowback-operated weapon which used a system whereby the round is fired while the bolt is still in forward motion. The bolt surrounded the rear end of the barrel at the moment of firing. The selector could be positioned for automatic fire, single shots or full safety. The was a grip safety and an extra safety was also located in the cocking-handle slide.

## Parabellum Mini-Uzi

| SPECIFICATION |
|---|
| **MANUFACTURER** Ta'as Israel Industries Ltd. |
| **CALIBRE** 9mm Parabellum |
| **MAGAZINE CAPACITY** 20, 25 or 32 |
| **ACTION** Blowback |
| **TOTAL LENGTH (STOCK EXTENDED)** 600mm/23.6in |
| **TOTAL LENGTH (STOCK RETRACTED)** 360mm/14.1in |
| **BARREL LENGTH** 197mm/7.8in |
| **WEIGHT UNLOADED** 2,700g/95oz metal stock |

As its name suggests, the Mini-Uzi, introduced in 1980, was essentially a more compact version of the standard Uzi submachine gun. One major difference in more recent versions of the Mini-Uzi was that it incorporated a closed-bolt firing mechanism with a floating firing pin. This weapon was ideal for any form of covert operation as it can be easily concealed. As it was a well-balanced weapon, it could be fired easily "from the hip" or, with the stock extended, from the shoulder.

## Micro-Uzi

| SPECIFICATION |
|---|
| **MANUFACTURER** Ta'as Israel Industries Ltd. |
| **CALIBRE** 9mm Parabellum |
| **MAGAZINE CAPACITY** 20 |
| **ACTION** Blowback |
| **TOTAL LENGTH (STOCK EXTENDED)** 460mm/18.1in |
| **TOTAL LENGTH (STOCK RETRACTED)** 250mm/9.84in |
| **BARREL LENGTH** 117mm/4.6mm |
| **WEIGHT UNLOADED** 1,950g/68.78oz metal stock |

The Micro-Uzi was introduced in the 1990s. It was, again, essentially the same as the Mini-Uzi in operation but in a smaller package. There was a tungsten insert in the bolt which was designed to increase the mass and reduce the rate of fire. The Micro-Uzi was intended for covert operations which required a weapon that can be easily concealed and deployed, while providing an effective rate of fire and accuracy. Another role intended for the Micro-Uzi was as a Personal Defence Weapon (PDW) for airborne and armoured crews in the Israeli Defence Forces.

# Egypt

**Egypt chose, along with the US armed forces, to adapt a version of the Swedish Carl Gustaf submachine gun. This was a simple, robust and effective weapon and also proved to be the inspiration for two separate Egyptian derivatives, the Port Said and the Akaba, a simpler version of the Port Said.**

## Port Said

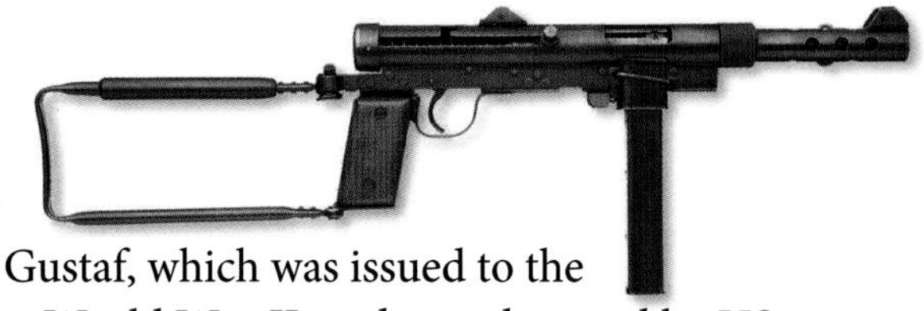

The Port Said was a close copy of the Swedish Carl Gustaf, which was issued to the Swedish armed forces after World War II, and was also used by US forces in Vietnam in the 1950s and 1960s. It was a fully automatic weapon, firing from an open bolt. The simplicity and efficiency of the design, allied to its sheer robustness, contributed to its success and explains why it was produced under licence not only in Egypt but also in Indonesia and the United States.

**SPECIFICATION**

**MANUFACTURER** Local Egyptian manufacturer
**CALIBRE** 9mm Parabellum
**MAGAZINE CAPACITY** 36 or 50
**ACTION** Blowback
**TOTAL LENGTH (STOCK EXTENDED)** 811mm/31.9in
**TOTAL LENGTH (STOCK RETRACTED)** 552mm/21.7in
**BARREL LENGTH** 212mm/8.35in
**WEIGHT UNLOADED** 3,900g/137.57oz

## Maadi Akaba

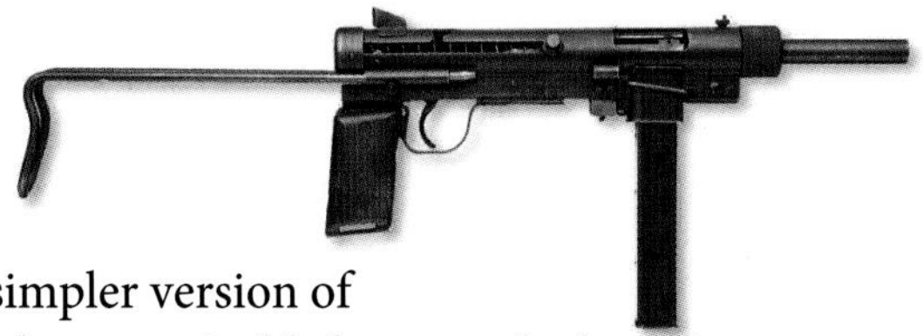

This submachine gun was developed in the 1970s as a simpler version of the Port Said. It is immediately recognizable because the barrel jacket was removed, and the barrel itself reduced in length to only 150mm/5.9in. The sights were also rearranged, the foresight having been removed from the end of the barrel jacket. Instead of a folding stock, the Akaba had telescoping wire stock not unlike that of the American M3. The model was produced in the 1970s and again in the mid-1990s.

**SPECIFICATION**

**MANUFACTURER** Local Egyptian manufacturer
**CALIBRE** 9mm Parabellum
**MAGAZINE CAPACITY** 36 or 50
**ACTION** Blowback
**TOTAL LENGTH (STOCK EXTENDED)** 737mm/29in
**TOTAL LENGTH (STOCK RETRACTED)** 482mm/19in
**BARREL LENGTH** 150mm/5.9in
**WEIGHT UNLOADED** 3,900g/137.57oz

# South Korea

**Production of a version of the American M3 "grease gun" was undertaken by the Daewoo Corporation, resulting in the K1, which was updated to the K2 and is in use today by military forces. Otherwise the country does not have a history of indigenous submachine-gun manufacture.**

## Daewoo K1A

The K1A was the first modern submachine gun developed by the Republic of Korea (South Korea) in the early 1980s. This was a gas-fired, selective-fire gun with an aluminium alloy receiver and a rotating-bolt locking system. It had a selection system that can be set on safety, full automatic, semi-automatic, and burst-fire. The K1A was the upgraded version of the K1, a version of the American M3 or "grease gun". All K1s in the South Korean military have been modified to K1A.

**SPECIFICATION**

**MANUFACTURER** Daewoo Telecom Ltd.
**CALIBRE** 5.56mm
**MAGAZINE CAPACITY** 20 or 30
**ACTION** Gas
**TOTAL LENGTH** 838mm/33in
**BARREL LENGTH (WITHOUT STOCK)** 653mm/25.7in
**WEIGHT UNLOADED** 2,870g/10oz

## XK9

**SPECIFICATION**

**MANUFACTURER** Daewoo Precision
**CALIBRE** 9mm Parabellum
**MAGAZINE CAPACITY** 30
**ACTION** Blowback
**TOTAL LENGTH (STOCK EXTENDED)** 680mm/27.8in
**TOTAL LENGTH (STOCK RETRACTED)** 590mm/23.2in
**BARREL LENGTH** 220mm/8.7in
**WEIGHT UNLOADED** 2,891g/102oz

Designed in 2003 and intended for use in tandem with the HK MP5 by the ROK Armed Forces, the gun never went into full production for reasons that remain uncertain. Despite this, the gun remains ready to be pushed into mass-production should the need ever arise. The XK9 has a rate of fire of 980 rounds per minute.

## Daewoo Telecom K7

**SPECIFICATION**

**MANUFACTURER** Daewoo Telecom and SNT Motiv
**CALIBRE** 9mm Parabellum
**MAGAZINE CAPACITY** 30 or 32
**ACTION** Blowback
**TOTAL LENGTH (STOCK EXTENDED)** 790mm/31.1in
**TOTAL LENGTH (STOCK RETRACTED)** 610mm/24in
**BARREL LENGTH** n/a (integrallly suppressed)
**WEIGHT UNLOADED** 3,288g/116oz

Based on the Daewoo K1A assault rifle, the K7 is an integrally suppressed submachine gun that uses a simple blowback design instead of the K1A's gas impingement system and it can fire semi-auto, three-round-burst, and full-auto. The gun was developed at the request of the ROK Army Special Warfare Command. Magazines from the Uzi and Beretta M12 can be used in the K7. The rate of fire is 1,100 rounds per minute, but sustained fire at that rate is detrimental to the suppressor's baffles.

# China

**Early Chinese guns were based on foreign designs such as the Soviet PPS-43, the American "grease gun" and the Russian Kalashnikov. The major producer of submachine guns for the Chinese armed forces is China North Industries Corporation, otherwise known as Norinco.**

## Type 36

The Type 36 (sometimes known as M36) was identical to the the American M3A1 (the "grease gun"), which was developed in the US during World War II as a cheaper version of the Thompson. It is thought that it was also produced at Mukden Arsenal in China during and after World War II. Although it was adopted by the Chinese in 1947, it never reached large-scale production because the factory was taken over by Chinese Communist forces in the late 1940s. Production started again on the island of Formosa (Taiwan) in 1950 where the model continued to be made, in 9mm Parabellum.

**SPECIFICATION**

**MANUFACTURER** Local Chinese manufacturers
**CALIBRE** .45 ACP
**MAGAZINE CAPACITY** 30
**ACTION** Blowback
**TOTAL LENGTH (STOCK EXTENDED)** 755mm/29.7in
**TOTAL LENGTH (STOCK RETRACTED)** 545mm/21.8in
**BARREL LENGTH** 203mm/8in
**WEIGHT UNLOADED** 3,375g/119oz

## Type 50

The Type 50 was a Chinese copy of the Soviet PPSh-41. It was used extensively by Chinese forces in close combat. Designed by Russian Georgii Shpagin, it was a simple but rugged design that was both effective and reliable. The Type 50 was designed specifically for ease of manufacture, and was slightly lighter than the PPSh-41. Produced from two or three plants in China, production started in 1950, shortly before the Korean War began, and continued until the mid-1950s.

**SPECIFICATION**

**MANUFACTURER** State Arsenals/local Chinese manufacturers
**CALIBRE** 7.62mm Tokarev
**MAGAZINE CAPACITY** 35 box or 71 drum
**ACTION** Blowback
**TOTAL LENGTH** 843mm/33.75in
**BARREL LENGTH** 269mm/10.75in
**WEIGHT UNLOADED** 3,630g/128oz

## Type 54

The Type 54 (also known as the M54) was a direct copy of the Soviet PPS-43. It went into production in China in 1953 with a distinguishing mark "K" on the grip. It had been designed by Russian Aleksei Sudaev in order to meet demand at the time of the Siege of Leningrad and was itself a stripped-down and simplified version of the PPSh-41. With its folding stock, it was adaptable for use in confined spaces. The PPS-43 was a blowback-operated weapon firing from an open bolt. The Type 54 quickly earned itself a good reputation under difficult circumstances. It was produced until 1956.

**SPECIFICATION**

**MANUFACTURER** State Arsenals/local Chinese manufacturers
**CALIBRE** 7.62mm Tokarev
**MAGAZINE CAPACITY** 35
**ACTION** Blowback
**TOTAL LENGTH (STOCK EXTENDED)** 808mm/32.25in
**TOTAL LENGTH (STOCK RETRACTED)** 606mm/24.25in
**WEIGHT UNLOADED** 3,330g/118oz

## Type 64

**SPECIFICATION**

**MANUFACTURER** State factories
**CALIBRE** 7.62mm Tokarev
**MAGAZINE CAPACITY** 30
**ACTION** Blowback
**TOTAL LENGTH (STOCK EXTENDED)** 843mm/33.3in
**TOTAL LENGTH (STOCK RETRACTED)** 635mm/25in
**BARREL LENGTH** 244mm/9.6in
**WEIGHT UNLOADED** 3,400g/120oz

Adopted by the Chinese military in the mid-1960s, the Type 64 was a simple blowback gun with an open-bolt system. It borrowed features from a number of other weapons, including the Soviet PPS-43 and the British Bren gun. Unusually for this type of weapon, it came with an integral steel silencer. Another unusual characteristic of the Type 64 was its high rate of fire, which could make the weapon difficult to control. The magazine was inserted into the receiver forward of the trigger guard. The bullet used was heavy and had a distinctive point. If standard rounds were used in this gun, it could suffer wear and be as loud as a standard weapon.

## Type 79

| SPECIFICATION | |
|---|---|
| MANUFACTURER | State factories/Norinco |
| CALIBRE | 7.62mm Tokarev |
| MAGAZINE CAPACITY | 20 |
| ACTION | Gas |
| TOTAL LENGTH (STOCK EXTENDED) | 740mm/29.1in |
| TOTAL LENGTH (STOCK RETRACTED) | 470mm/18.5in |
| BARREL LENGTH | 225mm/8.86in |
| WEIGHT UNLOADED | 1,900g/67oz |

The Type 79 submachine gun was first produced in 1979 and issued in large numbers to the People's Liberation Army and other Chinese security forces in 1983. Unlike many other weapons in its class, it was gas operated rather than blowback operated. It had a rotary bolt system and the gas piston is located above the barrel. The weapon had a fire-mode selector which could be set to full safety, single shots or automatic fire. The weapon had a foldable buttstock and could be fitted with both a tactical light and laser indicator.

## Type 85

The Type 85 was essentially an improved version of the Type 79, developed during the 1980s. Both the barrel and the bolt-carrying mechanism were redesigned to reduce noise and fit into a cylindrical receiver. It had a traditional blowback design with an open-bolt mechanism and a steel stock that could be folded. There was a selector above the trigger guard which allowed for selection of full safety, single shots or automatic fire. The magazine was the same as that used on the Type 79.

| SPECIFICATION | |
|---|---|
| MANUFACTURER | State factories/Norinco |
| CALIBRE | 7.62mm Tokarev |
| MAGAZINE CAPACITY | 30 |
| ACTION | Blowback |
| TOTAL LENGTH (STOCK EXTENDED) | 628mm/24.7in |
| TOTAL LENGTH (STOCK RETRACTED) | 444mm/17.48in |
| BARREL LENGTH | 275mm/10.83in |
| WEIGHT UNLOADED | 1,900g/67oz |

## Chang Feng

| SPECIFICATION | |
|---|---|
| MANUFACTURER | Jian Sheng |
| CALIBRE | 9mm Parabellum |
| MAGAZINE CAPACITY | 50 |
| ACTION | Blowback |
| TOTAL LENGTH (STOCK EXTENDED) | 588mm/123.15in |
| TOTAL LENGTH (STOCK RETRACTED) | 405mm/116in |
| BARREL LENGTH | 250mm/19.84in |
| WEIGHT UNLOADED | 2,100g/174oz |

Developed during the 1990s, this was a compact submachine gun with a blowback operation. The bolt wrapped around the barrel. The primary feed was from helical magazine made of polymer. The magazine was situated at the top of the weapon and is similar in design to the magazines of US Calico submachine guns. The gun had open sights and was also designed to take a night sight behind the main sight block. The barrel of the weapon was threaded to accept an optional detachable silencer.

## QCW-05

An integrally suppressed submachine gun that fires from an open bolt, the QCW-05 is a bullpup design where the magazine and action are located behind the trigger. This allows for a shorter overall length of 500mm/19.7in. Aluminum and polymer construction allows for a relatively light weight of just under 2,200g. It was designed to fire the same subsonic 5.8×21mm DCV05 ammunition as the integrally-suppressed QSW-06 pistol. The rate of fire is 900 rounds per minute.

| SPECIFICATION | |
|---|---|
| MANUFACTURER | China South Industries Group |
| CALIBRE | 5.8x21mm DCV05 |
| MAGAZINE CAPACITY | 50 |
| ACTION | Blowback |
| TOTAL LENGTH | 500mm/19.7in |
| BARREL LENGTH | 250mm/9.8in |
| WEIGHT UNLOADED | 2,182g/77oz |

## QCQ-171

**SPECIFICATION**

**MANUFACTURER** China South Industries Group
**CALIBRE** 9mm Parabellum
**MAGAZINE CAPACITY** 30
**ACTION** Blowback
**TOTAL LENGTH (STOCK EXTENDED)** 690mm/27.1in
**TOTAL LENGTH (STOCK RETRACTED)** 490mm/19.2in
**BARREL LENGTH** 216mm/8.5in
**WEIGHT UNLOADED** 2,778g/98oz

The QCQ-171 is the military designation for the CS/LS7. The gun was unveiled by the People's Liberation Army in the fall of 2019. The QCQ-171 fires from a closed bolt, has ambidextrous controls, and can be outfitted with either a fixed or a telescoping stock. There are handguard options that feature Picatinny rails in multiple different positions, as well as one option that includes a vertical foregrip like the one seen on the HK MP5K.

# Australia

**Australia produced both its adaptation of the English Sten gun, known as the Austen, and a completely home-grown weapon, the 9mm Owen. The Owen proved to be popular with the troops and remained in service through to the 1960s, since when Australia has bought an adapted version of the Steyr Aug.**

## Austen

This submachine gun was an Australian version of the Sten gun, which had been imported into Australia in 1941, but failed to impress. The Lithgow Small Arms Factory in New South Wales set about developing the gun, borrowing some of the features of the German MP40. The weapon was given a folding stock and two plastic pistol grips. The mainspring was also an MP40 design. The Austen could be set to either selective or automatic fire. Despite all the improvements, the Austen did not prove very popular. The required level of performance was to be achieved by another Australian weapon, the Owen.

**SPECIFICATION**

**MANUFACTURER** Small Arms Factory, Lithgow, NSW
**MAGAZINE** 28
**ACTION** Blowback
**TOTAL LENGTH (STOCK EXTENDED)** 845mm/33.25in
**TOTAL LENGTH (STOCK RETRACTED)** 552mm/31.75in
**BARREL LENGTH** 290mm/11.41in
**WEIGHT UNLOADED** 3,980g/140oz

## F1

The F1 was developed by the Lithgow Small Arms Factory and first produced in 1962. It proved to be a successful replacement for the Owen submachine gun and remained in service until the late 1980s, when it was replaced by a Steyr Aug adaptation, the F88. The F1 was a blowback-operated selective-fire weapon. The trigger mechanism included a lever that could be set in single-shot, automatic or safe modes.

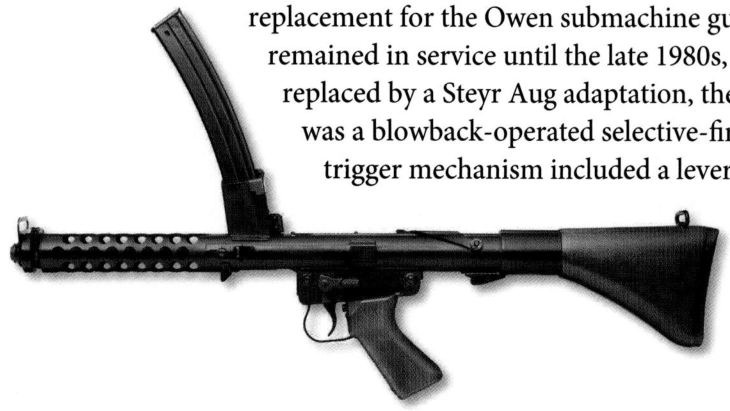

**SPECIFICATION**

**MANUFACTURER** Small Arms Factory, Lithgow, NSW
**CALIBRE** 9mm Parabellum
**MAGAZINE** 34
**ACTION** Blowback
**TOTAL LENGTH** 714mm/28.1in
**BARREL LENGTH** 213mm/8.38in
**WEIGHT UNLOADED** 3,270g/115oz

### Owen

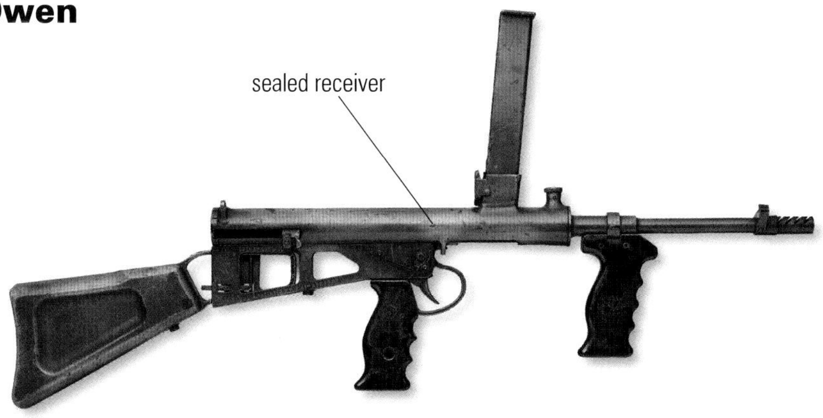


**SPECIFICATION**

**MANUFACTURER** John Lysaght (Australia) Ltd.
**CALIBRE** 9mm Parabellum
**MAGAZINE** 33
**ACTION** Blowback
**TOTAL LENGTH** 813mm/32in
**BARREL LENGTH** 250mm/9.84in
**WEIGHT UNLOADED** 3,980g/140oz

The Owen submachine gun was designed by Lieutenant Evelyn Owen and developed privately. It took some time for the weapon to be accepted by the Australian military, partly in view of the fact that the Austen was the official submachine gun programme. Once adopted, however, it proved to be both reliable and popular, with better performance than the Austen. The production run was 45,000, finishing in 1944. It was a select-fire, open-bolt design that carried the 9mm Parabellum round.

## Japan

**Japanese production of submachine guns was limited by the weak 8mm Nambu cartridge. Japanese manufacture of such weapons was in many respects the opposite of the manufacturing excellence that was to characterize Japanese industry in the post-World War II period.**

**SPECIFICATION**

**MANUFACTURER** Kokura Arsenal/Nagoya Arsenal
**CALIBRE** 8mm Nambu
**MAGAZINE CAPACITY** 30
**ACTION** Blowback
**TOTAL LENGTH** 890mm/35in
**BARREL LENGTH** 228mm/9in
**WEIGHT UNLOADED** 3,830g/135oz

### Nambu Type 100

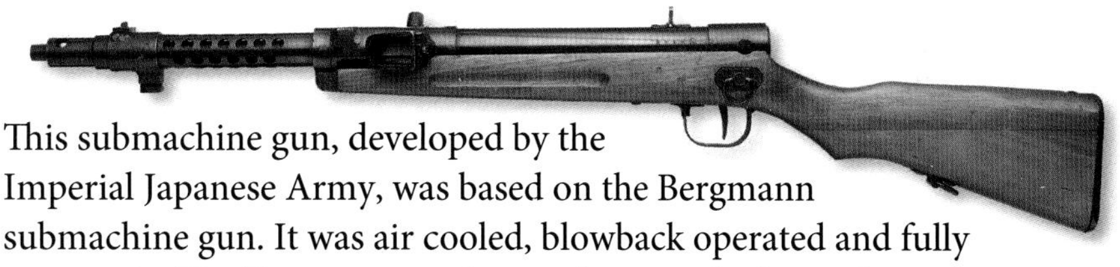

This submachine gun, developed by the Imperial Japanese Army, was based on the Bergmann submachine gun. It was air cooled, blowback operated and fully automatic. The Type 100 was designed primarily for use by paratroops. Although it was robust, the weapon had some problems with stoppages and the cartridge it fired was relatively weak. A modified version was introduced in 1944, which had a higher rate of fire.

**SPECIFICATION**

**MANUFACTURER** Shin Chuo
**CALIBRE** 9mm Parabellum
**MAGAZINE CAPACITY** 30
**ACTION** Blowback/selective fire
**TOTAL LENGTH (STOCK EXTENDED)** 762mm/30in
**TOTAL LENGTH (STOCK RETRACTED)** 501mm/19.72in
**BARREL LENGTH** 140mm/5.5in
**WEIGHT UNLOADED** 4,080g/14.39oz

### SCK Models 65 and 66

The SCK Model 65 was similar to the Swedish Carl Gustaf submachine gun and was introduced in 1965. A modified version was introduced in 1966 with a lower rate of fire. It had a conventional blowback operation. The weapon had a grip safety which had to be held down if the gun was to be either cocked or fired. The cocking handle had a safety system incorporated which would not allow it to be slip forward and fire the weapon unless it had first been pulled fully to the rear. The weapon had a buttstock that could be swung open or closed.

# Manufacturers

**Where information is available, listed below are details of the manufacturers whose arms are featured in the directories.**

### CANADA

**Para-Ordnance** Founded in 1985, its original products were based on aptations of the Colt M1911. Now it produces a wide range of handguns.

### UNITED STATES

**Auto-Ordnance Corp**. Founded in 1916 by John T. Thompson and others. Their products included various models of Thompson machine gun. The company was associated with Savage Arms Corp. from 1939 and then merged with Maguire Industries in 1944. Auto-Ordnance Corp. was bought out in 1999 by Saelio Enterprises Inc., parent company of Kahr Arms.

**Calico** Based in Oregon. Calico produces firearms that use the top-mounted, helical-feed magazine that can take between 50 and 100 rounds.

**Colt Manufacturing Co.** Founded in the 1840s in Connecticut, initially to produce revolvers. Products include the .45 Colt Single Action Army, Colt M1911 pistol and M4 Carbine. In 2002 the company was split between Colt Defense and Colt Manufacturing Company. In 2021, Colt was acquired by Czech company CZG-Ceská Zbrojovka Group.

**Harrington & Richardson** Founded in 1871 as Wesson and Harrington. The major production is of single-shot shotguns. The company went out of business in 1986. The new company H&R 1871 was formed in 1991. It was sold to Marlin Firearms in 2000. H&R was acquired by Remington in 2007. When Remington filed for bankruptcy in 2020, H&R was bought by JJE Capital Holdings, LLC. The company owns a number of firearms brands.

**High Standard Mfg. Co.** Founded in Connecticut in 1926. In 1932 the company purchased Hartford Arms and Equipment Company. In 1993, the company was acquired by High Standard Manufacturing Company Inc. of Houston, Texas.

**Intratec** Founded as a subsidiary of Interdynamic AB, then Interdynamic USA. Intratec produced the Tec-9 submachine gun. It folded in 2001.

**Marlin Firearms Co.** Founded in 1870 by John M. Marlin. In 1915 a New York syndicate bought the company and named it Marlin Rockwell Corporation. In 2000 Marlin bought the assets of H&R 1871. Marlin was acquired by Remington in 2007, and in 2020, Marlin was bought by Ruger Firearms.

**Remington Arms Co.** Founded in 1816 by Eliphalet Remington. They first made flintlock rifles. It continues to produce both arms and ammunition under the name RemArms for the forner and Remington Ammunition for the latter.

**Savage Arms Corp.** Founded in 1894 by Arthur Savage, it manufactured pistols, rifles and ammunition. The company grew through the acquisition of Stevens Arms, Page Lewis Co., Davis-Warner Arms, Crescent Firearms and A.H. Fox. In 1995 it became a private company.

**Smith & Wesson Inc.** Its origins lie in the partnership between Horace Smith and Daniel Wesson, dating from 1852. First success came in 1856 with manufacture of the .22 rimfire revolver. It is now the largest producer of handguns in the United States.

**Sturm, Ruger & Co Inc.** The company was founded in 1949 by William B. Ruger. The product line covers hunting, self-defence and law enforcement. It is now the largest manufacturer of firearms in the United States.

**Taurus International Manufacturing Inc.** Forjas Taurus was established in Brazil in Porto Alegre in 1937. It opened an affiliated company in Miami, USA, in 1968. Taurus began to produce Beretta pistols under licence. From the 1990s it began to produce its own range of pistols and revolvers in both countries.

### MEXICO

**Productos Mendoza S.A.** This company was established in 1911 and manufactures submachine guns and other products.

### CHILE

**Las Fábricas y Maestranzas del Ejército (FAMAE)** Founded in 1811, it produces a wide range of assault rifles and submachine guns.

### ARGENTINA

**Bersa S.A.** Founded in the 1960s. Its product line consists of pistols for various purposes, including self-defence and target shooting.

**Fábrica Militar de Armas Portatiles "Domingo Matheu"** This company used to produce weapons for FN Herstal of Belgium, under licence.

### BRAZIL

**Indústria de Material Bélico do Brasil (IMBEL)** This is a publicly owned company administered by the Brazilian Ministry of Defence, said to have strong ties with the Brazilian military establishment. From 1985 IMBEL entered into association with Springfield Armory of the United States.

**Mekanika Indústria e Comércio Lda** This company was set up to produce the Uru submachine gun from 1979 to 1988. It has made an arrangement with Rossi to continue producing the Uru.

**Rossi** Founded in 1889. From 1997, Rossi firearms were imported into the United States by BrazTech International. Forjas Taurus SA bought the rights to produce Rossi handguns.

### PORTUGAL

**Fábrica Militar de Braço de Prata** This major armament company manufactured the Heckler & Koch G3 under licence, among others.

**Indústrias Nacionais de Defesa (INDEP)** The main ordnance factory in Portugal, it produces mortars, artillery and small arms.

### SPAIN

**Astra-Unceta y Cia.** Unceta was founded in 1908 in Eibar, Spain, and then moved to Guernica in the Basque country. Today it is known by the name of Astra.

**Star Bonifacio Echeverría S.A.** Manufacturer of small arms in the Basque region 1905 to 1997.

**UNITED KINGDOM**

**Birmingham Small Arms Company (BSA)** This company was founded in 1861. During World War I, the gun business grew exponentially. In World War II, production was focused on the Lee Enfield rifle as well as on miltary folding bicycles and on motorcycles. In 1986 BSA Guns was liquidated and now trades as BSA Guns (UK) Ltd.

**Royal Ordnance** This was formed as a public corporation in 1985 but its roots in the Royal Ordnance factories extend back to the middle of the 16th century. The company was bought by British Aerospace, later BAE systems, and became part of BAE Systems Land and Armaments.

**Royal Small Arms Factory, Enfield** Founded in 1804 as one of the factories of the Board of Ordnance. Privatized in 1984 as part of Royal Ordnance Plc. Production included Bren and Sten guns as well as a modified version of the Webley service revolver.

**Webley & Scott** Founded around 1834 by Philip Webley as Webley & Sons. Production moved from percussion rifles to revolvers. In 1897 the firm amalgamated with W&C Scott & Sons. Production increased during the World Wars, but fortunes declined post-war and the company closed in 2005. It was bought by Airgunsport in 2006, which has kept the famous Webley name. In 2010, the company restarted production of shotguns.

**FRANCE**

**Hotchkiss et Cie.** This company was set up by Benjamin B. Hotchkiss of the United States in 1867 to produce a wide range of weaponry for both the French and the American armed forces. By the beginning of the 20th century, Hotchkiss was also manufacturing cars.

**Manufacture d'Armes de Bayonne (MAB)** Founded in 1920 by Leon Barthe. Initial production of pistols was based on the Browning M1906.

**Manufacture d'Armes de Châtellerault (MAC)** Founded 1819 on the banks of the River Vienne. Initial production was of tools and swords. In 1822 the factory began to produce firearms, which continued until 1968.

**Société Alsacienne de Construction Mécanique (SACM)** Founded in 1839. The company was mainly concerned with manufacture of locomotives.

**BELGIUM**

**Anciens Établissements Pieper** Located at Herstal, Belgium, Pieper was a manufacturer of small arms between 1907 and 1939. During this time it manufactured Bayard pistols.

**Charles Ph. Clement** A manufacturer based in Liège that patented an automatic pistol with no fixed cylinder head. The company ceased trading from the beginning of the German occupation of Belgium in 1914.

**Fabrique Nationale (FN) Herstal** This firm was first established in 1889 near Liège. The company began a successful association with John Moses Browning at the end of the 19th century which resulted in the famous Browning GP35 High-Power, among other designs. The firm continues to produce world-class small arms and also owns the US Repeating Arms Company (Winchester) and the Browning Arms Company.

**SWITZERLAND**

**B&T AG** Founded in 1991, B&T AG is a Swiss defence company that makes firearms, sound silencers and mounting rails.

**Hispano-Suiza S.A. (Suisse)** The company was founded in 1899 by Mark Birkigt in Catalonia and formed an alliance with Spanish banker Damian Mateu. It made famous cars and aircraft. It is now part of the huge SAFRAN Group.

**SIG** Founded in 1853 by Friedrich Peyer im Hof, Heinrich Moser and Conrad Nehrer. It won an order for the Prelaz-Burnand rifle from the Swiss Ministry of Defence. In the 20th century, the company developed a range of pistols, beginning with the P49. It had acquired J.P. Sauer by the early 1980s. SIGARMS was formed in the United States in 1985.

**GERMANY**

**Carl Walther Waffenfabrik GmbH.** This business was first founded in 1886 by Carl Walther to make hunting rifles. The first semi-automatic pistol was produced in 1908. The factory closed down at the end of World War II and re-opened again in West Germany.

**Heckler & Koch GmbH.** This firm began business in January 1950 and was first concerned with making parts for bicycles and sewing machines. In 1956 the company won the bid for the new West German general service rifle, the G3. In the mid-1960s, the MP5 was developed. In 1991 the company was bought by British Aerospace/Royal Ordnance. It produces the whole range of small arms, from pistols to grenades and machine guns.

**J.P. Sauer & Sohn GmbH.** Founded in 1751, the company received its first major order from the German Army in 1870. In 1976 SIG of Switzerland acquired the majority of Sauer's stock and completed acquisition at the beginning of the 1980s. The company continues to produce pistols and hunting rifles today.

**Korth GmbH.** Founded in 1940s by Willi Korth. The company is now Korth Germany and Korth USA, manufacturing revolvers and semi-automatic pistols.

**Rheinische Metallwaaren und Maschinefabrik** This company was established in 1889 by Heinrich Erhardt. Production increased during World War I. In 1941, the company was taken over by the German state. In 1997 weapons and ammunition division became Rheinmetall W&M GmbH. In 2002 the company acquired Oerlikon Contraves Pyrtotec AG.

**Waffenfabrik Mauser AG.** Oberndorf This company was founded in 1811 as a royal weapons factory in Oberndorf.

In 1867 Wilhelm and Paul Mauser developed a rifle with a rotating bolt system. In 1912 the company started producing pistols. In 1897 the factory became Waffenfabrik Mauser AG. The factory was dismantled by French authorities at the end of World War II but the firm was then re-established in the 1950s. In 2004 Mauser-Werke Oberndorf Waffensysteme GmbH incorporated into Rheinmetall Waffe Munition, GmbH.

**ITALY**
**Benelli Armi SpA.** The company was founded in 1911 with production f ocused on motorcycles. In the mid-1960s the firearms business was started. The company manufactures shotguns, rifles and pistols.

**Fabbrica d'Armi P. Beretta SpA.** This company had its roots in the early 16th century, beginning with the forging of arquebus barrels.Today it is one of the leading firearms producers in the world, providing issue service pistols to the United States, French, Italian and other armed forces. In 2021, Beretta acquired London gunmaker Holland & Holland.

**Fabbrica Nazionale d'Armi Brescia**
This firm was launched in 1935 and began producing sports and hunting rifles. In World War II, production was focused on military weapons. In 1958 the factory was bought by Beretta.

**Luigi Franchi SpA.** Founded in 1868 and now part of the Beretta group.

**DENMARK**
**Dansk Industri Syndikat, Madsen** This company was established in 1900 to produce light machine guns. In 1959 the shipping company Maersk acquired a controlling interest in the company. By 1963 arms production had ceased.

**AUSTRIA**
**Glock GmbH.** Founded in 1963 by Gaston Glock in Deutsch-Wagram, near Vienna. The product line consists of pistols, knives, and various typs of tools.

**Steyr Mannlicher GmbH. & Co. KG**
This firm incorporated the designs of Ferdinand Ritter von Mannlicher, who joined Steyr in 1866. It currently produces highly regarded assault rifles as well as sniper rifles and pistols.

**SWEDEN**
**Carl Gustaf Arms Co.** Formed as part of the original agglomeration of small arms producers that began in 1620 and centred on certain designated towns. It is now part of Bofors.

**Husqvarna Vapenfabriks AB.**
The company was founded in 1689 to produce muskets.

**CZECH REPUBLIC**
**Ceská/Ceskoslovenská Zbrojovka**
Established in 1919 as part of the famous Skoda Works. Post-World War II products carried the BRNO designation. In the 1990s it was re-established on a free-trade basis. It established a US subsidiary, CZ-USA.

**POLAND**
**Fabryka Broni Radom** Founded in 1922, the company became independent in 2000. Early production included the Nagant 95 pistol.

**HUNGARY**
**Fegyver es Gepgyar (FÉG)**
Founded in 1891, the company produced Frommer pistols and also hunting and sports weapons. In 2003 the company was privatized and at this present time still continues to produce small arms.

**SERBIA**
**Zastava Arms Co.** Founded in 1853 to manufacture cannons. It is the sole arms producer in Serbia and Montenegro, with production largely based around Kalashnikov designs.

**FINLAND**
**Valtion Kivaaritehdas (VKT), Jyvastalyla** A state factory which produced the Lahti pistol.

**ROMANIA**
**Cugir Arsenal** This arsenal has been producing small arms from World War II to the present day. It is now part of the Romaru National Company.

**RUSSIA**
**Izhevsk Machanical Plant (IZHMECH)**
This is the state-owned Russian plant at Izhevsk.

**Tula Arsenal** Founded in 1712 by Peter the Great. It has produced arms throughout Russia's modern history. Production has included the Mosin-Nagant rifle and the AK-47.

**ISRAEL**
**Israeli Military Industries (IMI)** Small Arms Division privatized in 2005 as Israel Weapons Industries. The product line includes Uzi submachine guns and the Galil assault rifle.

**Ta'as Israel Industries Ltd.** Established in 1933 and is the country's oldest defence industry. It grew substantially after the 1973 Middle East wars and produces a wide range of advanced defence equipment.

**CHINA**
**China North Industries Corp. (Norinco)** Established in 1980, Norinco makes a wide variety of equipment for defence, including submachine guns.

**AUSTRALIA**
**John Lysaght Ltd.** This firm was established in 1921, initially as a wholly owned subsidiary of a firm of the same name in England. Mainly concerned with the production of sheet steel, during World War II the company produced the Owen submachine gun.

**Lithgow Small Arms Factory**
Opened in 1912, having been set up with the assistance of exports from US-based Pratt & Whitney. The factory produced Lee-Enfield rifles during World War I and the Bren machine gun in World War II. The factory later diversified to produce sporting rifles, tools and other manufactured items.

**SOUTH KOREA**
**Daewoo Telecom Ltd.** This corporation was first founded in 1967 and is one of South Korea's leading industrial concerns, including cars in one of its product divisions.

**JAPAN**
**Nagoya Arsenal** This arsenal was opened in 1923 and ceased manufacture in 1945.

**Kokura Arsenal** Consisted of an extensive collection of military industries. It began operating in 1935 and was the intended target for the second atomic bomb to be dropped on Japan. Due to bad weather over Kokura Nagasaki suffered devastation instead.

# Glossary

**ACP** Abbreviation for "Automatic Colt Pistol". Used to designate certain cartridges that were first chambered in Colt pistols.
**Action** The working mechanism of the firearm which determines the way it is cocked, fired and reloaded.
**Arquebus** An early matchlock pistol which preceded the musket.
**Assault rifle** An automatic or semi-automatic rifle with a magazine.
**Backstrap** The part of the frame of a firearm exposed at the rear of the grip.
**Baffles** Devices that impede the movement of gas within a silencer.
**Barrel** The metal tube of a firearm.
**Beavertail** Describes the shape of some forms of trigger, safety catch or hammer guard.
**Blackpowder** The earliest type of propellant used in muzzleloaders and older breech-loading guns. Modern firearms use smokeless powder.
**Blish lock system** A breech-locking mechanism designed by John Bell Blish used in the original Thompson submachine gun. It was a form of retarded blowback based on the principle of static friction.
**Blowback** An operation system which the slide or breech block is driven to the rear by direct gas pressure on the cartridge case head.
**Bolt** Normally a mobile device that closes the breech of a weapon.
**Bolt action** A gun mechanism activated by manual operation of the breech block.
**Bore** The inside of the barrel of a gun, excluding the chamber. It is the channel through which the bullet is fired from the weapon.
**Box lock** When the firing mechanism (and sometimes the trigger) is concealed in the body of the pistol and only appears once the trigger is pulled.
**Box magazine** A rectangular compartment attached to, or placed into a firearm that holds cartridges stacked on top of one another ready for feeding into the chamber.
**Bramit device** A special silencer that was designed by Mitin brothers for the Nagant M1895 revolver and was mounted on the barrel.
**Breech** The rear part of the barrel of the firearm, sometimes used as an area for reloading.
**Breech block** The part of the firearm action that closes the breech of a weapon at the moment of firing.
**Breech loader** A gun that is loaded through the rear or breech.
**Bullet** The projectile expelled from a firearm.
**Burr-type hammer** A rounded, grooved hammer, rather than the more well-known spur shape.
**Butt/buttstock** In a handgun, the butt is the bottom part of the grip or grip frame. In submachine gun, it is the rear or shoulder end of the stock.
**Butt plate** A plate put on the butt end of a stock. May be used for comfort, positioning or may be purely decorative.
**Calibre** Measurement of the interior diameter of a gun barrel (the size of the bore). It also refers to the size of the cartridge used in a particular firearm. This is determined by the diameter of the cartridge, measured either in millimetres in the European system or in 100s of an inch in the American system.
**Cam** A mechanical device that uses a rotating motion in order to move another part of a mechanism in a particular way.
**Carbine** A lightweight rifle with a short barrel, which developed from muzzle-loading muskets.
**Cartridge case** A cylindrical case containing primer, charge and bullet. As the powder burns, the case expands to seal against the side of the chamber, forcing the expansion of gas down the barrel.
**Centrefire** A cartridge with its primer located in the centre of the base of the case.
**Chamber** The area of a firearm where a round rests prior to firing. A revolver has several chambers.
**Charger** A device that is used to load a magazine.
**Clip** A device for holding cartridges together, usually to facilitate loading. Technically, a magazine has a feeding spring, but a clip does not.
**Cocked and locked** The practice of carrying a semi-automatic pistol with a round in the chamber, the hammer cocked and the safety engaged.
**Cocking handle** A handle which compresses the spring behind the bolt.

**Combat range** The range at which a firearm is effective against a target.
**Crane** The swinging unit hinging the cylinder of a revolver with the frame.
**Cutts compensator** A device invented by Colonel Richard Malcolm Cutts that reduces the shock and rise of the muzzle when firing a firearm.
**Cyclic rate** The rate at which an automatic weapon goes through the full reload cycle after a round is fired.
**Cylinder** The part of a revolver that holds the chambers where rounds are inserted prior to firing.
**Delayed blowback** A variant of the blowback principle in which the blowback operation is deliberately retarded by some means.
**Discharge** To cause a firearm to fire.
**Disconnector** Part of trigger mechanism in a semi-automatic pistol that disconnects the trigger from the firing mechanism after each shot.
**Dot system** A system of marking fixed sights on semi-automatic handguns so that there is greater contrast between the sight and the target.
**Double action** A type of lockwork in either a revolver or semi-automatic pistol that permits the hammer to be cocked either by direct manual action or by a long pull on the trigger.
**Double-action only** Double-action only handguns function in much the same way as double-action handguns, except it is not possible to manually cock the hammer.
**Double-barrel** A firearm with two barrels, either side by side or one above the other.
**Drop safety** Designed to prevent the unintentional discharge of a handgun if it is dropped on the hammer.
**Dum-dum bullet** Originally referred to the British military jacketed .303 bullet with an exposed lead core, developed in India's Dum-Dum Arsena. It is also the name given to several types of expanding bullets.
**Ejection port** The opening where spent cartridge cases are ejected.
**Ejector** Mechanism that ejects the spent cartridge case.
**Extractor** Normally a claw-like

mechanism that pulls the empty cartridge case from the chamber so that it can be ejected by a separate mechanism (the ejector).
**Feed mechanism/system** The mechanism that feeds the new round into the chamber.
**Field stripping** The act of taking apart a firearm for regular maintenance and cleaning.
**Fire selective system** A system by which single shots or automatic fire can be manually selected by pushing a lever or button normally located on the side of the receiver.
**Firing pin** The mechanism that strikes the rear of the cartridge.
**Flash hider** A device attached to a gun to reduce the muzzle flash which occurs upon firing. The flash is caused by incandescence of the expanding gases produced by burning gunpowder.
**Flintlock** The action of early firearms where a piece of flint was held by the cock. When the trigger was pulled, the cock/flint struck the steel "frizzen" causing a shower of sparks to ignite fine gunpowder in a small pan next to the "touch-hole" in the barrel. The flash in the pan travelled through the touch hole and ignited the powder charge in the base of the barrel.
**Folding stock** Usually a metal shoulder piece that can be folded back against the main body of the weapon when not in use.
**Frizzen** The metal arm of a flintlock mechanism. The flint strikes the frizzen to create sparks in the flash pan.
**Full metal jacket** A bullet enclosed in copper or steel, which helps prevent damage and misfires.
**Full cock** The position of the hammer or striker when the firearm is ready to fire.
**Full-moon clip** A clip designed to hold ammunition to fill the cylinder in a revolver.
**Fulminate of mercury** A highly sensitive explosive used as a primer compound.
**Furniture** Parts of the weapon that facilitate handling – such as stock, butt and pistol grip.
**Gas-operation** An operating system in a firearm. Gas being bled off from the barrel and used against the bolt to drive it backwards and prepare the gun for the next round.
**Grip** The handle of a handgun.
**Grip safety** A device that prevents a handgun from being fired unless the handle is firmly gripped.
**Half-moon clip** A clip designed to hold ammunition to fill half of the cylinder in a revolver.
**Hammer** Part of a weapon that drives the firing pin forward.
**Hammer spur** The extension on an exposed hammer that acts as a cocking aid.
**High-capacity magazine** A non-technical term for a magazine that holds more rounds than average.
**LAM (laser aiming module)** A laser module set on a weapon to emit a laser beam parallel to the barrel. When fired, the bullet will hit the spot made by the laser.
**Loading gate** The hinged cover over the opening through which cartridges are inserted into the magazine or chamber on a revolver.
**Lock plate** A metal plate mounted on the stock of a firearm and on which the firing mechanism (traditionally in flintlock and percussion firearms) is attached.
**Locked breech** A firearms action in which the barrel and breechface remain locked together during the initial part of the firearm's discharge. Most powerful semi-automatic pistols use the locked-breech principle; most low-powered ones are blowbacks.
**Long recoil** A method of recoil in which the barrel and bolt recoil for a greater length than that of the entire cartridge.
**Magazine** A holder for cartridges prior to their being fed into the weapon chamber.
**Magazine catch** The catch that releases to open a firearm in order to insert the magazine.
**Magazine safety** A device that prevents a firearm from being discharged when the magazine has been removed.
**Magnum** A type of firearm that fires a heavily loaded metallic cartridge.
**Mainspring** The source of the energy needed to fire the gun. Cocking the hammer compresses the mainspring, generating potential energy.
**Match** A long cord soaked in saltpetre (potassium nitrate), which burns slowly and was used to ignite powder in an early firearm.
**Matchgrade trigger** A trigger found in some guns used for competitive shooting. The trigger is smoother and lighter than standard triggers.
**Matchlock** The action of early firearms that relied on an S-shaped (serpentine) piece of metal to hold a smouldering match. Once activated, the burning end of the match, held by the upper end of the serpentine, drops to the priming powder in the pan and ignites the powder charge in the barrel though the touch hole.
**Musket** A muzzle-loaded smoothbore gun, fired from the shoulder.
**Muzzle** The opening at the end of the barrel from which the projectile exits.
**Muzzle brake** A device attached to the muzzle which softens the recoil of the firearm.
**Muzzle climb** Upward movement of a firearm as a result of recoil.
**Muzzle velocity** The speed at which the bullet leaves the muzzle of a firearm.
**Needle gun** A rifle where the primer, placed against the bullet beyond the powder, was detonated by a needle passing through the powder when the trigger was pulled.
**Open bolt** A semi or fully automatic firearm fires from an "open bolt" when the bolt and working parts are held at the rear when ready to fire. When the trigger is pulled the bolt goes forward, feeding a round from the magazine into the chamber and firing it. The action is cycled by the energy of the shot; this sends the bolt back to the rear, ejecting the empty cartridge case and preparing for the next shot.
**Pan** The small container located on the side or top of a matchlock, wheel-lock or flintlock pistol, used to hold the priming powder.
**Parabellum** A type of 9mm ammunition. The word derives from a German arms manufacturer, who used the Latin maxim – *si vis pacem, para bellum*. This means "If you want peace, prepare for war."
**PDW (personal defence weapon)** A firearm designed for close-quarters defence rather than a firearm designed for active assault.
**Percussion cap** A small metal explosive-filled cup, which is placed over the nipple of a percussion firearm. The compound explodes when fired igniting a secondary charge of gunpowder or other explosive.
**Pinfire cartridge** A 19th-century cartridge where a pin would ignite the priming mixture and the explosion would cause the brass sheath containing the gunpowder and ball to expand, closing the breech.
**Ported barrel** The holes that are precision drilled in the forward

part of the barrel of a revolver (and the slide on pistols) to divert gases and so reduce the upward flip of the firearm.
**Primer** The ignition part of a cartridge, usually made up of a metallic fulminate or, currently, lead styphnate.
**Proof-mark** Official mark placed on a firearm after the barrel has been tested by a proof house.
**Rail attachment** A rail fixed to a firearm or integral to the frame that enables attachments such as lights or laser pointers to be fitted.
**Ramrod** A rod used to ram the charge and bullet into a muzzle-loading firearm.
**Receiver** Major part of the body of a firearm that houses its internal workings, including the barrel and bolt.
**Recoil** The rearward movement of internal parts of a gun as a result of the explosive force of the cartridge.
**Recoil operated** Operating system in which the firearm is cycled by the recoil-propelled force of the bolt and barrel when the firearm is fired. The bolt and barrel recoil together before the barrel stops and the bolt moves forwards to perform reloading and chambering.
**Repeater** A firearm which loads a new round as a result of the action created by the explosive force of the previous round.
**Revolver** A firearm with a revolving cylinder that holds the rounds. The cylinder is turned automatically after each round is fired to present a new round to the hammer.
**Rifled barrel** A barrel with a spiral pattern of grooves cut into its bore. This puts a spin on the projectile (bullet) as it is forced through it.
**Rim** The edge on the base of a cartridge case. The rim is the part of the case that the extractor grips in order to remove the cartridge from the chamber.
**Rimfire** A cartridge that has its primer located inside the rim of the case.
**Round** One shot fired by a gun. It is also one complete unit of ammunition or a cartridge which has all the parts needed to fire one shot.
**Safety** A device on a firearm designed to prevent accidental firing.
**Sear** A lever or catch connected to the trigger that holds back the firing pin.
**Select-fire trigger** A trigger mechanism that will allow either single shots or automatic fire.
**Selective fire** The ability of a firearm to be fired fully automatically, semi-automatically or in burst-fire mode at the option of the shooter.
**Self-loading** Operating system in which one pull of the trigger allows the gun to fire and reload in a single action. A semi-automatic pistol is self-loading. An automatic firearm would continue to fire.
**Semi-automatic** A firearm that loads a new round automatically after firing and just requires another squeeze of the trigger to fire the next round.
**Sight** Any of a variety of devices, mechanical and optical, designed to assist in the aiming of a firearm.
**Silencer** A device attached to a firearm's muzzle to suppress sound. The bullet emerges at a lower speed and the firearm makes less noise. Reducing the speed avoids a sonic crack as the speed is below the speed of sound.
**Single action** Mechanism by which the hammer is cocked, either manually or by the action of recoil and then released by the trigger.
**Single shot** A gun mechanism lacking a magazine. Separately-carried ammunition must be manually placed in the gun's chamber for each firing.
**Slide** Upper part of a gun that literally slides back, under the force of recoil, or by being manually pulled back in order to service the weapon.
**Slide safety** A device that blocks the firing mechanism of a firearm.
**Slide stop** This indicates when a handgun has expended all loaded ammunition, and helps reloading by removing the step of pulling back the slide to advance the first round of a new magazine.
**Small bore** Generally refers to a .22 firearm or rimfire ammunition (called a .22 calibre firearm).
**Smokeless powder** Propellent powder for cartridges normally containing mainly nitrocellulose or both nitrocellulose and nitroglycerine.
**Smooth bore** A firearm with a bore that is not rifled, such as a shotgun.
**Stock (wooden or wire)** The part of a firearm that is held against the shoulder to steady it for aiming and to absorb the force of recoil.
**Striker** An axially mounted, spring-propelled firing pin. A firing pin is an alternative term for striker used mainly when a firing pin is axially mounted and spring-propelled.
**Subcompact pistol** A pistol that is even smaller than the compact size.

**Suppressor** Similar to a silencer, but it only muffles the noise rather than affect the bullet's velocity.
**Telescopic mount** The means of attaching a telescopic sight to a firearm.
**Telescopic sight** An optical sight attached to a firearm that magnifies the user's view of a target.
**Three-dot sights** The part of the firearm used to line up a target. A white dot painted on the frontis lined up between a dot on each side of the rear sight notch. These are the three-dot sights.
**Touch-hole** A small hole, through which the propellant charge of a cannon or muzzle-loading gun is ignited.
**Tumbler** A steel cam attached to the axis shaft of the cock of a gun. It holds and releases the power of the mainspring and transmits it to the hammer.
**Toggle-lock pistol** A sophisticated device by which the bolt or breech lock of the Luger pistol is locked by a two-lever link. It is also found in the Maxim machine gun.
**Top-break system** A mechanism by which a revolver is broken open and hinges forward to reveal the cylinder for reloading.
**Trigger** The part of the firearm mechanism that releases the part of the action that fires the cartridge.
**Trigger guard** The metal loop around the trigger made to protect it and prevent the user accidentally touching the trigger.
**Wadcutter** A type of bullet used in target shooting. It is designed to make a clean hold in the target at the range, without ragged edges.
**Wheel-lock** An early firearm mechanism. A wheel with serrated edges is spun against a piece of iron pyrites.This sends sparks into the pan to ignite the charge.
**Windage** An allowance given in taking aim in order to compensate for the effect of wind on the bullet's flight. The rear sight adjustment is known as "windage."

# Index

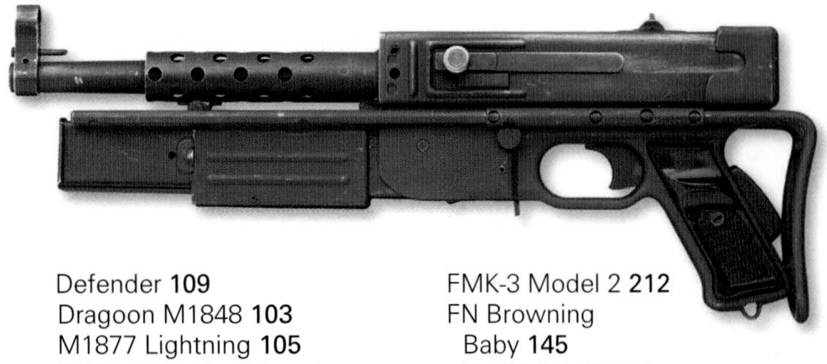

# Picture credits

The publisher would like to thank the following for kindly supplying photos for this book: Aaron Littlefield: 116t; Corbis: 17t, 34b, 36, 54b, 90t, 94, 95t, 95b; Gary Cooke: 105, 111t; Getty Images: 43, 79b, 37t; Horst Held: 49t; iStockphoto: 26b, 33b, 39t, 39tm, 65bl, 82b, 83t, 86m, 86b, 89b, 89t, 90b, 91r, 92; JupiterImages 33r, 39, Peter Newark's Military Pictures: 11t, 13b, 16b, 19b, 27b, 27t, 28bl, 29t, 31b, 31t, 37b, 38, 42, 47b, 63t, 75mr, 11b; Royal Armouries Picture Library: 15t, 17b, 18t, 20t, 21b, 21t, 22t, 24t, 25t, 26t, 33t, 35b, 41b, 44bl, 45b, 48, 53t; The Bridgeman Art Library: 6b, 23, 41t; The Kobal Collection: 87b; The Research House: 78b, 83b, 85t, 85b; TopFoto: 10, 15b, 19tr, 28t, 29b, 40t, 47t, 52b, 63b, 68bl; Will Fowler: 58b, 60b, 62b, 64b, 66b, 67b, 70b, 71b, 72b, 76b, 51b.

All other images are commissioned. With thanks to the Royal Armouries, Leeds in England for allowing access to their extensive collection of firearms for photography.

With thanks to the following companies for supplying images: Browning-Winchester, Glock, Heckler & Koch, Para-Ordnance, Ruger, Tangfoglio, Taurus International Manufacturing, Inc.

All commissioned pictures by Gary Ombler. All artwork by Peters & Zabransky Ltd., and Richard Peters.

With thanks to Cybershooters for their invaluable information about gun mechanics.

BONIFACIO ECHEVERRIA - EIBAR (ESPAÑA)